FIND IT
IN THE
TALMUD

FIND IT
IN THE
TALMUD

An ENCYCLOPEDIA of
JEWISH ETHICS and CONDUCT

Thousands of Talmudic Subjects, Stories & Expressions

MORDECHAI (MARTIN) JUDOVITS

URIM PUBLICATIONS
Jerusalem • New York

Find It in the Talmud:
An Encyclopedia of Jewish Ethics and Conduct

by Mordechai (Martin) Judovits
Edited by Rabbi Ben Sugerman

Typeset by Ariel Walden

Printed in Israel

First Edition

ISBN 978-965-524-146-4

Urim Publications, P.O. Box 52287, Jerusalem 9152102 Israel

www.UrimPublications.com

———————

Library of Congress Cataloging-in-Publication Data

Judovits, Mordechai.
    Find it in the Talmud : an encyclopedia of Jewish ethics and proper conduct
/ Mordechai (Martin) Judovits.
        p.   cm.
    Includes bibliographical references and index.
    Summary: "The Talmud — an ancient and seminal text central to Rabbinic
Judaism — is the focal point of this reference book. With more than 6,000
entries, this book serves as a path finder for those interested in the Talmud
and a useful tool when searching for a particular Talmudic subject" —
Provided by publisher.
    ISBN 978-965-524-146-4 (hardcover : alk. paper)   1. Talmud —
Encyclopedias. I. Title.
    BM500.5.J83 2014
    296.1'2003 — dc23   2014021673

THIS Sefer, *Find It in the Talmud*, is being dedicated
In loving memory of my אשת חיל

HELEN JUDOVITS · הנשא בת יוסף צבי

Born July 28, 1930 · ג' אב תר"צ
Died September 9, 2011 · י"א אלול תשע"א

ঙ্কৈ

Beloved wife, mother,

grandmother, and great-grandmother

HELEN was a Holocaust survivor,

she was taken to Auschwitz at age fourteen.

During her entire life she was a profile

in courage, friendship,

and generosity.

ת·נ·צ·ב·ה

THIS Sefer, *Find it in the Talmud*, is being dedicated
in honor of the JUDOVITS Family

To my son
ROBERT JUDOVITS
שלמה
And to my son
LAWRENCE JUDOVITS & NANCY JUDOVITS
יוסף צבי & חנה לאה
And to my daughter
JOYCE ISRAEL & RICKY DAVID ISRAEL
נחמה ריזל טובא & יהושע

And to my granddaughter
MAYAH JUDOVITS
מיה יעל
And to my granddaughter
TALYA RACHEL JUDOVITS
טליה רחל
And to my granddaughter
AMELIA JUDOVITS
אמיליה

And to my grandson
BENJAMIN GREGORY JUDOVITS
שלמה
And to my granddaughter
EMILY REBECCA JUDOVITS
רבקה

And to my grandson
NOAH ALEXANDER ISRAEL
נח משה
And to my grandson
JONAH OLIVER ISRAEL
יונה אברהם

And to my great grandchildren
MORDECHAI ARYEH ELKOUSS
מרדכי אריה
And
ARI ISAAC ELKOUSS
ארי יצחק

THE HOLOCAUST MEMORIAL photos on the following pages are a standing memorial near the main entrance of the Boca Raton Synagogue in the town of Boca Raton, Florida. It was dedicated in a ceremony in 2010. The memorial consists of six granite pillars, symbolizing the six million martyrs. The pillars are in the shape of candles (sliced in half – one side is round, the other side is flat) with electrified flames on top.

FOUR OF THE SIX PILLARS have on their flat side engravings of the names of the martyrs who died in the German extermination camps. Two pillars contain the names of Holocaust survivors who have died since the Holocaust. The names engraved are those of relatives of Synagogue members.

ON THE ROUND SIDE of the pillars are engravings consisting of words and maps describing the horror of the Holocaust.

The monument was planned and designed by Martin (Mordechai) Judovits.

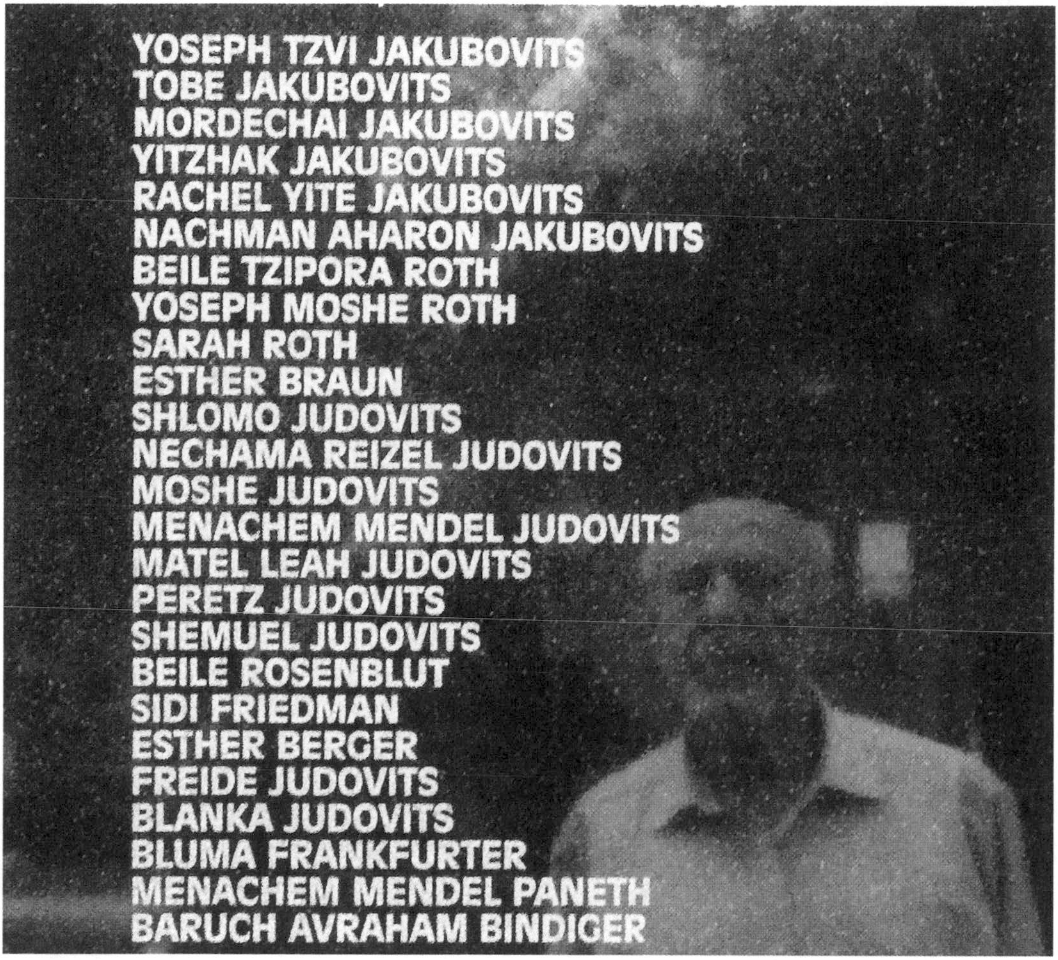

Photos by Dr. Sid Cohen

The Talmud Bavli is named such not only because it originated in Babylonia, but also because its contents are all *mevulbal*, mixed up. Mordechai Judovits's "Find it in the Talmud" is therefore an indispensable part of the library of any student of Talmud. This extraordinary Encyclopedia is well structured, highly organized and tremendously comprehensive thereby allowing any student, from the novice to the scholar, to find exactly what they are looking for in Judaism's most authoritative Rabbinic text, the Talmud. The author, R' Mordechai Judovits, is an outstanding personal example of the Talmud's morals, values and vision, that he so proficiently indexes in his book. For him, the Talmud's teachings and lessons are not esoteric or abstract law, but they represent a code of conduct and a way of life that have defined his incredible personal story. R' Mordechai displayed incredible perseverance and tenacity in surviving the Holocaust, but more than survive, he has thrived in rebuilding his family and becoming a transformational leader in the Jewish community. Thanks to him, whether you are looking for a Rabbinic quote, biographical information, or a timeless teaching, you can easily "Find it in the Talmud."

I wish R' Mordechai many more years of Torah learning and Torah teaching in good health and happiness, with nachas from his family.

With admiration and love,

Rabbi Efrem Goldberg

Dr. Israel Drazin
22164 Verbena Way
Boca Raton, Florida 33433
Phone 561-368-4350
IDDrazin@comcast.net
booksnthoughts.com

Find It in the Talmud is a comprehensive, clear, and informative collection of over a thousand entries that give readers, lay and scholar, the views of prominent Talmudic rabbis on many subjects in an enjoyable manner. Mordechai Judovits arranges his short, to-the-point entries of Talmudic subjects, stories, and expressions in alphabetical order. He summarizes what the Talmud says and gives the sources of the statements. He shows his deep love of the Talmud, which he showed previously in his *Sages of the Talmud*, a love which his writings make delightfully infectious. The book is easy to follow. He identifies subjects dealing with ethics, morality, charity, and justice with a Star of David, and anecdotes with the image of a book. The many other subjects receive no special mark. Judovits includes a separate section containing hundreds of interesting Talmudic expressions, such as "even though a Jew sinned, he is still a Jew." He also includes a brief history of the Talmudic sages. Readers will benefit by learning many details about Judaism as well as obtaining a comprehensive historical overview.

Rabbi Dr. Israel Drazin
Author of *Maimonides: The Exceptional Mind*
and co-author of the five-volume set *Onkelos on the Torah*

Contents

Acknowledgments / 17

Introduction / 19

Find It in the Talmud:
Subjects Entries Listed Alphabetically / 29

The Talmud:
An Overview of the Order of the Talmud / 445

Abbreviations / 487

Talmudic Expressions / 489

Acknowledgments

As a Holocaust survivor, I am grateful to Hashem for rescuing me from the extermination camps and from so many close calls with death, and for inspiring me and giving me strength to write this book.

Publishing this book is the culmination of over ten years of work, research, and study. It would not have been possible without the encouragement and patience of my beloved wife, Helen, *a"h*, who passed away two years ago, on the eleventh of Elul in the year 5771 (2011).

My thanks and appreciation to Rabbi Efrem Goldberg, the rabbi of the Boca Raton Synagogue, for his endorsement, and his Rebbetzin Yocheved Goldberg for their support and encouragement in all my efforts.

The environment of the Boca Raton Synagogue had a lot to do with enabling me to write this book; every waking hour in this synagogue is filled with Divrei Torah. It is considered to be one of the flagship synagogues in America.

It is with much appreciation that I thank Rabbi Dr. Israel Drazin, author of many books, for his encouragement and his endorsement.

I would also like to express my thanks and appreciation to Rabbi Ben Sugerman for editing my book, reading every word in my manuscript and for his many valuable suggestions. With a BA in Psychology from Yeshiva University and Rabbinic Ordination from Ohr HaChaim, Rabbi Sugerman has been in Jewish Education for over fifteen years. Currently, he is a Department Head at Weinbaum Yeshiva High School in Boca Raton and has been serving the school for over a decade. He has taught both formally and informally to high school, college, and adult education students, and his Daf Yomi can be heard daily on YUTorah.org. He and his wife Rebecca are the proud parents of eight delightful children.

Yasher Koach to Mr. Tzvi Mauer, publisher of Urim Publications, the publisher of two of my books: *Sages of the Talmud* and *Find It in the Talmud*.

I would also like to express my appreciation to my editor at Urim Publications, Mrs. Batsheva Pomerantz. Her input and meticulous editing of my book resulted in weeding out the imperfections and improving the quality of the book.

— Mordechai Judovits, Kislev 5774

Introduction

IT IS A GREAT HONOR and privilege to introduce my new book, *Find It in the Talmud*. This book is not a complicated Talmudic discourse, which can be the case in many books written about the Talmud. Rather it is a guide to students of the Talmud to locate a subject among the thousands of topics discussed in the Talmud.

The Talmud contains an immense number of topics which are spread throughout its sixty-three volumes. Even an experienced student would have difficulty finding a specific subject.

This book does not deal with the final Halachah. Halachic decisions have to be decided by rabbis of great scholarship who are recognized by other contemporary rabbis as the great halachic authorities of their generation.

THE ENTRIES

Most entries in this book are very brief – consisting only of the title of the topic and the description thereof. However, many entries consist of an event that took place or a complete story.

Subjects that deal with ethics, morality, charity, decency, and justice are symbolized with the Star of David. Its symbol, ✡, is placed at the start of the entry.

Entries of anecdotes and stories are symbolized with a book. Its image, 📖, is placed at the start of the entry.

The emphasis in this book is on ethics, morality, charity, decency, and justice.

Every entry in the book points the reader to at least one citation in the Talmud, where the subject is being discussed.

Some entries are duplicated under different headings. In most cases, entries are repeated to emphasize the ethical and proper conduct advocated by the Talmud.

The entries are alphabetically arranged according to the English alphabet, except the section of Talmudic expressions, which is arranged according to the Hebrew alphabet.

If the reader is looking for names or entries beginning with the letter ח (*het*), like "Cherem" or "Cheshbon," it is transliterated with "h" as "Herem" or "Heshbon."

*

Included in the book are photos of the Holocaust Memorial, designed and planned by the author, which stands near the entrance of the Boca Raton Synagogue.

It is an eyewitness account of the atrocities perpetrated against the Jewish people in Europe during World War II. The names of the families of the author and his wife, as well as hundreds of other martyrs who were murdered in the Holocaust, are engraved on the granite pillars of the monument.

The monument illustrates the lack of morality and decency that prevailed during that period. The continuation of the study of Talmud today is a victory of the spirit – with its emphasis on ethics and morality. This book facilitates and enhances the study of the Talmud.

*

The following entries illustrate the stories and anecdotes which have a message of ethics or morality.

Tree overhanging
It happened that Rabbi Yannai had a tree, which overhung on a public road. Another man in town also had a tree hanging over a public street. Some people who used the street objected, and the man was summoned to the court of R. Yannai.

R. Yannai said to them: "Go home and come back tomorrow." During the night, he had his workers cut down his own tree. On the next day when they came back for a decision, he ordered the man to cut down his tree. The man objected, saying to the rabbi: But you, sir, also have a tree hanging over?"

R. Yannai answered: "Go and see. If mine is cut down, then cut yours; if it is not, you need not cut yours."

What was R. Yannai's thinking? At first he thought that people would be happy to sit in the shade of the tree. (*Bava Batra* 60a)

Rabbis' field
Two rabbis negotiated to buy the same field; each rabbi was unaware of the other
On one occasion, Rabbi Giddal was negotiating to buy a certain field, but in the meantime R. Abba bought the field.

R. Giddal was unhappy and complained to R. Zera who in turn took the complaint to R. Yitzhak Nepaha, who lived in another town.

R. Zera said to R. Giddal: "Wait until he comes here for the festival."

When R. Yitzhak came, and he was presented with the case, he asked R. Abba: "If a poor man wants to buy a cake and examines it, but in the meantime another man comes and takes it away from him and buys it, what then?"

"He is called a wicked man," replied R. Abba."

"Then why did you buy the field that R. Giddal wanted to buy?"

"I did not know that he was negotiating for it."

R. Yitzhak suggested that now that he does know, he should let him have it.

"I cannot sell it to him, because it is the first field I ever bought, and it is not a good omen to sell it, but if he wants it as a gift, he can have it."

But R. Giddal refused to accept it as a gift, and R. Abba did not want it, because R. Giddal negotiated for it. And so no one took possession of the field, and it was called "the Rabbis' field." (*Kiddushin* 59a)

TALMUDIC EXPRESSIONS

The Talmud has many expressions and maxims, which are best expressed in Hebrew or Aramaic. This book has a separate section encompassing hundreds of these expressions – in Hebrew or Aramaic.

The following are illustrations of those expressions:

Self-incrimination אין אדם משים עצמו רשע

No man may declare himself wicked. (*Yevamot* 25b; *Ketubbot* 18b; *Sanhedrin* 9b, 25a)

אין גוזרין גזירה על הצבור אלא אם כן רוב הצבור יכולין לעמוד בה

No law may be imposed upon the public unless a majority of the people can endure it. (*Avodah Zarah* 36a; *Horayot* 3b; *Bava Kamma* 79b; *Bava Batra* 60b; *Horayot* 3b)

A Jew is a Jew is a Jew אף על פי שחטא ישראל הוא

R. Abba bar Zavda said: "Even though a Jew sinned, he is still a Jew. Thus people say, a myrtle, even when it is mixed in with reeds is still a myrtle and is so called." (*Sanhedrin* 44a)

דינא דמלכותא דינא

R. Shemuel said: "The law of the land is the law." One has to obey the laws of the land in which he lives. (*Bava Kamma* 113a; *Bava Batra* 54b; *Gittin* 10b; *Nedarim* 28a)

Shaming a person in public המלבין פני חבירו ברבים כאילו שופך דמים

A Tanna said before R. Nahman b. Yitzhak: "Anyone who shames another person in public is equal to shedding the blood of another person." (*Bava Metzia* 58b, 59a)

כוסו כיסו כעסו

R. Illai said: "One can recognize a person's character by three things: his cup, his purse, and his anger. (*Eruvin* 65b)

A certainty! פסיק רישא ולא ימות

Let his head be cut off, but let him not die. This is a dialectic term for a sure consequence of an act. (*Shabbat* 75a, 103a, 111b, 117a, 120b, 133a, 143a; *Ketubbot* 6b; *Bechorot* 25a)

קשוט עצמך ואחר כך קשוט אחרים

Resh Lakish said: "Correct yourself first before you correct others." (*Bava Metzia* 107b; *Bava Batra* 60b; *Sanhedrin* 18a, 19a)

תפסת מרובה לא תפסת

If you try to grasp a lot, you will not be able to hold on to it. If you try to do too much, you won't accomplish anything. (*Rosh Hashanah* 4b)

THE MISHNA AND THE GEMARA

The sixty-three volumes of books which are called the Talmud consist of two distinct separate component parts. One is called the Mishna and the other is known as the Gemara.

THE MISHNA

The Mishna is written in the Hebrew language and was authored by the rabbis known as Tannaim. Rabbi Yehuda HaNasi, who lived in the second and third centuries CE, was the final redactor of the Mishna.

To be more accurate, not all the authors of the Mishna are called Tannaim. The earlier authors were called The Men of the Great Assembly, Anshei Knesset HaGedolah. Some of the early authors worked in pairs and they are known by the title of Zugot –pairs.

THE ZUGOT

The following rabbis are known as the Zugot of the Talmud:

Rabbi Yosi ben Yoezer and Rabbi Yosi ben Yohanan; Rabbi Yehoshua ben Perahia and Rabbi Nittai HaArbeli; Rabbi Yehuda ben Tabbai and Rabbi Shimon ben Shetah; Rabbi Shemaya and Rabbi Avtalyon, and Rabbi Hillel and Rabbi Shammai.

THE GEMARA

The other component of the Talmud which is called the Gemara is written in the old Aramaic language, mixed with Hebrew words. It was authored by the rabbis known as Amoraim.

Rabbi Ashi (4th century CE), and R. Ravina (fourth and fifth centuries CE) were the final compilers and editors of the Gemara.

The Talmud is also referred to as the Shas, an acronym for the two words *shisha sedarim* (Hebrew for "six orders"), because the Mishna is divided into six categories of topics. These are further subdivided into several books on specific subjects, each of which is called a *masechet* (tractate). The tractates are divided into chapters called *perakim* (singular: *perek*), and then divided into smaller units, which are called *mishnayot* (singular: *mishna*).

Each mishna is accompanied by a Gemara text that sometimes dissects the mishna word by word and explains its meaning. At other times, when other sources might seem to contradict this mishna in question, the Gemara reconciles the other sources with it.

WHO IS RABBI YEHUDA OR RABBI SHIMON?

Who is Rabbi Yehuda and who is Rabbi Shimon? This question arises because the Talmud refers very frequently to a Tanna or Amora by his first name only.

For example, the Talmud will say when quoting: "Rabbi Yehuda said," or "Rabbi Yosi said," or "Rabbi Shimon said" – using their first name only.

The question is, which Rabbi Yehuda made this statement, since there are numerous rabbis by the name of Yehuda, and likewise, numerous rabbis named Yosi and Shimon.

WHO ARE THE RABBIS REFERRED TO BY THEIR FIRST NAME ONLY?

A little history is now necessary to show how the names of certain Tannaim fit into the picture. It will also reveal to which Rabbis the Talmud refers when it mentions only their first name.

In 132 CE, Bar Kochva, a Jewish warrior and hero, led a revolution in Eretz Yisrael against the Romans who occupied the Land of Israel. About 400,000 armed men joined him. They fought so successfully that Tinnius Rufus, the governor of Judea under Emperor Hadrian, had to give up fifty strongholds.

Hadrian sent his greatest general, Julius Severus. After three years, the revolt faltered, and the Romans destroyed 985 towns. Betar, where Bar Kochva made his last stand, fell in 135 CE.

After the revolt was suppressed, Hadrian issued many harsh decrees in Judea, forbidding the practice of Judaism. Judea was completely defeated. The revolt claimed the lives of 580,000 men, in addition to thousands of women and children who died of starvation. Many were sold as slaves.

The Sanhedrin was dissolved in 135 CE. Rabbi Akiva, who supported the revolt and disobeyed the edict against the teaching of Torah, was jailed for three years, and subsequently put to death.

Hadrian removed the Jewish population from Jerusalem, replaced the Jews with Syrians and Phoenicians. In 136 CE, he rebuilt Jerusalem and called the city Aelia Capitolina.

RABBIS ORDAINED UNDER THE PERIL OF DEATH

R. Yehuda ben Bava wanted to ordain his students, but there was a decree against it. Tinnius Rufus enforced the ban cruelly.

The Talmud relates how Rabbi Yehuda ben Bava became a martyr when he attempted to disobey the decree (*Sanhedrin* 14a):

During the Hadrian persecution, the authorities issued a decree stating the following: anyone ordaining a rabbi would be subject to the death penalty; anyone receiving ordination would be subject to the death penalty; the city where the ordination takes place would be demolished, and the boundaries around the city would be uprooted.

> In order to avoid causing the destruction of a city, Rabbi Yehuda b. Bava sat between two great mountains and between the two cities of Usha and Shefaram. Five prominent students sat before him: Rabbi Meir, Rabbi Yehuda, Rabbi Shimon, Rabbi Yosi, and Rabbi Eleazar ben Shammua. The ceremony was held and he ordained them. Rabbi Avia adds the name of Rabbi Nehemya to the list of those ordained. As soon as the ceremony was finished, they noticed the Romans approaching. Rabbi Yehuda told his students to flee. "What will happen to you?" his students asked. They wanted to take him with them, but he urged them to flee without him. "I would cause all of you to be caught. I am too old to run. I will lie before them like a stone." It was said that the Romans stabbed him 300 times. It is noteworthy that four out of the five students were named only by their first name. They are the same names repeated later on all over the Talmud without adding their father's name.

The following story appears in the Talmud in *Shabbat* 33b:

> Come and listen: When the rabbis entered the Kerem Be-Yavne, Rabbi Yehuda, Rabbi Eleazar b. Yosi and Rabbi Shimon were among those present, and a question was raised before them. The speaker who speaks first on all occasions was R. Yehuda b. Illai. He rose to answer the question.

The Talmud identifies here that R. Yehuda is the same as R. Yehuda b. Illai. The Talmud discusses the subject at hand, and later on asks why R. Yehuda is called the first speaker on all occasions. It answers with the following story:

R. Yehuda, R. Yosi, and R. Shimon were sitting together and a person by the name of Yehuda, a son of proselytes, was sitting next to them. Rabbi Yehuda was telling them how great the works of the Roman occupiers were. They created roads, built bridges, and established public baths. R. Yosi listened, but made no comment.

R. Shimon b. Yohai commented: "Whatever the Romans have done, they have done for their own benefit. They built neighborhoods to have places for their prostitutes; they built bathhouses in order to indulge their bodies, and they built bridges to levy tolls on them." Yehuda, the son of proselytes, repeated the discussion to friends and relatives. Eventually, it was repeated to the authorities. It was decreed that R. Yehuda, who praised the Romans, would be rewarded; R. Yosi, who was silent, should be punished and held in his own community of Sepphoris, and R. Shimon was condemned to death.

R. Shimon and his son R. Eleazar ran away and hid in the Bet Midrash. His wife brought them bread and water, but this did not last, because they were worried the Romans would discover them. They fled and hid in a cave. Miraculously, a carob tree grew near the cave and a water-well was revealed to them. They shed their clothing all day long and sat naked in the sand, up to their neck to prevent their clothing from wearing out. They studied all day long and put on their clothes every day – only for prayers. They hid in the cave twelve years. Eventually Eliyahu came to the entrance and called out: "Who will inform the son of Yohai that the Emperor is dead and the decrees have been annulled?" When they heard the good news, they came out from the cave. (*Shabbat* 33b)

In the beginning of the story, Rabbi Shimon is called by his first name only, but further on he is identified as Rabbi Shimon b. Yohai.

Although R. Yosi is again called only by his first name, it is obvious that the rabbi in question is R. Yosi b. Halafta. In the story above, he is banished to Sepphoris, the hometown of R. Yosi b. Halafta, and the home of his father and family.

These rabbis – Yehuda b. Illai, Shimon b. Yohai, Yosi b. Halafta, Eleazar ben Shammua, and Meir – were colleagues, all contemporary students of Rabbi Akiva and Rabbi Yehuda b. Bava.

They were the rabbis who emerged after the catastrophe of the failed Bar Kochva revolt to re-establish the religious life of a defeated nation. They gave their opinions and rulings, which were collected in the mishnayot. When they quoted one another, they did it by their first name only because they were colleagues. When they quoted older sources or other rabbis, they used their full names. Therefore, we can establish that when the Talmud quotes only the first name of:

Rabbi Yehuda, it refers to Rabbi Yehuda bar Illai; Rabbi Yosi is Rabbi Yosi ben Halafta, and Rabbi Shimon is Rabbi Shimon ben Yohai.

When Hadrian died in 138 CE, Antoninus Pius became emperor. In 139 CE, after the Hadrian persecution subsided somewhat, the students of R. Akiva assembled at Usha to re-establish the halachic authorities and to reinstitute the Sanhedrin. Among those assembled was R. Meir, R. Yehuda b. Illai, R. Yosi b. Halafta, and R. Shimon b. Yohai. At a subsequent meeting, they elected R. Gamliel as president, R. Nathan as vice president, and R. Meir as Hacham.

When the name of R. Eliezer is mentioned on its own, it refers to the Tanna R. Eliezer b. Horkynos.

When the name of R. Yehoshua is mentioned on its own, it refers to the Tanna R. Yehoshua b. Chanania.

As a rule, when the Talmud mentions the name Eleazar without mentioning the father's name, it refers to R. Eleazar b. Pedat, an Amora during the third century CE, and head of the academy in Tiberias. He was a colleague of R. Yohanan b. Nepaha.

This R. Eleazar is not to be mistaken with the Tanna R. Eleazar b. Shammua.

There were several Amoraim by the name of Rabbah, but when the Talmud mentions the name of Rabbah without referring to his father's name, it refers to Rabbah b. Nahmeni.

Rav was the name of the famous head of the Sura academy. But Rav is also a title for a rabbi as for instance: Rav Yehuda.

Rav Yehuda is R. Yehuda b. Yehezkel. He was the founder and the head of the academy in Pumbedita, and was a student of Rav.

WHERE ARE THE NAMES OF AVRAHAM, MOSHE, AHARON, DAVID OR SHLOMO?

These traditional Hebrew names are completely absent. Not even one of the hundreds of rabbis in the Talmud is named after Moshe, who was the greatest rabbi of them all.

In answering this question, we must consider the conditions under which the Jews lived. During the entire Talmudic period, they endured constant persecution. The people of Israel feared not only the foreign occupiers, but also their own leaders, such as the paranoid Herod, and even some of the earlier Hasmonean kings, who were insecure regarding their position. For many years, the Jews were under Syrian and Roman occupation, and circumcision was forbidden.

Parents naming their newborn children feared the authorities. They were already risking their children's and their own lives by circumcising their children. Giving the children traditional Hebrew names posed an added risk.

For example, the name Avraham is significant not only because it belonged to the founder of the Jewish faith, but also because it is associated with circumcision. If a child was named Avraham, the authorities would know for certain that he had been circumcised. A child named after Moshe – the greatest Jewish leader – might be considered a threat to anyone who aspired to be king. Naming a child Aharon could be interpreted as an act of defiance against all the high priests who were appointed by the foreign occupiers. To name a son after an actual Jewish king, like David or Shlomo, might be considered an act of outright rebellion.

The above answer is my own. While it is speculative, I believe that it is plausible.

IN WHAT TIME PERIOD DID THE VARIOUS TANNAIM AND AMORAIM LIVE?

The majority of the Tannaim lived in the first and second centuries CE, but some of the Tannaim mentioned in the Mishna lived earlier. The Anshei Knesset HaGedolah, who preceded the Tannaim, were active in the time of Ezra and Nehemia, in approximately the fifth century BCE.

The Amoraic period, which started in the 3rd century CE during Rav's time, lasted until the 5th century CE.

Rav was probably the last of the Tannaim and the first of the Amoraim. According to the Talmud (*Ketubbot* 8a), Rav may differ with a Tanna because he is also a Tanna, even though Rav is never quoted in the Mishna where only the Tannaim are quoted.

THE SACRIFICES THE SAGES MADE FOR TORAH STUDY

When we study the Talmud, we see only a glimpse of the great sacrifices made by the Sages in order to study Torah. These scholars, giants of the Talmud, ignored their own suffering and ignored their poverty in order to pass on this heritage to us. The following excerpts from the Talmud illustrate under what conditions they lived.

Rabbi Akiva's water spilled

> Rabbi Akiva was imprisoned, because he defied the Roman authorities by teaching Torah in public. R. Yehoshua HaGarsi attended to Rabbi Akiva in prison. Every day he brought him a certain quantity of water. One day the prison keeper said to him: "Your water today is much too much. Perhaps you want to use it to undermine the prison?"
>
> The prison keeper spilled out half of it and the rest he let R. Yehoshua take inside. When he brought the water to Rabbi Akiva who saw the small amount of water, Rabbi Akiva said: "Yehoshua, don't you know that I am an old man and my life depends on you?" Rabbi Yehoshua told him what happened.
>
> Rabbi Akiva said to him: "Give me some water to wash my hands before I eat bread."
>
> The other hesitated: "It will not even suffice for drinking, let alone for washing hands."

Rabbi Akiva answered him: "What can I do, for disobeying the words of the rabbis one deserves to die?"

He refused to taste any food until R. Yehoshua brought him water to wash his hands first. (*Eruvin* 21b)

Shema on Rabbi Akiva's lips when he died

When R. Akiva was taken out to be executed, it was the time for the recital of *Shema*. While they were tearing his flesh with iron combs, he was accepting upon himself the kingship of Heaven. His students asked him: "Rabbi, do you have to go to such extremes?"

He answered: "All my life I have been troubled by a verse in the Torah which says 'with all your soul.' I wondered when I would have the opportunity to fulfill this commandment. Now that I have the opportunity, shall I not fulfill it?" (*Berachot* 61b)

Another illustration is Rabbi Akiva's wife. She was the daughter of Kalba Savua, the richest man in Jerusalem. Her father was angry at her because she married R. Akiva against his will, and he cut her off from his will. On one occasion, she had to sell her hair to buy food.

These Talmudic giants ignored poverty, religious persecution, and all personal hardships in order to leave us a legacy and a guide to a way of life that no other nation possesses. There are hundreds of similar stories, anecdotes, and quotations in this book, *Find It in the Talmud*.

Subjects Entries Listed Alphabetically

This symbol 📖 denotes that the entry has a story or an anecdote with a message.
This symbol ✿ denotes that the entry is about ethics or a guide to proper conduct.

A

📖 Abandoned   הפקר
R. Yishmael b. R. Yosi was walking on the road and he met another man carrying a load of twigs. After a while, the man put his bundle down to rest; when he finished resting, he asked R. Yishmael to help him lift the bundle on his back. R. Yishmael asked him, "How much is it worth?" He said: "Half a *zuz*." R. Yishmael gave him a half a *zuz* and declared the bundle *hefker*.[1] The man took the *zuz* and declared: "I am re-acquiring the bundle; now please help me load it on my shoulder." R. Yishmael gave him another half a *zuz* and said, "I declare it *hefker* to everyone except you." (*Bava Metzia* 30b)

Abandoning the right of ownership מבטל את רשותו
One who gives up the right to the property (*Eruvin* 68b, 72b, 73b)

Abba   אבא
Amora from Eretz Yisrael

---

1. Disowned; it belongs to anyone who finds it.

3rd – 4th centuries CE (*Sanhedrin* 17b; *Bava Kamma* 117b)

Abba   אבא
Amora from Eretz Yisrael
3rd – 4th centuries CE (*Sotah* 40a)

Abba   אבא
Amora from Eretz Yisrael
4th – 5th centuries CE (*Bava Kamma* 27b)

Abba   אבא
Father of R. Yirmiyahu (*Shabbat* 56b)

✿ Abba Aricha
Rav was sometimes called Abba Aricha.
When Issi b. Hini came from Babylonia to Israel, R. Yohanan inquired, "Who is the head of the academy in Babylonia?" Issi answered, "Abba Aricha." "You simply call him Abba Aricha? I remember when I was sitting before Rebbe, seventeen rows behind Rav, sparks were flying from the mouth of Rebbe into the mouth of Rav and from the mouth of Rav into the mouth of Rebbe and I could not understand what they were saying, and you simply call him Abba Aricha?" (*Hullin* 137b)

Abba bar Avina   אבא בר אבינא
Amora from Eretz Yisrael
3rd century CE (*Shabbat* 60b)

Abba bar Kahana   אבא בר כהנא
Amora from Eretz Yisrael
3rd century CE (*Shabbat* 121b)

Abba bar Marta   אבא בר מרתא
Amora from Babylonia
3rd – 4th centuries CE (*Yoma* 84a)

Abba bar Memmel   אבא בר ממל
Amora from Eretz Yisrael
3rd – 4th centuries CE (*Ketubbot* 111a)

Abba bar Zavda   אבא בר זבדא
Amora from Eretz Yisrael
3rd century CE (*Sanhedrin* 44a)

Abba ben Abba HaKohen
                        אבא בן אבא הכהן
Amora from Babylonia
3rd century CE (*Berachot* 18b)

Abba Binyamin   אבא בנימין
Tanna from Jerusalem
1st century CE (*Bava Batra* 11a)

Abba Gurion Me-Sidon
                        צדיין אבא גוריון איש
Tanna from Eretz Yisrael
2nd century CE (*Kiddushin* 82a)

Abba Hilkiah   אבא חלקיה
Tanna from Eretz Yisrael
1st century CE (*Taanit* 23a–b)

Abba Kohen Bardella   אבא כהן ברדלא
Tanna from Eretz Yisrael
2nd century CE (*Bava Metzia* 10a)

Abba Shaul   אבא שאול
Tanna from Eretz Yisrael
2nd century CE (*Shabbat* 133b; *Niddah* 24b)

Abba Shaul b. Batnit אבא שאול בן בטנית
Tanna from Eretz Yisrael
1st century CE (*Betzah* 29a)

Abba Sikra   אבא סקרא
The head of the Biryoni in Jerusalem, and
nephew of R. Yohanan ben Zakkai
1st century CE[2] (*Gittin* 56a)

Abba Yosi b. Dostai   אבא יוסי בן דוסתאי
Tanna from Eretz Yisrael
2nd century CE (*Yoma* 22b)

Abba Yosi b. Hanan   אבא יוסי בן חנן
Tanna from Eretz Yisrael
1st century CE (*Middot* 2:6)

Abbaye   אביי
Amora from Babylonia
Head of the academy in Pumbedita
3rd – 4th centuries CE
(*Berachot* 56a; *Kiddushin* 31b; *Ketubbot* 65a)
Abbaye's wife's name was Huma.

Abbaye Kashisha   אביי קשישא
Amora from Babylonia
2nd – 3rd centuries CE (*Sanhedrin* 7a;
Ketubbot 96b)

Abbreviated prayers
Sometimes one may say the prayers in
abbreviated form.[3] (*Berachot* 3a, 28b)

Above and beyond   לפנים משורת הדין
To perform a mitzvah beyond the re-
quirement of the law (*Bava Kamma* 100a; *Bava
Metzia* 30b)

Abridged Hallel
The Psalms of *Hallel* should be recited
in its entirety during the prayers on holidays; however there are days when only

---

2. See entry, Escape from besieged Jerusalem.
3. See the story of R. Yosi.

an abridged *Hallel* is recited. (*Taanit* 28b; *Pesahim* 117a)

✿ Abrogate a ruling
By Rav and Shemuel

R. Nahman came to visit the town of Sura, and R. Hisda and Rabbah b. R. Huna went to see him; they asked him to abrogate a certain ruling by Rav and Shemuel.

He replied to them: "Do you think I have traveled this long distance to come here to annul a ruling of Rav and Shemuel?" (*Shevuot* 48b)

✿ Absence of Torah
R. Eleazar b. Azariah said: "Where there is no Torah there is no proper conduct; where proper conduct is absent there is no Torah."[4] (*Avot* 3:21)

📖 Absent from home
A scholar was absent from his home for twelve years to study Torah

It is related that R. Hanania went to the academy in Bene Berak and spent twelve years there. By the time he returned home, the streets of the town were altered and he was unable to find his way home. He decided to go to the riverbank to be oriented; there he heard people addressing a young girl: "Daughter of Hachinai, fill up your pitcher and let us go."

He didn't recognize her, but followed her and found his home where his wife was sifting flour. When she turned around and saw her husband, she was so overcome with joy that she fainted. (*Ketubbot* 62b)

Abstain not from Torah
R. Yehuda said in the name of Rav: "One should not abstain from the Bet Midrash even for a single hour." (*Shabbat* 83b)

Abstinence
Abstinence during the נדה *peri*

R. Meir said: "Why did the ?
that the duration of uncleanı
the menstruation period be sev
order that the absence will make their love even greater." (*Niddah* 31b)

📖 Abusers of power
Sectarians tortured R. Safra

R. Avohu praised R. Safra to the Minim[5] as a great scholar, and consequently they exempted him from paying taxes for thirteen years. One day they encountered him and they asked him to explain a passage in the Bible. He could not give them an answer. They took a scarf and wound it around his neck and tortured him.

When R. Avohu came and found him being tortured, he asked: "Why do you torture him?"

They answered: "Have you not told us that he is a great scholar? He cannot even explain the meaning of a verse in the Bible."

He replied: "I might have told you that he is a great scholar, but what I meant was that he is a scholar in Tannaitic learning, but not in scripture."

"But how is it that you do know scripture?"

"The rabbis and I who are with you frequently make it our business to study it thoroughly, but others do not." (*Avodah Zarah* 4a)

✿ Academy had tight quarters
R. Yohanan stated: "When we were studying at R. Oshaya, four of us sat cramped together in an area of one cubit." (*Eruvin* 53a)

📖 Academy in Heaven
The Talmud relates that there was some money belonging to orphans deposited at

---

4. See also entry, Bread without Torah

5. Sectarians.

Rabbi Shemuel's father. When his father passed away, Shemuel was not in town. Shemuel went to the cemetery and said, "I want to speak to my father."

They told him:[6] "He has gone up to learn in the Heavenly Academy." Shemuel noticed that the spirit of Rabbi Levi, who had passed away some time ago, was sitting outside. He asked him, "Why have you not gone up to the academy?" He replied: "I was told that for as many years that I did not attend the academy of Rabbi Afes and hurt his feelings, for that many years I will not be admitted to the Heavenly Academy."[7] (*Berachot* 18b)

Academy in Rome

R. Matya was born in Eretz Yisrael, and was a student of Rabbi Yohanan ben Zakkai, but in his later years he established a great academy in Rome. (*Sanhedrin* 32b)

✿ Academy in Sura rebuilt

R. Hisda spent a large sum of money to have the academy in Sura rebuilt. He renovated it when it became neglected and was in a rundown condition. (*Pesahim* 113a)

Academy students in great numbers

The Talmud states that when the majority of the rabbis departed from the academy of Rav in Sura, there still remained behind 1,200 students. When the students left the academy of R. Huna, there remained behind 800 students.

When R. Huna delivered a lecture thirteen interpreters assisted him.

When the students left the academy of Rabbah and R. Yosef in Pumbedita, there remained 400 students, and they described themselves as orphans. When the students left the academy of R. Abbaye, in Pumbedita, others say from the academy of R. Papa, and still others say from the academy of R. Ashi, there remained 200 rabbis, and they described themselves as orphans of the orphans.
(*Ketubbot* 106a)

Accessories on Shabbat

What accessories can women wear on Shabbat is discussed in *Bameh isha*, the 6th *perek* in *Shabbat*. (*Shabbat* 57a)

Acco עכו

The academy of Acco, also called Acre, is located in this coastal city in northern Israel, north of Haifa.

It was already an important town in the 15th century BCE and was best known in the old days for producing glass. R. Abba lived in Acco and was the head of the academy there. He lived in the 3rd – 4th centuries CE. (*Sotah* 40a)

According to his means השג יד

Heseg Yad (*Arachin* 5a, 17a)

✿ Accurate

Be accurate, do not estimate

R. Gamliel said: "Provide yourself a teacher and you will avoid making mistakes. Train yourself to be accurate and not to estimate." (*Avot* 1:16)

📖 Accused of arrogance

R. Eliezer Zera once put on black shoes[8] and stood in the marketplace of Nehardea. When the staff of the Resh Galuta saw him there, they said to him: "Why are you wearing black shoes?"

He replied: "I am mourning over Jerusalem."

"Who do you think you are to show such arrogance to mourn in public over Jerusalem?" They put him in jail.

"But I am a scholar," he said to them.

---

6. The spirits.
7. See also entry, Trustee for orphans.

8. A sign of mourning.

"Prove it."

He proved it by answering their questions. (*Bava Kamma* 59a–b)

Achievments ignored

R. Pinhas lamented: "Since the Temple was destroyed, scholars and noblemen were put to shame and they cover their faces. Men of achievements are disregarded; pushy men and loudmouth men gained the upper hand. There is no one to rely upon except our Father in Heaven." (*Sotah* 49a)

Achsadra אכסדרה

An open porch, it has halachic implications (*Bava Batra* 11b)

Acquiring land in Israel by a non-Jew
יש קנין לנכרי בארץ ישראל

A non-Jew can acquire land in Israel to free the crop from the obligation of tithing. (*Bava Metzia* 101a; *Gittin* 47a; *Menahot* 31a; *Bechorot* 11b)

Acquiring property

Act required to acquire an object

Abbaye and Rava stated that מסירה *mesirah*, meaning handing over, confers legal ownership in a public area or in a courtyard that belongs to neither of them; משיכה *meshichah*, meaning pulling, confers ownership in an alley or in a courtyard owned by both of them, and הגבהה *hagbahah*, lifting, confers ownership everywhere. (*Bava Batra* 76b)

Acquiring that which does not exist
אדם מקנה דבר שלא בא לעולם

One can transfer that which did not yet come to this world. The opinion of R. Meir (*Bava Metzia* 33b; *Bava Batra* 79b, 127b, 131a, 141b, 157a; *Yevamot* 93a; *Kiddushin* 62b; *Gittin* 13b, 42b)

Acrobatic feats

Rabbi Levi was often a guest at Rabbi Yehuda HaNasi, and he used to entertain his guests with acrobatic feats.

It is related that he used to juggle with eight knives in front of Rabbi Yehuda HaNasi, but at one time he dislocated his hip during a performance, which resulted in a permanent limp.

R. Shemuel used to juggle before King Shapur with eight glasses of wine, and Abbaye used to juggle before Rabbah with eight eggs, or some say with four eggs. (*Sukkah* 53a)

Act objectionable to others מראית עין

Do not flaunt doing things in public, which might be objectionable to your neighbors (*Avodah Zarah* 12a; *Shabbat* 64b)

Adda b. Abba אדא בר אבא
Amora from Babylonia
4th century CE (*Bava Batra* 22a)

Adda b. Ahava אדא בר אהבה
Amora from Babylonia
3rd century CE (*Berachot* 42b; *Kiddushin* 72a; *Bava Metzia* 47a)

Admon b. Gaddai אדמון
Tanna and judge from Eretz Yisrael
1st century CE (*Ketubbot* 105a)

Adam's sacrifice

R. Yehuda said: "The animal sacrificed by Adam was a one-horn animal." (*Shabbat* 28b)

Adasha עדשה
Lentil; a halachic measurement (*Bava Kamma* 25b; *Shabbat* 64a; *Bava Batra* 16b)

✿ Administrator of the community

R. Yohanan said in the name of R. Shimon b. Yehotzedek: A community should not appoint an administrator over its affairs unless he carries a basket of reptiles on his back. If he becomes arrogant the community can tell him, turn around. (*Yoma* 22b)

✿ Admiration for a colleague

Whenever R. Hisda and R. Sheshet met each other they trembled in admiration of each other. R. Hisda admired R. Sheshet's extensive knowledge of Mishna and R. Sheshet admired R. Hisda for his deep penetrating mind in *pilpul*. (*Eruvin* 67a)

✿ Admission to the Sanhedrin hall

It was learned that after they elected R. Eleazar b. Azariah as president of the Sanhedrin, they opened the doors on that day for all the disciples to enter the assembly. Prior to this Rabbi Gamliel had ordered that those students whose interior intellect does not match their exterior appearance may not enter (כל תלמיד שאין תוכו כברו לא יכנס).

Four hundred additional seats were brought in to accommodate the new students who entered the hall. (*Berachot* 27b)

✿ Admitting error

Rabbah b. Huna made a halachic statement, which R. Hisda questioned. After the correction, Rabbah b. Huna said through an interpreter. "A man does not fully understand the words of the Torah until he has been made to trip on the words." (*Gittin* 43a)

✿ Admitting mistake

R. Dimi quoted R. Yohanan with regards to a Halachah dealing with woven material. Later on when he came to Nehardea, he sent the following words: "The things I told you were erroneous," and he sent them the correct statement made by R. Yohanan. (*Shabbat* 63b)

Admitting in part   מודה במקצת

(*Bava Kamma* 107a; *Bava Metzia* 3a; *Ketubbot* 18a; *Gittin* 51b; *Shevuot* 42b)

Admitting to part of the claim
הודה מקצת הטענה

Admitting to part of the claim (*Bava Metzia* 4b; *Bava Batra* 128b)

Adrachta   אדרכתא

A halachic document of authorization to seize property (*Bava Batra* 169a; *Bava Kamma* 112b)

Adult

A minor versus an adult in Halachah (*Bava Kamma* 112a)

Advice

R. Baba b. Buta gave advice to King Herod to build the Temple.[9] (*Bava Batra* 4a)

✿ Advice to a son

The Talmud relates that Rav advised his son Hiyya: "Do not take drugs, do not leap in high jumps, and do not have your teeth extracted, do not provoke serpents, and do not provoke a Syrian woman." (*Pesahim* 113a)

Advice to a son[10]

(*Pesahim* 112a)

✿ Advice to Rabbah

Rabbah b. Nahmeni received a message from his brothers in Eretz Yisrael:

"Although you are a great scholar, you must admit that studying alone does not equal to studying with a master. And perhaps you think there is no one here with whom you could study; there is Rabbi Yohanan."

However, if you are not coming up to Eretz Yisrael, then we give you the following advice: "Do not sit too long, because sitting for a long time leads to abdominal troubles. Do not stand for a long time, because long standing is injurious

---

9. See entry, Herod building the Temple.
10. See entry, Akiva's instructions to his son.

to the heart. Do not walk too much, because excessive walking is harmful to the eyes. Rather divide your time into three thirds; one-third of the time sitting, one-third standing, and one-third walking. (*Ketubbot* 111a)

Advisors to Pharaoh
R. Hiyya b. Abba said in the name of R. Simai: "Pharaoh had three advisors: Bilam, Iyov (Job), and Yitro." (*Sotah* 11a)

📖 Advocate effective
R. Adda bar Ahava lived in the house of a proselyte. The proselyte and R. Bibi were in contention for the position of town administrator. They came before Rabbi Yosef, and R. Adda argued for the proselyte. After listening to both sides, Rabbi Yosef declared: "Let R. Bibi, who is a great man, give his attention to heavenly matters, like distributing charity, and let the proselyte pay attention to the affairs of the town." R. Abbaye remarked: "When one provides a scholar with housing, let him provide it for one like R. Adda bar Ahava, who is able to argue in his favor." (*Kiddushin* 76b)

Af Al Gav   אף על גב
Even though (*Shabbat* 7a)

Af Al Pi   אף על פי
Although (*Yevamot* 54b)

Afes   אפס
Amora from Eretz Yisrael
Head of the academy in Sepphoris
3rd century CE (*Berachot* 18b; *Ketubbot* 103b)

Afikoman   אפיקומן
Afikoman is a piece of matzah eaten at the end of the Seder; it is set aside earlier in the Seder meal for this purpose and no food is eaten after the *afikoman*. (*Pesahim* 119b)

After-meal blessing   ברכת המזון
Rava was a frequent visitor to the Exilarch and he said, "When we eat together at the Exilarch, we say *Birkat Hamazon* in groups of three." "Why not eat in groups of ten and say *Birkat Hamazon* in groups of ten?" "Because the Exilarch might hear them finish without waiting for him and get angry." (*Berachot* 50a)

After-meal blessing without bread
A meal where bread was not eaten, the blessing is usually that which includes the three blessings. (*Berachot* 44a, 37a)

After-meal fourth blessing
Rabbi Mathna said: "The fourth blessing after the meal was instituted in Yavne with reference to those who were slain in Betar."[11] (*Berachot* 48b; *Bava Batra* 121b; *Taanit* 31a)

Afternoon prayers
"A person should always be extra careful about the afternoon prayers. For the Prophet Eliyahu prayed in the afternoon and was answered favorably." (*Berachot* 6b)

Agav Orha   אגב אורחא
Incidentally, by the way (*Bava Metzia* 21b; *Sanhedrin* 95b)

Aggadata   אגדתא
R. Yehoshua b. Levi was an expert in Aggadata. (*Bava Kamma* 55a)

📖 Aggadata   אגדתא
R. Avohu and R. Hiyya b. Abba traveled to a place to deliver lectures. R. Hiyya b. Abba lectured on legal matters and R. Avohu lectured on Aggadah. The people left the hall where R. Hiyya was lecturing to go to listen to R. Avohu.[12] (*Sotah* 40a)

---

11. See also entry, Betar.
12. See also entry, Lecturers.

Aggadata

📖 **Aggadata** אגדתא **or Halachah**
The Talmud relates that when R. Ammi and R. Assi were sitting before R. Yitzhak Nepaha, one of them said to him: "Would you please tell us some Halachah." The other one said: "Would you please tell us some Aggadata."

He started speaking on Aggadata; one of them was not happy, and when he started instruction on Halachah, the other one was unhappy. He therefore stopped and told them; I will tell you a story. "A man had two wives, one young and one older. The young one used to pluck out his white hair, whereas the older one used to pluck out his black hair. At the end he was left bald on both sides. Therefore I will tell you something which will be interesting to both of you." (*Bava Kamma* 60b)

Agent
An agent appointed was asked to buy wheat. Instead, he bought barley. (*Bava Kamma* 102b)

✿ **Agent for R. Kahana**
R. Kahana gave money to an agent to buy him flax. In the meantime, the price of flax went up and the seller sold it on behalf of R. Kahana at a profit to R. Kahana. He came before Rav to ask if he can accept the deal. (*Bava Kamma* 103a)

Agent's power שלוחו של אדם כמותו
A man's agent is considered as himself. (*Bava Metzia* 96a; *Berachot* 34b)

Agent's power שלוחו של אדם אינו כמותו
A man's agent is not considered as himself. (*Bava Metzia* 96a)

📖 **Agility at eighty**
It was said of Rabbi Hanina that at the age of eighty he could stand on one foot and put on the shoe on the other foot. He credited the warm bath and the oil his mother

anointed him in his youth, with giving him this agility. (*Hullin* 24b)

Agra Pagra אגרא פגרא
Hire and loss: when leasing a boat, the lessee will be responsible if the ship is broken. (*Bava Metzia* 69b)

✿ **Agreement voided by Rava**
R. Papa and R. Huna bought sesame seeds on the bank of the Nahar Malka. They hired a boatman to bring the merchandise across the river, with a guarantee against any accident that might happen. However, the canal was stopped up and they couldn't deliver the merchandise. They told the boatman to hire donkeys and deliver, because he guaranteed it. The boatman appealed to Rava and he ruled against R. Papa and R. Huna. He said, "'White ducks that strip men of their clothing': This is an exceptional kind of situation." (*Gittin* 73a)

Agrippas אגריפס
King Agrippas was the last of the Herodean kings. (*Sotah* 41a; *Pesahim* 107b)

Agrippas the general
General Agrippas asked R. Gamliel. (*Avodah Zarah* 55a)

Agrippas's overseer
The overseer for King Agrippas asked R. Eliezer: "A person like me who eats only one meal a day, may I eat one meal in the *sukkah* and be exempt from the rest?"

He also asked R. Eliezer: "A person like me with two wives; one in Tiberias and one in Sepphoris; may I go from *sukkah* to *sukkah*?" (*Sukkah* 27a)

Agrippas took a census
King Agrippas wanted to take a census, but it was unpopular because the people feared that it meant new taxes. Agrippa

told the High Priest to take a kidney from each Pesach sacrifice. (*Pesahim* 64b)

Aguna עגונה

A deserted wife; a wife unable to get a divorce. (*Gittin* 33a)

Aha אחא

Amora from Eretz Yisrael
4th century CE (Talmud Yerushalmi *Shabbat* 6:9)

Aha Aricha b. Papa אחא אריכא

Amora from Babylonia
3rd – 4th centuries CE (*Berachot* 33a)

Aha bar Bizna אחא בר ביזנא

Amora from Eretz Yisrael
3rd – 4th centuries CE (*Berachot* 3b; *Sanhedrin* 16a)

Aha bar Hanina אחא בר חנינא

Amora from Eretz Yisrael
3rd – 4th centuries CE (*Sanhedrin* 41b)

Aha bar Rav אחא בר רב

Amora from Babylonia
4th – 5th centuries CE (*Hullin* 33a; *Sanhedrin* 76b)

Aha bar Yaakov אחא בר יעקב

Amora from Babylonia
3rd – 4th centuries CE (*Bava Kamma* 40a; *Kiddushin* 35a)

Aha Cartigna R. אחא קרטיגנא

(Hana Cartigna) (*Bava Kamma* 114b)

Ahadboi אחדבוי

The sons of Rabbi Mathna were Rabbi Ahadboi, Rabbi Tobi, and Rabbi Hiyya. (*Bava Batra* 151a)

Ahai b. Yoshaya אחי ברבי יאשיה

Tanna from Babylonia
2nd century CE (*Kiddushin* 72a)

Ahala אהלא

Aloe, used for medicinal purposes. (*Shabbat* 90a)

Aharon אהרון

High Priest, biblical figure, and brother of Moshe Rabbeinu (*Megillah* 25b)

Ahas Beta Gif אח״ס בט״ע גי״ף

A combination of letters in a code whereby the first letter is replaced with the 8th letter; as for instance, א is replaced with ח and so on. It is similar to At Bash א״ת ב״ש where the first letter is replaced with the last letter and the second from the first is replaced with the second from the last. (*Shabbat* 104a)

Ahashverosh אחשורוש

R. Abba b. Kahana said: "When King Ahashverosh removed his ring, it was a greater accomplishment than the accomplishments of forty-eight prophets and seven prophetesses. For all of them were not able to improve the lot of Israel as much as this one act." (*Megillah* 14a)

Ahav אחאב

King of Israel (*Bava Kamma* 17a)

Ahaz מלך אחז

King of Judea (*Avodah Zarah* 52b)

📖 Aher (Elisha ben Avuyah) אחר

Elisha b. Avuyah was a great scholar and R. Meir was one of his students. In his later years, Elisha became a non-believer.

Our rabbis taught: Once Aher was riding on a horse on the Shabbat, and Rabbi Meir was walking behind him to learn Torah from him. When they had gone a distance, Aher said to R. Meir, "Turn back, because by my measurement we have gone already to the limit of the *techum-Shabbat*." Rabbi Meir answered him: "You too turn back." Aher replied: "Have I not told you that I have heard from behind the heavenly curtain that there is a way back to Judaism for everyone except for Aher?"

But Rabbi Meir prevailed upon him and took him to a schoolhouse. Aher stopped a child in the school and asked: "Recite for me the verse you learned today." The child recited a verse from the Prophet Yeshaya.

"There is no peace for the wicked, says the Lord."

They went to another school and Aher asked a child to recite his verse. The child recited another verse, which was similar in rebuke to the wicked. They went to a total of thirteen schoolhouses and all the children quoted verses in a similar vein. The last child stuttered, and the word he used sounded like Elisha, with a rebuke. Aher, whose name was Elisha, got angry and said: "Had I a knife in my hand I would have cut him up." (*Hagigah* 15a)

Aher   אחר

Rabbi Yosef said: "Aher wouldn't have sinned had he interpreted the Torah verse as his daughter's son Rabbi Yaakov did." Others say, he saw the tongue of Hutzpit, the translator being dragged along with a swine and he exclaimed.

"The mouth that uttered pearls is licking the dust. Is this Torah and its reward?" He went away and sinned. After turning his back on Torah and Judaism, the rabbis did not refer to him by his name; they called him Aher.[13] But Rabbi Meir continued to discuss Torah with him and tried to bring him back to Judaism. (*Kiddushin* 39b)

✿ Ahitofel   אחיתופל

Ahitofel, advisor to King David, advised his sons on three things: Do not take part in quarrels, do not rebel against the government of King David, and if the

---

13. The other.

weather is good during the festival of Atzeret, plant wheat. (*Sanhedrin* 16b, 106b; *Bava Batra* 147a)

Ahiya   אחיה

Officer of the Temple (*Shekalim* 5:1)

Aibu   אייבו

Amora and Tanna from Eretz Yisrael and Babylonia
2nd – 3rd centuries CE
Father of Rav, and brother of R. Hiyya (*Sanhedrin* 5a; *Pesahim* 4a)

Aibu   אייבו

Amora from Babylonia
3rd century CE (*Pesahim* 113a)

Aibu   אייבו

Amora from Babylonia
3rd – 4th centuries CE (*Sukkah* 44b)

Air space inside a vessel

Uncleanness and impurity inside a vessel is discussed. (*Hullin* 24b)

Akalton

Roundabout road
(*Bava Kamma* 28a)

✿ Akavia was asked to retract

R. Akavia b. Mehalalel had halachic differences with his colleagues and was offered the position of Av Bet Din if he retracts his ruling. He refused by stating: "I would rather be called an idiot, but I will not transgress before God even for one hour." (*Eduyot* 7b, 5:6)

Akavia b. Mahalalel   עקביא בן מהללאל

Tanna from Eretz Yisrael
1st century BCE – 1st century CE (*Berachot* 19a; *Negaim* 1:4)

Akiva   עקיבא

Tanna from Eretz Yisrael

Head of the Academy in Bene Berak
1st – 2nd centuries CE (*Ketubbot* 62b)

Akiva and the glory of Torah
Since R. Akiva passed away the glory of the Torah came to an end. (*Sotah* 49a)

✿ Akiva as a shepherd
R. Akiva was a shepherd at Kalba ben Savua, who was one of the wealthiest men in Jerusalem. His daughter Rachel noticed how modest and noble Akiva conducted himself, and she said to him, "Were I to be betrothed to you would you go to study in a Talmudic academy?" He replied in the affirmative, and they were betrothed secretly. She married him that winter. When her father found out what she had done, he expelled her from his house and made a vow that she can't have any benefit from his estate. They lived in extreme poverty; she even sold her hair for food.

Upon her insistence to become a scholar. He left her and his job and spent twelve years in Lydda in the yeshivas of Rabbi Eliezer ben Horkynos and Rabbi Yehoshua ben Hanania. Upon arriving home, he overheard a wicked man talking with his wife Rachel and telling her: "Your father did the right thing; because your husband is inferior to you and he abandoned you to a living widowhood?" She replied: "If he would listen to me, he would spend another twelve years in the academy." He therefore departed again and spent another twelve years at the academy. When he finally returned the second time he was accompanied by twenty-four thousand students. Everyone came out to welcome him, and his wife Rachel also went out to meet him. When she approached him, his attendants tried to thrust her aside, but R. Akiva yelled at them, saying: "Leave her alone, what is mine and yours – really belongs to her."

Her father, Kalba Savua on hearing that a great man and scholar came to town, said to himself, I shall go to him; perhaps he will annul my vow. When he visited R. Akiva, he asked him if his vow could be annulled. R. Akiva asked him: "If you had known that she was marrying a great scholar would you have made the vow?" He replied: "If I had known that he knows one chapter or even one Halachah, I would not have made the vow." He annulled the vow and said to him, "I am the man she married." Kalba Savua fell on his face and kissed the feet of R. Akiva. He also gave him half of his wealth. (*Nedarim* 50a; *Ketubbot* 63a)

⊞ Akiva had no equal
When R. Hanania b. Ahi Yehoshua left for Babylonia he began to intercalate the years and to fix the new months outside of Israel. The Bet Din of Israel sent two scholars to stop him from doing it. They were R. Yosi b. Kippar and the grandson of R. Zechariah b. Kavutal.

Shortly after that, they were ruling against his declarations. He said to them: "Why do you declare everything clean which I declared unclean?"

They answered him, "Because you intercalate years and fix the new moon outside Israel." He retorted, "Did not R. Akiva b. Yosef intercalate years and fix the new month outside of Israel?" They answered him: "Do not cite R. Akiva,[14] who had no equal in Israel." (*Berachot* 63a)

⊞ Akiva imprisoned
Rabbi Akiva was imprisoned for teaching Torah openly in defiance of the decree. They also arrested Pappus b. Judah, and he was in the same prison. Rabbi Akiva asked him: "Why were you imprisoned?"

He replied: "Happy are you Akiva that they arrested you for occupying yourself

---

14. See entry, Intercalate outside Israel.

with teaching Torah, alas for Pappus who was arrested for occupying himself with idle things." (*Berachot* 61b)

Akiva in Nehardea
R. Akiva and R. Nehemia
The Talmud relates that Rabbi Akiva was saying. "When I visited Nehardea in Babylonia to declare a leap year I met with Rabbi Nehemia Ish Bet Deli. He told me I heard that in Eretz Yisrael they don't permit a woman to remarry on testimony of one witness." He went on to say that he learned from Rabban Gamliel otherwise. (*Yevamot* 116a, 122a)

✿ Akiva's daughter marries
Rabbi Akiva had a daughter who was about to be married, but R. Akiva was concerned because astrologers told him that on the day of her wedding she would be bitten by a snake and die. It happened that she was getting dressed for the wedding and she stuck a brooch needle into the wall. The next morning when she removed the brooch she found the needle was stuck in the eye of a dead serpent. R. Akiva asked her:

"Can you think of any good deed you did yesterday?"

She replied, "While everyone was busy with the wedding banquet, a poor man came to the door, but everyone ignored him. I took a portion from the banquet meal and gave it to the poor man." Rabbi Akiva praised her and then delivered a sermon on the topic of "Charity saves from death." (*Shabbat* 156b)

✿ Akiva's instructions to his son
The Talmud relates that Rabbi Akiva charged his son Yehoshua with seven instructions:

– Do not sit to study Torah at the highest point of the city.

– Do not live in a town where the leaders of the town are scholars, because they will neglect the needs of the town.

– Do not enter your house suddenly.

– Do not walk without shoes.

– Arise early in the summer on account of the heat, and in the winter on account of the cold.

– Treat your Shabbat like a weekday rather than be dependent on others.

– Be on good terms with the person on whom the hour smiles. (*Pesahim* 112a)

Akiva's sons
Rabbi Akiva lost two sons, both of them were bridegrooms, and people came from all over Israel to lament for them. Rabbi Akiva stood on a podium and addressed the people. "Even though these two sons were bridegrooms, I am consoled on account of the honor you have done to them." R. Akiva also had a son by the name of Yehoshua, and also a daughter who was married to R. Shimon ben Azzai (*Moed Katan* 21b)

📖 Akiva's students
Who revived the Torah
It is stated Rabbi Akiva had twelve thousand pairs of students. All of them died at the same time, because they did not treat each other with respect. A Tanna taught that all of them died between Pesach and Shavuot. And these were the remaining students of Rabbi Akiva who revived the Torah at that time: Rabbi Meir, Rabbi Yehuda bar Illai, Rabbi Yosi ben Halafta, Rabbi Shimon ben Yohai, and Rabbi Eleazar ben Shammua. (*Yevamot* 62b)

📖 Akiva's water spilled
R Akiva's water was spilled by the prison guard
A story is told that the Romans imprisoned Rabbi Akiva for disobeying their decree not to teach Torah, and Rabbi Yehoshua HaGarsi attended to him in

prison. Every day he brought him a certain quantity of water.

One day the prison keeper said to him: "Your water today is much too much. Perhaps you want to use it to undermine the prison?"

The prison keeper spilled out half of it, and the other half he gave to Rabbi Yehoshua. When he brought the water to Rabbi Akiva and gave it to him, he said to him: "Yehoshua, don't you know that I am an old man and my life depends on you?"

Rabbi Yehoshua told him what happened, but in spite of it Rabbi Akiva said to him: "Give me some water to wash my hands before I eat."

The other hesitated: "It will not even suffice for drinking, let alone for washing hands."

Rabbi Akiva answered him: "What can I do, for disobeying the words of the rabbis one deserves to die?"

He refused to taste any food until R. Yehoshua brought him water to wash his hands first. (*Eruvin* 21b)

Akiva was multilingual
R. Akiva was multilingual. (*Sanhedrin* 17b)

Alcohol influence
Rabbah ben R. Huna said: "A person who is under the influence of alcohol should not pray." (*Eruvin* 64a)

Aleph Bet   אל״ף בי״ת
Mem *and* samech *in the Tablets*
Rabbi Hisda stated: "The letters *mem* and *samech* in the Tablets of Moshe were suspended by miracle and the writing on the Tablets could be read from within and without or from both sides."[15] (*Shabbat* 104a)

---

15. The two letters mentioned have holes in the middle and would not hold without a miracle.

Aleph Bet   אל״ף בי״ת
The rabbis told R. Yehoshua b. Levi that each of the letters of the Aleph Bet has special meanings. (*Shabbat* 104a)

📖 Alexander and the Samaritans
The Talmud relates: "It was taught that on the twenty-fifth of Tevet, it is the day of Mount Gerizim." On that day no mourning is permitted. It is the day in which the Samaritans asked Alexander the Macedonian to give them permission to destroy the Temple, and he granted their request. Messengers came and informed Shimon HaTzaddik of the decree. He dressed up in his high-priestly garments, and took with him the noblemen of Israel. All of them were carrying lit torches and were walking all night; some were walking on one side of the road and some on the other side. When Alexander saw the lit torches in the night from a distance, he asked the Samaritans, "Who are those people walking?"

They told him that those are the Jews who had rebelled against him. The two camps met at Antipatris. When Alexander spotted Shimon HaTzaddik, he descended from his carriage and bowed down before him. They said to him.

"Should a great king like you bow down to a Jew?"

He answered. "It is his image that I see when I win all my battles."

He asked them, "For what reason have you come to see me?"

They said to him. "Is it possible that you would listen to the advice of star-worshippers to destroy the Temple in which we pray for you and your kingdom that it should never be destroyed?"

"Who are those star-worshippers?"

"They are the Samaritans who stand before you."

He answered. "They are delivered in your hands."

That day was made into a festive day. (*Yoma*, 69a)

📖 **Alexander the Macedonian king**
The rabbis taught:

On one occasion, the Egyptians came to Alexander to make a claim against the Israelites. They said, "It is written in the Torah: 'and God gave the people favor in the eyes of the Egyptians and they lent them gold and silver.'

"Now we want you to repay us for all that gold and silver." Geviha ben Pesisa asked permission from the rabbis to go before Alexander and argue against the Egyptians. He was granted permission. Geviha asked the Egyptians to bring proof for their claim. They gave him proof from the Torah, where it says that the Egyptians lent the Israelites gold and silver. Geviha answered, "I will also bring proof from the Torah that Israel does not owe anything to the Egyptians. The Torah says that the Israelites were slaves in Egypt for 400 years. Now pay us for the labor of 600,000 men working for 400 years." The Egyptians could not come up with an answer and they fled, leaving behind their planted fields and vineyards.

On another occasion, the children of Ishmael and the children of Ketura came before Alexander and made a claim against the children of Israel. They claimed that the land belongs to them just as much as it belongs to the Israelites, because they are also the children of Avraham. Geviha was given authority to argue before Alexander, and he said to them: "You bring your proof from the Torah, and I will bring proof from the Torah that you are wrong. The Torah says: 'And Avraham gave all that he possessed to Yitzhak, and to the children of his concubines, he gave gifts and he sent them away.'" (*Sanhedrin* 91a)

Alexandrian Synagogue
R. Yehuda stated: "Anyone who has not seen the double colonnade synagogue in Alexandria, Egypt has never seen the glory of Israel." It was like a huge basilica; it could accommodate thousands of worhippers. Some of the worshippers could not always hear the *hazan*; therefore, the attendant stood on a wooden platform with a scarf in his hand. When the time came to answer amen he would wave the scarf and the congregation would respond with Amen. (*Sukkah* 51b)

Aliyot　　　　　　　　　　　עליות
Number of Aliyot for Torah reading on the holidays
Who is called up first and second: On Rosh Hodesh, there are four *aliyot*, on Hol Hamoed, there are four *aliyot*, on Yom Tov, there are five *aliyot*, on Yom Kippur, there are six *aliyot*, and on Shabbat, there are seven *aliyot*. (*Megillah* 21a)

All Israel are guarantors
כל ישראל ערבים זה בזה
All of Israel are guarantors one for another (*Shevuot* 39a; *Sanhedrin* 27b)

Alley closed in
An alley that was closed in between a heap of rubbish and the sea. (*Eruvin* 99b)

Alleys
The usage of alleys during Shabbat (*Eruvin* 2a)

Alleys: one clean, one not clean
(*Taharot* 5:5)

Altar had a painted line in the middle
מזבח
There was a line painted in the middle of the altar in the Temple to separate the upper bloods from the lower bloods. (*Middot* 3:1)

Altar in the Temple   מזבח
The altar in the Temple measured thirty-two by thirty-two cubits. (*Middot* 3:1)

Altar stones in the Temple   מזבח
The stones for the altar in the Temple came from Bet Kerem and none of them were chiseled with an iron (*Middot* 3:4)

Altars   במות
Altars in high places for sacrifices
Before the Mishkan was set up, Bamot[16] were permitted, but after the Mishkan was set up, private altars were forbidden. (*Zevahim* 112b; *Bechorot* 4b)

Altering a contract
     המשנה ידו על התחתונה
The one who alters the contract is at a disadvantage. (*Bava Metzia* 76a, 77b; *Bava Kamma* 102a; *Avodah Zarah* 7a)

Am Haaretz   עם הארץ
According to R. Eliezer, a person who does not recite the *Shema* evening and morning is called an *am haaretz*; according to R. Yehoshua, a person who does not put on *tefillin*; according to Ben Azzai, a person who does not wear *tzitzis*; according to R. Nathan, a person that does not have a *mezuzah* on the door is considered an *am haaretz*. (*Berachot* 47b)

Am Haaretz   עם הארץ
Living in the same courtyard with an *am haaretz*.[17] (*Taharot* 8:1, 2)

Amalekite children spared
Rabbi Mani had an explanation as to why King Saul did not kill all the Amalekites. King Saul reasoned that since the children were innocent they should be spared. (*Yoma* 22b)

---

16. Private altars.
17. An uneducated person in halachic learning.

Ameimar   אמימר
Amora from Babylonia
Head of the academy in Mehuza
4th – 5th centuries CE (*Bava Batra* 31a)

Amen   אמן
R. Shemuel said: "Anyone who utters the word Amen after hearing an oath is equal as if he uttered the oath himself." (*Shevuot* 29b)

Amen   אמן
Resh Lakish said: "He who responds Amen with all his might will have the gates of Gan Eden opened for him." (*Shabbat* 119b)

Amidah
The *Amidah* has to be said in respectful awe. (*Berachot* 30b)

Amidah beginning
R. Yohanan said: "One begins the *Amidah* with ה' שפתי תפתח ופי יגיד תהילתך" (*Berachot* 4b, 9b)

Amidah
Shemona Esrei   שמונה עשרה
It has been taught: Shimon HaPakuli formulated the proper order of the eighteen blessings of the *Amidah* in the presence of R. Gamliel in Yavne. R. Yohanan said that it was stated in a Beraita: "A hundred and twenty elders – among them were many prophets – drew up eighteen blessings in a fixed order." (*Megillah* 17b; *Berachot* 28b)

Ammi b. Nathan   אמי בר נתן
Amora from Eretz Yisrael
Head of the academy in Tiberias
3rd – 4th centuries CE (*Berachot* 16a; *Nedarim* 40b)

Ammon and Moav
The rabbis were discussing the nations of Ammon and Moav. (*Yadayim* 4:3)

Ammonite proselyte
The dispute between R. Gamliel and R. Yehoshua with regards to an Ammonite proselyte (*Yadayim* 4:4)

Ammonites
A male Ammonite marrying a Jewish woman and an Ammonite woman marrying a Jewish man (*Yevamot* 76a)

📖 Ammonites in dispute
R. Yehoshua and R. Gamliel had many halachic differences: one halachic dispute between R. Gamliel and R. Yehoshua was over the Ammonites – whether they can be accepted into the Jewish community. Rabbi Yehoshua was in favor and Rabbi Gamliel was against. The Sanhedrin sided with Rabbi Yehoshua.[18] (*Berachot* 28a)

Amplification   ריבוי אחר ריבוי
An amplification following amplification[19] (*Bava Kamma* 45b)

Amplification and limitation
Rabbi Yohanan stated that R. Akiva who served R. Nachum Ish Gam Zu, who expounded the whole Torah on the principle of amplification and limitation, also expounded the Torah as his teacher by that same principle. (*Shevuot* 26a; *Sotah* 16b)

Amputee
What may an amputee carry on Shabbat? (*Shabbat* 65b)

Amram   עמרם
Amora from Babylonia
3rd century CE (*Bava Metzia* 20b; *Pesahim* 105a)

Amram   עמרם
Amora from Babylonia
4th century CE (*Bava Metzia* 38b)

Amulet   קמיע
(*Shabbat* 53b, 61a)

Amulet that was proven   קמיע מומחה
An amulet that has healed three times (*Shabbat* 61a)

Anan   ענן
Amora from Babylonia
3rd century CE (*Bava Metzia* 70a; *Kiddushin* 39a)

Androgynous
Sexually undefined (*Bikkurim* 4:1; *Sanhedrin* 66a)

Androgynous animal
A dedicated animal given to a Kohen that is androgynous or a *tumtum* (*Bechorot* 41b)

📖 Anemic child
R. Nathan said: "I once came to Cappadocia and was approached there by a woman who had circumcised her first and second sons, and they died. She brought her third son to me. I saw that the child had a greenish color. I examined him and found that the child was anemic, without blood for circumcision so I said to her, 'Wait until the blood will circulate in the body.' She waited and then circumcised her son and he lived. She named him Nathan the Babylonian after me."[20] (*Hullin* 47b)

📖 Angel of Death   מלאך המות
R. Hisda was sitting and studying in the academy. Consequently, when the time came for him to die, the Angel of Death could not take his life, because he was studying Torah. To interrupt his studies, the Angel of Death leaned on a cedar tree next to the academy and the cedar tree cracked under him, which interrupted R. Hisda's studies and the Angel was able to take his life. (*Makkot* 10a)

---

18. See entry, Appointment to the Sanhedrin.
19. One of R. Yishmael's thirteen principles.

20. See entry, Circumcision.

📖 Angel of Death gave time
מלאך המות

It is related, Rabbi Hanina bar Papi was about to die, and the Angel of Death was sent to his house with orders to carry out any wish of his. Rabbi Hanina said to the Angel:

"Allow me thirty days in order to revise my studies." He was granted the wish. It is said that when he died a pillar of fire formed a partition between him and the world. We have it as a tradition that such a partition by a pillar of fire is granted only to a person unique in his generation (*Ketubbot* 77b)

Angel of Death visits
מלאך המות

R. Bibi b. Abbaye had frequent visits by the Malach HaMavet and had conversations with him. (*Hagigah* 4b)

Angels

Even if 999 angels are in a person's disfavor and only one in his favor, he is saved. (*Shabbat* 32a)

Angels accompany on Shabbat

R. Yosi b. Yehuda said: "Two angels accompany a person on Shabbat eve on the way home from the synagogue." (*Shabbat* 119b)

Angels do not understand Aramaic

R. Yohanan said: "When one prays for his needs in Aramaic, the angels do not understand the prayers." (*Shabbat* 12b)

Angels placed crowns

R. Simai lectured: "When the Israelites gave the answer 'We will do, we will listen' 600,000 angels placed two crowns on each person at Mount Sinai – one for 'we will do,' and one for 'we will listen.' But as soon as the Israelites sinned they were removed by the angels." (*Shabbat* 88a)

Angels sing to God

R. Hananel said in the name of Rav: "Three groups of angels sing praises to God daily." (*Hullin* 91b)

Angels visit Avraham

The three angels that visited Avraham were Michael מיכאל, Gavriel גבריאל and Refael רפאל. Michael came to bring good news to Sarah that she would have a son, Refael came to heal Avraham, and Gavriel came to destroy Sodom. (*Bava Metzia* 86b)

📖 Angels: Why Torah to Israel

Rabbi Yehoshua ben Levi said: "When Moshe ascended to receive the Torah, the angels said to Hashem, 'What business has one born of woman amongst us?'

"'He came to receive the Torah,' came the answer.

"The angels asked in wonderment 'This great secret treasure which you have hidden for 974 generations before the world was created, you desire to give to men of flesh and blood?'

"Hashem said to Moshe, 'Give them an answer.'

"Moshe said to the angels, 'It is written in the Torah, "I am the God who took you out of Egypt." Have you gone down to Egypt, have you been enslaved by Pharaoh?' "Moshe further asked them, 'It is written in the Torah: "Honor thy father and mother." Do you have fathers and mothers?'

"Moshe asked them other questions. Finally the angels were convinced and conceded to Moshe. After this encounter, they became his friends." (*Shabbat* 88b)

✿ Anger

R. Mani b. Patish said: "Whoever becomes angry, heaven is not pleased with that person." (*Pesahim* 66b)

✡ Anger
Be not easily provoked to anger
One of Rabbi Eliezer's famous sayings was, "Let the honor of your fellow-man be as precious as your own; be not easily provoked to anger; repent one day before you die; warm yourself at the fire of the Sages, but beware of their glowing coals." (*Avot* 2:15)

✡ Anger
R. Shimon b. Eleazar said in the name of R. Hilfa b. Agra in the name of R. Yohanan b. Nuri: "One who tears his garments or breaks his vessels in anger is equal to an idol worshipper." (*Shabbat* 105b)

Anger management
Making R. Hillel angry was not easy
Two men wagered 400 *zuz* to provoke R. Hillel to make him angry; they did not succeed. (*Shabbat* 31a)

Angry person
Do not placate an angry person
R. Shimon b. Eleazar said: "Do not try to placate a person when he is angry, and do not comfort him while his dead lie before him." (*Avot* 4:18)

Animal and its young
Slaughtering an animal and its young on the same day is a transgression. (*Hullin* 78a)

Animal injured
Can an animal that had its legs cut off be slaughtered for food? (*Hullin* 42b, 57b, 76a)

Animal slaughtered
בהמה שנשחטה הרי היא בחזקת היתר
An animal slaughtered ritually is presumed to be permitted. (*Hullin* 9a; *Betzah* 25a)

Animals attacked by wolf
Animals attacked by a wolf that caused wounds in the animals, is a question of *kashrut*. (*Hullin* 52b)

Animals carrying on Shabbat
What objects animals can carry on Shabbat is discussed in *Bameh beheimah*, the 5th *perek* in *Shabbat*. (*Shabbat* 51b)

Animals in the wilderness
It is proper to breed small animals in the *midbar*. (*Bava Kamma* 79b)

Animals' tents
R. Huna owned sheep that needed the shade during daytime, but at nighttime they needed open air. On weekdays, it was arranged by spreading a mat over the area and removing it for the night, but on Shabbat, he was concerned this might be an act of building. He came to his teacher Rav, and asked him what to do. Rav advised him to roll up the mat on Friday evening before Shabbat, but to leave a handbreadth unrolled, and the next morning when the mat is unrolled he will only add to an existing temporary tent. (*Eruvin* 102a)

Animals to be reared
To rear small animals in Eretz Yisrael is not proper, because they spoil the crops of the field. (*Bava Kamma* 79b)

Animals while alive
בהמה בחייה בחזקת איסור עומדת
An animal while alive is presumed to be forbidden, and remains to be forbidden after death, until it becomes known that it was slaughtered ritually. (*Hullin* 9a; *Betzah* 25a)

Anniversaries and birthdays of kings
Observing birthdays and anniversaries of kings by burning objects is considered idol worship. (*Avodah Zarah* 8a, 11a)

Announcing in public
Found objects are to be announced in public. (*Bava Metzia* 21a, 28a)

Annul   מבטל
Idol images which are to be annulled,
how to annul items from an Ashera is discussed. (*Avodah Zarah* 49b, 43a; *Moed Katan* 3b)

Annul another court's ruling   מבטל
Rabbah b. b. Hana said in the name of R. Yohanan: In all matters, a Court can annul the decision of another Court except the eighteen things prohibited by the schools of Hillel and Shammai. (*Avodah Zarah* 36a; *Moed Katan* 3b; *Megillah* 2a; *Gittin* 36b)

Annulling vows
Annulling vows on Shabbat is discussed in *Mi she-hehshich*, the 24th *perek* in *Shabbat*. (*Shabbat* 147a)

Anointed a High Priest
The difference between a High Priest who was anointed and one that wears many garments: during the First Temple, the High Priest was known by the title "the Anointed Priest"; during the Second Temple, he was known as "the Priest with many garments." (*Horayot* 11b)

Anointing a king
A son of a king does not need to be anointed; he becomes king by inheritance. (*Horayot* 11b)

Anointing a king at a water fountain
(*Horayot* 12a)

Anointing oil
The anointing oil Moshe Rabbeinu used in the wilderness consisted of twelve *lugin*; the word "*zeh*" זה adds up to twelve. Many miracles occurred with the anointing oil from the beginning to the end. In what manner the anointing oil was applied is discussed. (*Horayot*11b, 12a)

Anointing oil was hidden away
King Yoshiyah hid away the following: the anointing oil, the Holy Ark, the jar of manna, Aharon's rod with the almond blossoms, and also the coffer the Philistines had sent as a gift to Israel. He did not want these precious things to be taken by the enemy. (*Horayot* 12a)

Anointing the body
Anointing the body on Shabbat is discussed in *Havit*, the 22nd *perek* in *Shabbat*. (*Shabbat* 147a)

Anointing with a horn
King David and King Solomon were anointed with oil from a horn. (*Horayot* 12a)

✿ Anonymous charity
R. Abba was a very charitable person. When he gave charity to the poor, he did not want to embarrass them by facing them; therefore, he used to wear a scarf with money in it slung towards his back. The poor could take what they needed without facing him. However, he kept an eye on would-be rogues. (*Ketubbot* 67b)

Anonymous Mishna
R. Yohanan said: "The author of an anonymous Mishna is R. Meir; of an anonymous Tosefta, R. Nehemia; of an anonymous Sifra, R. Yehuda b. Illai; of an anonymous Sifri, R. Shimon b. Yohai; and all are taught according to the views of R. Akiva." (*Sanhedrin* 86a)

Anonymous Mishna   סתם משנה
R. Yohanan said: "The Halachah is in agreement with the anonymous Mishna." (*Yevamot* 42b; *Shabbat* 46a; *Bava Kamma* 69a; *Eruvin* 92a)

Answer a non-believer

R. Eleazar said: "Be diligent in the study of Torah, and know what to answer a non-believer. Know before whom you toil, and be aware that your Employer can be relied upon to pay your earned wages." (*Avot* 2:19)

Antedated contracts and notes

The Talmud discusses contracts and notes that were antedated. (*Bava Metzia* 17a, 72a; *Sanhedrin* 32a; *Bava Batra* 157b, 171b)

Antigonus Ish Socho   אנטיגנוס איש סוכו

Tanna from Eretz Yisrael

2nd century BCE (*Avot* 1:3)

Antigonus Ish Socho

Antigonus Ish Socho said: "Do not serve your master with ulterior motives in mind." (*Avot* 1:3)

✡ Anti-social

R. Hillel said: "Do not separate yourself from the community, do not believe you know it all, and do not judge your friend until you have been put in his position." (*Avot* 2:4)

📖 Antoninus asks advice from Rebbe

Rabbi Yehuda was on good terms with the Roman emperors. During the reign of Emperor Antoninus, he once said to Rebbe: "It is my desire that my son A. should become emperor after me and that Tiberias should be declared a colony. But I am concerned that if I ask the Senate for one request, it will be granted, but if I ask for both, they will be denied."

Rebbe gave him advice by a demonstration. He brought two men, one riding on the shoulders of the other. He put a dove in the hand of the upper person and told the lower person to order the upper man to liberate the dove. Antonius perceived that he should ask the Senate to appoint A. to succeed him and to tell A. to make Tiberias a free colony.

On another occasion, Antoninus mentioned to Rebbe that some prominent Romans were annoying him. Rebbe again advised him by a demonstration. He took him into his garden, and in his presence he picked radishes, one at a time. The Emperor concluded that his advice was to get rid of them, one at a time, but not to get rid of them all at once. (*Avodah Zarah* 10a)

📖 Antoninus's exchange with Rebbe

The Emperor asked Rebbe: "The body and soul have a good argument to escape punishment. The body can plead that the soul has sinned, and the proof of it is that since the soul left me I lie in the ground like a stone in the grave, while the soul can plead that the body has sinned, and the proof of it is that since I left the body I fly in the air without committing sins." Rebbe replied: "It is compared to two watchmen: one being blind and one lame. The lame one is telling the blind one, 'I see beautiful figs in the orchard. Take me on your shoulders and I will pick some for us to eat.' The blind person carried the lame person on his shoulders and they ate the figs. Some time later the owner of the orchard inquired from his watchmen. 'Where are those beautiful figs you were supposed to watch in my orchard?' The lame watchman replied: 'Do I have feet to walk with?' And the blind man asked: 'Do I have eyes to see with?' The owner of the orchard told the lame one to ride on the shoulder of the blind one and then he judged them together."

In another exchange: Why does the sun rise in the east? Rebbe answered: "If it was the reverse, you would ask the same question." (*Sanhedrin* 91a–b)

📖 Ants
R Shimon b. Halafta is experimenting with ants

It is said of Rabbi Shimon ben Halafta that he was an experimenter in all things. Once he had a hen, which had no feathers at all. He put the hen into the oven, having first wrapped the hen in a warm blanket. When the hen came out, it grew feathers even larger than the original one. Why was he called an experimenter with flora and fauna? R. Mesharshia said because he personally experimented with all sorts of insects and plants. Once he went out to find out whether it is true that ants have no king. First he put a blanket over an anthill during the summer solstice to create a shade over the anthill. Next he removed the blanket and the sun beat down on the anthill. He kept watch over the ants during the experiment to come to a conclusion. (*Hullin* 57b)

Apes breeding
R. Yishmael said or R. Shimon b. Eleazar said: "It is permissible to breed village dogs, cats, and apes." (*Bava Kamma* 80a–b)

Aphrodite's statue
A statue of Aphrodite was in a public bath. (*Avodah Zarah* 44b)

Apikoros   אפיקורוס
What is an *apikoros*? It is someone who does not accept the teachings of the rabbis. Rav and R. Hanina both say an *apikoros* is a person who insults a scholar. (*Sanhedrin* 38b, 90a, 99b)

✿ Apology
R. Abba had a complaint against R. Yirmiyahu, and R. Abba felt insulted. R. Yirmiyahu went to R. Abba's home to apologize and sat down at his door. As he was sitting there, the maid poured out some water and some of it fell upon R. Yirmiyahu's

head. He remarked, "They made a dung heap of me." R. Abba heard what happened and came out apologizing. He said to R. Yirmiyahu: "Now I think you are the injured party and I have to ask your forgiveness." (*Yoma* 87a)

Apology
R. Gamliel went to the house of R. Yehoshua to apologize. (*Berachot* 28a)

Apostasy
R. Elisha b. Avuyah abandoned the observance of Judaism.[21] (*Hagigah* 15a)

Apostate for his appetite   מומר לתיאבון
An apostate to satisfy his appetite (*Avodah Zarah* 26b; *Hullin* 3a)

Apostate in defiance   מומר להכעיס
An apostate in defiance to provoke anger (*Avodah Zarah* 26b; *Hullin* 3a)

Apotiki   אפותיקי
Mortgaging a particular field (*Bava Kamma* 96a)

Apotropos   אפוטרופוס
An *apotropos* is a trustee appointed by the court to supervise an estate. (*Bava Batra* 144a; *Bava Metzia* 39a)

Appear in Jerusalem   ראיה
Who is obligated to appear in Jerusalem for the Three Festivals? (*Hagigah* 2a)

Applies only in such a case   זאת אומרת
The subject or rule discussed applies only. (*Hullin* 3a)

📖 Appointed Nasi of the Sanhedrin
R. Eleazar b. Azariah was elected as Nasi of the Sanhedrin

On one occasion a student asked Rabbi

---

21. See entry, Aher.

Yehoshua: "Is the evening prayer compulsory or optional?" Rabbi Yehoshua replied that it is optional. The same student asked Rabbi Gamliel the same question, and Rabbi Gamliel replied that it is compulsory. "But," said the student, "Rabbi Yehoshua told me it is optional." Rabbi Gamliel told the student to wait until the session of the assembly starts. The question was asked and Rabbi Gamliel said that it is compulsory. Rabbi Gamliel asked, "Is there anyone here who disagrees?"

"No," Rabbi Yehoshua replied.

"Did they not report to me that you said, 'It is optional'?

"Stand up, and let them testify against you." Rabbi Yehoshua stood up, while Rabbi Gamliel remained seated, and expounded for a long time. After a while, the scholars in the assembly began shouting at Hutzpit the interpreter: "Stop!" The interpreter stopped.

The members of the Sanhedrin said: "How long will Rabbi Gamliel go on insulting him? This is the third time he insulted him. Last year on Rosh Hashana he insulted him, in the affair of R. Tzadok he insulted him, and now he insults him again. Let us depose Rabbi Gamliel."

"Whom can we appoint? We can't appoint R. Yehoshua, because he is a party to the dispute; we can't appoint R. Akiva, because he has no ancestral merits. Let us appoint Rabbi Eleazar ben Azariah, who is wise, rich and a descendant of Ezra."

"He is wise to give the proper answer to a question. He is rich, so that if money is needed to pay the government he can do it. He is a descendant of Ezra and therefore he has great ancestral merit." They asked him: "Will you honor us to become the head of the academy?"

He replied: "I will consult the members of my family." He consulted his wife. She said to him:

"Maybe they will also depose you?"

He answered: "Let one use a cup of honor for one day, even if it be broken the next day." She said to him, "You have no white hair." He was eighteen years old, but a miracle happened and his beard turned white. He accepted the position.

It was learned that on that day the doors were opened for all the disciples to enter the assembly. Prior to this, Rabbi Gamliel had issued orders that those students whose exterior appearance does not match their interior intellect may not enter.

Four hundred additional seats were brought in to accommodate the new students who entered the hall.

It was taught that many testimonies were formulated on that day, and whenever there is mention "on that day" it refers to this particular day.

Rabbi Gamliel – in spite of his demotion – did not absent himself from the assembly even for one hour. (*Berachot* 27b)

Appraising
Valuation or appraising damages is the subject discussed. (*Bava Kamma* 14b)

Aramaean
An Aramaean saw a man fall from a roof ... (*Hullin* 56b)

Aramaic language
R. Yosi said: "Why use the Aramaic language in Babylon; use either the Holy tougue or Persian." (*Bava Kamma* 83a)

Aramaic prayers
R. Yohanan said: "When one prays for his needs in Aramaic, the Angels do not understand the prayers." (*Shabbat* 12b)

Arava if stolen
Is a stolen *arava* fit for performing the mitzvah on Sukkot? (*Sukkah* 33b)

Arbitration

The force of arbitration is greater than that of a legal judgment. (*Sanhedrin* 5b)

Ardashir and Ktesifon

Two neighboring towns next to the Tiger River were involved in measuring for an *eruv*. (*Eruvin* 57b)

Arioch   אריוך

R. Shemuel was also called Arioch. (*Shabbat* 53a; *Hullin* 76b)

Arise early in the morning

R. Akiva charged his son R. Yehoshua with seven things. Among them was to rise early in the morning. (*Pesahim* 112a)

Aristobulus

A Hasmonean king[22]
(*Sotah* 49b; *Bava Kamma* 82b; *Menahot* 64b)

Ark of the Temple was hidden

Tradition has it that the Ark was hidden underneath the Temple ground opposite the wood store. (*Shekalim* 6:1)

Army in Pumbedita

An army of occupation was once stationed in Pumbedita; Rabbah and R. Yosef fled the town. (*Hullin* 46a)

Army of occupation

The Nehardean Jewish quarters was occupied
An army was once stationed in Nehardea, and they took over the living quarters of the local population. Rabbi Nahman told his students to go out to the swamp and prepare a place for Shabbat by covering the area with reeds so they can sit there and study. (*Eruvin* 34b)

---

22. See Hasmonean.

Arona

A wealthy man in King David's time (*Avodah Zarah* 24b)

Arrest of two rabbis

Our rabbis taught: When Rabbi Eleazar ben Parta and Rabbi Hanania ben Teradion were arrested, R. Eleazar said to R. Hanania:

"Happy are you that they arrested you only on one charge, but woe to me, for I have been arrested on five charges." Rabbi Hanania replied:

"Happy are you that they brought five charges against you for learning Torah and for acts of benevolence, but you will be rescued, however woe to me for being arrested on one charge only, for learning Torah." Rabbi Eleazar was miraculously saved from being executed.
(*Avodah Zarah* 17b)

Arrested on suspicion

R. Eliezer b. Horkynos was arrested on suspicion of consorting with heretics. (*Avodah Zarah* 16b)

Arresting thieves

R. Eleazar b. Shimon b. Yohai accepted under compulsion an official position from the Romans to be in charge of apprehending thieves and robbers. It came about from a chance meeting between R. Eleazar and a Roman officer who was sent to arrest thieves. R. Eleazar asked him, "How can you tell which one is a thief? Perhaps you are arresting the innocent and the guilty are walking free?" The officer replied, "What can I do, I am commanded by the king?" R. Eleazar advised the officer to go to the tavern and talk to the people and find out what their occupations are. "If they don't have a trade and do not have a good answer as to how they make a living then they are thieves." The report of this conversation was brought to the authorities and the order was issued. "Let the advisor become the enforcer." They sent for R. Eleazar b. Shimon and they ordered him to go out and arrest the thieves, an order which he had to obey. R. Yehoshua b. Korha sent a reproving message. "Vinegar, son of wine, how long will you deliver the people of our God to slaughter?" R. Eleazar sent a reply. "I weed out thorns from the vineyard." R. Yehoshua retorted. "Let the owner of the vineyard come and weed out the thorns." (*Bava Metzia* 83b)

Arriving late for prayers
If one arrives late for prayers, how does one join the congregation? (*Berachot* 21b)

✿ Arrogant administrator
R. Yohanan said in the name of R. Shimon b. Yehotzedek: "A community should not appoint an administrator over its affairs unless he carries a basket of reptiles on his back. If he becomes arrogant the community can tell him, turn around."[23] (*Yoma* 22b)

Artisans
All artisans are deemed as paid guardians. (*Bava Metzia* 80b)

Arusah   ארוסה
A betrothed girl (*Sotah* 23b; *Yevamot* 58a; *Kiddushin* 27b)

Ascents and descents
R. Yehuda said in Rav's name: "A town that has too many ascents and descents shortens the life of its people and its animals." (*Eruvin* 56a)

Ascertain   אפשר לצמצם
It is possible to deduce or to ascertain. (*Bechorot* 17b; *Yevamot* 19a, 88a; *Shevuot* 32a)

Ascertain not   אי אפשר לצמצם
It is impossible to ascertain exactly. (*Bechorot* 17b; *Yevamot* 19a, 88a; *Shevuot* 32a)

✿📖 Ascetics   פרושין
Our rabbis taught: When the Second Temple was destroyed, a large number of Jews became ascetics; they abstained from meat and wine. R. Yehoshua had a conversation with them and asked them why they abstain from meat and wine. They answered: "How can we eat meat when it was offered on the altar in the Temple? How can we drink wine which was poured as a libation on the altar?" He told them, "If that is the reason, we should not eat bread either, because bread was also offered as a meal offering on the altar." They insisted that they would live on fruit. He said to them, "There was the first fruit offering. You should not drink water either because there is no longer the pouring of the water on the holiday of Sukkot." Finally he said to them: "My sons, not to mourn at all is impossible, but to mourn excessively is to impose on the community a hardship, which the majority could not endure." (*Bava Batra* 60b)

Asham Talui   אשם תלוי
Suspended guilt offering (*Keritut* 17b)

Ashamed of the sin committed
Rabbah b. Hanina Saba said in the name of Rav: "If one commits a sin and is ashamed of it, all his sins are forgiven." (*Berachot* 12b)

Asher Yatzar   אשר יצר
A blessing recited after leaving the toilet. Abbaye composed the very profound blessing of *Asher Yatzar*. This blessing is said when one exits from the toilet after attending to his needs and washing hands. (*Berachot* 60b)

---

23. See also entry, Administrator.

Asherah   אשרה
Certain trees that were made into idols
(*Avodah Zarah* 48a, 45b; *Eruvin* 79b)

Ashes from the inner altar
Does desecration apply to the ashes from
the inner altar of the Temple? (*Meilah* 11b)

Ashes on the groom's forehead
R. Yitzhak said: "The reason we put ashes
on the forehead of the groom are to remind us of the destruction of the Temple."
Abbaye said it is placed where the *tefillin*
are normally placed. (*Bava Batra* 60b)

Ashi   אשי
Amora from Babylonia
Head of academy in Sura
4th – 5th centuries CE (*Bava Metzia* 86a)

Ashi and Ravina
Ashi and Ravina are the two rabbis who
redacted and concluded the Gemara. (*Bava
Metzia* 86a)

Ashi's daughter
Rabbi Ashi's daughter had a stomach ailment, and Rabin from Naresh cured her
with herbal medicines. (*Gittin* 69b)

Ashrei   אשרי
R. Eleazar said in the name of Rabbi
Avina: "Whoever recites *Ashrei* and *Tehila
LeDavid* three times a day is sure to inherit
the World to Come." (*Berachot* 4b)

Ashrei   אשרי
The letter Nun missing
R. Yohanan said, there is a reason why the
letter *nun* is missing in the prayer *Ashrei*.
(*Berachot* 4b)

Asimon   אסימון
An unofficial coin of metal (*Bava Metzia* 47b)

✿ Asking forgiveness
An offense of insult or hurting another
person is not forgiven until he asks for
forgiveness, even though compensation
was paid. (*Bava Kamma* 92a)

Asleep on the road
A person traveling on Friday takes a nap
on the road, yet in the meantime it gets
dark, what does one do? (*Eruvin* 45a)

Asmachta   אסמכתא
An obligation undertaken in a commer-
cial transaction (*Bava Batra* 168a; *Ketubbot* 67a;
Bava Metzia 66b)

Asmachta   אסמכתא
A biblical support
A rabbinic enactment which relies on a
biblical text (*Hullin* 64b)

Asporak Gorion   גוריון דמאספורק
Gorion of Asporak
One of the rabbis of the Talmud (*Bava
Kamma* 65b, 93b; *Temurah* 30b)

📖 Ass not eating untithed food
R. Pinhas arrived at an inn, where they
put food in front of his ass, but the ass
would not eat. They asked R. Pinhas why
his ass would not eat. He told them: "Perhaps it was not tithed." They immediately
tithed the grain and the ass ate it. (*Hullin*
7a; *Shabbat* 112b)

Assembly   אסיפה
A gathering of notables (*Taanit* 64a)

Assets
R. Yitzhak said: "One should always divide his assets in three: one-third in real
estate, one-third in merchandise, and one-
third in cash at hand." (*Bava Metzia* 42a)

Assi[24] (*Bava Kamma* 60b)

Assi   אסי
Amora from Babylonia
3rd century CE (*Bava Kamma* 80a)

Assi   אסי
Amora from Eretz Yisrael
Head of the academy in Tiberias,
3rd — 4th centuries CE (*Sanhedrin* 17b;
Megillah 22a)

✡ **Associate with a wise person**
Choose for friends the wise and learned
R. Yosi b. Yoezer said: "Let your house
be a meeting house for the wise, and sit
amidst the dust of their feet, and drink in
their words with thirst." (*Avot* 1:4)

📖 **Astrologers' prediction**
Astrologers told the mother of R. Nahman bar Yitzhak that her son would be a
thief. Thereupon, she told her son to wear
a cover on his head all the time, so that
the fear of Hashem would be on him and
keep him from temptation. One day he
was studying while sitting under a palm
tree that was not his, an urge came upon
him, he climbed up and bit off a cluster of
dates. (*Shabbat* 156b)

Astrology
Mazal of the day or hour
It was recorded in R. Yehoshua b. Levi's
notebook that the day of the week on
which a person was born determines his
fate. When R. Hanina heard this he said
to his people, "Go and tell the son of Levi:
Not the *mazal* of the day, but the *mazal* of
the hour influences the fate."

A person born under the influence of
the sun will be distinguished, he will eat
and drink from his own provisions, and

his secrets will be revealed. If he becomes
a thief, he will not succeed.

A person who is born under Venus will
be wealthy and immoral.

A person born under Mercury will have
a retentive memory and will be wise.

A person born under the moon will suffer, he will build and demolish, he will
eat and drink that which is not his own,
his secrets will remain hidden, and if he
chooses to be a thief he will be successful.
A person born under Saturn will have his
plans frustrated. (*Shabbat* 156a)

✡ **Astronomy**
R. Shemuel was ahead of his time in san-
itary awareness. He was called Yarchina,
because he was knowledgeable in astronomy which helped him in halachic matters. (*Bava Metzia* 85b)

What is *zikin*?

R. Shemuel said it is a comet. R. Shemuel
also said: "I am as familiar with the paths
of heaven as with the streets of Nehardea."
(*Berachot* 58b)

📖 **Astronomy and Math**
Rabbis Eleazar Hisma and Yohanan ben
Nuri were very familiar with astrology
and mathematics.

Rabbi Gamliel and Rabbi Yehoshua once
traveled on board a ship. The food supply
of Rabbi Gamliel was quickly consumed
and he had to rely on the food which
Rabbi Yehoshua brought with him.

"Did you know that we would be delayed
that much that you brought additional
food with you?" asked Rabbi Gamliel

"A certain star appears every seventy
years and leads sailors to miscalculate
their position and I calculated that it was
due to appear," said Rabbi Yehoshua.

"You possess so much knowledge," complimented him Rabbi Gamliel, "and yet
you travel on board a ship."

"Don't marvel at me, rather be surprised

---

24. See the full story under Ammi.

at two of your students who live on land, like Rabbi Eleazar Hisma and Rabbi Yohanan ben Nuri, who can calculate how many drops of water there are in the sea, and yet they have neither bread to eat nor clothing to put on."

Rabbi Gamliel decided to appoint them as supervisors, and sent for them when he landed. They were reluctant to accept on account of their humility. But Rabbi Gamliel told them. "Do you imagine that I offer you rulership? It is servitude that I offer you." (*Horayot* 10a)

Assur Be-Hanaah   אסור בהנאה
Forbidden to have any benefit or enjoyment from it (*Bava Kamma* 41a; *Pesahim* 21a; *Hullin* 114b)

Asufi   אסופי
An *asufi* is one who was picked up from the street and knows neither his father nor his mother (*Kiddushin* 69a; *Yevamot* 85a)

At Bah   אטב"ח
According to R. Hiyya, this is a code of the Aleph Bet. (*Sukkah* 52b)

At Bash   א"ת ב"ש
A code written in cryptic letters based on the Hebrew alphabet of Aleph Bet. It exchanges the first letter for the last letter, and the second letter for the second from the end and so on. (Rashi, *Sanhedrin* 22a)

It is similar to *Ahas beta gif* אח"ס בט"ע גי"ף – a combination of letters in a code whereby the first letter is replaced with the eighth letter; as for instance א is replaced with ח and so on. (*Shabbat* 104a)

✿ Atonement for the nations
It has been taught, Rabbi Yohanan ben Zakkai said: "Just as the sin offering makes atonement for Israel, so does charity make atonement for the nations of the world." (*Bava Batra* 10b)

Attendant
To Rabbi Akiva and Rabbi Yishmael
Rabbi Yehoshua ben Levi said: "Whenever you find a statement in the Talmud, 'a student said it in the name of Rabbi Yishmael, in front of Rabbi Akiva,' it refers to Rabbi Meir, who was an attendant to both Rabbi Akiva and Rabbi Yishmael." (*Eruvin* 13a)

✿ Attending to his fields
Rabbi Assi working on his property
Rabbi Assi was a well-to-do person, who inspected his property daily. The Talmud relates that one day when Rabbi Assi was inspecting his property he noticed a pipe had burst and was flooding his property. He took off his coat, rolled it up, and plugged the pipe with it. (*Hullin* 105a)

✿ Attentive to your wife
Rabbi Papa advised people to be very considerate of their wives. "If your wife is short, bend down to listen to her." (*Bava Metzia* 59a)

Attestation of a deed   קיום השטר
(*Bava Batra* 154a)

Authors
Who authored the books of the Prophets
Who are the authors of the Prophets? Moshe wrote the Torah, and *Parshat Bilam*, and Iyov. Yehoshua authored the book called Yehoshua; Shemuel wrote the book named after him; he also wrote Shoftim and Ruth.

David wrote the book of Tehillim; Yirmiyahu wrote the book which bears his name, also Melachim and Kinot. The men of the Great Assembly wrote Yechezkel and also the twelve Minor Prophets, Daniel, and Esther. Ezra wrote the book that bears his name and Divrei Hayamim. Others name different authors. (*Bava Batra* 15a)

Av fifteen
The fifteenth day of Av was made into a holiday with celebrations because the restrictions on the land apportioned to the tribes were lifted, and all the tribes could intermarry. Hence the Jewish people became united. (*Taanit* 30a)

Avdan (Avidan)　　　　אבידן
Amora from Eretz Yisrael
He was a student of Rabbi Yehuda Ha-Nasi. He lived in the 2nd – 3rd centuries CE. (*Berachot* 27b; *Yevamot* 105b)

Avdimi b. Hama　　　אבדימי בר חמא
Amora from Babylonia
3rd – 4th centuries CE (*Shabbat* 88a)

Avdimi de-man Haifa　　אבדימי דמן חיפא
Amora from Eretz Yisrael
4th – 5th centuries CE (*Bava Batra* 12a; *Kiddushin* 33b)

Aveilut　　　　אבילות
Period of mourning (*Moed Katan* 20a; *Yevamot* 43b)

Avia　　　　אויא
Amora from Babylonia
4th century CE (*Berachot* 28b)

Avimi　　　　אבימי
Amora from Babylonia
3rd century CE (*Arachin* 22a; *Menahot* 7a)

Avimi b. Avohu　　　אבימי בר אבהו
Amora from Eretz Yisrael
4th century CE (*Sanhedrin* 99a; *Ketubbot* 85a)

Avimi b. Nazzi　　　אבימי בר נאזי
Father in law of Ravina (*Bava Kamma* 115a)

Avina　　　　אבינא
Amora from Babylonia
3rd – 4th centuries CE (*Berachot* 4b)

Avinu Malkenu　　　אבינו מלכנו
The Talmud states that R. Akiva prayed *Avinu Malkenu* during a severe drought. Since then, we recite those prayers during the ten days between Rosh Hashana and Yom Kippur, and also on fast days. (*Taanit* 25b)

Avira　　　　עוירא
Amora from Eretz Yisrael
3rd – 4th centuries CE (*Berachot* 20b)

Avira　　　　עוירא
Amora from Babylonia
4th century CE (*Berachot* 44a)

▭ Avlat
Persian friend of Shemuel
R. Shemuel said that Israel is immune from planetary influences.

R. Shemuel and his Persian friend Avlat were having a conversation near a meadow. Some people were walking to the meadows passing them. Avlat pointed to a man and said:

"That man is going to the meadows, but he will not return, because a snake will bite him and he will die."

R. Shemuel replied: "If he is an Israelite he will go and return."[25] (*Shabbat* 156b)

Avohu (Abbahu)　　　אבהו
Amora from Eretz Yisrael, Head of academy in Caesarea
3rd – 4th centuries CE (*Shabbat* 119a)

✿ Avoid embarrasing
Avoid embarrassing a poor person receiving charity.

R. Abba was a very charitable person. When he gave charity to the poor, he did not want to embarrass them by facing them. Therefore, he used to wear a scarf with money in it, which he slung towards

---

25. See also entry, Planetary influences.

his back, so that the poor could take what they needed without facing him. (*Ketubbot* 67b)

✿ Avoid hurting feelings
Be aware of sensibilities of others.[26] (*Sotah* 40a)

✿ Avoid in all circumstances
R. Abbaye asked R. Dimi: "What do people in Eretz Yisrael try to avoid the most?" He answered, "Putting another person to shame." (*Bava Metzia* 58b)

Avoidable accidents
What is the responsibility of a guardian in an avoidable accident (*Bava Metzia* 93b)

Avraham   אברהם
The patriarch was in prison
R. Hanan b. Rava said in the name of Rav: "Avraham was imprisoned for ten years; three in Kutha and seven years in Kardu." (*Bava Batra* 91a)

Avraham in the fiery furnace
Nimrod threw Avraham in the fiery furnace (*Pesahim* 118a; *Eruvin* 53a)

Avraham's mother
R. Hanan b. Rava stated in Rav's name: "The name of Avraham's mother was Amathlai; and her father's name was Karnevo." (*Bava Batra* 91a)

Avshalom
Avshalom, son of King David, gloried in his hair. (*Sotah* 9b)

Avtalyon   אבטליון
Tanna from Eretz Yisrael
1st century BCE (*Yoma* 35b)

---

26. See entry, Aggadah.

Avtolemus   אבטולמוס
Tanna from Eretz Yisrael
2nd century CE (*Eruvin* 3:4)

📖 Awe in the presence of Rebbe
On one occasion when Rav was still very young, he and R. Hiyya were having dinner at Rabbi Yehuda HaNasi's table. Rebbe said to Rav, "Get up and wash your hands." R. Hiyya saw that Rav was trembling. He said to him, "Son of Princes, he is telling you to prepare yourself to lead in the blessings after the meal." (*Berachot* 43a)

Axe
Borrowing an axe and breaking it (*Bava Kamma* 11a; *Bava Metzia* 96b)

Azarah
The Temple court in Jerusalem (*Shevuot* 14a)

Azariah   עזריה
Tanna from Eretz Yisrael
1st century CE (*Sotah* 21a)

Azariah   עזריה
In the fiery furnace
Hanania, Misha'el and Azariah were thrown into the fiery furnace by the order of Nebuchadnezzar. (*Sanhedrin* 92b; *Avodah Zarah* 3a)

B

Babel
The generation of dispersion, and the building of the Tower of Babel (*Sanhedrin* 109a)

Babylonia
Leaving Babylonia to Eretz Yisrael (*Shabbat* 41a; *Ketubbot* 110b; *Berachot* 24b)

Babylonian family purity
It was asked, how far does Babylon extend

– with regards to family purity? Rav and Shemuel differed.[27] (*Kiddushin* 71b)

Babylonian scholars
Rebbe asked Levi, after he returned from Babylonia, "What are the scholars of Babylon like?" "They are like the ministering angels." (*Kiddushin* 72a)

✿ Bachelor living in a large city
R. Yohanan said: "Three kinds of people earn special approval from Hashem: a bachelor who lives in a large city and does not sin, a poor man who returns lost property to its owner, and a rich man who tithes his produce in secret.

R. Safra was a bachelor living in a large city. When R. Safra heard this quotation, his face lit up. Rava said to him, "Rabbi Yohanan did not have in mind someone like you, but persons like R. Hanina and R. Hoshia. They are sandal makers in Eretz Yisrael and they live in a neighborhood of prostitutes. They make sandals for them, and when they deal with them they do not lift their eyes to look at the prostitutes. When the prostitutes take an oath, they do it 'by the life of the holy rabbis of Eretz Yisrael.'" (*Pesahim* 113a–b)

Backhanded manner   כלאחר יד
The back of the hand, not in the usual way (*Shabbat* 92a, 153b)

Backwards   למפרע
Reading backwards (*Berachot* 13a)

✿ Bad news
Avoid bringing bad news
Rav was a nephew of R. Hiyya. When he came to Eretz Yisrael from Babylonia, his uncle, R. Hiyya, asked him:
"Is your father Aibu alive?"

He answered: "Ask me if my mother is alive."

When he asked him about his mother, he gave him the same answer. When he heard all of this, he realized that his brother and sister died. (*Pesahim* 4a)

Bad news also requires a benediction
The blessing over bad news is discussed in *Haroeh* הרואה, the 9th *perek* in *Berachot*. (*Berachot* 54a)

Baker
Abba Shaul was the baker in R. Yehuda HaNasi's house. (*Pesahim* 34a)

Balak, King of Moab
R. Yosi b. Hanina said: "Ruth was a descendant of Eglon, the grandson of Balak, King of Moab." (*Sanhedrin* 105b; *Nazir* 23b)

Baldness in the head during mourning
Cutting the hair to make the head bald as a sign of mourning for the dead; it is a forbidden practice. (*Makkot* 20a)

Banquet in Jerusalem
There was a custom in Jerusalem: When a caterer was engaged to prepare a banquet, he had to indemnify the host if he spoiled the food, for the insult to him and his guests.[28] (*Bava Batra* 93b)

📖 Bar Hama
Bar Hama was accused of murder; he was defended by R. Papi
There was a case of a person by the name of Bar Hama, who was accused of murder. Two witnesses testified against him. However, two other witnesses came forward to disqualify one of the former witnesses. Rabbi Papi defended Bar Hama, and he was able to have him acquitted.

---

27. See also entry, Family purity in Babylonia.

28. See also entry, Caterers in Jerusalem.

Thereupon, Bar Hama kissed his feet and undertook to pay his taxes for the rest of his life. (*Sanhedrin* 27a–b)

Bar Kappara   בר קפרא
Tanna-Amora from Eretz Yisrael
2nd – 3rd centuries CE (*Moed Katan* 16a)

Bar Kappara
R. Yohanan visited the town of Parud, where Bar Kappara used to live. He had since passed away. R. Yohanan inquired whether any manuscripts or Mishna by Bar Kappara were left by him. R. Tanhum, from the same town, quoted a Halachah by Bar Kappara. (*Avodah Zarah* 31a)

▢ Bar Kochva
(Bar Koziba)
During the reign of the Roman Emperor Hadrian, there was a revolt led by a person called Bar Kochva. The Talmud recounts that Bar Koziba reigned two and a half years. He said to the rabbis: "I am the Mashiach," and the rabbis told him that it is written of the Mashiach that he smells and judges; let us see if you can do so." He could not. (*Sanhedrin* 93b)

Bar Pada   בר פדא
Yehuda b. Pedayah
Amora from Eretz Yisrael
3rd century CE (*Nedarim* 28b)

Bar Sheshach
Once Rava visited Bar Sheshach, a non-Jewish officer of the Persian King and a friend of Rava; he found him surrounded by naked women. He asked Rava, "Do you have anything like this in the World to Come?" Rava answered, "We have much finer. You have the fear of the ruling power, but for us there will be no fear of the ruling power." While they were sitting together the King's courier arrived, telling him, "The King requires your presence . . ." (*Avodah Zarah* 65a)

Barber
Is it proper to sit down in a barber shop to get a haircut before *Minha* prayer? (*Shabbat* 9b)

✿▢ Barber and idol worshipper
R. Hana b. Bizna was on the road towards Nehardea and he stopped at a barber to have his hair cut. The barber was an idol worshipper. R. Meir had said that a Jew should not have his hair cut by an idol worshipper. The barber made a remark to R. Hana: "Hana, Hana, your throat is very attractive to the scissors." R. Hana said: "I deserve this, because I transgressed on R. Meir's prohibition." (*Avodah Zarah* 29a)

Bardeles   ברדלס
Panther (*Bava Kamma* 15b)

Bareheaded
Walking bareheaded
R. Huna b. Yehoshua said, "May I be rewarded for never walking four cubits bareheaded." R. Huna b. Yehoshua would not walk four cubits bareheaded. (*Kiddushin* 31a; *Shabbat* 118b)

✿ Bareheaded
R. Hisda was praising R. Hamnuna to R. Huna, saying that he is a great man. Said R. Huna, "When he comes to you, bring him to me!"

When he came, he didn't wear a cap, customarily worn by married men. "Why have you no head cap?"

"I have no head cap, because I am not married." R. Huna turned his face away from him and said:

"See to it that you do not come before me before you are married." (*Kiddushin* 29b)

✡ Bareheaded

The mother of R. Nahman b. Yitzhak told her son, "Cover your head so that the fear of Heaven will be upon you.[29] (*Shabbat* 156b)

📖 Barred from academy

Rabbi Meir and Rabbi Nathan

The following instructions were issued in the days when Rabbi Shimon ben Gamliel was president of the Sanhedrin: Whenever the president of the Sanhedrin enters into the assembly, everyone should stand up, but when the Hacham enters and when the Av Bet Din enters only a limited number of the assembly should rise. Rabbi Meir was the Hacham and Rabbi Nathan was the Av Bet Din.

Rabbi Meir and Rabbi Nathan decided to engage in a discourse, in which Rabbi Shimon was not familiar. In consequence, he issued an order to have them removed from the Sanhedrin. When they were on the outside they wrote down difficult scholastic questions on slips of paper, which they threw inside. Many of the questions could not be answered inside, and they were sent back outside unanswered. They wrote down the answer and sent it back inside. Rabbi Yosi b. Halafta said to the assembly, "The Torah is outside and we are sitting inside." (*Horayot* 13b)

📖 Barred from R. Yehuda's academy

It is related that after Rabbi Meir passed away, Rabbi Yehuda b. Illai told his students, "Do not allow the students of Rabbi Meir to enter our academy, because they come only for disputations and to overwhelm me with citations from traditions, but not to learn Torah." Rabbi Sumchos forced his way into the academy. He quoted Rabbi Meir on an important halachic issue. Rabbi Yehuda became very angry and told his students, "Didn't I instruct you not to admit any of Rabbi Meir's students?" Rabbi Yosi responded: "People will say, Rabbi Meir is dead, Rabbi Yehuda is angry, and Rabbi Yosi is silent." (*Nazir* 49b, 50a; *Kiddushin* 52b)

Barrel broken on Shabbat

Food kept in a barrel was broken on Shabbat – what can be saved? (*Shabbat* 143b)

Barren woman   איילונית

A woman incapable of bearing children (*Gittin* 46b; *Ketubbot* 11a)

Baruch Shem   ברוך שם

The rabbis were discussing how to recite the words "*Baruch Shem.*" R. Avohu said it should be said aloud, because if it was said quietly the heretics might accuse the worshippers of cursing them in quiet. But in Nehardea, where there were no heretics, they said it in a low voice. (*Pesahim* 56a)

Basis for what is forbidden

בסיס לדבר האסור

A basis, a stand for that which is forbidden (*Shabbat* 117a)

Basis for what is permitted

בסיס לדבר המותר

A basis, a stand for that which is permitted[30] (*Shabbat* 117a)

Basket

On Shabbat, a basket in the street is a domain of its own. (*Shabbat* 8a)

Bastard marrying (*Yevamot* 78b)

📖 Bat Kol   בת קול

Heavenly voice

Rabbi Eliezer had halachic differences

---

29. See entry, Astrology.

30. Talmudic phrase.

with the rabbis; he brought forth every argument to prove his point, but the rabbis did not accept them. He declared: "If the Halachah agrees with me, let this carob tree prove it."

The carob tree uprooted itself. The rabbis retorted: "The carob tree couldn't prove the argument."

He then said to them: "If I am right, then let the stream of water prove it." Thereupon the stream of water started flowing in the opposite direction. The rabbis retorted: "The stream of water couldn't prove anything in this matter." Rabbi Eliezer then said:

"If I am right, then let the walls of this school prove it."

Thereupon the walls began to incline. Rabbi Yehoshua spoke up and rebuked the walls.

"When scholars are in a holy dispute, what business do the walls have to interfere?" The walls stopped to incline, but did not straighten out either. Rabbi Eliezer said:

"If I am right, let the heavens prove it." Thereupon a heavenly voice came forth. "The Halachah is like Rabbi Eliezer." Rabbi Yehoshua spoke up and said: "The Torah is not in heaven." Rabbi Yirmiyahu arose and declared:

"The Torah has already been given on Mount Sinai, it belongs here on earth and we do not pay attention to heavenly voices." He continued to say:

"It has been written in the Torah that the majority decides."

A postscript to the story: At a later time, Rabbi Nathan encountered Eliyahu and inquired:

"What did Hashem do during that hour?" He was happy laughing, "My sons have defeated Me, and My sons have defeated Me." (*Bava Metzia* 59b)

Bat Kol[31]   בת קול
(*Berachot* 17b; *Bava Metzia* 59b)

📖 Bat Kol and Hillel
Dispute between Bet Shammai and Bet Hillel
Rabbi Abba said in the name of Rabbi Shemuel: "For three years there was a dispute between Bet Shammai and Bet Hillel, each one claiming the Halachah is in agreement with their views." Then a Bat Kol[32] was heard announcing that both are the words of the living God, but the Halachah is in agreement with the rulings of Bet Hillel. (*Eruvin* 13b; *Gittin* 6b)

📖 Bat Kol in Yavne
The rabbis were meeting in the upper chamber in Yavne when they heard a heavenly voice say: "There is one amongst you who is worthy that the Shechina should rest upon him." The rabbis present directed their gaze on Shemuel HaKatan. (*Sanhedrin* 11a; *Sotah* 48b)

📖 Bat Kol replaces prophecy
Our rabbis taught: When Haggai, Zecharyah and Malachi died, the *Ruah Ha-Kodesh* departed from Israel. Nevertheless, they still had the Bat Kol to make use of. On one occasion when the rabbis were sitting in the upper chamber of Gurya's house in Jericho, a Bat Kol from heaven was heard saying: "There is in the midst of you a man who deserves that the Shechina should rest upon him but his generation is unworthy of it." The rabbis present directed their gaze on Rabbi Hillel the Elder. (*Sotah* 48b; *Sanhedrin* 11a; *Yoma* 9b)

Bathhouse
R. Gamliel encountered Pruklos, the son

---

31. See entry, Feeding the world.
32. Heavenly voice.

of a philosopher in a bathhouse. Pruklos asked him why he is bathing in a bathhouse where the statue of Aphrodite is present. R. Gamliel answered him that actually all the activities one does in the bathhouse are insulting the idol Aphrodite. (*Avodah Zarah* 44b)

Bathhouse
R. Yehuda HaNasi in the bathhouse (*Shabbat* 40b)

Bathhouse before Minha
Visiting a bathhouse before *Minha* praying (*Shabbat* 9b)

Bathhouse insult (*Bava Kamma* 86b)

Bathhouse in Tzippori
A person rented a bathhouse for a year and that year was a leap year. (*Bava Batra* 105a)

Bathhouse on Shabbat
A bathhouse heated on Shabbat by non-Jews (*Machshirin* 2:5)

Bathhouse praying
Praying or putting on *tefillin* in a bathhouse (*Shabbat* 10a)

Bathhouse thoughts
Having Torah thoughts in a bathhouse or toilet (*Shabbat* 40b)

Bathing a child on Shabbat (*Shabbat* 134b)

Bathing in Tiberias
Bathing in the hot waters of Tiberias on Shabbat is discussed in *Havit*, the 22nd *perek* in *Shabbat*. (*Shabbat* 143b)

Bathing on Erev Shabbat
R. Yehuda said in the name of Rav: This was the custom of R. Yehuda b. Illai on Erev Shabbat: A basin of water was brought to him and he washed his face,

hands and feet, and he wrapped himself in fringed linen ropes and he looked like an angel. (*Shabbat* 25b)

Bathing with preheated water
At first they allowed preheated water, but bath attendants took advantage and fooled people saying it was heated from before Shabbat when it wasn't; therefore, it was forbidden. (*Shabbat* 40a)

Bava ben Buta   בבא בן בוטא
Tanna from Eretz Yisrael
1st century BCE (*Betzah* 20a)

Be accurate
R. Gamliel said: "Do not estimate, do not guess, but be accurate." (*Avot* 1:16)

Be Biri and Be Narash
R. Huna b. Yehoshua remarked: "The hills between Be Biri and Be Narash contributed to make me old." (*Eruvin* 56a)

Beacons lit on the hills
To signal the arrival of the new month, they lit beacons on top of the hills. After the first beacon was lit on the hill, the nearest hill to it lit also its beacon and so on. (*Rosh Hashana* 22b)

Beam   קורה
A cross beam used to make an *eruv* for Shabbat (*Eruvin* 12b)

📖 Beams by miracle
Once a woman, a neighbor of R. Hanina b. Dosa, was building a house, but the beams were not long enough to reach the walls. She came to him with her problem. He asked her for her name, and she replied that her name is Aiku. He told her: "Aiku, may your beams reach your walls."

A Tanna taught that after that the beams projected one cubit on either side. Poleimu said: "I saw that house and its beams projected one cubit on either side and people told me: 'This is the house that was covered with beams by the prayers of R. Hanina b. Dosa.'" (*Taanit* 25a)

Bear
The danger of a bear and warning thereof is being discussed. (*Bava Kamma* 15b)

Beard-cutting
(*Makkot* 20b)

Bears and goats
R. Hanina b. Dosa; his goats brought in bears on their horns (*Bava Metzia* 106a)

Bears and lions
Selling bears and lions to non-Jews (*Avodah Zarah* 16a)

Beaten by his teacher
The father of Shemuel found one day Shemuel crying.
  "Why are you crying?"
  "Because my teacher beat me."
  "Why did he beat you?"
  "Because I fed his son without washing hands."
  "Why did you not wash hands?"
  "It was he that was eating, so why should I wash hands?" (*Hullin* 107b)

Bechi Yutan   בכי יותן
Bechi yutan is a Talmudic term for a situation where food became wet, but there was no intention to make the food wet, however the owner welcomed if the liquid fell upon the food. (*Hullin* 16a; *Machshirin* 1:1)

Beds' susceptibility to uncleanness
(*Kelim* 18:5, 19:1– 6)

Bedtime Shema
R. Yehoshua b. Levi said: "The *Shema* at bedtime is a religious act to recite even

when one recited it in the synagogue." (*Berachot* 4b)

Beehives and uncleanness (*Uktzin* 3:10)

Beer
Drinking beer with non-Jews
Rami b. Hama said in the name of R. Yitzhak: "Drinking beer with non-Jews is to be avoided; it might lead to intermarriages." (*Avodah Zarah* 31b)

Beer Manufacturer
R. Hisda was a beer manufacturer
R. Hisda said: "If I were not a beer manufacturer, I wouldn't have become a wealthy person." He was a very charitable person. An example of his generosity is the large sum of money he contributed to have the academy in Sura rebuilt when it became neglected and in a rundown condition.
  R. Hisda said: "The reason I have an advantage over my colleagues is because I was married at sixteen."
  He and his wife had seven sons and two daughters. (*Pesahim* 113a)

Bei Evyoni   בי אביוני
Name of a location (*Bava Kamma* 117a)

Beitus ben Zonan   ביתוס בן זונן
A merchant mentioned in the Talmud (*Avodah Zarah* 65b)

Believable, but some are unbelievable
R. Papa had a saying. "If you hear that your neighbor died, believe it. If you hear that your neighbor became wealthy, do not believe it." (*Gittin* 30b, 85a; *Ketubbot* 83b)

Ben Ahiya   בן אחיה
Officer of the Temple (*Shekalim* 5:1)

Ben Arza   בן ערזה
Officer of the Temple (*Shekalim* 5:1)

Ben Avtiah
Physically a big man, he was the son-in-law of R. Yohanan b. Zakkai. (*Bechorot* 37b)

Ben Azzai   בן עזאי
Tanna from Eretz Yisrael
2nd century CE (*Avot* 4:3)

Ben Azzai   בן עזאי
Since Ben Azzai passed away, industrious scholars ceased. (*Sotah* 49a)

Ben Bag Bag   בן בג בג
Tanna from Eretz Yisrael
1st century CE (*Avot* 5:22)

Ben Bevi   בן בבי
Officer of the Temple (*Shekalim* 5:1)

Ben Buchri   בן בוכרי
Tanna from Jerusalem
1st century CE (*Shekalim* 1:4)

Ben Gever   בן גבר
Officer of the Temple (*Shekalim* 5:1)

Ben Ha Ha   בן הא הא
Tanna from Eretz Yisrael
1st century CE (*Avot* 5:23)

Ben Ha Ha and Eliyahu
The Talmud mentions that Eliyahu spoke to Ben Ha Ha. (*Hagigah* 9b)

Ben Zoma   בן זומא
Tanna from Eretz Yisrael
2nd century CE (*Avot* 4:1)

Ben Zoma   בן זומא
Since Ben Zoma died, good interpreters ceased. (*Sotah* 49a)

Bene
R. Hiyya's brother's name was Bene. (*Ketubbot* 50b)

Bene Berak   בני ברק
During the second century CE in Tannaic times, Bene Berak became a center of Jewish learning. Rabbi Akiva ben Yosef established his academy there. Today, the community is located near Yaffo and Tel Aviv.

In the Haggadah, it is mentioned that R. Eliezer, R. Yehoshua, R. Eleazar b. Azariah, and R. Tarfon visited R. Akiva in Bene Berak. Such luminaries as Rabbi Meir, Rabbi Shimon ben Yohai, and Rabbi Yehuda bar Illai studied in the academy of Rabbi Akiva. (*Sanhedrin* 32b)

Bene Berak   בני ברק
Bathhouse meeting
It happened that R. Eleazar b. Azariah and R. Akiva were in the bathhouse; a question arose about the water being heated improperly. (*Shabbat* 40a)

📖 **Bene Berak academy**   בני ברק
It is related that R. Hanania went to the academy located in Bene Berak and spent twelve years there. By the time he returned home, the streets of the town were altered and he was unable to find his way home. (*Ketubbot* 62b)

Bene Betera Family   בני בתירא
The Bene Betera family were active from the 1st century BCE to the 2nd century CE. (*Bava Metzia* 85a)

Benedictions before and after
Eating or performing a mitzvah – when does one say the benediction? (*Niddah* 51b; *Berachot* 44b)

Benedictions' beginning and ending
All benedictions begin with *Baruch* and end with *Baruch*, except benedictions over fruit and *mitzvot*, and benedictions that are next to another benediction. (*Berachot* 46a; *Pesahim* 104b)

Benedictions before the Shema
The number of benedictions to be recited before and after the *Shema* (*Berachot* 11a)

✿ Benefactor
The Talmud relates that Rabbah said to Rafram b. Papa: "Tell me some of the good deeds Rabbi Huna had done."

He replied, "On cloudy days, they used to drive him in his golden carriage to survey every part of the city of Sura. When he saw walls that were unsafe he would order them to be demolished, and if the owner could not afford to rebuild them he would rebuild them at his own expense.

"On Friday afternoons, he would send messengers to the market and buy all the leftover vegetables.

"Whenever he discovered a new medicine, he would suspend it above his door with a jug of water next to it, and would put a notice with it, which stated that whoever needs it should come and get it.

"When he had a meal, he would open his doors wide open and declare. 'Whoever is in need of a meal, come and eat.'"
(*Taanit* 20b)

▭ Beneficial
All happenings are for good
R. Huna said in the name of Rav, who learned it from R. Meir, who learned it from R. Akiva: "A person should always say: 'Whatever happened, Hashem did it for something good.'"[33] (*Berachot* 60b)

Benefit derived without thanking
R. Hanina b. Papa said: "Anyone who benefits from this world without making a blessing is equal to a robber." (*Sanhedrin* 102a; *Berachot* 35b)

---

33. See entry, Whatever happened, Hashem did it for something good.

Benefit forbidden   אסור בהנאה
It is forbidden to have any benefit or enjoyment from it. (*Bava Kamma* 41a; *Pesahim* 21a; *Hullin* 114b)

Benefit for one party, but loss for other   זה נהנה וזה חסר
One party benefits and the other loses (*Bava Kamma* 20b)

Benefits for one, no loss for other   זה נהנה וזה לא חסר
One party benefits and the other has no loss (*Bava Kamma* 20b)

Benefiting a person in his absence   זכין לאדם שלא בפניו
A benefit can be conferred on a person in his absence. (*Eruvin* 81b; *Gittin* 11b; *Kiddushin* 23a)

Berachia (Berechiah)   ברכיה
Amora from Eretz Yisrael
4th century CE (*Taanit* 4a)

Beraira   ברירה
A subsequent selection reveals retrospectively what the original intent was. (*Bava Kamma* 51b; 69b; *Bava Batra* 27b; *Betzah* 39b; *Nedarim* 45b)

Beraita   ברייתא
A Beraita is similar to a Mishna in Talmudic learning, but not incorporated in the Talmud. The Talmud also refers to it as Matnita מתניתא (*Berachot* 2b; *Shabbat* 19b, 61a, 145b; *Eruvin* 19b; *Pesahim* 101b; *Gittin* 45a; *Eruchin* 30a)

Beraita   ברייתא
Rabbi Hiyya was particularly known for the Talmudic teachings called *Beraitot*, which he and his students compiled. He had interactions constantly with Rabbi Yehuda HaNasi, and they quoted each

other, but Rabbi Hiyya had his own Bet Midrash.

R. Hiyya is the author of the Beraita, which he taught in his own academy. As the Talmud says: "Abbaye says our Mishna is in accordance with R. Safra, who learned it in the academy of R. Hiyya on the subject of charging interest. R. Hiyya taught there are 24 principal kinds of damages." (*Bava Kamma* 4b)

Rav said: "I found a secret scroll of the scroll of the school of R. Hiyya." (*Shabbat* 6b)

R. Hiyya taught: "Issi b. Yehuda said, 'There are thirty-nine principal labors on Shabbat.'" (*Berachot* 24a; *Pesahim* 4a; *Bava Metzia* 62b–65b)

Beroka from Hozeah   ברוקא חוזאה
2nd century CE (*Taanit* 22a)

Berona   ברונא
Amora from Babylonia
3rd century CE (*Eruvin* 74a)

Beror Hayil academy   ברור חיל
Beror Hayil was a small community in southern Israel, southeast of Ashkelon.

In his later years, R. Yohanan b. Zakkai moved to that community and many students followed him there. R. Yohanan Ben Zakkai lived in the 1st century CE. (*Sanhedrin* 32b)

📖 Berurya   ברוריה
The Talmud relates that Berurya, Rabbi Meir's wife, was the daughter of Rabbi Hanania b. Teradion. Her sister was captured and placed in a brothel. Berurya told her husband, "I am ashamed to have my sister in a brothel. Can you do something to get her out of there?" So he took a bag full of *dinarim* and set out to ransom her. He offered the money to the watchman and he released her. The government found out what he had done and they were

looking to arrest him. For that reason he had to leave Eretz Yisrael and move to Babylonia. (*Avodah Zarah* 18a)

Berurya   ברוריה
Berurya was the wife of Rabbi Meir and the daughter of Rabbi Hanania ben Teradion. She was a great scholar. (*Pesahim* 62b)

📖 Berurya advises R. Meir
Once there were some Biryoni in the neighborhood of R. Meir, who caused him a lot of aggravation. R. Meir wanted to pray for them to die. But his wife Berurya said to him: "It is not a good idea; rather pray for them they should repent." He did pray and they repented. (*Berachot* 10a)

Berurya debates a sectarian (*Berachot* 10a)

📖 Berurya met R. Yosi HaGlili
R. Yosi HaGlili was once traveling, when he met Berurya, the wife of Rabbi Meir, and he asked her: "By which road do we go to Lydda?" She replied: "Foolish Galilean, didn't the rabbis teach that you should not engage in much conversation with a woman? You should have asked, 'by which to Lydda.'" (*Eruvin* 53b)

Besamim
Spices used at the end of the Shabbat day (*Berachot* 51b)

Beseech God
The most appropriate time for an individual to beseech God are the ten days between Rosh Hashana and Yom Kippur. (*Yevamot* 49b, 105a; *Rosh Hashana* 18a)

Best quality property   עידית
(*Gittin* 48b; *Bava Kamma* 7b)

Bet Avtinas   בית אבטינס
Officer of the Temple (*Shekalim* 5:1)

Bet Avtinas   בית אבטינס
A chamber at the Temple; it had an upper floor where the young priests kept watch. (*Tamid* 2a)

Bet Garmu   בית גרמו
Officer of the Temple (*Shekalim* 5:1)

Bet HaMoked   בית המוקד
A chamber in the Temple where the elders of the Priests slept; they had the keys to the different chambers. (*Tamid* 2a)

Bet HaNitzotz   בית הניצוץ
A chamber in the Temple; it had an upper floor where the young priests kept watch during the night. (*Tamid* 2a)

Bet HaPras   בית הפרס
An area of doubt about graves (*Ohalot* 17:1 *Niddah* 57a; *Berachot* 19b; *Eruvin* 30b)

Bet Hinu   בית הינו
A place in Jerusalem where the stores were located. The stores of Bet Hinu were destroyed before Jerusalem by three years. (*Bava Metzia* 88a)

Bet Shearim   בית שערים
Bet Shearim is an ancient city in the Lower Galilee, and was located not far from Tivon and Haifa. Rabbi Yehuda HaNasi took up residence there in 170 CE. He also moved his academy to that location. Consequently, Bet Shearim was the seat of the Sanhedrin during his tenure.

During Rabbi Yehuda HaNasi's time there were hundreds of students studying in his academy. The Mishna – upon which the whole Gemara is based – was redacted by Rabbi Yehuda HaNasi and he did most of his editing in Bet Shearim. The great Amoraim of Babylonia including Rav studied in the academy of Rabbi Yehuda HaNasi. Rav eventually established his own academy in Sura, Babylonia.

Rabbi Yehuda HaNasi is buried in Bet Shearim.

The area has been excavated and they found remains of large buildings. They also found many caves with burial places inside the caves.

R. Yehuda HaNasi lived in the 2nd – 3rd centuries CE. (*Sanhedrin* 32b; *Ketubbot* 103b)

Betar
There were three persons in Betar who could speak seventy languages. (*Sanhedrin* 17b)

Betar and After-meal blessing
Rabbi Mathna is one of the authors of the fourth blessing after meals. The benediction was instituted in Yavne with reference to those who were slain in Betar. For Rabbi Mathna said, "On that day permission was given to bury those slain, they ordained that 'Who is good and bestows good' הטוב והמטיב should be said." (*Berachot* 48b; *Taanit* 31a; *Bava Batra* 121b)

Betar fell
During the Bar Kochva war, the city of Betar fell to the Romans on the ninth day of Av. (*Taanit* 26b)

Betar martyrs buried
R. Mathna said: "The fifteenth of Av was the day the martyrs of Betar received their burial. (*Bava Batra* 121b)

📖 Betrayal
One Jew against another
Rabbi Kahana had to flee Babylonia, because of an incident. A man was brought before Rav; he wanted to denounce another Jew to the Persian authorities and to show them where the Jew is hiding his straw. Rav ordered the man not to show

it, but the man insisted. "I will show it."[34]
(*Bava Kamma* 117a)

Betrothal
A *peruta* is required to make a betrothal
binding. (*Bava Metzia* 55a)

Betrothal / Conversion
A man says to a woman: "Be betrothed to
me after my conversion." (*Bava Metzia* 16b;
Kiddushin 63a; *Ketubbot* 58b)

Betrothal for children
Negotiations for betrothal on Shabbat?
(*Shabbat* 12a)

Betrothed maiden   נערה מאורסה
Punishment for violating a betrothed
maiden (*Sanhedrin* 66b)

✡ Beware of authorities
R. Gamliel said: "Beware of the authorities, for they befriend people only for
their own benefit; they act friendly when
it benefits them, but are not there when
one needs them." (*Avot* 2:3)

▭ Beware of suspicious characters
R. Giddal said in the name of Rav: "If
someone from Naresh gives you a kiss,
then count your teeth; if a man from Nahar Pakod accompanies you, it is because
of the fine garments you wear; if a man
from Pumbedita accompanies you, then
change your address." (*Hullin* 127a)

Beyond Tehum Shabbat
Walking on Shabbat beyond the bound-
ary permissible to walk (*Eruvin* 52b)

Bibi (Bibai)   ביבי
Amora from Eretz Yisrael
3rd century CE (*Bava Kamma* 61a)

Bibi (Bibai)   ביבי
Amora from Babylonia
4th century CE (*Bava Metzia* 23b)

Bibi b. Abbaye (Bibai)   ביבי בר אביי
Amora from Babylonia
Head of Academy in Pumbedita
4th century CE (*Ketubbot* 85a)

Bikkur Holim
A student of R. Akiva took ill. (*Nedarim* 40a)

Bilam
The biblical figure who was asked by King
Balak to curse the Jewish people (*Sanhedrin*
105a–b, 106a)

Bilam advisor to Pharaoh
Bilam advised Pharaoh to destroy Israel;
Iyov was also an advisor, but he was silent;
Yitro was also an advisor, but he fled. He
did not want to be associated with the de-
cree. (*Sanhedrin* 106a)

Bilam's advice
Bilam advised King Balak to let loose his
women among the Israelites, because God
hates immorality. (*Sanhedrin* 106a)

Bilam's blessings
Bilam blessed Israel against his inclination. (*Sanhedrin* a–b)

Binyamin b. Yafet   בנימין בר יפת
Amora from Eretz Yisrael
3rd century CE (*Berachot* 33a)

Biram
A town near Pumbedita along the river
Euphrates (*Avodah Zarah* 57a)

Bird organs
What organ-injuries make a bird *trefa*?
(*Hullin* 56 a–b)

---

34. See entry, Lion has come up from Babylonia.

Bird slaughtering

Rebbe said: "Moshe Rabbeinu was in-structed about the esophagus and the windpipe in birds." (*Hullin* 85b, 28a; *Yoma* 75b)

Bird slaughtering by Halachah

יש שחיטה לעוף מן התורה

Some rabbis hold that *shehita* for a bird is from the Torah. (*Hullin* 20b)

Birds and Shehita

R. Yehuda said in the name of R. Yitzhak b. Pinhas: "Birds do not require to be slaughtered by the law of the Torah." (*Hullin* 20a, 85a, 27b, 4a; *Kiddushin* 71a; *Nazir* 29a)

✡ Birds for the Temple

It once happened that the price of a pair of birds in Jerusalem was inflated to a golden *dinarim*. R. Shimon b. Gamliel became upset and he exclaimed: "I shall not go to rest tonight until a pair of birds can be obtained for a silver *dinarim*." He entered the Bet Din and issued instructions that a woman who has five confinements brings only one sacrifice and she may eat sacri-ficial meat; she need not bring the rest. On that day, the price of a pair of birds went down to a quarter of a *dinar*. (*Bava Batra* 166a)

Bird's nest

Observance of this commandment is dis-cussed. (*Hullin* 142a; *Berachot* 33b)

Birta DeSatya

The Talmud relates that there is a town in Babylonia called Birta DeSatya. Once a fishpond overflowed on Shabbat and the people went out to catch the fish. When Rabbi Ahi found out, he declared a ban against the people who violated the Shab-bat. The people then renounced Judaism altogether. (*Kiddushin* 72a)

Birthing

Helping an animal and relieving her of pain when giving birth on Shabbat. (*Shabbat* 54b)

Bisa   ביסא

Tanna from Eretz Yisrael
2nd century CE (*Bava Batra* 59a)

Bishlama   בשלמא

It is well, it can be acceptable.[35] (*Shabbat* 7a)

Bitusian   ביתוסי

A Bitusian is a member of a sect similar to the Tzadokis. (*Shabbat* 108a)

Bitter herbs Maror   מרור

Bitter herbs used on Pesach at the Seder table (*Pesahim* 116b)

Bizna b. Zavda   ביזנא בר זבדא

Tanna from Eretz Israel
2nd – 3rd centuries CE (*Berachot* 55b)

Blasphemer

A blasphemer is not condemned unless he utters the divine name. (*Sanhedrin* 55b, 56a)

Blemished animal

One may not examine his own animal's blemish. (*Bechorot* 38b)

Blemished animals

Teaching students about the characteris-tics of blemished animals (*Bechorot* 38b)

Blemished firstling

Can a Kohen share a blemished animal with an Israelite or a non-Jew? (*Bechorot* 32b)

Blemishes in animals

Which blemishes disqualify an animal for offerings (*Bechorot* 37a)

---

35. Talmudic expression.

Blemishes in humans that matter
(*Bechorot* 43a, 3b; *Ketubbot* 85a)

Blessed be Mordechai
Rava said: "One should drink enough wine on Purim to become mellow until one does not know the difference between cursed be Haman and blessed be Mordechai." (*Megillah* 7b)

Blessed memory   זכור לטוב
When the name of the Prophet Eliyahu is mentioned, it is always followed by the words "of blessed memory." It is also used when someone did something special like Hanania b. Hezkiya. (*Berachot* 3a; *Shabbat* 13b)

Blessing after a meal
The commandment from the Torah to make the blessing after eating a meal (*Berachot* 48b)

Blessing after a meal
When can a large group split to bless separately? (*Berachot* 50a)

Blessing after the meal
The blessing after the meal is a commandment from the Torah. (*Berachot* 21a)

Blessing after the meal, if forgotten
Forgetting the blessing after the meal; dispute between Bet Shammai and Bet Hillel (*Berachot* 51b)

Blessing at dining
When three people dine together (*Berachot* 45a, 50a, 7th *perek*)

Blessing before and after Torah study
(*Berachot* 21a)

✿📖 Blessing for personal miracles
Mar b. Ravina was going through a valley called Aravot and was becoming dehydrated. By miracle, a well was created and he drank. Another time he was walking through a famous building in Mehuza and a wild camel was about to attack him. Just at that moment, one of the walls fell in and he was able to escape from the camel. Thereafter, whenever he passed these places he used to say a blessing and thank God for the miracles. (*Berachot* 54a)

📖 Blessing from a Sage
Rabbi Yitzhak was a guest at Rabbi Nahman and when he was about to leave Rabbi Nahman asked him, "Please bless me."

Rabbi Yitzhak replied: "Let me tell you a story. A traveler was crossing the desert and he was hungry and warm, but he had no more food and he longed for a little shade. All of a sudden, he came upon a fruit tree. He ate from the fruit, which were sweet; he rested under the shade and drank from the stream of water flowing beneath the tree. When he was about to continue on his journey, he said, 'O tree, with what should I bless you? Your fruits are already sweet, your shade is already pleasant, and the stream of water is already flowing beneath you. Therefore I bless you with this: May it be God's will that all the shoots taken from you should also be like you.' The same is with you. You are already blessed with many blessings, and here is one more: God should bless your children to be also like you." (*Taanit* 5b)

📖 Blessing from Rav
As a young man R. Huna was very poor, but in his later years he became wealthy.

One day R. Huna entered the academy of Rav with a string tied around his waist. Rav asked him, "What is the meaning of this?" He explained that he had no wine for *Kiddush* and had to pledge his girdle to buy wine. Rav blessed him:

"May it be the will of God that one day you shall have plenty of silk robes to be smothered in them."

On the day when R. Huna's son, Rabbah, was married, R. Huna, who was a short man, was lying on a couch and his daughters and daughters-in-law were selecting cloths for themselves and without noticing him, they threw silk dresses on the couch until he was smothered in silk dresses. When Rav heard of this, he remarked, "When I blessed you why did you not say, 'the same to you, Sir?'" (*Megillah* 27b)

✡ Blessing of a commoner
R. Hanina said, "Let not a blessing of a common man be taken lightly." (*Megillah* 15a)

Blessing over beer (*Bava Batra* 96b)

Blessing over bread exempts
R Hiyya said: "A blessing said over bread suffices for all kinds of food served during the meal, and a blessing over wine suffices for all kinds of drinks served at that meal." (*Berachot* 41b; *Hullin* 111b)

Blessing over food
In what order, which food has precedence
R. Hisda and R. Hamnuna were dining together. The attendants set before them dates and pomegranates. R. Hamnuna took some dates and said a blessing over them. R. Hisda asked him if he does not agree with the rabbis who say one should make a blessing on the fruit mentioned first in the Torah. He replied that the date is mentioned second following the word "*eretz*" and the pomegranates are mentioned fifth following the word "*eretz*." Rabbi Hisda remarked, "If we only had iron feet so that we could always run and listen to you." (*Berachot* 41b)

Blessing over vegetables – boiled
R. Hiyya b. Abba said in the name of R. Yohanan: "The blessing over boiled vegetables is *Pri Adama*." However, R. Binyamin b. Yafet said in the name of R. Yohanan: "The blessing over boiled vegetables is *Shehakol*." R. Nahman b. Yitzhak said: "Ulla made an error in accepting the word of R. Binyamin b. Yafet." R. Zera expressed astonishment: "How can you compare R. Binyamin b. Yafet with R. Hiyya b. Abba? R. Hiyya b. Abba was very particular to get the exact teachings of R. Yohanan, while R. Binyamin b. Yafet was not so careful. Furthermore, R. Hiyya b. Abba used to go over his learning with R. Yohanan every thirty days, while R. Binyamin did not." (*Berachot* 38b; *Hullin* 86b; *Keritot* 27a)

Blessing prior to performance
R. Yehuda said in the name of R. Shemuel: "All the benedictions for all the commandments are recited prior to the performance." (*Pesahim* 7b, 119b; *Menahot* 35b; *Megillah* 21b; *Sukkah* 39a; *Niddah* 63a)

Blessing when learning Torah
R. Yohanan Nepaha composed one of the blessings we recite when we learn Torah. (*Berachot* 11b)

Blessings
The fourth blessing in Birkat Hamazon
Rabbi Mathna is one of the authors of the fourth blessing after meals. The benediction was instituted in Yavne with reference to those who were slain in Betar. For Rabbi Mathna said, "On the day permission was given to bury those slain, they ordained that 'Who is good and bestows good' should be said.[36] (*Berachot* 48b; *Taanit* 31a; *Bava Batra* 121b)

Blessings After-meal
R. Zera said to R. Hisda: "Teach us about the blessings after the meal."

---

36. See also entry, Betar and After-meal blessing.

R. Hisda replied: "The blessings after the meal I do not know myself, how could I teach it to others?"

"What do you mean?" asked R. Zera.

"I was once in the house of the Resh Geluta and when I said the blessings after the meal R. Sheshet stretched out his neck at me like a serpent, because I left out some passages." (*Berachot* 49a)

Blessings after the meal
When one recites the blessing after a meal, what language may be used? (*Sotah* 32a; *Berachot* 40b; *Shevuot* 39a)

Blessings at weddings
R. Assi came to the wedding feast of Mar, the son of R. Ashi, and recited six benedictions. (*Ketubbot* 8a)

Blessings incorrect (*Berachot* 40a)

Blessings of the Kohanim   ברכת כהנים
The proper way to do the blessings and the proper participation of the congregation is discussed. (*Sotah* 39b)

Blessings of the Kohanim lifting hands
When do the Kohanim lift their hands to do the Priestly Blessings? (*Taanit* 26a; *Yoma* 87b)

Blessings of the Kohen Gadol
The proper ceremony and performance of the Kohen Gadol's Blessing (*Sotah* 40b; *Yoma* 68b)

Blessings on Har Eival   הר עיבל
How were the blessings and the curses pronounced? (*Sotah* 32a)

Blessings on Har Gerizim   הר גריזים
How were the blessings and the curses pronounced? (*Sotah* 32a)

Blessings over several fruits
When making a blessing over several fruits, which one is first? (*Berachot* 41a)

Blessings when acquiring a home
Also acquiring new garments, etc. (*Berachot* 54a)

Blessings when seeing a mountain
Also when seeing the seas, oceans, and deserts (*Berachot* 54a)

Blessings without mentioning the Divine name (*Berachot* 40b)

Blessings' words of the Kohanim
The proper form and pronunciation of the words used in the Blessings (*Sotah* 37b)

Blind
Blind persons performing mitzvot
R. Yosef said: "Formerly, I used to say that if anyone told me the Halachah is in accordance of R. Yehuda, who said a blind person is exempt from *mitzvot*, and I would have made a festive occasion for our rabbis. [R. Yosef was blind.] But now that I heard R. Hanina say that greater is the reward for those who are being commanded than of those who are not being commanded. (*Bava Kamma* 87a; *Kiddushin* 31a)

Blood   דם הקזה
First blood after slaughtering (*Keritot* 20a, 22a; *Pesahim* 65b; *Zevahim* 35a)

Blood   דם התמצית
Secondary blood after slaughtering (*Keritot* 20a, 22a; *Pesahim* 65b; *Zevahim* 35a)

Bloodletting
Bloodletting for medicinal purposes (*Avodah Zarah* 29a; *Nedarim* 54b)

📖 Blood of lust
Ifra Hormuz once sent some blood to

Rava to be examined while R. Ovadiah was present. He smelled it and declared: "This blood is from lust." When she heard what Rava said, she said to her son the king: "See how wise the Jews are."

The king replied, "He is guessing." She sent him sixty samples of different blood, and Rava identified all of them except one, which was lice blood. However, he sent her a comb, which exterminates lice. She exclaimed. "You Jews, you seem to know one's inner heart." (*Niddah* 20b)

Blood removal by salting
R Shemuel said: "Meat cannot be drained of its blood unless it has been salted very well and rinsed very well." (*Hullin* 97b, 111a, 113a; *Pesahim* 76a)

Bloodshed
On account of bloodshed, the Temple was destroyed and the Shechina removed itself from the people of Israel. (*Shabbat* 33a; *Yoma* 85a)

Blood stain (*Niddah* 52b)

Blue fringes   תכלת
The absence of blue fringes (*Menahot* 38a)

Blue yarn in the Tzitzit
The rabbis discuss the commandment of the blue yarn (תכלת) in the *tzitzit* of the *tallit*. (*Menahot* 38a)

📖 Boat endangered by a donkey
A certain man pushed his donkey on a ferryboat before the passengers had a chance to disembark. The boat was shaking and in danger of sinking. Another man who was on the boat came and pushed the donkey overboard and the donkey drowned. When the case came before Rabbah, he declared the man not guilty.

Abbaye said to Rabbah: "Didn't the man rescue himself with another man's money?"

Rabbah replied: "No, the owner of the donkey was from the beginning the pursuer." (*Bava Kamma* 117b)

Boat in a storm
A boat in the open sea being threatened by a storm and it becomes necessary to lighten the cargo; how the loss is apportioned to the passengers (*Bava Kamma* 116b)

Boat sale
When selling a boat – what is included? (*Bava Batra* 73a)

Bogeret   בוגרת
A young girl, 12.5-year old about to mature, adolescence (*Ketubbot* 39a; *Sanhedrin* 66b)

Bohayon
Our rabbis taught: Ben Bohayon gave the corners of his vegetable field to the poor. When his father came and saw the poor laden with vegetables, he told them, "Leave the vegetables and I will give you double from tithing." (*Pesahim* 57a)

Boiled vegetables
What is the blessing to be made?
R. Hiyya b. Abba said in the name of R. Yohanan: "The blessing over boiled vegetables is *Pri Adama*." (*Berachot* 38b)

Boiled wine   יין מבושל
Boiled wine is not suspected of idolatrous use.

Shemuel and Avlat were sitting together and boiled wine was being served. Avlat withdrew his hand,[37] Shemuel said to him: "Boiled wine is not suspected of idolatrous use." (*Avodah Zarah* 30a)

✿ Bold as a leopard
Yehuda b. Tema said: "Be bold as a leopard, light as an eagle, swift as a deer, and

---

37. Avlat was not Jewish.

strong as a lion – to carry out the will of your Father in Heaven." (*Avot* 5:20)

Bonds of indebtedness (*Bava Batra* 172a)

Bones
Removing bones from the table on Shabbat is discussed in *Notel* נוטל, the 21st *perek* in *Shabbat*. (*Shabbat* 141b)

Book of cures hidden
R. Levi said: "King Hizkiyahu hid the book of cures." (*Berachot* 10b)

Books not to read
R. Akiva said: "Anyone who reads books which are against the Jewish religion will not have a share in *Olam Haba*." (*Sanhedrin* 90a, 100b)

Books of the Prophets: their order
Our rabbis taught: The order of the Prophet books is Yehoshua, Shoftim, Shemuel, Melachim, Yirmiyahu, Yehezkel, Yeshaya, and the Twelve other Prophets. Others would have it in this order: Yeshaya, Yirmiyahu and Yehezkel. The order of the Ketuvim is Ruth, Tehillim, Iyov, Mishlei, Kohelet, Shir HaShirim, Kinot, Daniel, Esther, Ezra, and Divrei Hayamim. Others disagree and have a different order. (*Bava Batra* 14b)

Borer   בורר
Chosen judge: Disputes in monetary matters are judged by three, each litigant chooses one, and the two choose a third one. (*Sanhedrin* 23a; *Bava Metzia* 20a)

✿ Born against your will
R. Eliezer HaKappar said: "You were created against your will, you were born against your will, and against your will you live, against your will you will die, and against your will you are destined to give an account before the King of Kings."[38] (*Avot* 4:29)

Born to replace great person
Great men are born on the very day another great man dies
The Talmud states: "The day when R. Akiva died, Rebbe was born; when Rebbe died, Rav Yehuda was born; when Rav Yehuda died, Rava was born; when Rava, died R. Ashi, was born." (*Kiddushin* 72b; *Yoma* 38b)

📖 Born without parents
Abbaye's father died before he was born and his mother died at his birth. He was raised by Rabbah ben Nahmeni, his uncle, and by a foster mother, whom he called Mother. He studied first with his uncle, Rabbah b. Nahmeni, and then with Rabbi Yosef, who succeeded Rabbah as head of the academy in Pumbedita.

The Talmud relates a similar story about R. Yohanan. R. Yohanan's father died before he was born and his mother died on the day he was born. "But," asked someone, "Didn't Abbaye say: 'My mother told me'?" That was his foster mother. (*Kiddushin* 31b)

Borrower
What are the obligations of a borrower? (*Bava Metzia* 93a, 94a; *Shevuot* 49a)

📖 Borrower slow to pay
R. Abba b. Marta or Abba b. Minyumi owed money to Rabbah. Rabbah asked him for his money, but he was slow. Finally, after some years, he came with the money during a Shemittah year.

The Halachah is that in a Shemittah year all debts are cancelled. Rabbah said to him: "It is cancelled." So R. Abba took

---

38. See entry, Living and dying against your will.

the money, put it in his pocket and went home. (*Gittin* 37b)

Borrowing
Borrowing food on Shabbat is discussed in *Shoel*, the 23rd *perek* in *Shabbat*. (*Shabbat* 148a)

Borrowing a Torah (*Bava Metzia* 29b)

✡ Borrowing and not repaying
R. Shimon b. Nathanel said: "It is evil to borrow and not to repay, whether borrowing from man or from God." (*Avot* 2:9)

Botzra
Resh Lakish visited the town of Botzra; it displeased him to observe the Jews acting in a way that he thought to be improper. (*Avodah Zarah* 58b)

✡ Bowel movement
He who relieves himself at night in the same place as during daytime is a person who has modesty. (*Avodah Zarah* 47b)

📖 Bowels disorder
Rebbe once suffered from a disorder of the bowels. He asked, "Does anyone know whether apple cider from a heathen is permitted or prohibited?" R. Yishmael b. Yosi b. Halafta answered, "My father had once the same ailment, and he drank from a heathen apple cider that was seventy years old, and he was cured. They found a heathen who had seventy-year old cider. Rebbe drank it and recovered. (*Avodah Zarah* 40b)

Bowing during prayer
When and how to bow during prayers (*Berachot* 12a)

✡ Bragging
Once the wife of R. Avohu's interpreter said to R. Avohu's wife:

"My husband has no need to get instructions from your husband, and when he bows down to your husband he is merely being courteous."

His wife told R. Avohu what she said. He said to her, "Why should we worry about it? All that matters is that through the two of us God is praised." (*Sotah* 40a)

Bread and the blessing
On bread, one makes the blessing *hamotzi lehem* (*Berachot* 35a)

Bread exempts all other foods
(*Berachot* 41b)

✡ Bread on the ground
R. Gamliel was on the road after Pesach and stopped to pick up a loaf of bread.

From this experience, we learned three things: One may not leave eatables on the road; we assume the food was left on the road by the majority of the travelers who are non-Jews, and that one may derive benefit from leavened bread after Pesach which belongs to a non-Jew. (*Eruvin* 64b; *Bava Metzia* 23a)

✡ Bread to be left on the table
R. Eleazar said: "He who doesn't leave bread on the table after a meal will not see blessings." (*Sanhedrin* 92a)

✡ Bread of a whole loaf of bread
It is preferable to make the blessing over a whole loaf of bread. Mar b. Ravina used to put the broken piece under the whole loaf, then break and make the benediction. (*Berachot* 39b; *Shabbat* 61a)

Bread of two loaves   לחם משנה
R. Abba said: "On Shabbat, it is one's duty to break bread over two loaves." R. Ashi said: "I saw R. Kahana holding two loaves, but he broke only one of them." (*Shabbat* 117b; *Berachot* 39b)

✿ Bread without Torah
When bread is absent there is no Torah
R. Eleazar b. Azariah said: "If there is no bread, there is no Torah; if there is no Torah, there is no bread."[39] (*Avot* 3:21, 22)

✿ Break his word
R. Papi said, "Ravina told me that a rabbi by the name of Tavut, others say it was R. Shemuel b. Zutra, who declared: 'If I was given all the treasures in the world I would not break my word." (*Bava Metzia* 49a; *Sanhedrin* 97a)

Breakfast
The rabbis taught: There are thirteen good things about breakfast. (*Bava Metzia* 107b)

✿ Bribe rejected
A man once brought to R. Anan a load of fish. R. Anan asked him: "What is your business here?" The man answered: "I have a lawsuit before you." R. Anan did not accept the gift and told him: "I am now disqualified to try your case." The man said to R. Anan: "I do not expect you to be the judge in my case, but I would like you to accept my gift in order that it be a substitute for my first fruit offering."

"I had no intention to accept the gift, but since you have given me your reason, I will accept." He sent him to R. Nahman, who was also a judge, with a message. "Will you please try this case, because I am disqualified to be his judge."[40] (*Ketubbot* 105b)

Bribery
Bribery is forbidden – not only bribing with money, but also bribery with words. Meticulous judges disqualified themselves even for the slightest impression

that might be understood as bribery. (*Ketubbot* 105b)

✿ Bribery by familiarity
A person who once hosted Rav, came before him in a lawsuit against another man, and said to Rav: "Were you not once a guest in my house?"

"Yes, replied Rav. "What can I do for you?"
"I have a case before you."
"In that case, I am disqualified as your judge."[41] (*Sanhedrin* 7b, 8a)

✿ Bribing a judge
Imma Shalom, the wife of R. Eliezer, was the sister of R. Gamliel. In the vicinity lived a sectarian judge with a reputation that he did not accept bribes. In order to expose him, she brought him a golden lamp and said to him: "My father left an estate and I want to get my share of the inheritance."

The judge ruled in her favor. The next day, R. Gamliel brought to the judge a Libyan ass. Whereupon, the judge reversed his own ruling.[42] (*Shabbat* 116a)

Bribing King Shapur
Rava said to the rabbis: "Do you have an idea how much I send secretly to the Court of King Shapur?" In spite of it, the Court of King Shapur sent men to plunder and seized some of his property. (*Hagigah* 5b)

Bridal affairs on Shabbat (*Shabbat* 150a, 151b)

Bride
Interrupting learning Torah to escort a bride to the canopy (*Megillah* 29a)

Bride and Groom
Rabbi Akiva expounded: "When a

---

39. See entry, Livelihood combined with Torah.
40. See entry, Seder Eliyahu.
41. See entry, Lawsuit before Rav.
42. See entry, Judge exposed as a bribe taker.

husband and wife are worthy and love and respect each other, the Shechina is with them, but when they are not worthy fire consumes them. In Hebrew a man is called אִישׁ and a woman is called אִשָּׁה, the spelling is almost identical, except the word for man has a *yud* in it and the word for woman has a *hey* in it; the extra two letters spell out the name of God. If you remove these two letters you are left with the word אֵשׁ which means fire." (*Sotah* 17a)

Bridegroom and Shema
Is a bridegroom obligated to recite the *Shema*? (*Berachot* 16a; *Ketubbot* 6b)

📖 Bridge crossing
Two biers of great scholars are being carried across the bridge
When Rabbah b. Huna and R. Hamnuna died, they took their remains to Israel. As they arrived to a bridge, the camels stopped. An Arab who was there[43] asked those carrying the cortege: "What is that?" They answered: "The two rabbis are paying honor to one another." (*Moed Katan* 25b)

Bridge crossing danger
Any place of danger is to be avoided. (*Shabbat* 32a; *Taanit* 20b)

Brit   בְּרִית
Mentioning Brit in Haaretz
R. Illai said in the name of R. Yaakov b. Aha, in the name of Rabbeinu: "Whoever omits the mention of *Brit* and *Torah* in the blessing of *Haaretz*, which is part of *Birkat Hamazon*, has not fulfilled his obligation." (*Berachot* 49a)

Broken barrel
Handling a broken barrel on Shabbat to get food is discussed in *Havit*, the 22nd *perek* in *Shabbat*. (*Shabbat* 143b, 146a)

Broken glass
Hasidim of former generations hid their broken glasses in the ground. (*Bava Kamma* 30a)

Broken Tablets
On the seventeenth day of Tammuz, the Tablets were broken. (*Taanit* 26a)

Broken utensils
Handling broken utensils on Shabbat is discussed in *Kol hakelim*, the 17th *perek* in *Shabbat*. (*Shabbat* 122b)

Brother of R. Hiyya
Marta inherits jewels
When the wife of Rabbah b. Hana was on her deathbed, she said: "Those precious stones belong to Marta and to his daughter's family. Marta was the brother of Rabbi Hiyya. (*Bava Batra* 52a)

Brother of R. Hiyya
R. Banai was the brother of R. Hiyya. (*Ketubbot* 50b)

Brother unknown
A man came to Mari b. Isaac and said: "I am your brother and I am claiming my share of the inheritance." "I do not know you," was the reply. They went to R. Hisda to settle the matter.[44] (*Bava Metzia* 39 b, *Yevamot* 88a; *Ketubbot* 27b)

Brothers inherit
A case of two brothers dividing a property between them which they inherited, and a third brother returned from overseas (*Bava Batra* 106b)

---

43. He probably was a bridge attendant.

44. See entry, Inheritance claim.

Brothers inheriting a house
A case of two brothers inheriting a house, and one wanted to build a wall; the other objected. (*Bava Batra* 7a)

📖 Brothers, Kohanim
Eighty pairs of brothers, Kohanim, married to sisters, daughters of Kohanim
The Talmud relates when R. Yitzhak came from Eretz Yisrael to Babylonia, he said:

"There was a town in Eretz Yisrael by the name of Gofnit where eighty pairs of brothers, all priests, married eighty pairs of sisters, all from priestly families. The rabbis searched from Sura to Nehardea and could not find a similar case, except the daughters of R. Hisda, who were married to two brothers: Rami b. Hama and to Mar Ukva b. Hama. While the daughters of R. Hisda were priestesses, their husbands were not priests." (*Berachot* 44a)

Brothers, partners
A case of two brothers, partners to the inherited land, and one of them was appointed to work for the government, what to do with the earnings? (*Bava Batra* 144b)

📖 Build the Temple in Jerusalem
Herod asked Rabbi Bava ben Buta: "What could I do to amend for the sin of killing all the scholars?"

R. Bava answered: "You have extinguished the light of the world by killing the rabbis; you should attend to the other light of the world, the Temple."[45] (*Bava Batra* 4a)

Building
To build on Shabbat in any form is discussed in *Haboneh*, the 12th *perek* in *Shabbat*. (*Shabbat* 102b)

Building collapses
A case of a building collapsing that belonged to two owners (*Bava Kamma* 20b)

Building Temple
The Temple in Jerusalem cannot be built at night. (*Shevuot* 15b)

Building the Temple on Yom Tov
The Temple in Jerusalem cannot be built on Yom Tov. (*Shevuot* 15b)

Burial   קבורה
(*Bava Kamma* 100a; *Bava Metzia* 30b)

Burial in Israel
R. Anan said: "Whoever is buried in the Land of Israel is considered to be buried under the altar." (*Ketubbot* 111a)

Burial in Israel
R. Ulla was in the habit of visiting the Land of Israel frequently, but he passed away outside the Land of Israel. His body was brought to Israel to be buried. When R. Eleazar was informed that his coffin arrived, he remarked: "Receiving a man in his lifetime is not the same as receiving him after his death." (*Ketubbot* 111a)

Burial of R. Eleazar[46] (*Bava Metzia* 84b)

Burning
Burning down property by sending a deaf person, an idiot or a minor to set the fire (*Bava Kamma* 59b)

Burning articles at a funeral
A non-Jewish practice is to burn articles at a funeral of a non-Jewish king or prince. It is considered a mark of high esteem in the non-Jewish world. (*Avodah Zarah* 11a)

---

45. See also entry, Herod building the Temple.

46. See entry, Coffin in the attic.

Burning of the red heifer

The ceremony of burning the red heifer (*Parah* 3:1–11)

✿ Business partnership for a needy

R. Abba said in the name of Resh Lakish: "Forming a partnership with a needy person by providing the capital is the greatest charity." (*Shabbat* 63a)

📖 Business and Torah

Rabbi Ilfa and Rabbi Yohanan studied together, but they had no income. They spoke to each other about going into business, but Rabbi Yohanan had a dream not to do it and therefore he continued to study. However, Rabbi Ilfa decided to go to earn a living. Years later when Rabbi Ilfa returned to the community, Rabbi Yohanan presided already over his academy. The scholars were teasing R. Ilfa by telling him, "Had you remained here to study you might have been presiding over the academy." To prove to the scholars that he did study, Ilfa suspended himself from the mast of a ship and exclaimed: "If there is any one who will ask me a question from a Beraita of Rabbi Hiyya and Rabbi Oshaya, and if I fail to know the subject, then I will throw myself into the water to drown. An old man came forward and asked him a question. Rabbi Ilfa had the right answer for the question. (*Taanit* 21a)

Business dealings (*Bava Metzia* 65a)

Business transaction

R. Hiyya b. Yosef received a deposit from a buyer for salt. In the meantime, the price of salt went up. He wanted to deliver salt equal to the deposit received. The matter came before R. Yohanan. (*Bava Metzia* 48b)

✿ Businessman's generosity

Come and hear: There was a man who sold a plot of land to R. Papa; he needed the money to buy some oxen. Eventually he didn't need to buy the oxen. When R. Papa found out, he returned the land to the man. (*Ketubbot* 97a)

✿ Businessmen and rabbis

R. Papa and R. Huna were also businessmen

R. Papa and R. Huna bought sesame seeds on the bank of the Nahar Malka. They hired a boatman to bring the merchandise across the river, with a guarantee against any accident that might happen.[47] (*Gittin* 73a)

Businessman speculator

Speculating on price differentials

R. Hama was a businessman; he was speculating on price differentials from one market to the next at his own risk. (*Bava Metzia* 65a)

Butcher knives and vessels (*Hullin* 8b)

Buying

Buying from people who are employees (*Bava Kamma* 118b, 119a)

✿ Buying a field

Two rabbis bid on the same property, neither knowing about the other. Consequently when one bought it, he did not want to take possession. It was left ownerless.

On one occasion, Rabbi Giddal was negotiating for a certain field, but in the meantime, R. Abba bought the field. R. Giddal was unhappy and complained to R. Zera, who in turn took the complaint to R. Yitzhak Nepaha.[48] (*Kiddushin* 59a)

Buying a house in Israel

Can a transaction be taken on Shabbat? (*Bava Kamma* 80b)

---

47. See also entry, Agreement voided by Rava.
48. See also entry, Rabbis' field.

Buying a non-existent item
אדם מקנה דבר שלא בא לעולם
One can buy that which did not yet come to this world. The opinion of R. Meir (*Bava Metzia* 33b; *Bava Batra* 79b, 127b, 131a, 141b, 157a; *Yevamot* 32a; *Kiddushin* 62b; *Gittin* 13b, 42b)

Buying from a shepherd
Suspicion who owns the sheep (*Bava Kamma* 118b)

Buying property in Syria
A Jew buying property from a non-Jew in Syria (*Hullin* 136a)

✿ Buying wine
A man bought wine for a friend and it turnrd sour
A man asked his friend to buy him 400 barrels of wine. When he brought him the wine, it turned out to be sour. The man came to Rava to claim that his friend bought him sour wine. Rava said to the man who bought the wine, go and bring proof that when you bought the wine it was good wine, and then will you be free from liability. (*Bava Metzia* 83a)

Buying wine from a Cuthite
Buying wine from a Cuthite. They were not trusted to tithe their produce (*Bava Kamma* 69b; *Gittin* 25a)

C

Cabinet maker
A person entering a cabinet maker's shop and is injured by a piece of wood (*Bava Kamma* 32b)

Caesarea
The academy in Caesarea
Caesarea is an ancient city on the Mediterranean coast of Israel, located today between Tel Aviv and Haifa. In Hebrew, the city was called Kisri. In 96 BCE, King Alexander Yannai captured the city during the Hasmonean wars, and it remained a Jewish city for many years afterwards. At one time it was given as a present to Cleopatra by the Roman Emperor; however, Emperor Augustus returned it to Herod. Herod enlarged the city and surrounded it with a wall; he also built a deep-sea harbor. When Judea became a Roman province, Caesarea was the capital of the province. The disputes between the Jewish and gentile inhabitants were one of the causes that led to the war with Rome in 66–70 CE. Vespasian made Caesarea a Roman colony.

Rabbi Avohu, who lived in Caesarea, was the representative of the people to the Roman governor. Many well-known Talmudic rabbis lived in the city. They are: R. Abba, R. Adda, R. Ahava, R. Assi, R. Avohu, R. Hanina, R. Hezkiya, R. Hoshaya, R. Yannai, and R. Zera.

R. Avohu lived in the 3rd – 4th centuries CE. (*Eruvin* 76b; *Ketubbot* 17a)

Caesarean section
יוצא דופן
A child born by caesarean section or an animal giving birth by caesarean section. (*Bechorot* 19a; *Niddah* 40a)

Caesarean section in animals
Firstborn male animal born by caesarean section. (*Bechorot* 19a)

Cake and the like
On what food do we make the blessing *Borei minei mezonot* בורא מיני מזונות (*Berachot* 36b)

Calamity
R. Shemuel b. Nahmeni said in the name of R. Yonatan: "Calamity comes to the world only when there are wicked people in the world, and it always begins with the righteous." (*Bava Kamma* 60a)

Calendar calculations
By what calendar calculation are documents written (*Avodah Zarah* 10a)

Calendar fixing
Notice sent to the Jewish communities to add another month to the calendar
It once happened that R. Gamliel was sitting on a step on the Temple Mount, and Yohanan, the well-known scribe, was before him prepared with three sheets of parchment. R. Gamliel said to him: "Write instructions to our brethren in Upper Galilee, and to those in Lower Galilee, and to our brethren in the South, and the Exiles in Babylonia, and to those in Media, and to all the other exiled sons of Israel, saying: 'Peace shall be with you! It seems advisable to me and in the opinion of my colleagues to add thirty days to this year.'"[49] (*Sanhedrin* 11b)

Calendar fixing outside Israel
When R. Hanania b. Ahi Yehoshua left for Babylonia, he began to intercalate the years and to fix the new months outside of Israel. The Bet Din of Israel sent two scholars to stop him from doing it. They said to him: "If you listen, then all is well, but if you don't you will be excommunicated."
  They also empowered us to tell the community here in Babylonia that "if they listen to us, then all is well. However, if they don't listen, then let them go up the mountain, let Ahia build an altar, and Hanania play the harp. All of you will become deniers and will have no portion in the God of Israel." When the community heard this, they started crying and declared: "Heaven forbid."[50] (*Berachot* 63a)

Calves of R. Huna (*Shabbat* 52a)

Camel
A camel leading a wagon loaded with flax causing fire (*Bava Kamma* 22a, 62b)

Canaanites
The Canaanites came to Alexander with a petition[51] (*Sanhedrin* 91a)

Canaanite
It is written in the Torah: "Yehuda the son of Yaakov saw the daughter of a Canaanite" (*Bereishit* 38:2). R. Yirmiyahu said: "Is it possible that Avraham admonished Yitzhak and Yitzhak admonished Yaakov not to marry a Canaanite, and Yehuda would then marry a Canaanite? No, Canaanite means a merchant." (*Pesahim* 50a)

Candle lighting
For Shabbat (*Shabbat* 2nd *perek*)

Candle lighting is an obligation
Rav Nahman bar Rav Zavda said, others said Rav Nahmann Bar Rava said in the name of Rav that "candle lighting for Shabbat on Friday evening is an obligation." (*Shabbat* 25b)

Capital cases
Capital cases are adjudicated by twenty-three judges. (*Sanhedrin* 2a)

Capital cases
Monetary and capital cases require interrogation and examination by the court. (*Sanhedrin* 32a)

Capital cases meet during daytime
Court of judges in monetary and capital cases must meet during daytime. (*Sanhedrin* 34b; *Niddah* 50a; *Yevamot* 104a)

---

49. See also entry, Intercalation of the year.
50. See also entry, Intercalate outside Israel.

51. See entry, Alexander the Macedonian king.

Captive
Daughter of R. Hanania b. Teradion was held captive by the Romans
The Talmud relates that Berurya, Rabbi Meir's wife, was the daughter of Rabbi Hanania b. Teradion. Her sister was captured and placed in a brothel. She told her husband, "I am ashamed to have my sister in a brothel. Can you do something to get her out of there?" So he took a bag full of *dinarim* and set out to ransom her. He offered the money to the watchman and he released her. The government found out what he had done and they were looking to arrest him. For that reason, he had to leave Eretz Yisrael and move to Babylonia. (*Avodah Zarah* 18a)

✿ Captives
Jewish women captives were brought to Nehardea
R. Shemuel's father placed watchmen over the women captives. Asked R. Shemuel his father, "And who watched over them until now?" His father answered him: "If they had been your daughters, would you have spoken so lightly of them?" (*Ketubbot* 23a)

✿ Captives to be redeemed
The Talmud relates that a certain man, in order to save himself, handed over to the robbers the money designated to redeem captives. On his return, he was summoned before Rabbah and he found him not guilty of negligence[52] (*Bava Kamma* 117b)

Caravan
If a caravan is traveling in the wilderness and is threatened by robbers to pay a ransom or be killed, how much does each contribute? (*Bava Kamma* 116b)

Caravan
A traveling caravan during Shabbat (*Eruvin* 15b)

Card player as witness
A card player is unqualified as a witness. (*Shevuot* 31a)

Carmel
Mount Carmel in Haifa (*Shabbat* 35a)

Carmelit (*Shabbat* 6b, 7a)

📖 Carob tree and Honi HaMaagel
One day R. Honi HaMaagel was traveling on the road and he encountered a man planting a carob tree.

He asked the man: "How long does it take for the tree to bear fruit"?

The man replied: "It takes seventy years."

He asked him: "Are you certain you will live another seventy years?"

The man replied: "When I came upon this land I found already a grown carob tree, which my forefathers have planted for me. The same way, I will plant this for my children."

R. Honi HaMaagel went to lay down to rest in a cave and he fell asleep.[53] He slept hidden in a cave for seventy years. (*Taanit* 23a)

📖 Carob tree uprooted
Rabbi Eliezer had halachic differences with the rabbis; he brought forth every argument to prove his point, but the rabbis did not accept them. He declared: "If the Halachah agrees with me let this carob tree prove it."

The carob tree uprooted itself. The rabbis retorted: "The carob tree[54] couldn't prove the argument." (*Bava Metzia* 59b)

---

52. See entry, Robbed of redemption money.

53. See also entry, Seventy years Honi HaMaagel slept.
54. See also entry, Bat Kol.

📖 Carpenter R. Avin
R. Huna used to say: "A person, who lights his house well, will have scholarly sons." R. Huna used to frequently pass the house of R. Avin, the carpenter. He noticed that many lights were always lit in the house. He remarked: "Two great men will be born to him," and so it was. R. Idi b. Avin and R. Hiyya b. Avin were born to him. (*Shabbat* 23b)

Carrion renders other things unclean
Thirteen rules apply to the carrion of a clean bird to render other things unclean. (*Taharot* 1:1)

Carrying on Shabbat
Carrying objects on Shabbat from one domain to another (*Shabbat* 2a)

Carrying in an unusual way
Carrying on Shabbat in an unusual way is discussed in *Hamatznia*, the 10th *perek* in *Shabbat*. (*Shabbat* 92a)

Carrying on Shabbat by women
What are women permitted to carry on Shabbat (*Shabbat* 57a)

Casual eating   אכילת עראי
(*Sukkah* 26a)

Casual sleeping   שינת עראי
(*Sukkah* 26a)

Cat-clawing animal
R. Kahana asked Rav: "An animal being clawed by a cat, is there a consequence?" (*Hullin* 53a)

✿ Caterers in Jerusalem
Rabbi Shimon ben Gamliel said: "There was a fine custom in Jerusalem. If one entrusted the preparation of a banquet to a caterer and he spoiled it, the caterer had to indemnify the host for the insult to him and to his guests." Another fine custom was in Jerusalem. When there was a party in a home, they spread a cloth over the door entrance. So long as the cloth was spread over the door, guests could enter. When the cloth was removed, no guests could enter. (*Bava Batra* 93b)

Cats
To breed cats (*Bava Kamma* 80a)

Cattle characteristics
The Torah specifies the characteristics of the animals (*Hullin* 59a)

Cattle tithing
When does the law of tithing cattle apply? (*Bechorot* 53a)

📖 Cave dwellers for twelve years
Rabbi Shimon ben Yohai and his son Rabbi Eleazar went and hid in a cave for twelve years.[55] They had to hide because the Roman authorities issued orders to have them executed. After twelve years, when the Emperor Hadrian died, they came out, but due to some circumstances they returned for one more year. (*Shabbat* 33b)

Cave of Avraham
R. Bannah used to mark out the graves of the dead. When he came to the grave of Avraham, he met Eliezer, the servant of Avraham, standing at the entrance. (*Bava Batra* 58a)

Cave of Machpelah, Kiryat Arba
R. Yitzhak explained: "It is called *arba* because four couples are buried in the cave: Adam and Eve, Avraham and Sarah, Yitzhak and Rivkah, Yaakov and Leah. (*Eruvin* 53a)

---

55. See also entry, Hiding in a cave.

✿ Cemetery proper conduct

R. Hiyya and R. Yonatan were visiting a cemetery when R. Hiyya noticed that the blue fringes of R. Yonatan were trailing on the ground. Said R. Hiyya to him, "Lift your fringes so that the deceased should not say: 'Tomorrow they are coming to join us and today they are insulting us.'" (*Berachot* 18a)

Certainty   פסיק רישא ולא ימות

Let his head be cut off, but let him not die: a dialectic term for a sure consequence of an act. (*Shabbat* 75a)

Certainty trumps a doubt
אין ספק מוציא מידי ודאי

A doubt cannot set aside a certainty. (*Hullin* 10a)

📖 Chamber of Hanania ben Hezkiya ben Gurion

The Mishna tells a story that Rabbi Hanania was ill and the rabbis went to visit him. "And these are the rulings, which they instituted in the upper chamber of Hanania ben Hezkiya ben Gurion. They voted and the school of Shammai outnumbered those of the school of Hillel and they decided on eighteen matters that day." (*Shabbat* 13b)

Change   שינוי קונה

A change transfers ownership; it is debated. (*Bava Kamma* 66a, 67a, 94b, 95a)

Change of an object to another object
(*Bava Kamma* 93b)

Change of diet

R. Shemuel said: "A change of diet is the beginning of abdominal trouble." (*Ketubbot* 110b; *Nedarim* 37b; *Bava Batra* 146a; *Sanhedrin* 101a)

Change of name

The same object acquiring a new name, like a skin being called a table cover. (*Bava Kamma* 66b)

Changed his mind (*Bava Kamma* 73b)

Changing a contract
המשנה ידו על התחתונה וכל החוזר בו ידו על התחתונה

Whichever party changes the terms of the contract is at a disadvantage, and also, whichever party cancels the contract is at a disadvantage. (*Bava Kamma* 102a; *Bava Metzia* 76a; *Avodah Zarah* 7a)

Chanukah

What is Chanukah; the miracle of Chanukah is described. (*Shabbat* 21b)

Chanukah

Candles' placement and height required (*Bava Kamma* 62b; *Shabbat* 21b)

Chanukah

How many candles to light, in what order? (*Shabbat* 21b)

Chanukah

The location where to place the *menorah* (*Shabbat* 21b, 22a)

Chanukah

Commandments (*Shabbat* 23a)

Chanukah

Chanukah has to be mentioned during *Birkat Hamazon*. (*Shabbat* 24a)

Chanukah

Many things permitted on the street (*Bava Kamma* 30a, 62b)

Chanukah candle lighting

One lighting for the whole household

or each individual lights separately
(*Shabbat* 21b)

Chanukah candles
Lit outdoors (*Shabbat* 21b)

Chanukah candles
Lighting one candle from another
(*Shabbat* 22a)

Chanukah Torah reading (*Megillah* 30b)

✡ Character recognition
One of R. Illai's famous sayings:

"A man's character can be determined[56] by three things: by his cup, by his purse and by his anger. Some say also by his laughter." (*Eruvin* 65b)

Character recognition
R. Yosi b. Hanina said: "A woman recognizes a character of a guest better than a man." (*Berachot* 10b)

Characteristics in animals
The characteristics of animals and birds with regards to being kosher or not (*Hullin* 59a)

✡ Charitable
To the extreme
R. Yonah was a very charitable man. Once a person of a good family became very poor. Rabbi Yonah said to him: "I heard that you have been left an inheritance; take this money and you can pay me back when you receive your inheritance."

Once he accepted the money, he said to him: "I changed my mind; let it be a gift to you." (*Taanit* 23b)

📖 Charitable
Very discreet
Rabbi Ulla and Rabbi Hisda were walking and they passed the house of R. Hana b. Hanilai. R. Hisda sighed. Asked R. Ulla, "Why are you sighing?" He answered him, "How can I refrain from sighing? He used to have sixty cooks to cook and bake for the poor. He always had his purse ready to give charity. In time of scarcity, he put the grain and barley outside at nighttime for anyone to take – he did not want people to have to come inside to be embarrassed. Now it is all in ruins, shall I not sigh?" (*Berachot* 58b)

✡ Charity
Saves from death
Rabbi Akiva had a daughter who was about to be married. The next morning when she removed the brooch from the wall where she stuck it, she found it was stuck in the eye of a dead serpent. R. Akiva asked her, "Can you think of any good deed you did yesterday?"

She replied, "While everyone was busy with the wedding banquet, I took a portion from the banquet meal and gave it to the poor man at the door."[57] (*Shabbat* 156b)

Charity
R. Dostai taught that if one gives even a small amount of charity – that person is deemed worthy to be received by the Divine presence. (*Bava Batra* 10a)

Charitable[58] (*Taanit* 20b)

✡ Charitable
R. Abba was a very charitable person. When he gave charity to the poor, he did not want to embarrass them by facing

---

57. See entry, Akiva's daughter marries.
58. See entry, Philanthropy.

them; therefore he used to wear a scarf with money in it, which he slung towards his back, so that the poor could take what they needed without facing him. He traveled frequently to Babylonia, where he met with the Babylonian scholars. (*Ketubbot* 67b)

Charity
Tzedaka   צדקה
R. Assi said: Giving charity is equivalent to all other religious precepts combined. (*Bava Batra* 9a)

Charity
Deeds of charity (*Bava Kamma* 17a)

✡ Charity
R. Eleazar stated: "The performance of charity is greater than offering all the sacrifices."

R. Eleazar further stated: "The act of *gemilut hasadim* is greater than charity."

He also stated: "The reward of charity is dependent on the kindness in it." (*Sukkah* 49b)

Charity
R. Illai stated: "They ordained in Usha that a man should not give more than a fifth of his assets to charity." (*Ketubbot* 50a)

📖 Charity
It has been taught, R. Binyamin the Tzaddik was the supervisor of the charity fund. One day a woman came to him during a year of great famine and asked him for help. He said to her: "There is no money in the charity basket.

She replied to him: "Rabbi, if you don't help me, then a mother and her seven children will die." When he heard this he took his own money and gave her what she needed.

Some time at a later period, he became dangerously ill. The angels addressed the

Holy One. "You have decreed that he who saves one soul of Israel is equal to saving a whole world. Binyamin the Tzaddik saved a mother and her seven children, is it right that he should die at such a young age?" His sentence to die was immediately torn up and he lived another twenty-two years. (*Bava Bata* 11a)

Charity
Our rabbis have taught: The charity fund is collected by two persons and distributed by three. Food for the soup kitchen is collected by three and distributed by three. The collectors of charity are not permitted to separate from one another. (*Bava Batra* 8b)

✡ Charity donor hides from recipient
The Talmud relates: There was a poor man in Mar Ukva's neighborhood, and Mar Ukva used to throw four *zuz* at his door every day in such a way that he would not be seen. One day the poor man was curious to see who the person was. Mar Ukva was coming home with his wife and they threw the coins at his door. As soon as the man saw people approaching his door he went out after them. They fled and hid in the furnace room, where his feet almost got burned. (*Ketubbot* 67b)

Charity in secret   מתן בסתר
Giving charity in secret (*Bava Batra* 9b)

Charity overseer   גבאי צדקה
A person overseeing the charity fund (*Bava Metzia* 38a; *Bava Batra* 8b; *Pesahim* 13a)

✡ Chasing after honors
Eliezer HaKappar states: "Envy, greed, and chasing after honors take a man out of this world." (*Avot* 4:21)

Chastity (*Ketubbot* 23a)

✿ Cheerful reception to all people
Rabbi Yishmael said: "Show esteem toward a great person, and receive all people cheerfully." (*Avot* 3:12)

Cheese and meat
Cheese and meat at the same table (*Shabbat* 13a; *Hullin* 104b)

Cheese and poultry
To have on the same table cooked poultry and cheese (*Shabbat* 13a; *Hullin* 104b)

Cheruvim   כרובים
The space for the *Cheruvim* in the Sanctuary is discussed. (*Bava Batra* 99a)

Chewing bones
Abbaye blamed himself for the death of R. Adda, because R. Adda used to say to the students: "Instead of chewing on bones in the school of Abbaye, rather eat meat in the school of Rava." (*Bava Batra* 22a)

Chicken and cheese
On the same table (*Shabbat* 13a)

Chicken without feathers
R. Shimon b. Halafta had a hen whose feathers were completely gone. He wrapped the chicken in a warm leather bag and put the chicken into the oven. When he took her out, she grew feathers larger than the original one. (*Hullin* 57b)

Chickens
Chickens flying, causing damage (*Bava Kamma* 17b)

Chief labors   אב מלאכה
Chief labors forbidden on Shabbat (*Shabbat* 68a; *Keritot* 16b)

Child
One-day old child is entitled to inherit (*Bava Batra* 142a)

Child
Using a child to carry on Shabbat is discussed in *Notel* the 21st *perek* in *Shabbat*. (*Shabbat* 141b)

📖 Child aged six remembers
R. Nahman said: "My father was one of the scribes of Mar Shemuel's court when I was about six or seven, and I remember that they used to proclaim, 'Deeds of transfer found in the street should be returned to the owner.'" (*Bava Metzia* 16b)

Child buying in a store
If a little child is sent by the father to the store to buy oil (*Bava Batra* 87b)

Child circumcised by a non-Jew
A Jewish child circumcised by a non-Jew (*Avodah Zarah* 27a; *Menahot* 42a)

📖 Child in captivity
It is stated in the Talmud that when Rabbi Yehoshua ben Hanania visited Rome, he was told that there is a Jewish child in prison with beautiful eyes and good looks. Rabbi Yehoshua stood at the prison gate and asked in Hebrew: "Who gave Yaakov for spoil and Yisrael to the robbers?"

The child responded: "We have sinned to God and we didn't follow his way." Rabbi Yehoshua said: "I would not budge from here before I ransom this boy, whatever price may be demanded." It is reported that he paid a very high price to ransom the boy. The boy's name was Yishmael, who later became one of the great scholars of his time. He was a student of R. Yehoshua, where he studied for many years and he also studied under Rabbi Nehunia ben HaKana. (*Gittin* 58a)

Child of parents improperly converted
R. Yohanan said: "A child born by a Jewish woman and a non-Jew who was not

properly converted is considered to be a *mamzer* (*Avodah Zarah* 59a)

Child support
Rava used to tell the men brought before him for refusing to maintain their young children: "Will it please you that your children should be supported by the charity fund?" (*Ketubbot* 49b)

Child taken captive
Rav and Shemuel – both of them say that a child who was taken captive, and forgot that it was Shabbat, is a special case. (*Shabbat* 68a)

📖 Child testifying
A child testified before R. Yehoshua b. Levi, or before Rebbe: "I and my mother were taken captive among heathens and I was constantly watching over my mother." Rebbe permitted the woman to be married to a priest, on the strength of the child's testimony. (*Bava Kamma* 114b; *Ketubbot* 26a)

Childbirth
Rova declared, "Two rulings were given by the elders of Pumbedita." R. Haviva observed that the Elders of Pumbedita ruled one additional ruling, which is that "Rav Yehuda said in R. Shemuel's name that "it is permitted to light a fire on Shabbat for a woman in childbirth." (*Eruvin* 79b; *Shabbat* 129a)

Childbirth
A woman in hard labor during childbirth (*Ohalot* 7:4, 5)

✡ Childhood learning
Elisha ben Avuyah said: "When one learns as a child, it is like writing on new paper, but when one learns as an old man, it is like writing on blotted paper." (*Avot* 4:20)

📖 Children
Abbaye and Rava as Children
Abbaye and Rava were sitting before Rabbah when they were still young boys. Rabbah wanted to test them and he asked: "To whom do we say the benedictions?" They both answered: "To God."

"And where is God?" Rava pointed to the roof and Abbaye went outside and pointed to the sky. Rabbah said to them: "Both of you will become rabbis."

This is why people say: "Every pumpkin can be told from its stalk." (*Berachot* 48a)

Children died
To his sorrow, the children of R. Yosi b. Hanina died in his lifetime. (*Taanit* 13b)

Children to be trained to fast
Children do not have to fast on Yom Kippur, but they should be trained a year or two before they are obligated to fast. (*Yoma* 82a)

📖 Children very bright
When R. Shimon b. Gamliel and R. Yehoshua b. Korha were teaching in the academy, they sat on couches, while R. Eleazar b. Shimon and Rebbe sat in front of them on the ground asking questions and raising objections. The other students suggested and said: "Let seats be placed for them."

R. Shimon b. Gamliel objected. So Rebbe was put down again. R. Eleazar was also put down on the ground.

After this day, when Rebbe spoke, R. Eleazar said, "Your statement has no substance." Rebbe was humiliated and complained to R. Shimon b. Gamliel, his father.[59] "Let it not bother you, his father said to him, he is a lion and the son of a lion, whereas you are a lion and the son of a fox." (*Bava Metzia* 84b)

---

59. See also entry, Lion and son of a lion.

✿ Children's education
Highest priority
Resh Lakish said in the name of R. Yehuda Nesiah: "Children may not be deprived of their studies even for the building of the Temple." (*Shabbat* 119b)

Children's education
Neglecting children's education is the cause of destruction
R. Hamnuna said: "Jerusalem was destroyed because they neglected to educate the children." (*Shabbat* 119b)

📖 Children's education
Introduced in Israel
R. Yehoshua b. Gamla introduced a universal system of education,[60] which was adopted and took root in the country.

He ordained that schools and teachers should be appointed in each town, and that children should enter school at the age of six or seven. (*Bava Batra* 21a)

Children's growth
Rav said to R. Hamnuna: "Children are like the grass in the field. Some blossom and some fade." (Eruvin 54a)

📖 Choir in the Temple
It happened that Rabbi Yehoshua went to assist R. Yohanan ben Gudgeda to fasten the Temple doors, and Rabbi Yohanan told him. "Turn back, because you are one of the guys in the choir and not of the doorkeepers." (*Arachin* 11b)

Chosen judge
Borer   בורר
Disputes in monetary matters are judged by three, each litigant chooses one, and the two choose a third one. (*Sanhedrin* 23a; *Bava Metzia* 20a)

Chronological order
אין מוקדם ומאוחר בתורה
Is the Torah written in chronological order or not?
R. Menashye b. Tahlifa said in Rav's name: "The subject we discussed above is proof there is no chronological order in the Torah. R. Papa observed, 'This was said only of two different subjects, but if it is about the same subject what is written first is earlier, and what is written second is later. Otherwise the principle of: If a general proposition is followed by a specific proposition, the general proposition applies only to what is contained in the specific – could not be sustained.'" (*Pesahim* 6b)

Cinnamon logs of Jerusalem
Rabbah said in the name of R. Yehuda: The fuel logs of Jerusalem were taken from cinnamon trees, and when they burned they could smell their fragrance all over Israel. (*Shabbat* 63a)

Circumcision
A convert's circumcision[61] without immersion in the *mikveh* (*Yevamot* 46a)

Circumcision
Circumcision on Shabbat is discussed in *Rabbi Eliezer De-Milah*, the 19th *perek* in *Shabbat*. (*Shabbat* 130a)

📖 Circumcision
Circumcised too soon, a health issue
Rabbi Nathan said: "Once I arrived in a coastal town and I was approached there by a woman who had circumcised her first and second sons, and they died. She brought her third son to me. I saw that the child was red so I said to her, 'My daughter, wait until the blood will become absorbed in him.' She waited accordingly. Thereafter, the child was circumcised and

---

60. See entry, Education in Israel in Temple time.

61. See entry, Conversion incomplete.

Circumcision and immersion

he lived. They named the child Nathan HaBavli after me.

"On another occasion, when I traveled to Cappadocia, I was approached by a woman who had circumcised her first and second sons, and they died. She brought her third son to me. I saw that the child had a greenish color; I examined him and found that he was anemic. I said to her: 'My daughter, wait until the blood will circulate more freely.' She waited accordingly, and thereafter the child was circumcised and lived. They named the baby Nathan HaBavli." (*Hullin* 47b; *Shabbat* 134a)

Circumcision and immersion
R. Yohanan said: "Conversion to Judaism is not complete until there is circumcision and immersion in a kosher *mikveh*." (*Avodah Zarah* 59a; *Yevamot* 46a)

Circumcision by a non-Jew
A Jew circumcising a non-Jew or a non-Jew circumcising a Jewish baby (*Avodah Zarah* 26b)

Circumcision performed by a woman
(*Avodah Zarah* 27a)

Circumcision time limit
A child may not be circumcised before the eighth day and no later than twelve days. However, there are exceptions. (*Arachin* 8b; *Shabbat* 137a)

City
Enlarging a city requirements (*Shevuot* 14a; *Sanhedrin* 2a, 14b)

City dweller
Living in a large city without sins (*Pesahim* 113a–b)

City newly built
Rava b. Mehasya said in the name of R. Hama b. Gurya in Rav's name: "A man

should always prefer to live in a city which was recently established, because it is less sinful." (*Shabbat* 10b)

Claim by the Canaanites
The Canaanites[62] made a claim to the Land of Israel. (*Sanhedrin* 91a)

✿ Clean language
R. Yehoshua b. Levi said: "One should not utter gross expressions with his mouth." It was taught in the school of R. Yishmael: "One should always use clean language." (*Pesahim* 3a)

Clean trade
Rabbi Meir said: "A man should always teach his son a clean trade." (*Kiddushin* 82a)

✿ Clean trade
R. Bar Kappara stated: "When the merchandise is cheap, hurry to buy. In a place where there is no man, you be the man. A man should always teach his son a clean and easy trade." (*Berachot* 63a; *Kiddushin* 82a)

Cleaning hands
If one has no water to clean hands, one may use earth or sawdust. (*Berachot* 15a)

Cleansing of a leper
The procedure for cleansing the leper ritually (*Negaim* 14:1–13)

Clear mind
Under the influence of wine
R. Hiyya said: "Anyone who can keep a clear mind under the influence of wine has the characteristics of the seventy elders. The numerical value of *yayin* is seventy." (*Eruvin* 65a; *Sanhedrin* 38a)

Clearing a room
Clearing a room on Shabbat for guests is

---

62. See entry, Alexander.

discussed in *Mefanim*, the 18th *perek* in *Shabbat*. (*Shabbat* 126b)

✿ Clever Jewish girl

R. Yehoshua b. Hanania remarked: "No one has ever had the better of me except a woman, a little boy, and a little girl."

What was the incident with the little girl? "I was once walking on the road, and I saw a path through a field. I started walking across the field when a little girl called out to me.

"'Master, isn't it part of the field where you are walking?'

"'No,' I answered, 'this is a trodden path.'

"'Yes,' replied the girl, 'robbers like you have trodden it down.'"

R. Yehoshua thought to himself: *Happy are you, Israel, all of you are wise, both young and old.* (*Eruvin* 53b)

Clinging to God

"*V'atem Hadvekim*" mentioned in the Torah in *Parshat Va-Etchanan* can be fulfilled by supporting *talmidei Hachamim*. (*Ketubbot* 111b)

Closing the eyes of a corpse (*Shabbat* 151b)

Cloths and uncleanness

The susceptibility of cloths to uncleanness (*Kelim* 27:1–8)

Coded message was sent to Rava

A message was sent to Rava about intercalating the New Year. (*Sanhedrin* 12a)

Coded watchword

For the new moon
"David King of Israel is alive and enduring." (*Rosh Hashana* 25a)

Cohabit

Without a Ketubbah (*Bava Kamma* 89 a–b; *Ketubbot* 57a)

Coin of Avraham

The coin of Avraham had an old man and an old woman on one side, and a young man and a young woman on the other side. (*Bava Kamma* 97b)

Coin of Jerusalem

The coin of Jerusalem had the names inscribed of King David and King Solomon on one side; on the other side was inscribed the name Jerusalem (*Bava Kamma* 97b)

Coinage

Mentioned in the Torah (*Bava Kamma* 36b; *Kiddushin* 11a; *Bechorot* 50b)

Coins for redeeming the firstborn

(*Bechorot* 49b; *Kiddushin* 11b)

✿ Colleague to learn Torah

One of Rabbi Nehorai's sayings was: "If you have to move, move to a place of Torah, and do not expect the Torah to follow you. Make sure you have a colleague with whom to discuss it, because that way it will be fixed in your mind. Do not depend entirely on your own knowledge." (*Avot* 4:14)

✿ Colleagues to be respected

When R. Eliezer fell ill, his students came to visit him and they said to him: "Teach us the right path of life so that we may deserve the World to Come." He told them: "Give respect to your colleagues, and when you pray know before whom you are standing." (*Berachot* 28b)

✿ Collecting a debt

Some people in Mehuza owed money to R. Sheshet for items he sold them. R. Yosef b. Hama was traveling to Mehuza and R. Sheshet asked him to collect the money for him. They gave him the money and asked him for a receipt. At first he agreed, but then he changed his mind. When he returned, R. Sheshet said to him: "You acted correctly in refusing to assume responsibility. 'A borrower is the slave of the lender.'" (*Gittin* 14a)

✿ Combine Torah with work

Our rabbis taught: One should combine the study of Torah with a worldly occupation. This is the view of R. Yishmael. However Rabbi Shimon b. Yohai said: "If you plow in its season, and reap in its season, and so on, what will become of studying Torah?"

R. Abbaye said: "Many have followed the advice of R. Yishmael and it worked well, others have followed R. Shimon b. Yohai, and it had not been successful." (*Berachot* 35b)

Combining two desecrations

Two desecrations, but neither has the size to be considered a desecration, are combined to make the required size. (*Meilah* 15b)

Combining two prohibitions

כל איסורין שבתורה מצטרפין זה עם זה

R. Meir said: "All the prohibited things of the Torah are combinable together to create an amount required for transgressing." (*Avodah Zarah* 66a)

Combining two smaller amounts מצרף

Combining two smaller amounts to make up the size required. (*Shevuot* 21b)

Come O Bride

Welcoming Shabbat

Rabbi Yannai donned his robes on Friday evening and called out "Come O Bride, Come O Bride." (*Shabbat* 119a)

📖 Comfort extended

One scholar comforts a bereaved scholar

When R. Shimon b. Lakish died, R. Yohanan became grief-stricken.[63] The rabbis

sent R. Eleazar b. Pedat to comfort him. He went and sat before him and they learned together. Every dictum which R. Yohanan uttered, he was supported by R. Eleazar with a remark. "There is a Beraita which supports you." (*Bava Metzia* 84a)

✿ Comforting

R. Yitzhak said: "He who comforts a poor man with words will obtain eleven blessings." (*Bava Batra* 9b)

📖 Comforting words

To a colleague whose feelings were hurt[64]

R. Avohu and R. Hiyya b. Abba came to a place to deliver lectures. R. Hiyya lectured on legal matters and R. Avohu lectured on Aggadah. The audience left the hall of R. Hiyya to go to listen to R. Avohu. R. Avohu tried to comfort him with kind words, but he was still upset. (*Sotah* 40a)

Commanded mitzvah

R. Hanina said: "He who is commanded and does the mitzvah stands higher than one who is not commanded. (*Avodah Zarah* 3a; *Bava Kamma* 38a; *Kiddushin* 31a)

Commandments

Some commandments are not specifically in the Torah. Then how can we say in the blessings we recite before we perform a mitzvah that God commanded us? R. Avia and R. Nehemia give the answer. (*Shabbat* 23a)

Commandments, Six hundred and thirteen תרי"ג מצות

R Simlai was saying: "Six hundred and thirteen precepts were given to Moshe: 365 negative precepts, corresponding to the number of solar days in the year, and 248 positive precepts, corresponding to

---

63. See entry, Resh Lakish dies.

64. See also entry, Lecturers.

the number of organs in the human body. (*Makkot* 23b)

Commandments tied to the land
מצוה שהיא תלויה בארץ
Every precept which is dependent on the Land is practiced only in the Land. (*Kiddushin* 36b)

Commandments time-bound
מצוות עשה שהזמן גרמא
Mitzvot that have to be performed in a limited designated time. (*Kiddushin* 29a; *Shabbat* 62a; *Eruvin* 96b)

Commandments to bring benefit
R. Hanania b. Akashia said: "Hashem wanted Israel to have many merits; therefore he increased for them the Torah commandments." (*Makkot* 23b)

Commodities price fluctuation
What is the case if one sells wine or oil and the price for the commodity went up or down (*Bava Batra* 87a)

Common denominator הצד השוה שבהן
The feature common to them all, the common denominator (*Bava Kamma* 2a, 88a; *Bava Metzia* 4a, 87b; *Hullin* 114a)

Common man's blessing
R. Eleazar said in the name of R. Hanina: "Let not a blessing of a common man be taken lightly." (*Megillah* 15a)

Competition in the Temple
The priests in the Temple were competing with each-other for the privilege of performing the various services in the Temple. (*Yoma* 22a)

Completed the Mishna
Redactor of the Mishna
R. Yehuda HaNasi and R. Nathan concluded the Mishna; R. Ashi and Ravina concluded the Horaah (Gemara). (*Sotah* 49a; *Bava Metzia* 86a)

✿ Completing the job and not being idle
R. Tarfon said: "It is not your obligation to complete the job, but neither are you at liberty to be idle. If you studied much Torah, you will have great reward, because your Employer is faithful and you should know that the righteous will be rewarded in the time to come." (*Avot* 2:16)

Composer of blessing over Torah
R. Yohanan composed one of the blessings we recite when we learn Torah. (*Berachot* 11b)

Composer of prayer
Rabbi Gamliel asked for a volunteer to compose a prayer which reflects Jewish opposition to the sectarians and non-believers. Rabbi Shemuel HaKatan volunteered and composed the prayer called "*Ve-Lamalshinim.*" This prayer with the other eighteen prayers constitute the *Amidah* prayers. (*Berachot* 28b)

Conceited men
Rabbi Zeiri is quoted as saying in the name of Rabbi Hanina that the son of David will not come until there are no conceited men in Eretz Yisrael. (*Sanhedrin* 98a)

Concentrating during prayers
Rabbi Shimon b. Nathanel said, "Do not perform your prayers mechanically, but offer them as an appeal for mercy to the Almighty." (*Avot* 2:13)

✿ Concise language
R. Huna said in Rav's name, others say R. Huna said in Rav's name, which Rav heard from R. Meir: "One should always teach his student to use concise language and refined speech." (*Pesahim* 3b; *Hullin* 63b)

Conclusion incorrect והלא דין הוא
This cannot be so because a fortiori would point us to a different conclusion. (*Hullin* 22b)

Concluded Gemara
R. Ashi and Ravina concluded the Gemara. (*Bava Metzia* 86a)

Concubine
What is the difference between a wife and a concubine (*Sanhedrin* 21a)

Condemned city
A city cannot be declared condemned except by a court of seventy-one. (*Sanhedrin* 2a)

Condemned city
We have learned there never was a condemned city and never will it happen. (*Sanhedrin* 71a)

Condemned city not applicable to Jerusalem
Jerusalem can never be declared a condemned city. (*Bava Kamma* 82b; *Yoma* 23a; *Arachin* 32b)

Condemned to die
By the Roman authorities
It has been taught: When Turnus Rufus the wicked destroyed the Temple, Rabbi Gamliel was condemned to die.[65] A high officer came for him and stood up in the Bet Midrash and called out: "The nose man is wanted, the nose man is wanted." When R. Gamliel heard this, he hid himself. The officer went to him in secret and asked him: "If I save you, will you bring me into the World to Come?" Rabbi Gamliel promised him. The officer threw himself down from the roof and died. In the Roman Empire, there was a tradition

that when an officer dies during enforcing a Roman decree, that decree is annulled. A voice from heaven was heard declaring: "The officer is destined to enter the World to Come."

Rabbi Gamliel survived in hiding. (*Taanit* 29a)

Condition contrary to Torah Law המתנה על מה שכתוב בתורה
Making condition in a contract contrary to that which is written in the Torah (*Bava Metzia* 94a; *Kiddushin* 90b)

Conditional תנאי
On condition (*Ketubbot* 19b)

Confession ודוי
Confession before dying (*Shabbat* 32a)

Confiscated property (*Gittin* 55b)

Confounded
"The son of Uzziel confounded me"
It is related that a certain person disapproved of his children's conduct, and he left his estate to Rabbi Yonatan b. Uzziel. Rabbi Yonatan divided the estate in three parts: one part he sold, another part he consecrated, and the other part he gave to the sons of the deceased.

Rabbi Shammai came to him, objecting to the way he handled it. Rabbi Shammai felt that the father did not want his children to benefit from his estate. Rabbi Yonatan told him if you can get back what I consecrated and what I sold, then you can also get back what I gave to the sons. Rabbi Shammai admitted: "The son of Uzziel has confounded me; the son of Uzziel has confounded me." (*Bava Batra* 133b)

Consequences
Act only after consequences are considered
Shimon b. Nathanel said: "Before you act,

---

65. According to some, this refers to Rabbi Shimon b. Gamliel, his son.

make sure you foresee the consequences."
(*Avot* 2:9)

✿ Consequences
Of the destruction of the Temple
R. Eliezer said: "From the day the Temple was destroyed, the Sages began to be like school teachers, school teachers like synagogue attendants, synagogue attendants like common people, and the common people became more debased.".

"There will be none to ask, none to inquire. Who can we rely upon? We can rely only upon our Father in Heaven."

"Just before the arrival of Mashiach, insolence will increase, honor will be scarce. The vine will yield its fruit abundantly, but wine will be dear. The government will adopt a new religion and no one will disapprove."

"The meeting places will be used for immorality; Galilee will be destroyed, Gablan desolated, and the dwellers on the frontier will go begging from place to place without anyone taking pity on them."

"The wisdom of the scholars will degenerate, fearers of sin will be despised, and truth will be lacking. Youth will put old men to shame, the old will stand up in the presence of the young, a son will revile his father, and a daughter will rebel against her mother, a daughter-in-law against her mother-in-law."

"The members of one's household will be the enemies of the house."

"That generation will have a face of a dog; a son will not be ashamed before his father. Therefore, on whom can we rely? We can rely only upon our Father in Heaven." (*Sotah* 49a–b; *Sanhedrin* 97a)

📖 Consider family
"*When looking for a wife to marry, do not consider only beauty, but consider family.*"
Rabbi Shimon ben Gamliel said: "There were no happier days for Israel than the Fifteenth of Av and Yom Kippur. On those two days, the daughters of Jerusalem used to go out dressed in white garments, which were borrowed, in order not to shame those who had none. They used to dance in the vineyards and call out: 'Young man, lift your eyes and select for yourself. Do not consider only beauty, but consider family.'" (*Taanit* 26b; *Bava Batra* 121a)

Consolation
R. Avohu gave consolation to R. Hiyya b. Abba. (*Sotah* 40a)

Consolation to a mourner (*Moed Katan* 21b)

✿ Consult your teacher
R. Gamliel said: "Provide yourself a teacher and you will avoid making mistakes. Train yourself to be accurate and not to estimate." (*Avot* 1:16)

Consulting Eleazar the Kohen Gadol
(*Sanhedrin* 16b; *Yoma* 73b)

Consulting one rabbi after another
If the first rabbi declared the item unclean, do not consult a second rabbi who might declare it as clean (*Avodah Zarah* 7a; *Hullin* 44b; *Niddah* 20b)

Contract
Specifications in a contract when selling a house (*Bava Batra* 63b)

Contract
Signatures of witnesses (*Bava Batra* 160a; *Kiddushin* 49a)

Contract
That was burned or destroyed by others (*Bava Kamma* 33b, 98a)

Contract altered המשנה ידו על התחתונה

The one who alters the contract is at a disadvantage (*Bava Metzia* 76a, 77b; *Bava Kamma* 102a; *Avodah Zarah* 7a)

Contract date

A contract that is dated on Shabbat or Yom Kippur (*Bava Batra* 171a)

Contract dates

How dates were fixed on a contract (*Bava Batra* 164b)

Contract document גט פשוט

A plain contract document (*Bava Batra* 160a; *Kiddushin* 49a)

Contract erased (*Bava Batra* 168a)

Contract of arbitration (*Bava Batra* 168a)

Contract of betrothal (*Bava Batra* 168a)

Contract of a loan (*Bava Batra* 168a)

Contract of sale (*Bava Batra* 168a)

Contract of tenancy (*Bava Batra* 168a)

Contract that includes interest

A contract which has a clause with forbidden interest written into it (*Bava Kamma* 30b, 72a; *Bava Kamma* 30b; *Bava Batra* 94b)

Contracts

Antedated, postdated contracts (*Bava Metzia* 17a, 72a; *Sanhedrin* 32a)

Contradictory statements

One of the thirteen rules of R. Yishmael state that when two sentences contradict each other the Torah provides a third sentence to reconcile them. (See *Shemot* 40:38; *Vayikra* 1:1; *Bamidbar* 7:89) (*Beraita in Sifra*)

Contrary stipulations
מתנה על מה שכתוב בתורה

Stipulations in a contract contrary to Torah commandments is considered null and void. (*Ketubbot* 83a; *Bava Metzia* 94a)

Contrary to what was stated
אדרבה איפכא מסתברא

On the contrary, the logic is the reverse. (*Pesahim* 28a)

Controversy

Controversy for Gods sake will turn out to be of benefit. (*Avot* 5:17)

Conversion after betrothal

A man says to a woman: "Be betrothed to me after my conversion." (*Bava Metzia* 16b; *Kiddushin* 63a; *Ketubbot* 58b)

Conversion incomplete

Performing circumcision without mikveh immersion

R. Hiyya b. Abba once visited Gabla and he found that women were married to proselytes; their conversion was only by circumcision, without *mikveh* immersion. He also noticed that non-Jews were serving Jewish wine to Jews and they were eating a non-kosher animal. R. Hiyya did not say anything to them; he wanted to consult first with Rabbi Yohanan, his rabbi. After he spoke to him, R. Yohanan instructed him to tell them that their children are considered bastards, that their wine is *nesech* and forbidden, and the animal is not kosher. (*Yevamot* 46a; *Avodah Zarah* 59a)

Convert

A man wanted to convert in order to become the High Priest; he came to R. Shammai and to R. Hillel. (*Shabbat* 31a)

✿ Convert

A man came to R. Yehuda and told him: "I converted to Judaism privately." "Do you have witnesses?" "No," the man replied. "Do you have children?" "Yes." R. Yehuda told him, "You are trusted. You may be disqualified if it was just for you, but you cannot disqualify your children." (*Yevamot* 47a)

Converts
Treated with preference
R. Adda b. Ahava lived in the house of a proselyte. The proselyte and R. Bibi were in contention for the position of town administrator. They came before Rabbi Yosef, and R. Adda argued for the proselyte. After listening to both sides, Rabbi Yosef declared, "Let R. Bibi who is a great man give his attention to heavenly matters, like distributing charity, and let the proselyte pay attention to the affairs of the town." R. Abbaye remarked, "When one provides a scholar with housing, let him provide it for one like R. Adda b. Ahava, who is able to argue in his favor." (*Kiddushin* 76b)

Converts
Certain people like the Cordyenians, Tarmodites, and Kartuenians were discussed whether they are acceptable as converts. (*Yevamot* 16a)

Convert's inheritance
The proselyte Issur had twelve thousand *zuz* deposited for safekeeping with Rava, but the question arose whether Issur's son Mari is entitled to it. The problem was that when Mari was conceived, Issur was still not Jewish, but became Jewish before Mari was born. R. Ika b. R. Ammi suggested that Issur should declare that the money belongs to R. Mari. That is how the matter was solved by Issur declaring that the money belongs to his son Mari." (*Bava Batra* 149a)

Converts not accepted
In the time of Mashiach converts will not be accepted. (*Avodah Zarah* 3b)

Conviction of oneself is not valid
Rova said: "A person cannot make himself a wicked man or convict himself." (*Sanhedrin* 9b, 25a)

Cooked by a non-Jew (*Avodah Zarah* 38a)

Cooking a kid in its mother's milk
לא תבשל גדי בחלב אמו
It was taught in the school of R. Yishmael: The prohibition of cooking a kid in its mother's milk is stated three times in the Torah: One is a prohibition against eating, one a prohibition against deriving benefit from it, and one a prohibition against cooking it. (*Hullin* 115b; *Kiddushin* 57b)

Cooking on Shabbat
Deliberately (*Bava Kamma* 71a; *Shabbat* 38a; *Betzah* 17b; *Hullin* 15a)

Cooking on Shabbat
Cooking unintentionally on Shabbat (*Bava Kamma* 71a; *Shabbat* 38a; *Betzah* 17b; *Hullin* 15a)

Cooking on Shabbat
For a sick person (*Hullin* 15b)

Cooking on Shabbat intentionally
R. Yehuda and R. Yohanan HaSandlar said: "The food cooked on Shabbat intentionally may never be eaten." (*Bava Kamma* 71a; *Shabbat* 38a; *Betzah* 17b; *Hullin* 15a)

Cooking prohibition
איסור בשול
Prohibition against cooking meat in milk (*Hullin* 115b; *Kiddushin* 57b)

Copulating
Copulating with an animal (*Bava Kamma* 40b)

Cordial and respectful to each other

Rav and Shemuel and R. Assi once met at a *Brit*, some say it was a *Pidyon Haben*. Rav did not want to enter before Shemuel and Shemuel did not want to enter before R. Assi. Finally it was decided that Rav and R. Assi would enter together first and Shemuel would enter last. (*Bava Kamma* 80a; *Gittin* 6a)

Corners of the field

Rav and Shemuel both ruled: The proper measure to be given to the priest for the first of the fleece is one-sixtieth part, for *teruma* one-sixtieth part, and for the corner of the field to the poor, one-sixtieth part. (*Hullin* 137b)

Corners of the head

To cut hair to round it? (*Makkot* 20a)

Corners of the tree

Does the commandment of leaving the corners to the poor apply also to a tree? (*Hullin* 131b)

Coronets on Torah letters[66] (*Menahot* 29b)

Corpse

Rescuing a corpse on Shabbat from a fire (*Shabbat* 30b, 43b, 142b)

📖 Corpse in the attic

Eleazar b. Shimon b. Yohai

When R. Eleazar was about to die, he said to his wife, "I know that the rabbis are angry with me and they will not attend to me properly. Please let me lie in a room on the upper floor, and be not afraid of me." R. Shemuel b. Nahmeni said: "R. Yonatan's mother told me that she was told by the wife of R. Eleazar that she kept him in the upper floor from eighteen to twenty-two years. She used to walk up to examine his

hair and not a single hair had fallen out. One day she saw a worm crawl out from his ear, and she was very upset, but he appeared to her in a dream and told her that it was nothing. It happened because he once heard an insult to a scholar and did not protest. While his body was upstairs people used to come to the house with disputes between them; they stood near the door, each stating his case, and then a voice came from the upper chamber proclaiming: so and so is liable, and so and so is not. One day R. Eleazar's wife was quarreling with a neighbor and the other woman told her, "You deserve to be like your husband, not worthy of burial." It was said that R. Shimon b. Yohai appeared to the rabbis of the town in a dream and complained. "I have a pigeon amongst you and you refuse to bring it to me." Then the rabbis decided to attend to him, but the people of Akavaria refused to let him be taken away, because during all the years that R. Eleazar was kept in the upper floor of his house, no bad thing happened to the town. One day on Erev Yom Kippur, when the people were busy preparing for Yom Kippur, the rabbis took his bier and carried it to his father's grave. (*Bava Metzia* 84b)

Corpse uncleanness

Contact with a corpse makes the person ritually unclean. (*Ohalot* 1:1–8)

Corpse under a roof

A person under the same roof with a corpse (*Ohalot* 2:1)

Corpses can hear

R. Avohu said: "The dead person knows what is said in his presence until the top stone closes the grave." (*Shabbat* 152b)

✿ Correct and scrupulous

Once R. Shimi ben Ashi came to Abbaye

---

66. See story under, Moshe in Heaven.

and asked him to give him lessons in To-rah. R. Abbaye answered him:

"I have no time; I need my time to study for myself."

The other asked him:

"Then teach me at night."

Abbaye answered:

"At night I am also busy; I have to water my fields."

R. Shimi offered to water his fields during daytime and to get lessons at nighttime. Abbaye agreed and he studied with him.

However, one incident did not please Abbaye at all. R. Shimi went to the field-owners which were located above R. Abbaye's fields and declared to them that the field-owners below have first right to water the fields. He then went to the field-owners below Abbaye's fields and told them the field-owners above have the first right to water the fields. In the meantime, R. Shimi had all the water available for himself to irrigate the fields of Abbaye. When Abbaye found out what he had done, it displeased him very much, and he refused to eat of that year's produce. (*Gittin* 60b)

Correct yourself first
קשוט עצמך ואחר כך קשוט אחרים

Resh Lakish said: "Correct yourself first before you correct others." (*Bava Metzia* 107b; *Bava Batra* 60b; *Sanhedrin* 18a, 19a)

Correcting mistakes
During prayers (*Berachot* 5th *perek*)

Count money by Chanukah candles
Can one count money by the light of the Chanukah candles? (*Shabbat* 22a)

Court   בית דין
A court of judges (*Bava Metzia* 32a)

Court
The court: its composition and progres-sion[67] (*Sanhedrin* 88b)

Court case
Between a Jew and a non-Jew (*Bava Kamma* 113a)

Court composition
The large court called Sanhedrin con-sisted of seventy-one judges; the smaller court consisted of twenty-three judges. (*Sanhedrin* 2a, 3b)

Court does not exist of even numbers
אין בית דין שקול
No court is constituted with even number members. (*Sanhedrin* 3b, 13b)

Court impudent   בית דין חצוף
An impudent court (*Sanhedrin*, 3a, 5b, 30a, 87b; *Ketubbot* 22a)

Court in session
Ezra ordained that the Court should meet on Mondays and Thursdays. (*Bava Kamma* 82a)

Court is in session
R. Ammi and R. Assi were sitting and studying between the pillars of the syn-agogue in Tiberias. Every now and then, they knocked on the side of the door and announced: "If anyone has a lawsuit, let him come forward." (*Shabbat* 10a)

Court of expert judges   בית דין מומחין
A court of expert judges (*Bava Metzia* 32a)

Court of judges, three in Jerusalem
There were three courts of judges in Jeru-salem. (*Sanhedrin* 86b)

---

67. See details under, Strife in Israel.

Courts of judges
The difference between courts in capital cases and monetary cases and other matters is discussed in the Talmud. (*Sanhedrin* 87b)

Court of judgment
Earthly court and Heavenly court (*Bava Kamma* 56a)

Court of non-expert judges
בית דין הדיוטות
A court of non-expert judges (*Bava Metzia* 32a)

Court with odd number of judges
בית דין נוטה

(*Sanhedrin* 3b)

Court's decision
When a decision by the court has been reached, the litigants are admitted to the court room and the presiding judge declares: "So and so is liable and so and so is not liable." (*Sanhedrin* 42a)

Court's ruling to be annulled
אין ב"ד יכול לבטל דברי ב"ד חבירו אלא א"כ
גדול הימנו בחכמה ובמנין
A court is unable to annul the decision of another court, unless it is superior to it in wisdom and numerical strength. (*Avodah Zarah* 36a; *Megillah* 2a; *Gittin* 36b; *Moed Katan* 3b)

✿ Courtesy and respect
R Hezkiya stated that R. Hanina b. Avohu said it in the name of R. Avohu and R. Avdimi de-man Haifa: "When a scholar passes, one should rise for him from a distance of four cubits. When the head of a Bet Din enters the room, one should rise as soon as he is seen and to be seated when he passes four cubits, when the Nasi enters the room, one rises when he is seen and sits down only after he is seated." (*Kiddushin* 33b)

Courtyard
A courtyard acquires things for the owner. (*Bava Kamma* 49b; *Bava Metzia* 102a)

Courtyard
When selling a courtyard in a general contract, the intangible items in the courtyard are not included. (*Bava Batra* 67a)

Courtyard shared with a non-Jew
(*Eruvin* 61b)

Courtyard acquires property
חצרו של אדם קונה לו שלא מדעתו
R. Yosi b. Hanina stated: "A person's courtyard acquires property even without the person's knowledge." (*Hullin* 141b; *Bava Metzia* 11a, 102a, 118a; *Bava Kamma* 49b)

Covered hands
The question was raised, may one cover his hands with a cloth in place of washing hands? (*Hullin* 107a)

Covered the blood for a friend
Substituted for a friend during slaughtering (*Hullin* 87a)

Covering blood
What can be used to cover the blood after slaughtering? (*Hullin* 88a)

Covering the blood
כסוי הדם
Covering the blood with sand after slaughtering (*Hullin* 31a, 83b)

Covering the blood of many animals during slaughtering (*Hullin* 86b)

Cow gave birth to a donkey
(*Bechorot* 5b)

Cows from Egypt
It once happened that Rabbi Tarfon ordered a cow — whose womb was removed — to be fed to the dogs. When the matter

was brought before the Sages in Yavne, they permitted it for human consumption, because a prominent physician, Theodos, stated that no cow was allowed to leave Alexandria, Egypt unless her womb was cut out, to prevent her from having offspring. Thereupon exclaimed Rabbi Tarfon: "Here goes my donkey, meaning I will have to compensate the owner of the cow."

But Rabbi Akiva said to him: "You are not bound to make compensation, because you are publicly recognized as an expert in these matters." (*Sanhedrin* 33a; *Bechorot* 28b)

Created food on Shabbat
Food created by a Jew on Shabbat, can it be eaten? (*Bava Kamma* 71a; *Shabbat* 38a)

Creation with purpose
R. Yehuda said in the name of Rav: "Everything God created in this world, He created for a purpose." (*Shabbat* 77b)

Creations
Ten things were created on Erev Shabbat: The mouth of the earth that swallowed Korah, the mouth of the well which provided water for Israel in the desert, the mouth of the donkey which spoke to Bilam, the rainbow, the manna, the staff of Moshe, the *shamir* worm, the script form of the Hebrew alphabet, the instrument to inscribe the Tablets, and the first Tablets (that were later broken). (*Avot* 5:8)

Creations: seven
Seven things were created before the world was created: The Torah, repentance, the Garden of Eden, Gehinom, the Throne of Glory, the Temple, and the name of Mashiach. (*Pesahim* 54a; *Nedarim* 39b)

✿ Credit not wanted for praying
When there was a drought in the Land of Israel, R. Yonah, the father of R. Mani, would go into his house and say to his family: "Get me my sacks so I can go and buy grain for a *zuz*." He was so humble; he didn't want to let on to his family that he is the person praying for rain. He then went to a low area, put on sackcloth and prayed for rain, and rain came. When he returned home, his family asked him: "Did you bring grain?" He would answer: "Now that rain has come, the world will feel relieved." (*Taanit* 23b)

Creditors
Five kinds of creditors can collect. (*Bava Kamma* 95a; *Ketubbot* 51b)

Creditor's contract
When a contract for a debt is sold to another person and subsequently the creditor forgives the debt (*Bava Kamma* 89a; *Bava Metzia* 20a; *Bava Batra* 147b; *Ketubbot* 85b; *Kiddushin* 48a)

Critical of Priests
Rabbi Shaul ben Batnit was very critical of the priests in the latter days of the Temple.

It was taught, Abba Shaul said: "There were sycamore trees in Jericho and strong-arm-men seized them by force. Thereupon, the owners of the trees consecrated them to Heaven. Of these kinds of deeds, he used to say in the name of Abba Yosef b. Honin:

"Woe is to me because of the houses of Boethus, woe to me from their rods, woe to me because of the house of Hanin, woe to me because of their secret whisperings. Woe to me because of the house of Kathros, woe to me because of their pens, woe to me because of the house of Yishmael ben Phabi, woe to me because of their fists. For they are High Priests and their sons are Temple treasurers, and their sons-in-law are trustees, and their servants beat the people with rods." (*Pesahim* 57a)

Cross dressing (*Nazir* 59a)

Crowns of wisdom
When R. Eleazar b. Azariah died, the crowns of wisdom ceased. (*Sotah* 49b)

Crowns on Yaakov's coffin
R Avohu said: "When Yaakov was taken from Egypt to be buried in Hevron, Yosef placed his crown on the coffin of Yaakov. During the funeral march to Hevron, the nations of the area saw Yosef's crown on the coffin. They all joined and placed their crowns on the coffin and they added up to sixty-three crowns." (*Sotah* 13a)

Cruelty to animals   צער בעלי חיים
The prohibition of cruelty to animals is discussed. (*Bava Metzia* 32b; *Shabbat* 128b)

Crushed testicles (*Yevamot* 75a)

Crushing nuts
Crushing nuts on Shabbat is discussed in *Kol hakelim*, the 17th *perek* in *Shabbat*. (*Shabbat* 122b)

Cry for the mourners
בכו לאבלים ולא לאבידה
Weep for the mourners and not for the deceased. (*Moed Katan* 25b)

Crying
The Prophet Yirmiyahu uses double language for the word crying, prophesying the destruction of both Temples. (*Sanhedrin* 104b)

Cryptic messages sent
Secret intercalation took place with cryptic messages sent under Roman occupation. A message was sent to Rava. It read: "A couple arrived from Rakkas who were captured by an eagle. They were in possession of articles manufactured in Luz, such as purple. Through Divine

mercy they escaped safely. Further, the offspring of Nahshon wished to establish a Netziv, but the Edomites would not permit it. The members of the Assembly met and established a Netziv in the month in which Aharon the High Priest died."[68] (*Sanhedrin* 12a)

Cubit
The cubit was a measuring size the rabbis used. (*Kelim* 17:9)

📖 **Cup of honor**
"Let one use a cup of honor for one day, even if it be broken the next day."[69] (*Berachot* 27 a–b)

Cure for ailment
Rabbi Ashi's daughter had a stomach ailment, and Rabin from Naresh cured her with herbal medicines. (*Gittin* 69b)

📖 **Cured by others**
R. Yohanan fell ill and R. Hanina went to visit him. He said to R. Yohanan, "Are your sufferings welcome to you?" He answered him, "No, neither the suffering nor their reward are welcome." R. Hanina told R. Yohanan:

"Give me your hand." He gave him his hand and he cured him. R. Yohanan cured others, so why couldn't he cure himself? The rabbis replied, "A prisoner cannot free himself." (*Berachot* 5b; *Nedarim* 7b; *Sanhedrin* 95a)

---

68. Eagle was the symbol for the Roman legion; the Nasi of the Sanhedrin was a descendant of Nahshon, prince of Judah; Neziv could be a month; the name of Edom was used to describe the Romans; and Adar was the month in which Aharon died.
69. See also entry, Appointed Nasi of the Sanhedrin.

✡ Curse
Of an ordinary man
R. Yitzhak said, "The curse of an ordinary man should never be considered light in your eyes." (*Bava Kamma* 93a; *Megillah* 15a, 28a)

✡ Curse on the lips
R Nehunia b. HaKana was asked by his students: "By what merit did you reach such old age?"

His reply was. "Never in my life did I try to elevate myself at the expense of degrading others, never did I go to sleep with a curse on my lips against my fellow-men, and I have been generous with my money." (*Megillah* 28a)

Cursed be Haman
Rava said: "One should drink enough wine on Purim to become mellow until one does not know the difference between cursed be Haman and blessed be Mordechai." (*Megilla* 7b)

Cursing a judge (*Sanhedrin* 66a)

Cursing a Nasi (*Sanhedrin* 66a)

Cursing parents (*Sanhedrin* 66a)

Cursing the name (*Sanhedrin* 45b)

📖 Custom in Jerusalem
Rabbi Shimon ben Gamliel said, "There was a fine custom in Jerusalem. When there was a party in a home, they spread a sheet over the door entrance. So long as the cloth was spread over the door, guests could enter. When the cloth was removed, no guests could enter." (*Bava Batra* 93b)

Custom of the community
When leasing a field, follow the custom of the community. (*Bava Metzia* 103a)

Cut down date trees
A man cut down date trees of a neighbor; they came before the Resh Galuta. (*Bava Kamma* 58b)

Cut hair
Cutting one's hair at a barber who is an idol worshipper (*Avodah Zarah* 29a)

Cut in the flesh   קעקע
An incised imprint in the flesh (*Makkot* 21a)

Cuthite daughters (*Shabbat* 17a)

Cuthite slaughtered the animal
R. Nahman b. Yitzhak said in the name of R. Assi: "I saw R. Yohanan eating the flesh of an animal slaughtered by a Cuthite." (*Hullin* 5b)

Cuthites at Mount Gerizim
They found an image of a dove on top of Mount Gerizim which some Cuthites worshipped. (*Hullin* 6a)

Cuthites (*Sanhedrin* 85b)

Cuthites
R. Meir said: "Cuthites became converts for fear of lions." (*Bava Kamma* 38b; *Yevamot* 16a; *Niddah* 56b)

Cuthites
R. Shimon b. Gamliel said: "Whatever mitzvah the Cuthites have adopted, they observed it scrupulously, even more than Jews. (*Hullin* 4a; *Berachot* 47b)

Cuthites
Two Cuthites formed a partnership, and one of the partners divided the money without the knowledge of the other. They came before R. Papa to adjudicate. (*Bava Metzia* 69a)

D

Dalet ד
Abbaye said, "The *dalet* of the *tefillin* were given to Moshe on Sinai." (*Shabbat* 62a)

Dam Hatamtzit
The last blood draining out of the animal (*Pesahim* 65a)

Dama
Ben Dama, a nephew of R. Yishmael was bitten by a snake (*Avodah Zarah* 27b)

✿📖 Dama son of Natina
A certain non-Jewish man from Ashkelon by the name of Dama son of Natina had precious pearls for sale. A Jewish buyer came to buy them for the Ephod and offered him a great sum of money profiting him 600,000 *dinarim*, but the keys to the locker were under the pillow of his father who was asleep. He would not disturb his father, and let the buyer leave. A year later, a red heifer was born in his herd. A Jewish buyer came to buy the heifer and he told them, "I know I could get any amount I desire, but I want only the amount I lost because my father was asleep." (*Avodah Zarah* 23b, 24a)

Damage without a visible sign הזיק שאינו ניכר
(*Gittin* 41a, 44b, 53a; *Moed Katan* 13a; *Bechorot* 35a; *Bava Kamma* 5a)

Damages
Four principal categories of damages (*Bava Kamma* 2a; *Keritot* 2b)

Damages
Thirteen principal categories of damages, R. Oshaya (*Bava Kamma* 4b; *Keritot* 2b)

Damages
Twenty-four main categories of damages, Hiyya (*Bava Kamma* 4b; *Keritot* 2b)

Damages
Nezikin סדר נזיקין
The Tractate *Nezikin* contains the laws concerning damages, criminal, and civil law.

Danger with Chanukah candles
If lighting Chanukah candles outdoors is dangerous, what to do (*Shabbat* 21b)

Daniel
Rav said: "The wiriting on the wall by Daniel was written in *gematria*." (*Sanhedrin* 22a)

Daniel
Reading the book of Daniel
R. Zechariah ben Kebutal was a Kohen. He relates that on Yom Kippur he was reading for the High Priest from the book of Daniel. (*Yoma* 18b)

Daniel made a Gezera
Daniel made a *gezera* not to drink the wine and oil. (*Avodah Zarah* 36a)

Darchei Shalom דרכי שלום
For the sake of peace
When the rabbis instituted the *halachot*, they paid great attention for the sake of peace. (*Bava Metzia* 12a; *Gittin* 61a)

Darius
Let Darius come and testify for Daniel. (*Avodah Zarah* 3a)

Date Torah was given
Our rabbis have taught: "The Ten Commandments were given to Israel on the sixth day of Sivan."
R. Yosi said: "They were given on the seventh day of Sivan." (*Shabbat* 86b)

Dated contracts

Antedated contracts and various other contracts are discussed (Bava Metzia 17a; Sanhedrin 32a; Bava Batra 157b; Gittin 17)

Dates and grapes

R. Shemuel was concerned about violation of kilayim, mixture of fruits

Shemuel's field worker brought him some dates from his property. When Shemuel bit into the date, it had a wine taste. He asked why they tasted like wine; his worker told him that the date trees were next to the vines. He instructed his worker to cut out the roots of the dates because they are weakening the vines. (*Bava Kamma* 92a)

Dating documents

Calculating by Jewish kings and by the kingdom of Greece (*Avodah Zarah* 10a; *Rosh Hashana* 2a, 8a)

Daughter

R. Zeiri was a student of R. Yohanan. He offered his daughter in marriage to R. Zeiri. (*Kiddushin* 71b)

Daughter in captivity

R. Shemuel's daughter was taken captive

A daughter of Shemuel was taken captive, and she became pregnant from her captor. Later, he converted and married her; they had a son, R. Mari. (*Ketubbot* 69a, also see Rashi there; *Berachot* 16a; *Bava Batra* 149a)

Daughter of R. Hisda

The daughter of R. Hisda asked her father: "Would you like to sleep a little?"

He answered her: "Soon there will come a time for me when the days will be long and short, and I will have time to sleep long." (*Eruvin* 65a)

Daughter of rabbi captured

R. Hanania b. Teradion's daughter was captured and placed in a brothel

The Talmud relates that the sister of Berurya was captured and placed in a brothel. Berurya was Rabbi Meir's wife and the daughter of Rabbi Hanina b. Teradion.

Berurya told her husband: "I am ashamed to have my sister in a brothel. Can you do something to get her out of there?"

So he took a bag full of *dinarim* and set out to ransom her. He said to himself, *If she is clean, then a miracle will happen.* He disguised himself as a knight and came to the place where she was kept. He said to her: "Get ready for me."

She replied: "I am menstruating.".

He answered: "I am prepared to wait." She replied: "But there are here many prettier women than I am."

He determined that she probably had the same excuse for others. He offered the money to the watchman and he released her. The government found out what he had done and they were looking to arrest him. For that reason he had to leave Eretz Yisrael and move to Babylonia. (*Avodah Zarah* 18a)

Daughters in captivity

Daughters of R. Shemuel were taken captive

The daughters of Rabbi Shemuel were taken captive in Babylonia and taken to Eretz Yisrael. The captors brought them to Rabbi Hanina. Both daughters stated to R. Hanina that they were pure. R. Hanina said to R. Shimon b. Abba: "Go and take care of your relatives." (*Ketubbot* 23a)

Daughters and mother in captivity

A woman had three daughters; she and one daughter were taken captive, another one died. A small child was born to one of the children. (*Bava Metzia* 39b)

Daughter's inheritance

When a man dies and leaves sons and daughters, if the inheritance is large the sons inherit and the daughters receive maintenance. (*Ketubbot* 108b; *Bava Batra* 139b)

Daughter's inheritance

Ravina allowed the daughter of R. Ashi to collect her inheritance without an oath; her father left it to her from the property of R. Mar b. Ashi. (*Ketubbot* 69a)

Daughters of Israel

The daughters of Israel are beautiful, but it is poverty that makes them uncomely

It once happened that a man vowed not to marry his sister's daughter. But there were no other prospects and the family was in favor of it. They brought the girl to Rabbi Yishmael and he instructed his household to dress up the girl and beautify her. Rabbi Yishmael said to the prospective groom: "Is this the woman you vowed against?" He answered: "No."

Rabbi Yishmael then annulled his vow. In that same hour Rabbi Yishmael wept and said:

"The daughters of Israel are beautiful, but it is poverty that makes them uncomely." (*Nedarim* 66a)

Daughters of Jerusalem

Rabbi Shimon ben Gamliel said: "There were no happier days for Israel than the Fifteenth of Av and Yom Kippur. On those two days, the daughters of Jerusalem used to go out dressed in white garments, which were borrowed, in order not to shame those who had none. They used to dance in the vineyards and call out: 'Young man, lift your eyes and select for yourself. Do not consider only beauty, but consider family.'" (*Taanit* 26b; *Bava Batra* 121a)

Daughters of Tzelofhad

The daughters of Tzelofhad took three parts of the inheritance. (*Bava Batra* 116b)

David

Rav said: "R. Yehuda HaNasi who is a descendant of King David expounded on the merits of King David." (*Shabbat* 56a)

David

David put off the Angel of Death. (*Shabbat* 30b)

David

David's sins were forgiven. (*Shabbat* 30a)

David

Did he sin?

Rabbi Shemuel b. Nahmeni said in the name of Rabbi Yonatan: "Anyone who asserts that David sinned is in error, because it is written (I Samuel 18:14): 'God was with him.'" (*Shabbat* 56a)

David did not listen to gossip לשון הרע

R. Shemuel said: "David did not listen to gossip." (*Shabbat* 56a)

David fighting the Philistines

The Philistines were hiding in grain stacks belonging to Jews; David wanted to destroy the grain stacks. (*Bava Kamma* 60b)

David's children

R. Yehuda said in Rav's name: "David had 400 children and all were good looking; they had long locks of hair and drove golden carriages." (*Sanhedrin* 21a, 49a)

David's death (*Shabbat* 39a)

David's harp

Rabbi Aha bar Bizna said in the name of Rabbi Shimon Hasida: "A harp hung above David's bed, and at midnight a north wind came and blew and played the harp to wake him." (*Berachot* 3b; *Sanhedrin* 16a)

David's mother
The name of David's mother was Nitzevet, and she was the daughter of Adael.
  The mother of Shimshon was Tzelalfonit, and his sister's name was Nashyan." (*Bava Batra* 91a)

Dawn   עמוד השחר
Dawn is to be considered when fixing time for prayer. (*Berachot* 2a)

✿ Days are short
R. Tarfon's saying was: "The day is short, the task is great, the laborers are lazy, the reward is plentiful, and the master is pressing urgently." (*Avot* 2:15)

Days the Torah is read
The Torah is read on the following days: Monday, Thursday at the *Shaharit* service, and on Shabbat at the *Minha* service – where three people are called up. Rosh Hodesh and Hol Hamoed, four people are called up. On Yom Tov, five people are called up; on Yom Kippur, six people, and on Shabbat *Shaharit*, seven people are called up.
  These are some of the enactments by Ezra: The Torah should be read during the *Minha* service on Shabbat, also on Mondays and Thursdays during the *Shaharit* service. (*Bava Kamma* 82a; *Megillah* 21a)

Daytime departure
R. Yehuda said in the name of Rav: "One should always arrive and leave a town during daylight." (*Bava Kamma* 60 a–b)

Dead
The dead will live again.[70] (*Avot* 4:29)

---

70. See entry, Wisdom.

Dead are aware
R. Avohu said: "The dead person knows what is said in his presence until the top stone closes the grave." (*Shabbat* 152b)

Dead at a young age
A scholar of Torah dying young (*Shabbat* 13a)

Dead body
If one finds a dead body on the open road, it may be removed to the side of the road. (*Bava Kamma* 81b; *Eruvin* 17b)

Dead corpse
On Shabbat (*Shabbat* 30b, 43b, 142b)

Dead outside Israel
Resurrection
Rabbi Abba bar Memmel disagreed with some of his contemporary rabbis with regards to the dead outside Israel; he firmly believed they would be resurrected, and he based it on scripture. (*Ketubbot* 111a)

Dead person
Feelings
R. Yitzhak said: "The worm is as painful to the dead as a needle to the living." (*Berachot* 18b; *Shabbat* 13b, 152a)

Dead person
In Jerusalem, it was not allowed to keep a dead person overnight. (*Bava Kamma* 82b)

Dead person attendance
(*Shabbat* 150b, 151a)

Dead Sea
When R. Dimi came to Babylonia, he stated, that no one ever drowned in the Dead Sea. (*Shabbat* 108b)

Dead while still alive
It was taught: Four kinds of people may be regarded as dead: the poor, the

blind, the leper, and the childless. (*Avodah Zarah* 5a)

✿ Dead's presence
Rabbi Zerika said in the names of Rabbi Ami and Rabbi Yehoshua ben Levi: "Do not speak in front of a deceased about other matters except about him." (*Berachot* 3b)

Deaf-mute
Fire being sent with a deaf-mute (*Bava Kamma* 22b, 59b; *Kiddushin* 42b)

Death
903 causes of death (*Berachot* 8a)

Death
R. Ammi said: "There is no death without sin." (*Shabbat* 55a)

📖 Death approaching
Once R. Huna was very ill, and R. Papa went to visit him. When he saw that he was very sick, he said to the people:
"Make ready for his trip to heaven."
R. Huna recovered and R. Papa was embarrassed for thinking it was the end. He asked him: "What did you see?"
He answered him:
"You were right, it was indeed my end, but the Almighty said to the angels: 'He deserves to live longer, because he never insisted on his rights and is a forgiving person.'" (*Rosh Hashana* 17a)

📖 Death delayed
It is related, Rabbi Hanina bar Papi was about to die and the Angel of Death was sent to his house with orders to carry out any wish of his. Rabbi Hanina said to the angel:
"Allow me thirty days in order to revise my studies." He was granted the wish. It is said that when he died, a pillar of fire formed a partition between him and the world. We have it as a tradition that such

a partition by a pillar of fire is granted only to a person unique in his generation (*Ketubbot* 77b)

Death of sons in father's lifetime
Showing a tooth to the group, R. Yohanan said: "This bone is from my tenth son who died." (*Berachot* 5b)

📖 Death of the righteous
Big loss but not a complete loss
R. Hanina said: "Everything is in the hand of heaven except the fear of Heaven."
R. Eleazar further said in the name of R. Hanina: "A righteous person when he dies is a great loss to his generation, but is not really lost because his legacy remains. It is like when one loses a precious pearl; it is a loss only to the owner, but the pearl remains a pearl wherever it is." (*Berachot* 33b; *Megillah* 15a)

Death penalty
Four kinds of death penalty were vested in the court. (*Sanhedrin* 49b)

✿ Deathbed instructions
Rava instructed R. Papa and R. Huna b. Yehoshua: "When a written legal decision of mine comes before you and you find objection to it, do not tear it up before you speak to me. If I have valid reasons for my decision, I will tell it to you, and if not, I will withdraw it. After my death, you shall neither tear it up nor draw any conclusions from it. You shall not tear it up, because had I been there I might have given you my reasons, and do not draw any conclusions, because a judge must be guided by what he sees with his eyes." (*Bava Batra* 130b)

Debate
R. Gamliel debates the Emperor
R. Gamliel had debates about belief in God with unbelievers. (*Sanhedrin* 39a)

Debate
R. Tanchum debates the Emperor
R. Tanchum had debates about belief in God with the emperor. (*Samhedrin* 39a)

Debate, Rebbe and a non-believer
(*Hullin* 87a)

D'bei Eliyahu
It was taught in D'bei Eliyahu: The world is to exist 6,000 years; the first 2,000 years are to be void, the next 2,000 years are the period of Torah, and the following 2,000 years are the time of Mashiach. (*Avodah Zarah* 9a)

D'bei Eliyahu
A story about a scholar (*Shabbat* 13a)

D'bei Eliyahu
It was taught in the teachings of D'bei Eliyahu: Whoever learns *halachot* is assured to have a share in the World to Come. (*Megillah* 28b)

D'bei Hezkiya   דבי חזקיה
Rabbi Hezkiya is the author of the *Debei Hezkiya* (it was taught in the school of Hezkiya). (*Sanhedrin* 37b; *Ketubbot* 30a; *Sotah* 8b)

D'bei R. Yishmael   דבי רבי ישמעאל
The school of R. Yishmael taught: The Torah stated three times "You shall not cook a kid in its mother's milk" – one is a prohibition against eating, one against deriving benefit, and one against cooking it. (*Hullin* 115b)

📖 Debt paid by agent
The Talmud relates that Rabbi Avimi had some commercial transactions with Babylonia. Once he sent money to Hozai, Babylonia with Rabbi Hama b. Rabbah b. Avohu in payment for a debt to some people. After he gave them the money and asked for the note, the people claimed that the payment was for another debt. Rabbi Hama went to complain to Rabbi Avohu. R. Avohu asked him: "Do you have witnesses that you paid him?" R. Hama said, "No." "In that case, they could plead that you didn't pay at all; and therefore we must believe them that it is for another debt." (*Ketubbot* 85a; *Shevuot* 42a)

📖 Debt payment in a Shemittah year
R. Abba b. Marta owed money to Rabbah. Rabbah asked him for his money, but he was slow. Finally after some years, he came with the money during a Shemittah year.

The Halachah is that in a Shemittah year all debts are cancelled. Rabbah said to him: "It is cancelled." So R. Abba took the money, put it in his pocket and went home. Afterwards, R. Abbaye met Rabbah and found him to be in a bad mood.

"Why are you in a bad mood?" Rabbah told him what happened with R. Abba.

R. Abbaye went to R. Abba and asked him: "When you took the money to Rabbah, what did you say to him?"

"I offered to pay back the money I owed."

"And what did he say?"

"He said. 'It is cancelled.'"

"Did you say to him, 'Even so, take it?'"

"No, I did not."

Abbaye said to him:

"If you had said to him, 'All the same take it,' he would have taken it. Now go to him and offer him the money again, but make sure you say to him, 'All the same take it.'"

He did as he was advised and Rabbah took it from him and said: "This rabbinical student did have the sense to see this from the beginning."[71] (*Gittin* 37b)

Debts annulled (*Gittin* 37b)

---

71. See entry, Shemittah year debt payment.

Deceived
He who was deceived has the upper hand. He can say, "Give me back my money or give me what you overcharged me." (*Bava Metzia* 51a)

✿ Deceiving non-Jews is forbidden
R. Shemuel said: "It is forbidden to deceive non-Jews as well as Jews." (*Hullin* 94a)

✿ Decent and unselfish
The rabbis decided to appoint R. Avohu as head of the academy in Acco, but when R. Avohu saw that R. Abba of Acco had numerous creditors asking for payment, he said to the rabbis: "There is a greater scholar more suitable for the office." (*Sotah* 40a)

Decent language
The school of R. Yishmael taught: One should always speak in decent language. (*Pesahim* 3a)

Decree   גזרה
A decree or an Ordinance
R. Yishmael b. Elisha said: "We do not issue a *gezera* on the community unless the majority can endure it." (*Bava Batra* 60b)

Decree not imposed
R. Shimon b. Gamliel and R. Eliezer b. Tzadok made a dictum: "We impose no decrees upon the community unless the majority is able to abide by it." (*Avodah Zarah* 36a; *Bava Kamma* 79b; *Bava Batra* 60b; *Horayot* 3b)

Dedicated teacher
Rabbi Pereda was a very dedicated teacher, he taught one of his students so many times until he was able to master the subject. (*Eruvin* 54b)

Dedication of an item not owned
אין אדם מקדיש דבר שאינו שלו
One cannot dedicate what does not belong to him. (*Arachin* 26b)

Dedication of the Ohel Moed
Moshe celebrated twelve dedication days at the inauguration of the Ohel Moed in order to give honors to the twelve princes. (*Horayot* 6b)

Deed attestation   קיום השטר
Kiyyum Ha-Shtar (*Bava Batra* 154a; *Ketubbot* 22)

Deeds   איגרות שום
Deeds of valuation (*Bava Metzia* 13a, 19a, 20a; *Ketubbot* 100b)

Deeds   איגרות מזון
Deeds of maintenance (*Bava Metzia* 20a; *Ketubbot* 100b)

Deeds and contracts (*Bava Batra* 172a)

✿ Deeds based on wisdom
Eleazar b. Azariah said: "Anyone whose wisdom exceeds his deeds is like a tree whose branches are many but whose roots are few; such a tree when a wind comes and blows against it, the tree will be uprooted. However, anyone whose deeds exceed his wisdom is compared to a tree whose branches are few but whose roots are many; even if all the winds of the world come and blow against it, it cannot be uprooted." (*Avot* 3:22)

Deeds documents (*Bava Metzia* 16b)

✿ Deeds exceeding wisdom endures
Rabbi Hanina used to say: "He whose deeds exceed his wisdom, his wisdom will endure, but he whose wisdom exceeds his deeds, his wisdom will not endure." (*Avot* 3:9)

Deeds lost and found
R. Nahman said: "My father was one of the scribes of Mar Shemuel's court when I was about six or seven, and I remember

that they used to proclaim: 'Deeds of transfer found in the street should be returned to the owner.'" (*Bava Metzia* 16b)

Deer slaughtered on Yom Tov

During one of the Festivals, a deer was served at the table of the Exilarch. This was on the second day of the festival, but the deer was caught on the first day by a non-Jew and slain on the second day. Among the guests at the table were R. Nahman, R. Hisda, and R. Sheshet. R. Nachman and R. Hisda ate from the deer, but R. Sheshet would not eat from it. "What can I do with R. Sheshet who does not want to eat from the deer?"

"How could I eat from it?" retorted R. Sheishes, in view of what R. Assi quoted R. Yosi. (*Eruvin* 39b)

Defamation

It is discussed how many judges are required in a case of defamation. (*Sanhedrin* 2a)

Defecating before the idol Peor

Idol worshippers defecate in front of the idol Peor. (*Avodah Zarah* 44b)

Defects

Defects that make an animal *traifa* (*Hullin* 43a)

Defending one's own property

חזקה אין אדם מעמיד עצמו על ממונו

No man will let his property be taken without resistance. (*Sanhedrin* 72a; *Yoma* 85b)

✿ Deference for colleagues

Rav and Shemuel and R. Assi once met at a *brit*. Rav did not want to enter before Shemuel and Shemuel did not want to enter before R. Assi. Finally it was decided that Rav and R. Assi would enter together first and Shemuel would enter last. (*Bava Kamma* 80a)

✿ Deference to a colleague

In one instance, Rabbi Zera asked a question from Rabbi Yehuda HaNasi and he received a ruling, which was different from that of Rabbi Hiyya. When he told Rebbe that Rabbi Hiyya has a different opinion, he answered. "Abandon my reply and adopt that of Rabbi Hiyya." (*Avodah Zarah* 36b)

📖 Defied the Romans and taught Torah

Our rabbis taught: When Rabbi Yosi b. Kisma was ill, R. Hanania b. Teradion went to visit him. R. Yosi said to him: "I heard that you are defying them and teach Torah in public."

R. Hanania answered: "Heaven will show mercy."

R. Yosi said to him, "I am telling you plain facts and you tell me, 'Heaven will show mercy?' I would not be surprised if they burn you and the scroll of Torah together in one fire."

The Romans came upon R. Hanania b. Teradion sitting and teaching Torah in public. They took him and his scroll of Torah and wrapped the scroll around his body, placed bundles of wood around him, and set it on fire.[72] (*Avodah Zarah* 18a)

Degeneration

Destruction of the Temple brought degeneration.[73] (*Sotah* 49a–b)

Degrees of uncleanness

Uncleanness is transmitted and can become first degree, second degree, and third degree. (*Taharot* 2:2–8)

Deitiki   דייתיקי

A *deitiki*[74] is a gift from a dying person, dis-

---

72. See entry, Martyrdom.
73. See entry, Consequences.
74. A Talmudic expression.

position of property by will and testament (*Bava Batra* 152b)

Delayed report of a death

Shiva is observed one day only when news of it is delayed. (Pesahim 4a)

📖 Delegation sent to Rome to rescind

Roman authorities issued a decree
forbidding Jewish religious practices
The Talmud states that one time the Roman authorities issued a decree against Jewish religious practices. They forbade Jews to observe the Shabbat, or to circumcise their sons, or to observe the practice of family purity. When the edict was issued, a Jew living in Rome by the name of Reuben b. Istroboli dressed up to look like a Roman and mingled among the Romans. He convinced the authorities that to enact these restrictions would be a disadvantage to the Romans. On his advice, they annulled the laws. When it was found out that Reuben was a Jew, the authorities reinstituted the decrees. After the decree was reinstituted, the Jews in Judea decided to send a delegation to Rome to find a way for the law to be rescinded, and R. Shimon ben Yohai and R. Eleazar b. Yosi were chosen to travel to Rome. On the way to Rome, they were met by a demon named Ben Temalion. Rabbi Shimon wept and said, "My ancestor Avraham's maid, Hagar, was worthy to be met by angels thrice and I don't deserve to be met by an angel even once." But R. Shimon continued to pray, "Let a miracle happen no matter who the messenger is." The demon, Ben Temalion, advanced ahead of them and entered into the body of the Emperor's daughter. When R. Shimon arrived to the palace, there was great commotion because the daughter kept on calling the name of R. Shimon. When the palace guards found out that this man was Rabbi Shimon, they brought him to the palace and R. Shimon called out: "Ben Temalion, leave her. Ben Temalion, leave her!"

The demon exited from her body. The Emperor, grateful for the healing, told them to request whatever they desire. Their request was to tear up the decree, which was granted. While Rabbi Eleazar was in Rome, he saw the vessels plundered from the Temple, he also saw the splattered blood from the sacrifices on the curtain, which separated the Holy of Holies. (*Meilah* 17a–b)

Delinquent payer (*Gittin* 37b)

Delivering a newborn calf on Shabbat
(*Shabbat* 128b)

Delivering a newborn child on Shabbat (*Shabbat* 128b)

Delivering a baby
Delivering a newborn baby on Shabbat is discussed in *Mefanim*, the 18th *perek* in *Shabbat*. (*Shabbat* 126b)

Delivering a calf
Delivering a calf or any animal on Shabbat is discussed in *Mefanim*, the 18th *perek* in *Shabbat*. (*Shabbat* 126b)

Demolishing a synagogue
R. Hisda said: "A synagogue should not be demolished before another has been built to take its place." (*Bava Batra* 3b)

Demons   שדים
(*Sanhedrin* 67b)

Demons (*Kiddushin* 29b)

📖 Demons and R. Aha b. Yaakov
When Abbaye heard that R. Aha is coming, he told the town people not to offer hospitality to R. Aha so that he would be

forced to sleep in the schoolhouse. Abbaye had a reason. A certain demon was haunting the schoolhouse, and whenever the people entered the house, they were injured. Abbaye figured a miracle might happen on account of R. Aha. R. Aha was known to be a holy person. R. Aha spent the night in the schoolhouse and the demon appeared to him as a seven- headed dragon. Every time R. Aha fell to his knees in prayer, one head of the dragon fell off. The next day he reproached them: "Had not a miracle occurred, you would have endangered my life." (*Kiddushin* 29b)

📖 Demons encounter
R. Abbaye was walking along with R. Papa on his right and R. Huna b. Yehoshua on his left. When R. Abbaye noticed some demons coming along, he transferred R. Papa to his left and R. Huna to his right. R. Papa asked R. Abbaye: "What is different about me, that you were not afraid on my behalf?" R. Abbaye answered: "The time is in your favor." (*Pesahim* 111b)

Denier of Torah
Anyone who denies that the Torah was given from Heaven will not share in the World to Come. (*Sanhedrin* 90a; *Avodah Zarah* 18a)

Denying food to an ox
When an ox is working in the field, may one deny it food. (*Bava Metzia* 88b, 89a, 90b)

✿ Departing from this world
When a person departs from this world, the only thing that will accompany him is his reputation, Torah, and his good deeds.
The Mishna quotes R. Yosi b. Kisma as saying: "One day I was on the road and I met a person who greeted me with *Shalom*. He asked me, "Where are you from?," and I answered him, "I am from a large city, where they have many sages and scribes."

He said to me, "I would like you to come and live in our town, and I will give you thousands and thousands of golden dinars."
I answered him, "You can't give me enough money to move away from the place where I live; I would only live in a place where I can learn Torah. Furthermore, when a person departs from this world, neither silver nor gold, nor precious jewels, nor pearls will accompany him – except his reputation, Torah, and his good deeds." (*Avot* 6:9)

Departing with a boat
Embarking on a boat before Shabbat (*Shabbat* 19a)

Dependent on others (*Pesahim* 112a)[75]

Depth and height   עומקא ורומא
These are terms included in a contract when selling a house. (*Bava Basta* 64a)

Deputy High Priest
The deputy was standing on the right side of the Kohen Gadol
The Talmud relates that Rabbi Hanina explained the reason why the deputy stands on the right side of the high priest. If there is an accident and the high priest is invalidated, the deputy then steps in and officiates in his stead. (*Yoma* 39a)

Derisha V'Hakira   דרישה וחקירה
The process of enquiry and examination of witnesses (*Sanhedrin* 32a 2b; *Yevamot* 122b)

Derivative labor on Shabbat
תולדה מלאכה
A labor that is derived from a main category of labors which are forbidden on Shabbat. (*Shabbat* 68a; *Keritot* 16b)

---

75. See story under, Advice to a son.

Derivative uncleanness ולד הטומאה
A ritual uncleanness derived from an original uncleanness (*Taharot* 1:5)

Derogatory Remark
R. Eleazar b. Shimon b. Yohai made some derogatory remarks.[76] (*Taanit* 20a)

Descendant of David
R. Yehuda HaNasi was a descendant of David. (*Shabbat* 56a)

Descendants of Efraim
The dead Yehezkel revived were the children of Efraim.
  R. Eliezer b. R. Yosi HaGlili said: "The dead whom the Prophet Yehezkel revived went to Israel, married wives, and had children." R. Yehuda b. Betera rose up and said: "I am one of their descendants and these are the *tefillin* which my grandfather left me from them." Rav said: "The dead Yehezkel revived were the children of Efraim who miscalculated the years of bondage in Egypt and left prematurely; they were killed trying to leave Egypt." (*Sanhedrin* 92b)

📖 **Descendants of Eli HaKohen**
It is related in the Talmud that Rabbi Yohanan was very anxious to ordain Rabbi Hanina and Rabbi Hoshia, but somehow it never materialized because he couldn't get a quorum of three qualified rabbis to do it. When Rabbi Hanina saw that Rabbi Yohanan was distressed on account of it, he said to him: "Master, do not grieve, for we are the descendants of Eli, and because of that we are destined not to be ordained." (*Sanhedrin* 14a)

📖 **Descendants of Sanheriv**
Shemaya and his colleague Avtalyon were descendants of Sanheriv. They became converts and the greatest scholars in Judaism; Rabbi Hillel was one of their students. (*Gittin* 57b; *Sanhedrin* 96b)

📖 **Descendants of the resurrected**
R. Yehuda b. Betera said he was a descendant of the dead revived by Yehezkel
Rabbi Eliezer b. R. Yosi HaGlili said, "The dead whom Yehezkel revived went up to Eretz Yisrael, and married wives and had sons and daughters." Rabbi Yehuda b. Betera stood up and declared, "I am one of their descendants, and these are the *tefillin*, which belonged to them and my grandfather left them to me as an heirloom." (*Sanhedrin* 92b)

✡ **Despising**
Do not despise any person
Ben Azzai used to say: "Do not despise any person and do not disparage anything. For there is not a person who does not have his hour and there is not an object that does not have its place." (*Avot* 4:3)

✡ **Destiny**
R. Eliezer HaKappar said: "Let not your evil inclination mislead you that your grave will be an escape for you. Against your will you will die, and against your will you are destined to give an account before the King of Kings." (*Avot* 4:22)

Destroying בל תשחית
It is not permitted to be wasteful or to destroy. It is a commandment "You shall not destroy." (*Shabbat* 129a)

Dialectician or well-read
There is a difference of opinion who is superior, a well-read scholar or a dialectician who seeks the truth through debate. (*Horayot* 14a)

---

76. See story under, We all make mistakes.

📖 Dictum of Rav is precious
R Hisda[77] was holding two priestly gifts from an ox in his hand, and declared: "If someone will come and tell me a new dictum in the name of Rav, I will give him these gifts.

Rava b. Mehasya said to him:" Rav said the following: 'If one gives a gift to a neighbor he must inform him first.'" Upon hearing this, R. Hisda gave him the gifts. Rava asked him: "Is Rav's dicta so dear to you?"

"Yes," he replied.

"This illustrates what Rav said: 'A garment is precious to its wearer.'" "Did Rav really say this also? I like this saying even more than the first one, if I had another gift I would also give it to you." (*Shabbat* 10b)

✿ Did you deal honestly?
Rava said: "When one is led before the heavenly court, he is asked, "Did you deal honestly?" (*Shabbat* 31a)

📖 Died at a young age
There was a family in Jerusalem whose members died at the young age of eighteen. They told this to Rabbi Yohanan ben Zakkai, and he suggested, perhaps they are descendants of the family of Eli the High Priest, who had a curse on them. "Go and study Torah and you will live." They did and they lived. That family was known as Yohanan ben Zakkai's family even though they were not. (*Rosh Hashana* 18a)

Di'eved   דיעבד
An issue after the act was done is taken in consideration. (*Hullin* 2a)

Differences
R. Hillel and R. Shammai differed in three

halachic decrees out of eighteen decrees. (*Shabbat* 14b, 15a)

Differences
The differences between Shiloh and Jerusalem (*Megillah* 9b)

Differences
What is the difference between an anointed priest and a priest with many garments? (*Horayot* 11b)

Differences in vows   אין בין המודר
The differences in vows (*Nedarim* 32b)

Difference of two worlds
The difference between this and the world of Mashiach
R. Shemuel said: "The only difference between this world and the world of Mashiach is servitude to foreign powers." (*Shabbat* 63a; *Berachot* 34b, 151b)

Differences of Shabbat and Yom Tov
What are the differences between Shabbat and Yom Tov? (*Megillah* 7b)

Differences of Yom Kippur and Shabbat
What are the differences between Yom Kippur and Shabbat? (*Megillah* 7b)

Digging ditches
Digging ditches, pits or canals next to a neighbor's property (*Bava Batra* 17a)

Dignity
Violating one's dignity by slapping him (*Bava Kamma* 90b)

Dilemma   ממה נפשך
Dilemma; either way
In either case (*Bava Kamma* 31a, 38a)

Diligent Torah student
R. Eleazar said: "Be diligent in the study

---

77. R. Hisda was a Kohen.

of Torah, and know what to answer a non-believer. Know before whom you toil, and be aware that your Employer can be relied upon to pay your earned wages." (*Avot* 2:19)

Dimi   דימי
Amora from Babylonia
Lived in the 4th century CE (*Shabbat* 108b)

Dimi of Nehardea   דימי מנהרדעא
Amora from Babylonia
Head of the academy in Pumbedita Lived in the 4th century CE (*Bava Batra* 22a)

📖 Dining with R. Yehuda HaNasi
R. Yehuda and R. Hezkiya, the sons of R. Hiyya, were having dinner with Rebbe, and R. Hiyya, their father, was also present. The sons did not utter a word during the meal. Whereupon Rebbe said:

"Give the young men plenty of strong wine, so that they will open up and say something."

When the wine was having its effect, they started talking, and they said:

"The son of David cannot come until the two ruling houses of Israel shall come to an end."

To back it up they quoted a passage from scripture. Rebbe was annoyed and exclaimed:

"My children, you throw thorns in my eyes." R. Hiyya intervened and said: "Rebbe, be not angry; the numerical value of the Hebrew letters for 'wine' is the same as the Hebrew letters for 'secret.' When wine goes in the secret comes out." (*Sanhedrin* 38a; *Eruvin* 65a)

📖 Dining at the Nasi
When Rav was a very young man, he and his uncle, R. Hiyya, dined at R. Yehuda HaNasi One time R. Hiyya and Rav were dining at R. Yehuda HaNasi; Rav was still very young. At the end of the meal Rebbe said to Rav:

"Get up and wash your hands."

R. Hiyya saw that Rav was trembling, he therefore said to him: "Son, he is telling you to get ready for *Birkat Hamazon.*" (*Berachot* 43a, 46b)

Dipping twice
At the Seder on Pesach, they dip twice. (*Pesahim* 116a)

Disagreement between rabbis
R. Yaakov and R. Zerika said: "Whenever R. Akiva and one of his colleagues are in disagreement, the Halachah is in accordance to R. Akiva. When R. Yosi is in disagreement with his colleagues the Halachah is with R. Yosi. Between R. Yehuda HaNasi and one of his colleagues, the Halachah is like Rebbe." What practical difference does it make? R. Assi said: "General Halachah." R. Hiyya b. Abba said: "We are leaning in their favor." R. Yosi b. Chanina said: "They are seen as acceptable views."

R. Yaakov b. Idi said in the name of R. Yohanan: "In a dispute between R. Meir and R. Yehuda, the Halachah is like R. Yehuda; in a dispute between R. Yehuda and R. Yosi, the Halachah is like R. Yosi, and needless to say that a dispute between R. Meir and R. Yosi, the Halachah is like R. Yosi.

R. Assi said: "I also learn that a dispute between R. Yosi and R. Shimon, the Halachah is like R. Yosi.

R. Abba said in the name of R. Yohanan: "In a dispute between R. Yehuda and R. Shimon, the Halachah is like R. Yehuda. A dispute between R. Meir and R. Shimon was left unresolved. (*Eruvin* 46b; *Ketubbot* 84b, 51a; *Pesahim* 27a; *Bava Batra* 124b)

Dishes to be immersed in the mikveh
The proper way to immerse dishes in the *mikveh* (*Mikvaot* 10:1–5)

Dishonest business
A man mortgaged his orchard to a neighbor for ten years. The man was using the land and collected the fruit for three years, after which he told the owner: "Sell me the property, if not, I will claim the land is mine, because I have been on the land for three years." Thereupon, the owner transferred his property to his son, still a minor, and then sold it to him. (*Bava Metzia* 72a)

Dishonest marriage
A man bought a boatload of wine and was looking for a place to store it. A certain woman had a storage room, but she was not willing to rent it to him. He decided to marry her and was able to use her storage room for his wine. Soon after the marriage, he wrote her a bill of divorce and sent it to her. She hired carriers, paying them money from proceeds of selling some of this man's wine, and had the wine put out on the street. The matter came before R. Huna b. Yehoshua, who said: "As he did, so shall be done to him. She can say to him: 'To anybody else, I am willing to rent out the place, but not to you, because you are like a lion in ambush.'" (*Bava Metzia* 101b)

Disinherited his son
The Talmud relates that Rabbi Yosi b. Yoezer left his property to the Temple and left nothing to his son, because he considered him unworthy. (*Bava Batra* 133b)

✿ Disobeying order of judge
A certain man built his villa upon a ruined building belonging to orphans. R. Nahman, as judge, confiscated the villa from him. The defendant was advised beforehand to go and make a peaceful settlement, but he ignored it. Therefore R. Nahman confiscated the villa. (*Bava Kamma* 21a)

✿ Disparage
Do not disparage anything
Ben Azzai used to say: "Do not despise any person and do not disparage anything. For there is not a person who does not have his hour and there is not an object that does not have its place." (*Avot* 4:3)

Dispute over property
Brothers inherited questionable property (*Bava Kamma* 112a)

Disputes between Bet Shammai and Bet Hillel
Why is the Halachah according to Bet Hillel? (*Eruvin* 13b)

Disqualified as a witness
A gambler is not qualified as a witness. (*Sanhedrin* 24b, 27b; *Eruvin* 82a; *Rosh Hashana* 22a)

Disqualified as a witness
A person who lends his money and charges interest is not qualified as a witness. (*Sanhedrin* 24b, 27b; *Eruvin* 82a; *Rosh Hashana* 22a)

Disqualified Kohen יוסף בן אילים
Yosef b. Ailim from Sepphoris once substituted for the Kohen Gadol who for some reason was unable to perform the service. When the Kohen Gadol returned to his duties, Yosef b. Ailim was not permitted to serve in any capacity. (*Horayot* 12b)

Dispute between two rabbinic schools
Rabbi Abba said in the name of Rabbi Shemuel: "For three years, there was a dispute between the school of Bet Shammai and the school of Bet Hillel – each one

claiming the Halachah is in agreement with their views." Then a Bat Kol[78] was heard announcing that both are the words of the living God, but the Halachah is in agreement with the rulings of Bet Hillel. (*Eruvin* 13b; *Gittin* 6b)

📖 **Dispute with the Exilarch's officers**
One time, Rabbah b. R. Huna was having a disagreement with the officers of the Exilarch. He told them, "I do not derive my authority from your office, I hold it from my father, who received it from Rav, and he received it from R. Hiyya, and he received it from R. Yehuda HaNasi." (*Sanhedrin* 5a)

✿ **Disqualified himself as a judge**
On account of a courtesy
It happened that Shemuel was crossing a river on a ferry and a man offered him his hand to get off the ferry. R. Shemuel asked him: "What is your business here?"
   "I have a lawsuit, in which you will be the judge."
   R. Shemuel told him: "I am now disqualified to act as judge in your case." (*Ketubbot* 105b)

Disregarding the property of others
R. Avia visited Rava, but his boots were soiled with mud and he sat down on a bed. Rava was annoyed. Rava therefore wanted to show R. Avia that he was annoyed and asked him difficult halachic questions. (*Shabbat* 46a)

✿ **Disrespect for fellow students**
It is stated Rabbi Akiva had twelve thousand pairs of students. All of them died at the same time, because they did not treat each other with respect. A Tanna taught that all of them died between Pesach and Shavuot. And these were the remaining students of Rabbi Akiva who revived the Torah at that time: Rabbi Meir, Rabbi Yehuda bar Illai, Rabbi Yosi ben Halafta, Rabbi Shimon ben Yohai, and Rabbi Eleazar ben Shammua. (*Yevamot* 62b)

Distinguished person אדם חשוב
A very respected person (*Avodah Zarah* 28a)

Distinguished scholar ארי
A lion, a name bestowed upon a distinguished scholar (*Yevamot* 122b)

Disturbance in public
Causing nuisance or disturbance on public streets (*Bava Kamma* 30b)

Diumsit
A locality in Judea; it was known for its warm springs. (*Shabbat* 147b)

Dividing property
When dividing property and measurements, even the very minimum has to be taken in consideration. (*Bava Batra* 11a)

Divide your study
R. Tanhum b. Hanilai said: "Divide your study into three: one-third Scripture, one-third Mishna, and one-third Talmud. (*Avodah Zarah* 19b; *Kiddushin* 30a)

Divine name utterance
Abba Shaul said: "A person who pronounces the Divine name as it is spelled will not have a share in the World to Come." (*Sanhedrin* 90a, 101b)

Divorce
R. Eliezer said: "He who divorces his first wife, brings the altar to shed tears." (*Sanhedrin* 22a; *Gittin* 90b)

---

78. Heavenly voice.

📖 Divorce
Husband unwilling to pay ketubbah settlement
Once a man wanted to divorce his wife, but he didn't want to have to pay her the *ketubbah* settlement.[79] (*Gittin* 57a)

📖 Divorce
A woman appeared in the academy of Rabbi Meir and declared: "One of you rabbis has taken me as a wife by cohabitation." Rabbi Meir rose and gave her a bill of divorce. Thereupon, all the students stood up and did likewise. (*Sanhedrin* 11a)

Divorce   גט
If a messenger brings a document of divorce from overseas, he must state that it was signed and sealed before me. (*Gittin* 2a, 15a)

Divorce in war
R. Shemuel b. Nahmani said in the name of R. Yonatan: "Every soldier that went out in the wars of the House of David wrote a bill of divorce to his wife." (*Shabbat* 56a; *Ketubbot* 9b)

Divorce ink
What kind of ink may be used in a divorce (*Gittin* 19a)

Divorce paper
What kind of paper or parchment may be used to write a divorce on it (*Gittin* 19a, 21b, 22a)

Divorce parties with multiple names
A husband and wife getting a divorce and having multiple similar names in the community (*Gittin* 34b)

Divorce scribe
Who is qualified to wrte a divorce (*Gittin* 21a, 22b)

Divorce sent by messenger
If a man sent a divorce with a messenger and then changed his mind. (*Gittin* 32a; *Kiddushin* 59a)

Divrei Sofrim   דברי סופרים
Enactment by the scribes (*Yevamot* 9:3, 84a)

Divrei Hayamim
The author of the book *Divrei Hayamim* was the Prophet Ezra.[80] (*Bava Batra* 15a)

Do good to yourself
According to your abilities
Rav said to R. Hamnuna: "My son, do good to yourself and according to your ability – for there is no enjoyment in the grave, and death is not far away." "Children are like the grass in the field; some blossom and some fade." (*Eruvin* 54a)

✿ Do not depend on others
The Talmud relates that Rabbi Akiva charged his son Yehoshua with seven instructions:
One of them was: "Treat your Shabbat like a weekday rather than be dependent on others." (*Pesahim* 112a)

Do not enter suddenly
One is not to enter suddenly into his own house."[81] (*Pesahim* 112a; *Niddah* 16b)

✿ Do not enter your neighbor's property
Ben Bag Bag said: "If your belonging is on your neighbor's property, do not enter his property to take your belonging without permission." (*Bava Kamma* 27b)

---

79. See entry, False evidence planted.

80. Others name different authors.
81. See entry, Akiva's instructions to his son.

✿ Do not judge others
Until you have been put in their position
R. Hillel said: "Do not separate yourself from the community, do not believe you know it all, and do not judge your friend until you have been put in his position." (*Avot* 2:4)

Doctor non-Jewish
Circumcision by a non-Jew (*Avodah Zarah* 26b; *Menahot* 42a)

Documents lost
The Talmud relates a story: Rabbi Nahman said: "My father was a scribe for the court of Rabbi Shemuel. When I was about six or seven years old I remember that they used to make an announcement in public that any deed document found on the street should be returned to its owners." (*Bava Metzia* 16b)

Dog causing damage
Jumping causing damage (*Bava Kamma* 21b)

Dog in the house
(*Shabbat* 63a; *Bava Kamma* 15b)

Dogs, vicious
R. Nathan said: "One should not bring up a vicious dog in his house." (*Bava Kamma* 46a)

✿ Dogs chained
It is improper to breed dogs unless they are kept on a chain. (*Bava Kamma* 79b)

Dog's price   מחיר כלב
The price received for a dog is not permitted to be used for a dedication in the Temple. (*Temurah* 30a)

Domains
There are four domains for Shabbat. (*Shabbat* 6a)

Domains on Shabbat
Standing in one domain and bending over to drink in another on Shabbat (*Shabbat* 11a; *Eruvin* 20a, 99a)

Donkey
Braying, causing damages (*Bava Kamma* 18b; *Kiddushin* 24b)

Donkey
Donkey biting hand of a child (*Bava Kamma* 84a)

Donkey
With bad manners
The Talmud relates that R. Levi b. R. Huna b. Hiyya and Rabbah b. R. Huna were traveling together on a road, and R. Levi's ass went ahead of Rabbah. Afterwards R. Levi noticed that Rabbah seemed to feel insulted. To pacify him, R. Levi asked him a question. "Can a donkey like mine with bad manners be taken out on Shabbat wearing a halter?" (*Shabbat* 51b)

Donkey firstborn
The donkey is the only non-kosher animal whose firstborn needs to be redeemed. (*Bechorot* 5b)

📖 Donkey overboard
A certain man pushed his donkey on a ferry-boat before the passengers had a chance to disembark. The boat was shaking and in danger of sinking. Another man who was on the boat came and pushed the donkey overboard and the donkey drowned.[82] (*Bava Kamma* 117b)

📖 Donkey refuses to eat untithed food
Once R. Pinhas ben Yair arrived at an inn where they put food in front of his donkey,

---

82. See entry, Boat endangered by a donkey.

but the donkey would not eat. They asked R. Pinhas why his ass would not eat. He told them: "Perhaps it was not tithed." They immediately tithed the grain and the donkey ate it. (*Hullin* 7a)

Donkey rented out
A man rented out a donkey and told the man, "Do not travel on the road via Nehar Pekod where there is water, but take the road via Naresh where there is no water." The man took the road of Nehar Pekod and the donkey died. (*Bava Metzia* 81b; *Ketubbot* 27b)

Donkey with load
Donkey with load causing damages (*Bava Kamma* 17b)

Door keeper in the Temple
It happened that Rabbi Yehoshua went to assist R. Yohanan ben Gudgeda to fasten the Temple doors, and Rabbi Yohanan told him: "Turn back, because you are one of the guys in the choir and not of the doorkeepers." (*Arachin* 11b)

📖 Doors opened to all students
Sanhedrin doors were opened to all
It was learned that on that day when R. Eleazar b. Azariah was elected President of the Sanhedrin, the doors were opened for all the disciples to enter the assembly. Prior to this, Rabbi Gamliel had issued an ordinance that those students whose exterior appearance does not match their interior intellect may not enter.

To accommodate the new students who entered the hall, 400 additional benches, some say 700 benches,[83] were brought in to accommodate the new students who entered the hall. (*Berachot* 27b)

---

83. See entry, Appointed Nasi of the Sanhedrin.

📖 Dosa ben Horkynos was sick
R. Dosa is being visited by the great rabbis of his time
When R. Dosa b. Horkynos became old, his eyes dimmed and he was unable to come to the academy. There was an important ruling they needed to discuss with him. His colleagues discussed among themselves as to who should go to visit him, because he was a great scholar. R. Yehoshua said: "I will go." And who will go with him? R. Eleazar b. Azariah will go with him. And who else will go with them? R. Akiva. They went and stood by the door. The maid announced them to R. Dosa and when they entered he received them with great respect. (*Yevamot* 16a)

Dosa ben Horkynos (Harkinas)
דוסא בן הרכינס
Tanna from Eretz Yisrael
1st – 2nd centuries CE (*Rosh Hashana* 25a)

Dostai ben Yannai
דוסתאי בן ינאי
Tanna from Eretz Yisrael
2nd century CE (*Gittin* 14 a–b)

Double portion inheritance
Dealing with who gets a double portion of inheritance from a mother (*Bava Batra* 122b)

Doubt
When the doubt concerns a religious prohibition, we take the more stringent view, but when the doubt concerns a monetary matter, we take the more lenient view. (*Hullin* 134a; *Ketubbot* 73b; *Gittin* 63b; *Nedarim* 53a; *Bava Batra* 57b; *Niddah* 25a)

Doubt vs. certainty
אין ספק מוציא מידי ודאי
A doubt cannot set aside a certainty. (*Hullin* 10a; *Pesahim* 9a; *Avodah Zarah* 41b; *Niddah* 15b; *Yevamot* 19b, 38a)

Doubtful if tithed   דמאי
(*Pesahim* 35b; *Shabbat* 127b; *Berachot* 47a; *Eruvin* 37a)

Doubtful loan
A man says to his friend: "I am not certain if I borrowed from you." (*Bava Kamma* 118a)

Dough
Different kind of dough made on Pesach (*Pesahim* 37a)

Dough kneaded with wine, oil or honey, is it fit for Pesach?
R. Akiva, R. Gamliel, R. Yehoshua, R. Eliezer (*Pesahim* 36a)

Doves and pigeons
The age required for pigeons and doves to be qualified for offerings (Hullin 22a)

Dragging a bench
Or a bed on Shabbat (*Shabbat* 22a, 29b, 46b)

Drakon   דרקון
Dragon (*Avodah Zarah* 42b)

Dream interpreters of Jerusalem
R. Bizna b. Zavda said in the name of R. Akiva, who had it from R. Panda, who had it from R. Nachum, who had it from R. Birim, who said it in the name of an Elder by the name of R. Banah: "There were twenty-four interpreters of dreams in Jerusalem. R. Banah once had a dream and he went to all twenty-four, and each gave him a different interpretation, and all were fulfilled." (*Berachot* 55b)

Dreaming
With the letter *tet* (*Bava Kamma* 55a)

Dreaming
About a *hesped* = eulogy (*Bava Kamma* 55a; *Berachot* 57a)

Dreaming
When one has a dream, a prayer should be said during the blessings of the Kohanim. (*Berachot* 55b)

Dreaming of the heavenly world
Rabbi Zera relates that Rabbi Yosi Bar Hanina appeared to him in a dream. R. Zera asked him, "Near whom are you seated in the Heavenly Academy?" He answered, "Next to Rabbi Yohanan." (*Bava Metzia* 85b)

📖 Dreaming with a brother who died
Rava had a brother by the name of Rav Seorim. It is stated that while Rav Seorim was sitting next to Rava's bedside and noticed that he was going into a sleep to die, he bent over to him to hear him say something, and Rava said to his brother: "Please tell the Malach HaMavet not to torment me."

"Are you not his intimate friend?" asked Rav Seorim.

Rova answered: "Since my *mazal* has been turned over to him, he pays no attention to me."

Rav Seorim then requested his brother: "After you are gone, please show yourself to me in a dream."

He did show himself to his brother in a dream. Rav Seorim asked him: "Did you suffer pain?"

"I felt like being pricked by needles." (*Moed Katan* 28a; *Bava Metzia* 73b)

Dreams
Fasting when having a bad dream (*Shabbat* 11a; *Taanit* 12b)

Dreams
Rabbi Papa and Rabbi Huna both dreamt that they walked into a lake, but Rabbi Papa dreamt that he was carrying a drum while walking into the lake. On the other

hand, R. Huna was dreaming that he only walked into a lake. Rabbi Papa became the head of the academy in Naresh and Rabbi Huna became his deputy. (*Berachot* 57a)

Dreams, what is one to do
While the *Kohanim* chant the blessings, the congregation recites a prayer for dreams. (*Berachot* 55b)

Dreams and prayers
Prayer for good outcome of dreams
Ameimar, Mar Zutra, and R. Ashi were once sitting together.

They said: "Let each one of us say something that the others did not hear before."

One of them said: "If one had a dream and does not know what he dreamt; he should say the prayer for dreams, which starts with the phrase *Ribbono shel Olam*. It is said during the time when the Kohanim bless the congregation in the synagogue." The others also said something new. (*Berachot* 55b)

Dreams are suggested
R. Shemuel b. Nahmeni said in the name of R. Yonatan: "A man is shown in a dream only what is suggested by his own thoughts."

Rava said: "This is proven by the fact that no one dreams of a golden palm tree or an elephant going through the eye of a needle." (*Berachot* 55b)

Dreams interpreted for a fee favorably
Bar Hedya was an interpreter of dreams. If one paid him, he gave a favorable interpretation and if one did not pay him, he gave an unfavorable interpretation. R. Abbaye came to him with a dream and paid him a *zuz*. He interpreted the dream by saying: "Your business will prosper and you will not be able to eat from sheer joy."

Abbaye went to him many more

times with dreams and most of the time he received pleasant interpretations. (*Berachot*. 56a)

Dressing for Shabbat
R. Yehuda said in Rav's name: "This was the practice of Rabbi Yehuda bar Illai. Friday afternoon they put before him a basin of hot water. He washed his face, hands and feet, and wrapped himself in a fringed linen robe, and he looked like an angel of God. (*Shabbat* 25b)

Dried fig used as a measuring size
(*Kelim* 17:7)

✿ Drink the words of wise men
Yosi ben Yoezer of Jerusalem said: "Let your house be a meeting place for the wise, sit in the dust of their feet, and drink their words of wisdom with thirst." (*Avot* 1:4)

Drinking wine and legal decision
R. Yehuda stated in the name of Shemuel: "He who has drunk a quarter of a log of wine should not give a legal decision." (*Eruvin* 64a)

Drinking wine on Purim
Rava said: "Every man is obligated to mellow himself with wine on Purim until he cannot tell the difference between the cursed Haman and the blessed Mordechai." (*Megillah* 7b)

📖 Drought in Israel
When there was a drought in the Land of Israel, R. Yonah, the father of R. Mani would go into his house and say to his family: "Get me my sacks so I can go and buy grain for a *zuz*." He was so humble; he didn't want to let on to his family that he is the person praying for rain. He then went to a low area, put on sackcloth and prayed for rain, and rain came. When

he returned home his family asked him: "Did you bring grain?" He would answer: "Now that rain has come, the world will feel relieved." (*Taanit* 23b)

Drowned or not
If a person fell into a body of water and was not been seen since – is he presumed do be drowned and dead, is his wife permitted to marry? Is there a difference if the boundaries of the water can be seen or they are invisible like the oceans? (*Yevamot* 121a)

Drowning Egyptians
R. Shemuel b. Nahman said in the name of R. Yonatan: "In the hour when the Israelites were crossing the sea and the Egyptians were drowning, the angels wished to utter a song of praise to Hashem. Hashem rebuked them saying: 'My handiwork is drowning in the sea and you want to sing a song of praise to Me?'" (*Sanhedrin* 39b)

✿ Drunkard
One of R. Hisda's sayings was: "Leave the drunkard alone, he will fall of himself." (*Shabbat* 32a)

Drusai
One who eats in a hurry, like a robber (*Shabbat* 20a)

Dung hills in Jerusalem
Dung hills were not permitted in Jerusalem. (*Bava Kamma* 82b)

Dwell in same town with teacher
R. Hiyya b. Ammi also said in the name of R. Ulla: "A man should always live in the same town as his teacher." (*Berachot* 8a)

Dweling with a non-Jew
A Jew living in a courtyard with a non-Jew, can an *eruv* be made? (*Eruvin* 61b)

Dyer selling wool
Buying wool from a dyer (*Bava Kamma* 119b)

E

Ead   איד יום אידם
Idolaterous festival (*Avodah Zarah* 7b)

Earthquake
The blessing over an earthquake is discussed in *Haroeh*, the 9th *perek* of *Berachot*. (*Berachot* 54a)

Eating after the meal is finished
R. Papa was once visiting R. Huna b. Nathan. After they finished their meal, they brought some additional food to the table. R. Papa took some food and ate. They said to him:

"Don't you hold that after the meal is concluded it is forbidden to eat?"

He replied, "The proper term is 'when the food is removed.'"

Rabbah and R. Zera visited the Exilarch and they were served a nice meal. After they removed the trays, they brought in a basket of fruit, a gift from the Exilarch. Rabbah ate from the fruit, but R. Zera did not. R. Zera asked Rabbah: "Don't you hold that if the food has been removed it is forbidden to eat?"

Rabbah replied: "We can rely on the Exilarch that he usually sends a gift." (*Berachot* 42a)

✿ Eat, drink less than one can afford
R. Avira was quoted as saying the following, sometimes in the name of Rabbi Ammi and sometimes in the name of R. Assi. "A man should always eat and drink less than he can afford, clothe himself in accordance to his means, honor his wife and children more than he can afford, because they are dependent on him, and he depends on the Creator." (*Hullin* 84b)

Eating a limb from a living animal
אבר מן החי
(*Hullin* 101b; *Meilah* 16a)

Eating before praying
R. Yitzhak said in the name of R. Yohanan, also R. Yosi b. R. Hanina said in the name of R. Eliezer b. Yaakov: "It is improper to eat before praying." (*Berachot* 10b; *Shabbat* 9b)

Eating Teruma
Abba Shaul said: "If one eats *teruma* inadvertently, he is obligated to repay only if it was worth more than a *peruta*. (*Pesahim* 32b)

Eating time
Different people have different set times when to eat. (*Shabbat* 10a; *Pesahim* 12b)

Eating time for Hametz
Until what time may one eat unleavened bread on Erev Pesach? (*Pesahim* 11b, 12b)

Eating without a blessing
R. Yehuda said: "If one forgot to make a blessing before swallowing the food . . ." (*Berachot* 50b)

Edomites
Converted Edomites, what status do they have, are Jews permitted to marriy them? (*Yevamot* 76b; *Nazir* 23b; *Horayot* 10b)

Education in Israel in Temple time
R. Yehuda said in the name of Rav: "Yehoshua b. Gamla, the High Priest just before the destruction of the Temple, is to be praised and blessed." The system of education before the ordinance of R. Yehoshua b. Gamla was very inadequate: if a child had a father, his father taught him, if he had no father he didn't learn at all. This created many ignorant children and grownups. They made an ordinance that teachers should be appointed in Jerusalem. If a child had a father he would take the child to Jerusalem and leave him there to be taught, if he had no father he would not go to learn. This didn't work either. They issued a new ordinance that each district should appoint teachers and that boys should enter school to study at age sixteen or seventeen. This didn't work either because when a teacher was too strict, the children would leave school. Finally, Yehoshua b. Gamla the High Priest ordained that every subdivision of a district and every town should appoint teachers and the children should enter school at age of six or seven. (*Bava Batra* 21a)

Eduyot
עדיות
Testimony
A Tanna taught: Whenever the Talmud speaks of "That Day" it refers to the day when R. Eleazar b. Azariah was elected as Nasi of the Sanhedrin. On that day every Halachah that was in question before the rabbis was resolved. Even R. Gamliel didn't stay away from the assembly even for one hour, in spite of him being removed as president. (*Berachot* 28a; *Yadayim* 4:4)

Efraim Mikshaah
אפרים מקשאה
A student of R. Meir (*Bava Metzia* 87a)

Efraim the Scribe
A student of Resh Lakish (*Bava Metzia* 119a)

📖 Efremites
Rav said that the dead, whom the Prophet Yehezkel revived, were the Efremites, who left Egypt prematurely. They miscalculated in counting the 400 years – which were prophesied to Avraham – from a different beginning of time. They were intercepted and killed by the Egyptians.[84] (*Sanhedrin* 92b)

---

84. See entry, Revived.

Egg born on Shabbat
Placing a receptacle under a chicken on Shabbat to catch the eggs. (*Shabbat* 42b)

Egg mixed with sixty other eggs
Some say an egg is lost in sixty, others say it is lost in sixty-one. (*Hullin* 98a)

Eggs laid on Yom Tov (*Betzah* 2a)

Egg of a clean or unclean bird
(*Hullin* 64a)

Eggs used as a measuring size (*Kelim* 17:6)

Egg with a spot of blood (*Hullin* 64b)

Eggshell
An eggshell holding oil for Shabbat candles (*Shabbat* 29b)

Egla Arufa   עגלה ערופה
The heifer used in the ceremony when a person was found murdered between two communities. (*Parah* 1:1)

Egyptian new king
When the Torah says that a new king arose in Egypt, there is a debate between the rabbis whether it was a different person or the same person who changed his policies towards the Israelites. (*Sotah* 11a)

📖 Egyptians
Claiming compensation from Israel
The rabbis taught: On one occasion the Egyptians came to Alexander to make a claim against the Israelites. They said it is written in the Torah: "And God gave the people favor in the eyes of the Egyptians and they lent them gold and silver."
Now we want you to repay us for all that gold and silver. Geviha Ben Pesisa asked permission from the rabbis to go before Alexander and argue against the Egyptians. He was granted permission.

Geviha asked the Egyptians to bring proof for their claim. They gave him proof from the Torah, where it says that the Egyptians lent the Israelites gold and silver. Geviha answered, "I will also bring proof from the Torah that Israel does not owe anything to the Egyptians. The Torah says that the Israelites were slaves in Egypt for 400 years. Now pay us for the labor of 600,000 men working for 400 years." The Egyptians could not come up with an answer and they fled, leaving behind their planted fields and vineyards.[85] (*Sanhedrin* 91a)

Ehad prolonged   אחד
Ehad in the Shema
It has been taught that Sumchos said: "Whoever prolongs the word *Ehad* will have his days prolonged." R. Abba b. Yaakov said the stress is on the *dalet*. R. Yirmiyahu was once sitting before R. Hiyya b. Abba, and R. Hiyya noticed that R. Yirmiyahu was prolonging the *Ehad* very much. He explained to him how long to prolong it. (*Berachot* 13b)

Eight cases of doubt
R. Hisda stated and so did R. Hiyya teach: "Eight cases of doubt were cited in connection with a proselyte." (*Hullin* 134a)

✿ Eighteen
R. Yehuda b. Tema said: "At the age of eighteen it is the time for marriage." (*Avot* 5:21)

Eighteen benedictions
R. Gamliel said: "Every day a person should say eighteen benedictions." (*Berachot* 28b)

Eighteen blessings of Shemona Esrei
The *Amidah* consists of three sections. R. Yehuda said, "One should never petition

---

85. See entry, Alexander thr Macedonian.

for his personal requirements either in the first three benedictions or in the last three, but in the middle ones." (*Berachot* 34a)

Eighteen Halachic Ordinances
(*Shabbat* 13b)

📖 Eighty pairs of brothers
Marriages between eighty pairs of brothers and eighty pairs of sisters, all Kohanim
The Talmud relates when R. Yitzhak came from Eretz Yisrael to Babylonia, he said: "There was a town in Eretz Yisrael by the name of Gofnit where eighty pairs of brothers, all priests, married eighty pairs of sisters, all from priestly families."[86] (*Berachot* 44a)

Eilonit   איילונית
A woman incapable of childbirth (*Bava Metzia* 67a; *Yevamot* 113a; *Ketubbot* 100b)

Ein kinyan Le-Nochri Be-Eretz Yisrael
אין קנין לנכרי בארץ ישראל
A non-Jew cannot acquire land in Israel to free the crop from the obligation of tithing. (*Bava Metzia* 101a; *Gittin* 47a; *Menahot* 31a; *Bechorot* 11b)

Eisav (Esau) delays Yaakov's burial
Eisav wanted to prevent Yaakov from being buried in the Cave of Machpelah.

Hushim the son of Dan took a club and struck Eisav on the head. Both brothers had their funeral the same day. (*Sotah* 13a)

Elders of Rome
The Jewish Elders of Rome were asked by philosophers: "If God doesn't want idol worshipping, why doesn't he abolish the idols?" They answered: "Foolish people worship the sun, the moon, the stars, and planets which are useful to the world.

Should God abolish those on account of foolish people?"

They retorted: "Why doesn't he abolish those which are unnecessary?"

"Because then they would claim that they must be real idols if they were not abolished." (*Avodah Zarah* 54b)

Eleazar   אלעזר
Officer of the Temple (*Shekalim* 5:1)

Eleazar bar Avina   אלעזר בר אבינא
Amora from Babylonia
3rd – 4th centuries CE (*Berachot* 4b)

Eleazar ben Arach (Arakh)
אלעזר בן ערך
Tanna from Eretz Yisrael
1st century CE (*Avot* 2:9; *Shabbat* 147b)

Eleazar ben Azariah   אלעזר בן עזריה
Tanna from Eretz Yisrael
Head of the Sanhedrin in Yavne
1st – 2nd centuries CE (*Rosh Hashana* 2:9, 25a)

Eleazar ben Azariah
Eleazar b. Azariah declared: "I am like a seventy-year old man." (*Berachot* 12b)

Eleazar ben Azariah
Since R. Eleazar b. Azariah passed away, wealth departed from the Sages. (*Sotah* 49a)

Eleazar ben Damma   אלעזר בן דמא
Tanna from Eretz Yisrael
2nd century CE (*Berachot* 56b)

Eleazar ben Dolai   אלעזר בן דולעאי
Tanna from Eretz Yisrael
2nd century CE (*Mikvaot* 2:10)

Eleazar b. Dordia
A person by the name of Eleazar b. Dordia frequented houses of harlots, but he did *teshuva*. (*Avodah Zarah* 17a)

---

86. See entry, Brothers, Kohanim.

Eleazar ben Hanania

אלעזר בן חנניה בן חזקיה

Tanna from Eretz Yisrael
1st century CE (*Shabbat* 1:4, 13b)

Eleazar ben Hisma   אלעזר בן חסמא

Tanna from Eretz Yisrael
2nd century CE (*Horayot* 10a)

Eleazar ben Mahabai   אלעזר בן מהבאי

Tanna from Eretz Yisrael (*Bava Metzia* 27b)

Eleazar ben Parta   אלעזר בן פרטע

Tanna from Eretz Yisrael
2nd century CE (*Avodah Zarah* 17b)

Eleazar ben Pedat   אלעזר בן פדת

Amora from Babylonia and Eretz Yisrael
Head of the academy in Tiberias
3rd century CE (*Hullin* 111b; *Moed Katan* 28a)

Eleazar ben Shammua   אלעזר בן שמוע

Tanna from Eretz Yisrael
2nd century CE (*Sanhedrin* 14a)

Eleazar ben Tadai

Tanna from Eretz Yisrael
2nd century CE (*Eruvin* 71b)

Eleazar ben Shimon ben Yohai

אלעזר בן שמעון בן יוחאי

(*Eleazar b. Simeon*)
Tanna from Eretz Yisrael
2nd century CE (*Shabbat* 33b)

Eleazar ben Tzadok (I)   אלעזר בן צדוק

Tanna from Eretz Yisrael
1st – 2nd centuries CE (*Niddah* 48b)

Eleazar ben Tzadok (II)   אלעזר בן צדוק

Tanna from Eretz Yisrael
2nd century CE (*Sukkah* 44b)

Eleazar ben Yosi   אלעזר בן יוסי

Tanna from Eretz Yisrael
2nd century CE (*Meilah* 17a–b)

Eleazar ben Yosi HaGlili

R Yohanan said in the name of R. Eleazar
b. R. Shimon: "Wherever you find the
words of R. Eleazar b. Yosi HaGlili – pay
attention." (*Hullin* 89a)

Eleazar HaModai   אלעזר המודעי

Tanna from Eretz Yisrael
1st – 2nd centuries CE (*Shabbat* 55b; *Bava
Batra* 10b)

Eleazar Me-Hagronia   אלעזר מהגרוניא

R. Eleazar had a business deal with his
tenant. (*Bava Metzia* 69a)

Elephant drawn through the eye of a needle

Once it happened that R. Sheshet decided
a matter in Nehardea by referring to a Beraita, and R. Amram was arguing against
it. Said R. Sheshet to him, "Perhaps you
are from Pumbedita, where they draw
an elephant through the eye of a needle."
(*Bava Metzia* 38b; *Berachot* 55b)

✡ Elevating yourself is not proper

*Do not elevate yourself at the expense of
others*
R Nehunia b. HaKana was asked by his
students: "By what merit did you reach
such old age?"
His reply was. "Never in my life did I try
to elevate myself at the expense of degrading others, never did I go to sleep with a
curse on my lips against my fellow-men,
and I have been generous with my money."
(*Megillah* 28a)

Eli the Kohen

Discussion about Eli's sons Hofni and
Pinhas, and about sinning (*Shabbat* 55b)

Eliezer ben Diglai   אליעזר בן דגלאי

Tanna from Eretz Yisrael
1st – 2nd centuries CE (*Tamid* 3:8)

Eliezer ben Horkynos אליעזר בן הורקנוס
Tanna from Eretz Yisrael
1st – 2nd centuries CE (*Avot* 2:8; *Shabbat* 130b)

Eliezer ben Matya אליעזר בן מתיא
Tanna from Eretz Yisrael
2nd century CE (*Shekalim* 5:1)

Eliezer ben Yaakov אליעזר בן יעקב
Tanna from Eretz Yisrael
1st century CE (*Yoma* 16a)

Eliezer ben Yaakov אליעזר בן יעקב
Tanna from Eretz Yisrael
2nd century CE (*Negaim* 10:4)

Eliezer HaKappar אליעזר הקפר
Tanna from Eretz Yisrael
2nd century CE (*Avot* 4:21; *Megillah* 29a)

Eliezer
Making instruments for a circumcision permitted on Shabbat
In the place of R. Eliezer, they used to cut wood on Shabbat to make charcoal in order to forge an iron instrument for circumcision. (*Hullin* 116a)

Eliezer
R. Eliezer b. Horkynos was multilingual. (*Sanhedrin* 17b)

📖 **Eliezer b. Horkynos**
Our rabbis taught: When R. Eliezer fell sick, four Sages went to visit him: R. Tarfon, R. Yehoshua, R. Eleazar b. Azariah, and R. Akiva.

R. Tarfon said to him: "You are more valuable to Israel than rain; for the rain is valuable only in this world but you are valuable in this and in the next world."

R. Yehoshua said: "You are more valuable to Israel than the sun's disc, because the sun's disc is only for this world, but you are for this and the next world."

R. Eleazar b. Azariah said: "You are

better to Israel than a father and mother; for these are for this world only, but you are for this and the next world." But R. Akiva remarked: "Suffering is precious." R. Eliezer said to them: "Support me to get up so I can hear the words of Akiva my student." (*Sanhedrin* 101a)

Eliezer from Biria
Eliezer from Biria said: "People who dwell in huts are like those who dwell in graves." (*Eruvin* 55b)

Eliezer's student
R. Eliezer had a sudent who studied quietly and within three years he forgot his studies. (*Eruvin* 54a)

Eliezer Zera
R. Eliezer Zera once put on black shoes[87] and stood in the marketplace of Nehardea. When the staff of the Resh Galuta saw him there, they said to him: "Why are you wearing black shoes?" He replied: "I am mourning over Jerusalem." "Who do you think you are to show such arrogance to mourn in public over Jerusalem?" They put him in jail. "But I am a scholar," he said to them. "Prove it." He proved it by answering their questions. (*Bava Kamma* 59a–b)

Elimelech
R. Hanan b. Rava said in the name of Rav: "Elimelech, Salmon, Peloni Almoni, and Naomi's father were all the sons of Nahshon ben Aminadav. (*Bava Batra* 91a)

📖 **Elisha**
Man of wings
R. Yannai said, "*Tefillin* require a pure body like Elisha, the man of wings." He was called the man of wings, because the Roman government once decreed a prohibition on wearing *tefillin*. Elisha put them

_____
87. A sign of mourning.

on anyhow. A Roman soldier ran after him and caught him. He removed them and held them in his hand.

"What is that in your hand?"

"They are wings of a dove."

He opened his hand and there were wings of a dove in his hand.[88] (*Shabbat* 49a,130a)

Elisha ben Avuyah (Aher)

אלישע בן אבויה

Tanna from Eretz Yisrael
2nd century CE (*Kiddushin* 39b)

Eliyahu
Eliyahu spoke of Mashiach
Eliyahu said to Rav Yehuda the brother of R. Salla Hasida: The world will last not less than eighty-five Jubilees and in the last Jubilee the son of David will come. Eliyahu was asked: "Will it be in the beginning or in the end?" "He answered: "I do not know." R. Ashi said that his answer was: "Do not expect him before, but afterwards expect him." (*Sanhedrin* 97b)

Eliyahu
Rabbah b. Avuha met Eliyahu standing in a non-Jewish cemetery. He started a conversation with him and they discussed halachic matters, but Eliyahu was in a hurry. He told him: "I am pressed for time."

Eliyahu led him through Paradise and offered him to collect some of the leaves and take them with him in his robe.

Rabbah b. Avuha gathered them and took them away. As he was coming out, he heard voices. "Who would consume in this world his portion of the World to Come?" Therefore, he scattered the leaves and threw them away. But the fine fragrance remained and was absorbed in his robe. Someone bought it from him for 12,000 *dinarim*, which he distributed among his sons-in-law. (*Bava Metzia* 114b)[89]

Eliyahu (*Eduyos* 8:7; *Sukkah* 52b)

Eliyahu
D'bei Eliyahu
It was taught in D'bei Eliyahu: "Whoever learns *halachot* is destined to take part in the World to Come." (*Megillah* 28b)

Eliyahu frequent visitor at R. Anan
A man once brought to R. Anan a load of fish. R. Anan asked him: "What is your business here?" The man answered: "I have a lawsuit before you." R. Anan did not accept the gift and told him: "I am now disqualified to try your case." The man said to R. Anan: "I do not expect you to be the judge in my case, but I would like you to accept my gift in order to be a substitute for my first fruit offering."

"I had no intention to accept the gift, but since you have given me your reason I will accept." He sent him to R. Nahman, who was also a judge, with a message. "Will you please try this case, because I am disqualified to be his judge?" After reading the message R. Nahman thought the man was his relative. R. Nahman postponed another case which was a lawsuit of orphans to take this one and showed great consideration to this man. The man was greatly astonished at the consideration he was shown.

Until this incident, Eliyahu was a frequent visitor to R. Anan, whom he was teaching the *Seder Eliyahu*. After this incident Eliyahu stopped his visits. R. Anan spent his time in fasting and in prayers. Eventually, Eliyahu came to him again, but a fear came over R. Anan when Eliyahu appeared. In order not to be frightened he made himself a box and he sat

---

88. See entry, Man of wings.

89. See entry, Fragrance of Paradise.

inside it until he finished the *Seder Eliyahu*. This is the reason there is a *Seder Eliyahu Rabbah* and a *Seder Eliyahu Zuta* – one part is before this incident and one after.[90] ((*Ketubbot* 105b)

📖 **Eliyahu saves holy man from death**
The Talmud relates that R. Kahana went to the house of a Roman woman to sell baskets and she tried to seduce him. He excused himself to clean up first. He went to the roof and jumped. The Angel Eliyahu flew towards him and caught him in mid-air and saved him from being killed. Eliyahu complained to him: "You caused me to have to fly 400 *parsi* to save you." "What caused me to end up in this kind of situation; isn't it my poverty?" Thereupon Eliyahu gave him a *shifa* (utensil) full of *dinarim*. (*Kiddushin* 40a)

Eliyahu's arrival
It was learned that Eliyahu will not arrive on Erev Shabbat or Erev Yom Tov. (*Pesahim* 13a; *Eruvin* 43b)

✿ **Embarrass**
R. Eleazar HaModai said: "Anyone who embarrasses another person in public will not have a portion in the World to Come." (*Avot* 3:15)

✿ **Embarrass**
R. Zutra b. Toviya said in the name of Rav, according to others R. Hana b. Bizna said it in the name of R. Shimon Hasida, and others say it was said by R. Yohanan in the name of R. Shimon b. Yohai: "It is preferable for a person to jump into a fiery furnace than to shame another person in public." (*Berachot* 43b; *Bava Metzia* 59a)

📖 **Embarrass**
The Talmud relates, Rabbi Gamliel asked

his assistant to call seven certain rabbis to a meeting in the upper chamber. When Rabbi Gamliel arrived, he found eight rabbis. He declared, "The person that was not invited should leave." Rabbi Shemuel stood up and declared, "I am the one who came uninvited, but I didn't come to take part in the decision-making; I came only to learn how to intercalate the month." Rabbi Gamliel answered. "Sit down, my son, sit down; you are worthy to intercalate all the months of the year, but it was the decision of the rabbis to have only those present who were specially invited for this purpose."

But in reality it was not Rabbi Shemuel who was the uninvited party, it was another rabbi, but he wanted to save that person the humiliation, therefore he told them it was he who was uninvited. (*Sanhedrin* 11a)

✿ **Embarrass in public**
המלבין פני חבירו ברבים
R. Hanina said: "If one puts to shame another person in pubic, he will end up in Gehinom." (*Bava Metzia* 58b, 59a)

✿ **Embarrasser has no World to Come**
R. Eleazar HaMmodai's saying was: "Anyone who embarrasses another person in public will not have a portion in the World to Come." (Avot 3:11)

✿ **Embarrassment**
No rejoicing at the embarrassment of friends
The students once asked R. Adda b. Ahava: "To what do you attribute your longevity"? He replied: "I have never displayed my impatience at home, I have never walked in front of a man greater than myself, I have never had thoughts about Torah in a dirty place, I have never walked four *amot* without Torah thoughts, and I never fell asleep in the Bet Midrash. I never rejoiced at the embarrassment of

---

90. See entry, Seder Eliyahu.

my friends, and I never called my friends by a nickname." (*Taanit* 20b)

✿⊞ Embarrassment avoided
The story is related that a woman appeared in the academy of Rabbi Meir and declared: "One of you rabbis has taken me as a wife by cohabitation." Rabbi Meir rose and gave her a bill of divorce. Thereupon, all the students stood up and did likewise. (*Sanhedrin* 11a)

✿ Embarrassment in public
Rabbi Yannai once saw a man give a poor person a *zuz* in front of many people. He said to him: "It would have been better if you had not given him at all, because you embarrassed him in public." (*Hagigah* 5a)

Emet   אמת
In truth, R. Eleazar said: "Whenever it is stated in truth, it is the Halachah." (*Bava Metzia* 60a; *Shabbat* 92b)

Emet, Truth, Truth   אמת אמת
Repeating the word "*Emet*" after the *Shema* (*Berachot* 12a, 14b)

Emmaus   אימאוס
R. Akiva was in the marketplace of Emmaus; he met there R. Gamliel and R. Yehoshua. (*Hullin* 91b)

Emperor Antonius
Emperor Antonius had a secret tunnel to the residence of Rebbe. (*Avodah Zarah* 10b)

⊞ Emperor makes proposal
Let us all be one people
The Talmud relates a story: The Emperor proposed to Rabbi Tanchum, "Come, let us all be one people."

"Very well," he answered, "but since we are all circumcised, we cannot become like you. Therefore, the only way we can become all alike is if you will be circumcised."

The Emperor replied: "You have spoken well; nevertheless, anyone who gets the better of the Emperor in debate must be thrown into the lion's arena." So they threw Rabbi Tanchum to the lions, but he came out alive. A heretic remarked: "The reason he was not eaten was because the lions were not hungry." Thereupon, they wanted to test if this was true, and they threw the heretic to the lions and he was eaten. (*Sanhedrin* 39a)

⊞ Emperor wants to see God
The Talmud describes a conversation between the Emperor of Rome and Rabbi Yehoshua. The Emperor said that he wished to see the Jewish God. Rabbi Yehoshua told him, "That is impossible."

The Emperor insisted. Thereupon, Rabbi Yehoshua told the Emperor to look at the sun during the summer solstice. The Emperor cried out, "I cannot."

"Well, said Rabbi Yehoshua, if you can't look at one of the servants of God, how do you expect to be able to look at God himself?" (*Hullin* 59b, 60a)

Employees
It happened that some employees came for their pay and they were gored by the owner's ox. (*Bava Kamma* 33a)

Employer and employees
A man hiring employees, what is the customary deal? (*Bava Metzia* 83a)

Enactments
Ten enactments were ordained by Ezra. (*Bava Kamma* 82a)

Enactments for the repentant
תקנת השבים
Special Enactment of the rabbis was made for the repentant, to make it easier for them. (*Bava Kamma* 94b)

Enactments made in Usha אושא תקנת
Enactments of the rabbis when they met in Usha (*Bava Kamma* 89a–b; *Bava Batra* 139b)

Enactment of importance תקנה גדולה
A great enactment was established with regards to misappropriated articles. (*Bava Kamma* 103b)

Enactments of the Sages תקנת חכמים
Ordinance of the Sages (*Ketubbot* 10a)

📖 **Encounter of Berurya with R. Yosi**
R. Yosi HaGlili was once traveling when he met Berurya, the wife of Rabbi Meir, and he asked her: "By which road do we go to Lydda?" She replied: "Foolish Galilean, didn't the rabbis teach that you should not engage in much conversation with a woman? You should have asked, 'by which to Lydda?'" (*Eruvin* 53b; *Nedarim* 20a)

Encounters; Rebbe and Antonius
Rebbe and Emperor Antonius had a few encounters; they met secretly. (*Avodah Zarah* 10b)

Endurable mitzvah
There is a statement in the Talmud. The rabbis relied upon the words of R. Shimon ben Gamliel and R. Eleazar b. Tzadok who said: "No law may be imposed upon the public unless a majority can endure it." (*Horayot* 3b)

Enduring precepts
Rabbi Shimon ben Eleazar said: "Every precept for which Israel was willing to die during the time of royal decrees and persecution, those precepts are still held firmly in the minds of Jews." (*Shabbat* 130a)

Engaged in a mitzvah is exempt from other mitzvahs
R. Hisda and Rabbah b. Huna slept on the river bank of Sura when they were visiting the Exilarch during the Sukkot holiday. They said: "We are engaged in a religious errand and therefore we are exempt from the mitzvah of sleeping in the *sukkah*." (*Sukkah* 10b, 26a)

Engagement on Shabbat
The question whether it is permitted to have a betrothal on Shabbat (*Shabbat* 12a)

Engrossed in study is unaware of pain
Once a Tzadoki saw Rava engrossed in his studies, and Rava was completely unaware that his finger was under his foot bleeding.
"You are irrational people," he declared. "You consented to do at Mount Sinai with your mouth before you heard what was expected of you."
Rava answered him: "We are a people of integrity and we trusted that God would not ask us to do what was impossible." (*Shabbat* 88a; *Ketubbot* 112a)

Enjoying הנאה
To enjoy or to get some benefit from a forbidden object (*Bava Kamma* 41a)

Enjoying food or anything
To enjoy anything in this world without a benediction is forbidden. (*Berachot* 35a)

✿ **Enjoying in both worlds**
We have learned: These are the *mitzvot* for which one gets enjoyment in this world and will also receive rewards in the World to Come: honoring parents, practice of loving-kindness and making peace between people – while the study of Torah surpasses them all. (*Shabbat* 127a)

✿ **Enjoyment of this world**
R. Shemuel believed: It is a good thing to enjoy the wonderful things Hashem created in this world. R. Shemuel said to Rav Yehuda: "Hurry on and eat and drink,

because the world from which we must depart is like a wedding feast." (*Eruvin* 54a)

Enlarging a city (*Shevuot* 14a)

Enlarging a city in Israel
To enlarge a city, a court of seventy-one is required. (*Sanhedrin* 2a)

Entering uninvited
Someone entered another person's property without permission and he was gored by an ox. (*Bava Kamma* 23b)

Entrusting for safekeeping
If one entrusts to someone animals or objects for safekeeping, and they were stolen or lost (Bava Metzia 33b; Bava Kamma 108a)

Entrusting fruit for safekeeping
If one entrusts to someone fruits for safekeeping (*Bava Metzia* 38a, 40a; *Pesahim* 13a)

Entrusting money for safekeeping
If one entrusts to someone money for safekeeping and the money is lost (*Bava Metzia* 36a, 42a)

✿ Envy
R. Eliezer HaKappar said: "Envy, greed, and chasing after honors take a man out of this world." (*Avot* 4:21)

Epidemic in town
What should one do when there is an epidemic in town (*Bava Kamma* 60b)

Erased contract
Witnesses signing on a contract that was erased of other writings (*Bava Batra* 164a)

Erasing names
Certain names may not be erased. (*Shevuot* 35a)

Erev Pesach
Can one eat Erev Pesach in the late hours of the day? (*Pesahim* 99b)

📖 Erev Pesach on Shabbat
It is stated: The Bene Betera rabbis were the heads of the Sanhedrin and this Halachah was hidden from them. On one occasion, the fourteenth of Nisan fell on the Shabbat and they didn't remember whether the slaughter of the Paschal lamb overrides the Shabbat. They inquired. Is there any man who knows this Halachah? They were told:

"There is a man by the name of Hillel from Babylonia who studied under Shemaya and Avtalyon, the two greatest man of our time."

They summoned him and he was asked the question. He told the Sanhedrin: "Surely we have more than 200 Paschal lambs during the year, which override the Shabbat." He quoted sentences from the Torah and logic to prove to them that it does override the Shabbat. After this incident, the president of the Sanhedrin resigned in 30 BCE, and they elected Hillel president. (*Pesahim* 66a)

Erev Shabbat
One should say three things before the Shabbat sets in. (*Shabbat* 34a)

Erev Shabbat Shofar blasts
Six blasts were blown on the *shofar* on Erev Shabbat to bring in the Shabbat. (*Shabbat* 35b)

Erev Yom Kippur eating
Eating erev Yom Kippur is a mitzvah. (*Berachot* 8b; *Pesahim* 68b)

Erroneous sale   מקח טעות
A mistaken sale, a sale under false pretenses (*Bava Kamma* 46b; *Bava Batra* 92a; *Avodah Zarah* 71b)

Error admitted
R. Shila admitted his ruling was in error
On one occasion, Rav disapproved of R. Shila's ruling. It happened that a man supposedly drowned in the swamps, but there were no witnesses. Rabbi Shila permitted his wife to marry again. Rav said to Rabbi Shemuel. "Let us place him in *herem*.[91] Shemuel told Rav, "Let us first ask him to give us an explanation." When they discussed the merits of the case, Rabbi Shila admitted that he made a mistake. (*Yevamot* 121a)

Eruv
Figuring measurements for an eruv
With regards to an *eruv*, R. Hanina b. Antigonus ruled that the two thousand cubits are figured for a circular area and not a squared area. (*Eruvin* 49b)

Eruv
How is an eruv *made in a courtyard where Jews and non-Jews live together*
R. Eliezer b. Yaakov was in disagreement with his colleagues with regards to an *eruv* where Jews live with non-Jews in the same courtyard. Abbaye said to R. Yosef, "We have a tradition that the teachings of R. Eliezer b. Yaakov are few in quantity but well sifted."

Also Rav Yehuda said in the name of R. Shemuel: "The Halachah is in agreement with R. Eliezer b. Yaakov." (*Eruvin* 62b; *Bechorot* 23b; *Yevamot* 49b; *Gittin* 67a)

Eruv agent
Who may act as an agent to make an *eruv*. (*Eruvin* 31b)

Eruv food
What kind of food may be used to make an *eruv* of partnership for Shabbat (*Eruvin* 26b)

Eruv for a town
How is an *eruv* made for a town, especially when the houses are not in a straight line (*Eruvin* 52b)

Eruv ordained
R. Yehuda stated in the name of R. Shemuel: "When King Solomon ordained the laws of making an *eruv* and the washing of hands before eating bread a heavenly voice proclaimed: *"My son, if your heart be wise, my heart will be glad, even mine."* (*Eruvin* 21b; *Shabbat* 14b)

Eruv placement
When placing food for an *eruv*, where may it be placed? (*Eruvin* 32b)

Eruv preparation
How is an *eruv* made? (*Eruvin* 82a)

Eruv prepared
Rav Yehuda related a story in the name of Rav: "The daughter-in-law of R. Yoshaya went to the bathhouse on a Friday, but she was delayed and before she could go home, it got dark and Shabbat set in. She was in a place beyond the Shabbat *tehum*. However, her mother-in-law solved the problem by preparing an Eruv for her. (*Eruvin* 80a)

Eruv; the quantity of food required
R. Yohanan is the one who prescribed the quantity of food required for making an *eruv*. (*Eruvin* 8:2, 82b)

Eruv with conditions
Making an *eruv* on condition that it be used in different directions of the town (*Eruvin* 36b)

Escape from besieged Jerusalem
During the Roman occupation the Jewish people had two parties: one party wanted to sue for piece and the other was against

91. Under the ban.

it. Rabbi Yohanan ben Zakkai sent word to his nephew Abba Sikra to come to visit him in secret. When he came, R. Yohanan asked him:

"Why are you permitting to kill the people with starvation?"

He answered:

"What could I do? If I say a word they would kill me."

Rabbi Yohanan said to him: "Devise a plan so I can escape from the city and perhaps I can save for the people something."

He came up with a plan and advised him, "Pretend to be ill so that people will come to visit you. Put something with a terrible odor next to you so that people will say you are dead. Let your students carry you out in a coffin, but no one else, because people will notice you are lighter than a dead corpse." He listened to his advice and pretended to be dead. His students carried the coffin: Rabbi Eliezer on one side and Rabbi Yehoshua on the other side and smuggled him out from Jerusalem. Abba Sikra himself also accompanied the coffin. When the gatekeepers wanted to pierce through the coffin, Abba Sikra prevented them from doing it. He said to them: "Shall they say that they pierced their Rebbe?" After Rabbi Yohanan was out of Jerusalem, he met with Vespasian, who was the commander in charge. Rabbi Yohanan addressed Vespasian by the title of Emperor. When Vespasian corrected him, Rabbi Yohanan told him that according to scripture only a king could conquer Jerusalem. Shortly after that, a messenger arrived with the news from Rome that the Emperor died. Vespasian was also informed that the Senate wants him to be the next Emperor of Rome.

Rabbi Yohanan and Vespasian had a discussion and Vespasian realized that he was speaking to a very wise person. Finally Vespasian told Rabbi Yohanan: "I must

leave now, but make a request of me and I will grant it to you."

Rabbi Yohanan said:

"Give me Yavne and its wise men to be allowed to teach, allow the family chain of R. Gamliel to continue, and a physician to heal Rabbi Tzadok."

His wish was granted, and the Yavne Academy was established. (*Gittin* 56a)

✿ **Esteem to be shown**
Rabbi Yishmael said: "Show esteem toward a great person, and receive all people cheerfully." (*Avot* 3:12)

Esther Megillah
Levi b. Shemuel and R. Huna b. Hiyya were repairing the mantles for the scrolls at the school of Rav Yehuda. When they came to the scroll of Esther, they remarked: "This scroll does not require a mantle." He disapproved of their remark and said: "It sounds like a remark of an *apikoros*." (*Sanhedrin* 100a)

Estimation, guesswork אמדות
(*Avot* 1:6)

Et את
The word "et" in the Torah adds something
R. Shimon Hamsoni or R. Nehemia Hamsoni derived from every *et* in the Torah to add something, but when he reached the *et* of "to fear God" he could not find anything appropriate and he stopped.

His students said to him: "What will happen to all the other expositions that you have already given?"

He answered them: "Just as I have received reward for the expositions, so will I get reward for withdrawing them." Until R. Akiva came and expounded the *et* to mean all the Torah scholars. (*Bava Kamma* 41b; *Kiddushin* 27a, 57a; *Bechorot* 6b; *Pesahim* 22b)

✡ Etiquette at mealtime
The Exilarch said to R. Sheshet: "Even though you are a respected rabbi, the Persians have mastered a better etiquette at meal time." (*Berachot* 46b)

Etrog stolen
Is a stolen *etrog* fit for performing the mitzvah? (*Sukkah* 34b)

📖 Eulogy
Who will eulogize Rabbah?
Abbaye asked Rabbah: "It is known that the people of Pumbedita hate you because of your outspokenness. Now, that being a fact, who might be willing to deliver the eulogy for you?" Rabbah replied: "You and Rabbah b. R. Hanan will do just fine." (*Shabbat* 153a)

Eunuch from birth   סריס חמה
R. Akiva said: "A born eunuch does not perform *halitza* or *yibbum*." (*Bechorot* 42b; *Yevamot* 79b)

Evaluating
When property is evaluated (*Bava Kamma* 58b)

Evaluation   שומע
Evaluation of objects and property (*Bava Metzia* 16b, 20a, 35a)

Evening prayers   מעריב
The evening prayer was instituted by the Patriarch Yaakov. (*Berachot* 26b)

Evening prayers
Compulsory or optional[92] (*Berachot* 27b)

Evil eye   משום עינא
(*Bava Metzia* 30a)

---

92. Also see entry, Appointment of R. Eleazar b. Azaria.

✡ Evil inclination
R. Yehoshua said: "An evil eye and the evil inclination, and hatred of fellow creatures remove a man from his world." (*Avot* 2:16)

Evil neighbor
R. Nittai HaArbeli said: "Keep far away from an evil neighbor." (*Avot* 1:7)

Evilman to be avoided
Rabbi Yehuda HaNasi added this prayer: "O Lord our God, deliver us from impudent people and from evil men, etc." (*Berachot* 16b)

Exactness of a contract
The exact place where witnesses are to sign on a contract is discussed. (*Bava Batra* 162b)

Exaggerated allegories
On one occasion, R. Yehuda and Rabbah went to visit Rabbah bar b. Hana at his home while he was sick. They were having a nice visit and a discussion on a halachic matter when some fanatical fire-worshipping Persian gangs invaded his house. The gangs caused havoc and confiscated the lamps from the house. When Rabbah bar b. Hana was praying for relief, he was mentioning that it is hard to believe that the Persians are worse than the Romans. Rabbah achieved great fame with his legendary stories. Many of his stories were exaggerations and he was criticized by some of his colleagues for it, but others saw in the stories allegories and a hint to matters beyond our comprehension. (*Gittin* 16b, 17a)

Exaggerated terms
R Ammi said: "The Torah sometimes speaks in exaggerated terms." (*Hullin* 90b)

Examination of witnesses
The procedure used to examine witnesses (*Sanhedrin* 29a)

📖 Examined slaughtering knife

Once it happened that Ravina examined the *shohet*'s knife in Babylonia, but R. Ashi, who was the halachic authority in the area, was offended and said to him:

"Why are you acting in this manner?" Ravina answered: "Did not R. Hamnuna decide legal matters at Harta di Argiz during the lifetime of R. Hisda? And just like in their case, I am also your colleague and your student." (*Eruvin* 63a)

Excision כריתות

The halachic penalty of excision (*Keritot* 2a)

📖 Excommunicated

R. Eliezer had halachic differences with the rabbis; he was excommunicated

On that day, all objects which R. Eliezer ben Horkynos had declared clean were brought and burned in fire. Then they took a vote and excommunicated him. The rabbis said: "Who should go and inform him of the excommunication?"

"I will go," said R. Akiva. He donned black garments and sat at a distance of four cubits from R. Eliezer.

"Akiva," said R. Eliezer, "what has happened today?" R. Akiva replied, "Master, it appears to me that your companions are keeping a distance from you."

He rent his garments, removed his shoes, set aside his seat, and sat on the floor and tears flowed from his eyes. It was learned that great was the calamity on that day. Rabbi Gamliel was traveling in a ship, when a huge wave arose to drown him. Rabbi Gamliel was reflecting. It appears to me that this is on account of Rabbi Eliezer ben Horkynos. Thereupon he arose and exclaimed:

"Sovereign of the Universe, You know full well that I have not acted for my honor, or for the honor of my paternal house, but for Your honor, so that strife may not multiply in Israel." At that the raging sea subsided. (*Bava Metzia.* 59b; *Berachot* 19a)

Excommunication an error

R. Yehuda said: "Heaven forbid that it should be said that R. Akavia ben Mehalalel was excommunicated; for the Temple Court never had a more eminent person in wisdom and the fear of sin as was R. Akavia ben Mehalalel." (*Eduyot* 7b)

✿ Execution

Before a person is executed, a herald goes out to announce, "Such and such person is about to be executed for committing such and such an offense; whoever knows anything in his favor shall come forth to state it." (*Sanhedrin* 43a)

Execution by burning (*Sanhedrin* 75a)

Execution by strangling (*Sanhedrin* 84b)

Executions

Four kinds of executions have been entrusted to the Beit Din: stoning, burning, slaying by the sword, and strangulation. (*Sanhedrin* 49b)

Exempt

While performing a mitzvah, one is exempt from other mitzvahs.

R. Hisda and Rabbah b. Huna slept on the river bank of Sura when they were visiting the Exilarch during the Sukkot holiday, saying: "We are engaged in a religious errand and therefore we are exempt from the mitzvah of sleeping in the *sukkah*." (*Sukkah* 10b, 26a)

Exemption from judgment

R. Sheshet said in the name of R. Eleazar b. Azariah: "I could justify the exemption from judgment for all the generations of all the Jews who lived from the day the Temple was destroyed to the present day." (*Eruvin* 65a)

Exemptions
For mourners
In מי שמתו *Mi shemetu* the 3rd *perek* in Tractate *Berachot*, the exemptions for mourners are discussed. (*Berachot* 17b)

Exhuming the body of a Jew
It happened in Bene Berak that a person sold his father's estate and then died. The members of his family protested and claimed that he was still a minor. They came to R. Akiva and asked that the body be exhumed. He told them that it is not permitted to dishonor the dead; further-more, the signs after death undergo a change. (*Bava Batra* 154a)

Exilarch   ריש גלותא[93]
(*Shabbat* 48a; *Zevachim* 19a)

Exilarch
A man showed robbers where the Exilarch keeps a heap of grain. (*Bava Kamma* 116b)

Exile
What kind of persons go into exile (*Makkot* 7a)

📖 Exile and the Shechina
R. Shimon b. Yohai said: "Come and see how beloved Israel is in the sight of God – for wherever Israel was exiled to, the Shechina went with them. They were exiled to Egypt and the Shechina was with them, as it is written. They were exiled to Babylon and the Shechina was with them, as it is written. And when they will be re-deemed in the future, the Shechina will be with them, as it is written. Abbaye said:

"In Babylonia, the Shechina is in the syn-agogue of Huzal, and in the synagogue of Shaf Yativ, which is in Nehardea. But do not think it is in both places, but rather it is sometimes in one and sometimes in the other." R. Abbaye always prayed in that synagogue when he was in that town. (*Megillah* 29a)

📖 Exorcised the demons
The Talmud relates that certain people were carrying a barrel of wine and they put the barrel under a drainpipe to take a rest. Demons caused the barrel to burst. The people came to R. Mar b. Ashi. He brought trumpets and exorcised the de-mons that now stood before him. "Why did you break the barrel?"

The demon replied: "What else could I do, they placed the barrel on my ear?"

R. Mar asked them: "What business do you have in a public place? You are in the wrong and you must pay for the damage."

The demon asked for time to pay. A day was fixed for the payment to be made, but the demon did not keep his promise with the excuse that he can acquire only things, which are not tied, sealed or measured or counted, and he could not find other things. (*Hullin* 105b)

Expert advisor   מומחה לבית דין
An expert advisor to the court (*Sanhedrin* 5a)

📖 Expert analyst of menstrual blood
Ifra Hormuz once sent some blood to Rava to be examined while R. Ovadiah was present. He smelled it and declared. "This blood is from lust."[94] When she heard what Rava said, she said to her son the king: "See how wise the Jews are." (*Niddah* 20b)

---

93. See story under, Exilarch.

94. See entry, Blood of lust.

Expert on ritual uncleanness

Rabbi Avohu stated in the name of Rabbi Yohanan: "Rabbi Meir had a student by the name of Sumchos and he was able to supply forty-eight reasons in support for every rule of uncleanness." (*Eruvin* 13b)

Extension of wall downward

Gud Ahit גוד אחית

A wall or partition that does not reach the ground is deemed as continuing downward and touching the ground. (*Eruvin* 87a)

Extension of wall upward

Gud Asik גוד אסיק

A wall or partition that does not reach the ceiling is deemed as continuing upward and touching the ceiling. (*Sukkah* 4b)

Exterior appearance

כל תלמיד שאין תוכו כברו לא יכנס

Students whose exterior appearance does not match their interior intellect may not enter. (*Berachot* 27b; *Yoma* 72b)

Exterior looks and inner character

תוכו כברו

His inner character matches his exterior

R. Gamliel had issued an order: "No student whose inner character does not match his exterior may enter the academy." When R. Eleazar b. Azariah became president the order was revoked. (*Berachot* 28a; *Yoma* 72b)

Extinguishing

A light on Shabbat in fear of danger (*Shabbat* 20b, 29b)

Extinguishing

A non-Jew extinguishing a fire on Shabbat on property of a Jew (*Shabbat* 121a)

Eye for an eye means monetary compensation

עין תחת עין

R. Shimon b. Yohai said: "An eye for an eye means pecuniary compensation."

It was taught, Rabbi Dostai b. Yehuda, or Rabbi Yehuda b. Dostai said: "Eye for an eye commanded in the Torah means only monetary compensation." (*Bava Kamma* 83b, 84a; *Ketubbot* 38a)

Eye medicine

On Erev Shabbat (*Shabbat* 18a)

✿ Eye medicine

R. Yannai sent word to Mar Ukva: "Send me some of Mar Shemuel's eye medicine."

He sent him the medicine with instructions. This is what Shemuel recommends: "A drop of cold water in the morning, bathing the hands and feet in hot water in the evening is better than all the eye medicines in the world." (*Shabbat* 108b)

Ezra ordained ten enactments

These are some of the enactments by Ezra: The Torah should be read during the *Minha* service on Shabbat, also on Mondays and Thursdays during the *Shacharit* service. (*Bava Kamma* 82a)

F

Face is enhanced by beard   הדרת פנים

A man with a beard is enhancing his looks. (*Bava Metzia* 84a)

Facing the Holy of Holies during prayers

During prayers of the *Shemona Esrei*, one should turn and face towards the Holy of Holies. (*Berachot* 28b)

Falling on the face to pray   נפילת אפים

Falling with the face on the arms to pray special prayers called *Tahanun* (*Bava Metzia* 59b)

False evidence planted
Husband unwilling to pay ketubbah *settlement*

Once a man wanted to divorce his wife, but he didn't want to have to pay her the *ketubbah* settlement. The man invited his friends for a feast and made them drunk, and then he put them all in one bed. He brought the white of eggs and scattered it among them and brought witnesses to see it. He went to the Bet Din to claim that his wife was not faithful and therefore he is not obligated to pay the *ketubbah*. Rabbi Bava said that he learned from Rabbi Shammai that egg-white contracts when brought near the fire, but semen becomes faint from fire. They tested it and found that it was so. They brought the man to the Bet Din, flogged him, and made him pay for the *ketubbah*. (*Gittin* 57a)

False oaths (*Shabbat* 33a; *Shevuot* 21a)

False prophet
To judge a false prophet, a court of seventy-one is required. (*Sanhedrin* 2a)

False prophet (*Sanhedrin* 89a)

False witnesses (*Bava Kamma* 72b; *Makkot* 2a)

Familiar with the Temple service
Abba Yosi b. Hanan was familiar with the service in the Temple and describes the various gates and their functions in the Temple. He said: "They prostrated themselves opposite the thirteen gates; the southern gates were facing the western wall; the upper gate, the gate of burning, the gate of the firstborn, and the water gate; through it they brought in the pitchers of water for libation on the festival." (*Middot* 2:6)

Family purity in Babylonia
It was asked, how far does Babylon extend – with regards to family purity and to be married with the Jews of that region?

Rav said: "It extends as far as the River Azak."

Shemuel said: "It extends as far as the River Yoani."

"How far does it extend on the upper Tigris?"

Rav said: "It extends as far as Bagda and Awana."

Shemuel said: "It extends as far as Moscani."

"How far does it extend on the lower reaches of the Tigris?"

Shemuel said: "It extends as far as the lower Apamea."

"How far does it extend on the upper reaches of the Euphrates?"

Rav said: "It extends to Tulbakene." Shemuel said: "It extends to the bridge of Be-Pherat." (*Kiddushin* 71b)

Famine in town
When there is a famine in town, what does one do? (*Bava Kamma* 60b)

Famous
R. Dosa b. Horkynos said of R. Akiva: "He is famous from one end of the world to the other end." (*Yevamot* 16a)

Fast and prayer
Eliyahu was a frequent visitor to R. Anan, whom he was teaching the *Seder Eliyahu*. However, after an incident, Eliyahu stopped his visits. R. Anan spent his time in fasting and in prayers. Eventually, Eliyahu came to him again, but a fear came over R. Anan when Eliyahu appeared. In order not to be frightened, he made himself a box and he sat in it until he finished the *Seder Eliyahu*. This is the reason there is a *Seder Eliyahu Rabbah* and a *Seder Eliyahu Zuta* – one part is before this incident and one after.[95] (*Ketubbot* 105b)

---

95. See entry, Seder Eliyahu.

Fast days

What is the procedure for fast days (*Taanit* 15a)

Fast days with shofar blowing

The Talmud relates that in the town of Sepphoris in the days of Rabbi Halafta and Rabbi Hanania ben Teradion they prayed special prayers and blew the shofar on fast days. (*Taanit* 15b)

Fasting

Private fast as an atonement for hurting someone's feelings
When Rabbi Hisda was studying at Rabbi Huna, he once asked him:

"What of a student whose teacher needs him more?" Rabbi Hisda had traditions from other rabbis, which Rabbi Huna did not know. R. Huna took offense and there was coolness between them for a long time. On account of this, Rabbi Hisda fasted forty fast days, because he felt he insulted his rabbi. Rabbi Huna also fasted forty days, because in his thoughts he suspected his student Hisda of arrogance. After some time had passed, there was reconciliation. (*Bava Metzia*.33a)

Fasting by the hour

Is fasting by the hour considered fasting? (*Avodah Zarah* 34a)

Fasting is a remedy for a bad dream

(*Shabbat* 11a)

Fasting not proper

There are certain days that are not proper for fasting. (*Taanit* 15b)

Fat-tail

A Syrian non-Jew used to go to Jerusalem on Pesach time. He boasted to R. Yehuda b. Betera when he returned that he ate from the very best of the Paschal lamb in spite of the prohibition. R. Yehuda b.

Betera said to him: "Did they supply you with the fat-tail?" "No," he replied. The next time he was in Jerusalem on Pesach time he said to them: "Supply me with the fat-tail." "But the fat-tail belongs to the Most High," they replied, and asked him, "Who told you to ask for it?" He answered that it was R. Yehuda b. Betera. They investigated and found out that he was not an Israelite. They sent a message to R. Yehuda b. Betera: "Peace be with you, even though you are in Nisibis, your net is spread over Jerusalem." (*Pesahim* 3b)

📖 Father and son

Father and son disagreed about a halachic matter; the grandfather sides with grandson
There was a dispute between R. Hama and R. Oshaya. R. Hama, the father, ruled one way and R. Oshaya, the son, ruled differently. They went to ask R. Bisa, the grandfather, who decided in favor of R. Oshaya, his grandson. Rami b. Hama applied to them the verse: "A threefold cord is not easily broken," as exemplified by R. Oshaya the grandson, R. Chama the son, and R. Bisa the grandfather. (*Bava Batra* 59a; *Ketubbot* 62b)

✡ Father and son

The Talmud relates that Rav advised his son Hiyya: "Do not take drugs, do not leap in high jumps, and do not have your teeth extracted, do not provoke serpents, and do not provoke a Syrian woman." (*Pesahim* 113a)

Father and son

What if a father tells his son to do something contrary to Torah commandments? (*Bava Metzia* 32a; *Yevamot* 6a)

Father and son students

R. Yaakov b. Aha b. Yaakov was sent by his father to study at R. Abbaye. When the son returned, his father realized that his own learning is dull. He said to his son:

"You remain at home so that I can travel to R. Abbaye to learn." (*Kiddushin* 29b)

Father and teacher

If a father and teacher are in captivity, who is to be redeemed first? (*Bava Metzia* 33a)

Father does not recognize son

The Talmud tells us that Rabbi Hama left his home and spent twelve years in the academy to study Torah. When he returned home, he stopped at the local academy before going home. A young man entered the academy and sat down next to him and asked him a question on the subject of study. When R. Hama saw the great knowledge this young man possessed he became depressed. He was thinking, *Had I been here, I also could have had such a son.* After he finally went home, the young man followed him and knocked on the door. Believing that he came to ask him another question, he rose before him as he entered the house. His wife broke out in laughter. "What kind of father stands up before his son?" The young man that followed him happened to be Rabbi Oshaya, his son. It was said of them, "a threefold cord is not quickly broken." (*Ketubbot* 62b; *Bava Batra* 59a)

Father teaching his son

Child remembers his father immersing him in the *mikveh* so he could partake in eating *teruma*[96] (*Bava Kamma* 114b)

✿ Father's advice to son

The Talmud relates that Rabbi Akiva charged his son R. Yehoshua with seven instructions:

– Do not sit to study Torah at the highest point of the city.
– Do not live in a town where the leaders of the town are scholars, because they will neglect the needs of the town."

– Do not enter your house suddenly.
– Do not walk without shoes.
– Arise early in the summer on account of the heat, and in the winter on account of the cold.
– Treat your Shabbat like a weekday rather than be dependent on others."[97]
– Be on good terms with the person on whom the hour smiles. (*Pesahim* 112a)

Father's authority

A daughter is under her father's authority. (*Ketubbot* 46b)

Fathom the depths of his knowledge

R. Yohanan also stated: "R. Oshaya in his generation was like R. Meir was in his generation. His colleagues could not fathom the depth of his knowledge." (*Eruvin* 53a)

Fear of Heaven (*Avot* 3:21, 22)

Fear of Heaven

When R. Yohanan b. Zakkai fell ill, his students asked for a blessing. He said to them: "May it be God's will that the fear of Heaven shall be upon you like the fear of flesh and blood."

The students asked him: "Is that all?"

He answered them: "If you can attain that, you have achieved a great deal, because when a person does something wrong he fears most that another person sees him committing the wrong." (*Berachot* 28b)

✿ Fear of Heaven

A favorite saying of R. Abbaye was: "A man should always be in fear of Heaven, strive to be on best terms with his fellow-men and his relatives, even with men of other religions in order that he may be beloved above and below and acceptable to his fellow-creatures." (*Berachot* 17a)

---

96. See story under, When I was a child.

97. See entry, Akiva's instructions to his son.

Fear of Heaven

R. Hanina said: "Everything is in the hands of heaven except the fear of Heaven." (*Megillah* 25a; *Shabbat* 31b; *Berachot* 33b)

Fears strong men have

Our rabbis taught: There are five fears the strong fear from the weak. (*Shabbat* 77b)

Feed children

On Yom Kippur

When R. Aha finished the *Musaf* service on Yom Kippur, he would urge the congregation with these words: "People, who have children, go out and feed them and give them to drink to avoid exposing them to danger." (Yerushalmi *Yoma* 6:4)

Feeding animals

On Shabbat

Feeding animals on Shabbat is discussed in *Mi she-hehshich*, the 24th *perek* in *Shabbat*. (*Shabbat* 153a)

✡ Feeding animals

R. Yehuda said in the name of Rav: "It is forbidden to eat before feeding your own animals." (*Berachot* 40a; *Gittin* 62a)

Feeding a dog

On Shabbat (*Shabbat* 19a)

Feeding hametz to animals (*Pesahim* 21a)

✡ Feeding hired laborers

The Talmud relates that Rabbi Yohanan ben Matya told his son to hire laborers to work for them. He did as his father asked him and promised to supply for them food. When his father heard what he did, he told him: "Son, even if you should prepare them a banquet like King Solomon did, you would not meet your obligation towards them. Before they begin to work tell them that they can work only on condition that you feed them bread and pulse only." (*Bava Metzia* 49a, 83a)

✡📖 Feeding the hungry

In a year of scarcity

R. Yehuda HaNasi opened his storehouse of produce to the public with a proclamation: The storehouse is open to all who studied the Scripture, the Mishna, the Gemara, the Halachah, or the Aggadah. There is no admission for the ignorant." R. Yonatan b. Amram entered the storehouse and asked for food. Rebbe asked him: "My son, have you studied Scripture and Mishna?"

"No," he answered.

"How can I feed you? You don't qualify."

"Feed me as a dog or as a raven is fed." He gave him some food. After he left, Rebbe regretted giving him food, saying to his son, "I have broken my principle in giving food to an ignorant." R. Shimon, his son, said to him: "Perhaps he was your student R. Yonatan b. Amram who made it his principle not to derive material benefit from learning Torah." Inquiries were made and it was found that it was so. After this incident he proclaimed: "All may enter!" (*Bava Batra* 8a)

✡📖 Feeding the hungry

The Talmud relates that Rabbah said to Rafram b. Papa: "Tell me some of the good deeds Rabbi Huna had done." He replied, "On cloudy days, they used to drive him in his golden carriage to survey every part of the city of Sura. When he saw walls that were unsafe, he would order them to be demolished, and if the owner could not afford to rebuild them he would rebuild them at his own expense.

"On Friday afternoons, he would send messengers to the market and buy all the leftover vegetables."[98] (*Taanit* 20b)

---

98. See entry, Benefactor.

📖 Feeding the poor, right or wrong?

Turnus Rufus, the Roman governor, asked Rabbi Akiva: "If God loves the poor, why does He not support them?"

Rabbi Akiva replied: "God gave us the mitzvah of charity, in order to save us from the punishment of Gehinom."

"On the contrary," countered Rufus, "it is this deed of giving food to the poor, which condemns you to Gehinom. I will illustrate it to you. Suppose a king was angry with his servant and sent him to prison and ordered that no food should be given to him, and someone gave him food. Would the king not be angry with this man, would he not punish him?"

Rabbi Akiva retorted: "Suppose the king got angry with his son and put him in prison with orders not to feed him, and someone gave him food. Would the king not be grateful to this man and even send him a present?" (*Bava Batra* 10a)

Feeding the world

The world population is fed in his merit
Rav Yehuda said in the name of Rav: "Every day a Bat Kol goes out from Mount Horev and proclaims: 'The whole world is being fed for the merits of my son Hanina and yet my son Hanina is satisfied with a small measure of carobs from one Friday to the next Friday.'" (*Berachot* 17b; *Taanit* 24b; *Hullin* 86a)

Feet together when praying

R. Yitzhak said in the name of R. Yohanan, also R. Yosi b. R. Hanina said in the name of R. Eliezer b. Yaakov: "When praying the feet should be straight together." (*Berachot* 10b)

Felicitate newlyweds

R. Helbo said: "At a wedding, one should partake of the wedding meal and felicitate the newlyweds." (*Berachot* 6b)

📖 Fell into a pit

Daughter of Nehunia, the digger of wells, fell into a pit, saved by a holy man
It happened that the daughter of Nehunia fell into a deep pit. When the people informed R. Hanina b. Dosa, he told them during the first hour: "She is well." In the second hour, he said again: "She is well." In the third hour, he said: "She is out of the pit." They asked her: "Who brought you up from the pit?" She answered, "A ram helped me and an old man was leading the ram." They asked R. Hanina b. Dosa: "Are you a prophet?" He answered: "I am neither a prophet nor the son of a prophet." (*Bava Kamma* 50a; *Shekalim* 8b; *Yevamot* 121b)

Female children   בנן נוקבין

(*Ketubbot* 52b)

Fence

Making a fence around other properties
(*Bava Kamma* 20b; *Bava Batra* 4b)

Fence

To break down a neighbor's fence for animals to escape (*Bava Kamma* 55b)

Fence around the Law

Fences around the Torah Law (*Avot* 1:1)

📖 Festive meal

Yom Tov meal for a friend who was recuperating from an illness
R. Zera was once ill and R. Avohu went to visit him. R. Avohu made a commitment and said: "If the little one with burned legs recovers, I will make a Yom Tov meal for the rabbis." R. Zera did recover and R. Avohu made a feast in his honor. When the time came to begin the meal, R. Avohu said to R. Zera: "Would you please make the blessing and begin." But R. Zera said to him, "Don't you accept R. Yohanan's dictum, that the host begins the meal?"

R. Avohu began the meal with the

blessing. When it came to saying the blessings after the meal, R. Avohu said to R. Zera; "Would you lead us in the blessings?"

R. Zera said to him, "Don't you accept R. Huna's ruling, that the same person who said the blessings before the meal also does the blessing after the meal?" (*Berachot* 46a)

Festivities of idolaters
Prohibitions dealing with idolaters on those days (*Avodah Zarah* 2a)

Fetus in the mother's womb
עובר במעי אשה
Dead fetus in the womb of its mother (*Hullin* 72a)

Field in Syria
When one buys a field in Syria close to the Land of Israel (*Ohalot* 18:7)

Fields
R. Shemuel discusses selling ten fields in ten different countries. (*Bava Kamma* 12a; *Bava Batra* 67a; *Kiddushin* 27a)

Fields sold for 60 years
A field sold for sixty years, is it required to be returned during the Yovel year? (*Bava Metzia* 79a)

📖 Fifteenth day of Av
R. Shimon b. Gamliel said: "There were no happier days for Israel than the Fifteenth day of Av and the day of Yom Kippur; for on those days the daughters of Jerusalem used to go out dressed in white garments, borrowed in order not to shame the ones who had none. They went out and danced in the vineyards. They called out: 'Young man, lift up your eyes and see what you will select for yourself. Set not your eyes on beauty but fix your eyes on family. For grace is deceitful and beauty is vain.'" (*Taanit* 26b; *Bava Batra* 121a)

Fighting over a net
Two men were fighting over a fishnet (*Bava Kamma* 117a)

Finding
Obligatory notes or documents (*Bava Metzia* 12b, 17a, 19a; *Ketubbot* 59a)

Finding a purse on Shabbat
(*Avodah Zarah* 70a)

Finding an object
Two people got hold of an object and both claim to have found it first. (*Bava Metzia* 2a)

Fine imposed
קנס
How many judges are required to levy a double fine, or a fine of fourfold or fivefold? (*Sanhedrin* 8a)

Fingerbreadth
Three fingerbreadths used as a measuring tool (*Kelim* 28:1, 7)

Fire
Causing damage (*Bava Kamma* 2a)

Fire
Caused by camel loaded with flax (*Bava Kamma* 22a, 62b; *Shabbat* 21b)

Fire
Saving holy objects from a fire on Shabbat or telling a non-Jew what to do when there is a fire is discussed in *Kol kitvei*, the 16th *perek* in *Shabbat*. (*Shabbat* 115a, 121a)

📖 Fire broke out on Shabbat
A miracle happened and a heavy rain came
It once happened that a fire broke out in the courtyard of Yosef b. Simai in Sichin. Men of the garrison from Sepphoris came to extinguish it, because he was a high ranking officer of the King, but he did not permit it because it was Shabbat. A miracle

happened; a heavy rain came down and extinguished the fire. (*Shabbat* 121a)

First cup of wine
First of the four cups of wine at the Seder (*Pesahim* 114a)

First finder
Finding property in a public area, whoever is first acquires title. (*Bava Kamma* 30a–b)

First of the fleece   ראשית הגז
Rav and Shemuel both ruled: The proper measure to be given to the priest for the first of the fleece is one-sixtieth part, for *teruma* one-sixtieth part and for the corner of the field to the poor, one-sixtieth part. (*Hullin* 137b)

First to do a mitzvah
Always try to be first in performing a mitzvah. (*Bava Kamma* 38b)

✿ First to greet
The dictum of Matya ben Heresh was: "Be first to extend greetings to all people, be rather a tail to lions than a head to foxes." (*Avot* 4:15)

First speaker
Our rabbis taught: When the rabbis entered the vineyard of Yavne, there were among them R. Yehuda b. Illai, R. Yosi b. Halafta, R. Nehemia, and R. Eliezer the son of R. Yosi HaGlili. They all spoke about hospitality. R. Yehuda, the first of the speakers in every place, spoke in honor of the Torah. (*Shabbat* 33b; *Berachot* 63b; *Menahot* 23a)

First vessel and second vessel on Shabbat
With regards to cooking which is prohibited on Shabbat, one should take into consideration the vessel which is directly on the fire – called the first vessel. When the food is taken and placed in the next vessel – this is the second vessel. R. Yitzhak b. Avdimi said: "I once followed Rebbe to the bath and wanted to give him heated oil, he told me to put it in a second vessel." (*Shabbat* 40b)

Firstborn
One may be considered a firstborn for one thing but not for other things like inheritance. (*Bechorot* 46a)

Firstborn
The double portion of a firstborn is discussed. (*Bava Batra* 124a)

Firstborn animal
When buying an animal from a Jew the first calf is for sure a *bechor* (*Bechorot* 21b)

Firstborn by caesarean section
(*Bechorot* 47b)

Firstborn in doubt
An animal bought from a non-Jew (*Bechorot* 19b)

Firstborn twins in animals (*Bechorot* 17a)

Firstborn twins in animals
One male one female (*Bechorot* 17a)

Firstling
Exemptions and obligations when buying sheep from a non-Jew under an iron clad agreement צאן ברזל (*Bechorot* 16b)

Firstling
Testicles missing in a firstling (*Bechorot* 40a)

Firstling
A firstling having five legs or three legs (*Bechorot* 40a)

Firstling blemishes
What are the blemishes that apply to a firstborn? (*Bechorot* 37a)

Firstling bought
Bought a firstling and was found out that it was not shown to a scholar. (*Bechorot* 37a)

Firstling mixed with hundred
If a firstborn animal got mixed up with 100 other animals (*Hullin* 132a)

Firstling slaughter
Slaughter of a blemished firstling requires three persons present if no expert is present. (*Bechorot* 36b)

Fish
Scales and fins (*Niddah* 51b)

Fish and Shehita (*Hullin* 27b)

Fish and uncleanness
When do fish become susceptible to uncleanness (*Uktzin* 3:8)

Fish cooked by a non-Jew
(*Avodah Zarah* 38a)

Fish species
R. Avimi b. Avohu taught: There are 700 species of unclean fish in the waters. (*Hullin* 63b)

Fish without fins or scales
Fish that have no fins or scales at first, but grow them later (*Avodah Zarah* 39a)

Fishing
Fish may be caught with an angle in the Sea of Tiberias, but not with nets. (*Bava Kamma* 81b)

📖 **Fit to learn**
"Are you really fit to learn Torah from Rebbe?" asked Rabbi Avdan.
An event that happened in the academy of Rabbi Yehuda HaNasi is told in the Talmud. The students were having a discussion in the academy and Rabbi Yishmael b. Yosi b. Halafta came over to ask them what subject they are discussing. They told him that the subject was prayer. While this was going on, Rabbi Yehuda entered the academy. They all rushed to their seats, but Rabbi Yishmael, being on the heavy side could not move that quickly to his seat, and he squeezed himself through climbing over a few other students. Rabbi Avdan inquired who is the man climbing over the heads of the holy people.

"I am Yishmael the son of Rabbi Yosi, and have come to learn Torah from Rebbe."

"Are you really fit to learn Torah from Rebbe?" asked Rabbi Avdan.

"Was Moshe fit to learn Torah from the lips of God?" retorted Rabbi Yishmael.

"Are you Moshe?" asked Rabbi Avdan.

"Is Rebbe God?" asked Rabbi Yishmael. In the meantime a woman came to the academy to inquire about a matter, and R. Yehuda sent R. Avdan to attend to it. After Avdan went out Rabbi Yishmael gave the answer to Rebbe in his father's name, Rabbi Yosi ben Halafta.

Rebbe called after Avdan. "Come back, we already have the answer."

When Avdan came back, he was pushing himself through the students. Rabbi Yishmael said to him. "He who is needed by the holy people may stride over their heads, but how dare he stride over the heads of the holy people?" Rebbe told Rabbi Avdan. "Remain in your place where you are and sit down." (*Yevamot* 105b)

Five differences
There were five differences between the First and the Second Temple. (*Yoma* 21b)

Five gates to the Temple mount
These are the five gates on the Temple Mount: two Hulda gates on the south, the Kifonot gate on the west, the Tadi gate on the north, and the eastern gate where there was a depiction of Shushan. (*Middot* 1:3)

Five instances of no consecration
R Eleazar said: There are five instances where animals do not become consecrated. (*Bechorot* 42a; *Yevamot* 83b; *Temurah* 11a)

✿ Five students
Five students and five profound remarks
R. Yohanan b. Zakkai had five outstanding students. He said to them: "Go and discern which is the proper way that a person should follow."

R. Eliezer said a good eye; R. Yehoshua said a good friend; R. Yosi said a good neighbor; R. Shimon said one who considers the outcome of his actions, and R. Eleazar said a good heart.

On this, R. Yohanan b. Zakkai remarked: "I prefer the words of R. Eleazar b. Arach, because all your words are included in his words." (*Avot* 2:13)

Fixed place at prayer
R. Helbo said in the name of R. Huna: "A person who has a fixed place when he prays has the God of Avraham as his helper." (*Berachot* 6b)

Fixed time for commandment
מצות עשה שהזמן גרמא
A positive commandment bound by time (*Berachot* 20b)

Fixing
Calendar fixing outside Israel[99] (*Berachot* 63a)

Fixing halachah erroneously
When enacting Halachah, consideration should be taken what impression it will have on future generations. (*Berachot* 11a)

Flat-shaped utensils
Utensils that are shaped flat are not susceptible to uncleanness. (*Kelim* 15:1)

Flatter
R. Shimon b. Pazi was saying: "It is permitted to flatter the wicked in this world." (*Sotah* 41b)

Flavor not imparted אין בגידין בנותן טעם
R. Yishmael b. Beroka said that nerves cannot impart a flavor (*Hullin* 99b)

Flavor worsened טעם לפגם
Imparts a worsened flavor (*Avodah Zarah* 36a, 39a–b, 75b)

Flax
To color flax on Erev Shabbat (*Shabbat* 17b)

Flaying a firstling (*Bechorot* 33a)

Flaying animals on Yom Tov
(*Bechorot* 33a)

📖 Fleeing
Fleeing from Babylonia to Eretz Yisrael
Rabbi Kahana had to flee Babylonia, because of a tragic incident.[100] (*Bava Kamma* 117a)

Flogging
Which transgressions incur judicial flogging (*Makkot* 13a)

Flooding
By saving his friend's donkey, his own

---

99. See story under, Calendar.

100. See also entries, Lion has come up, and Rage.

donkey drowned – what is he entitled to receive? (*Bava Kamma* 115b)

📖 Flooding
R. Assi's property was flooded
R. Assi inspected his property daily. The Talmud relates that one day when Rabbi Assi was inspecting his property he noticed a pipe had burst and was flooding his property. He took off his coat, rolled it up and plugged the pipe with it. He then called out loud and people came to help him stop the flood. (*Hullin* 105a)

Flour permissible for matzot
One fulfills his obligation when eating *matzot* from certain flours. (*Pesahim* 35a)

Folding
Folding cloth on Shabbat
It is discussed in *Eilu kesharim*, the 15th *perek* in *Shabbat*. (*Shabbat* 111b)

Followed in the path of teacher Rav
Abbaye said: "His teacher Rabbah did everything according to Rav except three things." (*Shabbat* 22a, 40a; *Pesahim* 101a; *Menahot* 41b)

Follow your rabbi
Follow your rabbi to his academy:
R. Eliezer to Lydda, R. Yohanan b. Zakkai to Beror Hayil, R. Yehoshua to Peki'in, R. Gamliel to Yavne, R. Akiva to Bene Berak, R. Matya to Rome, R. Hanania b. Teradion to Sichnin, R. Yosi b. Halafta to Sepphoris, R. Yehuda b. Betera to Nisibis, R. Hanina to Exile, R. Yehuda HaNasi to Bet Shearim (*Sanhedrin* 32b)

Food cooked by a non-Jew בישולי נכרים
(*Avodah Zarah* 38a; *Eruvin* 65b)

Food for a dog
Giving food to a dog on Shabbat (*Shabbat* 19a)

Food kept warm on Shabbat
What may be used on Shabbat to keep food warm (*Shabbat* 47b)

Food not grown in the earth
What blessings are to be made over food not grown in the earth (*Berachot*, 6th *perek*)

Foodstuff and uncleanness
Some foodstuff need intent to become susceptible to uncleanness, others do not. (*Uktzin* 3:1)

Feet of animals causing damage
Warning for animals that cause damage by their feet (*Bava Kamma* 17a)

Foolish Babylonians
Rabin came up to Israel from Babylonia and quoted a dictum from R. Nahman to R. Yirmiyahu. R. Yirmiyahu remarked: "Foolish Babylonians – they dwell in a dark country." (*Bechorot* 25b)

Forbidden labors on Shabbat
Rav said: "I found a secret scroll of the school of R. Hiyya in which he discusses the thirty-nine principal labors forbidden on Shabbat. (*Shabbat* 6b, 69a, 96b)

Forbidden marriages
A Kohen is forbidden to a divorced woman or to a woman who performed *halitza*. A Kohen Gadol is forbidden to a widow, a divorced woman, and one that performed *halitza*. (*Yevamot* 59a)

Forbidden things on Yom Tov
In comparison to forbidden things on Shabbat (*Betzah* 36b)

✿ Forbidden to benefit
From a neighbor's property
R. Yohanan said: "In three places did R. Yehuda teach us that it is forbidden to

benefit from a neighbor's property without his knowledge." (*Bava Metzia* 117b; *Bava Kamma* 95a; *Avodah Zarah* 6b)

Forbidden on Yom Kippur
What is forbidden on Yom Kippur (*Yoma* 73b)

Forbidden to a Kohen
R. Amram quoted R. Sheshet with regards to a woman forbidden to a Kohen. (*Yevamot* 35a)

Foretold the time of his death
It is stated: "In the year in which Shimon HaTzaddik died, he foretold that he would die." When asked how he knew, he replied: "On every Yom Kippur when I entered the Holy of Holies, I would see a vision of an old man dressed in white joining me to enter and leave with me, but today I saw an old man dressed in black enter with me, but did not leave." (*Yoma* 39b; *Menahot* 109b)

Forged signature
A deed was produced by a man with the signature of Rava and R. Aha b. Adda. He came before Rava who said: "This is my signature, but I never signed it." The same was with R. Aha b. Adda. The man was arrested and he confessed. Rava asked him: "I can understand how you forged my signature, but how did you manage to forge R. Aha's signature whose hand trembles?" "I put my hand on a bridge made of ropes which trembles." (*Bava Batra* 167a)

Forgetting that it is Shabbat
(*Shabbat* 67b)

Forgiving person
Once R. Huna was very ill, and R. Papa went to visit him. When he saw that he was very sick, he said to the people:

"Make ready for his trip to heaven."

R. Huna recovered and R. Papa was embarrassed for thinking it was the end. He asked him: "What did you see?"

He answered him.

"You were right, it was indeed my end, but the Almighty said to the angels: 'He deserves to live longer, because he never insisted on his rights and is a forgiving person.'" (*Rosh Hashana* 17a)

Forgot
Forgetting the blessing after the meal is discussed in *Eilu devorim*, the 8th *perek* in *Berachot*. (*Berachot* 51b)

Forgot his learning
R. Eleazar b. Arach forgot his learning

Rabbi Helbo said the wines of Perugitha and the water of Diomsith caused the ten tribes of Israel to be cut off from their brethren. R. Eleazar b. Arach visited that place and was attracted and stayed there. Consequently, he forgot his learning. When he returned to his former home he tried to read from the Torah but didn't remember and read incorrectly. The rabbis who were his colleagues prayed for him and his memory returned. We have learned, R. Nehorai said: "If you have to move to another location, be sure you move to a place of Torah and do not say that Torah will follow you, and do not rely on your own understanding of the Torah." Some say his name was not Nehorai but R. Nehemia, others say his name was Eleazar b. Arach, and why was he called Nehorai, because he enlightened the eyes of the Sages with his knowledge of the law. (*Shabbat* 147b)

Forgot his learning
At one time, Rabbi Avimi forgot some of his learning, as is mentioned in the Talmud: R. Zera said R. Avimi was studying

the Tractate *Menahot* under R. Hisda.[101]
(*Arachin* 22a; *Menahot* 7a)

Forgotten fruit
Or produce (*Peah* 6:4)

Formula for prayer
The prayer the High Priest recited on Yom Kippur (*Yoma* 35b)

Forty-eight reasons
For the rule of uncleanness
Rabbi Avohu stated in the name of Rabbi Yohanan: "Rabbi Meir had a student by the name of Sumchos and he was able to supply forty-eight reasons in support for every rule of uncleanness." (*Eruvin* 13b)

Forty seah   ארבעים סאה
The *mikveh* requires forty *seah* to be fit for immersion. (*Avodah Zarah* 75b)

✡ Foul language
R. Nahman b. Yitzhak said: "When one hears obscene language and is silent, he will wind up in the Gehinom. (*Shabbat* 33a)

Found books
Is it permissible to read them without permission? (*Bava Metzia* 29b)

Found objects
Found objects are to be announced in public. (*Bava Metzia* 21a, 23b, 24a)

Found object in a store (*Bava Metzia* 26b)

Found Tefillin (*Bava Metzia* 29b)

Four brothers   ארבעה אחין
Four brothers marrying sisters – is the subject discussed? (*Yevamot* 26a)

Four craftsmen referred to
in Yehezkel
R. Hana b. Bizna said in the name of R. Shimon Hasida: "Who are the four craftsmen referred to in Yehezkel?" He answered: "They are: Mashiach b. David, Mashiach b. Yosef, Eliyahu, and the Kohen Tzedek." R. Sheshet objected: "It does not fit." To this R. Hana replied: "Read the end of the verse." R. Sheshet conceded, "Who am I to argue in Aggadata with R. Hana." (*Sukkah* 52b)

Four cubits   ארבע אמות
R. Abba Kohen Bardella is quoted by Rabbi Shimon ben Lakish that a man's four cubits acquire property for him everywhere. (*Bava Metzia* 10a–b)

Four cubits   ארבע אמות
In certain circumstances, one may not move on Shabbat more than four cubits. (*Eruvin* 41b)

Four cubits where Torah is learned
R. Hiyya b. Ammi said in the name of Ulla: "Since the Temple was destroyed, the most precious thing to God in this world are the four cubits of space where they learn Halachah." (*Berachot* 8a)

Four cups of wine at the Seder
(*Pesahim* 99b, 114a)

Four death sentences   ארבע מיתות
Four kinds of death sentences have been entrusted to the judges. (*Sanhedrin* 49b; *Yevamot* 46b)

Four domains
There are four domains in respect to Shabbat. (*Shabbat* 6a)

Four for atonement   ארבעה מחוסרי כפרה
There are four persons who require a ceremony of atonement. (*Keritot* 2b, 8b)

---

101. See entry, Memory loss.

Four general rules
R. Shimon b. Eleazar stated four general rules that apply to the laws of Torts. (*Bava Kamma* 14a)

Four kinds of damages
ארבעה אבות נזיקין
The principal categories of damages are four. (*Bava Kamma* 2a; *Shekalim* 8a; *Keritot* 2b)

Four kinds of guardians ארבעה שומרין
Four different responsibilities for watchmen (*Shevuot* 49a; *Bava Metzia* 93a, 94b)

Four New Year days ארבעה ראשי שנים
There are four New Year days: On the first of Nisan, on the first of Elul, on the first of Tishrei, and on the fifteenth of Shevat. (*Rosh Hashana* 2a, 8a; *Avodah Zarah* 10a)

Four principal causes of damage
The four principal causes of damage are: the ox, the pit, the tooth of animals, and fire. (*Bava Kamma* 2a)

Four Questions
The son asks the Four Questions at the Seder. (*Pesahim* 116a)

Four rules apply to vendors
(*Bava Batra* 83b)

Four seals in the Temple
There were four seals in the Temple with these inscriptions: עגל זכר גדי חוטא (*Shekalim* 5:3)

Four sisters' children circumcised
R. Hiyya b. Abba stated in the name of R. Yohanan: "It once happened to four sisters in Sepphoris. The first sister's child died when circumcised, the second also died, and the third child died too. The fourth sister came to R. Shimon b. Gamliel who told her: "You must not circumcise." (*Yevamot* 64b)

Four types of custodians
The four types of custodians are: the unpaid custodian, the borrower, the paid custodian, and the hirer. (*Bava Metzia* 93a)

Four types of vows ארבעה נדרים
Four types of vows have been invalidated by the rabbis. (*Nedarim* 20b; *Nazir* 11b)

Fourteenth of Nisan on Shabbat
(*Pesahim* 13a, 20b, 49a)

Fourth cup at the Seder (*Pesahim* 117b)

Fowl and milk
Bet Hillel is stricter than Bet Shammai in this instance. According to Bet Shammai, cheese and fowl may be put on the same table but not eaten, while Bet Hillel forbids both, not to eat and not to put them on the same table. (*Hullin* 104b)

Fowls
Fowls were not permitted to be reared in Jerusalem. (*Bava Kamma* 82b; *Hagigah* 26a; *Zevachim* 96a)

Fox clawing
Is there a consequence when a fox claws a kosher animal (*Hullin* 53a)

Fox in the Holy of Holies
R. Akiva, R. Gamliel, R. Eleazar b. Azariah, and R. Yehoshua were visiting Jerusalem and they saw a fox emerging from the Holy of Holies. (*Makkot* 24b)

📖 Fragrance of Paradise
Rabbah b. Avuha met Eliyahu standing in a non-Jewish cemetery. He started a conversation with him and they discussed halachic matters, but Eliyahu was in a hurry. He told him: "I am pressed for time."

Eliyahu led him through Paradise and offered him to collect some of the leaves and take them with him in his robe.

Rabbah b. Avuha gathered them and took them away. As he was coming out, he heard voices. "Who would consume in this world his portion of the World to Come?" Therefore, he scattered the leaves and threw them away. But the fine fragrance remained and was absorbed in his robe. Someone bought it from him for 12,000 *dinarim*, which he distributed among his sons-in-law. (*Bava Metzia* 114b)

Fragrant trees of Jerusalem
Rahava said in the name of R. Yehuda: "The logs used in Jerusalem for burning were of cinnamon trees and their fragrance pervaded the whole of Israel." (*Shabbat* 63a)

Frame of mind
One should not start praying unless he is in a reverent frame of mind. (*Berachot* 30b)

Fraud   אונאה
Overcharging is discussed. (*Bava Metzia* 49b, 55a)

Fraud with words
R. Yohanan said in the name of R. Shimon b. Yohai: "Fraud by word is worse than monetary fraud.

"Just as there is fraud in buying and selling, so is fraud with words: to ask a seller what is the price of the article when he has no intention of buying is fraud. Another instance: one should not remind a *baal teshuva*: 'Remember when you did such and such.'" (*Bava Metzia* 58b)

📖 Free food for Torah scholars
In a year of scarcity Rabbi Yehuda HaNasi opened up his storehouse and proclaimed: "Let those who studied Scripture, Mishna, and Halachah enter to get food for free. But there is no admission for the ignorant." R. Yonatan b. Amram entered and asked

for food. They asked him: "Have you learned the Torah?"

He answered: "No."

"Have you learned Mishna?"

He answered: "No."

He was refused food.

"Feed me as a dog or as a raven is fed." Rebbe gave him some food. After he left, Rebbe regretted giving him food, saying to his son: "I have broken my principle in giving food to an ignorant." R. Shimon, his son, said to him: "Perhaps he was your student R. Yonatan b. Amram who made it his principle not to derive material benefit from learning Torah." Inquiries were made and it was found that it was so.

After this incident, Rebbe changed the rules and declared: "All may enter and get free food."[102] (*Bava Batra* 8a)

Frequent and less frequent
תדיר ושאינו תדיר תדיר קודם
Whatever is more frequent takes precedence over a nonfrequent. (*Horayot* 12b)

Friday afternoon
One should avoid doing certain things Friday close to Shabbat. (*Shabbat* 11a)

Friend to the end
The Talmud relates that Rabbi Avina's friend Geniva was unfortunately sentenced to die. When the sentence was about to be carried out, he instructed the people to give Rabbi Avina 400 *zuz* from his wine estate. (*Gittin* 65b)

📖 Fright killed Rabbah
R. Kahana said: "R. Hama the son of the daughter of Hassa told me that Rabbah b. Nahmeni died of fear from persecution. An informer told the authorities that Rabbah keeps twelve thousand Israelites from paying the poll tax. It was the custom

---

102. See entry, Feeding the hungry.

for many Israelites to study two months every year in the academy. A royal officer was sent to arrest him, but could not find him. Rabbah fled from Pumbedita to Acra, from Acra to Agama, from Agama to Sahin, from Sahin to Zarifa, from Zarifa to Eina Damim, and then back to Pumbedita. There the officer found him. He locked him up in a chamber, but Rabbah managed to escape and fled to Agama where he died. Abbaye and Rava, his students, and the entire academy went to attend to his body, but they could not find it. When they finally found his body they mourned for him for seven days." (*Bava Metzia* 86a)

From now and further מכאן ואילך
(*Berachot* 9b)

From time to time מעת לעת
A twenty-four hour period (*Shabbat* 15a)

Fruit watchman selling merchandise
We may not buy fruits or wood from a person watching the fruits. (*Bava Kamma* 118b)

Fruits
Blessing over fruits, which fruit should be eaten first, and on which fruit should the blessing be made? (*Berachot* 40b, 41b)

Fruits and vegetables
The blessings on fruits, vegetables, and food not grown in the earth is discussed in *Keitzad mevorchin*, the 6th *perek* of *Berachot*. (*Berachot* 35a)

Fruits of the tree
On fruits of the tree, one makes the blessing *Borei pri ha-etz*. (*Berachot* 35a)

Full months
When the years are intercalated, there is always a minimum of four months in a year that are a full thirty days (*Arachin* 8b)

📖 Funds for captives
A man saved himself with the funds entrusted to him to save captives
The Talmud relates that a certain man was traveling to redeem some captives. He had the ransom money in a purse, but he was attacked by robbers. In order to save himself, he handed over to the robbers the money, and they let him go.[103] (*Bava Kamma* 117b)

Funeral
Buying cemetery plots for a funeral (*Bava Batra* 100b)

Funeral arrangements
Funeral arrangements on Shabbat are discussed in *Shoel*, the 23rd *perek* in *Shabbat*. (*Shabbat* 148b)

✿ Funeral attendance is important
Torah study suspended to escort a dead body
It was recorded: R. Yehuda b. Illai used to suspend the study of Torah for escorting a dead body to the cemetery. He also suspended the study of Torah for escorting a bride to the canopy on her wedding day. (*Megillah* 29a)

Funeral of R. Yosi b. Kisma
When R. Yosi died, all the dignitaries of Rome came to his funeral. (*Avodah Zarah* 18a)

Funeral on a rainy day
R. Nathan said: "Rain at a funeral is a good omen." (*Sanhedrin* 47a)

Future of the world
Predicting the future of the world
R. Hanan b. Tahlifa sent word to R. Yosef: "I once met a man who was in the possession of a *megillah* scroll in Hebrew." I asked him, "Where does it come from?"

---

103. See also entry, Robbed of redemption money.

Future world

He replied: "I joined the Roman mercenary army and I found it amongst the Roman archives. In the scroll, it was written that 4,231 years after Creation, the world will be in great distress. During the years following this, the world will be engaged in wars – some of them will be the wars of Gog U'Magog. The remaining years will be the era of Mashiach. Hashem will not renew the world only after 7,000 years." R. Aha b. Rava said: "It was after 5,000 years." (*Sanhedrin* 97b)

Future world   עולם הבא
Acquiring Olam Haba in a single hour
R. Hanania b. Teradion was condemned to die for violating the decree "not to teach Torah." While he was being burned to death, the executioner asked him, "If I ease your pain, would you take me to the next world with you?" R. Hanania answered him in the affirmative. When R. Yehuda HaNasi heard the news, he cried and said: "One may acquire *Olam Haba* in a single hour, others after many years." Rabbi Hanania ben Teradion became one of the Ten Martyrs.[104] (*Avodah Zarah* 17a, 18a, 10b)

Future world
Three kings and four commoners will not have a share in the World to Come. The kings are: Yerovam, Achav, and Menashe. R. Yehuda disagrees. The commoners are: Bilam, Doeg, Ahitofel, and Gehazi. (*Sanhedrin* 90a)

Future world reward
R. Yehoshua b. Levi said: "All the good deeds Israel does in this world will bear testimony in the World to Come." (*Avodah Zarah* 2a, 4b)

Futures
Buying produce in advance of the fixed price in the market (*Bava Metzia* 62b, 72b)

G

Gains
R. Papa said: "At the gate of gains there are many brothers and friends; at the gates of losses there are neither brothers nor friends." (*Shabbat* 32a)

Gamblers
Disqualified witness
One who is a gambler is disqualified as a witness. (*Sanhedrin* 24b)

Gamliel
It happened that R. Gamliel accidentally put out the eye of his slave Tovi. It made R. Gamliel sad, but at the same time also happy, because he wanted to free his very faithful slave. When he met R. Yehoshua and told him: "Do you know that my slave Tobi has obtained his freedom?", he told R. Gamliel that he disagrees with his conclusion and a discussion developed. (*Bava KamMa* 74b)

Gamliel and Proclos
R. Gamliel and the philosopher Proclos had a discussion. (*Avodah Zarah* 44b)

Gamliel ben Shimon D'Yavne

גמליאל בן שמעון דיבנה
Tanna from Eretz Yisrael
Head of the academy in Yavne
1st – 2nd centuries CE (*Berachot* 2:5, 16a)

Gamliel ben Yehuda HaNasi
גמליאל בן יהודה הנשיא
Amora from Eretz Yisrael
3rd century CE (*Ketubbot* 103a)

---

104. See also entry, Burned with his Torah together.

Gamliel HaZaken   גמליאל הזקן
Tanna from Eretz Yisrael
1st century CE (*Sanhedrin* 11b)

Gamliel HaZaken
Since R. Gamliel HaZaken died, the glory of the Torah ceased to exist. (*Sotah* 49a)

Gamliel in Syria
The rabbis taught: A year may be intercalated only with the approval of the Nasi. It once happened that R. Gamliel was away in Syria to meet with the governor, and his return was delayed. The year was intercalated without him, but subject to his approval. When he returned, he gave his approval and the fixed calendar held good. (*Sanhedrin* 11a; *Eduyot* 7:7)

R. Gamliel kisses R. Yehoshua
There was a dispute between R. Gamliel and R. Yehoshua. R. Gamliel ordered him to demonstrate that he abides by the ruling of his. R. Yehoshua did so and when he entered the Sanhedrin, R. Gamliel kissed him on his forehead and told him, come in peace, my teacher and my student. You are my teacher in wisdom and my student because you accepted my ruling. (*Rosh Hashana* 25a)

R. Gamliel and R. Yehoshua on a boat
R. Gamliel and R. Yehoshua once traveled on a boat. R. Gamliel had some bread with him, while R. Yehoshua had other provisions. When R. Gamliel's bread was consumed, he had to rely on the provisions of R. Yehoshua. He asked R. Yehoshua, "How did you know to bring adequate provisions?" He answered, "A certain comet appears every seventy years and confuses the sailors. I suspected that it would appear about this time."[105] (*Horayot* 10a)

Gamliel's daughter
R. Gamliel's daughter was married to R. Gamliel's brother, whose name was Abba, but he died without having children. (*Yevamot* 15a)

Gam Zu LeTova
Nahum Ish Gam Zu: The Talmud explains the reason why he was called Nahum Ish Gam Zu, because whatever befell him he would always say, "This also is for the best."

Once, the Jewish people of Eretz Yisrael wanted to send a gift to the Emperor. After debating who should take the gift, they chose Rabbi Nahum. The gift they sent was a bag full of precious stones and pearls. Overnight, he stayed at an inn, but while he slept some people emptied his bag and filled it with earth. In the morning, when he discovered that he was robbed, he declared: "This is also for the best."[106] (*Taanit* 21a; *Sanhedrin* 108b; *Berachot* 60b)

Garb of a scholar
R. Yehuda said in the name of Rav: "Anyone who is not a scholar but wears a garb usually worn by a scholar will not be admitted to the inner circle of Hashem." (*Bava Batra* 98a)

Garbage
Object found in the garbage – to whom does it belong? (*Bava Metzia* 24a, 25b)

Garbage removal
What is the customary way to remove the garbage? (*Bava Kamma* 30a, 81b; *Bava Metzia* 118b)

Garlic odor
It happened once that when Rabbi Yehuda HaNasi was delivering a lecture, he noticed a smell of garlic in the room. He

---

105. See entry, Scientific knowledge.

106. See entry, Nahum Ish Gam Zu.

told his students, "Let the person who ate garlic leave the room." R. Hiyya stood up and left the room, and then all the students left the room. The next morning, R. Hiyya was asked by R. Shimon, the son of R. Yehuda, "Was it you who caused annoyance to my father? Heaven forbid that such a thing should happen in Israel."

From whom did Rabbi Hiyya learn such conduct? It was from Rabbi Meir. The story is related that a woman appeared in the academy of Rabbi Meir and declared: "One of you rabbis has taken me as a wife by cohabitation." Rabbi Meir rose and gave her a bill of divorce. Thereupon all the students stood up and did likewise. (*Sanhedrin* 11a)

Garments for a scholar
The flesh of a scholar should not be visible beneath his garment. (*Bava Batra* 57b)

Garments of Moshe
Garments Moshe wore during the seven days of consecration (*Avodah Zarah* 34a)

Garments of the common Priest
The common Priest performed the Temple service in four garments. (*Yoma* 71b)

Garments of the High Priest
The High Priest performed the Temple service in eight pieces of garments. (*Yoma* 71b)

Gartel
R. Huna, who was a student of Rav, was a very wealthy man, but when he was still a student of Rav he was very poor. Once he came dressed with a string around his waist. When Rav saw him, he said to him: "What is the meaning of this?" He replied: "I had no money to buy wine for *Kiddush* so I pledged my silk *gartel* to buy wine." Rav blessed him: "May it be the will of Heaven that you may one day be smothered in

robes of silk." On the day when Rabbah the son of R. Huna got married, R. Huna, who was a short man, was lying on a bed. His daughters were selecting silk dresses and throwing the dresses on the bed without noticing that he was lying there. They kept on throwing silk dresses until he was smothered in silk. When Rav heard this, he remarked: "When I blessed you, why didn't you say 'the same to you, my Rebbe?'" (*Megillah* 27b)

Gate of Temple opening noise
The noise of the gate opening in the Temple could be heard in Yericho. (*Tamid* 30b)

Gates of
The Temple gates would not open. (*Shabbat* 30a)

Gave up comfort of his home
R. Hanania b. Hachinai gave up living at home with his family for twelve years so he could study Torah.[107] (*Ketubbot* 62b)

Gazit chamber in the Temple
In the chamber of the Temple called Gazit, was the seat of the Great Sanhedrin. (*Middot* 5:4)

Geese   אווז בית ואווז בר
Domestic and wild goose (*Bechorot* 8a; *Bava Kamma* 55a)

Gehinom
Giving charity to the poor saves a person from the punishment of the Gehinom. (*Bava Batra* 10a)

Gehinom
R. Shimon b. Lachish said: "There is no Gehinom in the World to Come, but Hashem brings out the sun from its sheath and the wicked are punished by it, while

---

107. See entry, Absent from home.

the righteous are healed by it." (*Avodah Zarah* 3b)

Gemara
Learning Gemara is like singing a song. (*Avodah Zarah* 32b; *Shabbat* 106b, 113a; *Betzah* 24a)

Gemara
The Talmud is called Gemara. Our rabbis have taught: there can be nothing more meritorious than learning Gemara. (*Bava Metzia* 33a)

Gemara concluded
R. Yehuda HaNasi and R. Nathan concluded the Mishna; R. Ashi and Ravina concluded the Horaah (Gemara). Rashi notes that prior to them, there was no particular order to the teachings of the Mishna. (*Bava Metzia* 86a)

Gematria   גימטריא
Numerical value of Hebrew letters (*Shabbat* 10b)

Genealogical classes of people
Ten genealogical classes of people came up from Babylon. (*Kiddushin* 69a)

Genealogical records
R. Shimon b. Azzai said: "I found a roll of genealogical records in Jerusalem and therein was written, 'So and so is a bastard, having been born from a forbidden union with a married woman.' In the record was also written 'The teaching of R. Eliezer b. Yaakov is small in quantity but thoroughly sifted.' In the records was also written 'Menashe killed Yeshayahu.'" (*Yevamot* 49b)

Genealogies
Rami b. R. Yuda declared: "Since the book of Genealogies was lost, the strength of the Sages has been weakened and the light of their eyes has been dimmed. (*Pesahim* 62b)

Genealogy
R. Yehuda HaNasi was a descendant of Shefatya b. Avital. Shefatya was David's son and Avital was David's wife. R. Hiyya was a descendant of Shimi, David's brother (*Ketubbot* 62b)

General and specific   כלל ופרט
Rabbi Yohanan stated that Rabbi Yishmael served and studied under Rabbi Nehunia b. HaKana, who expounded the Torah on the principles of generalization and specification and he also expounded by the same principles. R. Akiva who served R. Nahum Ish Gam Zu who expounded the whole Torah on the principle of amplification and limitation, also expounded the Torah as his teacher by the same principles. (*Shevuot* 26a; *Sotah* 16a)

General proposition
A general proposition needs specifications
As for instance: The Torah says that all firstborn are to be sanctified, but the Torah then specifies that it applies only to male animals. (*Bechorot* 19a)

General proposition followed
כלל ופרט אין בכלל אלא מה שבפרט
A general proposition followed by a specific instruction. In that case, the scope of the proposition is limited to that of the specific. This is one of the thirteen principles of R. Yishmael. (*Hullin* 88b; *Bechorot* 19a; *Bava Kamma* 54b, 62b, 64b; *Eruvin* 27b; *Nazir* 35b)

Generalization followed   כלל ופרט וכלל
Generalization followed by a specification, which was followed by another generalization.

It is one of the thirteen methods and principles of biblical interpretation by R. Yishmael. (*Bava Kamma* 54b, 62b, 64b; *Eruvin* 27b; *Nazir* 35b)

Generations of scholars

Parnach said it in the name of R. Yohanan: "If there are three generations of Torah scholars in the family, the Torah will never depart from that family." (*Bava Metzia* 85a)

◻✿ Generosity

On one occasion Rabbi Giddal was negotiating for a certain field, but in the meantime R. Abba bought the field. When R. Abba was made aware of it, he offered it as a gift to R. Giddal, but he refused to accept it as a gift, and R. Abba did not want it, because R. Giddal negotiated for it. And so no one took possession of the field, and it was called the Rabbis' Field.[108] (*Kiddushin* 59a)

✿ Generous above and beyond

Come and hear: There was a man who sold a plot of land to R. Papa. He needed the money to buy some oxen. Eventually he didn't need to buy the oxen. When R. Papa found out, he returned the land to the man. (*Ketubbot* 97a; *Berachot* 7a, 45b; *Bava Kamma* 99b; *Bava Matzia* 24b)

Geniva   גניבא

3rd – 4th centuries CE

Geniva was a close friend of R. Avina. When Geniva died, he left R. Avina an inheritance of 400 *zuz*.

R. Huna and R. Hisda were sitting together and Geniva was passing by. Said one to another: "Let us rise before him, since he is a learned man . . ." (*Gittin* 62a, 65b)

✿◻ Gentle as a reed

"A man should always be gentle as a reed and let him never be unyielding as the cedar."
R. Eleazar b. Shimon was coming home from the house of his teacher in Migdal Gedor. He was riding leisurely on his donkey by the riverside, and he was feeling happy and elated because he studied a lot of Torah. A man, who was very ugly-looking, was passing him, and he greeted him with: "Peace shall be upon you."

He did not return the greeting. Instead, he said to him:

"Raca, how ugly you are, are all your townspeople as ugly as you are?"

"I do not know," he answered, "but go and tell the craftsman who made me."

When R. Eleazar realized that he had done wrong, he dismounted from the donkey and bowed down before the stranger and said to him. "I am in your debt, please forgive me."

The man said: "I will not forgive you until you go to the craftsman who made me and you tell him. 'How ugly is the vessel which you have made.'"

They started walking and R. Eleazar was walking behind him until they reached the city where R. Eleazar lived. The townspeople came out and they greeted him with words: "Peace shall be upon you, Master and Teacher."

The man asked: "Whom are you addressing with those words?" They replied: "We are addressing the man walking behind you."

The man exclaimed: "If this man is a teacher, may there not be any more like him in Israel."

The people asked him, "Why?"

He replied: "He did to me such and such." They asked the man to forgive R. Eleazar, because he is a great scholar in the Torah.

The man replied, "For your sake I forgive him, but only on condition that he will never act again in the same manner." Soon afterwards R. Eleazar entered the Bet Midrash and delivered a speech on the subject. "A man should always be gentle as a reed and let him never be unyielding as the cedar." (*Taanit* 20a)

---

108. See entry, Rabbi's field.

Gentle like Hillel
Our rabbis taught: A person should always be gentle like Hillel and not impatient like Shammai. (*Shabbat* 30b)

Ger   גר
A convert making a contract with a Jew (*Bava Kamma* 49b)

✿ Get along with everyone
A favorite saying of Abbaye was, "A man should always be in fear of Heaven, strive to be on best terms with his fellow-men and his relatives, even with men of other religions in order that he may be beloved above and below and acceptable to his fellow creatures." (*Berachot* 17a)

✿ Get up early
Our rabbis have taught: one should get up early in the morning and eat breakfast – in the summer because of the heat, and in the winter because of the cold weather. (*Bava Kamma* 92b; *Pesahim* 112a)

Geviha Ben Pesisa   גביהא בן פסיסא
Pre-Tannaic personality
4th century BCE[109] (*Sanhedrin* 91a)

Geviha of Be-Katil   גביהא דבי כתיל
Amora from Babylonia
4th – 5th centuries CE (*Meilah* 10a; *Hullin* 64b)

Gezera   גזרה
A *gezera* against the Cuthites: R. Ammi and R. Assi and R. Avohu declared the Cuthites absolute heathens. (*Hullin* 6a)

Gezera Shava   גזירה שוה
Word analogy, similar words
It is one of the thirteen methods and principles of biblical interpretation of R. Yishmael (*Shabbat* 97a; *Pesahim* 66a)

---

109. See entry, Alexander the Macedonian king.

Gid Ha-Nasheh   גיד הנשה
There is a prohibition against eating the sciatic nerve.
  Gid ha-nasheh applies in the Land of Israel as well as outside Israel (*Hullin* 89b)

Giddal   גידל
Amora from Babylonia
3rd century CE (*Berachot* 49a)

Giddal bar Minyumi   גידל בר מניומי
Amora from Babylonia
3rd – 4th centuries CE (*Berachot* 49b)

Gift
When giving a gift to a friend, does he have to be notified first? (*Shabbat* 10b; *Betzah* 16a)

Gift giving
When giving a gift, one gives it with a good eye and a liberal spirit. (*Bava Batra* 53a, 65a, 71a)

✿ Gift not accepted
R. Eleazar would not accept a gift sent to him by the house of the Nasi. (*Hullin* 44b)

✿ Gift not accepted
Whenever R. Zera was sent a gift, he would not accept it. (*Hullin* 44b)

✿ Gifts, do not offer
R. Meir said: "Do not offer gifts to your friend when you know that he will not accept." (*Hullin* 94a)

📖 Gifts of movable property
A man from Meron came to Jerusalem; he had with him much movable wealth and he wanted to give it away as gifts. He was told, however, that movable property cannot be given away unless it is given away at the same time with land. He bought a rocky piece of land near Jerusalem and gave the following instructions: "The northern side I give to one and with it 100

sheep and 100 casks; the southern side I give to the other one with 100 sheep and 100 casks. When he died, the rabbis carried out his instructions." (*Bava Batra* 156b)

Gifts to Kohanim
Twenty-four gifts were granted to the priests (*Bava Kamma* 110b; *Hullin* 133b)

Gilgal   גלגל
The Tabernacle was in Gilgal for fourteen years. (*Zevachim* 112b; *Bechorot* 4b; *Megillah* 10a)

Gilgul Shevuah   גלגל שבועה
A rollover oath; if by chance an oath is imposed on a person in another lawsuit in a dispute with the same persons, the court makes him swear also in another case. (*Shevuot* 45a, 48b)

Ginzak
R. Akiva visited Ginzak and was asked several questions. (*Avodah Zarah* 34a)

Girdle of the High Priest (*Hullin* 138a)

✡ Give honor
To your colleagues
Our rabbis taught: When R. Eliezer fell ill, his students came to visit him. They said to him: "Teach us the way of life so that we should merit the World to Come." He advised them: "Give honor to your colleagues, keep your children from nonsense, and place them between the knees of scholars. When you pray, know before Whom you are standing. In this way, you will merit the World to Come." (*Berachot* 28b)

Giving up ever recovering item   מייאש
The owner of the object gave up on recovering it. (*Avodah Zarah* 43a)

Givon   גבעון
The Tabernacle was moved from Shiloh to Givon. (*Zevahim* 112b; *Bechorot* 4b; *Megillah* 10a)

Glassware
Pure or impure (*Shabbat* 15b)

Glassware
Objects of glass, flat or hollowed, mirrors with regards to uncleanness (*Kelim* 30:1, 2, 3, 4)

Glory of the Law
The Talmud says: "When Rabbi Akiva died, the glory of the Law came to an end." (*Sotah* 49a)

Glory of the Law
The Talmud states that when Rabban Gamliel the Elder died, the glory of the Law ceased. (*Sotah* 49a)

✡ Glutton
R. Huna b. Nathan said: "He who drinks his cup in one gulp is considered to be a glutton; in two gulps, shows good breeding; in three gulps, shows arrogance." (*Pesahim* 86b)

Goat
Jumping goat causing damage (*Bava Kamma* 21b)

Goat
A goat was providing warm milk for a sick *Hasid*. (*Bava Kamma* 80a; *Temurah* 15b)

Goats and bears
R. Hanina b. Dosa: His goats brought in bears on their horns. (*Bava Metzia* 106a; *Taanit* 65a)

Goat ate the dough
A woman entered the house of a neighbor to bake bread; the goat of the owner

ate the dough, got sick, and died. (*Bava Kamma* 48a)

God conferred favors
One of R. Hanania b. Akashia's well-known sayings is "God was pleased to confer favors on Israel; therefore, He multiplied for them His commandments, for which they will be rewarded." This passage is usually recited at the end of a learning session. (*Makkot* 23b)

God favors Israel
R. Avira was sometimes quoting R. Ammi and sometimes R. Assi: "The Angels said to God, 'Master of the Universe, it is written in Your Torah "He does not favor one person over the other and does not take bribes," but You do favor the Jewish people?' God's answer to the angels was: 'How could I not favor them? I wrote in my Torah "Eat, be satisfied and bless your God," and they are so meticulous that they bless God even on a quantity of an olive or an egg.'" (*Berachot* 20b)

God is in heaven
Children were asked, where is God
Abbaye and Rava were sitting before Rabbah when they were still young boys. Rabbah wanted to test them and he asked them: "To whom do we say the benedictions?" They both answered, "To God." "And where is God?" Rava pointed to the roof, and Abbaye went outside and pointed to the sky. Rabbah said to them, "Both of you will become rabbis." (*Berachot* 48a)

God laments for his children
R. Yitzhak b. Shemuel said in the name of Rav: "The night has three watches, and at each watch the Holy One sits, roars like a lion, and laments: 'Woe to my children; on account of their sins, I have destroyed My house, and burnt My Temple, and exiled them among the nations of the world.'" (*Berachot* 3a)

God provides
For every individual according to his habits
A man once came to Rava and applied for support.

Rava asked him: "What do your meals consist of?"

"They consist of fat chicken and old wine."

"Did you consider the burden of the community," asked Rava.

"Am I eating of theirs?" asked the man. "I am eating the food of God, Who provides for every individual according to his habits."

In the meantime, the Rava's sister, whom he had not seen for thirteen years, arrived. She brought with her a fat chicken and old wine.

"What a remarkable incident," said Rava. "I apologize. Come and eat." (*Ketubbot* 67b)

God's Tefillin
R. Avin b. R. Adda said in the name of R. Yitzhak: "How do we know that Hashem puts on *tefillin*? We know it from a passage in Yeshaya 62:8." (*Berachot* 6a)

God's will
R. Gamliel said: "Make His will your will so that He will treat your will as if it was His will." (*Avot* 2:4)

God would not ask the impossible
Once a Tzadoki saw Rava engrossed in his studies, and Rava was completely unaware that his finger was under his foot bleeding.

"You are irrational people," declared the Tzadoki. "You consented to do at Mount Sinai with your mouth before you heard what was expected of you."

Rava answered him: "We are a people of

integrity and we trusted that God would not ask us to do what was impossible." (*Shabbat* 88a; *Ketubbot* 112a)

Gog U'Magog   גוג ומגוג
R. Hanan b. Tahlifa sent word to R. Yosef: "I met a man who had a scroll of ancient writing which he found in Rome. It is written there that 4,231 years after creation, the world will be in great distress. After that, there will be wars with the great sea monsters and the wars of Gog U'Magog." (*Sanhedrin* 97b)

Gog U'Magog   גוג ומגוג
The wars of Gog U'Magog (*Avodah Zarah* 3b *Sanhedrin* 95b; *Berachot* 13a)

Gold and silver
Monetary exchanges of gold, silver and coins of monetary value (*Bava Metzia* 44a)

📖 Golden dishes of the queen defiled
Rav Yehuda said in Rav's name: "Once Queen Shal-Zion[110] made a banquet for her son, and all her utensils became defiled. She ordered[111] all her golden dishes to be melted down and new ones to be made of the molten gold." (*Shabbat* 16b)

Golel V'dofek   גולל ודופק
Stone covering the grave (*Hullin* 72a)

Gomel
The *Gomel* prayer is to be recited when crossing the sea or when one had a bad accident and managed to recuperate. (*Berachot* 54b)

Gomlin   גומלין
Showing partiality (*Avodah Zarah* 61b; *Ketubbot* 24a)

---

110. Salome Alexandra.
111. Probably on the advice of her brother R. Shimon b. Shetah.

✡ Good advice
Rabbi Hillel said: "The more Torah, the more life; the more thought, the more wisdom; the more counsel, the more understanding; the more righteousness, the more peace." (*Avot* 2:8)

Good deed
R. Shemuel b. Nahmeni said in the name of R. Yonatan: "Every good deed that one does in this world, proecedes that person to the World to Come (*Avodah Zarah* 5a; *Sotah* 3b)

Good deeds
R. Yohanan said in the name of R. Shimon b. Yohai: "Whoever studies Torah and does work of charity will be worthy of the inheritance of two tribes." (*Bava Kamma* 17a; *Avodah Zarah* 5b)

✡ Good deeds
R. Yehuda b. Shila said in the name of R. Assi in the name of R. Yohanan: "There are six good deeds from which one can derive benefits in this world and still get the rewards in the World to Come: hospitality to guests, visiting the sick, concentration during prayer, rising early for prayer, bringing up a son with Torah study. and to judge everyone as being upright." (*Shabbat* 127a)

Good in the Ten Commandments
The word "good" טוב appears only in the Ten Commandments of *Devarim*, but not in Shemot. (*Bava Kamma* 54b)

✡📖 Good manners
R. Huna b. Nathan, who was the Resh Galuta (the Exilarch) visited the home of R. Nahman b. Yitzhak.
    They asked him: "What is your name?"
    "Rav Huna."
    "Would you sit down?" He sat down. They offered him a cup to drink and he

accepted it without hesitation, but drank from it twice.

They asked him: "What is the reason you called yourself Rav Huna?"

"That is my name."

"What is the reason you sat down when asked?"

"Whatever the host asks, one should do." "What is the reason you accepted the drink on the first offering?"

"One must not show reluctance to a great man."

"Why did you drink twice?"

"He who drinks his cup in one gulp is considered to be a glutton; in two gulps, shows good breeding; in three gulps, shows arrogance." (*Pesahim* 86b)

Gored

A person entered someone else's court, without permission and was gored by an ox. (*Bava Kamma* 23b)

Gorion Asporak

There was a discussion between the rabbis about a product that was changed – for example, wheat becoming flour. Is that product still under the same prohibition? R. Yosef said: "R. Gorion Asporak learned that it is in dispute between Shammai and Hillel." (*Bava Kamma* 65b)

Government

The intricacies of government are so complex and very difficult to describe. (*Shabbat* 11a)

✿ Government
Beware of authorities

R. Gamliel said: "Beware of the authorities, for they befriend people only for their own benefit. They act friendly when it benefits them, but are not there when one needs them." (*Avot* 2:3)

Grace after a Meal

The format for ברכת המזון (*Berachot* 48b)

Grace after a Meal

The ברכת המזון is a Torah commandment. (*Berachot* 48b)

Grace after a Meal ברכת המזון

The authors of blessings after a meal (*Berachot* 48b)

Grace after a Meal

The mention of the *Brit*, Torah, and the Kingdom of David must be included in *Birkat Hamazon*. (*Berachot* 49b)

✿ Gracious

One of Abba Shaul's statements was that "One should strive to be gracious and merciful – as God is gracious and merciful." (*Shabbat* 133b)

Grains kosher for Pesach (*Pesahim* 35a)

Granted אי אמרת בשלמא

I grant you if you were to say (*Yoma* 17b)

Graves in a cave

(*Bava Batra* 100b, 101a–b, 102a)

✿ Grave is no escape

R. Eliezer HaKappar said: "The newborn are destined to die, the dead will live again, and the living will be judged. Know that everything is according to the reckoning. Let not your evil inclination mislead you that your grave will be an escape for you. You were created against your will; you were born against your will. Against your will you live, against your will you will die, and against your will you are destined to give an account before the King of Kings." (*Avot* 4:29)

Grave marking[112] (*Bava Metzia* 85b)

Grave of R. Huna
When R. Huna passed away, they brought his coffin to Tiberias, Israel, and they buried him next to R. Hiyya and his two sons: R. Yehuda and R. Hezkiya. (*Moed Katan* 25a)

Gravedigger's observation
It was taught, Abba Shaul stated: "I was once a gravedigger and I made a practice of carefully observing the bones of the dead. The bones of one who drinks undiluted wine are burned; the bones of one who drinks diluted wine excessively are dry, and those who drink wine properly mixed are full of marrow. The bones of a person whose drinking exceeds his eating are burned; the bones of one whose eating exceeds his drinking are dry, and those who eat and drink in a proper manner are full of marrow." (*Niddah* 24b)

Great Academy of Sura
The Talmud states that when the majority of the rabbis departed from the academy of Rav in Sura there still remained behind 1,200 students. When the students left the academy of R. Huna in Sura, there remained behind 800 students.[113] (*Ketubbot* 106a)

Great assembly
The Talmud refers to R. Shimon HaTzaddik as one of the last survivors of the Great Assembly. (*Avot* 1:2)

Great man
R. Assi said: "I received an explanation from a great man, to wit, R. Yosi b. Hanina." (*Bava Kamma* 42b)

Great man
Rava in his conversation with R. Nahman praised R. Aha b. Yaakov as a great man. He said to him: "When you meet him, bring him to me." (*Bava Kamma* 40a)

Great men
Torah learning and high office in one man
R. Adda b. Ahava stated: "From R. Yehuda HaNasi until R. Ashi, we do not find Torah learning and high office in one person. (*Sanhedrin* 36a)

Great mind
Rabbi Abba b. Hanina said: "In the generation of Rabbi Meir, there was none equal to him; then why was not the Halachah fixed in agreement with his views, because his colleagues could not fathom the depth of his mind." (*Eruvin* 13b, 53a)

Great person dies, another is born
The Talmud states: "The day when R. Akiva died, Rebbe was born; when Rebbe died, Rav Yehuda was born; when Rav Yehuda died. Rava was born; when Rava died, R. Ashi was born. This teaches that when a rightrous man dies another righteous man is born." (*Kiddushin* 72b; *Yoma* 38b)

Great respect for each other
Rav and Shemuel and R. Assi once met at a *Brit*, some say it was a *Pidyon Haben*. Rav did not want to enter before Shemuel and Shemuel did not want to enter before R. Assi. Finally it was decided that Rav and R. Assi would enter together first and Shemuel would enter last. (*Bava Kamna* 80a; *Gittin* 6a)

Great respect[114] (*Shevuot* 48b)

Great scholar[115] (*Bava Kamma* 117a)

---

112. See story under, Bat Kol.
113. See entry, Academies.

114. See entry, Abrogate a ruling.
115. See entry, Fleeing from Babylonia.

Great scholar
R. Eliezer b. Horkynos
Rabbi Yohanan ben Zakkai had a very high opinion of R. Eliezer b. Horkynos. He said, "If all the scholars of Israel were to be put in one side of the scale, and Rabbi Eliezer in the other, he would outweigh them all" (*Avot* 2:8).

Great tall man
Has come to Nehardea
Rav was told: "A great, tall and lame man has come to Nehardea and has lectured."

Rav remarked: "Who is great, tall and lame? It must be Levi, and it seems to me that R. Afes must have died and R. Hanina b. Hama became head of the academy in Eretz Yisrael. Consequently, R. Levi lost his study companion, for he used to study with R. Hanina. (*Shabbat* 59b)

Great teacher dies
When Rav died, his students accompanied his bier. After they returned, they said: "Let us eat a meal at the river Danak."

After they finished eating, they discussed a question of Halachah with regards to the blessing after a meal, for which they did not know the answer. R. Adda b. Ahava stood up and tore his garment from front to back and tore it once more and said:

"Our teacher Rav is dead and we have not learned the rules for the blessings after the meal!"

Finally, an old man solved their problem. (*Berachot* 42b)

📖 Grecian wisdom
R. Yehuda said that R. Shemuel stated in the name of R. Shimon b. Gamliel: "A thousand youth were in my father's house; 500 of them learned Torah and 500 learned Grecian wisdom." (*Bava Kamma* 83a; *Sotah* 49b; *Gittin* 58a)

Grecian wisdom
Ben Damma, the son of R. Yishmael's sister, once asked R. Yishmael a question. "A person like me who studied the whole Torah, may I study Greek wisdom?" His answer was, "If you can find time that is neither day nor night, then you can study Greek." (*Menahot* 99b)

Greece ruled in Eretz Yisrael
R. Yosi b. Halafta said: "Greece ruled in Eretz Yisrael 180 years during the existence of the Temple." (*Avodah Zarah* 9a)

✿ Greed
Eliezer HaKappar said: "Envy, greed, and chasing after honors take a man out of this world" (*Avot* 4:21).

Greek language
Rebbe said: "Why use the Syrian language in Eretz Yisrael? Use either *Lashon HaKodesh* or Greek." (*Bava Kamma* 83a)

✿ Greeting everyone first
Greeting first; Jews and Gentiles alike
R. Hisda conducted himself in a humble way, and went out of his way to greet everyone first in the marketplace, Jews or gentiles alike. (*Gittin* 62a)

✿ Greeting everyone first
It was related that no one was able to greet Rabbi Yohanan ben Zakkai first, because he was always greeting everyone first, even non-Jews. (*Berachot* 17a)

✿ Greeting everyone first
R. Matya b. Heresh said: "Be first to greet everyone with a salutation of peace." (*Avot* 4:15)

Greeting friends before praying
(*Berachot* 14a)

✿ Greeting people

R. Helbo said in the name of Rav Huna: "If one knows that his friend is used to greeting him, let him greet him first." (*Berachot* 6b)

Greeting people in a bathhouse

(*Shabbat* 10a)

✿ Greetings to a lender

To extend greetings to someone who lent you money is a form of paying interest with words. This is so if otherwise he does not greet him. (*Bava Metzia* 75b)

📖 Grief-stricken

R. Yohanan was grief-stricken when Resh Lakish died

When R. Shimon b. Lakish died, R. Yohanan became grief-stricken. The rabbis sent R. Eleazar b. Pedat to comfort him.

"You are no replacement for Resh Lakish," he complained. "When I stated a law, Resh Lakish raised twenty-four objections, to which I gave twenty-four answers. It led to a fuller understanding of the law. While you tell me that a Beraita supports me.[116] Do I not know myself that what I said is correct?" (*Bava Metzia* 84a)

📖 Grievance

Against Rava

R. Yosef had a grievance against Rava b. Yosef b. Hama and he felt hurt. A day before Yom Kippur, Rava went To R. Yosef to apologize. He found his attendant mixing him a cup of wine. R. Yosef was blind in his later years. Rava said to the attendant: "Give it to me and I will mix it." When R. Yosef tasted the wine, he said: "This mix of wine tastes like Rava used to mix it."

"I am here, Rava responded."

R. Yosef said to him: "Do not sit down until you interpret to me a Scriptural passage." (*Eruvin* 54a)

Grounds needed for intercalation

What are the grounds that can be used to intercalate the year (*Sanhedrin* 11a)

Guarantors   כל ישראל ערבים זה בזה

All Israel are guarantors one for another. (*Shevuot* 39a; *Sanhedrin* 27b)

Guard my tongue   נצור לשוני

Mar b. R. Avina used to finish the *Amidah* with a special prayer: "Keep my tongue from evil and my lips from speaking falsehood. May I be silent for those who curse me, and may I be to them like dust. Open my heart to Torah, and may I pursue your commandments . . .". Most congregations have adopted this prayer and they recite it at the conclusion of the *Amidah*. (*Berachot* 17a; *Yoma* 16b)

Guardians

There are four kinds of guardians: paid and unpaid guardians, borrower and renter. (*Bava Metzia* 93a; *Shevuot* 49a)

Guarding wine with one seal (*Avodah Zarah* 31a)

Guarding wine with two seals (*Avodah Zarah* 31a)

Gud Ahit   גוד אחית

A wall or partition that does not reach the ground is deemed as continuing downward and touching the ground. (*Eruvin* 87a)

Gud Asik   גוד אסיק

A wall or partition that does not reach the ceiling is deemed as continuing upward and touching the ceiling. (*Sukkah* 4b; *Eruvin* 89a)

---

116. See entry, Resh Lakish dies.

Guesswork, estimation   אמדות
(*Avot* 1:16)

📖 Guest
Rabbi Yitzhak was a guest at Rabbi Nahman. When he was about to leave, he asked him: "Please bless me."

Rabbi Yitzhak told him a story about a traveler and gave him this blessing: "God should bless your children[117] to be also like you." (*Taanit* 5b)

Guest
Is a guest obligated to light Chanukah candles? (*Shabbat* 23a)

Guilt offering of Hasidim
R. Eliezer said: "One may donate a suspensive guilt offering on any day and at any hour he desires. This is called the guilt offering of the Hasidim." (*Keritot* 25a)

Guilt offering
The Talmud relates that Rabbi Bava ben Buta used to offer a suspenseful guilt offering every day, except the day after Yom Kippur. (*Keritot* 25a)

✿ Guilt and innocence of litigants
R. Yehuda b. Tabbai said: "Act not the part of an advocate when you are a judge, and when the parties stand before you, consider them in your eyes as guilty, and when they leave regard both of them as innocent." (*Avot* 1:8)

Gurion Me'Aspurak
Amora 3rd century CE (*Bava Kamma* 65b, 94a)

H

Habit to touch purse
R. Yitzhak said: A person usually touches his purse frequently. (*Bava Metzia* 21b)

Hacham   חכם
Hacham was a title given to the leader in the academy next to the Nasi. When Rebbe was nearing his death, he told his attendants, "I would like to speak to my younger son." R. Shimon came in and Rebbe instructed him in the rules and regulations of being a Hacham. (*Ketubbot* 103b)

Hadas stolen
Is a stolen *hadas* fit for performing the mitzvah? (*Sukkah* 34b)

Hadassim on Sukkot
Regular prices for myrtle
Shemuel said to the merchants: "Sell the *hadassim* (myrtle) during Sukkot at regular prices. Otherwise, I will give a ruling to allow a lesser quality to be acceptable, like R. Tarfon, who was lenient regarding the myrtle." (*Sukkah* 34b)

📖 Hadrian prohibited ordination
Rabbi Yehuda became a martyr when he disobeyed the decree of the Roman authorities banning the ordination of rabbis. The decree issued by the authorities during the Hadrian persecution was that anyone who ordains a rabbi is subject to the death penalty, anyone who receives ordination is subject to the death penalty, the city where the ordination takes place is to be demolished, and the boundaries around the city are to be uprooted. In order to avoid the destruction of a city, Rabbi Yehuda b. Bava sat between two great mountains[118] and between the two

---

117. See entry, Blessing by a Sage.

118. See Martyrdom.

cities of Usha and Shefaram and ordained the rabbis. (*Sanhedrin* 14a)

Hadrianic coins (*Avodah Zarah* 52b)

Hadrianic earthenware (*Avodah Zarah* 32a)

Haggai   חגא
Amora from Eretz Yisrael
  3rd – 4th centuries CE (*Bava Batra* 19b)

Hagvash   חג״בש
חלב גבינה בצלים שחלים
After bloodletting, one should not eat milk, cheese, onions, and pepper. (*Avodah Zarah* 29a)

Ha-Hodesh Ha-Zeh   החדש הזה
When do they read *Parshat Ha-Hodesh Ha-Zeh*? (*Megillah* 29a)

Haircut
Can one get a haircut on Hol Hamoed? (*Moed Katan* 13b)

📖 Haircut
Similar to one worn by the High Priest
The son-in-law of Rebbe was Ben Eleasa. Rebbe was asked: "What kind of a haircut did the High Priest wear?" Rebbe answered; "Go and look at the haircut of my son-in-law Eleasa." It has been taught that R. Eleasa did not splurge his money for anything, but he spent money to learn the style of haircut the High Priest used to have. He did it to display and teach the style of haircut the High Priest had. (*Sanhedrin* 22b)

Haircut
Before praying (*Shabbat* 9b)

Halachah
R. Yohanan maintains that the Halachah is like the anonymous Mishna. (*Bava Kamma* 29b; *Shabbat* 46a)

Halachah
Halachah derived from learning or from actual cases. (*Bava Batra* 130b)

Halachah
Rabbah bar b. Hana said in the name of R. Yohanan: Wherever R. Shimon b. Gamliel's view is taught in the Mishna, the Halachah is according to him, except in several cases. (*Sanhedrin* 31a–b; *Gittin* 38a; *Bava Kamma* 69a; *Bava Batra* 174a; *Ketubbot* 77a; *Bava Metzia* 38a; *Bechorot* 24a)

Halachah
Rava said to R. Papa and to R. Huna b. Yehoshua: "When one of my legal decisions comes before you in writing and you have objections to it, do not tear it up before you have spoken to me. If I have a valid reason, I will explain it to you and if not, I will withdraw it. After my death, you shall neither tear it up nor infer any Halachah from it. Had I been alive, I might have given you a reason for it." (*Bava Batra* 130b)

Halachah according to Rav
Rabbah followed the Halachah according to Rav except in three cases where he followed them according to Shemuel. (*Shabbat* 22a, 40a; *Pesahim* 101a)

Halachah according to Rava
The Halachah is according to Rava except in six cases where they are according to Abbaye as indicated by an acronym in the Talmud. (*Bava Metzia* 22b; *Sanhedrin* 27a)

Halachah differs from written
R. Yohanan said in the name of R. Yishmael: "In three places, the Halachah is different from the scriptural text." (*Sotah* 16a)

Halachah disagreement between rabbis
R. Yaakov and R. Zerika said: "Whenever R. Akiva and one of his colleagues

are in disagreement, the Halachah is in accordance to R. Akiva. When R. Yosi is in disagreement with his colleagues, the Halachah is with R. Yosi. Between R. Yehuda HaNasi and one of his colleagues, the Halachah is like Rebbe." What practical difference does it make? R. Assi said: "general Halachah." R. Hiyya b. Abba said: "We are leaning in their favor." R. Yosi b. Hanina said: "They are seen as acceptable views."

R. Yaakov b. Idi said in the name of R. Yohanan: "In a dispute between R. Meir and R. Yehuda, the Halachah is like R. Yehuda; a dispute between R. Yehuda and R. Yosi, the Halachah is like R. Yosi, and needless to say that a dispute between R. Meir and R. Yosi, the Halachah is like R. Yosi."

R. Assi said: "I also learn that in a dispute between R. Yosi and R. Shimon, the Halachah is like R. Yosi."

R. Abba said in the name of R. Yohanan: "In a dispute between R. Yehuda and R. Shimon, the Halachah is like R. Yehuda. A dispute between R. Meir and R. Shimon was left unresolved." (*Eruvin* 46b; *Ketubbot* 84b, 51a; *Pesahim* 27a; *Bava Batra* 124b)

☐ Halachah forgotten
On one occasion, the fourteenth of Nisan fell on the Shabbat and the Bnei Betera, the rabbis who headed the Sanhedrin, did not remember whether the slaughter of the Paschal lamb overrides the Shabbat.[119] (*Pesahim* 66a)

Halachah is as given to Moshe on Sinai
הלכה למשה מסיני
It is a command by Moshe from Sinai. (*Kiddushin* 38b)

☐ Halachah or Aggadata
The Talmud relates that when R. Ammi and R. Assi were sitting before R. Yitzhak Nepaha, one of them said to him: "Would you please tell us some Halachah?" The other one said: "Would you please tell us some Aggadata?"[120] (*Bava Kamma* 60b)

Halachah questions
Halachah questions may be answered by a student only by his teacher's permission.

When Rabbah b. Hana was about to move to Babylonia, R. Hiyya, his uncle, said to Rebbe: "My brother's son is going to Babylonia. May he decide in ritual law, in monetary cases?" Rebbe answered in the affirmative. "May he declare firstborn animals fit for slaughter?" Rebbe answered, "He may."

When Rav was about to move to Babylonia, R. Hiyya, his uncle, said to Rebbe: "My sister's son is going to Babylonia. May he decide in ritual law?" "He may." "May he decide in monetary cases?" "He may." "May he declare firstborn animals fit for slaughter?" Rebbe answered: "He may not." (*Sanhedrin* 5a)

Halachic decision under influence
R. Yehuda b. Yehezkel said in the name of R. Shemuel: "He who has drunk a quarter of a log of wine should not render a halachic decision. (*Eruvin* 64a; *Ketubbot* 10b; *Nazir* 38a; *Sanhedrin* 42a)

☐ Halachic differences
Rabbi Eliezer had halachic differences with the rabbis. He brought forth every argument to prove his point, but the rabbis did not accept them. He declared: "If the Halachah agrees with me, let this carob tree prove it."

He then said to them: "If I am right, then let the stream of water prove it." "If I am right, then let the walls of this school prove it."

---

119. See entry, Erev Pesach on Shabbat.

120. See also entry, Aggadata.

"If I am right, let the heavens prove it."
Thereupon a heavenly voice[121] came forth:
"The Halachah is like Rabbi Eliezer."
Rabbi Yehoshua spoke up and said: "The
Torah is not in heaven." Rabbi Yirmiyahu
arose and declared:

"The Torah has already been given on
Mount Sinai, it belongs here on earth
and we do not pay attention to heavenly
voices." He continued to say:

"It has been written in the Torah that
the majority decides."[122] (*Bava Metzia* 59b;
Berachot 19a; *Eruvin* 7a; *Pesahim* 114a; *Yevamot* 14a)

Halachot stated
Halachot were discussed and eighteen
halachot were established in the upper
chamber of Hanania b. Hezkiya b. Gurion
when they went to visit him. (*Shabbat* 13b)

Halafta   חלפתא
Tanna from Eretz Yisrael
1st – 2nd centuries CE (*Taanit* 15b)

Halafta
R. Yosi said: "When my father Halafta
went to study Torah with R. Yohanan b.
Nuri, the question of testimony by con-
flicting witnesses was discussed." (*Bava
Kamma* 70a; *Bava Batra* 56b)

Halafta ben Dosa   חלפתא בן דוסא
Halafta b. Dosa Ish Kefar Hanania
Tanna from Eretz Yisrael
2nd century CE (*Avot* 3:6)

Halafta ben Shaul   חלפתא בן שאול
Amora from Eretz Yisrael
3rd century CE (*Zevahim* 93b)

Half-servant and half-free
חציו עבד וחציו בן חורין
Half-servant and half-free man. The

servant belongs to two persons: one freed
the slave and the other not. (*Bava Kamma*
90a; *Bava Batra* 50a; *Eduyot* 3a)

Halitza   חליצה
When one brother dies childless, then one
of the remaining brothers must marry the
widow. However, if he refuses, he must
perform the ceremony of *halitza* in place
of *yibbum*; it also involves taking off the
shoe. (*Yevamot* 2a, 35b; *Sanhedrin* 49b)

Halitza   חליצה
How many judges must be present when
the commandment of *halitza* is performed? (*Yevamot* 101a; *Shabbat* 66a, 112a)

Halitza footwear
What kind of footwear is required to
perform the commandment of *halitza* is
discussed. (*Yevamot* 101a; *Shabbat* 66a, 112a)

Halitza ritual
Consultation with the Bet Din is required.
(*Yevamot* 106b; *Sanhedrin* 49b)

Halitza spit
When spitting at the ceremony of *hal-
itza* – what is required to make it valid?
(*Yevamot* 104a)

Hall of Israelites in the Temple
The Hall of Israelites was 135 cubits long
by 11 cubits wide. (*Middot* 2:6)

Hall of the Kohanim in the Temple
The Hall of the Kohanim was 135 cubits
long by 11 cubits wide. (*Middot* 2:6)

Hallel
The Psalms of *Hallel* should be included
in the prayers at certain times. (*Pesahim* 117a;
Taanit 28b)

Hallel
Hallel is not said on Purim. R. Nahman

---

121. Bat Kol.
122. See also entry, Bat Kol.

said: "The reason is that the Megillah reading is its *Hallel*. (*Arachin* 10b)

Hallel
Hallel was recited in the Temple during the Pesach offering. If they finished *Hallel*, they repeated it again for the second division, and if necessary, they repeated it again for the third division. (*Pesahim* 64a)

Hallel daily
R. Yosi said: "May my portion be among those who recite *Hallel* daily." The Talmud explains that R. Yosi means the six Psalms of the morning prayers. (*Shabbat* 118b)

Hallel reading time
When is the proper time to read the *Hallel*? (*Megillah* 20b)

Hallucination
If a person was overcome with hallucination, and during his state of hallucination, he declared: "Write me a *get* for my wife" (*Gittin* 67b)

Hama   חמא
Amora from Babylonia
Head of Academy in Pumbedita,
4th century CE (*Bava Batra* 7b)

Hama bar Bisa   חמא בר ביסא
Tanna from Eretz Yisrael,
2nd – 3rd centuries CE (*Bava Batra* 59a)

Hama bar Gurya   חמא בר גוריא
Amora from Babylonia
3rd – 4th centuries CE (*Shabbat* 10b)

Hama bar Hanina   חמא בר חנינא
Amora from Eretz Yisrael,
3rd century CE (*Berachot* 32b)

Haman's mother
R. Hanan b. Rava stated in Rav's name: "The name of Haman's mother was

Amathlai, and her father's name was Orabti (*Bava Batra* 91a)

Hamavdil
The blessing recited at the end of Shabbat. (*Berachot* 33a; *Shabbat* 111a, 150b; *Pesahim* 105b)

Hamavdil forgot
What if one forgot to say *Hamavdil* – the blessing at the end of Shabbat? (*Berachot* 26b)

Hametz
Selling *hametz* to a gentile (*Shabbat* 18b; *Pesahim* 21a)

Hametz of a non-Jew
Benefitting from *hametz* after Pesach that belongs to a non-Jew (*Pesahim* 28a; *Eruvin* 64b)

Hamnuna   המנונא
Amora from Babylonia
3rd century CE (*Bava Kamma* 106a; *Eruvin* 16b)

Hamnuna   המנונא
Amora from Babylonia
4th century CE (*Yevamot* 17a)

Hamnuna Zuta   המנונא זוטי
Amora from Babylonia
4th century CE (*Berachot* 31a)

Hana bar Bizna   חנא בר ביזנא
Amora from Babylonia
3rd – 4th centuries CE (*Berachot* 7a)

Hana bar Hanilai   חנא בר חנילאי
Amora from Babylonia
3rd century CE (*Berachot* 58b)

Hana bar Katina (*Bechorot* 37b)

Hana Cartigna
R. Dimi stated that R. Hona of Kartigna or some say R. Aha of Kartigna[123] related

---

123. 3rd century CE.

a case brought before R. Yehoshua b. Levi or some say a case before Rebbe. A child was testifying for his mother and on the strength of that testimony the mother was permitted to marry a Kohen. (*Bava Kamma* 114b; *Ketubbot* 27b)

Hana Tzippori (Sepphoris)
חנה בר ציפוראה

Amora from Eretz Yisrael
3rd – 4th centuries CE (*Rosh Hashana* 34b)

Hanan bar Rava
חנן בר רבא

Amora from Babylonia
3rd – 4th centuries CE (*Bava Batra* 91a; *Shabbat* 121 a–b)

Hanan ben Avishalom
חנן בן אבישלום

Tanna and judge from Eretz Yisrael
1st century CE (*Ketubbot* 104b)

Hanan HaMitzri
חנן המצרי

(*Hanan Egyptian*)
Tanna from Alexandria
2nd century CE (*Ketubbot* 105a)

Hanania

Hanania, Misha'el, and Azariah were thrown into the fiery furnace by the order of Nebuchadnezzar. (*Sanhedrin* 92b)

Hanania ben Ahi Yehoshua
חניא בן אחי יהושע

Tanna from Eretz Yisrael and Babylonia
1st – 2nd centuries CE (*Berachot* 63a)

Hanania ben Akashia
חניא בן עקשיא

Tanna from Eretz Yisrael
2nd century CE (*Makkot* 23b)

Hanania ben Akavia
חניא בן עקביא

Tanna from Eretz Yisrael
2nd century CE (*Ketubbot* 78a)

Hanania ben Hachinai
חניא בן הכינאי

(*Hannah b. Hachinai, Hanina*)
Tanna from Eretz Yisrael
2nd century CE (*Ketubbot* 62b)

Hanania ben Hezkiya
חניא בן חזקיה

The book of Yehezkel was almost hidden, because it seemed to contradict the words of the Torah. However, R. Hanania b. Hezkiya reconciled the differences. (*Shabbat* 13b; *Hagigah* 13b; *Menahot* 45a)

Hanania ben Hezkiya ben Guryon
חניא בן חזקיה בן גוריון

Tanna from Eretz Yisrael
1st century CE (*Shabbat* 13b)

Hanania ben Teradion (Hanina)

Tanna from Eretz Yisrael
Head of the academy in Sichnin
2nd century CE (*Sanhedrin* 32b)

Hand washing

Blessings for washing hands (*Berachot* 60b)

Handbreadths of a person
ידו של אדם חשובה לו כד' על ד'

A man's hand is equal to his four by four *tefahim*. (*Shabbat* 5a; *Ketubbot* 31b)

Handbreadths measurements

(*Kelim* 27:10–12)

Hands impurity (*Shabbat* 14b)

Hanging tree

Tree hanging over neighbor's field (*Bava Kamma* 82a; *Bava Batra* 27b)

Hanina

R. Hanina stated: "A mitzvah that was commanded or a mitzvah that was not commanded, but is done only of free will, the commanded one has a greater reward. (*Avodah Zarah* 3a; *Bava Kamma* 38a, 87a; *Kiddushin* 31a)

Hanina   חנינא
Amora from Eretz Yisrael
3rd – 4th centuries CE (*Menahot* 79b;
Yevamot 58b)

Hanina bar Avohu   חנינא בר אבהו
Amora from Eretz Yisrael
3rd – 4th centuries CE (*Kiddushin* 33b)

Hanina bar Hama   חנינא בר חמא
Tanna and Amora from Eretz Yisrael
Head of the academy in Sepphoris
3rd century CE (*Ketubbot* 103b)

Hanina bar Papa   חנינא בר פפא
Amora from Eretz Yisrael
3rd – 4th centuries CE (*Kiddushin* 81a)

Hanina ben Antigonus   חנינא בן אנטיגנוס
Tanna from Eretz Yisrael
2nd century CE (*Bechorot* 38b)

Hanina ben Dosa   חנינא בן דוסא
Tanna from Eretz Yisrael
1st century CE (*Berachot* 34b)

Hanina ben Dosa
R. Hanina's prayers were usually answered.[124] (*Bava Kamma* 50a; *Berachot* 34b)

Hanina ben Dosa
Since R. Hanina b. Dosa died, men of
great deeds ceased to exist. (*Sotah* 49a)

Hanina ben Dosa
R. Yehuda said in the name of Rav: "Every
day a Bat Kol goes forth and proclaims:
'The whole world is fed only in the merit
of my son R. Hanina, while my son
Hanina is satisfied with a little carob fruit
from one Shabbat to the next. (*Hullin* 86a;
Taanit 24b; *Berachot* 17b)

Hanina ben Dosa
It happened that the daughter of Nehu-
nia, the digger of wells, fell into a deep pit.
When the people informed R. Hanina b.
Dosa, he told them during the first hour:
"She is well." In the second hour, he said
again: "She is well." In the third hour, he
said: "She is out of the pit."

They asked her: "Who brought you up
from the pit?"

She answered: "A ram helped me and an
old man was leading the ram."

They asked R. Hanina b. Dosa: "Are you
a prophet?"

He answered: "I am neither a prophet
nor the son of a prophet." (*Bava Kamma* 50a;
Shekalim 8b; *Yevamot* 121b)

📖 Hanina ben Dosa prayed
It happened that on one occasion Rabbi
Hanina ben Dosa went to study at Rabbi
Yohanan ben Zakkai in Arav. While he
was there, Rabbi Yohanan's child fell
gravely ill. He said to him, "Hanina, my
son, pray for him that he may live."

Rabbi Hanina put his head between his
knees and prayed for the recovery of the
child, and the child recovered. Said R.
Yohanan ben Zakkai: "If Ben Zakkai had
stuck his head between his knees all day
long they would not have noticed me." His
wife said to him: "Is Chanina greater than
you are?"

"No, but he is like a servant before the
king, – who has permission to enter any-
time – I am like a nobleman before a king."
(*Berachot* 34b)

Hanina ben Gamliel   חנינא בן גמליאל
Tanna from Eretz Yisrael
2nd century CE (*Moed Katan* 23a)

Hanina Hozaa
R. Hanina was from a town in Babylonia
called Hozaa. (*Avodah Zarah* 41b)

---

124. See story, Power of prayers.

Hanina Segan HaKohanim
חנינא סגן הכהנים
Tanna from Eretz Yisrael
1st century CE (*Avot* 3:2)

📖 Hardship
Hardship in the cave brought also benfits
Rabbi Shimon ben Yohai had to flee from the Roman authorities. He hid in a cave for thirteen years. When he came out of the cave, his son-in-law, Rabbi Pinhas ben Yair, went to meet him. He took him into the bath and massaged his body. Seeing the lumps in his body, he cried with tears running down from his eyes.

"Woe to me that I see you in such condition."

"No," he replied, "happy are you that you see me thus." Because before the cave experience, Rabbi Shimon would ask a question and Rabbi Pinhas would have thirteen answers, but now when Rabbi Pinhas raised a question, Rabbi Shimon had twenty-four answers. (*Shabbat* 33b)

✿ Hardship the community can't endure
Imposing a hardship on the community which the majority could not endure.[125]

The rabbis relied upon the words of R. Shimon ben Gamliel and R. Eleazar b. Tzadok who said: "No law may be imposed upon the public unless a majority can endure it." (*Horayot* 3b; *Bava Batra* 60b)

Harlot's hire
אתנן זונה
Money received by a harlot for her service (*Temurah* 29a)

Haroset
A specially mixed food eaten at the Seder (*Pesahim* 114a)

Haroset
No flour may be put into the *haroset*. (*Pesahim* 40b)

Harp over David's bed
R. Aha b. Bizna said in the name of R. Shimon Hasida: "A harp hung over David's bed and at midnight a northerly wind blew the strings of the harp and it began to play. David arose and studied Torah until dawn." (*Sanhedrin* 16a)

📖 Hashem's favorite
R. Shimon b. Shetah called Honi HaMaagel Hashem's favorite
Rabbi Shimon ben Shetah sent this message to Honi HaMaagel: "You deserve to be excommunicated for the things you do, and if you weren't Honi haMaagel, I would pronounce you excommunicated. But what can I do, since you are a favorite of Hashem? He accedes to your wishes, and you are like a son who is favored by his father." (*Berachot* 19a; *Taanit* 19a)

Hasid
חסיד
A man was very sick; the doctors prescribed warm goat milk. (*Bava Kamma* 80a; *Temurah* 15b)

✿ Hasid
The rabbis taught: One who invests the money of orphans at risk to the orphans, but no risk to himself, is called a wicked man, and one who invests the money of orphans in which the orphans will receive profits only and will not share in the losses, is called a pious man, and one who invests to share both in profits and losses is an average person. (*Bava Metzia* 70a)

Hasid
Wherever the Talmud says: "It once happened to a Chasid," it refers to either R. Yehuda b. Baba or R. Yehuda b. Illai. (*Bava Kamma* 103b; *Temurah* 15b)

---

125. See also entry, Ascetics.

Hasidim

The early *hasidim* used to hide their thorns deep in the ground. (*Bava Kamma* 30a)

Hasidim

The hasidim of former generations hid their broken glasses in the ground. (*Bava Kamma* 30a)

📖 Hasid's rebuke

Once a man was throwing stuff from his property into the public street. A hasid came by and said to him: "Fool, why do you throw stones from a property that is not yours to the property that is yours?" The man laughed at him. In years to come, the man had to sell his property and he walked on that public street and stumbled on the stones he had thrown. He said how well the hasid had spoken. (*Bava Kamma* 50b)

📖 Hasmonean family

The entire Hasmonean family was killed by Herod

King Herod wiped out the entire Hasmonean family, except one girl. Herod wanted to marry her, but she did not want to be his wife. She went up on the roof and called out: "Whoever claims to be from the Hasmonean family is a slave, since I alone am left from that family and I am throwing myself down from the roof." After she was dead, Herod preserved her body in honey for seven years. (*Bava Batra* 3b–4a)

📖 Hasmonean House divided

When the two brothers, Hyrcanus and Aristobulus of the Hasmonean House, were contending for the crown, war broke out between them. Hyrcanus was outside the city wall and Aristobulus was within the city of Jerusalem. They had no animals inside the city for sacrifices. Those on the inside lowered down buckets with money inside and in return they received cattle for the sacrifices. An old man advised the besiegers: "As long as they have sacrifices, they will not surrender." The next day when the bucket came down with the money, they sent up a swine. It was proclaimed on that occasion: "Cursed be the man who breeds swine."[126] (*Sotah* 49b; *Bava Kamma* 82b)

Hasmonean rule in Israel

R. Yishmael b. Yosi b. Halafta was ill. The rabbis sent word to him: "Tell us a few things you heard from your father." He told them: "One hundred and eighty years before the Temple was destroyed, Rome was ruling in Israel. The Hasmonean rule lasted 103 years during the existence of the Temple. (*Avodah Zarah* 9a)

Hasten to perform a good deed

R. Hiyya b. Avin said in the name of R. Yehoshua b. Korha: "One should always perform a good deed as early as possible." (*Horayot* 11a)

✿ Hate lording over others

Shemaya is quoted as saying: "Love to do labor, hate lording over others, and do not seek intimate relations with the ruling powers." (*Avot* 1:10)

✿ Hate not

Ben Azzai used to say: "Do not despise any person and do not disparage anything. For there is not a person who does not have his hour and there is not an object that does not have its place." (*Avot* 4:3)

---

126. In Tractate *Sotah* 49b, the Gemara states that Aristobulus was inside Jerusalem and his brother Hyrcanus was besieging the city from the outside, but in Tractate *Bava Kamma* 82b, the Gemara has it in reverse: Hyrcanus was trapped inside and Aristobulus was besieging the city from the outside.

✿ Hateful to Hashem

There are three kinds of people Hashem hates: a two-faced person, one who has evidence in favor of his neighbor but does not come forward to testify, and one who is the only witness against his neighbor and comes forward to testify. (*Pesahim* 113b)

📖 Hatred brings ruin

The Talmud relates that a certain wealthy man had a friend by the name of Kamza and an enemy by the name of Bar Kamza. The wealthy man made a big party and invited all the dignitaries of Jerusalem including all the scholars. He told his servant to invite his friend Kamza. By mistake the servant invited Bar Kamza. When the host noticed Bar Kamza in his house, he said to him. "I hear you tell tales about me, what are you doing here? I don't want you here. Get out!"

Bar Kamza did not want to be embarrassed in front of the guests. He said to him. "Since I am here, let me stay and I will pay you. I will give you half of the cost of the whole party."

"No," the host replied, and he grabbed him by his hand and pushed him out. Bar Kamza was very hurt. He was thinking to himself, *Since the rabbis were present and did not stop him, this shows they agree with him.* He decided to inform against them to the government. He told the authorities. "The Jews are rebelling against you."[127]

After the Temple was destroyed, Rabbi Yohanan remarked: "Through the scrupulousness of R. Zechariah and the unscrupulous Bar Kamza, Jerusalem was destroyed and the Jewish people were exiled from their land." (*Gittin* 55b, 56a)

Hatzitza   חציצה

A Talmudic term for when an object intervenes between the body and the pool

---

127. See entry, Kamza and Bar Kamza.

of water during immersion. (*Bava Kamma* 82a; *Eruvin* 4b; *Sukkah* 6a)

✿ Haughty

R. Ashi said: "Anyone who is haughty would in the end be degraded." (*Sotah* 5a)

Haughty

When Rebbe was praying, he also prayed to save him from the haughty. (*Shabbat* 30b)

Havdalah

R. Aha Aricha stated in the presence of Rav Hinena that if one recites *Hamavdil* in the prayer service, he is more praiseworthy than he who says it over a cup of wine. If he said it in both, may blessings be on his head. (*Berachot* 33a; *Shabbat* 11a)

Havdalah

Ulla visited Pumbedita, and R. Yehuda said to his son R. Yitzhak: "Go and offer him a basket of fruit and observe how he recites *Havdalah*." (*Pesahim* 104b)

Havdalah

Between Shabbat and Yom Tov (*Hullin* 26b; *Shabbat* 114b)

Havdalah before dark (*Berachot* 27b)

Havdalah for Yom Tov

Havdalah for Yom Tov in the middle of the week (*Hullin* 26b)

Havdalah in the Amidah

Havdalah is mentioned in the *Amidah* in the prayer *Ata Honen*. (*Berachot* 33a)

Havitim   חביתים

The griddle cakes of the High Priest in the Temple (*Menahot* 96a)

Haviva   חביבא

Amora from Babylonia
3rd – 4th centuries CE (*Eruvin* 79b)

Havivi
Havivi from Huzna
An Amora
4th – 5th centuries (*Bava Kamma* 72a)

Hazakah   חזקה
Presumptive title to property; a title to a property not supported by documents or witnesses, but based only on possession (*Bava Batra* 28a)

Hazakah   חזקה
R. Yehuda said: The three-year period fixed for *hazakah* was instituted in order to protect a person who traveled to Spain, while away another person occupied his land and stayed on the land one year. It would take one year to inform the traveler of what happened, and a third year for him to return to claim back his land. (*Bava Batra* 38a)

Hazakah   חזקה
Persons who may or may not claim *hazakah* (*Bava Batra* 47a)

Hazeh   חזה
Our rabbis taught: What counts as the breast of the animal – the portion that faces the ground. (*Hullin* 45a)

Head and body in the Sukkah
Sitting in the *sukkah* with only his head and the majority of his body inside the *sukkah*, however the table is not inside the *sukkah* (*Sukkah* 28a)

Head of Academy at Mehuza
Rava moved to Mehuza because Nehardea was destroyed by the Palmyra. He became head of the academy in Mehuza and was appointed a judge. (*Yevamot* 115b)

Head of animal that fell into the canal
Rav was once sitting on the bank of the Ishtatith canal when he saw a man washing an animal's head, but the head fell into the canal. The man took a basket to fish it out, and he brought up two heads (*Hullin* 93a–b)

Head of Sura academy
After Rabbi Huna passed away, Rabbi Hisda became the head of the yeshiva in Sura and served there the last ten years of his life. (*Berachot* 44a)

Head of the court   אב בית דין
Rabbi Nathan was the Av Bet Din of the Sanhedrin during the time when R. Shimon b. Gamliel was the Nasi. New protocol was established regarding the honor accorded to the Av Bet Din. (*Horayot* 13b; *Taanit* 15a)

Heal the sick   ורפא ירפא
R. Yishmael said: "From the words in the Torah 'heal the sick' ורפא ירפא, we learn that a doctor has the permission to heal the sick." (*Bava Kamma* 85a; *Berachot* 60a)

Healing by a non-Jew
Is it permitted for a Jew to be healed by an idol worshipper (*Avodah Zarah* 27a)

Healing by prayer
R. Yohanan fell ill and R. Hanina went to visit him. He asked him: "Are your sufferings welcome to you?" He answered him, "No, neither the suffering nor their reward are welcome." R. Hanina told R. Yohanan: "Give me your hand." He gave him his hand and he cured him.

    R. Yohanan cured others, so why couldn't he cure himself? The rabbis replied: "A prisoner cannot free himself." (*Berachot* 5b; *Nedarim* 7b)

Health
Suggestions for good health (*Shabbat* 41a)

Health advice
Rabbah b. Nahmeni received a message

from his brothers in Eretz Yisrael:

"Although you are a great scholar, you must admit that studying alone does not equal studying with a master. And perhaps you think there is no one here with whom you could study; there is Rabbi Yohanan.

"However, if you are not coming up to Eretz Yisrael, then we give you the following advice: "Do not sit too long, because sitting for a long time leads to abdominal troubles. Do not stand for a long time, because long standing is injurious to the heart. Do not walk too much, because excessive walking is harmful to the eyes. Rather divide your time into one-third of the time sitting, one-third standing, and one-third walking. (*Ketubbot* 111a)

📖 Health lectures
By R. Hisda

Rabbi Huna asked his son, Rabbah, "Why are you not attending the lectures of Rabbi Hisda, whose lectures are so sharp and enlightening?"

"Why should I attend, he talks about secular matters most of the time. He speaks about how one should behave in the toilet, not to sit down abruptly, not to force the rectum, because the glands might be dislocated."

R. Huna became annoyed with his son and said to him: "He is discussing health matters and you call them secular? There is even more reason that you should attend his lectures." (*Shabbat* 82a)

📖✿ Heard it from my teacher

It happened that R. Eliezer spent a Shabbat in the Upper Galilee and while there, they asked him thirty questions on the Halachah of Sukkot.

His answer was: "I heard the answer on twelve questions, but on eighteen questions, I did not hear the answer from my teachers."

R. Yosi b. Yehuda said: "Reverse the words; 'I heard the answer on eighteen questions, but on twelve questions I did not hear the answer.'"

They asked him: "Are all your answers on Halachah only words you heard from your teachers?"

He answered: "You are trying to make me say something I did not hear from my teachers. During my entire life no one ever preceded me to the Bet Midrash, never did I sleep or doze off in the Bet Midrash, never did I go out and leave anyone behind me in the Bet Midrash, nor did I ever utter profane language and never did I say anything which I did not hear from my teachers." (*Sukkah* 28a; *Megillah* 27b)

Heating

Heating indirectly on Shabbat (*Shabbat* 40b)

Heating food

Various ways of warming up food on Shabbat is discussed. (*Shabbat* 36–37)

Heavenly books

R. Keruspedai said in the name of R. Yohanan: "Three accounting books are opened in heaven on Rosh Hashana." (*Rosh Hashana* 16b)

Hebrew letters
Torah was given in Hebrew

Mar Zutra said, some say Mar Ukva said: "Originally, the Torah was given to Israel in the Hebrew language and Hebrew letters. Later, in the time of Ezra, it was also given in Assyrian square letters and Aramaic language. Finally, they selected the Assyrian script and the Hebrew language." (*Sanhedrin* 21b)

Hebrew recital only

The following may be recited only in the Holy Language: the first fruit recital, the *halitza* recital, the blessings and curses, the priestly benedictions, the benediction of the High Priest, the King's declaration, the breaking of the heifer portion, and the person who was anointed for battle when he addresses the people. (*Sotah* 32a)

Hebrew preferred
By R. Yehuda HaNasi
Rabbi Yehuda HaNasi preferred the Hebrew language. He declared: "What has the Syrian language have to do with Eretz Yisrael?

Why use the Syrian language in the Land of Israel? Either one should use the holy tongue or Greek." (*Bava Kamma* 82b, 83a; *Sotah* 49b)

Helbo   חלבו
Amora from Babylonia
3rd – 4th centuries CE (*Berachot* 6b)

Helen, the mother of King Monbaz
Queen Helen, the mother of King Monbaz, donated a golden candelabra to the Temple and a golden tablet on which the inscription read by the *sotah* was engraved. (*Yoma* 37a; *Gittin* 60a)

Help a fellow-man loading
(*Bava Metzia* 32a)

Helping a friend
A man carrying wood on his donkey has to remove his wood in order to save the flax of his friend whose donkey died. This is one of the conditions Yehoshua imposed on the Israelites when he divided the land. (*Bava Kamma* 81b, 114b)

✿ Helping the needy
Is greater than all the sacrifices
R. Eleazar stated: "The performance of charity is greater than offering all the sacrifices."

R. Eleazar further stated: "The act of *gemilut hasadim* is greater than charity."

He also stated: "The reward of char-

ity is dependent on the kindness in it." (*Sukkah* 49b)

📖 Hen without feathers
It is said of Rabbi Shimon ben Halafta that he was an experimenter in all things. Once, he had a hen which had no downs at all. He put the hen into the oven, having first wrapped the hen in a warm blanket. When the hen came out, it grew feathers even larger than the original one.[128] (*Hullin* 57b)

Hens (*Bava Kamma* 79b; *Taanit* 25a)

Herbal medicine
Rabbi Ashi's daughter had a stomach ailment, and Rabin from Naresh cured her with herbal medicines. (*Gittin* 69b)

Herbs for Pesach
One fulfills his obligation when eating the following herbs.

For specifics, read the text in the Gemara. (*Pesahim* 39a)

📖 Herem   חרם
Excommunication
Rabbi Eliezer had halachic differences with the rabbis; he brought forth every argument to prove his point, but the rabbis did not accept them.

On that day, all objects which R. Eliezer had declared clean were brought and burned in fire. Then they took a vote and excommunicated him. The rabbis said: "Who should go and inform him of the excommunication?"

"I will go," said R. Akiva. He donned black garments and sat at a distance of four cubits from R. Eliezer.

"Akiva, said R. Eliezer, "What has happened today?" R. Akiva replied, "Master,

---

128. See also entry, Ants.

it appears to me that your companions are keeping a distance from you."

He rent his garments, removed his shoes, set aside his seat, and sat on the floor and tears flowed from his eyes. It was learned that great was the calamity on that day. Rabbi Gamliel was traveling in a ship, when a huge wave arose to drown him. Rabbi Gamliel was reflecting, "It appears to me that this is on account of Rabbi Eliezer ben Horkynos." Thereupon, he arose and exclaimed: "Sovereign of the Universe, You know full well that I have not acted for my honor or for the honor of my paternal house, but for Your honor, so that strife may not multiply in Israel." At that, the raging sea subsided. (*Bava Metzia* 59b)

📖 Herem   חרם

Excommunication, Rabbi was put in Herem
Shila b. Avina decided a matter according to Rav. When Rav was on his deathbed, he said to R. Assi:

"Go and restrain him and if he does not listen, try to convince him." After Rav passed away R. Assi asked him to retract, because Rav had retracted his ruling.

R. Shila said: "If Rav had retracted, he would have told me." He refused to retract; thereupon R. Assi put him under the ban.

R. Shila asked him: "Are you not afraid of the fire?" He answered: "I am Issi b. Yehuda, who is Issi b. Gur-aryeh, who is Issi b. Gamliel, who is Issi b. Mahalalel, a copper mortar, which does not rust." The other retorted: "I am Shila b. Avina, an iron mallet that breaks the cooper mortar."

Soon after this incident R. Assi became very sick and died. R. Shila told his wife prepare my shrouds, "because I don't want him to have the opportunity to tell Rav things about me." When R. Shila departed, people saw a myrtle fly from one grave to the other. We may conclude that the rabbis have made peace. (*Niddah* 36b)

✿ Herem on himself first
Whenever Mar Zutra would have to issue a *herem* (a ban) on a colleague, he would first put himself in *herem* and then pronounce it on his colleague. (*Moed Katan* 17a; *Nedarim* 7b)

✿ Hermit
R. Hillel said: "Do not separate yourself from the community, do not believe you know it all, and do not judge your friend until you have been put in his position." (*Avot* 2:4)

Herod
The house of Herod
R. Yosi b. Halafta said: "The House of Herod's rule lasted 103 years during the time of the Temple. (*Avodah Zarah* 9a)

📖 Herod
King Herod wiped out the entire Hasmonean family, except one girl. Herod wanted to marry her, but she did not want to be his wife. She went up on the roof and called out: "Whoever claims to be from the Hasmonean family is a slave, since I alone am left from that family and I am throwing myself down from the roof." After her death, Herod preserved her body in honey for seven years. (*Bava Batra* 3b, 4a)

📖 Herod building the Temple
Herod asked his advisers: "Who are those that say that Israel can only have a Jew as a king?" They told him it is the rabbis. To eliminate criticism, he killed all the rabbis, except one – R. Bava ben Buta.

Herod asked Rabbi Bava b. Buta: "What could I do to amend for the sin of killing all the scholars?"

R. Bava answered: "You have extinguished the light of the world by killing the rabbis; you should attend to the other light of the world, the Temple."

Herod told him: "I am afraid of the government in Rome."

Bava b. Buta advised him to send an envoy to Rome to ask permission, and let the envoy take a year on the way, and let him stay a year in Rome and another year to come back. In the meantime, Herod should rebuild the Temple.

Herod followed his advice. He received the following reply from Rome:

"If you have not yet pulled down the old one, do not do so. If you have pulled it down, do not rebuild it. If you have pulled it down and already rebuilt it, you are one of those bad servants who do first and ask permission afterwards." (*Bava Batra* 4a)

Herod's Temple

It used to be said: "He who has not seen the Temple of Herod has never seen a beautiful building."

Rabbah said: "It was built of yellow and white marble. Herod had originally intended to cover it with gold, but the rabbis advised him to leave it as is, because it was more beautiful as it was. It looked like the waves of the sea." (*Bava Batra* 4a)

Heshbon

The city of Heshbon in the Torah was originally a Moabite City, but it was conquered by King Sichon. Hence, it was acceptable for Israel to conquer it. (*Hullin* 60b; *Bava Metzia* 46b)

Hesped dream   הספד

Dreaming a eulogy (*Bava Kamma* 55a; *Berachot* 57a)

Hevron   חברון

Hevron is a town of refuge. (*Makkot* 10a; *Bava Batra* 122b)

Hezkiya   חזקיה

Amora from Eretz Yisrael
4th century CE (*Zevachim* 75b)

Hezkiya

The rabbis taught: Six things did King Hezkiya enact; in three the rabbis agreed with him, but in three they did not. (*Pesahim* 56a; *Berachot* 10b)

Hezkiya bar Hiyya   חזקיה בר חייא

Amora from Eretz Yisrael
3rd century CE (*Megillah* 5b)

Hezkiya ben Gurion

Hezkiya b. Gurion was visited by the rabbis when he was sick, and eighteen *halachot* were voted and enacted that day. (*Shabbat* 13b)

Hezkiya King of Judea   חזקיה

At the funeral of Hezkiya King of Judea, 36,000 warriors marched before him. (*Bava Kamma* 17a)

Hidden scrolls of R. Hiyya

Rav said: "I have found secret scrolls hidden by the school of R. Hiyya." (*Bava Metzia* 92a)

Hidka   חידקא

Tanna from Eretz Yisrael
2nd century CE (*Bava Batra* 119a)

📖 Hiding in a cave

R. Shimon b. Yohai and his son R. Eleazar were hiding in a cave for twelve years

Rabbi Shimon ben Yohai and his son Rabbi Eleazar went and hid in a cave for twelve years. They had to hide because on one occasion Rabbi Yehuda, Rabbi Shimon, and Rabbi Yosi were making remarks to an audience. Rabbi Yehuda b. Illai remarked how fine the works of the Romans are – they built bridges, they built bathhouses, etc. Rabbi Yosi b. Halafta was silent, but Rabbi Shimon b. Yohai commented: "Whatever they built, they did for themselves. They built bridges to levy tolls on them, and they built bathhouses to indulge their bodies in them." Someone conveyed his words to the Romans. They decreed that Rabbi Yehuda shall be rewarded, Rabbi Yosi shall be exiled to Sepphoris, and Rabbi Shimon shall be executed. Rabbi Shimon and his son Rabbi Eleazar went and hid in a cave. By miracle, a carob tree grew nearby and they found a well in the cave, which served them as nourishment. To save their clothes, they would sit during the day naked in the sand and study Torah. After twelve years, when the Emperor Hadrian died, they came out, but due to some circumstances they returned for one more year. (*Shabbat* 33b)

📖 Hiding in a cave
The Judeans were hiding in a cave during one of the severe persecutions. They decreed that no one could leave, but they discovered a shoe print going out of the cave and they all rushed to the exit. Many were killed. (*Shabbat* 60a)

Hiding objects
If one hides objects in the wall of a friend and the friend destroyed the wall (*Bava Kamma* 30a)

Hiding to commit a prohibited act
בצנעא
A prohibited act done in hiding (*Avodah Zarah* 54a)

High Priest   כהן גדול
To judge a High Priest in Israel requires a court of seventy-one (*Sanhedrin* 2a)

High Priest
Story of a convert and R. Hillel (*Shabbat* 31a)

📖 High Priest
Marries widow
R. Yehoshua b. Gamla was married to Marta the daughter of Boethus, the wealthiest person in Jerusalem. She was a widowed woman, but in spite of it, King Yannai appointed him High Priest. The marriage was nevertheless consummated in spite of the fact that she was a widow. (*Yevamot* 59a, 61a)

📖 High Priest
Office of the High Priest bought
It is related that Rabbi Assi said: "Marta, the daughter of Boethus, gave King Yannai a basketful of dinars to nominate Yehoshua ben Gamla as High Priest. He is credited with perpetuating Jewish studies in Eretz Yisrael." (*Yoma* 18a)

High Priest
Procedure to prepare the High Priest for Yom Kippur (*Yoma* 2a)

High Priest's woolen cap
It has been taught: Upon the head of the High Priest there was a woolen cap upon which was placed the golden *tzitz*. (*Hullin* 138a)

📖 High Priests
The High Priests of the First Temple and of the Second Temple
Rabbah bar b. Hana said: "What is the meaning of the passage, 'the fear of God prolongs the days, but the years of the wicked shall be shortened.'? The first part refers to the First Temple, which lasted 410 years, and was served by only 18 High Priests. The second part refers to the Second Temple, which lasted for 420 years, but was served by more than 300 High Priests. Deduct from the 420 years of the Temple's existence the 40 years served by Shimon HaTzaddik. Deduct also 80 years

served by Yohanan, and 10 years served by Yishmael b. Phabi. Some say, 11 years served by Eleazar b. Harsum. After the deductions, you will come to the conclusion that the rest of the High Priests didn't complete a full year in service." (*Yoma* 9a)

High Priest's entrance
When the High Priest entered the Sanctuary (*Tamid* 33b)

Hilfa b. Agra
2nd century CE (*Shabbat* 105b)

Hillel   הלל
Amora from Eretz Yisrael
3rd century CE (*Bava Batra* 83b)

Hillel   הלל
Nasi of Sanhedrin from Eretz Yisrael
4th century CE

Hillel
His humility (*Shabbat* 17a)

Hillel bar R. Vallas   הילל בר וולס
(*Avodah Zarah* 52)

📖 Hillel elected president of Sanhedrin
It is stated: "The B'nei Betera rabbis didn't remember whether the slaughter of the Paschal lamb overrides the Shabbat."

They were told: "There is a man by the name of Hillel from Babylonia, who studied under Shemaya and Avtalyon, the two greatest men of our time."

They summoned him and he told the Sanhedrin: "Surely we have more than 200 Paschal lambs during the year, which override the Shabbat. He quoted sentences from the Torah and logic to prove to them that it does override the Shabbat. After this incident, the president of the Sanhedrin resigned in 30 BCE, and they elected Hillel president.[129] (*Pesahim* 66a; *Sanhedrin* 82a)

📖 Hillel frozen on the roof
Rabbi Hillel used to work daily at hard work to earn one tropek.[130] He split his earnings, half of it he gave to the guard to admit him to the house of learning, the other half he spent on food and necessities. One day, he had no earnings and the guard would not let him enter. He climbed up on the roof and from the window of the roof he listened to the lectures of Rabbis Shemaya and Avtalyon. That day happened to be on a Friday of winter solstice. Rabbi Hillel fell asleep on the roof and snow fell and covered him. The next morning on Shabbat, Shemaya said to Avtalyon: "Every day about this time the room is bright with light, but today it is dark, is it perhaps a cloudy day?" They looked up and they saw a human figure in the window. They climbed up and found Hillel covered with three cubits of snow. They removed him, bathed and anointed him, and they sat him next to the fire. They said;

"For this man it was worth to desecrate the Shabbat."

From then on, he gained permanent admittance to their school. (*Yoma* 35b)

Hillel and Shammai
In six cases Hillel is more stringent
R. Yehuda lists six cases in which the school of R. Hillel is more stringent than the school of Shammai. R. Yosi also lists six different cases in which the school of Shammai is more lenient than the school of Hillel. R. Yishmael lists three cases in which the school of Shammai is more lenient than the school of Hillel, and R.

---

129. See entry, Erev Pesach on Shabbat.
130. An amount which equals half a dinar.

Eliezer lists two cases in which the school of Shammai is more lenient (*Eduyot* 5:1–4)

📖 Hillel's first partner
At first, it was Rabbi Hillel and Rabbi Menaham, but Rabbi Menahem left and Rabbi Shammai took his place. According to some, Menahem went into the service of King Herod, others say he withdrew into seclusion. (*Hagigah* 2:2, 16a)

Hillel HaZaken   הלל הזקן
Tanna from Eretz Yisrael
Head of the Sanhedrin in Jerusalem
1st BCE – 1st centuries CE (*Yoma* 35b)

Hillel's students
Our rabbis taught: Hillel the Elder had eighty students; the greatest of them was Yonatan b. Uzziel, the least of them was R. Yohanan b. Zakkai. (*Bava Batra* 134a)

Hinena   חיננא
Amora from Babylonia
4th century CE (*Berachot* 33a)

Hiring a cow
If one hired a cow and lent it to a friend, and the cow died. (*Bava Metzia* 35b)

Hiring employees
The prohibition of hiring employees on Shabbat is discussed in *Shoel*, the 23rd *perek* in *Shabbat*. (*Shabbat* 148b)

Hiring laborers on Shabbat
(*Shabbat* 150a)

Hisda   חסדא
Amora from Babylonia
Head of the academy in Sura
3rd – 4th centuries CE (*Bava Kamma* 91b)

Hisda's sons
Mar Yanuka and Mar Kashisha were the sons of R. Hisda. (*Bava Batra* 7b)

Hishamer, Pen, Al   השמר פן אל
R. Avin said in the name of R. Illai: "Whenever it is written in the Torah the words: *hishamer, pen*, and *al* – it is a negative precept." (*Eruvin* 96a)

History
Seder Olam
The authorship of the book *Seder Olam* is attributed to Rabbi Halafta or to his son R. Yosi b. Halafta: "Come and hear, it was taught in the book *Seder Olam*, and so on." The book is a history in chronological order; it begins with creation and ends with the Bar Kochva revolt. (*Shabbat* 88a; *Yevamot* 82b; *Niddah* 46b)

History
R. Yishmael b. R. Yosi b. Halafta cited some history in the name of his father, R. Yosi. (*Shabbat* 15a)

History
It is stated that Rabbi Hillel and his descendants, Shimon, Gamliel, and his son Shimon, were the heads of the Sanhedrin that lasted for one hundred years during the Temple's existence. (*Shabbat* 15a)

Hitting one's parents (*Bava Kamma* 85b, 87a)

Hiyya   חייא
Tanna from Eretz Yisrael
2nd century CE (*Ketubbot* 5a; *Bava Metzia* 5a; *Shabbat* 3b)

Hiyya
Rav asked a question from Rebbe. Afterwards R. Hiyya said to Rav: "Have I not told you that when Rebbe is engaged in one tractate, you must not ask him a question about another subject?" (*Shabbat* 3b)

Hiyya
R. Hiyya and his brothers
A master said Aibu and Hona, Shila and Marta and R. Hiyya were the sons of Abba b. Aha Karsela of Kafri. Rav was also the son of R. Hiyya's sister. (*Sanhedrin* 5a)

Hiyya
R. Hiyya was born in Kafri
Rabbi Hiyya bar Abba was born in Kafri, a community near Sura in Babylonia, but left Babylonia and moved to Eretz Yisrael. (*Ketubbot* 5a)

Hiyya author of Beraitot
R. Hiyya is the author of the Beraita, which he taught in his own academy. As the Talmud says, "Abbaye says our Mishna is in accordance with R. Safra, who learned it in the academy of R. Hiyya on the subject of charging interest." R. Hiyya taught there are twenty-four principal kinds of damages. (*Bava Kamma* 4b)

Rav said: "I found a secret scroll of the scroll of the school of R. Hiyya." (*Shabbat* 6b; *Berachot* 24a; *Pesahim* 4a; *Bava Metzia* 62b–65b)

Hiyya bar Abba
חייא בר אבא
Amora from Eretz Yisrael
3rd – 4th centuries CE (*Berachot* 5a)

Hiyya bar Ammi
חייא בר אמי
Amora from Eretz Yisrael
3rd – 4th centuries CE (*Berachot* 8a)

Hiyya bar Avin
חייא בר אבין
Amora from Babylonia
4th century CE (*Kiddushin* 58a)

Hiyya bar Rav
חייא בר רב
Amora from Babylonia
3rd century CE (*Pesahim* 113a)

Hiyya's family
He and his wife Yehudit had twin sons, Yehuda and Hezkiya.

Rabbi Hiyya and his wife also had twin daughters, Pazi and Tavi. (*Yevamot* 65b; *Berachot* 21b)

Hizkiyahu
חזקיה
King of Judea (*Bava Kamma* 17a)

Hizkiyahu
Our rabbis taught: King Hizkiyahu enacted six things; the rabbis approved of three and three they disapproved. (*Berachot* 10b)

Hol Hamoed
What kind of work is permitted and what is not permitted to perform on Hol Hamoed? (*Moed Katan* 2a)

Hol Hamoed
Can one be married on Hol Hamoed? (*Moed Katan* 8b)

Hol Hamoed haircut
Can one get a haircut on Hol Hamoed? (*Moed Katan* 13b)

✿ Hol Hamoed mistake
R. Yannai had an orchard of fruits which ripened during the week of the festival and his workers picked the fruit during Hol Hamoed. The next year many people waited to pick their fruits until the festival. He realized that people were misled by his action and therefore he renounced the rights to the fruits of his orchard for a whole year. (*Moed Katan* 12b)

Holding court
R. Ammi and R. Assi were sitting and studying between the pillars of the Bet Midrash in Tiberias. Every now and then, they would stop studying. They would knock on the door and announce: "If anyone has a lawsuit, let him come in." (*Shabbat* 10a)

Hole in the skull

R. Yosi b. Hamshulam said: "It happened that a man had a hole in his skull and they put over it a plaster and he recovered." (*Hullin* 57b)

Holidays

Seder Moed   סדר מועד

The *Seder Moed* contains the laws of Shabbat and other Festivals.

Holy Ark   ארון

When King Solomon finished building the Temple, he desired to take the Holy Ark into the Holy of Holies, but the doors would not open. (*Shabbat* 30a)

Holy Ark

When Rabbi Shimon ben Yohai visited Rome, Rabbi Matya consulted with him on an important halachic issue.

Rabbi Shimon asked him about the Holy Ark of the Temple. (*Meilah* 17a; *Yoma* 53b)

Holy Ark was hidden away

King Yoshiyah hid away the anointing oil, the Holy Ark, the jar of manna, Aharon's rod with the almond blossoms, and also the coffer the Philistines had sent as a gift to Israel. He did not want these precious things to be taken by the enemy. (*Horayot* 12a)

Holy inspiration   רוח הקודש

The Talmud relates that immediately after Pesach, R. Gamliel was riding on a donkey from Acco to Kheziv, and R. Illai was behind following him. R. Gamliel saw an expensive loaf of bread on the ground and he said to R. Illai, "Please pick up the loaf of bread." Riding on further on the road, they met a non-Jew by the name of Mavgai.

R. Gamliel called Mavgai by name and told him to take away the loaf of bread.

R. Illai approached the stranger and asked him: "Where are you from?"

"I am an attendant at the station-house."

"And what is your name?"

"My name is Mavgai."

"Did you ever meet R. Gamliel?"

"No," answered Mavgai.

From this experience, we became aware that R. Gamliel had *Ruah Ha-Kodesh*. We also learned three things: One, one may not leave eatables on the road; two, that we assume the food was left on the road by the majority of the travelers, who were non-Jews, and three, that one may derive benefit from leavened bread after Pesach which belongs to a non-Jew. (*Eruvin* 64b; *Pesahim* 28a; *Bava Metzia* 23a)

Holy of Holies repair work

There were openings in the upper chamber of the Holy of Holies from where they lowered the artisans into the chamber in closed boxes to do repair work. (*Pesahim* 26a; *Middot* 37a)

Holy things

Seder Kodshim   סדר קדשים

Seder Kodshim contains laws concerning Holy things, sacrifices, and Temple services.

Holy tongue   לשון הקודש

Where may one use the Holy Tongue (ancient Hebrew) (*Shabbat* 40b)

📖 Hometown changed

It is related that at the conclusion of the festivities of R. Shimon b. Yohai's wedding, R. Hanania b. Hachinai was about to leave to the academy in Bene Berak. R. Shimon said to him: "Wait for me until I am able to join you." But R. Hanania didn't wait for him and spent twelve years there. By the time R. Hanania returned home, the streets of the town were altered and he was unable to find his way home. He decided to go to the riverbank to find his way home. There he heard people addressing a young girl. "Daughter of Hachinai, fill up your pitcher and let us go."

He didn't recognize her, but followed her and found his home. He saw his wife sifting flour. When she turned around and saw her husband, she was so overcome with joy she fainted. (*Ketubbot* 62b)

✿ Honest labor

R. Hiyya b. Ammi said in the name of R. Ulla: "A man who lives from the labor of his hands, instead of relying on others to support him, is greater than one who fears God, but relies on others to support him." (*Berachot* 8a)

📖✿ Honesty

R. Safra's honesty was legendary. A story is told that once a person who wanted to buy his donkey approached him, and made him an offer. Rabbi Safra did not answer him because he was in the middle of prayers. The person offered him a higher price because he thought the first offer was not satisfactory. He kept on raising the offer a few times. Finally, when R. Safra finished praying he insisted on selling the donkey for the first price offered. (*Makkot* 24a, Rashi)

✿ Honesty and integrity

Rava said: "When a man dies and goes up to heaven, he is asked:

'Did you deal honestly and with integrity with your fellow-men?

'Did you set a time regularly for learning Torah?

'Did you engage in procreation?

'Did you wish constantly for redemption?

'Did you enter into discussions of intellect?

'Were you able to deduce one thing from another?'" (*Shabbat* 31a)

Honesty

Found objects must be announced in public. (*Bava Metzia* 21a, 28a)

✿ Honesty

On the eve of a holiday, Abba Shaul b. Batnit would fill up his measuring devices with his products and give it to his customers. He did this in order to give his customers a full measure down to the last drop due to them. (*Betzah* 29a)

Honey as a preservative

Herod killed all the descendants of the Hasmonean family except one maiden. When she found out that he wanted to marry her, she threw herself down from a roof. He preserved her body in honey for seven years. (*Bava Batra* 3b, 4a)

Honi HaMaagel   חוני המעגל

Tanna from Eretz Yisrael

1st century BCE (*Berachot* 19a)

Honi HaMaagel

And R. Shimon b. Shetah

Rabbi Shimon ben Shetah sent this message to Honi HaMaagel: "You deserve to be excommunicated for the things you do, and if you weren't Honi HaMaagel I would pronounce you excommunicated. But what can I do since you are a favorite of Hashem? He accedes to your wishes, and you are like a son who is favored by his father." (*Berachot* 19a, 23a; *Taanit* 19a)

Honi HaMaagel

How he died

There are different versions how he died. According to Josephus, he died during the war between the two Hasmonean brothers Aristobulus II and Hyrcanus II, in 65

BCE. Hyrcanus's men ordered him to pray for their side to win the battle, and Rabbi Honi prayed for both sides. Thereupon, he was stoned to death. However, the story in the Talmud differs.

R. Honi HaMaagel went to lay down to rest in a cave and he fell asleep. He slept hidden in a cave for seventy years. When he awoke he came to the conclusion that he slept seventy years. When he returned home, he enquired: "Is the son of Honi HaMaagel still alive?" The people told him that his son is no longer alive, but his grandson is still living. He declared: "I am Honi HaMaagel," but no one believed him. He went to the house of study, where he overheard the rabbis say: "The Halachah is as clear as in the days of Honi HaMaagel, which he made very clear to us. When Honi HaMaagel used to come to the house of study he would settle every difficulty the rabbis had." When he heard this, he declared to the rabbis: "I am Honi," but the rabbis did not believe him, and they did not give him the honor due to him. This hurt him greatly and he prayed for death, and he died. (*Taanit* 23a)

📖 Honi HaMaagel
Prays for rain
It once happened that the greater part of the month of Adar passed by without rain, and the people were concerned that there would be no grain to harvest. They sent word to R. Honi to pray for rain. He prayed and no rain fell. He drew a circle around himself on the ground where he stood and exclaimed to God: "Master of the Universe, Thy children have turned to me, because they are under the impression that I am a member of Your house. I swear by Your great name that I will not move from here until You have mercy upon them."

Rain began to drip, but the people said to him: "This rain is only to release you

from your oath; we look to you to save us from death."

He exclaimed: "I did not pray for this, I prayed for rain that will fill the cisterns, the ditches and the caves."

The rain came down excessively with great force, and the people were concerned there would be flooding. He exclaimed: "Master of the Universe, I did not pray for this, but for rain of benevolence and blessing." After his praying, the rain came down normally, but it continued to come down without stop, and the people had to go up to the Temple Mount to escape the rain. The people said to him: "Please pray for the rain to cease, just as you prayed for the rain to come down."

He answered them: "I have it as a tradition that we may not pray for an excess of good." (*Taanit* 23a)

✿ Honor
Ben Zoma said: "Who is wise? A wise person is one who learns from all people. Who is strong? A strong person is one who subdues his passions. Who is rich? A rich person is one who is happy with his portion. Who is honored? An honored person is one who honors his fellow-men." (*Avot* 4:1)

✿ Honor
R. Eliezer HaKappar said: "Envy, greed, and chasing after honors take a man out of this world." (*Avot* 4:21)

Honor of your fellow-man
Let the honor of your fellow-man be as precious as your own
One of Rabbi Eliezer's famous sayings was: "Let the honor of your fellow-man be as precious as your own; be not easily provoked to anger; repent one day before you die; warm yourself at the fire of the Sages, but beware of their glowing coals." (*Avot* 2:15)

✿ Honor of your friend

R. Eliezer said: "Let the honor of your friend be as precious to you as your own." (*Avot* 2:10)

✿ Honor your colleague

R. Eleazar b. Shammua said: "Let the honor of your student be as precious to you as your own, and the honor of your colleague as the reverence for your teacher's, and have reverence for your teacher as the fear of Heaven." (*Avot* 4:12)

✿ Honor your wife

R Helbo said: "One should always observe the honor due to his wife because the blessings given to a home is always on account of his wife." (*Bava Metzia* 59a)

✿ Honor your wife

R. Avira was quoted as saying the following, sometimes in the name of R. Ammi and sometimes in the name of R. Assi: "A man should always eat and drink less than he can afford, clothe himself in accordance with his means, and honor his wife and children more than he can afford, because they are dependent on him, and he depends on the Creator." (*Hullin* 84b)

Honoring parents (*Yevamot* 5b)

Honoring parents

R. Yosi ben Akavia also known as R. Issi ben Yehuda was of the opinion that honoring a father takes precedence over performing another mitzvah, provided that someone else takes his place. Rabbi Mathna agreed with him (*Kiddushin* 32a)

✿ Honoring parents

R. Tarfon carried respect for his mother to the extreme. When she wished to mount her bed, he would lie down on the floor so she could step on him and mount the bed. (*Kiddushin* 31b)

Honoring parents

When performing another mitzvah

R Eliezer b. Matya is quoted saying: "If my father orders me, 'Give me a drink of water,' while I have a mitzvah to perform, I disregard my father and perform the mitzvah, because my father and I are bound to fulfill the mitzvah. (*Kiddushin* 32a)

📖✿ Honoring parents

A certain non-Jewish man from Ashkelon by the name of Dama son of Natina had precious pearls for sale.[131] A Jewish buyer came to buy them for the Ephod and offered him a great sum of money profiting him 600,000 *dinarim*, but the keys to the locker were under the pillow of his father, who was asleep. He would not disturb his father, and let the buyer leave. (*Avodah Zarah* 23b, 24a)

📖 Honoring Shabbat

R. Hiyya b. Abba related a story: "I was once a guest in a house in Lodokia where they served the host on a golden table, which was carried by sixteen men with sixteen silver chains. On it were plates, goblets, pitchers, and bottles. In those utensils, were all kinds of delicious foods and spices. I said to him, 'What did you do to merit all this?" He replied, 'I was a butcher, and every time I came across a fine piece of meat, I put it aside for Shabbat.'" (*Shabbat* 119a)

📖 Honoring Shabbat with special foods

R. Abba used to buy thirteen cuts of the finest meat from thirteen different butchers, and then handed the meat over to his servants, urging them to hurry, make haste: prepare for Shabbat. (*Shabbat* 119a)

---

131. See entry, Dama son of Natina.

Hope
Never lose faith
R. Yohanan and R. Eleazar stated: "Even if a sharp sword rests on ones neck, do not desist from praying." (*Berachot* 10a)

Hopping
Poultry hopping causing damages (*Bava Kamma* 18b)

Hormin
The name of a demon (*Bava Batra* 73a)

📖✿ Hormuz Ifra
The mother of King Shapur, Ifra Hormuz, sent 400 *dinarim* to R. Ammi, but he would not accept it. She then sent the money to Rava and he accepted it. He accepted it in order not to offend the government. When R. Ammi heard this, he was indignant. Rava defended himself on the ground that he did not wish to offend the government and the queen. R. Ammi did not want to accept the money because he would have had to distribute it also to non-Jews. Rava did indeed distribute it to non-Jews as well. R. Ammi claimed that it was not made very clear to him how to dispose of the money. (*Bava Batra* 10b)

Horse
R. Yishmael quoted his father, R. Yosi, regarding animals on Shabbat, like a horse, mule, camel, and ass. (*Shabbat* 52a)

Horse Neighing
A horse neighing causing damages (*Bava Kamma* 18b)

Hoshia (Hoshaiah)   הושעיא
Amora from Babylonia
3rd–4th centuries CE (*Gittin* 25a; *Bechorot* 37b)

✿ Hospitality
R. Dimi said: "Hospitality to guests is a greater mitzvah than the mitzvah of arriving early at the Bet Midrash." (*Shabbat* 127a)

✿ Hospitality to guests
R. Yehuda b. Shila said in the name of R. Assi in the name of R. Yohanan: "There are six good deeds from which one can derive benefits in this world and still get the rewards in the World to Come: hospitality to guests, visiting the sick, concentration during prayer, rising early for prayer, bringing up a son with Torah study, and to judge everyone as being upright." (*Shabbat* 127a)

✿ Hosting a scholar
It is stated: Rabbi Yosi son of Rabbi Hanina said in the name of Rabbi Eliezer ben Yaakov: "If a man is hosting a scholar in his home and lets him use his possessions, he is compared to offering the daily sacrifices." He also said: "A man should not stand on a high platform when he prays." (*Berachot* 10b)

House beams
In Jerusalem, house beams were not allowed to project. (*Bava Kamma* 82b)

House buying
When buying a house in Israel, can the deed be written on Shabbat? (*Bava Kamma* 80b)

House of partners collapsed
A house that belonged to partners collapsed; how do they settle? (*Bava Metzia* 117a; *Bava Kamma* 20b)

✿ House of prayer with windows
R. Hiyya b. Abba said in the name of R. Yohanan: "A person should always try to pray in a house with windows." (*Berachot* 31a, 34b)

House of study   בית המדרש
(*Megillah* 27a)

House sale
When selling a house, what is included?
(*Bava Batra* 61a)

House sold
R. Yehoshua b. Levi said: "A house is sold when the key is handed over." (*Bava Kamma* 52a)

✿ House very ornate
Leave a small area bare
After the destruction of the Temple, the rabbis were concerned about having a house which is very ornate. However, the rabbis declared that a house may be plastered, but one should leave a small area bare. How much of an area?

R. Yosef said: "It should be a square cubit."

R. Hisda said: "It should be by the entrance." (*Bava Batra* 60b)

House well-lit
The rabbis believed that a house well-lit would have blessings (*Shabbat* 23b)

Houses taller than the Synagogue
Houses that are taller than the height of the synagogue are not a good omen. (*Shabbat* 11a)

Housing a scholar
To house a scholar in your home (*Kiddushin* 76b)

How do we arrive at this conclusion   מה"מ מנא הני מילי
(*Horayot* 10a)

How many Torahs
R. Hillel was asked by a non-Jew, how many Torahs do you have? (*Shabbat* 31a)

Hugras ben Levi   הוגרס בן לוי
Officer of the Temple (*Shekalim* 5:1)

Huma
The name of Abbaye's wife was Huma. (*Ketubbot* 65a)

Human being
With regards to giving warnings, a human being is always considered to be warned. (*Bava Kamma* 3b, 26a; *Sanhedrin* 72a)

✿ Human dignity
R. Hisda attached great importance to human dignity. He conducted himself in a humble way, and went out of his way to greet everyone first in the marketplace, Jews or gentiles alike. (*Gittin* 62a)

✿ Humble
R. Levitas is quoted as saying, "Be exceedingly humble, because in the end we all have to die." He was a contemporary of Rabbi Yohanan ben Beroka and Rabbi Akiva. (*Avot* 4:4)

Humble
R. Hiyya was the uncle of Rav, but he was a humble person as illustrated by his following the Halachah according to Rav. (*Pesahim* 8b)

📖 Humble
R. Hanina b. Hama
When Rabbi Yehuda HaNasi died, he left instructions. One of them was: R. Hanina bar Hama shall preside at the Academy. However, R. Hanina did not accept, because R. Afes was two and a half years older, hence R. Afes became president of the Academy. R. Hanina did not attend inside the Academy, but instead studied outside in the company of Rabbi Levi. When Rabbi Afes passed away, R. Hanina bar Hama took over the presidency. Rabbi Levi had no one to study with. As

a consequence, he moved to Babylonia. (*Ketubbot* 103b)

✿ Humble

When there was a drought in the Land of Israel, R. Yonah, the father of R. Mani, would go into his house and say to his family: "Get me my sacks so I can go and buy grain for a *zuz*." He was so humble that he didn't want to let on to his family that he was the person praying for rain. He then went to a low area, put on the sackcloth and prayed for rain, and rain came. When he returned home, his family asked him: "Did you bring grain?" He would answer: "Now that rain has come, the world will feel relieved." (*Taanit* 23b)

Humble

The wife of R. Avohu's interpreter once said to the wife of R. Avohu:

"My husband has no need to get instructions from your husband, and when he bows down to your husband he is merely being courteous."

The wife of R. Avohu told her husband what she said. R. Avohu said to her, "Why should we worry about it? All that matters is that through the two of us God is praised." (*Sotah* 40a)

📖 Humble

Once R. Huna had a great loss: 400 jars of wine turned sour. He was visited by Rav Yehuda, the brother of R. Sala Hasida and the other rabbis. But some say it was R. Adda b. Ahava and other rabbis who visited him. They said to him: "Master you ought to examine your actions."

He asked them: "Am I suspicious in your eyes?"[132]

They answered him: "Is God suspect of punishing without justice?"

He declared: "If somebody has heard any misdeed against me, then let him speak."

They replied: "We heard that the master does not give his tenant his lawful share of vine twigs."

He replied: "Does he leave me any? He steals all of them."

They said to him: "That is exactly what the proverb says. 'If you steal from a thief, you also have a taste of it.'"

He said to the rabbis: "I take upon myself to give him his share in the future."

It was reported that after this visit the vinegar became wine again. Others say that the price of vinegar went up so high that R. Huna sold the vinegar for the same price as wine. (*Berachot.* 5b)

📖✿ Humble

Spared humiliation for colleague

R. Shemuel HaKatan was a very humble person. The Talmud relates, Rabbi Gamliel asked his assistant to call seven certain rabbis to a meeting in the upper chamber. When Rabbi Gamliel arrived he found eight rabbis. He declared: "The person that was not invited should leave." Rabbi Shemuel stood up and declared: "I am the one who came uninvited, but I didn't come to take part in the decision-making. I came only to learn how to intercalate the month." Rabbi Gamliel answered: "Sit down, my son, sit down. You are worthy to intercalate all the months of the year, but it was the decision of the rabbis to have only those present who were specially invited for this purpose."

But in reality it was not Rabbi Shemuel who was the uninvited party, it was another rabbi, but he wanted to save that person the humiliation. Therefore, he told them it was he who was uninvited. (*Sanhedrin* 11a)

✿ Humble and considerate

The rabbis decided to appoint R. Avohu

---

132. See entry, Reproval accepted.

as head of the academy in Acco, but when R. Avohu saw that R. Abba of Acco had numerous creditors pressing him for payment, he said to the rabbis: "There is a greater scholar more suitable for the office." (*Sotah* 40a)

📖 Humble people
It was stated, Rabbi Yehuda HaNasi said: "Three prime examples of humble people are these: my father, the Bene Betera, and Yonatan the son of King Saul." The Bene Betera rabbis were the presidents of the Sanhedrin during Herod's reign. It happened once on the day before Pesach when the Sanhedrin under the Bene Betera was not sure what the Halachah was. Rabbi Hillel proved to the Sanhedrin that the Paschal lamb overrides the Shabbat. After that incident, around 30 BCE, the president of the Sanhedrin resigned and they elected Hillel as President. (*Bava Metzia* 85a; *Pesahim* 66a)

📖 Humility
Rabbi Hanina ben Dosa was a student of Rabbi Yohanan ben Zakkai in Arav. While he was there, Rabbi Yohanan's child fell gravely ill. He said to him: "Hanina my son, pray for him that he may live."

Rabbi Hanina put his head between his knees and prayed for the recovery of the child, and the child recovered. R. Yohanan ben Zakkai made a remark: "If Ben Zakkai had stuck his head between his knees all day long, no one would have noticed."[133] (*Berachot* 34b)

📖 Humility
Rabbi Gamliel and Rabbi Yehoshua once traveled on board a ship. The food supply of Rabbi Gamliel was quickly consumed and he had to rely on the food which Rabbi Yehoshua brought with him. R. Gamliel complimented him.

R. Yehoshua said to him: "Don't marvel at me, rather be surprised at two of your students who live on land, like Rabbi Eleazar Hisma and Rabbi Yohanan ben Nuri, who can calculate how many drops of water there are in the sea, and yet they have neither bread to eat nor clothing to put on."

Rabbi Gamliel decided to appoint them as supervisors, and sent for them when he disembarked. They were reluctant to accept on account of their humility. But Rabbi Gamliel told them. "Do you imagine that I offer you rulership? It is servitude that I offer you."[134] (*Horayot* 10a)

Humility
R. Avohu said: "I used to think that I was humble, but when I saw R. Abba from Acco offer one explanation and his interpreter another, and he did not object, I figured that I was not humble at all." (*Sotah* 40a)

Humility
R. Eleazar b. Shammua said: "Let the honor of your student be as precious to you as your own, and the honor of your colleague as the reverence for your teacher's, and have reverence for your teacher as the fear of Heaven. (*Avot* 4:12)

Humility
Rebbe stated: "It was childishness on my part to be presumptuous in the presence of R. Nathan the Babylonian." (*Bava Batra* 131a)

✡ Humility
In one instance, Rabbi Zera asked a question from Rabbi Yehuda HaNasi and he received a ruling which was different from that of Rabbi Hiyya. When he told

---

133. See also entry, R. Hanina ben Dosa prayed.

134. See entry, Star appears every 70 years.

Rebbe that Rabbi Hiyya has a different opinion, he answered: "Abandon my reply and adopt that of Rabbi Hiyya." (*Avodah Zarah* 36b)

Humility

R. Meir said: "Do a little less work and use that time to study Torah and be humble before all men." (*Avot* 4:10)

✿ Humility

R. Yehoshua b. Levi said: "Humility is the greatest of all character traits." (*Avodah Zarah* 20b; *Arachin* 16b)

Humility ceased

When Rabbi Yehuda HaNasi died, humility and the fear of sin ceased." (*Sotah* 9:15, 49a)

Huna

R. Huna from Diskarta (a small town near Bagdad) (*Bava Metzia* 47a)

Huna   הונא

Amora from Babylonia
Head of the academy in Sura
3rd century CE (*Megillah* 27b)

Huna   הונא

Amora from Babylonia
2nd century CE (*Sanhedrin* 7a)

Huna bar Nathan   הונא בר נתן

Amora from Babylonia

Resh Gelutha

4th – 5th centuries CE (*Zevahim* 19a)

Huna bar Yehoshua   הונא בר יהושע

Amora from Babylonia
4th century CE (*Berachot* 57a)

Huna from Sepphoris   הונה ציפוראה

Amora from Eretz Yisrael
3rd – 4th centuries CE (*Rosh Hashana* 34b)

Huna's bier

The people wanted to place a *Sefer Torah* on the bier of R. Huna, but Rabbi Hisda stopped them, because Rabbi Huna would not have approved of it.

He was buried in the cave of Tiberias next to R. Hiyya. (*Moed Katan* 25a; *Menahot* 32b)

Hunting

Hunting on Shabbat is discussed in *Haoreg*, the 13th *perek* in *Shabbat*. (*Shabbat* 105a)

📖 Hurt feelings

R. Avohu and R. Hiyya b. Abba traveled to a place to deliver lectures. R. Hiyya lectured on legal matters and R. Avohu lectured on Aggadah. The people left the hall where R. Hiyya was lecturing to go to listen to R. Avohu.

It was the habit of R. Hiyya to accompany R. Avohu every day to his lodging, but on this day, R. Avohu reversed the role and he accompanied R. Hiyya to his lodging. He tried to make him feel better, but he was still upset.[135] (*Sotah* 40a)

📖 Hurt feelings

The Talmud relates that R. Levi b. R. Huna b. Hiyya and Rabbah b. R. Huna were traveling together on a road, when R. Levi's ass went ahead of Rabbah. Afterwards R. Levi noticed that Rabbah seemed to feel insulted. To pacify him, R. Levi asked him a question: "Can a donkey like mine with bad manners be taken out on Shabbat wearing a halter?" (*Shabbat* 51b)

Hurt feelings

Ima Shalom was the wife of Rabbi Eliezer and the sister of Rabbi Gamliel. R. Eliezer was put in *herem*. From the time of this incident and onwards, she did not allow him to fall on his face to say *Tahanun*, because she feared that her husband's hurt feelings

---

135. See also entry, Lecturers.

would cause him to pray, and her brother R. Gamliel would die. However, one day a poor man came to the door, and she was occupied giving him food. When she came back, she found her husband fallen on his face. "Arise," she cried to him, "you have slain my brother." Soon thereafter an announcement was made from the house of R. Gamliel that he died.[136] (*Bava Metzia* 59b)

 Hurt feelings

Close friends hurt each others feelings

Rabbi Yohanan once inadvertently insulted Resh Lakish by a slip of the tongue, when he expressed himself thus:

"A robber knows his trade."

One word led to another and they hurt each other's feelings. When Resh Lakish fell ill, his wife, who was R. Yohanan's sister, came to R. Yohanan and cried, asking him to forgive her husband.

She pleaded: "Forgive him for the sake of my son."[137] (*Bava Metzia* 84a)

Husband of Yalta

R. Nahman bar Yaakov was married to Yalta, the daughter of the Exilarch. (*Chullin* 124a)

Husband traveled overseas

A husband who traveled overseas and his wife was told that he died. She remarried and then the first husband returned home. (*Yevamot* 87b)

Husband's jealousy

When a husband is suspicious of his wife's fidelity, they go through the ceremony of *sotah*. (*Sotah* 2a)

Hutzpit   חוצפית

(*Huzpit HaMeturgeman*)

Tanna from Eretz Yisrael in the 1st century CE. He was the main *meturgeman* (explainer) in the Sanhedrin. (*Berachot* 27b)

Huzal

Walled city or not

Rabbi Assi read the Megillah in Huzal on the fourteenth and on the fifteenth, because he was in doubt whether his town was walled in the time of Yehoshua. According to another report, R. Assi said: "Huzal of the house of Binyamin was walled in the days of Yehoshua Bin Nun." (*Megillah* 5b)

 Hyrcanus war

War between the two Hasmonean brothers; Aristobulus and Hyrcanus

Hyrcanus and Aristobulus were brothers and princes of the Hasmonean dynasty. They were fighting each other for the throne.

Aristobulus was trapped inside the besieged city of Jerusalem, while his brother Hyrcanus was on the outer part of the besieged city.[138] (*Sotah* 49b; *Bava Kamma* 82b)

I

Idi bar Avin   אידי בר אבין

Amora from Babylonia

4th century CE (*Pesahim* 101b; *Bava Metzia* 35b)

Idiot

Fire being sent with an idiot (*Bava Kamma* 22b, 59b)

---

136. See entry, Excommunicated.
137. See entry, Resh Lakish dies.

138. See also entry, Hashmonean house divided. In Tractate *Sotah* 49b, the Gemara states that Aristobolus was inside Jerusalem and his brother Hyrcanus was besieging the city from the outside, but in Tractate *Bava Kamma* 82b, the Gemara has it in reverse: Hyrcanus was trapped inside, and Aristobulus was besieging the city from the outside.

Idith עידית
Best quality property (*Bava Kamma* 7b)

Idol images (*Avodah Zarah* 40b)

Idol pedestals בימוסיאות
Idol worship pedestals (*Avodah Zarah* 54a)

Idol worship
The Jewish Elders of Rome were asked: "If God does not want idol worshipping why doesn't he abolish the idols?"

They answered: "Foolish people worship the sun, the moon, the stars, and planets which are useful to the world. Should God abolish those on account of foolish people?"

They retorted: "Why doesn't he abolish those which are unnecessary?"

"Because then they would claim that the others must be real idols if they were not abolished." (*Avodah Zarah* 54b)

Idol worship in public
Worshipping an idol in public under the threat of death (*Avodah Zarah* 27b)

Idol worshippers
It is not permitted to have commercial dealings with them on the days next to their holidays. (*Avodah Zarah* 2a)

Idol worshippers
Things belonging to idol worshippers are forbidden to use. (*Avodah Zarah* 29b)

If I am not for myself אם אין אני לי מי לי
R. Hillel said: "If I don't look out for myself, who will?" (*Avot* 1:14)

If not now, when אם לא עכשו אימתי
R. Hillel said: "If not now, when?" (*Avot* 1:14)

Ifra Hormuz
Queen Ifra Hormuz, mother of King Shapur[139] (*Bava Batra.* 10b)

Ignorants become more foolish
R. Yishmael b. R. Yosi stated: "The older the scholars get, the more wisdom they acquire, but the reverse is true about the ignorant – the older they get, the more foolish they become." (*Shabbat* 152a)

✿ Ignoring abuses
There was a man who used to say: "Happy is a person who hears abuse of himself and ignores it; for hundreds of evils pass him by." On this R. Shemuel said to R. Yehuda: "It is hinted in a verse in Scripture." (*Sanhedrin* 7a)

Ika b. Ammi איקא בר אמי
Amora from Babylonia
3rd – 4th centuries CE (*Bava Batra* 149a)

Ilfa אילפא
Amora from Eretz Yisrael
3rd century CE (*Zevahim* 13b)

Illai אלעי
Tanna from Eretz Yisrael
1st – 2nd centuries CE (*Eruvin* 65b)

Illai אלעי
Amora from Eretz Yisrael
3rd – 4th centuries CE (*Shabbat* 5a)

Illish
Rava said R. Illish is a great man. (*Bava Metzia* 68b)

Ilmaleh אלמלא
If not (*Sanhedrin* 49a)

---

139. See entry, Hormuz Ifra.

Ilonut   איילונות
A sexually underdeveloped woman (*Ketubbot* 11a)

Images of the moon
R. Gamliel had images of the moon on a tablet and on the wall to use for examination of witnesses. (*Rosh Hashana* 24a)

📖 Imma Shalom
Imma Shalom was R. Eliezer's wife and the sister of R. Gamliel.[140] (*Bava Metzia* 59b)

Immersed person of that very day
     טבול יום

Someone requiring immersion in the *mikveh*; that person has a special status on the day of his immersion and is called *tevul yom*. (*Parah* 8:7)

There is an entire tractate dedicated to this topic called *Tevul Yom*.

Immersion
Immersion for a *niddah* refers to a woman after menstruation who goes to the ritual bath (*mikveh*) to attain ritual purification. (*Niddah* 1–10)

Immersion
When a woman immerses in the *mikveh*, there shall be nothing intervening between her body and the water. (*Bava Kamma* 82a; *Eruvin* 4b; *Sukkah* 6a)

Immersion
Twilight immersion for Kohanim (*Shabbat* 35a)

Immersion in general (*Shabbat* 14a)

Immersion required
Everyone entering the Temple court including Kohanim are required to immerse in a *mikveh*. (*Yoma* 30a, 19a, 31a, 71a; *Zevahim* 19b)

📖 Immoral act resisted
There is a story about R. Zadok, told as follows: A Roman woman, who was politically powerful, made an immoral proposition to R. Zadok. To reject her would have put him in danger. He said to her, "I am hungry." She offered him non-kosher meat. He said to her; "What is the meaning of this, 'he who commits one immoral act can commit other non-permissible acts?'"

She lit the fire and put the non-kosher food into it. He then climbed himself into the fire. She said to him, "Had I known that it was so heinous to you, I would not have tormented you." (*Kiddushin* 40a)

Impaired document   איתרע שטרא
Faulty document (*Shevuot* 42a)

Imparts a taste   נותן טעם
(*Avodah Zarah* 66a)

✿ Impatience not displayed
The students once asked R. Adda b. Ahava: "To what do you attribute your longevity?"[141] He replied: "I have never displayed my impatience at home." (*Taanit* 20b)

Impose a hardship
We do not impose a hardship on the community which the majority cannot endure. (*Bava Batra* 60b)

Impossible to measure exactly
     אי אפשר לצמצם

A dispute between the rabbis whether it is possible to measure exactly (*Bechoros* 17a; *Yevamot* 19a, 88a; *Shevuot* 32a)

---

140. See entry, Excommunicated.

141. See entry, Longevity.

Impoverished
A Jew who became impoverished
R. Abbaye said: "R. Shimon b. Gamliel, R. Shimon, R. Yishmael, and R. Akiva, all maintain that all Israelites are princes.

For we have learned, if one was a debtor for a thousand *zuz* and he wore a robe costing a hundred *maneh*, he is stripped of that robe and dressed in a less expensive robe. R. Yishmael and R. Akiva disagreed, because all Israel are worthy of that robe."
(*Bava Metzia* 113b; *Shabbat* 128a)

✡ Impoverished person
A Jewish person becoming poor is entitled to continue in his lifestyle
One time there was a person from a fine family, who became impoverished. Hillel obligated himself to provide him with a horse to ride upon and a slave to run before him. On one occasion, he could not find a slave to run before him, so he himself ran before him for three miles.
(*Ketubbot* 67b)

Improper behavior
R. Avia visited Rabbah, but his boots were soiled with mud and he sat down on a bed. Rabbah was annoyed. He therefore wanted to show him that he is annoyed and asked him difficult halachic questions.
(*Shabbat* 46a)

📖 Improper conduct
There was a man whose sons did not conduct themselves in a proper manner. The father was upset with them and he left his estate to R. Yonatan b. Uzziel. R. Yonatan did not keep the estate, instead he sold one-third, consecrated one-third and returned a third to the sons. R. Shammai disapproved. R. Yonatan said to R. Shammai: "If you can take back what I have sold and what I have consecrated, then you can also take back what I have returned to the sons. If you can't take it back, then neither can you take back what I have returned to the sons." R. Shammai exclaimed: "The son of Uzziel has confounded me; the son of Uzziel has confounded me." (*Bava Batra* 133b)

✡ Improper dress
R. Hiyya b. Abba said: "It is improper for a scholar to walk in patched shoes."
(*Berachot* 43b)

Improving the world
R. Yohanan said: "Torah scholars are engaged all their days in improving the world." (*Shabbat* 114a)

Impudence
To be saved from impudent men, one recites a prayer. (*Berachot* 16b)

Impudence abound
In the time before Mashiach, the generations will degenerate
R. Nehorai said: "In the generation when Mashiach comes, young men will insult the old, old men will stand before the young, daughters will rise against their mothers, and daughters-in-law against their mothers-in-law. The people will be dog-faced, and a son will not be embarrassed in his father's presence."

R. Nehemia said: "In the generation just before Mashiach is coming, impudence will increase, esteem will be considered wrong, the vine will yield its fruit but will be expensive, and the kingdom will become non-believers and no one will rebuke them. (*Sanhedrin* 97a; *Sotah* 49b)

Impudent person   עזות פנים
Rebbe added a prayer to the morning service to save us from brazen and impudent men. (*Shabbat* 30b; *Berachot* 16b)

Impurities
First degree impurities, second, and third degree (*Shabbat* 14a–b)

Impurity of holy scripts
Impurity was decreed on parchments. (*Shabbat* 14a)

📖 In touch with Jews in exile
R. Gamliel the elder is in touch with Jews in Israel and in exile
It once happened that R. Gamliel was sitting on a step on the Temple Mount, and Yohanan, the well-known scribe, was before him prepared with three sheets of parchment. R. Gamliel said to him: "Take one sheet and write instructions to our brethren in the Upper Galilee and to those in the Lower Galilee, saying: 'Peace shall be with you! We are pleased to inform you that the time has arrived for removal of tithing from the olive heaps.'

"Take another sheet and write to our brethren in the South. 'Peace shall be with you! We are pleased to inform you that the time has arrived for removal of the tithing from the corn sheaves.'

"Take another sheet and write to our brethren, the Exiles in Babylonia and to those in Media, and to all the other exiled sons of Israel, saying: 'Peace shall be with you for ever! We are pleased to inform you that the doves are still tender and the lambs still too young and the crops are not yet ripe. It seems advisable to me and in the opinion of my colleagues to add thirty days to this year.'" (*Sanhedrin* 11b)

📖 Incense in Temple
The Talmud mentions that Rabbi Eliezer talked about the use of incense in the Temple. He was stressing the fact that the incense had a strong aroma. Even though the Temple was a long distance away from his father's place, the goats his father had on the Mountain of Michvar used to sneeze every time the incense was grinded in the Temple. (*Tamid* 3:8)

Incense left over in the Temple
It is taught that Bar Kappara said: "Once every sixty or seventy years, the accumulated incense leftovers were enough for a half-year supply for the Temple." (*Keritot* 6; Yerushalmi *Yoma* 4:5)

Inciting
To incite a dog to bite (*Bava Kamma* 23b, 24b; *Sanhedrin* 15b)

Inclusive or exclusive   עד ועד בכלל
When the Talmud says, "It is up to a certain day or hour," is the day or hour included or excluded? (*Berachot* 26b; *Hullin* 46a)

✿ Incomplete man
Without a wife – a man is incomplete
R. Eleazar said: "Any man who has no wife is not a complete man." (*Yevamot* 63a)

Increase peace
Torah scholars increase peace
It was Rabbi Eleazar who transmitted in the name of Rabbi Hanina the famous saying: "The wise scholars of Torah increase the peace in the world." (*Berachot* 64a)

Indirect monetary value
Any indirect money value is considered like money. (*Pesahim* 5b, 29b; *Ketubbot* 34a; *Bava Kamma* 71b)

Inferior quality property   זיבורית
(*Bava Kamma* 7b; *Gittin* 48b)

📖 Inflated prices
It once happened in Jerusalem that the price of a pair of pigeons was inflated to a golden dinar. R. Shimon b. Gamliel declared: "I will not rest this night until the price drops to a silver dinar." He was very upset at the merchants for charging such

a high price. He issued a decree, which reduced the number of pigeons required and the price dropped that very same day. (*Keritot* 1:7, 8a)

Inform the buyer

Four periods of the year, the seller must inform the buyer that he sold a cow that gave birth to a calf which was also sold to a different buyer. (*Hullin* 83a)

📖 Informer

Against Rabbah

R. Kahana said: R. Hama the son of the daughter of Hassa told me Rabbah b. Nahmeni died from fear of persecution. An informer told the authorities that Rabbah keeps 12,000 Israelites from paying the poll tax two months every year. It was the custom for many Israelites to study two months every year in the academy. A royal officer was sent to arrest him, but could not find him. Rabbah fled from Pumbedita to Acra, from Acra to Agama, from Agama to Sahin, from Sahin to Zarifa, from Zarifa to Eina Damim, and then back to Pumbedita. There the officer found him. He locked him up in a chamber, but Rabbah managed to escape and fled to Agama where he died. Abbaye and Rava, his students, and the entire academy went to attend to his body, but they could not find it. When they finally found his body, they mourned for him for seven days. (*Bava Metzia* 86a)

Inhabitant of Nehar Pekod

R. Giddal said in the name of Rav: "If an inhabitant of Naresh kisses you, then count your teeth. If an inhabitant of Nehar Pekod accompanies you, it is because of the fine garments he sees on you. If an inhabitant of Pumbedita accompanies you, then change your quarters." (*Hullin* 127a)

Inheritance

Order of inheritance (*Bava Batra* 115a)

Inheritance

Leaving the inheritance to a stranger when there are sons and daughters (*Bava Batra* 130a)

Inheritance

R. Ravina allowed the daughter of R. Ashi to collect her inheritance from her brother Mar without an oath. He gave her permission to choose from his medium-grade properties. But from her brother Sama, he allowed her to collect property only with an oath, and a lower-grade property. (*Ketubbot* 69a)

Inheritance

When a man dies and leaves sons and daughters, if the inheritance is large, the sons inherit and the daughters receive maintenance. (*Ketubbot* 108b; *Bava Batra* 139b)

📖 Inheritance

The Talmud relates that R. Avina's friend Geniva was unfortunately sentenced to die. When the sentence was about to be carried out he instructed the people to give Rabbi Avina 400 *zuz* from his wine estate. (*Gittin* 65b)

📖 Inheritance

The proselyte Issur had 12,000 *zuz* deposited for safekeeping with Rava, but the question arose whether Issur's son Mari is entitled to it. The problem was that when Mari was conceived, Issur was still not Jewish, but became Jewish before Mari was born. R. Ika b. R. Ammi suggested that Issur should declare that the money belongs to R. Mari. That is how the matter was resolved by Issur declaring that the money belongs to his son Mari. (*Bava Batra* 149a)

Inheritance

When one inherits the property of a proselyte, if he wants to merit holding on to it, he should buy a Torah (*Eruvin* 64a)

📖 Inheritance claim

A man came to Mari b. Isaac from Be-Hozai claiming that he is his brother, and he wanted to share in the inheritance of their father.

"I do not know you," said R. Mari. The case came before R. Hisda.

R. Hisda said to R. Mari: "He speaks the truth," but R. Hisda also said to the brother: "Go and produce witnesses that you are his brother." "I have witnesses, but they are afraid to testify on account that he is a powerful man."

R. Hisda then said to R. Mari: "You go and bring witnesses that you are not his brother."

"Is that justice?" exclaimed R. Mari? Subsequently, witnesses came to testify that he was his brother. (*Bava Metzia* 39b; *Ketubbot* 27b)

Inheritance

The daughters of Tzelofchad received three shares of the land taken from the Canaanites when the land was divided. (*Bava Batra* 116b)

Inheritance

Rav and Shemuel have a disagreement on the matter of inheritance. (*Bava Kamma* 9a; *Bava Metzia* 107a)

Inheritance

R. Yirmiyahu b. Abba said: "There is a Mishnaic ruling that if a father assigns his possessions to his son to take effect after his death neither can sell the property." (*Bava Kamma* 88b; *Yevamot* 56a; *Bava Batra* 156b)

Inheritance

Which relatives are entitled to inheritance? (*Bava Batra* 108a)

📖 Inheritance

A man made a will leaving to his three sons the following: "I leave a barrel of dust to one of them, a barrel of bones to my other son, and a barrel of fluff to my third son." No one could make out what he meant and they came to R. Banaah to consult him. He told them, "Do you have land, do you have cattle, and do you have fine mattresses and cushions?" They replied, "Yes." "In that case, this is what he meant: one son will get the land, the other son will get the cattle, and the third son will get the fine mattresses and cushions." (*Bava Batra* 58a)

📖 Inheritance dispute

The mother of Rami b. Hama gave her property in writing to Rami b. Hama in the morning, but in the evening she gave it in writing to Mar Ukva b. Hama. Rami b. Hama came to R. Sheshet, who confirmed his inheritance. Mar Ukva then went to R. Nahman, who confirmed Mar Ukva in his inheritance.

R. Sheshet thereupon went to R. Nahman and said to him: "What is the reason you acted this way in this matter?"

R. Nahman replied: "And what is the reason you acted in this matter this way?"

R. Sheshet answered: "Because the will of R. Rami was written first."

R. Nahman replied: "Are we living in Jerusalem, where the hours are recorded? We live in Babylonia, where the hours are not recorded."

R. Sheshet asked: "And why did you act the way you did?"

"I treated it as a case to be decided at the discretion of the judges," replied R. Nahman.

R. Sheshet then retorted: "I also treated

it as a case to be decided at the discretion of the judges."

But R. Nahman replied: "I am a judge, and you are not, and furthermore, you did not at first say that you treated it as a case to be decided by a judge." (*Ketubbot* 94b; *Bava Batra* 151a)

📖 Inheritance invested
By brother
The father of R. Safra left a large sum of money. R. Safra took the money and invested it into business. His brothers took him before Rava's court and demanded a share in the profits. Rava told them that since R. Safra is a great scholar he is not expected to leave his studies in order to make a profit for others. (*Bava Batra* 144a)

Inheritance money
R. Yohanan said: "If one inherited from his parents a fortune and wishes to lose it, etc." (*Bava Metzia* 29b; *Hullin* 84b)

Injuring a fellow-man (*Bava Kamma* 83b)

Injuring a slave (*Bava Kamma* 87a)

Injuring a son (*Bava Kamma* 87b)

Injuring oneself (*Bava Kamma* 91b)

Ink preparation
Preparing ink on Erev Shabbat (*Shabbat* 17b)

Inner character
R. Gamliel had issued an order: "No student whose inner character does not match his exterior may enter the academy." When R. Eleazar b. Azariah became president the order was revoked. (*Berachot* 28a)

📖 Innocents might be arrested
In an attempt to save innocents, R. Eleazar wound up to become the arresting officer.

"Let the advisor become the enforcer." They sent for R. Eleazar b. Shimon and ordered him to go out and arrest the thieves, an order which he had to obey.[142] R. Yehoshua b. Korha sent a reproving message: "Vinegar, son of wine, how long will you deliver the people of our God to slaughter?" R. Eleazar sent a reply. "I weed out thorns from the vineyard." R. Yehoshua retorted: "Let the owner of the vineyard come and weed out the thorns." (*Bava Metzia* 83b; *Sanhedrin* 82a, 96a)

Inscribed in the Heavenly books
R. Keruspedai said in the name of R. Yohanan: "Three books are opened in heaven on Rosh Hashana: one for the completely wicked, one for the completely righteous, and one for those in between. The completely righteous are forthwith inscribed to life, the completely wicked are forthwith inscribed to death, and the fate of those in between is suspended from Rosh Hashana till Yom Kippur: if they deserve it, they are inscribed to life, if not, they are inscribed to death. (*Rosh Hashana* 16b)

Inscription on Tefillin worn by God
The great scholar Rabbi Nahman b. Yitzhak asked Rabbi Hiyya b. Avin to explain to him a question that bothered him. "What is inscribed on the *tefillin* worn by the Ruler of the Universe?"

R. Avin replied: "The *tefillin* of the Ruler of the Universe are inscribed with these words 'And who is like your people Israel?'" (*Berachot* 6a)

Inserting
Additional prayers (*Berachot*, 5th *perek*)

Inserting prayers
If one forgot to insert prayers (*Berachot* 29b)

---

142. See entry, Arresting thieves.

Inspecting property daily

R. Shemuel's maxim was: "He who inspects his property daily will find a silver coin." (*Hullin* 105a; *Taanit* 20b)

✿ Inspecting property

R. Assi used to inspect his property daily. One day he saw that an irrigation pipe had burst on his land. He took off his coat, rolled it up and stuffed it into the hole. He then raised his voice and people came to help him (*Hullin* 105a)

Insult

R. Yitzhak said: "If one insults another person, he must ask his forgiveness." (*Yoma* 87a)

Insult according to the social position of the insulted and the insulter

הכל לפי המביש והמתבייש

(*Bava Kamma* 83b; *Ketubbot* 40a)

📖 Insulted

R Abba felt insulted

R. Yirmiyahu had a dispute with R. Abba and R. Abba felt insulted. R. Yirmiyahu went to R. Abba's home and sat down at his door.[143] (*Yoma* 87a)

Insulting the dead

Do not insult the dead by wearing *tefillin* in the cemetery. (*Berachot* 18a)

Insulting

A blind person (*Bava Kamma* 86b)

Insulting

A naked person (*Bava Kamma* 86b)

Insulting

A sleeping person (*Bava Kamma* 86b)

✿ Insulting

Or hurting another person

If one insults or hurts another person's feelings, even though he made monetary compensation, the offense is not forgiven until he asks for forgiveness. (*Bava Kamma* 92a)

📖✿ Insulting mindlessly

Another person

R. Eleazar b. Shimon was coming home from the house of his teacher in Migdal Gedor. He was riding leisurely on his donkey by the riverside, and he was feeling happy and elated because he studied a lot of Torah. A man, who was very ugly-looking, was passing him, and he greeted him with: "Peace shall be upon you."

He did not return the greeting. Instead, he said to him:

"Raca, how ugly you are.[144] Are all your townspeople as ugly as you are?" (*Taanit* 20a)

✿ Insulting the dead

R. Hiyya and R. Yonatan were visiting a cemetery when R. Hiyya noticed that the blue fringes of R. Yonatan were trailing on the ground. Said R. Hiyya to him, "Lift your fringes so that the deceased should not say: 'Tomorrow they are coming to join us and today they are insulting us.'" (*Berachot* 18a)

Intangible property

מטלטלין

Movables versus real estate (*Bava Metzia* 48b; *Kiddushin* 26b; *Bava Batra* 156b)

Integrity[145] (*Shevuot* 48b)

Intent

Transgression according to intent (*Hullin* 102b)

---

143. See also entry, Apology.

144. See entry, Gentle as a reed.
145. See story under, Abrogation.

Intention to use
If one intended to use the money which was entrusted to him for safekeeping (*Bava Metzia* 43b)

Intercalate
How many judges are required to intercalate the month, the year (*Sanhedrin* 2a)

Intercalate
While in prison
R. Shimon said: "One time while R. Akiva was in prison, he intercalated three years one after another." (*Sanhedrin* 12a)

Intercalate
Our rabbis taught: R. Simai and R. Tzadok traveled to Lydda to intercalate the year. (*Hullin* 56b)

📖 Intercalate
The year cannot be intercalated unless the Nasi of the Sanhedrin gives his consent. Once R. Gamliel was away in Syria to meet with the governor and he was delayed there. The Sanhedrin intercalated the year on condition that R. Gamliel would approve. When he returned, he said: "I approve," and the intercalation was considered correct. (*Sanhedrin* 11a; *Eduyot* 7:7)

📖 Intercalate outside Israel
R. Safra said that R. Avohu used to tell this story:

When R. Hanania b. Ahi Yehoshua left for Babylonia, he began to intercalate the years and to fix the new months outside of Israel. The Bet Din of Israel sent two scholars to stop him from doing it. They were R. Yosi b. Kippar and R. Zechariah b. Kavutal. When R. Hanania saw them, he asked them:

"Why have you come?"

"We have come to learn Torah from you," they answered.

When he heard that, he proclaimed to the community: "These men are the great scholars of our generation. They and their ancestors have served in the Temple. As we have learned, Zechariah b. Kavutal said: 'Many times have I read from the book of Daniel.'"

Shortly after that, the two scholars were ruling against R. Hanania. Everything he called unclean, they declared clean; what he had forbidden, they permitted. R. Hanania became upset and announced to the community: "These men are false and worthless."

R. Yosi b. Kippar and R. Zechariah b. Kavutal said to him: "You have already built our reputation and you cannot destroy it; you have made already fences and you cannot break them down."

R. Hanania said to them: "Why do you declare everything clean, which I declared unclean?"

They answered him: "Because you intercalate years and fix the new moon outside Israel."

He retorted: "Did not R. Akiva b. Yosef intercalate years and fix the new month outside of Israel?"

They answered him: "Do not cite R. Akiva who had no equal in Israel."

He retorted: "I also left no equal in the Land of Israel."

They said to him: "The kids which you left behind in Israel have become goats with horns, and they sent us to tell you in their name. If you listen, then all is well, but if you don't, you will be excommunicated.

"The Bet Din of Israel also empowered us to tell the community here in Babylonia that if they listen to us then all is well. However, if they don't listen, then let them go up the mountain, let Ahia build an altar, and Hanania play the harp. All of you will become deniers and will have no portion in the God of Israel." When the community heard this, they started crying and declared "Heaven forbid." (*Berachot* 63a)

Intercalate place and time
Our rabbis have taught: The place to intercalate the year is in Judea, Transjordan, and the Galilee, and it has to be done in daytime. (*Sanhedrin* 11b)

Intercalated year
When the years are intercalated, there is always a minimum of four months during a year that are a full thirty days. (*Arachin* 8b)

Intercalation
Secret intercalation took place with cryptic[146] messages sent under Roman occupation. (*Sanhedrin* 12a)

Intercalation of the year
It once happened that R. Gamliel was sitting on a step on the Temple Mount, and Yohanan, the well-known scribe, was before him prepared with three sheets of parchment. R. Gamliel said to him: "Take the sheets and write instructions to our brethren:[147] It seems advisable to me and in the opinion of my colleagues to add thirty days to this year." (*Sanhedrin* 11b)

Interceded to nullify the harsh decree
The Romans decreed to ban Torah study
Rabbi Yehuda ben Shammua is credited with successfully interceding with the Roman authorities to nullify the decree forbidding the study of Torah. The Roman authorities issued a decree that the Jews should not study Torah, shall not circumcise their sons, and should not observe the Shabbat. Rabbi Yehuda ben Shammua consulted a Roman matron who had many influential Roman friends. She advised

him how to get the decree annulled. (*Rosh Hashana* 19a; *Taanit* 18a)

Interception in the air
קלוטה כמי שהומחה
Interception in the air[148] is equal as resting on the ground. (*Shabbat* 4b)

Intercourse
Abnormal and forbidden intercourse (*Sanhedrin* 54b)

Interest
ריבית
Money lent with interest (*Bava Metzia* 60b, 62a)

Interested parties
It has been taught: If a Torah belonging to the inhabitants of the town was stolen, the judge of that town may not judge the case, nor may the inhabitants of the town give testimony. (*Bava Batra* 43a)

Interest prepaid
ריבית מוקדמת
(*Bava Metzia* 75b)

Interest postpaid
ריבית מאוחרת
(*Bava Metzia* 75b)

Interested parties
נוגעין בעדותן
Interested parties, prejudiced witnesses (*Bava Batra* 43a)

Interior intellect matching exterior
It was learned that prior to the election of R. Eleazar b. Azariah as president of the Sanhedrin, Rabbi Gamliel had issued an ordinance that those students whose exterior appearance does not match their interior intellect may not enter.

After R. Eleazar was elected, 400 additional seats were brought in to

---

146. See entry, Cryptic messages sent.
147. See entry, In touch with Jews in exile.

148. It has halachic implications on Shabbat.

accommodate the new students who entered the hall.[149] (*Berachot* 27b)

📖 Interpreter

As a young man, Rav came to the place where R. Shila was teaching. One day there was no interpreter available and Rav offered to be one. Rav interpreted the words "*Keriat hageber*" as the call of man. R. Shila said to him: "Would you change that to the call of the rooster?"

Rav replied: "A flute is a nice musical instrument for the educated, but give it to weavers and they will not accept it. When I interpreted this word as meaning a man before R. Hiyya, he did not object to it."

R. Shila asked Rav to sit down. (*Yoma* 20b)

Interpreters of dreams

R. Bizna b. Zavda said in the name of R. Akiva, who had it from R. Panda, who had it from R. Nachum, who had it from R. Birim, who said it in the name of an Elder by the name of R. Banah: "There were twenty-four interpreters of dreams in Jerusalem. R. Banah once had a dream and he went to all twenty-four, and each gave him a different interpretation, and all were fulfilled. (*Berachot* 55b)

Interrupting to say the Shema

R. Eleazar b. Zadok said: "When we were engaged in intercalating the year, we didn't break for the *Shema*." (*Shabbat* 11a)

Interruptions during prayers

Permissible and forbidden interruptions during prayers (*Berachot*, 2nd *perek*; *Berachot* 13a)

Intoxication

A walk or a little sleep helps remove the effects of wine. (*Eruvin* 64b)

---

149. See also entry, Appointed Nasi of the Sanhedrin.

Intoxication

A person who is intoxicated bought or sold merchandise. His sale and purchase are valid. (*Eruvin* 65a)

Investigating and examining   חקירות ובדיקות

R. Kahana and R. Safra studied at Rabbah. They encountered Rami b. Hama and they were discussing the difference between *hakirot* and *bedikot*. (*Sanhedrin* 41b)

Investigating witnesses   חקירת עדים

The process of examining and investigating the witnesses (*Rosh Hashana* 25b)

Invitation to dine

R Meir said: "Do not invite a friend to dine if you know that he will decline." (*Hullin* 94a)

Invitation to dine was declined

R. Pinhas b. Yair was invited for dinner by R. Yehuda HaNasi, but he excused himself for many reasons. (*Hullin* 7b)

Iron clad agreement   צאן ברזל
(*Bechorot* 16b)

Irreverence in the Temple   מעילה
Misappropriation

Desecration by the slightest deviation from the prescribed ceremony is considered a *meilah*. (*Meilah* 2a)

Ishboren   אישבורן

An area holding water in a flat area where the water can become stagnant. (*Pesahim* 42a)

📖 Ishmaelites

Rebbe asked R. Levi after he returned from Babylonia: "What are the Persians like?" "They are like the armies of the House of David." "What are the Guebers fire-worshippers like?"[150] "They are like the destroying angels." "What are the Ishmaelites like?" They are like the demons of the outhouse." "What are the scholars of Babylon like?" "They are like the ministering angels." (*Kiddushin* 72a)

Iska   עיסקא

The Nehardeans said: "An *iska* is a semi-loan and a semi-trust." (*Bava Metzia* 104b)

📖 Israel beloved in the sight of God

R. Shimon b. Yohai said: "Come and see how beloved Israel is in the sight of God – for wherever Israel was exiled to, the Shechina went with them. They were exiled to Egypt and the Shechina was with them, as it is written. They were exiled to Babylon and the Shechina was with them, as it is written. And when they will be redeemed in the future, the Shechina will be with them, as it is written." Abbaye said: "In Babylonia, the Shechina is in the synagogue of Huzal, and in the synagogue of Shaf Yativ, which is in Nehardea. But do not think it is in both places, but rather it is sometimes in one and sometimes in the other." R. Abbaye always prayed in that synagogue when he was in that town. (*Megillah* 29a)

📖 Israel immune

From planetary influences

R. Shemuel said that Israel is immune from planetary influences.

R. Shemuel and his Persian friend Avlat were having a conversation near a meadow. Some people were walking to the meadows and they were passing by them. Avlat pointed to a man and said:

"That man is going to the meadows, but he will not return, because a snake will bite him and he will die."

---

150. The Guebers are a fanatical sect of Persian fire-worshippers.

R. Shemuel replied: "If he is an Israelite he will go and return."

They were still having a conversation when the man – who went to the meadows – returned from the meadow. Avlat was surprised, and he walked over to the man, took his carrying case, opened it and found in it a snake cut in two pieces. R. Shemuel asked the man:

"Is there anything that you may have done to merit this?"

The man answered: "Every day all of us in the group pooled and shared our food equally. However, today the man next to me had no food to share and he was embarrassed. I told the group I am going to collect the food from everyone. When I came to him, I pretended to take food from him to avoid embarrassment for him." (*Shabbat* 156b)

Israelite woman eating Teruma

An Israelite woman married to a Kohen, may she eat from *teruma*? (*Yevamot* 86b)

Issachar of Kefar Barkai

An interaction that happened between Issachar and the Hasmonean king and queen (*Pesahim* 57a)

Issar Italki

An Italian coin (*Bava Metzia* 44b; *Kiddushin* 12a)

Issur L'Hag   איסור לחג

Binding to the holiday, adding another day of joy to the holiday (*Sukkah* 45b)

Issur the convert

Issur left an inheritance to his son Mari, but there were complications. (*Bava Batra* 149a)

📖 Istroboli

Reuben ben Istroboli

The Talmud relates that one time the Roman authorities issued a decree against

It all depends on me alone

Jewish religious practices. They forbade Jews to observe the Shabbat, or to circumcise their sons, or to observe the practice of family purity. When the edict was issued, a Jew living in Rome by the name of Reuben b. Istroboli dressed like the Romans do and mingled among the Romans, so that they thought he is a Roman. He convinced the authorities that to enact these restrictions would be a disadvantage to the Romans. On his advice, they annulled the laws.[151] (*Meilah* 17a–b)

📖 It all depends on me alone
אין הדבר תלוי אלא בי

R. Eleazar b. Dordia frequented many houses of ill repute. Once he was told that there was a harlot in a town by the sea who charges a purse of *dinarim* for her services. He crossed seven rivers for her sake. When he was with her, she expressed her conviction that Eleazar b. Dordia will never be forgiven for his sins. After this incident, he went to sit between two mountains and called out to the mountains, "Please plead for mercy for me." The mountains replied: "We need to plead for ourselves." He pleaded with heaven and earth and received the same reply. He pleaded with the sun and moon and received the same reply. He then pleaded with the stars and constellations and received the same reply. Finally, he said: "The matter of repentance really depends on me alone." He placed his head between his knees and cried aloud until his soul departed. A Bat Kol was heard proclaiming: "Rabbi Eleazar b. Dordia is destined for the life of the World to Come."

Rebbe remarked: "One may acquire eternal life after many years and another may acquire it in one hour." (*Avodah Zara* 17a)

---

151. See entry, Delegation sent to Rome to rescind.

📖 It is for my benefit

R. Huna said in the name of Rav, who learned it from R. Meir, who learned it from R. Akiva: "A person should always say: 'Whatever Hashem does is for the good.'" The following story illustrates this:

"R. Akiva was traveling on the road with a rooster, a donkey, and a lamp. When he arrived in a certain town, he looked around for lodging, but none was available. He said to himself, *Whatever Hashem does is for the good*, and he slept in the open field. A strong wind came and blew out the lamp, a wild cat came and ate the rooster, and a lion came and ate the donkey. He said again, *Whatever Hashem does, it is for the good*. During the same night, a gang of terrorists came and captured all the inhabitants of the town and carried them away. He expressed himself thus: "Did I not say, '*Whatever Hashem does, it is for the good*'?" The light of the lamp and the noise of the rooster and donkey would have revealed his presence. (*Berachot* 60b; *Taanit* 21a)

Itliz
איטליז

R. Gamliel and R. Yehoshua in the meat market of Emmaus (*Hullin* 91b)

Iyo
איו

Tanna from Eretz Yisrael
2nd century CE (*Eruvin* 36b)

Iyov

R. Yohanan and R. Eleazar stated that Iyov was one of those who returned from the Babylonian exile. His house of study was in Tiberias. Much more is written about Iyov in the Talmud. (*Bava Batra* 15a–b, 16a; *Sotah* 27b)

Izgedar King of Persia

Rabbi Ashi related what he was once told by Rabbi Huna: "I was standing next to

Izgedar, King of Persia, and my girdle[152] was pushed high up. He reached over and pulled my girdle down, observing to me, 'It is written of you, "You shall be unto Me a kingdom of priests and a holy nation".'" (*Zevahim* 19a)

J

📖 Jailer deserves the World to Come
Eliyahu pointed out a man to R. Beroka. "That man has a share in the World to Come."

R. Beroka ran after him and asked him: "What is your occupation?"

"I am a jailer,[153] and I keep the men and women separated by placing my bed between them. When I see a Jewish girl and I see the non-Jewish guys cast their eyes on her, I risk my life to save her from them. (*Taanit* 22a)

Jerusalem
Jerusalem can be enlarged only by the authority of seventy-one judges. (*Sanhedrin* 2a)

📖 Jerusalem
Our rabbis taught: Anyone who has not seen the Water-drawing[154] at the Temple in Jerusalem has not seen rejoicing in his life. Anyone who has not seen Jerusalem in its splendor has never seen a lovely city. Anyone who has not seen the Temple in Jerusalem when it was fully rebuilt has never seen a beautiful building in his life. (*Sukkah* 51b; *Bava Batra* 4a)

📖 Jerusalem
Siege of Jerusalem in 70 CE
R. Yohanan b. Zakkai was smuggled out of Jerusalem[155] in order to meet with Vespasian. He thought he could save something for the Jewish people.

Rabbi Yohanan and Vespasian had a discussion and Vespasian realized that he was speaking to a very wise person. Finally Vespasian told Rabbi Yohanan: "I must leave now, but make a request of me and I will grant it to you."

Rabbi Yohanan said:

"Give me Yavne and its wise men to be allowed to teach, allow the family chain of R. Gamliel to continue, and a physician to heal Rabbi Tzadok."

His wishes were granted, and the Yavne Academy was established. (*Gittin* 56a)

Jerusalem
Jerusalem can never be declared a condemned city. (*Bava Kamma* 82b; *Yoma* 23a; *Arachin* 32b)

Jerusalem and a dead body
In Jerusalem, it was forbidden to keep a dead person overnight. (*Bava Kamma* 82b; *Yoma* 23a; *Arachin* 32b)

Jerusalem gardens
The garden of roses existed from the days of the first Prophets. (*Bava Kamma* 82b)

Jerusalem had no hot springs
R. Dostai b. Yannai said: "There are no hot springs in Jerusalem similar to the hot springs in Tiberias so that the pilgrims coming to Jerusalem would not be able to say, 'I went up to Jerusalem to enjoy the hot springs.'" (*Pesahim* 8b)

Jerusalem houses that were sold
Houses sold in Jerusalem should not be liable to become irredeemable. (*Bava Kamma* 82b; *Yoma* 23a; *Aruchin* 32b)

---

152. The insignia of the Exilarch.
153. See entry, Eliyahu.
154. See entry, Water-drawing rejoicing.

155. See entry, Escape from besieged Jerusalem.

Jerusalem; its regulations
Ten regulations were applied in Jerusalem. (*Bava Kamma* 82b; *Yoma* 23a; *Arachin* 32b)

Jerusalem of the future
R. Levi said in the name of R. Papi in the name of R. Yehoshua De-Sachni: "Jerusalem of the future will be three times the size of the present Jerusalem and the houses will be thirty stories high." (*Bava Batra* 75b)

Jerusalem redeemed
Ulla said: "Jerusalem will be redeemed only by righteousness." (*Sanhedrin* 98a)

📖 Jester
Deserves a share in the World to Come
Eliyahu pointed out two men to R. Beroka. "These two have a share in the World to Come."

R. Beroka ran after them and asked them: "What is your occupation?"

They replied: "We are jesters.[156] When we see people depressed, we cheer them up. When we see two people quarreling, we try to make peace between them." (*Taanit* 22a)

✿ A Jew is a Jew is a Jew
אף על פי שחטא ישראל הוא
R. Abba bar Zavda said, "Even though a Jew sinned, he is still a Jew. Thus people say, a myrtle, even when it is mixed in with reeds is still a myrtle and is so called." (*Sanhedrin* 44a)

Jewelry
To carry jewelry on Shabbat (*Shabbat* 46b; *Moed Katan* 12b)

Jewish captives redeemed
Once R. Tanhum with the assistance of Rabbi Aha redeemed Jewish captives for

a great sum of money. These captives were brought to Tiberias from Armenia. (*Yevamot* 45a)

Jewish people are united on the 15th of Av
The 15th day of Av was made into a holiday with celebrations because the restrictions on the apportioning of land to the tribes was lifted, and all the tribes could intermarry – hence, the Jewish people were united. (*Taanit* 30a)

Jewish property (*Bava Kamma* 13b, 37b)

Jewish wine served by non-Jews
(*Yevamot* 46a; *Avodah Zarah* 59a)

Jews
All Jews have a share in the World to Come. (*Sanhedrin* 90a)

Job   איוב
R. Gamliel buried the book of Job under the bricks. (*Shabbat* 115a)

Job   איוב
When the report of the spies was given, Yehoshua and Calev reported that the protector of the cities died, namely, Job, who was their protector, died. (*Bava Batra* 15a)

✿ Job nearby
A job nearby with less pay is preferable to a job far away with more pay
Rav instructed his son Aibu with the following: "It is preferable to earn a smaller amount near your home, over a job earning a larger amount far from your home." (*Pesahim* 113a)

Joyous month of Adar
משנכנס אדר מרבין בשמחה
R. Yehuda b. R. Shemuel b. Shilat in the name of Rav said: "Just as from the beginning of the month of Av we curtail

---

156. See entry, Eliyahu.

rejoicing, so it is the opposite with the month of Adar: from the beginning of Adar, rejoicing is increased." (*Taamit* 29b)

Jubilee arrival to be considered

The years before and after the Jubilee have to be considered when signing a contract for land. (*Arachin* 24a)

Jubilee year

Exile comes to the world on account of the sin of non-observance of the Jubilee year. (*Shabbat* 33a)

📖 Judean king must be Jewish

Herod heard rumors that people were saying a king of Judea must be a Jew. He asked his advisers: "Who are they who teach that a king can be chosen only from thy brethren?"

They told him, "It is the rabbis." He therefore killed all the rabbis except R. Bava b. Buta, but he blinded him. One day, Herod pretended to be a commoner and sat before R. Bava b. Buta and complained, saying:

"This former slave, Herod, does wicked things."

"What do you want me to do to Herod?" asked R. Bava b. Buta.

"I want you to curse him," said Herod.

"It is written in scripture that even in thy thoughts you should not curse a king," replied R. Bava b. Buta.

Herod tested him with more suggestions, but R. Bava did not fall into his trap. Finally he said:

"I am Herod. Had I known that the rabbis were so circumspect, I wouldn't have killed them." (*Bava Batra* 4a)

Judge

Must be guided by what he sees
Rova instructed R. Papa and R. Huna b. Yehoshua: "When a written legal decision of mine comes before you and you find objection to it, do not tear it up before you speak to me. If I have valid reasons for my decision, I will tell it to you, and if not, I will withdraw it. After my death, you shall neither tear it up nor draw any conclusions from it. You shall not tear it up, because had I been there I might have given you my reasons, and do not draw any conclusions, because a judge must be guided by what he sees with his eyes." (*Bava Batra* 130b)

Judge accedes to ruling of another judge

The relatives of R. Yohanan seized a cow that belonged to orphans. They were brought before R. Yohanan who ruled the seizure lawful, but when they appealed to Resh Lakish, he ruled that they must return the cow. They appealed again to R. Yohanan, who said to them: "What can I do when one of equal authority differs from me?" (*Ketubbot* 84b)

📖✿ Judge by example

Require no more from others than from yourself
It happened that Rabbi Yannai had a tree, which overhung a public road. Another man also had a tree hanging over a public street. Some people who used the street objected, and the man was summoned to the court of R. Yannai. R. Yannai said to them, "Go home and come back tomorrow." During the night he had his workers cut down his own tree. On the next day when they came back for a decision, he ordered the man to cut down his tree. The man objected, "But you, sir, also have a tree hanging over?"

R. Yannai answered: "Go and see. If mine is cut down, then cut yours; if it is not, you need not cut yours." What was R. Yannai's thinking? At first he thought that people would be happy to sit in the shade of the tree. (*Bava Batra* 60a)

✡ Judge disqualifies himself

Ameimar, as a judge, was in the middle of a trial when a bird flew down and landed on his head. A man approached and removed the bird. "What is your business here?" asked Ameimar. "I have a lawsuit going on," replied the man. "In that case, I am disqualified to act as a judge." (*Ketubbot* 105b)

✡ Judge everyone as being upright

R. Yehuda b. Shila said in the name of R. Assi in the name of R. Yohanan: "There are six good deeds from which one can derive benefits in this world and still get the rewards in the World to Come: hospitality to guests, visiting the sick, concentration during prayer, rising early for prayer, bringing up a son with Torah study, and to judge everyone as being upright." (*Shabbat* 127)

📖 Judge exposed as a bribe taker

Imma Shalom, the wife of R. Eliezer, was the sister of R. Gamliel. In the vicinity, lived a sectarian judge with a reputation that he did not accept bribes. In order to expose him, she brought him a golden lamp and said to him: "My father left an estate and I want to get my share of the inheritance."

The judge ordered the estate to be divided so that she gets her share. R. Gamliel argued that according to Torah Law, if there are sons, then they inherit, but a daughter does not inherit. The judge replied, since the day you were exiled from your land, the law of the Torah has been superseded by other laws, which give a daughter an equal inheritance. The next day R. Gamliel brought to the judge a Libyan ass. Whereupon the judge reversed his own ruling by declaring, "I found at the end of the book it is written, 'I came neither to destroy the Law of Moshe nor to add to it.'

"And it is written therein, 'A daughter does not inherit where there is a son.'"

Imma Shalom said to the judge: "Let your light shine forth like a lamp." R. Gamliel said to him: "An ass came and knocked the lamp over." (*Shabbat* 116a–b)

Judge feels he must disqualify himself

Mar b. R. Ashi said: "I am unqualified to be a judge when one litigant is a Torah scholar, because he is as dear to me as I am to me." (*Shabbat* 119a; *Ketubbot* 105b)

Judge is loved or hated

Rava remarked: "At first I thought that all the people of Mehuza love me. When I was appointed a judge, I thought that some people would hate me and some would love me. But my observation is that a litigant may lose today and win tomorrow. Therefore, my conclusion is that if I am loved, they all love me, and if I am hated, they must all hate me. (*Ketubbot* 105b)

✡ Judge not exterior

R. Meir said: "Do not judge a wine by the jug it is in, but by its contents." (*Avot* 4:27)

✡ Judge not your fellow-man

R. Hillel the grandson of R. Yehuda Ha-Nasi said: "Do not judge your fellow-man until you are in his position." (*Avot* 2:4)

✡ Judge people

Judge all people in the scale of merit (*Avot* 1:6)

Judges

The rabbis have taught: The total number of judges in Israel was 78,600. (*Sanhedrin* 18a)

Judges

Judges in Israel and judges in Babylonia differed in certain cases. (*Bava Batra* 70b)

Judges for monetary cases

The number of judges required for

monetary cases, larceny or other cases (*Sanhedrin* 2a)

Judges in Jerusalem

The Talmud says: Two judges of civil law were in Jerusalem, Admon and Hanan b. Avishalom. Somewhere else the Talmud states that there were three Judges – Hanan HaMitzri was the third. The Talmud reconciles the discrepancy. His decisions are quoted in the Talmud, and Rabbi Gamliel is quoted as agreeing with Rabbi Admon. (*Ketubbot* 105a; *Shevuot* 38b)

Judges in Tiberias

R. Ammi and R. Assi were sitting and studying between the pillars in Tiberias. Every now and then, they would stop studying. They would knock on the door and announce: "If anyone has a lawsuit, let him come in." (*Shabbat* 10a)

Judges of Eretz Yisrael

When the Talmud states: "The judges of Eretz Yisrael" – this refers to Rabbi Ammi and Rabbi Assi. (*Sanhedrin* 17b)

Judges to ignore personalities

The Torah demands that judges must ignore personalities. (*Sanhedrin* 7b)

Judge's compensation

Karna, who was a judge, used to take a fixed fee from both parties before informing them of his decision.

Karna received compensation for loss of work, for he was occupied regularly as a wine taster and smeller for which he was paid a fee.

The Talmud questions whether this is against Torah prohibition. The Talmud explains that Karna received compensation for the loss of his time at work. Karna was regularly employed in a wine store, therefore when he took time out to act as a judge, he incurred a loss of time and

money. This is similar to the case of R. Huna. When a lawsuit was brought before him, he used to tell the litigants: "Provide me a man who will draw the water for my fields and I will be a judge for you." (*Ketubbot* 105a; *Kiddushin* 58b; *Bechorot* 29a)

Judge's mistake in student's presence

When a student sees his Rebbe making a mistake in judgment between two litigants (*Shevuot* 31a; *Sanhedrin* 6b)

Judges' discretion[157] (*Ketubbot* 94b; *Bava Batra* 151a)

Judging

R. Hisda and R. Rabbah b. Huna were sitting in judgment all day long and their hearts grew faint. (*Shabbat* 10a)

✿ Judging alone

R. Yishmael said: "Judge not alone for none may Judge alone save one." (*Avot* 4:8)

Judging for pay (*Bechorot* 29a)

✿ Judging other people

R. Yishmael said: "One who avoids judging people removes from himself hatred, robbery, and unnecessary oaths but one who is too self-confident in judging others is a fool, wicked, and arrogant." (*Avot* 4:7)

Judgment day

Rava said: "When a person dies and comes before the heavenly Judge he is asked several questions." (*Shabbat* 31a)

Judgment day

R. Keruspedai said in the name of R. Yohanan: "Three books are opened in heaven on Rosh Hashana: one for the completely wicked, one for the completely

---

157. See entries, Last will, and Inheritance dispute.

righteous, and one for those in between. The completely righteous are forthwith inscribed to life, the completely wicked are forthwith inscribed to death, and the fate of those in between is suspended from Rosh Hashana until Yom Kippur. If they deserve it, they are inscribed to life, if not, they are inscribed to death." (*Rosh Hashana* 16b)

Judgment in the heavenly court
R. Yehoshua b. Levi said: "There are four acts for which one is exempt from judgment by fellow-men, but guilty in the heavenly courts." (*Bava Kamma* 55b)

✿ Judgmental
R. Hillel said: "Do not separate yourself from the community, do not believe you know it all, and do not judge your friend until you have been put in his position." (*Avot* 2:4)

Judicial court
How large a population is required for a city to have its own court (*Sanhedrin* 2b)

✿ Jug of wine
Don't judge wine by the jug it is in
R. Meir said: "Do not judge a wine by the jug it is in, but by its contents." (*Avot* 4:27)

📖 Jugglers
R. Levi used to juggle before R. Yehuda HaNasi with eight knives. He did it on the occasion of the Water-drawing celebration.

R. Shemuel used to juggle before King Shapur with eight glasses of wine.

R. Abbaye used to juggle before Rabbah with eight eggs, but some say four eggs. (*Sukkah* 53a)

✿ Jump into a fiery furnace
R. Zutra b. Toviya said in the name of

Rav, according to others R. Hana b. Bizna said it in the name of R. Shimon Hasida, and others say it was said by R. Yohanan in the name of R. Shimon b. Yohai: "It is preferable for a person to jump into a fiery furnace than to shame another person in public." (*Berachot* 43b; *Bava Metzia* 59a)

📖 Jump into the sea
Nahshon ben Aminadav was the first to jump into the sea before it split
What did Yehuda, the son of Yaakov, do that he merited a special blessing from Yaakov? We have learned: R. Meir used to say" "When the Israelites stood by the Reed Sea, the tribes were arguing about who is to jump first into the sea. Then men from the tribe of Benjamin jumped in first, and the princes of Yehuda hurled stones at them, because they wanted to be first."

R. Yehuda said to R. Meir: "That is not the story I heard, but this is what happened. The tribes were not willing to jump into the sea, but Nahshon ben Aminadav, who was a prince from the tribe of Yehuda, came forward and jumped in first. At that time Moshe was busy praying to God. Hashem said to Moshe: "My children are drowning and you are prolonging in prayer?"

"What should I do?" Moshe asked. Hashem answered him: "Lift up your rod and stretch it over the sea and go forward."

As they marched into the water, the sea split. As a reward the kings of Israel belong to the tribe of Yehuda. (*Sotah* 36b, 37a)

📖 Jumps from the roof
To avoid temptation
The Talmud relates that when R. Kahana came to the house of a Roman woman to sell his baskets he was peddling, she tried to seduce him. He excused himself to clean up first. He went to the roof and jumped.

The Angel Eliyahu flew towards him and caught him in mid-air and saved him from being killed. Eliyahu complained to him: "You caused me to have to fly 400 parsi to save you."

"What caused me to end up in this kind of situation; isn't it my poverty?" Thereupon Eliyahu gave him a *shifa* full of *dinarim*. (*Kiddushin* 40a)

✿ Justice

R. Shimon b. Gamliel said: "The world rests on three foundations: truth, justice, and peace." (*Avot* 1:18)

Juxtaposition of text in the Torah

R Eleazar said: "Whence is the rule of proximity derived from the Torah?" (*Yevamot* 4a; *Berachot* 10a, 21b)

K

Kaaka   קעקע
Writing an incision in the flesh (*Makkot* 21a)

Kaddish
The world endures because during the recital of Kaddish, the entire congregation recites יהא שמה רבא. (*Sotah* 49a)

Kafri
Rabbi Hiyya bar Abba was born in Kafri, a community near Sura in Babylonia, but left Babylonia and moved to Eretz Yisrael. (*Ketubbot* 5a)

Kahana I   כהנא
Amora from Babylonia
2nd – 3rd centuries CE (*Sanhedrin* 36b; *Nazir* 19a; *Betzah* 6a, 37b)

Kahana II   כהנא
Amora from Babylonia
3rd century CE (*Bava Kamma* 117a)

Kahana III   כהנא
Amora from Babylonia
3rd century CE (*Moed Katan* 13b; *Hullin* 19b)

Kahana IV   כהנא
Amora from Babylonia
4th century CE (*Sanhedrin* 41b)

Kahana V   כהנא
Amora from Babylonia
Head of the academy in Pum Nahara
4th century CE (*Berachot* 39a)

📖 Kaiser wants to see God
The Kaiser asked R. Yehoshua b. Hanania: "I want to see your God."

R. Yehoshua replied: "You can't see God."

"Indeed, I insist."

He took the Kaiser in front of the sun during the summer solstice and said to him: "Look up at the sun."

"I cannot," said the Kaiser.

"If you can't look at the sun which is only one of the servants of God, how do you presume to look at the Divine presence?" (*Hullin* 60a)

📖 Kalba Savua
The daughter of Kalba Savua, one of the richest men in Jerusalem, betrothed herself to R. Akiva. When her father found out, he disinherited her of his property. She married him that winter. They were so poor, they had to sleep on straw. She had to pick out the straws from his hair.

Upon her insistence that he become a scholar, he left her and spent twelve years in Lydda in the yeshivas of Rabbi Eliezer ben Horkynos and Rabbi Yehoshua ben Hanania, and at one time he studied with Rabbi Tarfon.

Her father, Kalba Savua, on hearing that a great man and scholar came to town, said to himself, *I shall go to him, perhaps he will invalidate my vow.* When he came, R. Akiva asked him: "If you had known that she was marrying a great scholar would you have made the vow?"

He replied: "If I had known that he knows one chapter or even one Halachah, I would not have made the vow." He annulled the vow and said to him: "I am the man she married." Kalba Savua fell on his face and kissed the feet of R. Akiva. He also gave him later half of his wealth. (*Nedarim* 50a)

Kal VaHomer   קל וחומר
Light and stringent
Fortiori = inference from a minor to a major
It is one of the thirteen methods and principles of biblical interpretation by R. Yishmael. (*Hullin* 12:5, *Sanhedrin* 73a; *Bava Kamma* 25a; *Bava Metzia* 88b)

Kameia   קמיע
Amulet (*Shabbat* 53b, 61a)

📖 Kamza and Bar Kamza
The Talmud relates a certain wealthy man had a friend by the name of Kamza and an enemy by the name of Bar Kamza. The wealthy man made a big party and invited all the dignitaries of Jerusalem including all the scholars. He told his servant to invite his friend Kamza to the party. By mistake the servant invited Bar Kamza. When the host noticed Bar Kamza in his house, he said to him: "I hear you tell tales about me. What are you doing here? I don't want you here. Get out!"

Bar Kamza did not want to be embarrassed in front of the guests, he said to him: "Since I am here, let me stay and I will pay you for whatever I eat and drink." The host replied, "I don't want you here. Get out!"

"I will give you half of the cost of the whole party."

"No," the host replied, and he grabbed him by his hand and pushed him out. Bar Kamza was very hurt and he was thinking to himself: *Since the Rabbis were present and did not stop him, this shows they agree with him.* He decided to inform against them to the government. He told the authorities: "The Jews are rebelling against you."

"How can you tell?"

He replied, "Send them an offering and see if they will offer it on the altar."

The Roman general sent a fine calf in the name of the Emperor. On the way to the Temple, Bar Kamza made a blemish in a place where it made the animal unfit for an offering. The Rabbis were inclined to offer it in order not to offend the Emperor. Rabbi Zechariah ben Avkulos objected. "People will say blemished animals are offered on the altar."

Some proposed to kill Bar Kamza to prevent him from informing the authorities. Again R. Zechariah objected. After the Temple was destroyed, Rabbi Yohanan remarked: "Through the scrupulousness of R. Zechariah and the unscrupulous Bar Kamza, Jerusalem was destroyed and the Jewish people were exiled from their land." (*Gittin* 55b, 56a)

Kankantum in ink
It was taught that Rabbi Meir said:
"When I was with Rabbi Yishmael, I used to put a chemical called *kankantum* into the ink, and he didn't object to it. But when I was with Rabbi Akiva and I tried to do the same thing, he forbade it." (*Eruvin* 13a; *Sotah* 17b)

Karet   כרת
Rabbah said, "If one dies at the age of between fifty to sixty years, that is death by *karet.* (*Moed Katan* 28a; *Keritut* 2a)

Karmelit   כרמלית
A domain, neither private nor public
(*Shabbat* 7a *Eruvin* 87a)

Karna   קרנא
Amora from Babylonia
3rd century CE (*Shabbat* 108a)

Karpaf   קרפף
An enclosure outside the town line for the storage of wood, etc. It has halachic implications. (*Shabbat* 7a; *Eruvin* 57a, 67b)

Kashisha
Son of R. Hisda
Mar Yanuka and Mar Kashisha were the sons of R. Hisda. (*Bava Batra* 7b)

Kedushah   קדושה
The *Kedushah* prayer is to be said with a *minyan* of ten. (*Berachot* 21b)

Keitzad Mevorchin   כיצד מברכין
What blessing is said over fruit?
(*Berachot* 35a)

Kerem Be-Yavne   כרם ביבנה
A building in the vineyard of Yavne where the Sanhedrin held their meetings. (*Shabbat* 33b; *Bava Batra* 131b)

Keritot   כריתות
The penalty of excision or cutting off
(*Keritot* 2a)

Keruspedai   כרוספדאי
Amora from Eretz Yisrael
3rd century CE (*Rosh Hashana* 16b)

Ketubbah
R. Shimon b. Shetach instituted a new way to deal with women's dowry. (*Shabbat* 14b, 16b; *Ketubbot* 82b)

Ketubbah absent
Living with a wife without a *ketubbah*.
(*Bava Kamma* 89a)

Kezayit   כזית
Food the size of an olive – is used as a halachic measuring device. (*Eruvin* 4b; *Keilim* 17:8)

Ki   כי
Resh Lakish said: "The word '*ki*' can be used to have four meanings: if, perhaps, but, and because." (*Gittin* 90a)

Kiddush
Are women obligated to make *Kiddush*?
(*Berachot* 20b; *Shevuot* 20b)

Kiddush Levana text
Blessing text for *Kiddush Levana*
(*Sanhedrin* 42a)

Kiddush over wine
R. Zutra b. Toviya said in the name of Rav: "Kiddush to sanctify Shabbat or Yom Tov must be made on wine that is fit to be brought upon the altar." (*Bava Batra* 97a)

Kiddush over wine or bread
R. Berona said in the name of Rav: "If one washed his hands for bread, he should not make *Kiddush* over wine." R. Yitzhak b. Shemuel b. Mata said to them: "Rav barely died and we have already forgotten his ruling? I stood many times before Rav; sometimes he preferred bread and made *Kiddush* over bread and at other times he preferred wine and made *Kiddush* over wine." (*Pesahim* 106 a–b)

Kiddush wine for the community
R. Ilfa lived in a community where no wine was available. He made sure to find wine to make *Kiddush* for the whole community. (*Taanit* 24a)

Kidnapping another Jew (*Sanhedrin* 85b)

Kilayim
Kilayim is a term used to describe a mixture of animals forbidden in the Torah. (*Bava Kamma* 55a; *Bechorot* 8a; an entire tractate is dedicated to this topic – *Kilayim*.)

Killed unintentionally
Rabbi Kahana had to flee Babylonia, because of the following incident. A man was brought before Rav; he wanted to denounce another Jew to the Persian authorities and to show them where the Jew was hiding his straw. Rav ordered the man not to show it, but the man insisted. "I will show it." Rabbi Kahana was present during this incident and he became enraged that this man is defying Rav. In the argument, R. Kahana accidentally killed the man.[158] (*Bava Kamma* 117a)

Killing a louse on Shabbat
R. Eliezer said: "Killing a louse on Shabbat is equal to killing a camel." (*Shabbat* 12a)

Kind and does good　　הטוב והמטיב
The One Who is kind and Who deals with kindness – it is a blessing recited on special occasions. (*Taanit* 31a; *Berachot* 48b; *Bava Batra* 121b)

King
The king may not be given a seat in the Sanhedrin. (*Sanhedrin* 18b)

King
A king can marry eighteen wives
A king may take eighteen wives. He should write himself a Torah. When he goes to war, he should take the Torah with him. (*Sanhedrin* 21a–b)

King as a witness
A king cannot be a witness. (*Shevuot* 31a)

King Hizkiya
Six things enacted Hizkiya, King of Judea. (*Pesahim* 56a; *Berachot* 10b; *Sanhedrin* 47a)

King Izgedar
Rabbi Ashi said, Rabbi Huna b. Nathan (the Exilarch) once told me:
"I was standing next to Izgedar, King of Persia and my girdle [the insignia of the Exilarch] was pushed high up. He reached over and pulled my girdle down, observing to me: 'It is written of you, "You shall be unto Me a kingdom of priests and a holy nation."'" (*Zevahim* 19a)

King leading the army to war
A king may lead his army into war by the decision of the Sanhedrin. (*Sanhedrin* 20b)

King of Israel
A king of Israel may not be a judge nor be judged, but the kings of the House of David can be both. The reason for this is an enactment by the rabbis, because of an incident.

A slave of King Yannai killed a man. R. Shimon b. Shetah said to the assembled rabbis: "Set your eyes boldly upon him and let us judge him."

They sent a messenger to the king saying: "Your slave has killed a man." He sent the slave to be tried, but the rabbis insisted that the king himself must come. The king came and sat down.

R. Shimon b. Shetah said to him: "Stand on your feet and let the witnesses testify against you."

The king replied: "I will not do what you tell me to do. Let your colleagues give instructions." The king looked at them and they turned their gaze to the ground. After this incident, they enacted the rule that a king may not be judged nor be a judge. (*Sanhedrin* 18a, 19a)

---

158. See entry, Uncontrolled rage.

📖 King of Judea consults R. Gamliel

It once happened that the king and queen instructed their servants to slaughter the Pesach-offering on their behalf.[159] There was some question whether it was done properly. The king and queen sent the servants to ask Rabban Gamliel. On another occasion, a lizard was found in the Temple area. Again the king and queen sent the servants to Rabban Gamliel to inquire what to do. (*Pesahim* 88b)

King Shapur

Shemuel was asked by King Shapur: "You say that Mashiach will arrive riding on a donkey; I would much rather send him one of my white horses." R. Shemuel answered: "Do you have a steed with hundred hues?" (*Sanhedrin* 98a)

📖 King Yannai and R. Shimon b. Shetah

King Yannai and his queen were sitting at the table having a meal together. There was no one to say a blessing for them, because he had killed the rabbis. He expressed a wish to his queen to have someone give a blessing. She said to him: "Swear to me that if I bring you a rabbi, you will not harm him."

He swore, and she brought her brother Rabbi Shimon ben Shetah to the palace and seated him between herself and the king. She said to him: "See what honor I pay you?"

He replied: "It is not you who honor me, but the Torah which honors me." The king said to her: "You see he still does not recognize authority." (*Berachot* 48a)

King Yezdegird of Persia

Ameimar, Mar Zutra, and R. Ashi were sitting at the gate of King Yezdegird ... (*Ketubbot* 61a)

Kings

Show respect to kings, run to have a look at a king when he comes into town. (*Berachot* 9b, 19b, 58a)

King's declaration

Procedure of reading the portion by the king (*Sotah* 41a)

King's greetings

During the *Amidah*, there should be no interruptions, even if the king greets you. (*Berachot* 30b)

King's mountain

When Ravin came from Eretz Yisrael to Babylonia he stated: "There was a city belonging to King Yannai in the king's mountain where they were chopping down fig trees. They needed a great amount of salted fish to feed the workers."

He also stated: "King Yannai had a tree on the king's mountain, from which they used to take down every month forty young pigeons from three broods."

When R. Dimi came from Eretz Yisrael to Babylonia he stated that King Yannai had a city in the king's mountain where they used to feed from Friday to Friday sixty huge vessels of salted fish to the men chopping down the fig trees. (*Berachot* 44a)

King's throne

No one may sit on the king's throne. (*Sanhedrin* 22a)

Kinot author

The author of the book of Kinot was the Prophet Yirmiyahu.[160] (*Bava Batra* 15a)

✿ Kippa

The mother of R. Nahman b. Yitzhak was told by astrologers that her son would be a thief. For that reason, she did not let him

---

159. Most likely it was Agrippas II.

160. Others name different authors.

go bareheaded, saying to him, "Cover your head so that the fear of Heaven will be upon you." (*Shabbat* 156b)

Kippa

A headcap customarily worn by married men

R. Hisda was praising R. Hamnuna to R. Huna, saying that he is a great man. Said R. Huna, "When he comes to you, bring him to me." When he came, he didn't wear a cap customarily worn by married men. "Why have you no headcap?"

"I have no headcap, because I am not married." R. Huna turned his face away from him. "See to it that you do not come before me before you are married." (*Kiddushin* 29b)

Kiryat Arba

R. Yitzhak said: "It is called Kiryat Arba because four couples are buried there: Adam and Eve, Avraham and Sarah, Yitzhak and Rivka, and Yaakov and Leah. (*Sotah* 13a)

Kissing

When greeting relatives, is kissing permitted? (*Shabbat* 13a)

Kissui Ha-Dam   כסוי הדם

Covering the blood after slaughtering (*Hullin* 83b)

Kiyyum Ha-Shtar   קיום השטר

Deed attestation, contract certification (*Bava Batra* 154a)

Kli Rishon   כלי ראשון

The pot with food directly on the fire cooking is called the first vessel. (*Shabbat* 42b)

Kli Sheni   כלי שני

Boiled food in a vessel not directly on the fire is called the second vessel. (*Shabbat* 42b)

Klal u'frat   כלל ופרט

Generalization and specification

It is one of the thirteen methods and principles of Biblical interpretation of R. Yishmael. (*Hullin* 88b; *Bechorot* 19a; *Bava Kamma* 54b, 62b, 64b; *Eruvin* 27b; *Nazir* 35b)

Knives for a Shohet (*Hullin* 8b)

Knock on door on Shabbat

One Shabbat, R. Ulla visited R. Menashye. During the visit, he heard a knock on the door. "Who is the person knocking on the door on Shabbat? It is a desecration of the Shabbat." Rabbah told him: "Only a musical sound is prohibited." (*Eruvin* 104a)

Knots

Making knots on Shabbat is discussed in *Eilu keshorim*, the 15th *perek* in *Shabbat*. (*Shabbat* 111b)

Knots on the Tefillin

It was quoted in the name of Rabbi Shimon Hasida: "The Torah hints that God showed Moshe the knots on the *tefillin*." (*Berachot* 7a; *Menahot* 35b)

✿ Know it all, not so

Do not believe, you know it all

"Do not separate yourself from the community, do not believe you know it all, and do not judge your friend until you have been put in his position." (*Avot* 2:4)

✿ Know what is above you

R. Yehuda HaNasi said: "Which path is the proper one to choose? Whatever is honorable to you and earns you the esteem of your fellow-men. Be as scrupulous in performing a minor good deed as a major one, for one does not know which one has a greater reward. Consider three things and you will avoid sinning: Know what is above you; an eye that sees an ear that hears, and all your deeds are recorded in the book." (*Avot* 2:1)

✿ Know where you come from
Akavia b. Mehalalel said: "Reflect upon three things: know whence you come from, where you are going, and before whom you will have to give an account of your life." (*Avot* 3:1)

Knowledge absent[161] (*Avot* 3:21, 22)

✿ Knowledge to be increased
These are the sayings of Rabbi Hillel: "He that does not add to his knowledge decreases it. He who does not study deserves to die. He who uses the crown of Torah for unworthy purposes shall waste away." (*Avot* 1:13)

✿ Knowledge to be shared
Do not depend entirely on your own knowledge
One of Rabbi Nehorai's sayings was: "If you have to move, move to a place of Torah, and do not expect the Torah to follow you. Make sure you have a colleague with whom to discuss it, because that way it will be fixed in your mind. Do not depend entirely on your own knowledge." (*Avot* 4:14)

Known fact   איגלאי מלתא
The fact became known[162] (*Sanhedrin* 109b)

Kodashim   סדר קדשים
The order *Kodashim* is one of the six orders of the Talmud. It contains laws concerning Holy things, sacrifices and Temple services.

Kohanim
R. Yehoshua spoke about two prominent families in Jerusalem: Bet Tzevaim of Ben Achmai and Bet Kuppai of Ben Mekoshesh. Some of them became High Priests. (*Yevamot* 15b)

Kohanim ages
Kohanim at age twenty-five start to study and train; at the age of thirty they perform the service. (*Hullin* 24a)

Kohanim called Levi'im
R. Yehoshua b. Levi said: "In twenty-four places the kohanim were called Levi'im." (*Hullin* 24b; *Bechorot* 4a; *Tamid* 27a; *Yevamot* 86b)

Kohelet
The Sages wanted to hide the book Kohelet. (*Shabbat* 30b)

Kohen
A Kohen marrying a divorcee (*Yevamot* 20a; *Sanhedrin* 53b)

Kohen
If a Kohen accepts the teachings of the Torah except one (*Bechorot* 30b)

Kohen butcher
R. Hisda said: "A Kohen who is a butcher has to give the priestly gift to another Kohen." (*Hullin* 132b)

Kohen Gadol
Can a Kohen Gadol be a judge, and can he be judged? (*Sanhedrin* 18a)

Kohen Gadol
Can a Kohen Gadol be married to a widow? (*Yevamot* 20a; *Sanhedrin* 53b)

Kohen Gadol Hyrcanus
Hyrcanus was Kohen Gadol for eighty years
Yohanan Kohen Gadol, also called John Hyrcanus King of Judea, was the son of Shimon the Hasmonean, and a grandson

---

161. See entry, Absence of Torah.
162. A Talmudic expression.

of the famous Matityahu, who started the Chanukah revolt against Antiochus Epiphanes.

He lived to a very old age. According to the Talmud, he was Kohen Gadol for eighty years. King Yohanan enlarged the kingdom by subduing the Edomites and the Samaritans, but spent many years at war, freeing the country from many of its enemies. (*Berachot* 29a; *Yoma* 9a)

Kohen Gadol to excel
The Kohen Gadol is to excel in beauty, strength, wisdom, and wealth. (*Horayot* 9a)

Kohen Mashiach   כהן משיח
The anointed High Priest (*Horayot* 6b)

Kohen Mashiach sinning
A Kohen Mashiach who committed a sin (*Horayot* 9b)

Kohen Talmid Hacham
Difference between a Kohen who is a *talmid hacham* and an ignorant one (*Bechorot* 36a)

Kohen Tzedek
R. Hana b. Bizna quoted R. Shimon Hasida: "The four craftsmen are Mashiach the son of David, Mashiach the son of Yosef, Eliyahu, and the Kohen Tzedek.[163] (*Sukkah* 52a–b)

Kohen's daughter
A daughter of a Kohen married to an Israelite, may she eat *teruma*? (*Yevamot* 87a)

Kohen's qualification to serve
A Kohen that grew two hairs is qualified for service. (*Hullin* 24a)

---

163. Rashi identifies the Kohen Tzedek as Shem the son of Noah or alternately Malki-Tzedek who came to meet Avraham when he returned from the war against the four kings.

Kol shehu   כל שהוא
A minute quantity (*Shevuot* 21b)

Kometz   קומץ
A handful of flour which the priest takes from the meal-offering (*Meilah* 10a)

📖 Korah
Rabbah bar b. Hana said: "I was traveling on the road when I met an Arab. He told me, 'Come, I want to show you where the men of Korah were swallowed up.' I followed him and saw two cracks in the ground from where smoke was coming forth. He took a piece of wool, soaked it in water, then attached it to the point of his spear, and passed it over the cracks and the wool was singed. I said to him, 'Listen to what I hear.' A voice was heard from below: 'Moshe and his Torah are true, but we are liars.'" (*Sanhedrin* 110a; *Bava Batra* 74a)

Kosher in animals
What makes an animal kosher or *trefa* (*Hullin* 45a, 46a, 54a, 57b)

✡ Kosher meat to be salted
In addition to other requirements
R. Shemuel said: "Flesh cannot be drained of its blood unless it has been salted very well and rinsed very well."

R. Shemuel also said: "One may not salt raw meat except in a vessel with holes in it." (*Hullin* 97b, 111b, 112a, 113a; *Pesahim* 76a)

Kosher slaughtering
Who may slaughter to be kosher? (*Hullin* 2a, 31a)

Kuee   כוי
R. Yosi and Rav Yehuda said: "A *quee* is a separate creature of animal." (*Hullin* 80a; *Yoma* 74a–b; *Keritut* 21a)

Kum Aseh   קום עשה
A positive duty to do a commandment (*Bava Metzia* 62a)

Kuti   כותים גרי אריות הן
Sectarian non-Jews living in the Land of Israel. They are considered to be forced conversions כותים גרי אמת הן (*Hullin* 3b; *Kiddushin* 75b; *Bava Kamma* 38b; *Sanhedrin* 85b; *Niddah* 56b; *Yevamot* 24b)

L

✿ Labor ethics
R. Tarfon said: "It is not your obligation to complete the task, but neither are you at liberty to idle from it." (*Avot* 2:16)

✿ Laborer
R. Hiyya b. Ammi said in the name of R. Ulla: "A man who lives from the labor of his hands is greater than one who fears God." (*Berachot* 8a)

📖 Laborer; R. Hillel
The Talmud tells us that Rabbi Hillel used to work as a laborer to earn one *tropek*[164] He split his earnings to be admitted to the house of learning. The other half he spent on food and necessities. One day he had no earnings and the guard would not let him enter, so he climbed up on the roof to listen in to the lectures from the window on top of the roof.[165] (*Yoma* 35b)

Labors forbidden on Shabbat
Principal creative labor categories forbidden on Shabbat – they are thirty-nine. (*Shabbat* 6b, 49b, 69a, 70b, 73a, 96b; *Bava Kamma* 2a)

Labors on Shabbat   חילוק מלאכות
If one does many labors on Shabbat, he is liable for each labor, and the rabbis discuss whether it applies also on Yom Tov. (*Makkot* 21b)

Ladder
Broken ladder in the house
One should not keep a shaky ladder in his house. (Bava Kamma 46a, 15b; *Ketubbot* 41b)

Lamed Vav Tzaddikim   ל"ו צדיקים
Abbaye said: "In each generation, the world must contain no less than thirty-six righteous men who merit the sight of the Shechina." (*Sanhedrin* 97b; *Sukkah* 45b)

Land   קרקע
Land, real estate (*Bava Metzia* 48b)

Land of Israel
When they entered the Land of Israel, Yehoshua divided the land by consulting the *Urim Ve-Tumim* on the chest of the High Priest Eleazar and the *Ruah Ha-Kodesh* guided them. (*Bava Batra* 122a)

Land of Israel
The land that was divided among the Israelite tribes was according to their numbers when they left Egypt. (*Bava Batra* 117a)

Land-bound mitzvah
מצוה שהיא תלויה בארץ
Every precept which is dependent on the land is practiced only in the Land of Israel. (*Kiddushin* 36b, 39a)

✿ Land returned to seller
A generous act
Come and hear: There was a man who sold a plot of land to R. Papa. He needed the money to buy some oxen. Eventually, he didn't need to buy the oxen. When R. Papa found out that he did not need to buy oxen, he returned the land to the man. (*Ketubbot* 97a)

---

164. An amount equal to a half a dinar.
165. See entry, Hillel frozen on the roof.

Lands exempt from tithing

R. Yehuda said in R. Shemuel's name: "All the lands God showed to Moshe are subject to tithing. These are excluded: Kenite, Kenizite, and Kadmonite." R. Meir said, "These are the Nabateans, Arabians, and Salmoeans." R. Eliezer said, "They are Mount Seir, Ammon, and Moab." R. Shimon said, "They are Ardiskis, Asia, and Aspamia." (*Bava Batra* 56a)

Language of benedictions (*Berachot* 40b)

Language of Torah

לשון תורה לעצמה לשון חכמים לעצמו

The Torah language is distinct and the language of the Sages is distinct. (*Avodah Zarah* 58b; *Hullin* 137b)

Language one may use for blessings

אלו נאמרין

The following may be recited in any language: certain blessings, obligatory readings, etc. (*Sotah* 32a; *Berachot* 40b; *Shevuot* 39a)

Language student used

Two students sat before Rav. One remarked: "This discussion has made us tired as an exhausted swine." The other said: "This discussion has made us tired as an exhausted kid." After that, Rav would not speak again to the first student. (*Pesahim* 3b)

Languages of the Torah

Rebbe said that the Torah can be recited in all languages. (*Megillah* 17b)

Larceny

Larceny cases require three judges. (*Sanhedrin* 2a)

📖 Lashes

For a serious violation

R. Shila ordered lashes for a man who had intercourse with an Egyptian woman.

The man went to the authorities and told them:

"There is a man among the Jews who acts like a judge without permission from the government." An official was sent to investigate. When he came, he asked R. Shila: "Why did you flog that man?" He answered, "Because he had intercourse with a female donkey."

"Do you have witnesses?"

"I have."

Eliyahu came in the guise of a man and gave evidence. The investigator said to R. Shila: "In that case he deserves the death penalty."

R. Shila responded: "Since we have been exiled, we have no authority to impose the death penalty."

While the official was considering the case, R. Shila praised God in Hebrew. They asked him what he said, and he replied: "I was saying 'Blessed is the All Merciful who invested the earthly royalty with love for justice.'" For this they handed him a staff and told him that he may act as a judge. (*Berachot* 58a)

Lashon Hara   לשון הרע

R. Sheshet said in the name of R. Eleazar b. Azariah: "Whosoever tells tales of *lashon hara* or listens to *lashon hara* deserves to be thrown to the dogs." (*Makkot* 23a)

Last will

The Talmud relates that Geniva was unfortunately sentenced to die by the non-Jewish authorities. When the sentence was about to be carried out, he instructed the people to give Rabbi Avina 400 *zuz* from his wine estate. (*Gittin* 65b)

📖 Last will

The mother of Rami b. Hama gave her property in writing to Rami b. Hama in the morning, but in the evening she gave it in writing to Mar Ukva b. Hama. Rami b.

Hama came to R. Sheshet, who confirmed his inheritance. Mar Ukva then went to R. Nahman, who confirmed Mar Ukva in his inheritance.

R. Sheshet thereupon went to R. Nahman and said to him: "What is the reason you acted this way in this matter?"

R. Nachman replied: "And what is the reason you acted in this matter this way?"

R. Sheshet answered: "Because the will of R. Rami was written first."

R. Nahman replied: "Are we living in Jerusalem, where the hours are recorded? We live in Babylonia, where the hours are not recorded."

R. Sheshet asked: "And why did you act the way you did?"

"I treated it as a case to be decided at the discretion of the judges," replied R. Nahman.

R. Sheshet then retorted: "I also treated it as a case to be decided at the discretion of the judges."

But R. Nahman replied: "I am a judge, and you are not, and furthermore, you did not at first say that you treated it as a case to be decided by a judge." (*Ketubbot* 94b; *Bava Batra* 151a)

Last will
Three people visiting a dying person and writing his last will (*Bava Batra* 113b, 114a)

📖 Last will of Rebbe
Our rabbis taught: When Rebbe was about to expire he said: "I would like to have my sons present." When they came, he instructed them: "Take care to show respect to your mother. The light shall continue to burn in its usual place, the table shall be set in its usual place, and my bed shall be made up in its usual place."

He designated R. Hanina to be Rosh Yeshiva, but R. Hanina did not accept, because R. Afes was older by two and a half years, and so R. Afes presided.

Rebbe said: "I would like to speak to my younger son." R. Shimon came in and Rebbe instructed him in the rules and regulations of being a Hacham.

Rebbe then said: "I would like the presence of my elder son." R. Gamliel entered, and he instructed him in the traditions and regulations of the Patriarchate. "My son," he said, "conduct your Patriarchate with high caliber men and keep strong discipline among your students." (*Ketubbot* 103a–b)

Launderer
R. Shimon b. Gamliel said: "In my father's house, they gave the cloths to launder three days before Shabbat." (*Shabbat* 18a)

Laundry for Shabbat
R. Tzadok said: "This was the custom of the house of R. Gamliel: They used to give the white garments to be washed three days before Shabbat." (*Shabbat* 19a)

Lavan
Let Lavan the father-in-law of Yaakov come and testify that Yaakov could not be suspected of theft. (*Avodah Zarah* 3a)

Laver in the Temple
At first the laver in the Temple had only two spigots. A person by the name of Ben Katin made a donation to change that to twelve spigots. (*Yoma* 37a, 25b; *Zevahim* 20a)

Lavud   לבוד
Lavud is a halachic law regarding a wall that has a gap of less than three handbreadths apart. It is considered halachically as connected. (*Shabbat* 97a; *Eruvin* 9a, 16a, 79b)

Law cannot be taken in own hands
לא עביד איניש דינא לנפשיה
No man may take the law into his own hands for the protection of his interests. (*Bava Kamma* 27b)

Law may not be imposed

אין גוזרין גזירה על הצבור אלא אם כן רוב
צבור יכולין לעמוד בה

The rabbis relied upon the words of R. Shimon ben Gamliel and R. Eleazar b. Tzadok who said: "No law may be imposed upon the public unless a majority can endure it." (*Horayot* 3b; *Avodah Zarah* 36a)

Law of the land   דינא דמלכותא דינא

R. Shemuel said: "The law of the land is the law. One has to obey the laws of the land in which he lives." (*Bava Kamma* 113a; *Bava Batra* 54b; *Gittin* 10b; *Nedarim* 28a)

Law repeated in the Torah

A Tanna of R. Yishmael taught that whenever a law is repeated in the Torah, it is to teach something new. (*Bechorot* 43a; *Shevuot* 19a; *Bava Kamma* 64b; *Sotah* 3a)

Lawless men

Befriended by R. Zera

R. Zera lived in a neighborhood where lawless men resided. He was on friendly terms with them in the hope that they would repent, but the rabbis were annoyed with him on account of it. When R. Zera passed away, the lawless men lamented: "Until now the man with the burned short leg prayed for us, who will pray for us now?" Thereupon they felt remorse in their hearts and repented. (*Sanhedrin* 37a)

Laws forgotten

R. Yehuda said in the name of R. Shemuel: "Three thousand *halachot* were forgotten during the period of mourning for Moshe Rabbeinu." (*Temurah* 15b)

📖 Lawsuit before Rav

Rav disqualified himself

A former host of Rav came before him in a lawsuit against another man, and said to Rav:

"Were you not once a guest in my house?"

"Yes," replied Rav. "What can I do for you?"

"I have a case before you."

"In that case, I am disqualified as your judge."

Rav turned to R. Kahana and told him: "You be the judge for this case." R. Kahana noticed that the man was relying too much on his acquaintance with Rav. Therefore, he told the man: "If I am going to be your judge, you must put Rav out of your mind." (*Sanhedrin* 7b, 8a)

Laying books on other books

The laying of Holy Books one on top of each other; what is permitted and what is not? (*Megillah* 27a)

📖 Leap year in Nehardea, Babylonia, declared by R. Akiva

The Talmud relates that Rabbi Akiva said: "When I visited Nehardea in Babylonia to declare a leap year I met with Rabbi Nehemia Ish Bet Deli. He told me, 'I heard that in Eretz Yisrael they don't permit a woman to remarry on testimony of one witness.' He went on to say that he learned from Rabban Gamliel otherwise." (*Yevamot* 16:7, 115a, 122a)

Learn and teach

Rabbi Yishmael ben Yohanan ben Beroka said: "He who learns in order to teach will be granted the means to learn and teach; and he who learns in order to practice, will be granted the opportunity to learn, teach, practice and to observe." (*Avot* 4:5)

✿ Learned from students

Rebbe said: "I have learned much Torah from my teachers, more from my fellow students and I learned the most from my students." (*Makkot* 10a)

✿ Learning

One of Aher's[166] famous sayings was: "Learning while young is like writing on clean paper, but learning in old age is like writing on blotted paper." (*Avot* 4: 20)

✿ Learning from an expert

R. Yosi said: "One who learns from the young and immature is likened to one who eats unripe grapes or drinks unseasoned wine from his vat. But one who learns from an old and matured person is likened to one who eats ripe grapes or drinks aged wine." (*Avot* 4:20)

✿ Learning little at a time

Rava said in the name of R. Sehora in the name of R. Huna: "If a person studies too much at a time, his learning decreases, but if he studies a little at a time, his knowledge increases. Rabbah remarked: "The rabbis were aware of this advice, but disregarded it." R. Nahman b. Yitzhak said: "I acted on this advice and it benefited me greatly." (*Eruvin* 54b; *Avodah Zarah* 19a)

Learning not shared

Rabbi Meir used to say: "He who studies Torah, but does not teach it to others is diminishing the word of Torah." (*Sanhedrin* 99a)

Learning Torah daily כל השונה הלכות

It was taught in the Tanna D'bei Eliyahu: He who studies Torah Laws every day will be destined to have a place in the World to Come. (*Megillah* 28b; *Niddah* 73a)

Leasing a field

When one leases a field, what are the obligations if they are not specified? (*Bava Metzia* 103a)

---

166. Elisha b. Avuya.

Leavened bread, benefit not permitted

R. Hezkiya said: "One may not benefit from leavened bread on Pesach . . ." (*Pesahim* 21b)

Leavened bread on Pesach

בל יראה ובל ימצא

Regarding leavened bread on Pesach – it shall not be seen and it shall not be found. (*Pesahim* 46b)

📖 Leaving Eretz Yisrael?

R. Assi had an old mother. She asked for ornaments and he bought her ornaments. She said to him: "I want a husband." He told her: "I will take care of you." When she told him, "I want a good-looking husband like you," he left her and moved to Eretz Yisrael. When he heard that she is following him to Eretz Yisrael, he went to R. Yohanan and asked him: "May I leave Eretz Yisrael to go abroad?" He answered him that it is forbidden.

"May I leave to meet my mother?"

He answered, "I do not know."

He waited a while and asked him again. R. Yohanan answered:

"Assi, I see you are determined to go – may God bring you back in peace."

He went to R. Eleazar and said to him: "Perhaps, God forbid, he was angry?" He answered him: "Had he been angry, he would not have blessed you." (*Kiddushin* 31b)

📖 Leaving Eretz Yisrael to Babylonia

Nephew of R. Hiyya, Rabbah b. Hana moving to Babylonia

When Rabbah b. Hana was leaving to Babylonia, R. Hiyya said to Rebbe: "My brother's son is going to Babylonia, may he decide monetary cases?"

"He may."

"May he decide on firstborn animals?"

"He may."

When Rav left for Babylonia, R. Hiyya

said to Rebbe: "My sister's son is going to Babylonia, may he decide on matters of ritual law?"

"He may". "May he decide on monetary cases"?

"He may".

"May he decide on firstborn animals"? "He may not." (*Sanhedrin* 5a)

📖 Leaving Babylonia

R. Yehuda b. Yehezkel expressed the view that whoever leaves Babylonia for Eretz Yisrael transgresses a positive commandment.

It is related that Rabbi Zera was evading Rabbi Yehuda, because he wanted to immigrate to Eretz Yisrael, and he knew that R. Yehuda expressed a view, that whoever leaves Babylonia for Eretz Yisrael transgresses a positive commandment. R. Zera disagreed with his teacher. He interpreted the scriptural passages differently. (*Ketubbot* 110b; *Shabbat* 41a; *Berachot* 24b)

Leaving a synagogue

R. Helbo said: "When a man leaves the synagogue, he should not be in a hurry." (*Berachot* 6b)

📖 Lecturers

Two different styles of lectures

R. Avohu and R. Hiyya b. Abba traveled to a place to deliver lectures. R. Hiyya lectured on legal matters and R. Avohu lectured on Aggadah. The people left the hall where R. Hiyya was lecturing to go to listen to R. Avohu.

R. Hiyya became upset. Said R. Avohu to him: "I will give you a parable. Two salesmen are selling merchandise: one sells precious jewels and the other sells various kinds of small knick-knacks. To whom do the people flock? Is it not to the one who sells the knick-knacks?"

It was the habit of R. Hiyya to accompany R. Avohu every day to his lodging,

but on this day R. Avohu reversed the role and he accompanied R. Hiyya to his lodging. He tried to make him feel better, but he was still upset.[167] (*Sotah* 40a)

📖 Lecture on Shabbat

It is related that R. Nahman, who was the regular lecturer on Shabbat, was about to deliver his lecture this Shabbat. However, it was his custom to review his lecture with R. Adda b. Abba before delivering it, and only then would he deliver his lecture.

But this Shabbat, R. Papa and R. Huna b. Yehoshua got hold of R. Adda b. Abba. They asked him to repeat for them the lecture they missed the day before. He took the time with them and repeated for them the whole lecture. But in the meantime, R. Nahman was waiting for R. Adda to review with him his lecture, and the hour was getting late. The rabbis who came to hear his lecture told R. Nahman:

"Come and lecture. It is late and why are you still sitting?" He said to them, "I am waiting for R. Adda's coffin." He was sarcastic, because he was angry. Soon after this happening, R. Adda b. Abba passed away and R. Nahman blamed himself for his death. (*Bava Batra* 22a)

📖 Lectures on health

Rabbi Huna asked his son Rabbah, "Why are you not attending the lectures of Rabbi Hisda, whose lectures are so sharp and enlightening?"

"He is discussing health matters and you call them secular? That is even more reason that you should attend his lectures." (*Shabbat* 82a)

📖 Left home to study

The Talmud tells us, that Rabbi Hama left his home and spent twelve years in the academy to study Torah. When he

---

167. See entry, Hurt feelings.

returned home, he stopped at the local academy before going home. A young man entered the academy and sat down next to him and asked him a question on the subject of his study. When R. Hama saw the great knowledge this young man possessed, he became depressed. He was thinking, *Had I been here, I also could have had such a son.* After he finally went home, the young man followed him and knocked on the door. Believing that he came to ask him another question, he rose before him as he entered the house. His wife broke out in laughter. "What kind of father stands up before his son?" The young man that followed him happened to be Rabbi Oshaya, his son.[168] It was said of them, a threefold cord is not quickly broken. (*Ketubbot* 62b)

Leftover vegetables Friday afternoon
Bought by R. Huna
On Friday afternoons, R. Huna would send messengers to the market and buy all the leftover vegetables. (*Taanit* 20b)

Leftovers נותר
Leftovers from Temple offerings (*Meilah* 6b)

Legal decision under influence
R. Yehuda said in the name of R. Shemuel: "He who has drunk a quarter of a log of wine should not render a halachic decision." (*Eruvin* 64a; *Ketubbot* 10b; *Nazir* 38a; *Sanhedrin* 42a)

Lehem Ha-Panim לחם הפנים
The time to consume the showbread in the Temple (*Arachin* 8b)

Lender
The lender demanded wheat, and the borrower admitted to barley. (*Bava Kamma* 35b; *Bava Metzia* 5a; *Shevuot* 38b)

---

168. See entry, Father does not recognize son.

Lender holding pledge
A lender holding a borrower's pledge is deemed a paid guardian. (*Bava Metzia* 80b)

✿ Lender living in borrower's house
A lender may not live in the house of a borrower at a reduced rate – it is considered usury. (*Bava Metzia* 64b)

Lending in the presence of a witness
(*Shevuot* 41a)

Lending money against a pledge
(*Shevuot* 43a; *Bava Metzia* 34b)

Lending with interest
A lender who took interest for the loan and he repented. (*Bava Kamma* 94b; *Hagigah* 26a)

Lending to a gentile Erev Shabbat
(*Shabbat* 18b)

✿ Lending to the needy
R. Abba also said in the name of Resh Lakish: "To lend money to a person in need is greater than giving charity. And to enable someone to go into business and then split the profits is greater than all charities." (*Shabbat* 63a)

Leniencies and stringencies מקיל ומחמיר
(*Moed Katan* 20a)

Leniencies of R. Shammai (*Eduyot* 6a)

Lenient for others
R. Gamliel was lenient for others but strict on himself
With regards to observing a mitzvah, R. Gamliel was lenient for others, but very strict on himself. (*Berachot* 16a)

Leopard
Is a leopard considered to be an animal that is warned? (*Bava Kamma* 15b)

Leprosy in houses
Symptoms for leprosy and infection in houses (*Negaim* 12:1–7)

Leprosy inspection
Inspecting the colors of leprosy (*Negaim* 1:1)

Leprosy symptoms (*Negaim* 2:4)

Less sinful city
Rava b. Mehasya said in the name of R. Hama b. Gurya in Rav's name: "A man should always prefer to live in a city which was recently established, because it is less sinful." (*Shabbat* 10b)

Lessee not conforming to contract
A man leased a field to plant sesame, but the lessee sowed wheat. (*Bava Metzia* 104b)

Letters
Mailed Erev Shabbat (*Shabbat* 19a)

Letter Tav ת in the Aleph Bet
R. Abba b. Hanina quoted from the Prophet Yehezkel, chapter 9, the following: "The angel Gabriel was told to go and inscribe with ink the letter ת *tav* upon the forehead of the righteous so the destroying angel would have no power over them, and inscribe the letter *tav* with blood on the wicked in order that the destroying angel would have power over them. (*Shabbat* 55a)

📖 Letters by R. Gamliel
To the Jewish community
It once happened that R. Gamliel was sitting on a step on the Temple Mount, and dictating to Yohanan, the well-known scribe. "Write instructions to our brethren in the Upper Galilee and to those in the Lower Galilee, the Exiles in Babylonia and to those in Media, and to all the other ex-iled sons of Israel, saying:[169] 'Peace shall

---

169. See entry, In touch with Jews in exile.

be with you for ever! We are pleased to inform you that the doves are still tender and the lambs still too young and the crops are not yet ripe. It seems advisable to me and in the opinion of my colleagues to add thirty days to this year." (*Sanhedrin* 11b)

Lettuce at the Seder (*Pesahim* 114a)

Levi · לוי
Amora from Eretz Yisrael and Babylonia 2nd – 3rd centuries CE (*Berachot* 49a)

Levi · לוי
Amora from Eretz Yisrael 3rd – 4th centuries CE (*Bava Batra* 88b)

Levi and Shimon
R. Shimon the son of R. Yehuda HaNasi and R. Levi studied together. (*Avodah Zarah* 19a)

Levi in Babylonia
After Rabbi Yehuda HaNasi died, R. Hanina did not attend the studies inside the academy, but instead studied outside in the company of Rabbi Levi. When Rabbi Afes passed away, R. Hanina bar Hama took over the presidency, and R. Levi was left without a partner to study. As a consequence, he moved to Babylonia. (*Ketubbot* 103b)

Levianus family of Rome
Levianus preferred to drink wine follow-ing the After-meal blessing rather than receiving forty gold coins.
   A certain Tzadoki said to Rebbe: "It seems to me from reading Scriptures that the mountains and the wind were not cre-ated by the same God."
   Rebbe told him: "You are a fool, read the end of the verse." At the end of the discus-sion, Rebbe asked him to stay for dinner which he accepted. After the meal Rebbe asked him: "Would you rather drink the

cup of wine over which the benedictions of the after-meal have been said or would you prefer forty gold coins?"

He replied: "I would rather drink the cup of wine." The family of that Tzadoki is still to be found amongst the notables of Rome: their name is Bar Levianus.[170] (*Hullin* 87a; *Sanhedrin* 39a)

Leviathan   לויתן
Rabbah said in the name of Rabbi Yohanan: "In the future, Hashem will make a banquet for the righteous, and will serve them the flesh of the Leviathan." (*Bava Batra* 74a–b, 75a)

Leviathan   לויתן
R. Yosi b. Durmaskith said: "The Leviathan is a clean fish." (*Hullin* 67b)

Levirate marriage   יבום
When one of the brothers dies without having any children, it is incumbent upon the oldest brother to marry the widow; it is called *yibbum*. (*Yevamot* 24a, 39a; *Betzah* 37a)

Levitas Ish Yavne   לויטס איש יבנה
Tanna from Eretz Yisrael
2nd century CE (*Avot* 4:4)

Levites singing Psalms
At the Temple in Jerusalem, the Levites sang each day to the words of a different Psalm
It has been taught: R. Yehuda said in the name of R. Akiva: "On the first day of the week, they chanted to Psalm 24 – 'God is the owner of the earth.'

"On the second day of the week, they sang to Psalm 48 – 'Great is the Lord and highly to be praised.'

"On the third day of the week, they chanted to Psalm 82 – 'God stands in the congregation of God.'

"On the fourth day of the week, they sang to Psalm 94 – 'O Lord, to whom vengeance belongs.'

"On the fifth day of the week, they chanted to Psalm 81 – 'Sing aloud to God who is our strength.'

"On the sixth day of the week, they sang to Psalm 93 – 'The Lord reigns, He is clothed in majesty.'

"On Shabbat, they chanted to Psalm 92 – 'A song for the day of Shabbat.'" (*Rosh Hashana* 31a; *Tamid* 33b)

Liability when one hires   יש לשכירות מתחילה ועד סוף
There is liability from the beginning to the end when one hires. (*Bava Kamma* 99a)

✿ Liars
A saying in the Talmud is attributed to Rabbi Hiyya: "Such is the punishment of a liar, that even when he tells the truth he is not believed." (*Sanhedrin* 89b)

Libations in the Temple (*Menahot* 89a)

Libyan ass
What is permitted to be put on a Libyan ass on Shabbat (*Shabbat* 51a)

Lice killed on Shabbat
R. Eliezer said: "Killing lice on Shabbat equals to killing a camel on Shabbat (*Shabbat* 12a, 107b)

Life cycle
Being born and dying (*Avot* 4:29)

Life of the hour   חיי שעה
Life of the hour is to be considered. (*Avodah Zarah* 27b)

✿ Lifting a hand
To hit another person
Resh Lakish and R. Hanina said that if a man lifts a hand to hit another man, he is

---

170. The story in *Sanhedrin* is different.

called a sinner, even if he didn't hit him. (*Sanhedrin* 58b)

Light as an eagle
Yehuda b. Tema said: "Be bold as a leopard, light as an eagle, swift as a deer, and strong as a lion – to carry out the will of your Father in Heaven. (*Avot* 5:20)

Light fire on Shabbat
Lighting a fire on Shabbat for a woman in childbirth (*Eruvin* 79b; *Shabbat* 129a)

Light lit for a Jew
A non-Jew who lit a light for a Jew (*Shabbat* 122a)

Lighted house
R. Huna used to say: "A person who lights his house well will have scholarly sons." R. Huna used to pass frequently the house of R. Avin the carpenter. He noticed that many lights were always lit in the house. He remarked: "Two great men will be born to him," and so it was – R. Idi b. Avin and R. Hiyya b. Avin were born to him. (*Shabbat* 23b)

▢ Lighted torches
The Talmud describes Rabbi Shimon ben Gamliel in a most colorful way: When R. Shimon b. Gamliel rejoiced at the Water-drawing festivities, he used to take eight lighted torches, throw them up in the air and catch them one after another, and they did not touch one another. And when he prostrated himself, he used to dig his two thumbs into the ground, bend down, kiss the ground, and draw himself up again – a feat no one else could duplicate. (*Sukkah* 53a)

Lighting
To take fire from one candle to light another on Chanukah (*Shabbat* 22a; *Menahot* 41b)

Lighting Chanukah candles
Lighting one candle the first day or lighting eight candles the first day; dispute between the rabbis (*Shabbat* 21b)

Lighting fire
What distance is required (*Bava Kamma* 61b)

Lighting materials
What lighting materials may be used to light Shabbat candles (*Shabbat* 20b)

Lighting Shabbat candles
Rav said: "Lighting Shabbat candles is an obligation." (*Shabbat* 25b)

Lightning
The blessing over Lightning is discussed in *Haroeh*, the 9th *perek* of *Berachot*. (*Berachot* 54a)

✡ Likable person
R. Hanina b. Dosa used to say: "A person who pleases humankind is also pleasing to God, but a person who is disliked by humankind is not pleasing to God." (*Avot* 3:13)

Limb of a living animal   אבר מן החי
Eating a limb from a living animal (*Hullin* 101b)

Limitation followed by another limitation   מיעוט אחר מיעוט
(*Bava Kamma* 86b; *Yoma* 43a)

▢ Limp
R. Levi was limping
Rabbi Levi was often a guest at Rabbi Yehuda HaNasi, and he used to entertain his guests with acrobatic feats.

It is related that he used to juggle with eight knives in front of Rabbi Yehuda HaNasi. At one time he dislocated his hip during a performance, resulting in a permanent limp. (*Sukkah* 53a; *Megillah* 22b; *Taanit* 25a)

Lines for a mourner
People standing in line to comfort a mourner at the gravesite (*Berachot* 17b)

Lion
Objects saved from a lion – to whom do they belong (*Bava Metzia* 24a)

📖 Lion and son of a lion
When R. Shimon b. Gamliel and R. Yehoshua b. Korha were learning in the academy, they sat on couches, while R. Eleazar b. Shimon and Rebbe sat in front of them on the ground asking questions and raising objections. The other students objected. They said: "We are drinking from their water, but they are sitting on the ground, let seats be placed for them."

They placed seats for them. R. Shimon b. Gamliel objected: "I have a pigeon amongst you and you want to destroy it?" So Rebbe was put down again. R. Yehoshua b. Korha was not happy and he said: "Shall he who has a father live, while he who has no father die?" Thereupon, R. Eleazar was also put down on the ground. R. Eleazar was hurt and expressed himself by saying:

"You have made him equal to me."

Until this incident, whenever Rebbe made a statement, R. Eleazar supported him, but after this day when Rebbe spoke, R. Eleazar said, "Your statement has no substance." Rebbe was humiliated and complained to R. Shimon b. Gamliel, his father. "Let it not bother you," his father said to him, "he is a lion and the son of a lion, whereas you are a lion and the son of a fox." (*Bava Metzia* 84b)

📖 Lion followed
A caravan, in which R. Safra was traveling, was followed by a lion. Every night they had to abandon one donkey to satisfy the lion. When it came to give up R. Safra's donkey, the lion would not eat it, and R. Safra reclaimed his donkey. (*Bava Kamma* 116a)

📖 Lion has come up
A scholar from Babylonia
Rabbi Kahana had to flee Babylonia. Rav advised R. Kahana to move to Eretz Yisrael and to study at Rabbi Yohanan, but he also made him promise that for seven years he would not give Rabbi Yohanan a hard time with his sharp questions.

When R. Kahana arrived, he found Resh Lakish with the young rabbis going over the lecture. He pointed out the difficult points in the lecture and also provided some of the answers. Resh Lakish went to R. Yohanan and told him:

"A lion has come up from Babylonia; be well prepared for tomorrow's lecture." The next day, R. Kahana was seated in the first row, because they thought that he must be a scholar. He kept quiet for a long while as he promised Rav. Consequently they demoted him and seated him in the seventh row.

R. Yohanan said to Resh Lakish: "The lion turns out to be a fox"

Rabbi Kahana prayed that the seventh row insult should be considered like the seven years he had promised.

The next day when Rabbi Yohanan lectured, Rabbi Kahana threw out one question after another, and quoted sources in contradiction. They seated him again in the first row. (*Bava Kamma* 117a)

Lion of the group
Rava was discussing a Halachah with his colleagues and he said, "I and the lion of the group, explained it." And who is the lion among us? It is R. Hiyya b. Avin. (*Shabbat* 111b; *Sanhedrin* 8b)

Lion of the group
Rava said, "I and the lion of the group." Who is the lion? It is R. Zera. (*Bava Batra* 88a)

Lions encountered

Once Rabbi Shimon ben Halafta was on the road and he encountered lions roaring at him. He quoted a passage from Psalms 104 and two lumps of meat descended from heaven. The lions ate one and left the other. He brought the other lump of meat to the schoolhouse, and questioned whether the meat is clean or not. The scholars answered: "Nothing unclean descends from heaven." (*Sanhedrin* 59b)

Liquids facilitate imparting impurities

These liquids facilitate the imparting of impurity. (*Machshirin* 1:1)

Liquids mixed

A colored liquid falls into water or a *mikveh* and changes the color of the water (*Hullin* 26a)

Lishca לשכה

Temple treasury chamber (*Shekalim* 3:2)

List of thirty-nine main labors (*Shabbat* 6b, 49b, 69a, 70b, 73a, 96b; *Bava Kamma* 20a)

Litigants both present

A judge should not hear one litigant without the other being present. (*Shevuot* 21a)

Litigants to stand

Our rabbis taught that the two litigants should be standing. R. Yehuda said: "I heard that they can both be seated, but both litigants have to be the same – seated or standing." (*Shevuot* 30a)

📖 Litigation

Dispute in a transporting case

R. Papa and R. Huna bought sesame seeds on the bank of the Nahar Malka. They hired a boatman to bring the merchandise across the river, with a guarantee against any accident that might happen. However, the canal was stopped up and they couldn't deliver the merchandise. Rava ruled against R. Papa and R. Huna. He said: "White ducks that strip men of their clothing."[171] (*Gittin* 73a; *Ketubbot* 85a)

✿ Live within means

R. Avira used to say sometimes in the name of R. Ammi and sometimes in the name of R. Assi: "A person should always eat and drink less than he can afford; clothe himself accordance to his means, and honor his wife and children more than he can afford, for they are dependent on him and he is dependent on God." (*Hullin* 84b)

✿ Livelihood combined with Torah

R. Eleazar b. Azariah said: "Where there is no Torah, there is no proper conduct; where proper conduct is absent, there is no Torah. If there is no wisdom, there is no fear of God; if there is no fear of God, there is no wisdom. Where there is no knowledge, there is no understanding, where there is no understanding, there is no knowledge. If there is no bread, there is no Torah; if there is no Torah, there is no bread." (*Avot* 3:21)

✿ Living and dying against your will

R. Eliezer Hakapar said: "The newborn are destined to die, the dead will live again, and the living will be judged. Know that everything is according to the reckoning. Let not your evil inclination mislead you that your grave will be an escape for you. You were created against your will, you were born against your will, and against your will you live, against your will you will die, and against your will you are destined to give an account before the King of Kings." (*Avot* 4:29)

---

171. See entry, Agreement voided by Rava.

Living extravagantly

Mar Zutra b. R. Nahman said: "The Torah teaches us that a father should not teach his son to live on meat and wine." (*Hullin* 84a)

📖 Lizard

Our rabbis taught: In a certain place, a lizard was injuring people. They came to tell R. Hanina b. Dosa. He said to them, "Show me its hole." They did, and he put his heel over the hole. The lizard came out and bit him and the lizard died. R. Hanina put the dead lizard on his shoulder and brought it to the Bet Midrash and said to them. "See my sons, it is not the lizard that kills – it is sins that kill." On that occasion, they said: "Woe to the man who meets up with a lizard, but woe to the lizard which meets up with R. Hanina b. Dosa." (*Berachot* 33a)

Loaf of bread on a corpse

When King David died, he was outdoors studying Torah, as he did every Shabbat. His son Solomon asked the rabbis: "My father is dead and lying outside in the sun. Can I bring him in?" The rabbis answered: "Put a loaf of bread or a child on him and carry him in." (*Shabbat* 30b, 142b)

📖 Loan repaid

In a Shemittah year

R. Abba b. Marta owed money to Rabbah, but he was slow to make payment. When he finally came with the money it was during a Shemittah year. According to Halachah, in a Shemittah year all debts are cancelled.[172] (*Gittin* 37b)

Loans with a note of indebtedness (*Bava Batra* 175a)

---

172. See entry, Shemita year debt payment.

Location of Menorah

Placing the *menorah* at the door, which side (*Shabbat* 22a)

Locust species

R. Avimi b. Avohu taught: There are 800 species of unclean locust in existence. (*Hullin* 63b)

Longevity

The students once asked R. Adda b. Ahava: "To what do you attribute your longevity?" He replied: "I have never displayed my impatience at home, I have never walked in front of a man greater than myself, I have never had thoughts about Torah in a dirty place, I have never walked four *amot* without Torah thoughts, and I never fell asleep in the Bet Midrash. I never rejoiced at the embarrassment of my friends, and I never called my friends by a nickname." (*Taanit* 20b; *Megillah* 28a)

Longevity

R. Hisda lived to a ripe old age of 92. There were 60 marriage feasts in the house of R. Hisda. (*Moed Katan* 28a)

Longevity

When R. Eleazar b. Shammua was asked by his students to what he attributed his longevity, his answer was, "I have never taken a shortcut through a synagogue, I never stepped over the heads of the holy people, and I never lifted my hands to do the priestly benedictions without first making a *beracha*." Rabbi Eleazar is mentioned among the Ten Martyrs during the Hadrianic persecutions. (*Sotah* 39a; *Megillah* 27b)

✿ Longevity

R. Nehunia b. HaKana was asked by his students: "By what merit did you reach such old age?"

His reply was: "Never in my life did I try

to elevate myself at the expense of degrading others, never did I go to sleep with a curse on my lips against my fellow-men, and I have been generous with my money." (*Megillah* 28a)

✿ Losses have no friends

R. Papa said: "At the gates of shops, there are many brothers and friends, but at the gates of loss – there are neither brothers nor friends." (*Shabbat* 32a)

✿ Lost and found

Our rabbis taught: After the destruction of the Temple, they instituted that an article that was found should be announced in the synagogue. (*Bava Metzia* 28b)

Lost article

An article lost by father and son – who has priority (*Bava Metzia* 33a; *Sanhedrin* 64b)

Lost article keeper   שומר אבידה

Keeper of a lost article waiting for its owner and the responsibility thereof for watching it (*Bava Metzia* 29a, 82a; *Bava Kamma* 56b; *Shevuot* 44a; *Nedarim* 33b)

Lost articles

Articles found must be announced in public. (*Bava Metzia* 21a, 23a)

Lost in sixty

A forbidden mixture is considered nullified if mixed in one of sixty times more than the other (*Hullin* 97b)

Lost in a vineyard

If one sees a person lost in a vineyard (*Bava Kamma* 81b)

📖 Lost Ketubbah

The sister of R. Rami b. Hama was married to R. Avia, but her *ketubbah* was lost. They came to R. Yosef to obtain a ruling, whether they can continue to live together without a *ketubbah*. He told them that it is a dispute between R. Meir and the Sages. According to the Sages, in such a case, a man may live with his wife for two to three years without a *ketubbah*. R. Abbaye objected and R. Yosef told him: "In that case, go and write her a new *ketubbah*." (*Ketubbot* 56b, 57a)

Lost objects in a flood

R. Yohanan said in the name of R. Yishmael b. Yehotzedek: "A lost article found in a flood may be retained." (*Bava Metzia* 22b)

📖 Lost ten sons

Once R. Eleazar was sick and R. Yohanan went to visit him. He saw R. Eleazar crying. He asked him: "Why are you crying? Are you crying because you have no children?" R. Yohanan took a bone from his pocket, showed it to him and said, "This is the tooth from my tenth son who died." (*Berachot* 5b)

Lots in the Temple made of gold

The lots for the two goat offerings on Yom Kippur were originally made of ebony, but the High Priest Ben Gamla donated new ones made of gold. (*Yoma* 37a)

Lots were cast in the Temple

The job assignment for the priests was done by lots. (*Tamid* 30a)

📖 Love God with all your soul

When R. Akiva was taken out to be executed, it was the time for the recital of *Shema*. While they were tearing his flesh with iron combs, he was accepting upon himself the kingship of Heaven. His students asked him: "Rabbi, do you have to go to such extremes?" He answered, "All my life I have been troubled by a verse in the Torah which says 'with all your soul.' I wondered when I would have the opportunity to fulfill this commandment. Now that I have the opportunity, shall I not fulfill it?" (*Berachot* 61b)

Love peace, pursue peace
R. Hillel said: "Love peace and pursue peace." (*Avot* 1:12)

✿ Loved by Hashem
There are three kinds of people that Hashem loves: One who does not display temper, one who does not become intoxicated, and one who does not insist on his rights. (*Pesahim* 113b)

Loving-kindness   גמילות חסדים
R. Eleazar stated: "The performance of charity is greater than offering all the sacrifices."

R. Eleazar further stated: "The act of *gemilut hasadim* is greater than charity."

He also stated: "The reward of charity is dependent on the kindness in it." (*Sukkah* 49b; *Bava Kamma* 100a)

Lower Court and the Higher Court
R. Yehoshua b. Levi said: "Three things were enacted by the lower court, and the higher court assented." (*Makkot* 23b)

📖 Lulav on a ship
One lulav *only for four rabbis*
The Talmud relates that R. Gamliel, R. Yehoshua, R. Eleazar b. Azariah, and R. Akiva were traveling together on a ship. Only R. Gamliel owned a *lulav* which he bought for 1,000 *zuz*. R. Gamliel performed the mitzvah of waving the *lulav*. When he finished, he gave it as a gift to R. Yehoshua. R. Yehoshua did likewise and then gave it as a gift to R. Eleazar b. Azariah who performed the mitzvah, and when he finished, he gave it as a gift to R. Akiva. R. Akiva performed the mitzvah and then returned it to R. Gamliel. (*Sukkah* 41b)

Lulav stolen
Is a stolen *lulav* fit for performing the mitzvah? (*Sukkah* 29b)

Lulav ties
What can be used to tie a *lulav*? (*Sukkah* 36b)

Lulav waving
Where in the prayers do they wave the *lulav*? (*Sukkah* 37b)

Lulav waving time
When is the proper time to wave the *lulav*? (*Megillah* 20b)

Luminaries
On the day a luminary died, another was born
The Talmud states: "The day when R. Akiva died, Rebbe was born; when Rebbe died, Rav Yehuda was born; when Rav Yehuda, died Rava was born; when Rava died R. Ashi was born." (*Kiddushin* 72b)

Lunar images
We have learned: R. Gamliel had hanging on the wall drawings and images of the moon in various positions. (*Avodah Zarah* 43a; *Rosh Hashana* 24a)

Lydda academy   לוד
Lydda, also called Lod, is a community located today south of Tel Aviv and Yaffa. During Talmudic times, it was the seat of the Sanhedrin for a while. Several great Talmudic scholars taught in Lydda. Among them were: R. Tarfon, R. Eliezer Horkynos, R. Akiva, R. Yehoshua ben Levi, R. Eleazar b. Kappara, and R. Hanina b. Hama.

Demetrius II gave the city to King Yonatan the Hasmonean.

Many Jews in the city suffered great tragedies during the wars with Rome. There was a time when the city was detached from Judea by the order of the Roman governor. Cestius Gallus, the Roman proconsul, burned the city on his way to Jerusalem.

Julius Caesar granted some privileges to the Jews of Lydda.

During the period when Septimus Severus was emperor, he changed the name of the city to suit his purposes.

Yehoshua b. Levi was the head of the academy in Lydda. He lived in the 3rd century CE.

M

Ma Nafshach   מה נפשך
Which way will you have it? Whatever your assumption is – it does not fit in. (*Horayot* 5a; *Avodah Zarah* 31b)

Ma Nishtana   מה נשתנה
The first words of the Four Questions a son asks his father at the Seder table (*Pesahim* 116a)

Maamadot   מעמדות
The early Prophets established twenty-four guard divisions consisting of Kohanim, Levites, and Israelites. When the time came for a particular guard division to go up, it was the Kohanim and the Levites that went up to Jerusalem while the Israelites of that division assembled in their own towns and they were reading the chapter of creation. (*Taanit* 26a)

Maamar   מאמר
Betrothal by word in connection with *yibbum* (*Yevamot* 17a, 18b)

Maariv service
On one occasion, a student asked Rabbi Yehoshua: "Is the evening prayer compulsory or optional?" Rabbi Yehoshua replied that it is optional. The same student asked Rabbi Gamliel the same question.

And Rabbi Gamliel replied that it is compulsory. "But," said the student, "Rabbi Yehoshua told me it is optional." Rabbi Gamliel told the student to wait until the assembly starts its session. The question was asked and Rabbi Gamliel said that it is compulsory. After this, R. Gamliel took R. Yehoshua to task. (*Berachot* 27b; *Shabbat* 9b)

Magrefa   מגריפה
A drum-like instrument producing a very loud noise. It was used in the Temple as a signal for the priests to go to their posts. (*Tamid* 33a)

Mahaah   מחאה
A protest taken against an action. (*Bava Batra* 38b, 39a)

Mai Ika L'meimar   מאי איכא למימר
What is there to say (*Hullin* 4a)

Mailing a letter
It is related that R. Yosi HaKohen never sent a letter with a non-Jew, for fear that he might deliver it on Shabbat. (*Shabbat* 19a)

Mailing a letter Erev Shabbat
Sending a letter with a non-Jew on Erev Shabbat (*Shabbat* 19a)

Main labors prohibited on Shabbat
The thirty-nine main labors forbidden on Shabbat are discussed in *Kelal gadol*, the 7th *perek* in *Shabbat*. (*Shabbat* 73a)

Maintenance for children
Rava used to tell the men brought before him for refusing to maintain their young children: "Will it please you that your children should be supported by the charity fund?" (*Ketubbot* 49b)

Major loss   הפסד מרובה
(*Bava Kamma* 117a; *Shabbat* 154b)

📖 Majority decides in halachic matters

Once R. Gamliel and the Elders were sitting in an upper chamber in Jericho. They were served dates. R. Gamliel gave permission to R. Akiva to say the blessings. R. Akiva said one blessing, which included three. R. Gamliel disapproved and said to him: "How long will you stick your head into quarrels which go against me?" R. Akiva replied:

"My teacher, you say this way and the rabbis say differently, and you have taught us that when an individual takes issue with the majority the Halachah is decided according to the majority." (*Berachot* 9a, 37a)

Majority determines in ritual matters
כי אזלינן בתר רובא באיסורא בממונא לא

Shemuel said: "We follow the majority only in ritual matters, but not in monetary." (*Bava Kamma* 27b, 46b; *Bava Batra* 92b)

Majority prevails

Majority prevails only if it is in front of us, like ten butcher stores – nine of them are kosher and one is not. (*Bechorot* 19b)

Make-up
No make-up – still beautiful

R. Dimi told his colleagues that the custom in Eretz Yisrael is to sing before the bride a song with the words of, "No powder, no paint, and no making the hair into locks, and still a beautiful gazelle." (*Ketubbot* 17a)

✿ Making a living
From the labor of own hands

R. Hiyya b. Ammi said in the name of R. Ulla: "A man who lives from the labor of his hands is greater than one who fears God." (*Berachot* 8a)

Making up the prayers

If one forgot to pray, can one make up

with another prayer? Can two *Maariv* prayers make up for *Minha*? (*Berachot* 26a,b)

Makkot   מכות

The number of lashes administered; the place and position of the lashes (*Makkot* 22a)

Makkot endurance   מכות

Endurance is taken into consideration when lashes are meted out. (*Makkot* 22a–b)

Male children   בנין דכרין
(*Bava Kamma* 89b)

Male children

R. Hiyya b. Abba said in the name of R. Yohanan: "If one makes *Havdalah* on wine at the termination of Shabbat, that person will have male children." (*Shabbat* 18b)

Male prostitute (*Sanhedrin* 54b)

Malshinim   מלשינים
Author of the prayer Ve-Lamalshnim

Rabbi Gamliel asked for a volunteer to compose a prayer which reflects Jewish opposition to the sectarians and non-believers. Rabbi Shemuel volunteered and composed the prayer called "*Ve-La-malshinim*." This prayer with the other eighteen prayers constitute the *Amidah* prayers. (*Berachot* 28b)

Mamzerim   ממזרים

Children born and conceived by forbidden relationships (*Yevamot* 49a)

📖 Man blessed with all

A blessing from a Sage for a person who is already blessed[173] (*Taanit* 5b)

Man desires
A man is consumed with a passion

R. Yehuda said in the name of Rav: "It

---

173. See entry, Blessing from a Sage.

happened that a man fell in love with a certain woman. He got sick because he was consumed by his passion for her. The doctors who were consulted said that he would die unless he could have her. However, the rabbis ruled that he should die rather than her submitting to his desires." (*Sanhedrin* 75a)

📖 **Man from Meron**

A man from Meron came to Jerusalem. He had with him much movable wealth and he wanted to give it away as gifts. He was told however that movable property cannot be given away unless it is given away at the same time with land. He bought a rocky piece of land near Jerusalem and gave the following instructions: "The northern side I give to one of my friends and with it I give him 100 sheep and 100 casks, the southern side I give to my other friend and with it I give him 100 sheep and 100 casks. When he died, the rabbis carried out his instructions. (*Bava Batra* 156b)

✿ **Man honors the place**

R. Nahman b. Yitzhak was seated among the ordinary people, and R. Nahman b. Hisda said to him: "Would you please come and sit closer to us?" R. Nahman b. Yitzhak replied: "We have learned that R. Yosi said: 'It is not the place that honors the man, but it is the man who honors the place.'" (*Taanit* 21b)

Man nursing a child

The Talmud relates a story that a woman died and left a child to be nursed. Her husband could not afford to pay for a wet nurse and a miracle happened – his breasts opened and produced milk like it does for a woman. Rabbi Yosef commented: "How great this man must be that such a miracle happened to him."

Rabbi Nahman observed: "The proof is that miracles do happen, but food is rarely created miraculously." (*Shabbat* 53b)

Man of knowledge
R. Yohanan b. Nuri

R. Gamliel and R. Yehoshua traveled on a boat. "You possess so much knowledge," Rabbi Gamliel complimented him, "and yet you travel on board a ship?"

"Don't marvel at me, rather be surprised at two of your students who live on land, like Rabbi Eleazar Hisma and Rabbi Yohanan ben Nuri, who can calculate how many drops of water there are in the sea, and yet they have neither bread to eat nor clothing to put on."

Rabbi Gamliel decided to appoint them as supervisors and sent for them when he landed. They were reluctant to accept on account of their humility. But Rabbi Gamliel told them. "Do you imagine that I offer you rulership? It is servitude that I offer you." (*Horayot* 10a)

📖 **Man of wings**

R. Yannai said, "*Tefillin* require a pure body like Elisha, the man of wings." He was called the man of wings because the Roman government once decreed a prohibition on wearing *tefillin*. Elisha put them on anyhow. A Roman soldier ran after him and caught him. Elisha removed the *tefillin* and held them in his hand.

"What is that in your hand?"

"They are wings of a dove."[174]

He opened his hand and there were wings of a dove in his hand. (*Shabbat* 32a, 49a)

Man was forced to show the wine

Non-Jews forced a Jew to show the wine of a fellow Jew (*Bava Kamma* 117a)

Mani   מני
Amora from Eretz Yisrael

---

174. See entry, Tefillin.

Head of the academy in Sepphoris
4th century CE (*Taanit* 23b)

Manna was hidden away

King Yoshiyahu hid away the anointing oil, the Holy Ark, the jar of manna, Aharon's rod with the almond blossoms, and also the coffer the Philistines sent as a gift to Israel. He did not want these precious things to be taken by the enemy. (*Horayot* 12a)

✿ Man's character

One of R. Illai's famous sayings: "A man's character can be determined by three things: by his cup, by his purse, and by his anger. Some say also by his laughter." (*Eruvin* 65b)

Man's hand

"ידו של אדם חשובה לו כד" על ד

A man's hand is equal to him as an area of four by four handbreadths (*tefahim*). (*Shabbat* 5a; *Ketubbot* 31b)

Manure on the street

Taking out manure in the street (*Bava Metzia* 118b)

Mar bar Rav Ashi   מר בר רב אשי

Amora from Babylonia
Head of academy in Sura
5th century CE (*Bava Batra* 12b)

Mar bar Ravina   מר בר רבינא

Amora from Babylonia
4th century CE (*Pesahim* 68b)

Mari bar Isaac   מרי בר איסק

Amora from Babylonia
3rd – 4th centuries CE (*Bava Metzia* 39b; *Ketubbot* 27b)

Mari bar Issur   מרי בר איסור

Amora from Babylonia
4th century CE (*Bava Batra* 149a)

Mari bar Rachel   מרי בר רחל

The son of a Jewish woman and a proselyte father, but he was conceived before conversion. (*Bava Metzia* 73b)

Mar Ukva Exilarch

Mar Ukva was the head of the Bet Din in the town of Kofri.
3rd century CE (*Kiddushin* 44b)

Mar Ukva's sons

Mar Ukva had two sons: Mari and Nathan. (*Hullin* 43b; *Berachot* 13b)

Marital duties

R. Yehuda said in the name of R. Shemuel: "Scholars are obligated to perform their marital duties every Friday night." (*Ketubbot* 62b; *Bava Kamma* 82a)

Marital intercourse

When there is a Torah in the room, there should not be marital intercourse. (*Berachot* 25b)

Marital relations in daytime

R. Yohanan stated: "It is forbidden to have marital relations in daytime." (*Niddah* 16b)

📖 Market privileges for rabbis

It is related that R. Dimi from Nehardea brought a load of figs in a boat. The Exilarch said to Rava: "Go and see if he is a scholar, and if so, reserve the market for him." The scholars had privileges; they could dispose of their merchandise before the rest of the merchants, so that they could then go and study. (*Bava Batra* 22a)

📖 Marking graves

To prevent priests from becoming defiled
Resh Lakish was marking the burial caves of the rabbis in order to prevent the priests from becoming defiled. But he could not locate the grave of R. Hiyya. He felt humiliated. He called out: "Sovereign of the

Universe, did I not debate on the Torah like R. Hiyya did?" A heavenly voice responded, "You did indeed debate like he did, but you did not spread the Torah as he did."

R. Hiyya prepared scrolls upon which he wrote the Five Books of Moshe. Then he went to a town where there were no teachers and he taught the five books to five children, and the six orders of the Mishna to six children. He told them: "Until I return, teach each other what I taught you," and thus he preserved the Torah from being forgotten.

This is what Rebbe meant when he said: "How great are the works of R. Hiyya." "Are they greater than yours?" asked R. Yishmael b. R. Yosi. "Yes," replied Rebbe. (*Bava Metzia* 85b)

Markings
Identifying markings on a lost article (*Bava Metzia* 22b, 23a)

Maror   מרור
Bitter herbs used on Pesach at the Seder (Pesahim 116b)

Marriage
A woman can be acquired as a wife in three ways. (*Kiddushin* 2a)

Marriage
Once a woman was annoyed by her son over something. She swore and declared: "Whoever offers to marry me, I will not refuse him." Some unsuitable person made her an offer. It was brought before the rabbis. They ruled that she certainly did not intend to marry an unsuitable person. (*Bava Kamma* 80a)

Marriage
Rabbi Akiva expounded: "When a husband and wife are worthy, and love and respect each other the Shechina is with

them, but when they are not worthy fire consumes them. In Hebrew a man is called איש and a woman is called אשה, the spelling is almost identical, except the word for "men" has a *yud* in it, and the word for "women" has a *hey* in it; the extra two letters spellout the name of God. If you remove these two letters you are left with the word אש which means fire." (*Sotah* 17a)

Marriage at sixteen
R. Hisda said: "The reason I have an advantage over my colleagues is because I was married at sixteen."

He and his wife had seven sons and two daughters. (*Pesahim* 113a)

⌂ Marriage insincere
A man bought a boatload of wine and was looking for a place to store it. A certain woman had a storage room, but she was not willing to rent it to him. He decided to marry her[175] and was able to use her storage room for his wine. Soon after the marriage, he wrote a bill of divorce and sent it to her. (*Bava Metzia* 101b)

⌂ Marriage offered
R. Yohanan offered his daughter in marriage to R. Zeri
Rabbi Yohanan must have thought of R. Zeri as very worthy, because he offered him his daughter in marriage. However, for his own reasons he did not accept the offer. One day, Rabbi Yohanan and Rabbi Zeri were traveling on the road, and they came to a pool of water, whereupon Rabbi Zeri carried Rabbi Yohanan on his shoulder. Rabbi Yohanan remarked: "It seems our learning is fit, but our daughters are not fit for you?" (*Kiddushin* 71b)

Marriage proposal with conditions
(*Kiddushin* 60a)

---

175. See entry, Dishonest marriage.

Married
To daughter of R. Hisda
R. Rami b. Hama was married to the daughter of R. Hisda. (*Berachot* 44a)

Married
R. Yannai's daughter was married to R. Yehuda, R. Hiyya's son
R. Yehuda was a son of Rabbi Hiyya. The daughter of R. Yannai was married to him. (*Ketubbot* 62b)

Marror
Which herbs may one eat on Pesach to fulfill the obligation of eating bitter herbs? (*Pesahim* 39a)

Marrying on Hol Hamoed
Can one be married on Hol Hamoed? (*Moed Katan* 8b)

✿ Marrying a daughter to an old man
Giving a daughter in marriage to an old man is profanity
R. Eliezer said: "When the Torah says do not profane your daughter, it means do not give your daughter in marriage to an old man." (*Sanhedrin* 76a)

▭ Martyrdom
Rabbi Yehuda ben Bava became a martyr when he disobeyed the decree of the Roman authorities banning the ordination of rabbis. The decree issued by the authorities during the Hadrian persecution was that anyone who ordains a rabbi is subject to the death penalty, anyone who receives ordination is subject to the death penalty, and the city where the ordination takes place is to be demolished, and the boundaries around the city are to be uprooted. The ceremony was held anyhow and he ordained them.[176] Five prominent students

sat before him: Rabbi Meir, Rabbi Yehuda bar Illai, Rabbi Shimon, Rabbi Yosi, and Rabbi Eleazar ben Shammua. Rabbi Yehuda told his students to flee. They wanted to take him with them, but he urged them to flee without him. "I would cause all of you to be caught; I am too old to run. I lie before them like a stone." It was said that the Romans stabbed him 300 times. (*Sanhedrin* 14a; *Avodah Zarah* 8b)

Mashehu   משהו
Very little (*Hullin* 102b)

Mashiach
אין בין העוה"ז לימות המשיח אלא שעבוד מלכיות
R. Shemuel said: "There is no difference between this world and the world of Mashiach except bondage of foreign powers." (*Berachot* 34b; *Shabbat* 63a, 151b; *Pesahim* 68a)

Mashiach
When will Mashiach come?
R. Yehoshua b. Levi met Eliyahu standing at the entrance to the tomb of Rabbi Shimon ben Yohai. He asked him:
"When will Mashiach come?"
Eliyahu answered, "Go and ask him yourself."
"Where will I find him?"
"He is sitting at the entrance of the city of Rome."
"How will I recognize him?" asked R. Yehoshua.
"He is sitting among the poor lepers. All the lepers untie their bandages all at once and treat their wounds all at once, but the person that unties his bandages one at a time and treats his wounds one at a time – he is the Mashiach. He does it that way, because just in case he is called to appear as the Mashiach, he wants to be ready and not cause a delay."
R. Yehoshua went over to him and greeted him with "Shalom, my Rebbe

---

176. See entry, Ordination of rabbis.

and Master." Mashiach replied, "Shalom to you son of Levi."

He asked: "Mashiach, when will you come?"

Mashiach replied: "I am coming today."

When R. Yehoshua returned to Eliyahu, he asked R. Yehoshua: "What did he tell you?"

"He told me: 'Shalom upon you son of Levi.'"

Eliyahu said to R. Yehoshua: "In this answer, he assured you that your father and you will have *Olam Haba*."

But R. Yehoshua was not happy. "He lied to me. He told me he was coming today and he didn't."

Eliyahu answered, "His promise was conditional upon whether the people of Israel would listen to his voice." (*Sanhedrin* 98a)

Mashiach

R. Yohanan said: "The son of David will come only in a generation that is either altogether righteous or altogether wicked." (*Sanhedrin* 98a)

Mashiach ben David

R. Zeiri said: "Mashiach will not come until there are no conceited men in Israel." (*Sanhedrin* 98a)

Mashiach ben Yosef

Mashiach son of Yosef (*Sukkah* 52a–b)

Mashiach delayed

Mashiach will come when the two ruling houses of Israel cease

R. Yehuda and R. Hezkiya, the sons of R. Hiyya, were having dinner with Rebbe, and R. Hiyya, their father, was also present. When the wine was having its effect, they started talking, and they said:

"The son of David cannot come until the two ruling houses of Israel shall come to an end." To back it up they quoted a passage from Scripture.

Rebbe said: "My children, you throw thorns in my eyes."

R. Hiyya intervened and said. "Rebbe, do not be angry; the numerical value of the Hebrew letters for 'wine' is the same as the Hebrew letters for 'secret.' You had them drink wine – when wine goes in the secret comes out."[177] (*Sanhedrin* 38a; *Eruvin* 65a)

Mashiach on a donkey

R. Shemuel was asked by King Shapur: "You say that Mashiach will be riding on a donkey. I would much rather send him one of my white horses." R. Shemuel answered: "Do you have a steed with hundred hues?" (*Sanhedrin* 98a)

Mashiach's name

What is Mashiach's name? The school of R. Shila says that his name is Shiloh; the school of R. Yannai says it is Yinnon; the school of R. Hanina says it is Hanina; others say it is Menahem b. Hezkiya. (*Sanhedrin* 98b)

Mashiach's time   חבלו של משיח

R. Eliezer said: "Just before the arrival of Mashiach insolence will increase, honor will be scarce. The vine will yield its fruit abundantly, but wine will be dear. The government will adopt a new religion, and no one will disapprove."

"The meeting places will be used for immorality; the Galilee will be destroyed, Gablan desolated, and the dwellers on the frontier will go begging from place to place without anyone taking pity on them.

"The wisdom of the scholars will degenerate, fearers of sin will be despised, and truth will be lacking. Youth will put old men to shame, the old will stand up in the presence of the young, a son will revile his father, and a daughter will rebel against

---

177. See entry, Dining with R. Yehuda HaNasi.

her mother; a daughter-in-law against her mother-in-law.

"The members of one's household will be the enemies of the house.

"That generation will have a face of a dog; a son will not be ashamed before his father. Therefore, on whom can we rely? We can rely only upon our Father in Heaven." (*Sotah* 49a–b; *Sanhedrin* 97a)

Mashiach's time   חבלו של משיח
The birth pangs before Mashiach comes (*Sanhedrin* 98b)

Mashiach's time   חבלו של משיח
R. Avimi b. Avohu stated: "The Mashiach of Yisrael will come after 7,000 years." (*Sanhedrin* 99a–b)

Master in Babylon
R. Yohanan used to address Rav in his letters as: "Greetings to our Master in Babylon." (*Hullin* 95b)

Mata Mehasya
Ravina said: "Mata Mehasya is a place where they go out to collect debts after they did the purchases."

Abbaye used to buy meat from two partners and paid each of them, but afterwards he brought them together to square the account with both. The academy of Torah learning was located there. (*Yoma* 86a)

Mata Mehasya, academy
Mata Mehasya is a town in Babylonia near the town of Sura, and situated on the banks of the Euphrates River. Rabbi Ashi lived there and headed the academy. R. Ashi lived in the 4th – 5th centuries CE. (*Ketubbot* 55a; *Shabbat* 11a; *Bava Metzia* 68a)

Match made in Heaven
R. Yehuda said in the name of Rav: "Forty days before an embryo is formed, a heavenly voice calls out to say: 'The daughter

of so and so is a match for so and so.'" (*Sanhedrin* 22a)

Matchmaking
Rabbah bar b. Honah said in the name of R. Yohanan: "To affect a union between a man and a woman is as difficult as the parting of the Reed Sea." (*Sanhedrin* 22a)

Mathna   מתנא
Amora from Babylonia
3rd century CE (*Eruvin* 6b; *Shabbat* 24a)

Mathna II   מתנא
Amora from Babylonia
4th century CE (*Ketubbot* 35b; *Kiddushin* 32a)

Matnita   מתניתא
It was learned in a Beraita
A *matnita* is similar to a Mishna in learning, but not incorporated in the Talmud. (*Shabbat* 19b)

Matya ben Heresh   מתיא בן חרש
Tanna from Eretz Yisrael and Rome
2nd century CE (*Sanhedrin* 32b)

Matityahu ben Shemuel
מתתיה בן שמואל
Officer of the Temple (*Shekalim* 5:1)

Mathna's sons
The sons of Rabbi Mathna were Rabbi Ahadboi, Rabbi Tobi, and Rabbi Hiyya (*Bava Batra* 151a)

Matzot
On the first night of Pesach, it is an obligation to eat *matzot*; on the other six days, it is *reshut*. (*Pesahim* 120a)

Matzot with cooled water
R. Yehuda said: "One must knead *matzot* only with water cooled down overnight." (*Pesahim* 42a)

Mavoi   מבוי
A closed alley
An entrance to a closed alley with a cross beam on top (*Eruvin* 2a)

Mazal
Rava said: "How long a life one lives, whether one will have children, and whether one will have sustenance does not depend on merit, but rather on *mazal*. For instance: Rabbah and R. Hisda – both were rabbis and *tzaddikim*, R. Hisda lived to ninety-two, while Rabbah lived only to the age of forty. In the house of R. Hisda, they celebrated sixty weddings, while in the house of Rabbah they had sixty bereavements. In the house of R. Hisda, they fed the dogs with the finest food, while in the house of Rabbah there was barely enough food for humans." (*Moed Katan* 28a)

Mazal of the hour
It was recorded in R. Yehoshua b. Levi's notebook that a man's fate is determined by the day of the week on which he was born in. R. Hanina said to his people: "Go and tell the son of Levi: Not the *mazal* of the day, but the *mazal* of the hour influences the fate."[178] (*Shabbat* 156a)

Mazal Mazalot   מזל מזלות
Planet, planets (*Avodah Zarah* 42b)

Meal at the end of Shabbat
R. Hanina said: "One should always set his table at the end of Shabbat." (*Shabbat* 119b)

Meal before Minha
Sitting down to eat a meal before Minha prayer. (*Shabbat* 9b)

Meal of three people
R. Shimon said: "Three people that shared a meal and did not discuss Torah is

---

178. See entry, Astrology.

comparable to eating at a table of corpses." (*Avot* 3:3)

Meals and blessings
Differences between Bet Shammai and Bet Hillel (*Berachot* 51b)

Meals on Shabbat
According to Rabbi Hidka, one is obligated to have four meals on Shabbat. (*Shabbat* 117b)

Mealtime hours
The hour of mealtime for different professions (*Shabbat* 10a)

Meaning deduced from context
                              דבר הלמד מעניינו
The meaning of a subject is sometimes deduced from its context. (*Hullin* 63a)

Measurements
R. Yohanan said: "Standard measures and penalties were fixed by the law given to Moshe on Sinai." (*Yoma* 80a)

Measurements
When the son of R. Mesharshia was going to visit R. Papa, R. Mesharshia told him to ask R. Papa this question about measurements:
    "When the rabbis established measurements, did they have the same standard measurement for everyone or was it determined by the size of each individual? Does a large person have a different measurement than a small person?" (*Eruvin* 48a)

Measurements
Given to Moshe Rabbeinu
R. Hanina said: "Moshe Rabbeinu was given all the measurements for the vessels of the Temple." (*Sukkah* 5a)

Measures and weights
R. Levi said: "The punishment for false

measures is more severe than those for marrying forbidden relatives." (*Yevamot* 21a; *Bava Batra* 88b)

Measuring device
Measuring devices of fifty cubits used to measure for an *eruv* (*Eruvin* 57b)

Measuring devices
The measuring devices in the Temple (*Menahot* 87a)

Measuring devices
Cleaning the measuring devices at certain intervals (*Bava Batra* 88a)

Measuring exactly אי אפשר לצמצם
Impossible to measure exactly (*Bechorot* 9a, 17a)

Meat and milk בשר בחלב
Boiling or eating meat and milk together (*Hullin* 103b; *Shabbat* 13a)

Meat between the teeth
R. Aha b. Yosef asked R. Hisda: "What about the meat between the teeth, can one eat dairy?" (*Hullin* 105a)

Medicine
The rabbis in the Talmud were discussing applying medicine for the eyes on Shabbat. It was mentioned that R. Shemuel must have heard it from his father. (*Shabbat* 108b)

Medicine free for the needy
The Talmud relates that Rabbah said to Rafram b. Papa: "Tell me some of the good deeds Rabbi Huna had done." He replied: "Whenever he discovered a new medicine, he would suspend it above his door with a jug of water next to it, and would put a notice with it, which stated that whoever needs it should come and get it." (*Taanit* 20b)

Medicine on Shabbat
R. Shemuel discusses medicines permitted or not permitted on Shabbat. (*Avodah Zarah* 28b)

Medium quality property בינונית
(*Bava Kamma* 7b; *Gittin* 48b)

Megillah reading
When is the proper time to read the Megillah? (*Megillah* 20b)

Megillah reading in walled cities
On which day do they read the Megillah in a walled city? (*Megillah* 2a)

Megillat Esther
The authors of Megillat Esther were the Men of the Great Assembly. (*Bava Batra* 15a)

Megillat Taanit
The scroll Megillat Taanit, which deals with fasting, was authored by Hanania b. Hezkiya and his associates. (*Shabbat* 13b)

Mehuza
The inhabitants of Mehuza are students of Torah. (*Avodah Zarah* 58a)

Mehuza; Academy מחוזא
Mehuza is a town in Babylonia on the banks of the Tigris River. It is also next to the Nahar Malka which connects the Euphrates with the Tigris. There were many Jewish farmers in Mehuza; they owned orchards and fields, and also reared cattle and traded in grain. During Talmudic times, the town was located on a central trading route, and many caravans passed through.

Mehuza became a place of learning when the Nehardean academy was destroyed in 259 CE by Papa ben Nasser, the commander-in-chief of Palmyra. But it gained more prominence after the death of Rabbi Abbaye, who was the head of the academy in Pumbedita. Rava lived in

Mehuza and headed the academy for four-teen years. The large Jewish community in Mehuza constituted a majority of the town's population. When Rabbi Abbaye visited there, he was surprised that there were no *mezuzot* on the town's gates. Em-peror Julian destroyed the city in 363 CE, but it was rebuilt.

The Exilarch Mar Zutra II led a revolt against the Persians in 513 and defeated them. He established an independent Jewish state in the area and Mehuza was its capital.

The following were the heads of the academy in Mehuza: Rabbah bar Avuha, who lived in the 3rd century CE; Rava, who lived in the 3rd – 4th centuries CE; Ameimar, who lived in 4th – 5th centuries CE. (*Berachot* 59b; *Yoma* 11a)

Meilah מעילה
Desecration or misappropriation or the slightest deviation from the prescribed ceremony is a *meilah*. (*Meilah* 2a)

Meir מאיר
Tanna from Eretz Yisrael
2nd century CE (*Horayot* 13b)

Meir מאיר
Since R. Meir passed away, the composers of parables ceased. (*Sotah* 49a)

R. Meir had to leave Eretz Yisrael for Babylonia[179] (*Avodah Zarah* 18a)

Melaveh Malkah
R. Hanina said: "One should always pre-pare a meal for after Shabbat even if not hungry." (*Shabbat* 119b)

Melika מליקה
Kosher slaughtering of a bird without a knife. (*Hullin* 19b, 28a)

Melog מלוג
A wife's estate in which the husband has the fruits without the responsibility for the losses (*Yevamot* 66a)

Mem and Samech ם, ס
In the Tablets
Rabbi Hisda stated: "The letters *mem* and *samech* which were in the Tablets were suspended by miracle and the writing on the Tablets could be read from within and without or from both sides." (*Shabbat* 104a)

Mema'enet ממאנת
Refusal – a minor who was given in marriage by her mother or brother has the right to repudiate the contract. (*Yevamot* 108a)

▭ Memory loss
At one time, Rabbi Avimi forgot some of his learning, as is mentioned in the Tal-mud. R. Zera said: "R. Avimi was studying the Tractate *Menahot* under R. Hisda.

But wasn't it the reverse? Was it not R. Hisda studying under R. Avimi? And did not R. Hisda say, "I received many beat-ings from R. Avimi?"

The answer is that he had forgotten this tractate and went to his student Rabbi Hisda to refresh his memory. Why did he not send for him to come to him? He thought that by going to him, he would get more out of it. (*Arachin* 22a; *Menahot* 7a)

Men of excellence in every generation
R Hiyya b. Abba said: "Three men of ex-cellence come forth in Israel in every gen-eration. These men plead in Israel's favor in every generation." (*Hullin* 92a)

Men of the Great Assembly
אנשי כנסת הגדולה
(*Avot* 1:1)

---

179. See entry, Berurya.

Menahem מנחם
Tanna from Eretz Yisrael
1st century BCE (*Hagigah* 2:2, 16a)

Menahem ben Yosi ben Halafta
מנחם בן יוסי בן חלפתא
Tanna from Eretz Yisrael
2nd century CE (*Yoma* 4:4)

Menahem replaced
At first, Rabbi Hillel's partner was Rabbi Menahem, but Rabbi Menahem left and Shammai took his place. According to some, R. Menahem went into the service of King Herod, others say he withdrew into seclusion. (*Hagigah* 2:2, 16a–b)

Menahem ben Simai
Menahem b. Simai was called "the son of the holy" because he would not gaze at the image of a *zuz*. (*Avodah Zarah* 50a; *Pesahim* 104a)

Menashe
R. Yohanan said: "Anyone who says that Menashe will not have a share in the World to Come undermines the hands of the *baalei teshuva*." (*Sanhedrin* 103a–b)

Menashe traveling to Torta
Traveling to Torta, R. Menashe encountered on the way a band of thieves. They asked him for his destination and he purposely deceived them by telling them he was traveling to Pumbedita which was far away. The thieves were unhappy and called him and his teacher names. (*Avodah Zarah* 26a)

Menashye bar Tahlifa מנשיא בר תחליפא
Amora from Babylonia
3rd century CE (*Pesahim* 6b)

Menorah location
Placing the *menorah* at the door; which side (*Shabbat* 22a)

Menorah replica with five branches
A *menorah* with five or six branches (*Avodah Zarah* 43a; *Rosh Hashana* 24a; *Menahot* 28b)

📖 Menstrual blood
Halachic Expert
Why was R. Eleazar described as the supreme authority in the Land of Israel? Because a woman once brought to R. Eleazar some blood to be examined while R. Ammi was present. R. Eleazar smelled it and declared: "This is blood of lust." After she went out, R. Ammi followed the woman to question her, and she admitted, "My husband was away on a trip and I desired him." (Niddah 20b)

Menstruation, regular period וסת
A woman who has a regular date for the menstrual period. (*Niddah* 63a)

Mental neglect היסח הדעת
Mental distraction (*Pesahim* 34a)

Mention Rosh Hodesh
Where to mention Rosh Hodesh in the daily prayers (*Shabbat* 24a)

Mentioning rain
One mentions the power of rain in the *Amidah*. (*Berachot* 33a; *Taanit* 2a)

Merciful
One of Abba Shaul's statements was that "One should strive to be gracious and merciful as God is gracious and merciful." (*Ketubbot* 111a)

Mercurius
A Greek deity (*Avodah Zarah* 50a)

Mereimar מרימר
Amora from Babylonia
Head of the academy in Sura
4th – 5th centuries CE (*Yevamot* 75b)

Meriting the World to Come

Rav Yehuda said in the name of Rav: "Every day a Bat Kol goes out from Mount Horev and proclaims: 'The whole world is being fed for the merits of my son Hanina, and yet my son Hanina is satisfied with a small measure of carobs from one Friday to the next Friday.'" (*Berachot* 17b)

📖 Merriment

Excessive merriment
Mar bar Ravina made a wedding feast for his son, and when he saw that the rabbis became very merry he took a cup worth 400 *zuz* and broke it in front of them. This shocked them and they became serious. (*Berachot* 30b, 31a)

Mesharshia   משרשיא
Amora from Babylonia
4th century CE (*Eruvin* 48a)

Messenger with marriage proposal
If one sends a woman a marriage proposal with a messenger and he proposes to her for himself (*Kiddushin* 58b)

Metal candle holder
To handle on Shabbat (*Shabbat* 44a)

Metal vessels and uncleanness (*Kelim* 11:1)

Metal vessels made Kosher
Metal vessels to be made kosher must have hot boiling water. (*Avodah Zarah* 75b)

Method used to examine witnesses
(*Rosh Hashana* 23b)

Meticulous student
Rabbi Hiyya b. Abba was very particular to get the exact teachings from Rabbi Yohanan, his teacher. He used to go over what he learned every thirty days with his teacher Rabbi Yohanan. (*Berachot* 33b, 38b; *Hullin* 86b)

Mezuzah
A *mezuzah* must be written in Hebrew. (*Megillah* 8b)

Mezuzah
A *mezuzah* for doorposts needs to be placed in a home, on the court doorpost, and on the town's gate. (*Yoma* 11a)

Mezuzah
R. Huna used to say: "A person who lights his house well will have scholarly sons. A person who is observant in placing a *mezuzah* on the door of his house will merit a beautiful home. A person who is observant in wearing *tzitzit* will merit a beautiful garment. A person who is observant in making *Kiddush* will merit full barrels of wine." (*Shabbat* 23b)

Mezuzah and Onkelos
Onkelos converted to Judaism. The Emperor sent soldiers to arrest him. As he was passing the door with a *mezuzah*, he pointed to the *mezuzah* and asked the soldiers, "What is this?" They told him, "You tell us." He replied that according to universal custom the emperor dwells inside and the soldiers guard him from the outside. Not so with the King of the Universe – His servants are within and He guards them from the outside. That is the idea of the *mezuzah*. The soldiers converted to Judaism. (*Avodah Zarah* 11a)

Miasha   מיאשא
Amora from Eretz Yisrael
3rd – 4th centuries CE (*Ketubbot* 85b)

✿ Midday wine
One of Rabbi Dosa's sayings was: "Morning sleep, midday wine, children's talk,

and sitting in companoy of the ignorant, remove a man from this world." (*Avot* 3:10)

✿ Middot
Good character traits
R. Eliezer said: "During my entire life, no one ever preceded me to the Bet Midrash, never did I sleep or doze off in the Bet Midrash, never did I go out and leave anyone behind me in the Bet Midrash, nor did I ever utter profane language, and never did I say anything which I did not hear from my teachers." (*Sukkah* 28a; *Megillah* 27b)

Midwives
Jewish and non-Jewish (*Avodah Zarah* 26a)

Migu מיגו Since
A Talmudic expression: Since he could have claimed more, therefore, a lesser claim is convincing. (*Bava Metzia* 5b; *Sanhedrin* 24a)

Mikvaot
Two *mikvaot* – one above the other or side by side (*Mikvaot* 6:8)

Mikveh
How much drawn water makes a *mikveh* unfit (*Eduyot* 2a; Mishna 3)

Mikveh for dishes
The proper way to immerse dishes in the *mikveh* (*Mikvaot* 9:5, 10:1–5)

Mikveh intervention
The immersion into the *mikveh* must be done without any object intervening between the body of the person and the water. (*Mikvaot* 9:1)

Mikveh of forty
A mikveh that had less than forty *se'ah*. (*Mikvaot* 2:2)

Mikveh unfit
Two weavers came through the Dung Gate of Jerusalem and testified in the name of Shemaya and Avtalyon what makes a *mikveh* unfit. (*Shabbat* 15a)

Mikveh with drawn water in it
A *mikveh* that was mixed with drawn water (*Mikvaot* 2:3)

Milah
A Jewish scholar must learn three things
R. Yehuda said in the name of Rav: "A scholar must learn three things: writing, *shehita* (kosher slaughtering), and circumcision." R. Hanania b. Shalmaya said in the name of Rav: "They also have to know how to make a knot in the *tefillin*, the blessings at a wedding, and how to bind the *tzitzit* (*Hullin* 9a)

Milah
A Jew circumcising a non-Jew or a non-Jew circumcising a Jewish baby (*Avodah Zarah* 26b)

Milk and chicken
In the community of R. Yosi HaGlili, they ate the flesh of fowl with milk. (*Hullin* 116a; *Yevamot* 14a)

Milk and meat
The benefits derived from milk and meat – are they permitted or not (*Hullin* 113a)

Milk and meat, three prohibitions
דבי רבי ישמעאל
The school of R. Yishmael taught: The Torah stated three times, "You shall not cook a kid in its mother's milk." One is a prohibition against eating, one against deriving benefit, and one against cooking it." (*Hullin* 115b)

Milking
When a non-Jew is milking a kosher animal and a Jew is watching, is it permissible (*Avodah Zarah* 39b)

Millennium
The seventh millennium for the world
It has been taught according to R. Kattina: Just as the seventh year is one year of release, so is the world: 1,000 years out of seven shall be fallow.

D'bei Eliyahu teaches: The world is to exist 6,000 years. (*Sanhedrin* 97a)

📖 Millenniums
Predicting the future of the world
R. Hanan b. Tahlifa sent word to R. Yosef: "I once met a man who was in the possession of a *megillah* scroll in Hebrew. I asked him: 'Where does it come from?' He replied: 'I joined the Roman mercenary army and I found it amongst the Roman archives. In the scroll was written that 4,231 years after Creation, the world will be in great distress. During the years following, the world will be engaged in wars – some of them will be the wars of Gog U'Magog. The remaining years will be the era of Mashiach. Hashem will not renew the world – only after 7,000 years.'" R. Aha b. Rava said: "It was after 5,000 years." (*Sanhedrin* 97b)

Mine is mine
There are four character traits in people: What is mine is mine and what is yours is yours. What is mine is yours and what is yours is mine. What is mine is yours and what is yours is yours. What is mine is mine and what is yours is also mine. (*Avot* 5:10)

Minha service, Torah reading
Ezra ordained that the Torah should be read on Shabbat at the Minha service and also on Monday and Thursday at the morning services. (*Bava Kamma* 82a)

Minha services   מנחה
Services for the afternoon are called Minha, and were instituted by the Patriarch Yitzhak. (*Berachot* 26b)

Minim Sectarians
Versus Jewish scholars
R. Avohu praised R. Safra to the Minim[180] as a great scholar, and consequently they exempted him from paying taxes for thirteen years. One day they encountered him and they asked him to explain a passage in the Bible. He could not give them an answer. They took a scarf and wound it around his neck and tortured him. When R. Avohu came and found him being tortured, he asked:

"Why do you torture him?" They answered: "Have you not told us that he is a great scholar? He cannot even explain the meaning of a verse in the Bible."

He replied:" I might have told you that he is a great scholar, and who he is, but what I meant was that he is a scholar in Tannaitic learning, but not in Scripture." "But how is it that you do know Scripture?"

"The rabbis and I who are with you frequently make it our business to study it thoroughly, but others do not." (*Avodah Zarah* 4a)

Miniscule amount   כל שהוא
A minute quantity (*Shevuot* 21b)

Ministering angels   מלאכי השרת
(*Hullin* 91b)

Minor causing fire
Fire being sent with a minor (*Bava Kamma* 22b, 59b; *Kiddushin* 42b)

Minor age
The use of a device to prevent pregnancy

---

180. Sectarians.

by a minor female (*Yevamot* 12b; *Ketubbot* 39a; *Niddah* 45a; *Nedarim* 35b)

Minor girl is instructed
To refuse marriage
R. Nahman said: "R. Yehuda ben Bava testified about five things: that they instruct an orphan girl who is a minor to refuse marriage; a woman may remarry on the evidence of one witness; a rooster was stoned in Jerusalem because it killed a human being; that wine forty days old was poured as an offering on the altar; that the daily offering was brought at four hours in the morning." (*Berachot* 27a)

Minor loss הפסד מועט
(*Bava Kamma* 117a; *Shabbat* 154b)

Minors and Grace after a Meal
Is a minor obligated to say Grace after a Meal? (*Berachot* 17b, 20a)

Minors and a Mezuzah
Is a minor obligated to have a *mezuzah*? (*Berachot* 17b, 20a)

Minors and prayers
Is a minor obligated to pray? (*Berachot* 17b, 20a)

Minors and Shema
Is a minor obligated to recite the *Shema*? (*Berachot* 17b, 20a)

Minors and Tefillin
Is a minor obligated to put on *tefillin*? (*Berachot* 17b, 20a)

Minor has intent (*Hullin* 12b, 13a)

Minyan
A *minyan* consists of a minimum of ten males praying together. (*Megillah* 23b)

Minyan
According to R. Huna, nine men and the Torah ark can be considered a valid *minyan*. (*Berachot* 47a)

Miracle
The mentioning of "God of R. Meir, answer me" was used by people when they were in distress. (*Avodah Zarah* 18b)

Miracles
The blessing over miracles is discussed in *Haroeh*, the 9th *perek* of *Berachot*. (*Berachot* 54a)

Miracles
Do not rely on miracles
R. Yannai used to say: "A man should never stand in a place of danger and say a miracle will happen." (*Shabbat* 32a; *Taanit* 20b)

Miriam
Miriam stayed and watched over Moshe. (*Sotah* 9b)

Miriam the daughter of Bilgah
The rabbis taught: Miriam the daughter of Bilgah (of the Watch group Bilgah) left Judaism and married a Greek officer. When the Greeks entered the Temple she stamped with her feet on the Altar crying out: "How long will you accept Israel's money and not help Israel when they are being oppressed." (*Sukkot* 56b)

Miriam's well
If one wants to see Miriam's well ascend to the top of the Carmel Mountain and gaze down to the sea. (*Shabbat* 35a)

Mi She-Meto מי שמתו
If one has to deal with a dead person (*Berachot* 17b)

Misappropriation

Irreverence in the Temple מעילה
Desecration by the slightest deviation from the prescribed ceremony is considered a *meilah* (*Meilah* 2a)

✿ Misfortune of others

Never rejoice in the misfortune of others
The students asked Rabbi Zera, "To what do you attribute your old age?" He replied. "Never have I been harsh with my household, never have I stepped in front of one greater than I, never have I studied Torah in a filthy place, never have I rejoiced in the misfortune of others, and never have I called people by their nickname." (*Megillah* 28a; *Taanit* 20b)

Misha'el, Hanania, and Azariah
מישאל חנניה עזריה

Let Nebuchadnezzar come and testify that they did not bow down to the idols. (*Avodah Zarah* 3a)

Misha'el, Hanania, and Azaria
מישאל חנניה עזריה

Hanania, Misha'el, and Azariah were thrown into the fiery furnace by the order of Nebuchadnezzar. (*Sanhedrin* 92b)

Mishkan

Before the Tabernacle in the wilderness, private altars were permitted, but when the Tabernacle was built, private altars were forbidden. (*Zevahim* 112b; *Megillah* 10a)

Mishkan

Hidden beneath the crypts of the Temple
Rabbi Hisda transmitted a tradition in the name of Rabbi Avimi: "The Tent of Meeting built by Moshe during their wanderings in the wilderness including its boards, hooks, bars, pillars, and sockets were stored away after the first Temple was erected by King Solomon." Where were they stored? R. Hisda said in the name of

R. Avimi: "They stored them beneath the crypts of the Temple." (*Sotah* 9a)

Mishkan vessels

R. Hanina said: "All the Mishkan vessels which Moshe made, he received the measurements from heaven, their length, their width, and their height. (*Sukkah* 5a)

Mishlei

The Sages wanted to hide the book of Mishlei. (*Shabbat* 30b)

Mishna

Rabbi Yohanan said: "The author of an anonymous Mishna is Rabbi Meir; of an anonymous Tosefta, Rabbi Nehemia; of an anonymous Sifra, Rabbi Yehuda; of an anonymous Sifri, Rabbi Shimon; and all are taught according to the views of Rabbi Akiva." (*Sanhedrin* 86a; *Eruvin* 96b; *Gittin* 4a)

Mishna

Run to study Mishna. (*Bava Metzia* 33b; *Bava Kamma* 94b)

Mishna conclusion

R. Yehuda HaNasi and R. Nathan concluded the Mishna, R. Ashi and Ravina concluded the Horaah (Gemara). Rashi notes that prior to them there was no particular order to the teachings of the Mishna. (*Bava Metzia* 86a, 87a; *Avodah Zarah* 3a; *Kiddushin* 31a)

Mishna is not in its original order
אין סדר למשנה

The Mishna has not retained its original order. A general statement is sometimes first, then there are different opinions quoted later. (*Avodah Zarah* 7a)

Mishum Eineh
משום עינא

Evil eye (*Bava Metzia* 30a)

Misunderstanding in business

The Talmud relates that Rabbi Avimi had some commercial transactions with Babylonia. Once he sent money to Hozai, Babylonia with Rabbi Hama b. Rabbah b. Avohu in payment for a debt. After he gave them the money and asked for the note, the people claimed that the payment was for another debt. Rabbi Hama went to complain to Rabbi Avohu. R. Avohu asked him: "Do you have witnesses that you paid him?" R. Hama said, "No." "In that case, they could plead that you didn't pay at all, and therefore, we must believe them that it is for another debt." (*Ketubbot* 85a)

✿ Misusing the Torah

R. Eleazar b. Tzadok said: "Do good deeds for the sake of your Maker. Do not make a crown for yourself from your Torah learning, or a spade to dig with. (*Nedarim* 62a)

Mitzri

A converted Mitzri (Egyptian) – is it permitted to marry them [after 3 generations]? (*Yevamot* 76b; *Nazir* 23b)

Mitzvah

A mitzvah that was commanded is preferred to a non-commanded mitzvah. (*Bava Kamma* 38a, 87a; *Avodah Zarah* 3a)

Mitzvah

One who is occupied performing a Mitzvah
R. Yosi HaGlili said: "A person who is occupied with the performance of a mitzvah is free from the performance of other religious duties." (*Sukkah* 26a)

Mitzvah dependent on time

מצות עשה שהזמן גרמא
Mitzvot that have to be performed in a limited designated time (*Kiddushin* 29a; *Berachot* 20b; *Shabbat* 62a; *Eruvin* 27a; *Hagigah* 4a; *Rosh Hashana* 30a; *Menahot* 43a)

Mitzvah exemption

R. Hisda and Rabbah b. Huna slept on the river bank of Sura when they were visiting the Exilarch during the Sukkah holiday, saying: "We are engaged in a religious errand and therefore we are exempt from the mitzvah of sleeping in the Sukkah." (*Sukkah* 26a)

Mitzvah messenger

R. Eleazar said: "A messenger on his way to perform a mitzvah will not suffer harm, neither on their way going nor upon returning." (*Pesahim* 8b)

Mitzvah of Kiddush

Once there was no rain and Rabbi Yehuda HaNasi ordained a fast, but no rain fell. R. Ilfa went before the ark and recited the prayers for rain and rain fell.

Rebbe asked him: "What is your special merit?"

He answered: "I live in a poverty-stricken remote neighborhood, where wine for *Kiddush* and *Havdalah* is hard to come by. I make sure that I have wine and this way I help others to fulfill the mitzvah of Kiddush." (*Taanit* 24a)

Mitzvah tied to the Land of Israel

מצוה שהיא תלויה בארץ
Every precept which is dependent on the Land is practiced only in the Land. (*Kiddushin* 36b)

Mitzvot

מצוות
R. Yehoshua b. Levi said: "All good deeds and *mitzvot* performed in this world will testify for that person in the World to Come. (*Avodah Zarah* 4b)

Mitzvot

Six hundred and thirteen commandments
R. Hamnuna said: "Moshe Rabbeinu brought us down the Torah with 613 commandments. The [numerical value of

the] letters of the word 'Torah' equals 611, which Moshe brought us, and the other two were spoken by Hashem himself." (*Makkot* 23b)

Mitzvot and rewards
Hanania b. Akashya's well-known saying is: "God was pleased to confer favors on Israel. Therefore, he multiplied for them his commandments, for which they would be rewarded." This passage is usually recited at the end of a learning session. (*Makkot* 23b)

Mixing a remedy
On Shabbat
Rabbi Shimon said in the name of Rabbi Meir that one could mix oil and wine on Shabbat for a remedy. Once Rabbi Meir was suffering internally and his students wanted to mix wine and oil for him, but he would not let them.

They said to him: "Your words shall be nullified in your own lifetime."

He replied to them: "Even though I ruled that it is permissible, my colleagues ruled otherwise. I have never presumed to disregard the words of my colleagues."

He was stringent in respect to himself, but for all others he ruled that it is permissible. (*Shabbat* 134a)

Mixing dates with vines
R. Shemuel's laborer brought him some dates, which tasted like wine. He asked the man why the dates tasted of wine. He answered that the date trees were growing between vines. He said to him, "Bring me their roots tomorrow." (*Bava Kamma* 92a)

Mixture of forbidden things
Rav and Shemuel both said: "All forbidden things in the Torah which are mixed together with a non-forbidden thing and both are of the same kind, even if the forbidden thing is only a minute quantity,

it makes all of it forbidden." (*Pesahim* 29b; *Avodah Zarah* 73b)

Mixtures of same substances
מין במינו לא בטיל
Homogeneous substances cannot neutralize each other when mixed together. (*Hullin* 98b, 99b, 100a, 109a; *Yevamot* 82a; *Zevahim* 79b; *Menahot* 22b)

Moabites
The descendants of the Moabites are discussed. (*Bava Kamma* 38b)

Moabites
A male Moabite marrying a Jewish woman and a Moabite woman marrying a Jewish man. (*Yevamot* 69a, 76a, 88b)

Moav and Ammon
The rabbis were discussing Ammon and Moav. (*Yadayim* 4:3)

Mocking someone
Rabbi Nathan said: "Do not mock your neighbor for a blemish you yourself have." (*Horayot* 13b)

Modesty   צנוע
(*Avodah Zarah* 47b; *Berachot* 62a)

Modesty
Rava said: "I made from Heaven three requests: two were granted and one was not. I prayed for the scholarship of R. Huna and the wealth of R. Hisda which were granted to me, but the modesty of Rabbah b. Huna was not granted to me. (*Moed Katan* 28a)

Modesty
A man married a woman who was missing one hand, but he didn't notice until the day she died. (*Shabbat* 53b)

Modesty

The bride turns her face away: What is the reason? R. Hiyya b. Abba said in R. Yohanan's name: "It shows modesty."

R. Huna b. Nathan, who was the Exilarch, visited the home of R. Nahman b. Yitzhak. He did everything they asked him to do. (*Pesahim* 86b)

✿ Modify a statement

Rabbi Illai said in the name of Rabbi Eleazar ben Shimon: "One may modify a statement in the interest of peace."[181] Rabbi Nathan said: "It is a commandment." (*Yevamot* 65b)

Modim D'Rabbanan

A prayer recited in the *Shemona Esrei* by the congregation while the *hazan* recites the regular *Modim*. (*Sotah* 40a)

Mondays and Thursdays

The Torah is read, also on Shabbat during Minha

The Torah is read on the following days: Monday, Thursday and Shabbat at *Minha*: three people are called up. (*Megillah* 21a)

Monetary cases

Court of judges in monetary and capital cases must meet during daytime. (*Sanhedrin* 34b)

Monetary cases inquiry   דרישה וחקירה

Monetary cases require inquiry and examination by the court (*Sanhedrin* 2b, 32a; *Yevamot* 122b)

Monetary coins

Exchanges of silver into gold or vice versa (*Bava Metzia* 44a)

Monetary disputes

Monetary disputes require three judges; each litigant chooses one, and the two judges choose a third one. (*Sanhedrin* 23a; *Bava Metzia* 20a)

Monetary Halachah

The study of Halachah on monetary matters makes a person wise

R. Yishmael said: "If one desires to be wise from learning, then one should study the Halachah on monetary judgment, since no subject in the Torah surpasses this. It is like a perpetual fountain." (*Berachot* 63b; *Bava Batra* 175b)

Monetary loss   דררא דממונא

(*Bava Metzia* 2b)

Monetary matters

In monetary matters, R. Hiyya gave judgments as a single judge by himself. (*Sanhedrin* 5a)

Money

Belonging to other people, can one save himself with that money? (*Bava Kamma* 60b)

Money

Money kept in the mattress on Shabbat (*Shabbat* 44b)

Money belonging to orphans[182]

(*Berachot* 18b)

Money claim is like money

דבר הגורם לממון כממון דמי

A matter where money is to be extracted is equivalent to money. (*Shevuot* 32a, 33a; *Ketubbot* 34a; *Bava Kamma* 71b, 98b, 105b; *Pesahim* 5b, 29b)

Money claimed by two parties

The Talmud states that Rav Yehuda said in the name Shemuel: "It is a ruling by

---

181. A white lie.

182. See story under, Communicating with the spirits of the dead.

Sumchos that money claimed by two parties whose ownership is in doubt must be shared by both parties. The rabbis, however, say it is a fundamental principle that if one has the money and the other makes a claim – the claimant has to bring proof." (*Bava Kamma* 35b, 46a; *Bava Metzia* 2a, 98b)

Money deposited

Money deposited for safekeeping at a money changer (*Bava Metzia* 43a; *Meilah* 21b)

Money found

Money found in the river, the rabbi ruled that it must be publicized

A man found a sum of money in the Biran River, which was tied up in a kerchief. He came to R. Yehuda to ask what to do with the money. He told him to go and publicize it. The man asked: "Is this not similar to retrieving it from the sea?" R. Yehuda answered him that the Biran River is different, because people don't give up on it." (*Bava Metzia* 24b)

Money found in Jerusalem

Money found in Jerusalem can be considered *hullin*, but it depends on where it was found. (*Pesahim* 7a)

Money found in the synagogue (*Bava Metzia* 21b)

Money hired out

R. Hama used to hire out his money for a small amount per day. As a result, his money evaporated. (*Bava Metzia* 69b)

Money in his hand

כל שהכסף בידו ידו על העלינו

He who has the money in his hand has the upper hand. (*Bava Metzia* 44a, 47b, 49b, 74b)

Money invalidated

The state cancelled the money. (*Bava Metzia* 46b)

Money not your own, guard it

R. Yosi said: "Let the money or property of your fellow-man be as precious to you as your own." (*Avot* 2:12)

Money to be stored away

Abbaye said: "The rabbis wanted to store away the Hadrianic and the Trajan dinars because they were from Jerusalem." (*Avodah Zarah* 52b)

☐ Monbaz

King of Adiabene donated gold vessels to the Temple

On Yom Kippur, two he-goats were waiting and next to them was an urn containing two box-wood tablets used for lots, but Ben Gamla donated gold tablets to replace the wooden ones. For this he was praised.

King Monbaz of Adiabene had all the vessels used on Yom Kippur made of gold. His mother Helene donated a golden candlestick for the door of the Heichal. She also donated a golden tablet. The tablet had the inscription the *sotah* had to read. (*Yoma* 37a; *Gittin* 60a)

☐ Monbaz

King Monbaz was the king of the Adiabene kingdom in the 1st century. He embraced Judaism.

Our rabbis taught that King Monbaz gave away his fortune and his father's fortune in the years of scarcity. His brothers came to him with a deputation of his staff and told him: "Your father saved treasures and added to the treasures of their father, but you have squandered away all that treasure." He replied to them: "My father stored up below and I am storing up for above." (*Bava Batra* 11a)

Mordechai   מרדכי

Amora from Babylonia
3rd – 4th centuries CE (*Shabbat* 99b)

More flesh, more worms
R. Hillel said: "The more flesh, the more worms." (*Avot* 2:7)

✿ More of everything
R. Hillel, the grandson of R. Yehuda Ha-Nasi, said: "The more possessions, the more anxiety." (*Avot* 2:7)

✿ Morning arise
The rabbis said: "Arise early in the morning and eat: in the summer on account of the heat and in the winter on account of the cold." (*Bava Metzia* 107b; *Pesahim* 112a; *Bava Kamma* 92b)

Morning prayers, time limit
תפלת השחר

Until what time can one say the morning prayers? (*Berachot* 26a)

Morning services called Shaharit שחרית
The morning services were instituted by the Patriarch Avraham. (*Berachot* 26a)

Morning sleep
One of Rabbi Dosa's sayings was: "Morning sleep, midday wine, children's talk, and sitting in company of the ignorant remove a man from this world." (*Avot* 3:10)

Moshe carries bones of Yosef
Moshe personally attended to carry out of Egypt the bones of Yosef. (*Sotah* 9b)

Moshe celebrated
Moshe celebrated twelve dedication days at the inauguration of the Ohel Moed in order to give honors to the princes. (*Horayot* 6b)

Moshe did three things
Moshe did three things on his own initiative and Hashem agreed: He separated from his wife, he broke the Tablets, and he added one day to the preparation for receiving the Torah. (*Yevamot* 62a; *Shabbat* 87a)

📖 Moshe in Heaven
The Talmud tells us that R. Yehuda said in the name of Rav:

When Moshe ascended up high to receive the Torah, he found the Almighty engaged with placing coronets over the letters of the Torah. Moshe said to the Lord of the Universe: "Is not the Torah perfect as it is – is anything missing from the Torah that additions are needed?"

He answered: "In future years, there will be a man by the name of Akiva ben Yosef, who will expound on this subject and will derive something from each point or elevation."

Moshe said. "Lord of the Universe, permit me to see this person."

He replied. "Turn around!"

Moshe turned around and found himself in the yeshiva of Rabbi Akiva. He went and sat down at the end of eight rows, where Rabbi Akiva's students were sitting. He listened to the discussion going on, but could not follow what they were arguing about. He felt ill at ease, but then a student asked:

"Where do we know this from?"

Rabbi Akiva replied. "This is the law according to Moshe given to him on Mount Sinai."

When Moshe heard this he was comforted. Moshe went back and addressed the Lord of the Universe. "You have there such a great man as Rabbi Akiva, and You give the Torah through me?"

He replied: "Be silent, do not question me, such is My decree." (*Menahot* 29b; *Shabbat* 89a)

📖 Moshe in Heaven
R. Yehoshua b. Levi said that when Moshe ascended on high, the Angels asked God: "What business has one born of woman amongst us?"

God answered them: "He has come to receive the Torah."

The Angels asked: "That secret treasure which has been hidden for 974 generations before the world was created – You want to give to flesh and blood?"

God told Moshe: "Give them an answer."

Moshe said: "I fear they will consume me."

God told Moshe: "Hold on to the Throne of Glory and give them an answer."

Moshe asked the Angels: "Did you go down to Egypt?

"The Torah says not to worship idols – do you have idols in heaven?

"The Torah says you should rest on Shabbat – do you work six days that you need to rest?

"The Torah says you should honor your father and mother – do you have a father and mother?"

Moshe asked them other questions. After hearing all these questions, they became his friend. (*Shabbat* 88b, 89a)

Moshe to Rebbe
From Moshe to Rebbe we do not find such greatness
Rabbah b. Rava stated, others say it was R. Hillel b. Wallas: "From Moshe until R. Yehuda HaNasi, we do not find Torah learning and secular greatness in one person." (*Sanhedrin* 36a)

Mother bird taken   נוטל אם על הבנים
Taking the mother bird together with the young (*Hullin* 141a; *Makkot* 16a, 17a)

Mother bird to be sent away, Shiluah ha-ken   שילוח הקן
Letting the mother bird go from the nest. (*Hullin* 138b)

Mother of Avraham
R. Hanan b. Rava stated in Rav's name: "The name of Avraham's mother was Amathlai, and her father's name was Karnevo." (*Bava Batra* 91a)

Mother of David
R. Hanan b. Rava said in the name of Rav: "The name of David's mother was Nitzevet, and she was the daughter of Adael." (*Bava Batra* 91a)

Mother of Haman
R. Hanan b. Rava said in the name of Rav: "The name of Haman's mother was Amathlai, and *she was the daughter of Orbati.*" (*Bava* Batra 91a)

Mother of R. Yohanan
Mother of R. Yohanan died when she gave birth to him
The Talmud relates: R. Yohanan's father died before R. Yohanan was born, and his mother died on the day he was born. (*Kiddushin* 31b)

Mother of Shimshon
R. Hanan b. Rava said in the name of Rav: "The mother of Shimshon was Tzelalfonit, and his sister's name was Nashyan." (*Bava Batra* 91a)

Motherly care
The mother of Mar b. Ravina prepared for him seven clean garments every week in order for his mind to be at ease for studying. (*Eruvin* 65a)

Motzeh, Matza   מוצא מצא
Finding a wife (*Berachot* 8a)

Motzi
On bread, one makes the blessing *hamotzi lehem.* (*Berachot* 35a)

Mount Carmel
R. Nehemia said: "Twilight is as long as walking a half a mil after sunset." R. Hanina said: "If one wants to know what

that distance is, it is walking from Mount Carmel to the sea." (*Shabbat* 35a)

📖 Mount Gerizim

The Talmud relates: It was taught that the twenty-fifth of Tevet is the day of Mount Gerizim. On that day no mourning is permitted. It is the day on which the Samaritans asked Alexander the Macedonian to give them permission to destroy the Temple, and he granted their request. Shimon HaTzaddik dressed up in his garments of the High Priest, and took with him the noblemen of Israel.

When Alexander met them, he asked them: "For what reason have you come to see me?"

They said to him: "Is it possible that you would listen to the advice of star-worshippers to destroy the Temple in which we pray for you and for your kingdom – never to be destroyed?"

"Who are those star-worshippers?"

"They are the Samaritans[183] who stand before you."

Alexander answered: "They are delivered in your hands."

That day was made into a festive day. (*Yoma* 69a)

📖 Mountain held over Israelites

R. Dimi said: "When the Israelites were standing at Mount Sinai, the Holy One, blessed is He, suspended the mountain over the Israelites like a vault and said to them: 'If you accept the Torah, it will be well with you, but if you don't, there will be your grave." (*Avodah Zarah* 2b; *Shabbat* 88a)

Mountains as idols

Some idol worshippers are using mountains as idols. (*Avodah Zarah* 45a)

Mourner   אונן אוננת

The persons mourning immediately after a close relative passes away are thus designated. (*Ketubbot* 53a; *Bava Metzia* 18a; *Yevamot* 29b; *Sanhedrin* 28b; *Moed Katan* 14b)

📖 Mourner

Notice of death received after thirty days

When Rav, who was a nephew of R. Hiyya, came to Eretz Yisrael from Babylonia, his uncle asked him:

"Is your father Aibu alive?"

He answered: "Ask me if my mother is alive."

R. Hiyya asked: "Is your mother alive?"

He answered: "Ask me if Aibu is alive."

When R. Hiyya heard all of this, he realized that his brother and sister died. Thereupon, he said to his servant:

"Take off my shoes and afterwards bring my things to the bathhouse." R. Hiyya wanted to teach his students the Halachah. From this, three things can be learned: a mourner is forbidden to wear shoes, one mourns only one day on a notice of death received after thirty days, and part of the day is considered like a whole day." (*Pesahim* 4a)

Mourners

The proper procedure for comforting the mourner (*Sanhedrin* 19a)

Mourners

When is a mourner exempt from prayers and putting on *tefillin*? (*Berachot* 17b, 18a)

Mourners

Comforting mourners on Shabbat (*Shabbat* 12b)

Mourning

Over Jerusalem (*Bava Kamma* 59b)

---

183. See entry, Samaritans.

📖 Mourning
When a stranger dies and there is no one to mourn

There was a man who died in the neighborhood where R. Yehuda lived, but there were no one to mourn after him. R. Yehuda assembled ten men every day and they sat *shiva* for seven days. After seven days, the man who died appeared to R. Yehuda in a dream and told him: "Your mind will be at peace because you have set my mind at peace." (*Shabbat* 152a–b)

Mourning   אנינות
Period of deep mourning (*Kiddushin* 80b)

Mourning on Shabbat   אין אבילות בשבת
There is no mourning on the Shabbat.
(*Moed Katan* 24a; *Ketubbot* 4a)

Mourning period   אבילות שבעה
Mourning time is seven days. (*Moed Katan* 24a)

Mourning period
Arriving to the mourning place three days late or seven days late (*Hullin* 50a)

Mouse which is half flesh and half earth (*Hullin* 127a)

Mouth can prohibit and permit
    הפה שאסר הוא הפה שהתיר
The mouth that prohibited is the mouth that permitted. (*Ketubbot* 16a)

Mouth cleaned with bread
R. Zera said: "Cleaning the mouth to eat meat after eating milk must be done by bread." (*Hullin* 105a)

Movable property   מטלטלין
Movables versus real estate

We have learned that movable property is acquired only by pulling. (*Bava Metzia* 48b; *Bava Batra* 156b; *Kiddushin* 26b; *Bava Batra* 86a)

Move to a place of Torah
We have learned that R. Nehorai said: "If you have to move to another location, be sure you move to a place of Torah and do not say that Torah will follow you, and do not rely on your own understanding of the Torah." (*Shabbat* 147b; *Avot* 4:14)

📖 Moving
Moving to Israel

Rabbi Abba, and also R. Zera, avoided being in the presence of Rabbi Yehuda, his teacher, because he wanted to move to Eretz Yisrael in spite of Rabbi Yehuda's prohibition against doing so. For Rabbi Yehuda said: "Whoever goes up from Babylonia to Eretz Yisrael is transgressing on a positive precept." R. Abba decided to go and listen to the lecture from outside the academy in order to avoid facing his Rebbe. When he left the lecture, he was satisfied and said: "Had I come only to learn only one thing, what I heard today – was already worthwhile." (*Berachot* 24b; *Ketubbot* 110a; *Shabbat* 41a)

Moving a dead body on Shabbat
A dead body was laying in Drukeret, and R. Nahman b. Yitzhak permitted the body to be carried out into the *karmelit* on Shabbat. (*Shabbat* 94b)

Moving an object is acquired by the mover   משיכה קונה
(*Bava Metzia* 46b; *Kiddushin* 1:4)

Moving objects   יציאות השבת
Moving objects on Shabbat is discussed in the first *perek* of the Tractate *Shabbat*. (*Shabbat* 2a)

Moving to Israel, Moving to Jerusalem
All may be compelled to move to Israel, but no one may be compelled to leave Israel.

All may be compelled to move to

Jerusalem, but no one may be compelled to leave Jerusalem. (*Ketubbot* 110b; *Arachin* 3b)

Muad   מועד

An animal which is on notice to cause damages – what is considered to be a *muad*? (*Bava Kamma* 15a, 16b, 23b; *Yevamot* 65a)

Muad   מועד

A human being is always considered to be warned. (*Bava Kamma* 26a)

Mufna   מופנה

A Talmudic term, meaning free and not used for other teachings. In a *gezera shava* where similar words are used to teach us a Halachah, the words must be *mufna* – free and not used for some other Halachah. (*Bava Kamma* 25b; *Sanhedrin* 40b; *Shabbat* 64a)

Mukkat Etz   מוכת עץ

Loss of virginity through an accident (*Ketubbot* 11a, 13a)

Muktza   מוקצה

An object made forbidden to handle on Shabbat for various reasons (*Shabbat* 43b, 44b, 45b)

Mules (*Shabbat* 52a; *Hullin* 114b)

Mules sold

What is included in a sale of a mule (*Bava Batra* 77b; *Hullin* 114b)

Multilingual

Members of Sanhedrin

Rav Yehuda said in Rav's name: "A Sanhedrin may not be established in a city which does not have at least two persons who can speak seventy languages and one who understands them. In the city of Betar there were three, and in Yavne there were four: Rabbi Eliezer, Rabbi Yehoshua, Rabbi Akiva, and Shimon HaTimni. (*Sanhedrin* 17b)

Multilingual

Rabbi Sumchos was a student of Rabbi Meir at the yeshiva in Tiberias. He spoke many languages, was fluent in Greek, and lived a very long life. (*Bava Metzia* 6:5, 80a; *Nazir* 8b)

Mumar   מומר

An apostate, one who abandons his faith (*Avodah Zarah* 26b; *Hullin* 3a)

Mumar

R. Huna said: "A person that desecrates Shabbat in public is regarded as an Israelite *mumar*." (*Eruvin* 69a)

Murder

On one occasion, Ulla was in danger of being murdered by one of his fellow travelers. It happened when on his return trip to Eretz Yisrael two inhabitants from Hozai joined him. During an argument, one of them killed the other. The murderer asked Rabbi Ulla: "Did I do well?"

"Yes," Ulla replied.

When Rabbi Ulla came before Rabbi Yohanan, he asked: "Maybe, Heaven forbid, my reply gave encouragement to a murderer?"

Rabbi Yohanan replied. "You have saved your life." (*Nedarim* 22a)

Musaf prayer time

When is the proper time to pray the *Musaf* service? (*Megillah* 20b)

Musaf service

Should Chanukah be mentioned in the *Musaf* service? (*Shabbat* 24a)

Music these days

An inquiry was made to Mar Ukva to find out the source where it is written that it is forbidden these days to listen to song and music. (*Gittin* 7a)

Musical instruments in the Temple
(*Arachin* 10a)

Mutual admiration
Whenever R. Hisda and R. Sheshet met, they trembled in admiration of each other. R. Hisda admired R. Sheshet's extensive knowledge of Mishna. R. Sheshet admired R. Hisda for his deep penetrating mind in *pilpul*. (*Eruvin* 67a)

Mute and hard of hearing students
In the academy of Rebbe
There were two mute men in the neighborhood of Rebbe, sons of R. Yohanan b. Gudgeda's daughter. Others say they were his sister's sons. They sat in the academy of Rebbe and nodded their heads and moved their lips. Rebbe prayed for them and they were cured. It was found out that they were versed in Halachah and in the whole Talmud. (*Hagigah* 3a)

Muzzle   בל תחסום
You shall not muzzle. (*Bava Metzia* 90a)

My benefit
R. Huna said in the name of Rav, who learned it from R. Meir, who learned it from R. Akiva: "A person should always say: 'Whatever Hashem did, must be for something good.'" (*Berachot* 60b; *Taanit* 21a)

Mysteries of Chariots
Once R. Yohanan said to R. Eleazar: "Come, I will teach you the mysteries of the Chariots."
"I am not old enough," he answered.
However, when he was old enough, R. Yohanan died.
R. Assi said to R. Eleazar: "Come I will teach you the mysteries of the Chariots." "Had I been worthy, I would have learned it from R. Yohanan, your master." (*Hagigah* 13a)

N

Nahman bar Yaakov   נחמן בר יעקב
Amora from Babylonia
3rd – 4th centuries CE (*Bava Metzia* 16b)

Nahman bar Yitzhak   נחמן בר יצחק
Amora from Babylonia
3rd – 4th centuries CE (*Shabbat* 140a)

🕮 Nahshon
What did Yehuda the son of Yaakov do that he merited a special blessing from Yaakov?
We have learned that R. Meir used to say: "When the Israelites stood by the Reed Sea, the tribes were arguing about who would jump into the sea first. Then men from the tribe of Benjamin jumped in first, and the princes of Yehuda hurled stones at them, because they wanted to be first."
R. Yehuda said to R. Meir: "That is not the story I heard, but this is what happened. The tribes were not willing to jump into the sea, but Nahshon ben Aminadv, who was a prince from the tribe of Yehuda, came forward and jumped in first."
At that time Moshe was busy praying to God. Hashem said to Moshe:
"My children are drowning and you are prolonging in prayer?"
"What should I do?" asked Moshe. Hashem answered him: "Lift up your rod and stretch it over the sea and go forward."
As they marched into the water, the sea split. For that reason, the kings of Israel belong to the tribe of Yehuda. (*Sotah* 36b)

Nahshon's sons
R. Hanan b. Rava said in the name of Rav: "Elimelech, Salmon, Peloni Almoni, and Naomi's father were all the sons of Nahshon ben Aminadav." (*Bava Batra* 91a)

Nahum HaMadai   נחום המדי
Tanna from Eretz Yisrael
1st century CE (*Ketubbot* 105a)

Nahum Ish Gam Zu   נחום איש גם זו
Tanna from Eretz Yisrael
1st – 2nd centuries CE (*Berachot* 22a)

📖 Nahum Ish Gam Zu
The Talmud explains the reason why he was called Nahum Ish Gam Zu – because whatever befell him, he would always say, "This is for my benefit, it is for the best."

Once, the Jewish people of Eretz Yisrael wanted to send a gift to the Emperor. After debating who should take the gift, they chose Rabbi Nachum. The gift they sent was a bag full of precious stones and pearls. Overnight he stayed in an inn. While he slept, some people emptied his bag and filled it with earth. In the morning, when he discovered that he was robbed, he declared:

"This is also for the best."

When he arrived at the Emperor and the officers opened his bag, they found the bag was full of earth. The Emperor became furious.

"The Jews are mocking me," he declared, and he wanted to kill the entire delegation. The Prophet Eliyahu appeared in the guise of one of the king's ministers and said. "Perhaps this is some of that legendary earth from their father Avraham? For when he threw earth at his enemies it turned into swords."

The Emperor ordered it to be tested and it turned out to be a potent weapon. They bestowed honors on Rabbi Nahum, and they filled his bag with precious stones and pearls. On his return trip, he slept again in the same inn. The people asked him.

"What did you take to the Emperor that he honored you so much?"

He replied, "I took to him what was in my bag." Thereupon the innkeepers rushed to the same spot from where they had dug up the earth. They dug up more earth and filled several bags. They came before the Emperor and explained to him that this is the same earth that Rabbi Nahum brought to him. They tested the earth and they found it to be ineffective. The Emperor condemned the innkeeper to be killed. (*Taanit* 21a; *Sanhedrin* 108b, 109a)

Nakdimon ben Gurion
Wealthy person
Rav Yehuda related in the name of Rav: "The daughter of Nakdimon b. Gurion, whose husband died, was granted by the rabbis an allowance of 400 gold coins for her perfume basket. She said to them: 'May you grant such allowances for your own daughters.' They answered her: 'Amen.'" (*Ketubbot* 66b)

Nakdimon ben Gurion
Our rabbis taught: It happened when all the people of Israel came to Jerusalem on a pilgrimage, but there was no water available for drinking. Nakdimon b. Gurion spoke to a heathen and asked him: "Lend me twelve wells for the pilgrims and I will repay you twelve wells of water and if I do not I will give you twelve talents of silver." They fixed a time of repayment. When the time came for repayment and no rain had yet fallen, he sent a message to Nakdimon: "Return to me either the water or the money you owe me. Nakdimon replied: "I still have time all day." In the afternoon, the heathen went to the bath in a happy mood figuring that it had not rained all year, so it surely would not rain that day. Nakdimon entered the Temple in a depressed mood and started to pray: "Master of the universe, it is well-known to You that I have not done this for my honor but for your honor." Immediately the sky became covered with clouds and rain fell until twelve wells were filled and

even overflowed. The heathen came out of the bath and still demanded the money. He argued the sun had already set and therefore the rain came past the time they had set. Nakdimon entered the Temple again to pray and the clouds dispersed and the sun came out. (*Taanit* 19b, 20a)

Naked

One should not touch a Torah while naked. (*Shabbat* 14a; *Megillah* 32a)

Naked person

The consequences for insulting a naked person (*Bava Kamma* 86b)

Name of Mashiach

The school of R. Shila said that his name is Shiloh; the school of R. Yannai said that his name is Yinon; the school of R. Hanina said that his name is Hanina; others say his name is Menahem the son Hezkiya. (*Sanhedrin* 98b)

Names

Which names may not be erased? (*Shevuot* 35a)

Nap

When the daughter of R. Hisda asked her father to take a nap, he answered her: "Soon the days in the grave shall be long and short, and I shall have plenty of time to sleep long." (*Eruvin* 65a)

Naphtali

The Sea of Tiberias was given to the tribe of Naphtali. (*Bava Kamma* 81b)

Naresh academy   נרש

Naresh is a town in Babylonia on the banks of the Euphrates, and south of the old city of Babylon and south of Sura. Naresh was situated in a hilly district and spread over a wide area. The Jews of Naresh were farmers. One of the famous products made in

Naresh was a thick felt-cloth and blankets. Naresh was well-known in Talmudic circles because Rabbi Papa established an academy there. Many students flocked to the academy to learn with Rabbi Papa. R. Huna b. Yehoshua was the head of the Kallah כלה.[184] R. Papa lived in the 4th century CE. (*Eruvin* 56a; *Yoma* 69a)

Naresh

R. Giddal said in the name of Rav: "If an inhabitant of Narash kisses you, then count your teeth; if an inhabitant of Nehar Pekod accompanies you, it is because of the fine garments he sees on you; if an inhabitant of Pumbedita accompanies you, then change your quarters." (*Hullin* 127a)

Nasi of Sanhedrin – 100 years

It is stated that Rabbi Hillel and his descendants – Shimon, Gamliel, and his son Shimon – were the heads of the Sanhedrin that lasted for 100 years during the Temple's existence. (*Shabbat* 15a)

📖 Nasi of Sanhedrin

Eleazar ben Azariah is elected Nasi

The Sanhedrin wanted to replace Rabbi Gamliel as Nasi. "Whom can we appoint? Let us appoint Rabbi Eleazar ben Azariah, who is wise, rich, and a descendant of Ezra. He is wise to give the proper answer to a question. He is rich, so that if money is needed to pay the government he can do it. He is a descendant of Ezra and therefore he has great ancestral merit."

They asked him. "Will you honor us to become the head of the academy?"

He replied: "I will consult the members of my family." He consulted his wife. She

---

184. *Kallah* is the name of the assemblies taking place in the months of Elul and Adar for students to study the laws of the festivals. (*Shabbat* 114a; *Kiddushin* 49b)

said to him: "Maybe they will also depose you?"

He answered: "Let one use a cup of honor for one day, even if it be broken the next day." He accepted the position.[185]

She said to him: "You have no white hair." He was eighteen years old, but a miracle happened and his beard turned white. (*Berachot* 27b)

Nathan ben Shila

Nathan ben Shila was the chief slaughterer in Sepphoris. (*Hullin* 50b)

Nathan   נתן

Amora from Eretz Yisrael
4th century CE (*Pesahim* 117b)

Nathan HaBavli   נתן הבבלי

Tanna from Eretz Yisrael and Babylonia
2nd century CE (*Shabbat* 12b; *Pesahim* 48a)

Nathan HaBavli, the Mohel

R. Nathan said: "I once came to a coastal town and was approached there by a woman who had circumcised her first and second sons, and they died. She brought her third son to me. I saw that the child was red, so I said to her, 'Wait until the blood will be absorbed in him.' She waited and then circumcised her son, and he lived. She named him Nathan HaBavli after me." (*Hullin* 47b; *Shabbat* 134a)

Nazir   נזיר

A Nazirite drinking wine (*Makkot* 21a; *Kiddushin* 77b; *Hullin* 82b; *Nazir* 38b, 42a)

Nazirite vow

A vow to become a Nazir without a time limit is for thirty days. (*Nazir* 5a, 39a; *Nedarim* 4b; *Taanit* 17a; *Sanhedrin* 22b; *Moed Katan* 19b)

---

185. See also entry, Appointed Nasi of the Sanhedrin.

Nazirite vow for a non-Jew

The Nazarite vow does not apply to a non-Jew. (*Nazir* 61a)

Nazirite woman

A woman who made a vow to become a Nazarite (*Nazir* 21b, 23a; *Nedarim* 83a)

✿ Near is now distant

Rebbe asked R. Shimon b. Halafta: "Why didn't we have the pleasure of your visit on the festival as our parents used to receive your parents?" He replied: "The rocks have grown tall, the near has become distant, two have turned into three, and the peacemaker of my home has ceased." (*Shabbat* 152a)

Nebuchadnezzar

Hanania, Misha'el, and Azariah were thrown into the fiery furnace by the order of Nebuchadnezzar. (*Sanhedrin* 92b, 95b)

Nebuchadnezzar (*Avodah Zarah* 3a; *Hullin* 89a)

Neck of animal

R. Hiyya b. Yosef said in the presence of R. Yohanan: "The entire neck is the appropriate place for slaughtering." (*Hullin* 45a)

Need a meal

The Talmud relates that Rabbah said to Rafram b. Papa: "Tell me some of the good deeds Rabbi Huna had done."

He replied: "When he had a meal, he would open his doors wide open and declare: 'Whoever is in need of a meal, come and eat.'" (*Taanit* 20b)

Needle found in the animal

R. Safra told Abbaye: "Have you seen the scholar who came from Israel? His name is Avira. He relates that a case came before Rebbe where a needle was found in the animal." (*Hullin* 51a)

📖 Needy person

A man once came to Rava and applied for support.

Rava asked him: "What do your meals consist of?"

"They consist of fat chicken and old wine."

"Did you consider the burden of the community?" asked Rava.

"Am I eating of theirs?" asked the man. "I am eating the food of God, who provides for every individual according to his habits."

In the meantime, the sister of Rava arrived, whom he had not seen in thirteen years. She brought with her a fat chicken and old wine.

"What a remarkable incident," said Rava. "I apologize, come and eat." (*Ketubbot* 67b)

Negative injunction deduced from a positive injunction

לאו הבא מכלל עשה עשה

A negative injunction deduced from a positive is considered a positive injunction. (*Pesahim* 41b; *Yevamot* 54b, 68a, 73b; *Zevahim* 34a; *Hullin* 81a)

Negative precept   לאו שיש בו מעשה

A negative precept in the Torah that involves action (*Shevuot* 21a)

Negative precept

R. Avin said in the name of R. Illai: "Whenever it is written in the Torah the words: **השמר פן אל** – *hishomer, pen*, and *al* – it is a negative precept." (*Eruvin* 96a; *Makkot* 13b; *Shevuot* 4a, 36a; *Sotah* 5a; *Avodah Zarah* 51b; *Zevahim* 106a; *Menahot* 99b)

Negligence with charity money

A purse of money was brought to Pumbedita. R. Yosef gave it to a person in town to guard it. However, the person was negligent and it was stolen. R. Yosef held the person liable. (*Bava Kamma* 93a)

Nehardea; the academy in the town

נהרדעא

The town of Nehardea is located southwest of Baghdad on the Euphrates River, at its junction with the Malka River. It was surrounded by walls and protected on one side by the Euphrates River. Jewish presence in the town goes back to before the destruction of the Temple. According to tradition, the first settlers came when they were exiled from Eretz Yisrael in the sixth century BCE, during the time of Yehoyachim, King of Judah. According to tradition, they erected a synagogue with stones and earth brought from Jerusalem.

They named the synagogue Shav Veyativ. Nehardea was the seat of the Exilarch and his Bet Din. Nehardea was well-known in the Jewish world because of its great academy. Its influence was widespread, especially during the period when Rabbi Shemuel was the head of the academy,

Many great Amoraic scholars lived in Nehardea. Among them: R. Karna, R. Shila, and Abba b. Abba, who was R. Shemuel's father.

The town of Nehardea and its academy was destroyed in the year 259 CE by Papa b. Nasser, the commander-in-chief of Palmyra. The scholars fled and built a new academy in Pumbedita.

The inhabitants of Nehardea were not students of Torah. (*Bava Kamma* 12a; *Bava Metzia* 16b; *Megillah* 29a; *Shabbat* 59b; *Ketubbot* 54a; *Avodah Zarah* 58a)

Nehardea meeting

R. Akiva and R. Nehemia met in Nehardea

The Talmud relates that Rabbi Akiva said: "When I visited Nehardea in Babylonia to declare a leap year, I met with Rabbi Nehemia Ish Bet Deli. He told me: 'I heard that in Eretz Yisrael they don't permit a woman to remarry on testimony of one witness.'" He went on to say that he learned from Rabban Gamliel otherwise. (*Yevamot* 16:7, 122a)

Nehemia
The name of the brother of the Resh Galuta was Nehemia. (*Shabbat* 20b)

Nehemia   נחמיה
Tanna from Eretz Yisrael
2nd century CE (*Ketubbot* 67b)

Nehemia Ish Bet Deli   נחמיה איש בית דלי
Tanna from Babylonia
2nd century CE (*Yevamot* 16:7, 122a)

Nehorai   נהוראי
Tanna from Eretz Yisrael
2nd century CE (*Shabbat* 147b)

Nehorai
A Tanna taught: His name was not R. Nehorai but Nehemia, while others say that his name was R. Eleazar ben Arach. Why did they call him Nehorai? Because he enlightened the eyes of the Sages in Halachah. This Nehorai is not the same as Rabbi Meir, whose name was also Nehorai. In *Pirkei Avot*, we have sayings quoted right next to each other of both these Sages. (*Shabbat* 147b; *Eruvin* 13b)

Nehunia   נחוניה
Officer of the Temple (*Shekalim* 5:1)

Nehunia ben Elinatan
R. Nehunia ben Elinatan was in disagreement with R. Eliezer. (*Eduyot* 6:3)

Nehunia ben HaKana   נחוניה בן הקנה
Tanna from Eretz Yisrael
1st century CE (*Megillah* 28a)

Nehunia Ish Bikat Bet Hortan
נחוניה איש בקעת בית חורתן
Amora from Eretz Yisrael
3rd century CE (*Sukkah* 44a)

✿ Neighbors
Nittai HaArbeli said: "Keep away from bad neighbors." (*Avot* 1:7)

✿ Neighbor's property
Ben Bag Bag said: "Do not enter your neighbor's property without his knowledge even to retrieve something that belongs to you, because he may think you are a thief." (*Bava Kamma* 27b)

Neighbor's view blocked
Building a wall on one's own property, but thereby blocking the light of his neighbor. (*Bava Batra* 7a)

Neilah   נעילה
One of the prayer services on Yom Kippur; if it is Shabbat, one is to mention Shabbat in the prayer. (*Shabbat* 24b)

Neshama
In the morning when Hashem returns the *Neshama*, a blessing is recited. (*Berachot* 60b)

Netz Ha-Hama   נץ החמה
Sunrise (*Berachot* 9b)

Netzor Leshoni   נצור לשוני
Mar b. Ravina used to finish the *Amidah* with a special prayer: "Keep my tongue from evil and my lips from speaking falsehood. May I be silent for those who curse me, and may I be to them like dust. Open my heart to Torah and may I pursue your commandments, etc." Most congregations have adopted this prayer, reciting it at the conclusion of the *Amidah*. (*Berachot* 17a)

Nevela   נבלה
Non-kosher meat; it became non-kosher on account of being dead and decaying flesh. (*Hullin* 32a)

Never happened   לא היו דברים מעולם
This never happened; what you claim
never happened. (*Shevuot* 41b)

✿ **Never rejoice at embarrassment**
At the embarrassments of friends
The students once asked R. Adda b.
Ahava: "To what do you attribute your
longevity?"

He replied: "I have never displayed my
impatience at home, I have never walked
in front of a man greater than myself, I
have never had thoughts about Torah in a
dirty place, I have never walked four *amot*
without Torah thoughts, and I never fell
asleep in the Bet Midrash. I never rejoiced
at the embarrassment of my friends, and
I never called my friends by a nickname."
(*Taanit* 20b)

Nevuzradan
Son of Sanheriv and brother of Nebuchadnezzar (*Sanhedrin* 95b, 96b; *Shabbat* 26a)

New city
It is preferable to live in a city that was
recently built. (*Shabbat* 10b)

New month
Time limit to make the blessing over a
new moon (*Sanhedrin* 41b)

New month
Sanctifying the new moon
Rabbi Hiyya once saw the descending
moon early in the morning on the twen-
ty-ninth day of the month. Rabbi Hiyya
was not speaking to anyone in particular,
but to himself. He was saying to the moon:
"Tonight we want to sanctify the new
month and you are still here? Go and hide
yourself." Rebbe must have overheard him
and said: "Go to Ein Tov and sanctify the
month and send me the following watch-
word: 'David King of Israel is alive and
enduring.'" (*Rosh Hashana* 25a)

📖 **New month**
Fixing the day for the new month
On one occasion, Rabbi Dosa ben
Horkynos and Rabbi Yehoshua ben Hanania had a halachic dispute with Rabbi
Gamliel regarding which day to fix the
new month on the calendar. R. Gamliel
as head of the academy ordered R. Yehoshua to appear before him with his staff
and money on the day that R. Yehoshua
determined Yom Kippur according to his
calculation. R. Dosa b. Horkynos agreed
with R. Yehoshua. However, R. Gamliel
did not take any action against R. Dosa b.
Horkynos. R. Yehoshua went to R. Dosa
to talk to him about the matter. R. Dosa
told R. Yehoshua: "You may be right in
your calculation, but if we want to argue
against the Court of R. Gamliel, then we
could argue against every Court that has
arisen from the days of Moshe Rabbeinu
until now." R. Yehoshua did as he was ordered; he took his staff and his money and
went to Yavne to R. Gamliel on the day
which was Yom Kippur by R. Yehoshua's
calculation. R. Gamliel rose and kissed
him on his head and said to him: "Come
in peace, my teacher and my disciple: my
teacher – in wisdom, and my disciple –
because you have accepted my decision.[186]
(*Rosh Hashana* 2:9, 25a)

New moon
R. Aha b. Hanina said in the name of R.
Assi, in the name of R. Yohanan: "Blessing
the moon in its proper time is almost equal
as being in the presence of the Shechina."
(*Sanhedrin* 42a)

New moon
In the school of R. Yishmael, it was taught
that the privilege of blessing the moon once
a month would have sufficed. (*Sanhedrin* 42a)

---

186. See also entry, Appointed Nasi of the Sanhedrin.

New moon text for blessing
The text for the blessing of the new moon (*Sanhedrin* 42a)

Niddah נדה
Period and duration of menstruation (*Niddah* 2a–b)

Niddah and the meat of a firstborn
There is a dispute between Hillel and Shammai whether a *niddah* may eat the meat of a *bechor*, a firstling (*Bechorot* 33a)

Night of the fourteenth of Nisan
Bodek Hametz בודק חמץ
A search is made for leavened bread. (*Pesahim* 2a)

Night of the Spies' Report
"The people wept that night"
Rabbah said in the name of R. Yohanan: "That night was the night of the ninth of Av." (*Taanit* 29a; *Sotah* 35a)

Nimrod (*Avodah Zarah* 3a; *Hullin* 89a)

Nishga נשג"א
נדה שפחה עובדת כוכבים אשת איש
An acronym for different transgressions (*Avodaj Zarah* 36b; *Sanhedrin* 82a)

Nishgaz נשגז
נדה שפחה עובדת כוכבים זונה
Abbreviation for different transgressions (*Avodah Zarah* 36b; *Sanhedrin* 82a)

Nishmat Kol Hai נשמת כל חי
This prayer is recited on Shabbat and Yom Tov. R. Yohanan called it "the song of the blessing." (*Pesahim* 118a)

Nittai HaArbeli נתאי הארבלי
Tanna from Eretz Yisrael
2nd century BCE (*Avot* 1:6)

Nitzevet
Nitzevet was David's mother, and she was the daughter of Adael. (*Bava Batra* 91a)

Nitzivin; Academy נציבין
Nitzivin or Nisibis was a community in Northeastern Mesopotamia.

R. Yehuda b. Betera established an academy there. Yehuda b. Betera II lived in the 2nd century CE. (*Sanhedrin* 32b)

✡ No bread, no Torah
R. Eleazar b. Azariah said: "Where there is no Torah, there is no proper conduct; where proper conduct is absent, there is no Torah. If there is no wisdom, there is no fear of God; if there is no fear of God, there is no wisdom. Where there is no knowledge, there is no understanding; where there is no understanding, there is no knowledge. If there is no bread, there is no Torah; if there is no Torah, there is no bread." (*Avot* 3:21)

No choice
The Talmud says: R. Avdimi b. Hama b. Hasa stated that when the Jewish people stood at Har Sinai, the Almighty uprooted the mountain and held it over their heads and said to them: "If you accept the Torah, it is well; if not, there will be your burial place." (*Shabbat* 88a; *Avodah Zarah* 2b)

✡ No drugs
Father's advice to a son
The Talmud relates that Rav advised his son Hiyya: "Do not take drugs, do not leap in high jumps, and do not have your teeth extracted, do not provoke serpents, and do not provoke a Syrian woman." (*Pesahim* 113a)

No man is so brazen
אין אדם מעיז פניו בפני בעל חובו
No man is so brazen as to deny a claim in the presence of a creditor. (*Bava Kamma*

107a; *Shevuot* 42b; *Bava Metzia* 3a; *Ketubbot* 18a; *Gittin* 51b)

✿ No nonsense
Keep your children from nonsense
Our rabbis taught: When R. Eliezer fell ill, his students came to visit him. They said to him: "Teach us the way of life so that we should merit the World to Come." He advised them: "Give honor to your colleagues, keep your children from nonsense, and place them between the knees of scholars. When you pray, know before Whom you are standing. In this way you will merit the World to Come." (*Berachot* 28b)

No obligation imposed
אין חיבין לאדם שלא בפניו
No obligation may be imposed on a person in his absence. (*Eruvin* 81b; *Kiddushin* 23a)

No preference for one son
Rava b. Mehasya said in the name of R. Hama b. Gurya in Rav's name: "A man should never show preference for one son over the others, because our ancestor Yaakov preferred Yosef over his brothers and they became jealous. Consequently, our ancestors wound up in Egypt as slaves." (*Shabbat* 10b; *Megillah* 16b)

No self-incrimination
אין אדם משים עצמו רשע
Rava said: "No person can make himself a wicked man, or incriminate himself." (*Sanhedrin* 9b, 25a; *Ketubbot* 18b; *Yevamot* 25b)

Noge'a Be-Eduto   נוגע בעדותו
A witness with interest in the matter (*Sanhedrin* 23b; *Bava Batra* 43a)

Noahide Laws
Seven Noahide laws
Our rabbis taught that the children of Noah were given seven commandments:

social justice, and to refrain from the following: blasphemy, idol worship, adultery, bloodshed, robbery, and the eating of flesh cut from a living animal.

In the school of Menashe, it was taught: The seven laws given to the sons of Noah are: to refrain from idolatry, adultery, murder, robbery, flesh cut from a living animal, emasculation, and forbidden mixtures. (*Sanhedrin* 56a; *Avodah Zarah* 2b)

Non-Jew acquires
יש קנין לנכרי בארץ ישראל
A non-Jew can acquire land in Israel to free the crop from the obligation of tithing, rabbis disagree. (*Bava Metzia* 101a; *Gittin* 47a; *Menuhot* 31a; *Bechorot* 11b)

📖 Non-Jew eating Pesach sacrifice
A certain non-Jewish Syrian used to go to Jerusalem to partake of the Pesach sacrifices. He was boasting to Rabbi Yehuda b. Beteira that in spite of the prohibition, he was still eating it. Rabbi Yehuda asked him: "Did they supply you with a fat tail?"

The next time he went to Jerusalem, he asked for the fat tail. They investigated and found out that he was not Jewish. They sent a message to Rabbi Yehuda: "Peace be with you, even though you are in Nisibis, Babylonia, your net is spread in Jerusalem." (*Pesahim* 3b, 84b)

Non-Jew learning
R. Meir said: "Even a non-Jew who is busy studying Torah is compared to the High Priest." (*Bava Kamma* 38a; *Sanhedrin* 59a; *Avodah Zarah* 3a)

✿ Non-Jews
Deceiving non-Jews is forbidden
R. Shemuel said: "It is forbidden to deceive non-Jews as well as Jews." (*Hullin* 94a)

Non-Jews atonement
R. Yohanan b. Zakkai said: "Just as a sin

offering brings atonement for Israel, so does charity bring atonement for a non-Jew." (*Bava Batra* 10b)

Non-Jewish prophets
Names of non-Jewish prophets (*Bava Batra* 15b)

📖 Not a prophet
Our rabbis taught: Once, the son of R. Gamliel became ill. He sent two scholars to R. Hanina b. Dosa to ask him to pray.

R. Hanina went up to the upper chamber and prayed. When he came down, he said to them: "Go home, the fever has left him."

They asked him, "Are you a prophet?" He replied, "I am neither a prophet, nor the son of a prophet, but I learnt this from experience. If my prayer is flowing, I know that my prayers are accepted, but if the prayers are not smooth, then I know that my prayers have not been accepted." (*Berachot* 34b)

Not all witnesses are equal
Giving evidence
On giving evidence about a dead person, Rabbi Yehuda was of the opinion that not all men or all places or all times are equal. (*Yevamot* 16:3, 121b)

Not excommunicated
We have learned that R. Yehuda said: "Heaven forbid for us to think that R. Akavia was excommunicated – that was a mistake. For the doors of the Temple hall never held any man in Israel who was the equal of Rabbi Akavia ben Mahalalel in wisdom, in purity, and in fear of God. But the case was that they excommunicated Eleazar ben Hanoch, who raised doubts about washing the hands." (*Berachot* 19a; *Pesahim* 64b)

Not in the usual way   כלאחר יד
The back of the hand, not in the usual way (*Shabbat* 92a)

Not owned – he would not eat
It is related that R. Pinhas b. Yair never ate a piece of bread that was not his own. (*Hullin* 7b)

Not to hurry when leaving
R. Helbo said: "When a man leaves the synagogue, he should not be in a hurry." (*Berachot* 6b)

Not yet existing
אין אדם מקנה דבר שלא בא לעולם
One cannot acquire or transfer that which did not yet come to this world. The opinion of the rabbis. (*Bava Metzia* 33b; *Bava Batra* 79b, 127b, 131a, 141b, 157a; *Yevamot* 32a; *Kiddushin* 62b; *Gittin* 13b, 42b)

Nov   נוב
The Tabernacle was moved from Shiloh to Nov. (*Zevahim* 112b)

Nullification of idols
Who can nullify idols? (*Avodah Zarah* 52b)

Nullified transaction   ביטול מקח
Deal nullification in a business transaction (*Bava Metzia* 50b *Kiddushin* 42b)

Nullifying
The quantity required to nullify forbidden things (*Hullin* 98a)

Nullifying Hametz
When searching for unleavened bread, one must also nullify the *hametz*. (*Pesahim* 6b)

Numeric value of word "Torah"
Equals number of commandments
R. Hamnuna stated that Moshe brought down from Mount Sinai 613 commandments. The numeric value of the word

"Torah" is 611. The two missing commandments are the first two, which the people of Israel heard from God Himself. (*Makkot* 2b)

Nun
The letter nun *is omitted*
R. Yohanan said: "The *nun* is omitted from *Ashrei*, because it bodes misfortune, and the word *nafal* begins with the letter *nun*. (*Berachot* 4b)

Nursing a Jewish child
A non-Jew nursing a Jewish child (*Avodah Zarah* 26a)

Nursing a child of idol worship
A Jewish woman nursing a child of idol worshipping parents (*Avodah Zarah* 26a)

O

Oath
The language which makes it an oath (*Shevuot* 20a; *Nedarim* 12a, 14a)

Oath concerning deposits (*Shevuot* 31b, 36b)

Oath language
When witnesses take an oath, in what language is it done? (*Sotah* 32a; *Shevuot* 39a; *Berachot* 40b)

Oath of this nature was instituted by the rabbis שבועה זו תקנת חכמים היא
This oath is a ruling of the rabbis (*Bava Metzia* 3a, 5b)

Oath the judges imposed
An oath is imposed by the judges on a debtor. (*Shevuot* 38b; *Bava Metzia* 55a; *Kiddushin* 11b)

Oath unrelated to the case גלגול שבועה
An oath is imposed on a person in an unrelated case when he is already required to make an oath. (*Shevuot* 45a, 48b, 49a)

Obligation not imposed אין חיבין לאדם שלא בפניו
No obligation may be imposed on a person in his absence. (*Eruvin* 81b; *Kiddushin* 23a; *Bava Metzia* 12a)

Obligation to help
It is an obligation to help a fellow-man load a heavy item
R. Yishmael b. R. Yosi was walking on the road and he met another man carrying a load of twigs. After a while, the man put his bundle down to rest. When he finished resting, he asked R. Yishmael to help him lift the bundle on his back.

R. Yishmael asked him: "How much is it worth?"

He said: "Half a *zuz*."

R. Yishmael gave him a half a *zuz* and declared the bundle *hefker*.[187]

The man took the *zuz* and declared: "I am re-acquiring it, and help me load it on my shoulder."

R. Yishmael gave him another half a *zuz* and said: "I declare it *hefker* to everyone except you." (*Bava Metzia* 30b)

Obscene language
R. Nahman b. Yitzhak said: "When one hears obscene language and is silent, he will wind up in the Gehinom." (*Shabbat* 33a)

Observing dead corpses[188] (*Niddah* 24b)

✿ Occupation
In combination with Torah study
It was the view of Rabbi Yishmael that the Torah demands that a person should

---

187. It belongs to anyone who finds it.
188. See entry, Gravediggers observation.

combine both an occupation to make a living with the study of Torah. However, Rabbi Shimon ben Yohai held the opposite view. (*Berachot* 35b)

✿ Occupation
Abba Gurion Me-Sidon said: "A man should not teach his son the occupation of an ass driver, camel driver, barber, sailor, shepherd, or tavern keeper, because it is a trade of robbers." (*Kiddushin* 4:14, 82a)

✿ Occupation combined with Torah
R. Gamliel said: "Torah study together with an occupation is excellent. All Torah study that is not in combination with work is for naught. All who occupy themselves with community needs should do it for the sake of heaven." (*Avot* 2:2)

Occupied doing other Mitzvot
If one is on his way to slaughter the Pesach sacrifice or is occupied with some other mitzvah, and remembered that he left unleavened bread in the house (*Pesahim* 49a)

Occupy yourself with Torah
R. Yehuda said in Rav's name: "One should always occupy himself with Torah and *mitzvot* even not for their own sake, because eventually it will be for the sake of Torah. (*Sanhedrin* 105b; *Pesahim* 50b; *Sotah* 22b; *Arachin* 16b)

Offended
When Rabbi Hisda was studying at Rabbi Huna, he once asked him:
"What of a student whose teacher needs him more?" Rabbi Hisda had traditions from other rabbis, which Rabbi Huna did not know. R. Huna took offense and their relationship was reserved for a while. On account of this, Rabbi Hisda fasted forty days, because he felt he insulted his rabbi. Rabbi Huna also fasted forty days, because in his thoughts, he suspected his student Hisda of arrogance. There was reconciliation after some time had passed. (*Bava Metzia* 33a)

Offering to the Temple by a non-Jew
(*Shekalim* 7:6)

Offerings of seventy bulls
The offering of seventy bulls on Sukkot was for the seventy major nations in the world during the time of the Temple. (*Sukkah* 55a)

Officers of the Temple
The officers appointed to serve in the Temple were: Yohanan b. Pinhas overseer of the seals, Ahiya over the libations, Matityahu b. Shemuel over the lots, and Petahia over the bird-offerings.
Petahia is the same as Mordechai. Why was he called Petahia? Because he opened up and explained many subjects. He knew seventy languages. (*Shekalim* 5:1)

Offspring follows
Offspring follows sometimes the father, sometimes the mother
Different situations differ; sometimes it is after the father and sometimes after the mother. (*Kiddushin* 66b; *Temurah* 5b)

Oil or wine sold, but price changed
If one sold wine or oil and the price went up or it went down (*Bava Batra* 87a)

Oils and fuels
Oils for Shabbat candles are discussed in *Bameh madlikin*, the 2nd *perek* in *Shabbat*. (*Shabbat* 20b)

Oils variety
Oils; variety of different kinds of oils with strange names (*Shabbat* 21a)

Old age
R. Yehoshua was blessed to live to a very old age.

Rabbi Yehuda HaNasi once asked him: "To what do you contribute your long life?"

He replied: "Do you begrudge me my long life?"

Rebbe answered him: "Heaven forbid, rather it is a question of Torah. I need to learn from it."

Rabbi Yehoshua answered: "Never in my life have I looked a wicked man into his face."

Rabbi Yehuda said to him: "Give me a blessing."

His blessing was: "May it be God's will that you should live to half my age." (*Megillah* 28a)

Old age
The Emperor asked R. Yehoshua ben Hanania: "Why didn't you come to the *avidan*?[189] R. Yehoshua answered: "The mountain is snowy, it is surrounded by ice, the dog does not bark, and the grinders do not grind." He was cryptic, and meant, "I am too old." (*Shabbat* 152a)

Old woman
At what age is a woman considered to be an old woman regarding the menstrual period? (*Niddah* 7b)

Oleh Regel
Festival pilgrimage: R. Yonah's wife attended the Festival pilgrimage and the rabbis did not prevent her from doing so. (*Eruvin* 96b)

Olive oil for Shabbat candles
R. Tarfon said: "Shabbat candles may be lit only with olive oil." R. Yohanan b. Nuri objected: "What should the Babylonians do, and what should the Medeans do, the Alexandrians, and the people of Cappadocia – they have other fuels only." (*Shabbat* 26a)

Olive oil on Chanukah
R. Yehoshua b. Levi said: "All oils are proper for Chanukah candle lighting, but olive oil is preferable." (*Shabbat* 23a)

Olive size used as a measuring device
כזית

A halachic measurement (*Eruvin* 4b; *Kelim* 17:8)

Omer
עומר

The meal offering in the Temple called Omer. The Omer was once brought from the gardens of Tzerifin. (*Menahot* 64b, 76b; *Bava Kamma* 82b)

Omit even one letter
A world can be destroyed by omitting one letter

A story was related by Rav Yehuda in the name of Rabbi Shemuel in the name of Rabbi Meir: "When I was a student at Rabbi Akiva, I used to put *kankantum* into the ink and he didn't tell me not to do it. But when I came to study at Rabbi Yishmael, he asked me: 'What is your profession?'

"I answered him: 'I am a scribe.'

"Upon this, Rabbi Yishmael said to me: 'Be meticulous in your work, because your work is heavenly sacred. Should you omit one letter or add one letter you could cause a situation where a world is destroyed.'[190]

"I told him: 'I put *kankantum* in the ink,

---

189. A debating club between sectarians.

190. Rashi comments that by adding one letter to a word, one can change that word from singular to plural, and when speaking of God that would be blasphemous.

which makes the ink permanent immediately.'" (*Eruvin* 13a, *Sotah* 20a)

✿ On best terms
It is important to be on best terms with his fellow-men, even with people of other religions
A favorite saying of R. Abbaye was: A man should always be in fear of Heaven, strive to be on best terms with his fellow-men and his relatives, even with men of other religions, so that he may be beloved above and below, and acceptable to his fellow creatures. (*Berachot* 17a)

On, son of Pelet, son of Reuven און בן פלת
Originally, he was part of the rebellion with Korah, however on the advice of his wife he withdrew. (*Sanhedrin* 109b)

▭ On that day
When they elected R. Eleazar b. Azaria as Nasi
It was learned that on that day the doors were opened for all the disciples to enter the assembly. Prior to this, Rabbi Gamliel had issued an ordinance that those students whose exterior appearance did not match their interior intellect would not enter.

Four hundred additional seats were brought in to accommodate the new students who entered the hall.

It was taught that many testimonies were formulated on that day, and whenever it is mentioned "on that day" – it refers to this particular day. (*Berachot* 27b)

On the contrary הוה אמינא אדרבה
I might have said on the contrary. (*Pesahim* 77a)

One angel in favor
In judgment before the heavenly court, even if only one angel out of 1,000 argues in his favor, he is saved. (*Shabbat* 32a)

One-horned animal
R. Meir said: "The animal *tahash* from the days of Moshe had only one horn." (*Shabbat* 28b)

One witness
Rabbi Yehuda testified regarding five opinions: One of them was that a woman may marry again on the say of one witness. (*Eduyot* 6:1)

One witness for a Kohen
One witness testifies that his friend is a Kohen. (*Ketubbot* 23b; *Bava Batra* 31b)

Onias Temple בית חוניו
The Temple erected by Onias the 4th in Leontopolis, Egypt was modeled after the Temple in Jerusalem. (*Avodah Zarah* 52b; *Menahot* 109a)

Onkelos אונקלוס
Tanna from Eretz Yisrael
1st – 2nd CE (*Gittin* 56b)

Onkelos
R. Yirmiyahu said, some say R. Hiyya b. Abba said: "The Targum on the Torah was authored by Onkelos the proselyte under the guidance of R. Eliezer and R. Yehoshua." (*Megillah* 3a)

▭ Onkelos
Convert to Judaism and nephew of Emperor Titus
Rabbi Onkelos was the son of Kalonikus and the son of the sister of Titus, the Roman emperor. Onkelos had in mind to convert to Judaism; he therefore went to a magician who speaks to the dead through a medium. The magician raised the spirit of Titus and asked him.

"Who is most honored in the heavenly world?"

Titus answered: "It is Israel, but its observances are burdensome and you will not be able to carry them out."

He converted to Judaism anyhow after coming in contact with Rabbi Yehoshua ben Hanania and Rabbi Eliezer ben Horkynos, whose student he was for many years.

His conversion angered the Roman emperor. (*Gittin* 56b)

Onkelos

The Roman emperor sent soldiers to arrest him, Onkelos convinced them to convert

The Talmud relates that the emperor[191] sent a contingent of Roman soldiers to stop Onkelos, but he convinced the soldiers to convert. The emperor sent two more contingents and he was able to convince them not to arrest him. He showed the soldiers the *mezuzah* on the door post and asked them: "What is this?"

They replied: "You tell us."

He told them: "According to universal custom, the mortal king dwells inside his palace, and the soldiers guard his palace outside. But in this case, the servants are inside the house and God guards them from outside." The guards did not arrest him and the emperor sent no more soldiers. (*Avodah Zarah* 11a; *Menahot* 33b)

Open your house

To the poor (*Avot* 1:5)

Open your mouth and learn

R. Shemuel said to his student R. Yehuda "Shinena" (an endearing nickname): "Open your mouth when you study Scripture, Talmud, so that your studies will be retained and that you may live long." (*Eruvin* 54a)

Oral Torah

A non-Jew came to Shammai and asked him: "How many Torahs do you have?"

Shammai answered: "We have two: the written Torah and the oral Torah."

The non-Jew said to Shammai: "I accept the written Torah, but not the oral Torah; make me a Jew on condition that you teach me only the written Torah."

R. Shammai became angry and chased him out of his house. The same man came to Hillel with the same request and Hillel accepted him. On the first day he taught him *aleph, bet, gimmel, dalet*, but the following day he taught him the reverse: *dalet, gimmel, bet, aleph*.

The non-Jew complained to Hillel: "Yesterday you taught me differently?"

Hillel replied: "You must rely on me not only on what is written, but also on what I tell you. The same is with the Torah. You must rely not only on the written Torah, but also on the oral Torah." (*Shabbat* 31a)

Oral Torah

Our rabbis learned: What was the procedure for teaching the Oral Law? Moshe learned the lesson directly from Hashem, Aharon learned it from Moshe, then Aharon's sons entered and Moshe taught them the lesson, then the Elders entered and Moshe taught them, then the entire people were taught by Moshe. After this procedure, Aharon taught them again the same lesson, then Aharon's sons were teaching. Then the Elders were teaching. Thus the lesson was taught four times to everyone. (*Eruvin* 54b)

Orchard workers

Workers in an orchard picking figs, may they eat grapes growing in the orchard? (*Bava Metzia* 91b)

---

191. Probably Domitian.

Order of prayers
The proper order for the prayers on Rosh Hashana (*Rosh Hashana* 32a)

Ordinance   גזרה
Majority must be able to endure
R. Yishmael b. Elisha said: "We do not issue a *gezera* on the community unless the majority can endure it." (*Bava Batra* 60b)

Ordinary man   הדיוט
A man who is not educated or a high ranking official (*Megillah* 12b)

Ordinary man's blessing
R. Eleazar b. Hanania said:[192] "Do not take lightly a blessing of an ordinary man, for two great men received blessings from ordinary men and they were fulfilled. They were David and Daniel." (*Megillah* 15a; *Berachot* 7a)

Ordination
No opportunity to ordain R. Hanina and R. Hoshia
It is related in the Talmud that Rabbi Yohanan was very anxious to ordain Rabbi Hanina and Rabbi Hoshia, but somehow it never materialized, because he couldn't get a quorum of three qualified rabbis to do it. When Rabbi Hanina saw that Rabbi Yohanan was distressed on account of it, he said to him.

"Master, do not grieve, for we, the descendants of Eli, are destined not to be ordained."

Rabbi Hanina and Rabbi Hoshia were both Kohanim, and descendants of Eli the Kohen. Rabbi Hanina and Rabbi Hoshia earned a living from making sandals. (*Sanhedrim* 14a)

Ordination
Once a great man ordains a rabbi, it remains so. (*Sanhedrin* 30b)

Ordination avoided
R. Zera used to hide to avoid ordination, because R. Eleazar said: "Remain always obscure and you will live with peace of mind."

But later, when he heard R. Eleazar say, "One does not obtain greatness unless all his sins are forgiven," he himself strove to obtain ordination. (*Sanhedrin* 14a)

Ordination of R. Meir
By R. Akiva
Rabbah bar b. Hana said in the name of R. Yohanan: "Anyone who says R. Meir was not ordained by R. Akiva is in error, because R. Akiva certainly ordained him, but he was also ordained by R. Yehuda b. Bava." (*Sanhedrin* 14a)

Ordination of rabbis
During the Hadrian persecution period, ordination of rabbis was forbidden
Rabbi Yehuda b. Bava became a martyr[193] when he disobeyed the decree of the Roman authorities banning the ordination of rabbis. The decree issued by the authorities during the Hadrian persecution was that anyone who ordains a rabbi is subject to the death penalty, anyone who receives ordination is subject to the death penalty, the city where the ordination takes place is to be demolished, and the boundaries around the city are to be uprooted. (*Sanhedrin* 14a; *Avodah Zarah* 8b)

Ordination of Yehoshua
The ordination of Yehoshua and of rabbis (*Sanhedrin* 13b)

---

192. Perhaps this saying is by R. Eleazar b. Pedat in the name of R. Hanina.

193. See entry, Martyrdom.

Ordination outside Israel
R. Yehoshua b. Levi said: "There is no ordination outside Israel." (*Sanhedrin* 14a)

📖 Ornaments on the Torah letters
The Talmud tells us: R. Yehuda said in the name of Rav:

"When Moshe ascended up high to receive the Torah[194] he found the Almighty engaged with placing coronets over the letters of the Torah. Moshe said to the Lord of the Universe.

'Is not the Torah perfect as it is – is anything missing from the Torah that additions are needed?'

"He answered. 'In future years there will be a man by the name of Akiva ben Yosef, who will expound on this subject and will derive something from each point or elevation.'" (*Menahot* 29b; *Shabbat* 89a)

Orphan girl
Who is still a minor
R. Nahman said: "R. Yehuda ben Bava testified about five things; one of them was: that they instruct an orphan girl –minor – to refuse marriage." (*Berachot* 27a)

Orphans
Some orphans inherited from their father a bond for a debt owed to him, however the borrower produced a receipt that it was paid. R. Hama ruled that we neither enforce payment on the strength of the bond, nor do we tear it up. We don't tear it up, because it is possible that when the orphans grow up, they will find more conclusive evidence. (*Bava Batra* 7b)

✿ Orphans boy or girl – who comes first
The rabbis taught: If two orphans need to be fed and there is enough only to feed one, the girl is fed first. (*Ketubbot* 67b)

✿ Orphans protected
The Talmud relates that there was some money belonging to orphans deposited at Rabbi Shemuel's father. When his father passed away, Shemuel was not in town. Shemuel went to the cemetery where his father was buried, and said: "I want to speak to my father."

They told him:[195] "He has gone up to learn in the Heavenly Academy." Meanwhile Shemuel's father arrived. Shemuel noticed that he was weeping and laughing.

"Why are you weeping?"

"Because I am told that you will be coming to this world soon."

"Why are you laughing?"

"Because they tell me that you are highly respected in the heavenly world." He asked his father: "Where is the money that belongs to the orphans?"

His father told him:[196] "The money is hidden in the wrap that covers the millstones. There are three bundles of money: the upper and lower belong to us, and the middle bundle belongs to the orphans."

Shemuel asked his father: "Why did you do it that way?"

He replied: "Because if thieves find it, they will take mine, and if the earth destroys some of it, that would also be mine." (*Berachot* 18b)

Orphans and usury
R. Anan said in the name of R. Shemuel: "Orphan's money, may it be lent out at interest?" (*Bava Metzia* 70a)

Orphan's money
The rabbis taught: One who invests the money of orphans at risk to the orphans, but no risk to himself – is called a wicked man. One who invests the money of orphans for which they will receive profits

---

194. See entry, Moshe in Heaven.

195. The spirits.
196. See story under, Trustee for orphans.

only but will not share in the losses – is called a pious man. One who invests to share both in profits and losses is an average person. (*Bava Metzia* 70a)

✿ Orphans to be married
Our rabbis taught if an orphan applied for assistance to marry, a house must be rented for him, a bed and household items must be prepared for him, and then a wife is given to him in marriage. (*Ketubbot* 67b)

Orphans
If a male orphan and a female orphan apply for a marriage grant, the girl orphan is to be helped first. (*Ketubbot* 67b)

Oshaya ben Hama   אושעיא בן חמא
Amora from Eretz Yisrael
2nd – 3rd centuries CE (*Ketubbot* 62b; *Bava Batra* 59a)

Ostentatious
Refrain from ostentatious living, a reminder of the destruction of the Temple
After the destruction of the Temple, the rabbis were concerned that Jewish people should not indulge in ostentatious living. They declared that during a lavish banquet something should be left out.

R. Papa said to leave out the hors d'oeuvre.

R. Yitzhak said: "On the day of the wedding, burnt ashes should be put on the head of the bridegroom as a reminder of the destruction of the Temple."

R. Papa asked R. Abbaye: "In which spot of the head should the ashes be placed?"

R. Abbaye answered him: "It should be placed on the spot where the *tefillin* are usually placed." (*Bava Batra* 60b)

✿ Outcome
Considering the outcome of an action
R. Yohanan b. Zakkai said: "Go and discern what is the proper way that a person should follow."

R. Shimon said: "One who considers the outcome of his actions." (*Avot* 2:13)

Outnumbered
On one occasion, R. Hillel was outnumbered by the disciples of R. Shammai. They took a count and the view of R. Shammai prevailed. (*Shabbat* 16b)

Outspoken
Abbaye asked Rabbah: "It is known that the people of Pumbedita hate you, because of your outspokenness. Now, since this is a fact, which person might be willing to deliver the eulogy for you?"

Rabbah replied: "You and Rabbah b. R. Hanan will do just fine." (*Shabbat* 153a)

Ovens and uncleanness (*Kelim* 5:1)

Overcharging   אונאה
(*Bava Metzia* 49b, 55a, 56b)

Overrides Shabbat
R. Akiva laid down a general principle: All labor that is needed in order to perform a positive commandment – like circumcision – if the labor could have been done on the eve of the Shabbat (Friday), it does not override Shabbat, but what cannot be done on the eve of the Shabbat (Friday), overrides the Shabbat. (*Shabbat* 130a; *Menahot* 72a, 96a; *Yevamot* 14a; *Pesahim* 69b)

Overseer of charity, Rabbi Akiva
Rabbi Akiva was also greatly concerned with the plight of the poor. He was appointed their overseer, and he made numerous trips to collect funds on their behalf. (*Kiddushin* 27a)

Own sake
R. Yehuda said in Rav's name: "One should always occupy himself with the

study of Torah and good deeds – even if at the beginning it is not for its own sake. Eventually, it will be done for its own sake." (*Sanhedrin* 105b; *Pesahim* 50b; *Arachim* 16b; *Sotah* 22b, 47a; *Horayot* 10b; *Nazir* 23b)

Ox
An ox belonging to a Jew has gored an ox belonging to a non-Jew. (*Bava Kamma* 37b, 38a)

Ox
One ox chasing another ox (*Bava Kamma* 35a)

Ox
An ox belonging to a Jew gored an ox belonging to the Temple. (*Bava Kamma* 37b)

Ox biting
An ox biting the hand of a child (*Bava Kamma* 84a)

Ox goring (*Bava Kamma* 2a)

Ox goring a donkey (*Bava Kamma* 37a)

Oxen
Two tame oxen injure each other (*Bava Kamma* 33a)

Oxen gifts offered
R. Hisda, who was a Kohen, offered two priestly gifts of the oxen to anyone who would tell him a new dictum by Rav. (*Shabbat* 10b)

P

Paired while still in the womb
R. Yehuda said in the name of Rav: "Forty days before the embryo is formed, a heavenly voice calls out to say: 'The daughter of so and so is to be the wife of so and so.'" (*Sanhedrin* 22a; *Sotah* 2a; *Bava Kamma* 18b)

Papa   פפא
Amora from Babylonia
  Head of the academy in Naresh
4th century CE (*Berachot* 20a; *Eruvin* 51a)

Paphunia
R. Aha b. Yaakov had a school in the city of Paphunia in Babylonia, a place near Pumbedita. (*Kiddushin* 35a; *Bava Kamma* 54b)

Papi   פפי
Amora from Babylonia
4th century CE (*Hullin* 110a)

Papi   פפי
Amora from Eretz Yisrael
4th century CE (*Bava Metzia* 109a)

Papiyas   פפייס
Tanna from Eretz Yisrael
1st – 2nd centuries CE (*Eduyot* 7:6)

Pappus b. Yehuda   פפוס בן יהודה
Tanna from Eretz Yisrael
1st – 2nd centuries CE (*Berachot* 61b)

📖 Pappus and Rabbi Akiva
Fox story parable
The Talmud relates the following story: Pappus b. Judah came to Rabbi Akiva and found him teaching Torah in a public gathering. He said to him: "Aren't you afraid of the government?" He replied. "Let me explain it to you with a parable. A fox was once walking on the riverbank, and he saw fish swimming away from the bank. 'From what are you fleeing?' the fox asked.

"They replied: 'From the nets people cast into the water to catch us.'

"He said to them, 'Come up to the dry land and live with me in safety.'

"They said to him: 'Are you the one they call the cleverest of all the animals? You are not clever, but foolish. If we are afraid in the element in which we live, how much more would we be endangered in the elements strange to us?'

"So it is with us Jews. If such is our condition when we study Torah, which is our natural environment, if we neglect the Torah, how much worse off shall we be?" (*Berachot* 61b)

Parables

Rabbi Yohanan said: "When Rabbi Meir used to deliver his public discourses, it would consist of one-third Halachah, one-third Aggadata and one-third of parables."

R. Meir also had 300 parables of foxes, but we have only three left. (*Sanhedrin* 38b)

Parah פרה

When do they read *Parshat Parah* (*Megillah* 29a)

Parah Aduma פרה אדומה

The red heifer was used to purify people who became ritually unclean. (*Parah* 1:1)

Parapet

Building a parapet on the roof (*Bava Batra* 6b)

Parchment for a Sotah

Writing the text for a *sotah* on a proper parchment (*Sotah* 17a–b)

Pardes

Four went into the Pardes
The rabbis taught: Four went into the Pardes: Ben Azzai, Ben Zoma, Aher, and R. Akiva. R. Akiva said to them: "When you reach the pure marble stones do not say 'water, water.'"

The story continues that Ben Azzai glanced and died; Ben Zoma looked and became stricken; Aher became a disbeliever, and R. Akiva emerged unharmed. (*Hagigah* 14b)

Parochet of the Temple פרוכת

Description of the Temple curtain (*Shekalim* 8:5)

Parsha in the Torah

Some *parashot* in the Torah are open and some are closed by tradition. (*Shabbat* 103b)

Part of the day

In some instances, a part of the day is considered like a full day
Rav was a nephew of R. Hiyya. When Rav came to Eretz Yisrael from Babylonia, R. Hiyya asked him:

"Is your father Aibu alive?"

He answered: "Ask me if my mother is alive."

He asked him: "Is your mother alive?"

He answered: "Ask me is Aibu alive?"

When R. Hiyya heard all this, he realized that his brother and sister died. Thereupon, he said to his servant: "Take off my shoes, and afterwards bring my things to the bathhouse."

R. Hiyya wanted to teach his students the Halachah. From this event, three things can be learned: a mourner is forbidden to wear shoes; one mourns only one day on a death notice received after thirty days, and part of the day is considered like a whole day. (*Pesahim* 4a; *Moed Katan* 20a; *Bechorot* 21a)

Partial payment

Debt owed, paid with a partial payment (*Bava Batra* 168a, 170b)

Partial to oneself אדם קרוב אצל עצמו

Rava said: "Every person is partial to himself; a man is his own relative." (*Sanhedrin* 9b, 19a, 25a; *Ketubbot* 18b; *Yevamot* 25b)

Parting from a friend

Mari b. Huna said: "The best form of parting from a friend is to tell him a point of Halachah, because this way he will remember him for it." (*Eruvin* 64a)

Partners
Partners owning a pit; responsibilities (*Bava Kamma* 51a)

Partners owning property (*Bava Batra* 2a)

Partners to a building
When partners to a dilapidated two-story house have no money to rebuild – Rabbi Nathan ruled the owner of the lower floor gets two-thirds of the land and the owner of the upper floor gets one-third. Others ruled differently. Came along Rabbah and said: "Hold fast to Rabbi Nathan's ruling, because he is a judge, and has penetrated to the depths of civil law." (*Bava Metzia* 117b; *Bava Kamma* 39a, 53a)

Partnership
Issur and R. Safra formed a business partnership. After a while, R. Safra divided the worth of the business in front of two witnesses without the knowledge of Issur. The matter came before Rabbah b. R. Huna and he ruled that R. Safra should produce the witnesses. (*Bava Metzia* 31b)

Partnership
A Jew and a non-Jew in partnership (*Avodah Zarah* 22a; *Sanhedrin* 63b)

Parud academy
Bar Kappara must have had an academy in a community called Parud, because when Rabbi Yohanan was in Parud, he inquired if there was a Mishna manuscript from Bar Kappara. Rabbi Tanhum, a local resident, quoted him a certain Mishna. (*Avodah Zarah* 31a)

Pass in front of a prayer
When one is standing engaged in prayer, may another person pass in front of him? (*Berachot* 27a)

Passage next to the altar
R. Yishmael b. Yohanan b. Beroka said: "There was a small passage between the altar and the stairway in the Temple." (*Pesahim* 34a)

Passing between women
Ten things adversely affect one's study; one of them is passing between two women. (*Horayot* 13b)

Passing wind
One should not pass wind when wearing *tefillin*. (*Shabbat* 49a)

Passion
R. Yehuda said in the name of Rav: "It happened that a man desired a woman to such an extent that he got sick over it. He was consumed by his passion for her. The doctors who were consulted said that he would die unless he would have her. However, the rabbis ruled to let him die rather than she should submit to his desires." (*Sanhedrin* 75a)

Passivity is not natural
חזקה אין אדם מעמיד עצמו על ממונו
Rava said: "No man will let his property be taken without resistance." (*Sanhedrin* 72a; *Yoma* 85b)

Pastures until it is blemished
ירעה עד שיסתאב
Left to pasture until it develops a blemish (*Yoma* 62a; *Bechorot* 19b)

Patched shoes
R. Hiyya b. Abba said: "It is improper for a scholar to walk in patched shoes." (*Berachot* 43b)

📖✿ Patience
There are many stories, which illustrate the patience of Rabbi Hillel. One such story is that a heathen came before

Shammai and asked him to convert him to Judaism and to teach him the Torah while he stands on one leg. Shammai chased him away with a builder's ruler. The man came to Hillel with the same request. Rabbi Hillel told him: "I will convert you, and this is what the Torah and Judaism are all about: 'What is hateful to you, do not impose on your neighbor.' That is the whole Torah, while the rest is commentary. Now go and learn the rest." (*Shabbat* 31a)

Patient
Patient like Hillel and impatient like Shammai (*Shabbat* 30b)

Patriarchate: traditions
Our rabbis taught: When Rebbe was about to expire he said:[197] "I would like to have my sons present." When they came, he instructed them: "Take care to show respect to your mother. The light shall continue to burn in its usual place, the table shall be set in its usual place, and my bed shall be made up in its usual place. Yosef of Haifa and Shimon of Efrat who attended to me in my lifetime shall attend on me when I am dead."

Rebbe said: "I would like to speak to my younger son." R. Shimon came in and Rebbe instructed him in the rules and regulations of being a Hacham.

Rebbe then said: "I would like the presence of my elder son." R. Gamliel entered, and he instructed him in the traditions and regulations of the Patriarchate. "My son," he said, "conduct your Patriarchate with high-caliber men and keep strong discipline among your students." (*Ketubbot* 103a–b)

Pay attention
R. Yohanan said in the name of R. Eleazar b. R. Shimon: "Wherever you find the words of R. Eleazar b. Yosi HaGlili, pay attention." (*Hullin* 89a)

Pay wages on same day (*Bava Metzia* 112a)

Paying promptly
Rav was very meticulous about paying promptly for his purchases. He considered it a desecration to buy meat from the butcher without paying him right away. Abbaye said: "If the custom in the community is to collect afterwards, then it is acceptable." Ravina said: "Mata Mehasya is a place where they go out to collect afterwards." Abbaye used to buy meat from two partners and paid each of them. Afterwards, he brought them together to square the account with both. (*Yoma* 86a)

Paying respect
Great scholar died, rabbis pay respect
When R. Huna passed away, they brought him to Eretz Yisrael. People told R. Ammi and R. Assi that R. Huna had come. They remarked: "When we were in Babylonia, he was so great that we could not raise our heads on account of him, and now that we are here, he has come after us?" They were then informed that it was his coffin that had arrived. When they heard the sad news, R. Ammi and R. Assi went out to pay respect to him. (*Moed Katan* 25a)

✿ Paying with non-kosher
R. Shemuel was once crossing on a ferry boat and he told his attendant to pay the boatman. Afterwards R. Shemuel became angry. Why was he angry? Because the attendant paid him with a *trefa* hen. (*Hullin* 94a)

✿ Peace
R. Hillel said: "Love peace and pursue peace." (*Avot* 1:12)

---

197. See entry, Last will of Rebbe.

Peace
Keeping peace between husband and wife
Once a woman broke two candles on the head of Baba b. Buta. When he asked her why she did it, she answered:

"My husband ordered me to do it." He blessed her; he didn't want to cause trouble between her and her husband. (*Nedarim* 66b)

✡ Peace
R. Shimon b. Gamliel said: "The world rests on three foundations: truth, justice, and peace." (*Avot* 1:18)

✡ Peace
In the interest of peace
Rabbi Illai said in the name of Rabbi Eleazar ben Shimon: "One may modify a statement in the interest of peace." Rabbi Nathan said: "It is a commandment." (*Yevamot* 65b)

Peace sake   דרכי שלום
When the rabbis instituted the Halachah, they paid great attention for the sake of peace. (*Bava Metzia* 12a; *Gittin* 59b, 61a; *Shevuot* 41a)

✡ Peace to be made between people
R. Beroka used to frequent the market in Be-Lapat where he frequently met with Eliyahu. Once he asked Eliyahu:[198] "Is there anyone in this market who merits the World to Come?"

Eliyahu replied: "No."

While talking to Eliyahu, two men passed by and Eliyahu said to R. Beroka: "These two have a share in the World to Come."

R. Beroka ran after them and asked them: "What is your occupation?"

They replied: "We are jesters, when we see people depressed, we cheer them

up. When we see two people quarreling, we try to make peace between them." (*Taanit* 22a)

Peah   פיאה
R. Shimon said: "There are four reasons the Torah commanded not to harvest the corners of the field." (*Shabbat* 23a)

Pearls
R. Miasha was a grandson of R. Yehoshua b. Levi. A man once deposited seven pearls, wrapped in a sheet, with R. Miasha. When R. Miasha died, without a will, the heirs to the man came before R. Ammi to claim the pearls. R. Ammi said to the heirs of R. Miasha: "I know that R. Miasha was not a wealthy man, and secondly, the man did give the recognizable clues." (*Ketubbot* 85b)

Pebbles
Damage caused by flying pebbles; R. Sumchos said full payment must be paid. (*Bava Kamma* 18a)

Peki'in; Academy   פקיעין
According to Jewish tradition, Peki'in is a community in Israel where Rabbi Shimon ben Yohai and his son Rabbi Eleazar hid in a cave for thirteen years during the Hadrianic persecutions.

After the destruction of the Temple, Rabbi Yehoshua ben Hanania settled in Peki'in and established there a Yeshiva, which he headed.

The grave of Rabbi Yosi from Peki'in is located in the village, but according to other sources it is between Yavne and Lydda.

Yehoshua ben Hanania lived in the 1st – 2nd centuries CE. (*Sanhedrin* 32b)

Peloni Almoni
R. Hanan b. Rava said in the name of Rav: "Elimelech, Salmon, Peloni Almoni,

---

198. See entry, Eliyahu.

and Naomi's father were all the sons of Nahshon ben Aminadav." (*Bava Batra* 91a)

Penalties
R. Yohanan said: "Standard measures and penalties are fixed according to the law given to Moshe on Sinai." (*Yoma* 80a; *Eruvin* 4a; *Sukkah* 5b)

Penitence
R. Hama b. Hanina said: "Great is penitence, because it brings healing to the world." (*Yoma* 86a)

Perfume
Erev Shabbat (*Shabbat* 18a)

Perfume in the shoes
The girls in Jerusalem carried perfume in their shoes. (*Shabbat* 62b)

Persecuted
R. Avohu said: "It is preferable to be a man who is persecuted than one who is the persecutor." (*Bava Kamma* 93a)

Persia
Persia is asking a share in the World to Come. (*Avodah Zarah* 2b)

Persian fire worshippers
On one occasion, R. Yehuda and Rabbah went to visit Rabbah bar b. Hana at his home while he was sick. They were having a nice visit and a discussion on a halachic matter when some fanatical fire-worshipping Persian gangs invaded his house. The gangs caused havoc and confiscated the lamps from the house. When Rabbah bar b. Hana was praying for relief, he was mentioning that it is hard to believe that the Persians are worse than the Romans. (*Gittin* 16b, 17a)

Persian language
Rebbe said: "Why use the Syriac language

in Eretz Yisrael – either use the Holy Tongue or the Greek language." R. Yosi said: "In Babylonia, why use the Aramaic language – either use the Holy Tongue or the Persian language." (*Bava Kamma* 83a)

Persian rule in Eretz Yisrael
R. Yishmael b. Yosi b. Halafta was ill. The rabbis sent word to him: "Tell us a few things you heard from your father."

He told them: "One hundred and eighty years before the Temple was destroyed, Rome was ruling over Israel. Forty years before the destruction of the Temple, the Sanhedrin moved from the Temple to the Hanut. The Persian rule lasted thirty-four years after the building of the Temple. Greece ruled 180 years during the existence of the Temple. The Hasmonean rule lasted 103 years during the existence of the Temple." (*Avodah Zarah* 9a)

Persians
Rebbe said to Levi after he returned from Babylonia: "What are the Persians like? They are like the armies of the House of David. What are the Guebers fire-worshippers like? They are like the destroying angels. What are the Ishmaelites like? They are like the demons of the outhouse. What are the scholars of Babylon like? They are like the ministering angels." (*Kiddushin* 72a)

Perugitha
R. Helbo said: "The wine of Perugitha and the water of Diomsith caused the ten tribes of Israel to be cut off from their brethren." (*Shabbat* 147b)

Pesach, historical first and those that followed
What are the differences between the first Pesach of Mitzrayim and the following Pesahim for generations? (*Pesahim* 96a)

Pesach offering
The Pesach offering in the Temple was done in three divisions. (*Pesahim* 64a)

Pesach offering and Shabbat
Certain work required to do for the Pesach offering supersede Shabbat. (*Pesahim* 65b)

Pesach offering for a single person
(*Pesahim* 91a; *Kiddushin* 42a)

Pesach Seder
R. Gamliel used to say: "Whoever does not mention these three things on Pesach is not fulfilling the mitzvah of Pesach: Pesach, Matzah, and Maror." (*Pesahim* 116a)

Pesach, the first and the second
What differences are there in observance between the first Pesach and the Pesach which is observed as a substitute when one cannot observe the first? (*Pesahim* 95a)

Pesach Torah reading (*Megillah* 30b)

Petahia   פתחיה
Officer of the Temple (*Shekalim* 5:1)

Petica   פתיחא
A legal document like a warrant, an opening of a legal proceeding (*Bava Kamma* 112b)

Petzua Daka   פצוע דכא
A man's testicles, crushed or wounded (*Yevamot* 70a, 75a)

Pharisees and King Yannai
King Yannai was not well-disposed towards the Pharisees, and he persecuted them for a long time – he had many of them put to death. Many rabbis fled the country, but after some time Rabbi Shimon ben Shetah was able to bring reconciliation between the rabbis and the king.

Rabbi Shimon restored the Torah to its former glory.

After King Yannai died, his queen, Salome Alexandra, acceded to the throne. Rabbi Shimon b. Shetah was the brother of the queen, and through his influence Pharisees were victorious over the Tzadokis. (*Kiddushin* 66a)

Philanthropy
The Talmud relates that Rabbah said to Rafram b. Papa: "Tell me some of the good deeds Rabbi Huna had done."

He replied: "On cloudy days, they used to drive him in his golden carriage to survey every part of the city of Sura. When he saw walls that were unsafe, he would order them to be demolished, and if the owner could not afford to rebuild them, he would rebuild them at his own expense.

"On Friday afternoons, he would send messengers to the market and buy all the leftover vegetables.

"Whenever he discovered a new medicine, he would suspend it above his door with a jug of water next to it, and would put a note with it which stated that whoever needs it should come and get it.

"When he had a meal, he would open his doors wide open and declare: 'Whoever is in need of a meal, come and eat.'" (*Taanit* 20b)

Philistines and King David
R. Huna said: "When David was at war with the Philistines, they hid themselves in stacks of barley belonging to Israelites. David asked the rabbis whether it was permissible to destroy another person's property in order to save his army. He was told that it was not permissible. "However, you are a king, and a king has the right to break the fences and go through another's property to make way for his army and nobody is entitled to stop him." (*Bava Kamma* 60b)

Philosophers asked

The philosophers asked the Jewish Elders of Rome: "If God does not want idol worshipping, why doesn't he abolish the idols?"

They answered: "Foolish people worship the sun, the moon, the stars, and planets, which are useful to the world. Should God abolish those on account of foolish people?"

They retorted: "Why doesn't he abolish those which are unnecessary?"

"Because then they would claim that the others must be real idols if they were not abolished." (*Avodah Zarah* 54b)

Philosophic discussions

Rabbi Yehoshua b. Hanania had scientific and philosophical discussions with the Roman Emperor and the wise men of Athens. (*Bechorot* 8b)

Philosophy

R. Gamliel conducted philosophical debates with the Roman philosophers.

A philosopher asked R. Gamliel questions. (*Avodah Zarah* 44b, 54b)

📖 Physician R. Shemuel and Rebbe

R. Shemuel was Rebbe's physician. Rebbe had an eye disease. R. Shemuel offered to bathe his eyes with a lotion, but Rebbe said: "I can't tolerate it."

R. Shemuel suggested: "I will apply an ointment to the area around the eye."

But Rebbe said, "I can't tolerate that either."

R. Shemuel placed some chemicals in a bag under his pillow and he was healed. (*Bava Metzia* 85b)

Pierced organs

R. Hiyya b. Rav said: "There are eight cases of *trefot* included under the heading of 'Piercing.'" (*Hullin* 43a)

Pig

Burrowing of a pig causing damage (*Bava Kamma* 17b)

Pigeon flyer

Racing pigeons against others (*Shevuot* 45a)

Pigeons

Rav Hisda, who was a Kohen, was holding two pigeons in his hand and declared: "If someone will come and tell me a new dictum in the name of Rav, I will give him these pigeons."

Rava b. Mehasya said to him: "Rav said the following: 'If one gives a gift to a neighbor he must inform him first.'"

Upon this, R. Hisda gave him the pigeons.

Rava asked him: "Are Rav's dicta so dear to you?"

"Yes," he replied. (*Shabbat* 10b)

Pigeons and doves

What is the age required for pigeons and doves to be qualified for offerings (*Hullin* 22a)

Pigul   פיגול

The Torah has an expression for Temple offerings that are offered with the wrong intentions or eaten beyond their prescribed time or prescribed place. It is called "*pigul.*" (*Zevahim* 36b)

Pigs

It is improper to rear pigs in any place whatsoever. (*Bava Kamma* 79b, 82b)

Pikuah Nefesh   פיקוח נפש

R. Yaakov b. Idi said in the name of R. Yohanan: "One may do any work on Shabbat to save a life." (*Ketubbot* 5a; *Shabbat* 150a)

Pilgrimages

Ulla said: "The fifteenth of Av is the day

King Hoshea removed the guards from the roads which King Yerovam b. Nevat placed there to prevent the people from pilgrimages to Jerusalem." (*Bava Batra* 121b)

Pinhas   פנחס
Officer of the Temple (*Shekalim* 5:1)

Pinhas ben Eleazar
Pinhas the High Priest who slew Zimri was initially not spoken of in a nice manner, but God approved of him and everything changed. (*Sanhedrin* 82b)

Pinhas ben Hama HaKohen
פנחס בן חמא הכהן
Amora from Eretz Yisrael
4th century CE (*Bava Batra* 116a)

Pinhas ben Yair   פנחס בן יאיר
Tanna from Eretz Yisrael
2nd century CE (*Hullin* 7a)

Pinhas ben Yair
R. Pinhas b. Yair declined an invitation by Rebbe to dine with him
When Rebbe heard of the arrival of R. Pinhas b. Yair, he went out to meet him and he invited him to dinner. R. Pinhas excused himself with the explanation that he is occupied with a mitzvah to redeem captives. (*Hullin* 7b)

📖 Pinhas ben Yair
When R. Shimon b. Yohai came out from the cave where he was hiding, his son-in-law, R. Pinhas b. Yair, came to meet him. He took him to the bath and massaged his body. Seeing the lumps in his body he wept with tears: "Woe to me to see you in such a state."

  R. Shimon answered: "Happy are you to see me in this condition for I have learned a lot during this time. Originally, when I raised a difficult question, you would give me thirteen answers, but now when you raise a difficult question, I can give you twenty-four answers." (*Shabbat* 33b)

Pious men
Whenever the Talmud talks about a certain pious man, it refers to either Rabbi Yehuda ben Bava or Rabbi Yehuda bar Illai. (*Bava Kamma* 103b; *Temurah* 15b)

Pirchus   פירכוס
Sign of vitality during slaughtering (*Hullin* 38a)

Pit
A pit causing damages; responsibility to animals when they are falling into a pit; responsibility of having a pit next to a neighbor's property; digging a pit on his own property next to a neighbor's pit (*Shabbat* 22a; *Bava Kamma* 2a, 29b, 50b; *Bava Batra* 17a)

Pit is a domain of its own
A pit on Shabbat is its own domain (*Shabbat* 8b)

📖✿ Place is not the honor
The place is not the honor, but the person is.

  In Drukeret, a city that supplied 500 foot soldiers, there were three deaths in one day. Therefore, R. Nahman b. Hisda ordered a public fast. R. Nahman b. Yitzhak supported the fast, citing R. Meir in support of it. Upon this, R. Nahman b. Hisda said to him: "Please, take a seat nearer to us." The other replied: "We have learned that R. Yosi said: 'It is not the place that honors the man, but it is the man that honors the place.'" (*Taanit* 21b)

Placing a receptacle to catch the oil
Placing a receptacle under a candle on Shabbat to catch the oil (*Shabbat* 42b)

Placing a Sefer Torah on the bier

The people wanted to place a Sefer Torah on the bier of R. Huna, but Rabbi Hisda stopped them. He said: "Rabbi Huna would not have approved of it." (*Moed Katan* 25a)

Plain meaning of Torah verses
אין מקרא יוצא מידי פשוטו

One cannot depart from the plain meaning of the Torah. (*Shabbat* 63a; *Yevamot* 11b, 24a)

Planetary cycles

R. Shimon b. Pazi said in the name of R. Yehoshua b. Levi on the authority of Bar Kappara: "He who knows how to calculate the cycles and planetary courses, but does not do it, of him scripture has sharp words." (*Shabbat* 75a)

📖 Planetary influences

It was recorded in R. Yehoshua b. Levi's notebook that the day of the week on which a person was born determines his fate. When R. Hanina heard this, he said to his people: "Go and tell the son of Levi. Not the *mazal* of the day,[199] but the *mazal* of the hour influences the fate." (*Shabbat* 156a)

📖 Planetary influences

R. Shemuel said that Israel is immune from planetary influences.

R. Shemuel and his Persian friend Avlat were having a conversation near a meadow. Some people were walking to the meadow, and they were passing by them. Avlat pointed to a man and said:

"That man is going to the meadows, but he will not return, because a snake will bite him and he will die."

R. Shemuel replied: "If he is an Israelite, he will go and return."[200] (*Shabbat* 156b)

Planetary influences
Israel is immune from planetary influences

R. Hanina said: "The planets influence wisdom and wealth, and Israel is also under planetary influences." R. Yohanan maintains that Israel is immune from planetary influences. (*Shabbat* 156a)

✿ Pleases mankind

R. Hanina b. Dosa used to say: "A person who pleases mankind – pleases also God, but a person who is disliked by mankind – is not pleasing to God." (*Avot* 3:10)

✿ Pleasing no one

Trying to please everyone will please no one.[201] (*Bava Kamma* 60b)

Pledge
משכון

Pledge: taking a pledge when lending money to another person (*Bava Metzia* 48b, 49a, 113a, 114b)

Pledge from a minor (*Bava Batra* 52a)

Pledge honored (*Rosh Hashana* 4b)

Plowing

Plowing on Shabbat in any form is discussed in *Ha-boneh*, the 12th *perek* in *Shabbat*. (*Shabbat* 102b)

Plowing a grave field

The size that becomes a grave field (*Ohalot* 17:1–5)

Pocket search
On Friday evening just before Shabbat

It was learned that R. Hanania said: "One must examine his garment pockets on Friday before Shabbat." R. Yosef observed: "This is an important Shabbat law." (*Shabbat* 12a)

---

199. See also entry, Astrology.
200. See entry, Israel immune.

201. See entry, Aggadah.

Pogem   פוגם
A slaughtering knife with a notch in it
(*Hullin* 10a, 43b)

Poison
To put poison in front of someone else's
animals (*Bava Kamma* 47b, 56a)

📖 Poking fun of a blind person
Rabbi Sheshet was blind and physically
frail. Once the king came to town and all
the people went out to see him. R. Sheshet
also went to see him and on the way he
met a Tzadoki who poked fun at him.

He said: "The pitchers which are whole
go to the river, but where do the broken
ones go?"

R. Sheshet replied: "I can show you that
even while I am blind, I know more than
you."

The first contingent of troops passed by
and a loud shout could be heard. "The
king is coming," said the Tzadoki. "He is
not coming," replied R. Sheshet.

A second contingent of troops passed by
and a loud shout could be heard. "Now the
king is coming," said the Tzadoki. "The
king is not coming," replied R. Sheishes.

A third contingent of troops passed
by and there was silence. "Now," said R.
Sheshet, "the king is coming." When the
king passed R. Sheshet said a blessing over
him. (*Berachot* 58a)

Pomegranates
Pomagrantes used as a measuring size
(*Kelim* 17:4)

Poor
R. Akiva said: "Even the poor in Israel
deserve dignity." (*Bava Kamma* 86b, 90b)

Poor man finds lost property and returns it to its rightful owner
R. Yohanan said: "Three kinds of people

earn special approval from Hashem: a
bachelor who lives in a large city and
does not sin, a poor man who returns lost
property to its owner, and a rich man who
tithes his produce in secret." (*Pesahim* 113b)

Poor people
Are loved by God
Turnus Rufus, the Roman governor, asked
Rabbi Akiva:

"If God loves the poor, why does He not
support them?"

Rabbi Akiva replied. "God gave us the
mitzvah of charity, in order to save us
from the punishment of Gehinom."

"On the contrary," countered Rufus.
"It is this deed of giving food to the poor,
which condemns you to Gehinom. I will
illustrate it to you. Suppose a king was
angry with his servant and sent him to
prison and ordered that no food should
be given to him, and someone gave him
food. Would the king not be angry with
this man, would he not punish him?"

Rabbi Akiva retorted. "Suppose the
king got angry with his son and put him
in prison with orders not to feed him, and
someone gave him food. Would the king
not be grateful to this man and even send
him a present?" (*Bava Batra* 10a)

Poor person
We have learned: The minimum to be
given to a poor person who is on his way
from one place to another is a loaf of
bread. If he stays over for Shabbat, he is
given food for three meals. (*Bava Batra* 9a)

Positive and Negative precepts
עשה ולא תעשה
(*Shabbat* 25a; *Betzah* 8b)

Positive precept   אין דיחוי אצל מצוות
A positive precept cannot be invalidated
on account of a happening; like if the

object of the precept was unintention-ally changed. (*Hullin* 87a; *Sukkah* 33a; *Avodah Zarah* 47a)

Positive precept with a fixed time
Women are exempt from observing a posi-tive precept for which there is a fixed time. (*Berachot* 20b; *Kiddushin* 29a)

Positive vs. positive and negative
אין עשה דוחה לא תעשה ועשה
When two mitzvah precepts are to be per-formed at the same time, and one mitzvah was given only in the positive, while the other was given in the positive and neg-ative precepts, the positive and negative precepts supersede the precept given in the positive only. (*Shabbat* 25a; *Sanhedrin* 19a)

✿ Possessions
The more possessions, the more anxiety
R. Gamliel b. R. Yehuda HaNasi said: "The more flesh, the more worms; the more possessions, the more anxiety."

Rabbi Hillel said: "The more Torah, the more life; the more thought, the more wisdom; the more counsel, the more un-derstanding; the more righteousness, the more peace." (*Avot* 2:7, 8)

Postdated contracts
(*Bava Metzia* 17a, 72a; *Sanhedrin* 32a; *Bava Batra* 157b, 171b)

Pot
Returning pot to a preheated stove on Shabbat
A heated pot on Shabbat on a preheated stove (*Shabbat* 36b, 38b)

Pot used to cook meat
A pot in which meat was cooked may not be used to boil milk; imparting flavor is an important factor. (*Hullin* 97a, 111b; *Zevahim* 96b)

Potifar
The wife of Potifar will give testimony that Yosef was not the transgressor. (*Avodah Zarah* 3a)

Potters
People stumbling on loose broken pottery, causing damage (*Bava Kamma* 31a, 47a)

Poverty
R. Eleazar b. Zadok said: "When I was studying at R. Yohanan b. HaHorani, I noticed that in a year of scarcity he used to eat dry bread dipped in salt." (*Yevamot* 15b)

Poverty
Pinhas b. Hama HaKohen said that "poverty in a man's house is worse than fifty plagues." R. Pinhas b. Hama also said: "When there is a sick person in the house, they should go to a Sage who is also a saintly person who will pray for mercy." (*Bava Batra* 116a)

📖 Poverty
Two rabbis; great scholars but very poor
Rabbis Eleazar Hisma and Yohanan ben Nuri were very familiar with astrology and mathematics.

Rabbi Gamliel decided to appoint them as supervisors, and sent for them. They were reluctant to accept on account of their humility. But Rabbi Gamliel told them: "Do you imagine that I offer you rulership? It is servitude that I offer you."[202](*Horayot* 10a)

📖 Power of prayers
Rabbi Hanina ben Dosa was a student of Rabbi Yohanan ben Zakkai in Arav. While he was there, Rabbi Yohanan's child fell

---

202. See entries, Star appears every 70 years, and Jobs offered.

Practical advice

gravely ill. He said to him: "Hanina my son, pray[203] for him that he may live."

Rabbi Hanina put his head between his knees and prayed for the recovery of the child, and the child recovered. (*Berachot* 34b)

✿ Practical advice
R. Aibu was the son of Rav. Rav said to his son Aibu: "I have worked hard to teach you studies, without success. Therefore, come and I will teach you worldly wisdom:

"Sell your merchandise while the sand is still in your feet. Everything you may sell and have regrets, because you might have sold it for more, except wine, which might become sour. Pocket the money first – before you open your sack of merchandise. It is preferable to earn a smaller amount near your home, than to earn a larger amount far from your home. When you harvest dates and they are in your bag, run to the brewery to make beer, before you consume them yourself." (*Pesahim* 113a)

✿ Practice and learn
Rabbi Yishmael ben Yohanan ben Beroka said: "He who learns in order to teach will be granted the means to learn and teach; and he who learns in order to practice, will be granted the opportunity to learn, teach, practice, and observe." (*Avot* 4:5)

📖 Practiced his studies forty times
Resh Lakish was a very diligent student and prepared himself well before studying with Rabbi Yohanan. He systematically went over the text forty times, corresponding to the forty days Moshe spent on Mount Sinai to receive the Torah, and only then did he come for his lecture. (*Taanit* 8a)

Praising
Rava was praising R. Aha b. Yaakov to

R. Nahman that he is a great man. (*Bava Kamma* 40a)

Pray for own needs in Amidah
Nahum HaMadai said: "One may ask for one's own needs during the *Amidah* in the blessing entitled '*Shomea Tefila*' שומע תפלה." (*Avodah Zarah* 7b)

✿ Pray for your government's welfare
R. Hanina Segan HaKohanim said: "Pray for the welfare of the government, for without the fear of the government men would swallow each other alive." (*Avodah Zarah* 4a; *Avot* 3:2)

Pray from a low spot
R. Yosi b. R. Hanina said in the name of R. Eliezer b. Yaakov: "When praying, do not stand in a high place." (*Berachot* 10b)

Pray reverently
When praying, one should be in a reverent frame of mind. (*Berachot* 30b)

Pray towards Jerusalem
When praying, one should face in the direction of Jerusalem. (*Berachot* 30a)

Pray with heart to Heaven
When praying, direct your heart to Heaven. (*Berachot* 31a)

Prayer
R. Shimon said: "When you pray, do not do it mechanically. Put meaning and feeling to it." (*Avot* 2:13)

Prayer
"If two people enter a synagogue to pray and one finishes first, he should wait for the other to finish, otherwise his prayers are for naught." (*Berachot* 5b)

Prayers after a meal
One should not say from memory

---

203. See also entry, R. Hanina ben Dosa prayed.

the prayers after a meal. (*Berachot* 15b; *Megillah* 19b)

Prayers are heard
When one puts his soul into his or her prayers, they are heard. (*Taanit* 8a)

Prayer before going to sleep
קריאת שמע על מטתו
R. Yitzhak said: "If one recites the Shema on his bed, the demons keep away from him." (*Berachot* 5a)

Prayer time
R. Yohanan said in the name of R. Shimon b. Yohai, and R. Aha b. R. Hanina also said: "The most acceptable time to pray is when the congregation prays." (*Berachot* 8a)

Prayer when traveling   תפלת הדרך
R. Yaakov and R. Hisda said: "When one travels on the road, the prayer *Tefillat Ha-Derech* should be said." (*Berachot* 29b)

Prayers
R. Abba Binyamin believed that only in the synagogue are prayers listened to. (*Berachot* 6a)

Prayers
Exemptions for mourners (*Berachot* 3rd *perek*)

Prayers
Exemptions for women and minors (*Berachot* 3rd *perek*)

📖 Prayers
Long or short
Once a student was leading the services in the presence of R. Eliezer, and he stretched out the prayers for a very long time. The students said to R. Eliezer: "Rabbi, this student is extremely long."

He replied to them: "He is not any longer than Moshe was when he was on the mountain for forty days and forty nights."

Another time a student was leading the services in front of R. Eliezer, and he cut the prayers very short. The students complained to R. Eliezer: "This student is extremely brief."

He replied to them: "He is not any shorter than Moshe when he prayed for Miriam with few words." (*Berachot* 34a)

Prayers for good outcome of dreams
Ameimar, Mar Zutra, and R. Ashi were once sitting together.

They said: "Let each one of us say something that the others did not hear before."

One of them said: "If one had a dream and does not know what he dreamt, he should say the prayer for dreams which starts with the phrase, '*Ribbono shel Olam.*' It is said during the time when the Kohanim bless the congregation in the synagogue." The others also said something new. (*Berachot* 55b)

Prayers for rain
One of the prayers in the *Amidah* is for rain. (*Berachot* 33a)

Prayers for rain
When do they begin prayers for rain (*Taanit* 2a)

Praying
R. Ashi said: "When there was suffering in the world, I saw R. Kahana remove his cloak, clasp his hands, and pray." (*Shabbat* 10a)

Praying
R. Yehoshua b. Levi said: "When the time to pray *Minha* arrives, it is forbidden to eat." (*Shabbat* 9b; *Berachot* 28b)

Praying
The rabbis of the Talmud – each had a distinct way of praying. (*Shabbat* 10a)

Praying alone

R. Ada b. Ahava said: "A person praying by himself does not say the *Kedushah*." (*Berachot* 21b)

Praying and eating

R. Yosi b. Hanina said in the name of R. Eliezer b. Yaakov: "One should not eat before praying first."

He also said in the name of R. Eliezer b. Yaakov: "One should pray with feet next to each other, and erect." (*Berachot* 10b)

Praying and holding a knife in hand

Holding in hand any object that will be a distraction while praying (*Berachot* 23b)

Praying and holding a Torah in hand

(*Berachot* 23b)

Praying at sunrise

R. Hiyya b. Abba said in the name of R. Yohanan: "It is a mitzvah to pray with the first and last appearance of the sun." (*Berachot* 29b; *Shabbat* 118b)

Praying for a friend

The rabbis said if one prays for a friend and he himself is in need of the same thing, his needs are answered first. (*Bava Kamma* 92a)

Praying for rain

(*Bava Metzia* 28a; *Taanit* 10a)

Praying for rain

In Eretz Yisrael and Babylonia

R. Zerika said to R. Safra: "Come and see the difference in approach between the good men of Eretz Yisrael and the pious men of Babylonia. When the world was in need of rain, the pious men of Babylonia – R. Huna and R. Hisda – came forward and said: 'Let us pray, perhaps the Almighty might be reconciled and send us rain.' But the great men of Eretz Yisrael – like R. Yonah, the father of R. Mani – would go and stand in a low spot dressed in sackcloth and pray for rain." (*Taanit* 23b; *Hullin* 122b; *Megillah* 28b)

Praying for rain

Once there was no rain and Rabbi Yehuda HaNasi ordained a fast, but no rain fell. R. Ilfa went before the ark and recited the prayers for rain and rain fell.

Rebbe asked him: "What is your special merit?"

He answered: "I live in a poverty-stricken remote neighborhood, where wine for *Kiddush* and *Havdalah* is hard to come by. I make sure that I have wine and this way I help others to fulfill the mitzvah of *Kiddush*." (*Taanit* 24a)

Praying for the sick

When praying, pray for every Jewish person

When one prays for a sick person, one should pray for the person together with prayers for all the Jewish people. (*Shabbat* 12b)

Praying in the bathhouse (*Shabbat* 10a)

Praying in a synagogue (*Berachot* 8a)

Praying interruption

R. Yohanan and R. Eleazar stated: "Even if a sharp sword rests on ones neck, do not desist from praying." (*Berachot* 10a)

Praying interruption

During the *Amidah*, there should be no interruptions, even if the king greets you. (*Berachot* 30b)

Praying language (*Sotah* 32a)

Praying time

Me'ematai מאימתי, the first *perek* in

Berachot, deals with proper time for prayer, and how many benedictions before the *Shema*. (*Berachot* 2a)

Praying without Minyan
R. Adda b. Ahava said: "How do we know that a person praying by himself does not say the *Kedushah*?" (*Berachot* 21b; *Megillah* 23b)

Precedence Kohen and Levi
A Kohen takes precedence over a Levite and a Levite over an Israelite. (*Horayot* 13:a)

Precedence Kohen and Mamzer
A *mamzer* who is a *Talmid Hacham* takes precedence over a Kohen Gadol. (*Horayot* 13a)

Precious gifts
R. Shimon b. Yohai said: "God gave Israel three precious gifts: the Torah, the Land of Israel, and the World to Come. (*Berachot* 5a)

Precious to God
R. Hiyya b. Ammi said in the name of Ulla: "Since the Temple was destroyed, the most precious thing to God in this world are the four cubits of space where they learn Halachah." (*Berachot* 8a)

Predictions
R. Huna used to pass the house of R. Avin. He predicted that two great scholars would be born to him and so it was. They were R. Idi and R. Hiyya. (*Shabbat* 23b)

Predicting the weather
R. Abba said to R. Ashi: "For weather information, we rely on R. Yitzhak b. Avdimi. (*Bava Batra* 147a)

Prefer new city
Rava b. Mehasya said in the name of R. Hama b. Gurya in Rav's name: "A man should always prefer to live in a city which was recently established, because it is less sinful." (*Shabbat* 10b)

✿ Preferable to earn less near home
R. Aibu was the son of Rav. Rav said to his son Aibu: "I have worked hard to teach you without success. Therefore, come and I will teach you worldly wisdom:
"It is preferable to earn a smaller amount near your home, than to earn a larger amount far from your home. (*Pesahim* 113a)

Preference for one child
Rava b. Mehasya said in the name of R. Hama b. Gurya in Rav's name: "A man should never show preference for one son over the others, because our ancestor Yaakov preferred Yosef over his brothers and they became jealous. Consequently, our ancestors wound up in Egypt as slaves." (*Shabbat* 10b)

Preferred oil
R. Yehoshua b. Levi said: "All oils are permissible for Chanukah lighting, but olive oil is preferable." (*Shabbat* 23a)

Preferred son
Leaving the inheritance to the preferred child (*Bava Batra* 130a)

Prefers Torah over sacrifices
R. Yehoshua b. Levi said: "God prefers one day of Torah study over a thousand sacrifices." (*Makkot* 10a)

Pregnancy prevention
The use of a device to prevent pregnancy is discussed. (*Yevamot* 12b; *Ketubbot* 39a; *Niddah* 45a; *Nedarim* 35b)

Pregnant woman
Encounter with a dog (*Shabbat* 63b; *Bava Kamma* 83a)

Prejudiced witnesses נוגעין בעדותן
Interested parties (*Bava Batra* 43a)

📖 **Preparing for Shabbat**
R. Hiyya b. Abba related a story: "I was once a guest in a house in Lodokia where they served the man on a golden table, which was carried by sixteen men with sixteen silver chains. On it were plates, goblets, pitchers, and bottles. In those utensils, were all kinds of delicious foods and spices. I said to him: 'What did you do to merit all this?' He replied: 'I was a butcher, and every time I came across a fine piece of meat, I put it aside for Shabbat.'" (*Shabbat* 119a)

Preparing for Shabbat
R. Yehuda said in Rav's name: "This was the practice of Rabbi Yehuda bar Illai. Friday afternoon they put before him a basin of hot water. He washed his face, hands, and feet, and wrapped himself in a fringed linen robe, and he looked like an angel of God." (*Shabbat* 25b)

✿ **Preparing for Shabbat**
Physical work preparation
Rabbah and R. Yosef used to chop wood on Friday to prepare for Shabbat. He wanted to do something physical to welcome the Shabbat. (*Shabbat* 119a)

Preserving food
On Shabbat
Preserving food on Shabbat in a pit is discussed in *Havit*, the 22nd *perek* in *Shabbat*. (*Shabbat* 143b)

Pressured to say "yes"
כופין אותו עד שיאמר רוצה אני
He is subjected to pressure until he says: "I am willing." This tactic is used by the rabbis in divorce cases and in *halitza*. (*Yevamot* 106a; *Arachin* 21a; *Kiddushin* 50a; *Bava Batra* 48a)

Pri Ha-Adama פרי האדמה
On vegetables, one makes the blessing *pri ha-adama*. (*Berachot* 35a)

Pri Ha-Etz פרי העץ
On fruits of the tree, one makes the blessing *pri ha-etz*. (*Berachot* 35a)

Pri Ha-Gefen פרי הגפן
On wine, one makes the blessing *pri ha-gefen*. (*Berachot* 35a)

Price-fixing on fruits (*Bava Metzia* 62b, 72b)

Price fluctuation
When one sells wine or oil and the price for the commodity went up or down (*Bava Batra* 87a)

✿ **Pride**
Rabbi Eleazar was very poor, but he refused to accept gifts. (*Taanit* 25a)

✿ **Pride**
When R. Yehuda HaNasi sent a present to R. Eleazar, he did not accept it, and when he was invited he would not go. He quoted a passage in Scripture for his reason. (*Megillah* 28a)

✿ **Priest and a scholar in need**
R Yosef said: A Kohen living in a neighborhood with a Torah scholar in great need, may assign to him the priestly gifts even if they have not come into his hands. (*Hullin* 133a)

Priest not familiar with priestly gifts
A priest who is not conversant with the twenty-four priestly gifts. (*Hullin* 132b)

Priestly dues
May anyone sell priesty dues (*Hullin* 138b)

Priestly gift

R. Shemuel b. Nahmani said in the name of R. Yonatan: "One should not give the priestly gift to a *Kohen am haaretz*, uneducated in Torah." (*Hullin* 130b)

Priestly gift not yet given

Rabbah b. bar Hana said in the name of R. Yohanan: "It is forbidden to eat from an animal from which the priestly dues have not been taken." (*Hullin* 132b)

📖 Priests competing

To perform their services at the Temple

It once happened that two priests were competing and running up the ramp to do the service, and one of them reached the altar first. The other one took a knife and stabbed him. Rabbi Zadok HaKohen mounted the platform and addressed the priests.

"On whose behalf shall we offer the heifer whose neck is to be broken, on behalf of the city or on behalf of the Temple court?" All the people burst out weeping. (*Yoma* 23a)

📖 Priests and marriages

Many brothers, all priests marrying sisters, all daughters of priests

The Talmud relates when R. Yitzhak came from Eretz Yisrael to Babylonia, he said: "There was a town in Eretz Yisrael by the name of Gofnit where eighty pairs of brothers, all priests, married eighty pairs of sisters, all from priestly families. The rabbis searched from Sura to Nehardea and could not find a similar case, except the daughters of R. Hisda, who were married to Rami b. Hama and to Mar Ukva b. Hama – brothers. While the daughters of R. Hisda were priestesses, because their father was a priest, their husbands were not priests. (*Berachot* 44a)

Primary sources of uncleanness (*Kelim* 1:1)

Principal labor categories אבות מלאכות

R. Hanina b. Hama said: The thirty-nine principal labor categories on Shabbat correspond to the forms of labor performed in the Tabernacle. (*Shabbat* 49b, 68a)

Principles

R. Akavia b. Mahalalel testified with regards to four principles, but the rabbis disagreed with him and told him to reverse his position. If he had done so, they would appoint him as head of the court of Israel. He replied: "I would rather be called a fool then to do something what I think is contrary to my principles." (*Eduyot* 5:6)

📖 Principles to uphold

Retraction refused, sticking to principles

R. Shila b. Avina decided a matter according to Rav.

When Rav was on his deathbed, he said to R. Assi: "Go and restrain him and if he does not listen try to convince him." After Rav passed away, R. Assi asked him to retract, because Rav had retracted his ruling.

R. Shila said: "If Rav had retracted, he would have told me," and refused to retract. Thereupon, R. Assi put him under the ban.

R. Shila asked him: "Are you not afraid of the fire?"

He answered: "I am Issi b. Yehuda, who is Issi b. Gur-aryeh, who is Issi b. Gamliel, who is Issi b. Mahalalel, a cooper mortar, which does not rust."

The other retorted: "I am Shila b. Avina, an iron mallet that breaks the cooper mortar."

Soon after this incident, R. Assi became very sick and died. R. Shila told his wife: "Prepare my shrouds, because I don't want him to have the opportunity to tell

Rav things about me." When R. Shila departed, people saw a myrtle fly from one grave to the other. We may conclude that the rabbis have made peace. (*Niddah* 36b)

📖 Prison conversation

Our rabbis taught: When Rabbi Eleazar ben Parta and Rabbi Hanania ben Teradion were arrested, R. Eleazar said to R. Hanania: "Happy are you that they arrested you on only one charge, but woe to me, for I have been arrested on five charges."

Rabbi Hanania replied: "Happy are you that they brought five charges against you – for learning Torah and for acts of benevolence, but you will be rescued. However, woe to me for being arrested on one charge only – for learning Torah." Rabbi Eleazar was miraculously saved from being executed. (*Avodah Zarah* 17b)

✿ Private property

Ben Bag Bag had this to say about private property: "Do not enter your neighbor's property without his knowledge, even to retrieve something that belongs to you, because he may think you are a thief." (*Bava Kamma* 27b)

Private town

Converted to a public town (*Eruvin* 59a)

📖 Privileges for scholars

It is related that R. Dimi from Nehardea brought a load of figs in a boat to be sold on the market. The Exilarch said to Rava: "Go and see if he is a scholar, and if so, reserve the market for him."[204]

The scholars had privileges; they could dispose of their merchandise ahead of the rest of the merchants in order for them to then go and study. Rava sent R. Adda

---

204. See entry, Market privileges.

b. Abba to test his scholarship. He put to him the following question.

"If an elephant swallows a basket and then passes it out with excrement, is it still considered to be a basket, still subject to uncleanness?"

R. Dimi could not give an answer. He asked R. Adda: "Are you Rava?"

R. Adda answered, "Between Rava and me there is a great difference, but at any rate, I can be your teacher and therefore, Rava is the teacher of your teacher." Consequently, they did not reserve the market for him, and his figs were a total loss. He appealed to Rabbi Yosef, by saying:

"See how they have treated me?"

It so happens that shortly afterwards, R. Adda died. R. Dimi aggravated himself and said: "It is through me that he has been punished, because he made me lose my figs." (*Bava Batra* 22a)

Proclos b. Philosophos

Proclos had a discussion with R. Gamliel in a bathhouse in Acco. (*Avodah Zarah* 44b)

Procreate

Ben Azzai is quoted as saying that anyone who does not procreate is considered as though he shed blood. (*Yevamot* 63b)

Profanation of the Name   חילול השם
(*Avodah Zarah* 28a)

✿ Profane language

It happened that R. Eliezer spent a Shabbat in the Upper Galilee. While there, he was asked thirty questions on the Halachah of Sukkot.

His answer was: "I heard the answer on twelve questions from my teachers. But on eighteen questions, I did not hear the answer from my teachers."

R. Yosi b. Yehuda said: "Reverse the words: 'I heard the answer on eighteen questions, but on twelve questions I did not hear the answer.'"

One of those answers was: "Never in my entire life did I utter profane language, and never did I say anything which I did not hear from my teachers." (*Sukkah* 28a)

✿ Profane language
It was said about Rabbi Yohanan ben Zakkai that during his whole life he never uttered profane talk, nor walked four *amot* without studying Torah, or without *tefillin*. No one arrived to the academy before him, nor did he leave the academy before everyone left. He never dozed off in the academy, nor did he think of holy thoughts in a filthy alley. He was always sitting and learning and he opened the door for his students. He always quoted his teacher, and never said it was time to stop learning, except on Erev Pesach and Erev Yom Kippur. (*Sukkah* 28a)

✿ Profit has many friends
R. Papa said: "At the gate of profit, there are many brothers and friends, but at the gate of loss, there are neither brothers nor friends. (*Shabbat* 32a)

Prohibited act done in public or in hiding   בצנעא בפרהסיא
A hidden prohibited act or a forbidden act in public (*Avodah Zarah* 54a)

Prohibiting something not owned
אין אדם אוסר דבר שאינו שלו
One cannot prohibit something that is not his. (*Avodah Zarah* 54b)

Prohibition applied upon another
אין איסור חל על איסור
R. Shimon said: "A prohibition cannot fall upon another prohibition." (*Pesahim* 35b)

Prohibition derived from a positive
לאו הבא מכלל עשה
A negative prohibition derived from a positive commandment. (*Pesahim* 41b; *Yevamot* 54b, 56b, 68a; *Zevahim* 34a; *Hullin* 81a)

Prohibitions neutralized
כל איסורין שבתורה בטלין בשישתין
R. Hiyya b. Abba said in the name of R. Yehoshua b. Levi who said it in the name of Bar Kappara: "All prohibited substances of the Torah are nullified by sixty-fold." (*Hullin* 98a)

Prohibition of meat and milk
לא תבשל גדי בחלב אמו
It was taught in the school of R. Yishmael: The prohibition of cooking a kid in its mother's milk is stated three times in the Torah: one is a prohibition against eating, one a prohibition against deriving benefit from it, and one a prohibition against cooking it. (*Hullin* 115b; *Kiddushin* 57b)

Prohibition is applied on another
איסור חל על איסור
A prohibition may apply on a prohibition already in force. (*Hullin* 113b; *Yevamot* 32a; *Kiddushin* 77b; *Sanhedrin* 81a; *Keritut* 14a; *Meilah* 16a)

Prohibition is not applied on another
אין איסור חל על איסור
A prohibition does not apply on a prohibition already in force. (*Yevamot* 13b, 20a; *Hullin* 113b)

Prohibition of certain cooking
איסור בשול
(*Hullin* 115b)

Prohibition without action
R. Yaakov said: "No lashes are given for a transgression without action." (*Hullin* 83a)

Projecting beams
In Jerusalem, projecting beams were not allowed. (*Bava Kamma* 82b; *Yoma* 23a; *Arachin* 32b)

Promise little
R. Eleazar said: "The righteous promise little and perform much, the wicked promise much and do not perform even little." (*Bava Metzia* 87a; *Nedarim* 21b)

Prompt payment (*Yoma* 86a)

Proof of a deed
Proof of a deed is established by witnesses, according to R. Huna. (*Bava Batra* 154a)

Proper conduct
Proper behavior when visiting the sick (*Shabbat* 12b)

✿ Proper behavior
R. Avira was quoted as saying the following, sometimes in the name of R. Ammi and sometimes in the name of R. Assi. "A man should always eat and drink less than he can afford, clothe himself in accordance to his means, honor his wife and children more than he can afford because they are dependent on him, and he depends on the Creator." (*Hullin* 84b)

✿ Proper behavior
R. Yohanan b. Zakkai had five outstanding students: R. Eliezer b. Horkynos, R. Yehoshua b. Hanania, R. Yosi HaKohen, R. Shimon Netanel, and R. Eleazar b. Arach.

He said to them: "Go forth and investigate to see, what is the most proper way that a person should follow?" R. Eliezer said a good eye; R. Yehoshua said a good friend; R. Yosi said a good neighbor; R. Shimon said one who considers the outcome of his actions, and R. Eleazar said a good heart.

On this, R. Yohanan b. Zakkai remarked, "I prefer the words of R. Eleazar b. Arach, because all your words are included in his words." (*Avot* 2:13)

Proper dress for a scholar
R. Hiyya b. Abba said in the name of R. Yohanan: "It is a disgrace for a Torah scholar to go to the marketplace in patched shoes." (*Shabbat* 114a; *Berachot* 43b)

Proper places for the Temple offerings
The offerings in the Temple had different designated places where a particular offering was to be offered on the altar. (*Zevahim* 47a)

Proper respect for the leaders
It is related in the Talmud that Rabbi Yohanan said: "The following instructions were issued in the days when Rabbi Shimon ben Gamliel was president of the Sanhedrin. Whenever the president of the Sanhedrin enters into the assembly everyone, should stand up, but when the Hacham enters and when the Av Bet Din enters only a limited number of the assembly should rise." (*Horayot* 13b)

✿ Property inspected
R. Shemuel said: "In the matter of inspection, I am as vinegar is to wine compared to my father. My father used to inspect his property twice a day, but I inspect only once a day." (*Hullin* 105a)

Property law
Rabbi Yishmael said: "He that desires to become wise should study property law, because it is like a welling spring, and the best place to study it is to be a student of Rabbi Shimon ben Nanas." (*Bava Batra* 10:8, 175b)

Property owner
A certain woman owned a palm tree on

the property of R. Bibi. Whenever she went to cut it, he showed annoyance. She transferred ownership to him, but only during his lifetime. After he died, it would revert to her. However, he in turn transferred it to his little son. (*Bava Batra* 137b)

Property recognized

A person recognized his property in someone else's possession. (*Bava Kamma* 114b)

Property sold

Someone sold property, but there were complications involved in the sale. (*Bava Kamma* 8b; *Ketubbot* 92a)

Prophecy

The Talmud relates that Rabbi Yohanan said: "Since the Temple was destroyed, prophecy was taken from prophets and given to fools and children."

One day Mar b. R. Ashi was present in a certain place in Mehuza, when he overheard a well-known town-idiot exclaim: "The man who signs his name Tavyomi is to be elected as head of the academy in Mata Mehasya."

Mar said to himself, *It must be my time has come*. He rushed to Mata Mehasya. When he arrived, he found that the rabbis of the academy were in favor of electing Rabbi Aha Me-Difti. Mar invited the rabbis to see him and he gave them a discourse, expounding on the Torah and Halachah. They changed their mind and elected him as head of the academy. (*Bava Batra* 12b)

Prophecy

The Talmud states: "Since the day the Temple was destroyed, prophecy has been taken from the prophets and given to the wise." (*Bava Batra* 12a)

Prophecy

R. Shemuel HaKatan prophesied the persecutions that were to follow.

Unfortunately, they all came true. He was eulogized by the leading rabbis of his time, including Rabbi Gamliel. (*Sanhedrin* 11a)

Prophecy

All the prophets looked through dimmed glass, but Moshe looked through a clear glass. (*Yevamot* 49b)

Prophetic inspiration

Our rabbis taught; since the death of the last Prophets – Haggai, Zechariah, and Malachi – the prophetic inspiration departed from Israel, but they could still hear a Bat Kol making prophesies. Once when the rabbis met in the upper chamber of Gurya's house in Jericho, a Bat Kol was heard saying: "There is one amongst you who is worthy that the Shechina should rest on him." The rabbis looked around, and they all looked at R. Hillel the Elder. (*Sanhedrin* 11a)

Prophets, its authors

Who are the authors of the Prophets: Moshe wrote the Torah, *Parshat Bilam* and Iyov. Yehoshua authored the book called Yehoshua; Shemuel wrote the book named after him, also Shoftim and Ruth. David wrote the book of Tehillim. Yirmiyahu wrote the book which bears his name, Melachim, and Kinot. Hezkiya and his aids wrote Yeshaya, Mishlei, Shir HaShirim, and Kohelet. The men of the Great Assembly wrote Yehezkel, the Twelve Minor Prophets, Daniel, and Esther. Ezra wrote the book that bears his name and Divrei Hayamim. Others name different authors. (*Bava Batra* 14a, 15a)

Prophets exaggerate sometimes

R. Ammi said: "The Prophets spoke sometime in exaggerated terms." (*Hullin* 90b)

Prophets books' order

Our rabbis taught: The order of the books

of the Prophets is Yehoshua, Shoftim, Shemuel, Melachim, Yirmiyahu, Yehezkel, Yeshaya, and the other Twelve Prophets. Others would have it in this order: Yeshaya, Yirmiyahu and Yehezkel. The order of the Ketuvim is Ruth, Tehillim, Iyov, Mishlei, Kohelet, Shir HaShirim, Kinot, Daniel, Esther, Ezra, and Divrei Hayamim. Others disagree and have a different order. (*Bava Batra* 14b)

Prosbul

The Prosbul is a Halachic device to facilitate the borrowing and lending of money to the poor. Biblical law cancels all debts in the seventh year. This law became a hardship, because the rich refused to lend money to the poor. Hillel the Elder created the Prosbul, whereby the debt was paid to the court. (*Gittin* 34b, 36a; *Bava Kamma* 12a)

Prosbul

Rabbi Hillel[205] is quoted teaching that a Prosbul has to be made a certain way. (*Gittin* 37a; *Bava Kamma* 36b)

Proselyte

Contract dealings with a proselyte (*Bava Kamma* 49b)

Proselyte

If a proselyte accepts the teachings of the Torah except one. (*Bechorot* 30b)

Proselyte settler   גר תושב

A gentile who renounces idolatry (*Avodah Zarah* 64b, 65a)

📖 Proselyte's inheritance

The proselyte Issur had 12,000 *zuz* deposited for safekeeping with Rava, but the question arose whether Issur's son Mari was entitled to it. The problem was that

when Mari was conceived, Issur was still not Jewish, but became Jewish before Mari was born. R. Ika b. R. Ammi suggested that Issur should declare that the money belongs to R. Mari. That is how the matter was solved by Issur declaring that the money belongs to his son Mari. (*Bava Batra* 149a)

Proselytes

A proselyte[206] circumcised without *mikveh* immersion (*Yevamot* 46a; *Avodah Zarah* 59a)

Protecting the property of others above own (*Berachot* 18b)

Proving the case falls on claimant
המוציא מחבירו עליו הראיה

The onus of proving the case falls on claimant; he who claims from the other has to produce proof. (*Bava Kamma* 35b, 46a; *Bava Metzia* 2b; *Hullin* 134a)

Psalms at the Temple

It has been taught that R. Yehuda said in the name of R. Akiva: "On the first day of the week, they chanted to Psalm 24 – 'God is the owner of the earth.'

"On the second day of the week, they sang to Psalm 48 – 'Great is the Lord and highly to be praised.'

"On the third day of the week, they chanted to Psalm 82 – 'God stands in the congregation of God.'

"On the fourth day of the week, they sang to Psalm 94 – 'O Lord, to whom vengeance belongs.'

"On the fifth day of the week, they chanted to Psalm 81 – Sing aloud to God who is our strength.'

"On the sixth day of the week, they sang to Psalm 93 – 'The Lord reigns, He is clothed in majesty.'

"On Shabbat, they chanted to Psalm 92

---

205. Rashi comments on the same page that this Rabbi Hillel was an Amora.

206. See entry, Conversion.

– 'A song for the day of Shabbat.'" (*Rosh Hashana* 31a)

Public announcements for lost documents

The Talmud relates a story: Rabbi Nahman said: "My father was a scribe for the court of Rabbi Shemuel. When I was about six or seven years old, I remember that they used to make an announcement in public that any deed document found on the street should be returned to its owners." (*Bava Metzia* 16b)

Public domain

When one leaves a pitcher on public property which was broken by another person (*Bava Kamma* 27a)

Public road

A public road which traverses a private field (*Bava Batra* 99b)

Public roads

What is considered a public road: A highway, a great open space, open alleys, and the desert (*Shabbat* 6b)

Public streets

Throwing stones into public streets[207] (*Bava Kamma* 29b, 50b)

Public transgressions

R. Yaakov said in the name of R. Yohanan: "A transgression that is to be called a public transgression must have a minimum of ten people present." (*Sanhedrin* 74b)

Publicizing found objects

Which found objects must be publicized in public places? (*Bava Metzia* 21a)

Publicizing the miracle of Chanukah
פרסומי ניסא

(*Shabbat* 23b; *Berachot* 14a)

Pumbedita

Choosing a leader for the adademy of Pumbedita

The Talmud relates that they were about to choose a leader for the yeshiva in Pumbedita – the choice was between Rabbah and R. Yosef. The elders of Pumbedita sent a query to Eretz Yisrael asking which one to choose: "One is 'Sinai' – R. Yosef, and one is an 'up-rooter of mountains' – Rabbah."[208]

The answer came from Eretz Yisrael that Sinai is preferred, because everyone is in need of the knowledge of Sinai. However, R. Yosef declined, because the astrologers told him that he would serve as head of the yeshiva for only two years. Rabbah took the position and he served for twenty-two years. After that R. Yosef served for two and a half years. During the whole term of Rabbah as head of the academy, R. Yosef did not summon anyone to his house, but went to the person himself. (*Berachot* 64a; *Horayot* 14a)

Pumbedita

R. Giddal said in the name of Rav: "If an inhabitant of Narash kisses you, then count your teeth. If an inhabitant of Nehar Pekod accompanies you, it is because of the fine garments he sees on you. If an inhabitant of Pumbedita accompanies you, then change your quarters. (*Hullin* 127a)

Pumbedita; Academy   פומבדיתא

Pumbedita is a town in Babylonia,

---

207. See story under, Hasid's rebuke.

208. Resh Lakish explained his point of view with such excitement, as if he were "uprooting mountains" – *oker harim*.

In this case, "Sinai" means a rabbi who has at his command and in his memory a vast amount of laws given at Sinai.

northwest of Baghdad. It is situated on the bank of the Euphrates River, near the canal Shunya-Shumvatha, and near the canal Papa. According to some sources, the town had already a Jewish settlement in the time of the Second Temple. In 259 CE, Nehardea and its academy were destroyed by Papa ben Nasser, the Commander in Chief of Palmyra. The scholars from Nehardea fled and established an academy in Pumbedita under the leadership of Rabbi Yehuda b. Yehezkel. This academy was the central religious authority for Babylonian Jewry for many centuries.

The following were the heads of the academy in Pumbedita:

Yehuda bar Yehezkel, 3rd century CE;
Rabbah, 3rd – 4th centuries CE;
Yosef b. Hiyya, 3rd – 4th centuries CE;
Abbaye, 3rd – 4th centuries CE;
Bibi bar Abbaye, 4th century CE;
Hama, 4th century CE;
Dimi of Nehardea, 4th century CE;
Rafram b. Papa, 4th – 5th centuries CE;
Rehumei II, 5th century CE. (*Gittin* 60b; *Yoma* 77b; *Bava Kamma* 12a; *Bava Metzia* 18b)

Pum Nahara; Academy   פום נהרא
R. Kahana escorted R. Shimi b. Ashi from Pum Nahara to Bei Tzenitha of Babylonia. When they arrived, he asked him: "Do people really say that these palm trees are from the time of Adam?"

R. Kahana V was the Head of the academy in Pum Nahara. He lived in the 4th century CE. (*Yevamot* 16b; *Hullin* 95b; *Berachot* 31a)

Punctillious people   ותיקין
(*Berachot* 9b)

✿ Punishment for liars
A saying in the Talmud is attributed to Rabbi Hiyya: "Such is the punishment of a liar, that even when he tells the truth, he is not believed." (*Sanhedrin* 89b)

Punishment for Shabbat violation
(*Sanhedrin* 78b)

Punishment in the world
R. Shemuel b. Nahmeni said in the name of R. Yonatan: "Punishment comes to the world only when there are wicked people in the world, and it always begins with the righteous." (*Bava Kamma* 60a)

✿ Purim charity money mixed-up
Our rabbis taught: When Rabbi Yosi b. Kisma was ill, R. Hanania b. Teradion went to visit him. R. Yosi said to him:

"Don't you know that Heaven ordained that the Romans would destroy our Temple and rule over us? I heard that you are defying them and teach Torah in public."

R. Hanania asked R. Yosi:

"How do I stand in the World to Come?"

"Is there any particular act you are concerned about?"

"Yes, once I mistakenly mixed up the Purim money with the ordinary charity." Rabbi Yosi replied: "I wish your portion would be my portion."[209] (*Avodah Zarah* 18a)

Purim Torah reading (*Megillah* 30b)

Purity   סדר טהרות
The Tractate *Taharot* contains laws concerning purity and impurity.

Purse of charity money
A purse of money was brought to Pumbedita. R. Yosef gave it to a person in town to guard it. However, the person was negligent, and it was stolen. R. Yosef held the person liable. (*Bava Kamma* 93a)

Purse given to a gentile on Friday
One of the enactments on that day was that a traveler should give his purse to a

---

209. See entry, Burned with his Torah together.

Gentile when it gets dark Friday evening (*Shabbat* 17b; 153a)

Putting down the head in prayer (*Bava Metzia* 59a, 59b)

Q

Qualification for kosher slaughtering
Who is qualified to be a *shohet*? (*Hullin* 2a)

Qualified person to read Megillah
Who is qualified to read the *Megillah*? (*Megillah* 19b)

Quality of mankind receding
R. Eliezer the Great said: "From the day the Temple was destroyed, the Sages began to be like school-teachers, school-teachers like synagogue attendants, synagogue attendants like common people, and the common people became more debased. There was none to ask, none to inquire. Who can we rely upon? We can rely only upon our Father in Heaven.

"Just before the arrival of Mashiach insolence will increase, honor will be scarce. The vine will yield its fruit abundantly, but wine will be dear. The government will adopt a new religion and no one will disapprove.

"The meeting places will be used for immorality. Galilee will be destroyed, Gablan desolated, and the dwellers on the frontier will go begging from place to place without anyone taking pity on them.

"The wisdom of the scholars will degenerate, fearers of sin will be despised, and truth will be lacking. Youth will put old men to shame, the old will stand up in the presence of the young, a son will revile his father, and a daughter will rebel against her mother, a daughter-in-law against her mother-in-law.

"The members of one's household will be the enemies of the house.

"That generation will have a face of a dog; a son will not be ashamed before his father. Therefore, on whom can we rely? We can rely only upon our Father in Heaven." (*Sotah* 49a–b)

Quee   כוי
A strange animal; the rabbis differ on what it is.

R. Yehuda said: "A *quee* is a creature of its own and not a hybrid of other two animals." (*Hullin* 79b, 80a)

Quee herds
R. Shimon b. Gamliel said: "The *quee* is a species of cattle and the house of Doshai used to breed herds and herds of them." (*Hullin* 80a)

Queen Shabbat
Rabbi Hanina used to dress up in the finest garments on Friday evening and call out: "Let's go out and welcome the Queen Shabbat." (*Shabbat* 119a)

Queen Shal-Zion
Rav Yehuda said in Rav's name. Once Queen Shal-Zion[210] made a banquet for her son, and all her utensils became defiled. She ordered[211] all her golden dishes to be melted down and to have new ones made of the molten gold. (*Shabbat* 16b)

Question
Rabbah bar b. Hana put a question to R. Yohanan. However, R. Yohanan went first to the washroom, washed his hands, put on *tefillin*, made a benediction, and only then did he give him an answer. (*Bava Kamma* 17a)

---

210. Salome Alexandra.
211. Probably on the advice of her brother, R. Shimon b. Shetah.

Question asked by R. Akiva
R. Akiva asked a question in the meat-market of Emmaus from R. Gamliel and R. Yehoshua. (*Hullin* 91b)

Question at inappropriate time
Rav asked a question from Rebbe. Afterwards, R. Hiyya said to Rav: "Have I not told you that when Rebbe is engaged in one tractate, you must not ask him a question about another subject?" (*Shabbat* 3b)

Question before the rabbis
A student asked Rabbi Gamliel and Rabbi Yehoshua: "Is the *Maariv* service obligatory or not?" The student asking the question was Rabbi Shimon b. Yohai (*Berachot* 28a)

Question to R. Hanina
A man once came to ask R. Hanina a halachic question while R. Yehuda b. Zevina was sitting at the doorstep. (*Hullin* 99b)

Questions are asked about Pesach
שואלין ודורשין בהלכות הפסח
Questions are asked and lectures are given on the laws of Pesach. (*Pesahim* 6a)

Quoting his mother
Abbaye quoted his mother about healing ailments, she was his step-mother. (*Avodah Zarah* 28b)

Quoting name carefully
R. Nahman b. Yitzhak was very careful with properly quoting the names of the rabbis. One of the rabbis was quoting R. Giddal Deman Naresh. Said R. Nahman b. Yitzhak: "I call him neither Giddal b. Menashye nor Giddal b. Minyoni, but simply Giddal." (*Pesahim* 107a)

✿ Quoting others by name
R. Eleazar said in the name of R. Hanina: "Whoever quotes another person by name brings Redemption to the world." (*Megillah* 15a; *Hullin* 104b)

R

Rabbah   רבה
Amora from Babylonia
Head of academy in Pumbedita
3rd – 4th centuries CE (*Rosh Hashana* 18a)

📖 Rabbah
Rabbah had to flee; the authorities wanted to arrest him
R. Kahana said: "R. Hama, the son of the daughter of Hassa, told me that Rabbah b. Nahmeni died of fear from persecution. An informer told the authorities that Rabbah keeps 12,000 Israelites from paying the poll tax two months every year. It was the custom for many Israelites to study two months every year in the academy. A royal officer was sent to arrest him, but could not find him. Rabbah fled from Pumbedita to Acra, from Acra to Agama, from Agama to Sahin, from Sahin to Zarifa, from Zarifa to Eina Damim, and then back to Pumbedita. There the officer found him. He locked him up in a chamber, but Rabbah managed to escape and fled to Agama where he died. His students Abbaye and Rava and the entire academy went to attend to his body, but they could not find it. When they finally found his body, they mourned for him for seven days." (*Bava Metzia* 86a)

Rabbah and Yosef
Rabbah was a keen dialectician who debated as long as it took to arrive at the truth, and R. Yosef was a well-read scholar. (*Horayot* 14a)

Rabbah bar Avuha   רבה בר אבוה
Amora from Babylonia

Head of the academy in Mehuza
3rd century CE (*Shabbat* 129b)

Rabbah bar bar Hana רבה בר בר חנה
Amora from Babylonia
3rd century CE (*Pesahim* 51a)

Rabbah bar Hana רבה בר חנה
Amora from Babylonia
3rd century CE (*Sanhedrin* 5a)

Rabbah bar Huna רבה בר הונא
Amora from Babylonia
Head of academy in Sura
3rd – 4th centuries CE (*Bava Batra* 136b; *Eruvin* 49a)

Rabbah bar Shila רבה בר שילא
Amora from Babylonia
3rd – 4th centuries CE (*Shabbat* 81a)

Rabbi Akavia
R. Akavia ben Mehalalel testified about four matters. (*Eduyot* 7b)

Rabbi and businessman
In addition to being a great scholar, Rabbah b. Hana was also a wine merchant and a businessman. (*Bava Metzia* 83a)

📖 **Rabbi and farmer**
R. Assi was a well-to-do person, who inspected his property daily. The Talmud relates that one day when Rabbi Assi was inspecting his property, he noticed a pipe had burst and was flooding his property. He took off his coat, rolled it up and plugged the pipe with it. He then called out loudly, and people came to help him stop the flood. (*Hullin* 105a)

Rabbi was blinded
In his old age
R. Yosef was very ill most of his life. In his later years, he became blind. He was so ill that he forgot a lot of his learning. Abbaye,

his student, had to relearn with him everything he had forgotten. (*Nedarim* 41a)

Rabbi Eliezer lists
Two leniencies of R. Shammai were listed by R. Eliezer. (*Eduyot* 7a)

Rabbi Yehuda lists
Six leniencies of R. Shammai were listed by R. Yehuda. (*Eduyot* 7a)

Rabbi Yishmael lists
Three leniencies of R. Shammai were listed by R. Yishmael. (*Eduyot* 7b)

Rabbi Yosi lists
Six leniencies of R. Shammai were listed by R. Yosi. (*Eduyot* 7a)

Rabbinai
Rabbi Hiyya had a brother. His name was Rabbinai. (*Berachot* 21b)

Rabbinic Mitzvot
Mitzvot instituted by the rabbis also require the blessing of "You commanded us." Where did Hashem command us? R. Avia and R. Nehemia give sources in the Torah. (*Shabbat* 23a)

Rabbinical teachings
Greater stringency applies to rabbinical teachings than to the teachings of the Torah. (*Sanhedrin* 88b)

Rabbis are familiar in the sciences
"You possess so much knowledge," said Rabbi Gamliel to R. Yehoshua and yet you travel on board a ship."
   "Don't marvel at me, rather be surprised at two of your students who live on land, like Rabbi Eleazar Hisma and Rabbi Yohanan ben Gudgeda,[212] who can calculate how many drops of water there are in the

---

212. Perhaps it was R. Yohanan b. Nuri.

sea, and yet they have neither bread to eat nor clothing to put on."

Rabbi Gamliel decided to appoint them as supervisors. When he landed, he sent for them to offer them those positions, but they did not show up. They were reluctant to accept on account of their humility.

But Rabbi Gamliel sent for them again and told them: "Do you imagine that I offer you rulership? It is servitude that I offer you." (*Horayot* 10a)

Rabbis differ

Dispute[213] developed between R. Shimon b. Gamliel, R. Meir, and R. Nathan. (*Horayot* 13b)

▢✿ Rabbis' field

Two rabbis negotiated to buy the same field; each rabbi was unaware of the other

On one occasion, Rabbi Giddal was negotiating to buy a certain field, but in the meantime R. Abba bought the field. R. Giddal was unhappy and complained to R. Zera who in turn took the complaint to R. Yitzhak Nepaha, who lived in another town.

R. Zera said to R. Giddal: "Wait until he comes for the festival." When R. Yitzhak came and he was presented with the case, he asked R. Abba: "If a poor man wants to buy a cake and examines it, but in the meantime another man comes and takes it away from him and buys it, what then?"

"He is called a wicked man," replied R. Abba.

"Then why did you buy the field that R. Giddal wanted to buy?"

"I did not know that he was negotiating for it."

R. Yitzhak suggested that now that he does know, he should let him have it. "I cannot sell it to him, because it is the first

field I ever bought, and it is not a good omen to sell it, but if he wants it as a gift, he can have it."

But R. Giddal refused to accept it as a gift, and R. Abba did not want it, because R. Giddal negotiated for it. And so no one took possession of the field, and it was called "the Rabbis' field." (*Kiddushin* 59a)

Rabbis of the Talmud referred to by another designation

When it is mentioned in the Talmud that "it was argued before the Sages," it refers to R. Levi arguing before Rebbe.

When it is mentioned that "it was discussed before the Sages," it refers to R. Shimon b. Azzai, R. Shimon b. Zoma, Hanan the Egyptian, and Hanania b. Hachinai. R. Nahman b. Yitzhak adds also the name of R. Shimon HaTimni.

When it is stated "our rabbis in Babylon," it refers to Rav and Shemuel.

When it is stated "as our rabbis in Eretz Yisrael," it refers to R. Abba.

"The judges in exile" refers to R. Karna.

"The judges in Eretz Yisrael" refers to R. Ammi and R. Assi.

"The judges of Pumbedita" refers to R. Papa b. Shemuel.

"The judges of Nehardea" refers to R. Adda b. Minyomi.

"The Elders of Sura" refers to R. Huna and R. Hisda.

"The Elders of Pumbedita" refers to R. Yehuda and R. Aina.

"The keen intellects of Pumbedita" refers to Efa and Avimi b. Rehavah.

"The Amoraim of Pumbedita" refers to Rabbah and R. Yosef.

"The Amoraim of Nehardea" refers to R. Hama.

"Those of Neharbelai taught" refers to Rammi b. Beribi.

"It was said in the school of Rav" refers to R. Huna or R. Hamnuna.

---

213. See story under, Sanhedrin Decorum.

"It was said in the West" refers to R. Yirmiyahu. (*Sanhedrin* 17b; *Shevuot* 47a; *Meillah* 9b; *Menuhot* 80b)

Rabbis to be followed

Follow your rabbi to his academy: R. Eliezer to Lydda, R. Yohanan b. Zakkai to Beror Chayil, R. Yehoshua to Peki'in, R. Gamliel to Yavne, R. Akiva to Bene Berak, R. Matya to Rome, R. Hanania b. Teradion to Sichnin, R. Yosi b. Halafta to Sepphoris, R. Yehuda b. Betera to Nisibis, R. Hanina to Exile, and R. Yehuda HaNasi to Bet Shearim. (*Sanhedrin* 32b)

Rachel gave signals to Leah

Rachel told Yaakov that her father is a trickster. She warned him that he would fool him by not giving her to him as a wife. Therefore, Yaakov gave Rachel secret signals which she would have to know at night in the dark. But when Rachel saw that Lavan placed Leah in her stead to be Yaakov's wife, Rachel did not want to embarrass her sister, and she passed on to her the secret signals. (*Megillah* 13b; *Bava Batra* 123a)

▢ Rachel
Wife of Rabbi Akiva
Rachel[214] was the wife of R. Akiva and the daughter of Ben Kalba Savua, who was one of the wealthiest men in Jerusalem. (*Nedarim* 50a; *Ketubbot* 62b, 63a)

Rachish bar Papa
Amora and student of Rav (*Hullin* 55a)

Rafram bar Papa   רפרם בר פפא
Amora from Babylonia
Head of the academy in Pumbedita
4th – 5th centuries CE (*Yoma* 78a)

---

214. See also entry, Akiva.

▢ Rage can lead to ugly consequences
Rabbi Kahana had to flee Babylonia, because of an incident. A man was brought before Rav; he wanted to denounce another Jew to the Persian authorities and to show them where the Jew was hiding his straw. Rav ordered the man not to show it, but the man insisted: "I will show it." Rabbi Kahana was present during this incident and he became enraged that this man is defying Rav. In the argument, R. Kahana accidentally killed the man. Rav advised R. Kahana to move to Eretz Yisrael and to study at Rabbi Yohanan, but he also made him promise that for seven years he would not give R. Yohanan a hard time with his sharp questions.

When R. Kahana arrived, he found Resh Lakish with the young rabbis going over the lecture. He pointed out to them the difficult points in the lecture and he gave some of the answers. Resh Lakish went before R. Yohanan and told him.

"A lion has come up from Babylonia, be well prepared for tomorrow's lecture." The next day R. Kahana was seated in the first row, because they were thinking that he must be a scholar. He kept quiet for a long while as he had promised Rav. Consequently, they demoted him and seated him in the seventh row.

R. Yohanan said to Resh Lakish: "The lion turns out to be a fox."

Rabbi Kahana prayed that the seventh row insult should be considered like the seven years he had promised.

The next day when Rabbi Yohanan lectured, Rabbi Kahana threw out one question after another, quoting sources in contradiction. They seated him again in the first row. (*Bava Kamma* 117a)

Railing
Building a railing on one's roof to guard against accidents (*Bava Batra* 6b)

Rain and drawn water for a mikveh
When rain and drawn water were mingled in a *mikveh* (*Mikvaot* 4:4)

📖 Rain or the lack of it
Prayers for rain
Once there was an urgent need for rain, and the rabbis sent two scholars to ask Rabbi Abba Hilkiah to pray for rain. When they got to his house, they didn't find him at home. They went after him to the fields where they found him hoeing the earth. They greeted him, but he took no notice. At the end of the day, he gathered some wood and put it on his shoulder to go home. Throughout his journey he walked barefoot, but when he reached a stream, he put on his shoes. When he reached the city, his wife came out to meet him, bedecked with jewels. He sat down to eat, but did not offer the scholars to eat. He shared his meal with his children, giving one portion to the older child, and two portions to the younger child. When he finished his meal, he said to his wife: "I know the scholars have come on account of rain. Let's go up on the roof and pray." They went up on the roof; he stood in one corner and she in another. At first, clouds appeared in the corner where she stood. When he came down he said to the scholars: "Why have you come to me?"

They replied, "The rabbis sent us to ask you to pray for rain."

He said to them: "Blessed is God that you are no longer dependent on me to pray for rain."

But they answered him: "We know that the rain has come on account of your prayers, but tell us the meaning of your mysterious behavior? Why did you pretend not to notice us when we greeted you first?"

He answered: "I was a paid laborer. I could not steal my employer's time to greet you."

"Why did you walk barefoot on the road and put on your shoes when you entered the stream?"

"Because I could see what was on the road, but could not see what was in the water."

"Why did your wife come out bedecked with jewels to greet you?"

"She did it in order that I should not set my eyes on any other woman."

"Why didn't you ask us to join you in the meal?"

"I could not ask you, because there was not enough food to feed all of us."

"Why did you give only one portion to your older son and two portions to the younger?"

"I did that, because one stays at home and the other is away in the synagogue."

"Why did the clouds appear first in the corner where your wife prayed?"

"Her prayers were answered first, because my wife stays home and feeds the poor, which food they can enjoy immediately. I give them money, which they can't enjoy immediately." (*Taanit* 23b)

📖 Rain or the lack of it
It once happened that the greater part of the month of Adar passed by without rain, and the people were concerned that there would be no grain to harvest. They sent word to R. Honi[215] to pray for rain. (*Taanit* 23a)

Rain while sitting in the Sukkah
When can one leave the *sukkah* if it starts raining (*Sukkah* 28b)

Rami bar Hama   רמי בר חמא
Amora from Babylonia
4th century CE (*Ketubbot* 56b, 57a)

---

215. See entry, Honi HaMaagel.

Rami b. Tamri visits Sura

Rami b. Tamri, also known as Rami b. Dikuli from Pumbedita, once happened to be in Sura. Many of the things that were forbidden, he violated and did not conform to the laws adopted in Sura. He was brought before R. Hisda and his answer for every question was that in his town of Pumbedita, R. Yehuda ruled differently. R. Hisda asked him: "Don't you accept the rule that when a person visits a town, he must adopt the restrictions of the town he has left and also the restrictions of the town he has entered?" (*Hullin* 110a)

Ransom money

Man carrying money to redeem captives was robbed

The Talmud relates that a certain man was traveling to redeem some captives. He had the ransom money in a purse, but he was attacked by robbers. In order to save himself, he handed over the money to the robbers and they let him go. On his return, he was summoned before Rabbah who found him not guilty of negligence.

Abbaye said to Rabbah: "Didn't this man rescue himself with another man's money?"

Rabbah replied: "There could hardly be a case of redeeming captives more urgent than this." (*Bava Kamma* 117b)

Rasha   רשע

The rabbis taught: One who invests the money of orphans at risk to the orphans, but no risk to himself is called a wicked man. One who invests the money of orphans so that they will receive profits only, but will not share in the losses, is called a pious man. One who invests to share both in profits and losses is an average person. (*Bava Metzia* 70a)

Rational person   דבר שיש בו דעת לישאל

A being that is rational, has a mind of his own, and can be interrogated. (*Sotah* 28b; *Pesahim* 19b)

Rationed water for R. Akiva spilled

Rabbi Yehoshua HaGarsi was a student of Rabbi Akiva and a very devoted and loyal friend. He brought him food and water daily.

One day, the prison keeper said to him, "Your water[216] today is much too much, perhaps you want to use it to undermine the prison?"

The prison keeper spilled out half of it, and he let R. Yehoshua take the rest inside. (*Eruvin* 21b)

Rav   רב

Amora from Babylonia
Founder, head of the Academy in Sura
3rd century CE (*Sanhedrin* 5a)

Rav   רב

Rav was probably the first Amora, but he was also considered to be a Tanna. (*Ketubbot* 8a; *Eruvin* 50b)

Rav as a young boy

On one occasion, when Rav was still very young, he and R. Hiyya were having dinner at Rabbi Yehuda HaNasi's table. Rabbi said to Rav: "Get up and wash your hands." R. Hiyya saw that Rav was trembling. He said to him: "Son of Princes, he is telling you to prepare yourself to lead in the blessings after the meal." (*Berachot* 43a)

Rav bar Sheva   רב בר שבא

Amora from Babylonia
4th century CE (*Eruvin* 33b)

Rav turned his face away

Rav turned his face away when he heard Shemuel's ruling. (*Eruvin* 94a)

---

216. See entry, Akiva's water spilled.

📖 Rav travels to Babylonia

Shemuel and Karna were sitting by the bank of the Nahar Malka. They saw the water rising and becoming discolored. Shemuel said to Karna: "A great man is arriving from Eretz Yisrael, who suffers from stomach trouble. Go and smell his bottle."

The man who arrived was Rav. Karna went and asked him several tricky questions to test his knowledge. Subsequently, Shemuel took him into his house and gave him barley bread, fish and strong liquor, but did not show him where the outhouse was. (*Shabbat* 108a)

📖 Rav visits Tatelfush

Rav once visited the town of Tatelfush where he overheard a woman asking her neighbor: "How much milk is required to cook a *riva* cut of meat?"

Rav was astonished: *Don't they know that meat cooked in milk is forbidden?* He therefore stayed there for some time to teach them. (*Hullin* 110a)

📖 Rav was unknown

R. Hiyya b. Yosef was quoting Rav about a Halachah in front of R. Yohanan and Resh Lakish. Resh Lakish retorted: "Who is this Rav? I do not know him."

R. Yohanan answered: "Don't you remember a student who attended lectures at R. Yehuda HaNasi and R. Hiyya? That student sat before his teachers and I remained standing. He excelled in everything." Immediately Resh Lakish remembered. (*Hullin* 54a)

Rav's dictum

R. Hisda offered two priestly gifts of oxen to anyone who would tell him a new dictum by Rav. (*Shabbat* 10b)

📖 Rav's humility

R. Huna, who was a student of Rav, was a very wealthy man, but when he was still a student of Rav he was very poor. Once he came dressed with a string around his waist. When Rav saw him, he said to him: "What is the meaning of this?" He replied: "I had no money to buy wine for *Kiddush* so I pledged my silk *gartel* to buy wine." Rav blessed him: "May it be the will of Heaven that you may one day be smothered in robes of silk." On the day when Rabbah the son of R. Huna got married, R. Huna, who was a short man, was lying on a bed. His daughters were selecting silk dresses and throwing the dresses on the bed without noticing that he was lying there. They kept on throwing silk dresses until he was smothered in silk. When Rav heard this, he remarked: "When I blessed you, why didn't you say 'the same to you, my Rebbe?'" (*Megillah* 27b)

Rava   רבא
Amora from Babylonia
Founder and head of the Academy at Mehuza (Mahoza)
3rd – 4th centuries CE (*Berachot* 48a)

Rava bar Mathna   רבא בר מתנא
Amora from Babylonia
3rd – 4th centuries CE (*Pesahim* 34a)

Rava bar Mehasya   רבא בר מחסיא
Amora from Babylonia
3rd – 4th centuries CE (*Shabbat* 10b)

Rava bar Zimuna   רבא בר זימונא
(Abba bar Zemina)
Amora from Eretz Yisrael
4th century CE (*Shabbat* 112b)

Rava Me-Barnish   רבא מברניש
Amora from Babylonia
4th – 5th centuries CE (*Shabbat* 28a)

Rava married R. Hisda's daughter
When she was still a child, the daughter of

R. Hisda was sitting on her father's lap. In front of R. Hisda, were his two students, Rava and Rami b. Hama. R. Hisda asked the little child: "Which one do you like?"

She replied: "I like both of them."

On this, Rava said: "Let me be the second." (*Bava Batra* 12b)

Rava was wealthy

Rava, the head of the academy in Mehuza, became a wealthy person. He owned fields and vineyards, and traded in wine. (*Bava Metzia* 73a)

Ravin bar Adda   רבין בר אדא

Amora from Babylonia

3rd century CE (*Berachot* 6b)

Ravina I   רבינא

Amora from Babylonia

4th – 5th centuries CE (*Berachot* 20b)

Ravina II   רבינא

Amora from Babylonia

Head of the academy in Sura

5th century CE (*Berachot* 39b)

Ravina's children

Ravina had a son. The Talmud relates that Ravina was engaged in preparations for his son's wedding at the house of R. Hanina.

He also had a daughter, as mentioned in the Talmud. Ravina was writing a large amount for his daughter's dowry. (*Niddah* 66a; *Bava Metzia* 104b)

Recital in any language

The following readings may be recited in any language: The reading of the *sotah*, the reading for the tithing, the reading of the *Shema*, the prayers of the day, the blessing after a meal, the oath of witnesses, and the oath concerning a deposit. (*Sotah* 32a)

Redemption of captives

Captives should not be redeemed for excessive amounts of money to prevent abuses. It would whet the appetite of the captors to take more captives. (*Gittin* 45a)

Reading of Torah on Mondays and Thursdays

Ezra ordained that the Torah should be read during *Shacharit* services on Mondays and Thursdays. (*Bava Kamma* 82a)

Real estate transactions (*Bava Kamma* 8b; *Ketubbot* 92a)

Real estate property

We have learned that real estate property is acquired by money, or a deed, or *hazaka*. (*Bava Batra* 86a)

Rebbe and R. Hiyya

R. Yehuda b. Kenusa was walking ahead of Rebbe and R. Hiyya; he was their student. (*Bava Kamma* 81b)

Rebellious Elder   זקן ממרא

An elder rebelling against the ruling of the Bet Din (*Sanhedrin* 86b)

Rebellious son   בן סורר ומורה

A stubborn and rebellious son

R. Shimon said: "It never happened and will never happen. Why did the Torah write it, so that one studies it and receives a reward. At what age can a child become a rebellious son?" (*Sanhedrin* 68b, 71a, 89a)

📖 Rebuilt unsafe walls

When R. Huna saw walls that were unsafe, he would order them to be demolished, and if the owner could not afford to rebuild them, he would rebuild them at his own expense. (*Taanit* 20b)

✿ Receive everyone cheerfully

One of R. Shammai's dictums was: "Make

the study of Torah a steady habit, say little and do much, and receive every person with a cheerful countenance." (*Avot* 1:15)

Recitations in the Temple
The superintendent said to the Kohanim: "Recite one blessing," and they recited. Then they read the Ten Commandments, the *Shema* and "*Ve-haya im shamoa.*" Next, they recited three benedictions: *Emet v'yatziv*, the *Avodah* Blessing, and the Priestly Blessing. (*Tamid* 32b)

✿ Recused himself as judge
Ameimar, as a judge, was in the middle of a trial when a bird flew down and landed on his head. A man approached and removed the bird. "What is your business here?" asked Ameimar.

"I have a lawsuit going on," replied the man.

"In that case, I am disqualified to act as a judge." (*Ketubbot* 105b)

Red heifer hair color
Different color hairs found in the red heifer (*Parah* 2:5; *Avodah Zarah* 24a)

Redactors of the Mishna
R. Yehuda HaNasi and R. Nathan concluded the Mishna; R. Ashi and Ravina concluded the *Horaah*. (Gemara). (*Bava Metzia* 86a)

📖 Redeeming captives
Miracles are happening
Once R. Pinhas ben Yair was on his way to redeem captives. When he arrived at the Ginnai River, he said: "O river, part your waters so I may pass."

The river replied: "You are about to do the commandments of God, and I, too, am doing the will of God. You may or may not succeed in accomplishing your purpose. I am sure of accomplishing my purpose."

Rabbi Pinhas replied: "If you do not

divide yourself, I will decree that no water ever flow again in your bed." Thereupon, the river parted.

In another case, there was a certain man who was carrying wheat for Pesach. R. Pinhas asked the river to divide itself for he is engaged in a mitzvah, and the river obeyed and parted.

When an Arab joined them on the journey, R. Pinhas again asked the river to part, so that he would not say: "This is the treatment of Jews for a fellow traveler." The river parted.

In another case, R. Pinhas arrived at an inn, where they put food in front of his ass, but the ass would not eat. They asked R. Pinhas why his ass would not eat. He told them: "Perhaps it was not tithed." They immediately tithed the grain and the ass ate it. (*Hullin* 7a)

✿ Redeeming captives   פדיון שבוים
The rabbis had a maxim that the redemption of captives is a religious duty of very great importance. (*Bava Batra* 8b)

Redemption
Redeeming captives[217] and risking arrest (*Avodah Zarah* 18a)

Redemption after repenting
R. Eliezer said: "If Israel will repent, they will be redeemed." (*Sanhedrin* 97b)

Redemption immediately
R. Shimon b. Yohai said: "If Israel would keep two Shabbatot according to the laws, they would be redeemed immediately." (*Shabbat* 118b)

Redemption in time to come
We have learned that R. Eliezer said: "Redemption will come in the month of Tishrei." R. Yehoshua said: "Redemption

---

217. See entry, Captives.

will come in the month of Nisan." (*Rosh Hashana* 11a)

Reduced prices for fruits
R. Shemuel's father used to sell his fruit immediately after the harvest, when prices were low. On the other hand, R. Shemuel kept the fruit until later when prices were higher, but he sold them at the low prices of the season. Word was sent from Israel to Babylonia that the father's practice was preferable because when prices are reduced, they remain so. (*Bava Batra* 90b)

Reeds for Sukkah
R. Hanina stated: "When I traveled to Babylonia, I met an old man who told me that a reed may be used as a *sukkah* roof. When I returned, I spoke about it to my uncle R. Yehoshua and he agreed." (*Sukkah* 20b)

Reeds
R. Hisda said in the name of R. Yitzhak: "Five rules have been laid down with regards to using reeds on account of splinters." (*Hullin* 16b)

Reference name
The Talmud does not always refer to a rabbi by name, but instead it uses a reference term. The following rules apply:
When the Talmud states:
"The judges of Eretz Yisrael," refers to Rabbi Ammi and Rabbi Assi.
"It was discussed before the rabbis" refers to R. Shimon ben Azzai, Rabbi Shimon ben Zoma, Rabbi Hanan HaMitzri, and R. Hanania ben Hachinai. (*Sanhedrin* 17b)

✿ Refined speech
R. Huna said in Rav's name, others say R. Huna said in Rav's name, which he heard from R. Meir: "One should always teach his student to use concise language and refined speech." (*Pesahim* 3b)

✿ Reflect upon three things
Akavia b. Mehalalel said: "Reflect upon three things: Know whence you come from, where you are going, and before whom you will have to give account." (*Avot* 3:1)

Refuge towns
Six towns of refuge (*Makkot* 9b)

Refuge towns
The roads leading to the towns of refuge were marked with signs. If the road split into two roads, then the road leading to the town of refuge was marked with a sign: "This way to the refuge town." (*Makkot* 10b)

Refuge towns
There were three towns of refuge east of the Jordan as well as west of the Jordan in spite of having nine and a half tribes on the west. Murders were more common on the east bank. (*Makkot* 9b)

Refusal   מיאון
Refusal; a fatherless girl of minor age who was given away by her mother or brother can refuse the continuance of the marriage. (*Hullin* 26b; *Ketubbot* 36a)

📖 Refused to abrogate
A ruling by Rav and Shemuel
R. Nahman was visiting in the town of Sura. R. Hisda and Rabbah b. R. Huna went to see him. They asked him to abrogate a certain ruling by Rav and Shemuel. He replied to them: "Do you think I have traveled this long distance to come here to annul a ruling of Rav and Shemuel?" (*Shevuot* 48b)

✿ Refused gifts
Rabbi Eleazar b. Pedat was very poor, but he refused to accept gifts. (*Taanit* 25a)

✿ Regrets expressed by fasting
When Rabbi Hisda was studying at Rabbi Huna, he once asked him:

"What of a student whose teacher needs him more?"

Rabbi Hisda had traditions from other rabbis, which Rabbi Huna did not know. R. Huna took offense and there was coolness between them for a while. After the incident, Rabbi Hisda fasted forty fast days, because he felt he insulted his rabbi. Rabbi Huna also fasted forty days because in his thoughts, he suspected his student Hisda of arrogance. There was reconciliation after some time had passed. (*Bava Metzia* 33a)

Regrets for four creations
R. Hana b. Aha said that it was said in the school: "Hashem regrets four creations: Exile, the Chaldeans, the Ishmaelites, and the Evil Inclination." (*Sukkah* 52b)

Regulations in Jerusalem
Ten regulations were applied to Jerusalem: A house if sold in Jerusalem could be redeemed; they never broke a heifer's neck in Jerusalem; Jerusalem could never be made a condemned city; the houses in Jerusalem would not become defiled through leprosy; beams and balconies were not allowed to project; no dunghills in Jerusalem; no kilns; no new gardens, except the garden of roses which existed from the days of the former prophets; no hens or roosters should be reared, and no dead person should be kept overnight in Jerusalem. (*Bava Kamma* 82b)

Rehumei I   רחומי
Amora from Babylonia
4th century CE (*Pesahim* 39a)

Rehumei II   רחומי
Amora from Babylonia

Head of the academy in Pumbedita
5th century CE (*Yoma* 78a)

Rehumei dies when roof collapses
R. Rehumei was at the school of Rava at Mehuza. He was sitting and studying on the roof, and suddenly the roof collapsed and killed him. (*Ketubbot* 62b)

Reiyah   ראיה
Who is obligated to appear in Jerusalem for the Three Festivals? (*Hagigah* 2a)

✿ Rejoice
Do not rejoice at the misfortune of others
R. Shemuel HaKatan said: "Control your emotions. Do not rejoice at the misfortune of your enemy." (*Avot* 4:19)

✿ Relations with non-Jews
A favorite saying of R. Abbaye was: "A man should always be in fear of Heaven, strive to be on best terms with his fellow-men, even with men of other religions, in order that he may be beloved above and below, and acceptable to his fellow creatures." (*Berachot* 17a)

Relatives
List of forbidden relatives to marry (*Yevamot* 21b)

Relatives unqualified witnesses
List of relatives who are considered too close and are unqualified to be witnesses in the case. (*Sanhedrin* 27b)

✿ Relieving the suffering of animals
It is a mitzvah to relieve the suffering of an animal. (*Bava Metzia* 33a)

Relying on taste of a gentile
If meat and milk are mixed, can we rely on the taste of a gentile for halachic purposes? (*Hullin* 97a)

Remarks, derogatory

R. Yehoshua b. Levi said: "A person who makes derogatory remarks about a dead scholar will go to Gehinnom." (*Berachot* 19a)

Remarry on evidence of one witness

R. Nahman said: "R. Yehuda ben Bava testified about five things: one of them was that a woman may remarry on the evidence of one witness." (*Berachot* 27a)

Remedies

Folk remedies of various kinds (*Avodah Zarah* 29a)

Reminder of the Temple destroyed

After the destruction of the Temple, the rabbis were concerned that Jewish people should not indulge in ostentatious living. They declared that during a lavish banquet something should be left out. R. Papa said to leave out the hors d'oeuvre.

R. Yitzhak said: "On the day of the wedding, burnt ashes should be put on the head of the bridegroom as a reminder of the destruction of the Temple." R. Papa asked R. Abbaye: "In which spot of the head should the ashes be placed?" R. Abbaye answered him: "It should be placed on the spot where the *tefillin* are usually placed." (*Bava Batra* 60b)

Reminders

One should remind himself on Fridays to do things for Shabbat. (*Shabbat* 20b)

Rending garments

Rending clothes on Shabbat when in mourning is discussed in *Ha-oreg*, the 13th *perek* in *Shabbat*. (*Shabbat* 105a)

Rending garments for a Kohen Gadol

(*Horayot* 12b)

Rending one's clothing for a teacher

When Rav died, his students accompanied his bier. After they returned, they said: "Let us eat a meal at the Danak River."

After they finished eating, they discussed a question of Halachah with regards to the blessing after a meal, for which they did not know the answer. R. Adda b. Ahava stood up and tore his garment from front to back, and tore it once more and said:

"Our teacher Rav is dead and we have not learned yet the rules for the blessings after the meal!" Finally, an old man solved their problem. (*Berachot* 42b)

Renouncing own property

Can one donate, renounce, give away his own property? (*Arachin* 28a)

Rent clothing for a scholar

The scholars in Babylon rent their garments for each other. (*Bava Metzia* 33a)

Rent increase

Is it halachically permissible to increase the amount of rent to be paid? (*Bava Metzia* 65a)

Renting a house

The obligations and responsibilities of the landlord and the tennant (*Bava Metzia* 101b)

Renting a house

Renting a house for a year or for a month (*Bava Metzia* 102a)

Renunciation יאוש

Giving up hope of ever recovering a lost item or lost property (*Bava Kamma* 66a, 67a–b, 68a, 114a; *Bava Metzia* 21b)

Renunciation without knowledge יאוש שלא מדעת

Unconsciously giving up (*Bava Metzia* 21b)

Repairman entrusted with an item
An object entrusted to a repairman (*Bava Kamma* 98b)

Repeated Parsha
R. Yishmael said: "Every *parsha* repeated in the Torah is there to make a new point." (*Bava Kamma* 64b; *Sotah* 3a; *Shevuot* 19a; *Menuhot* 10a)

Repeated his studies every thirty days
Rabbi Zera said: "Rabbi Hiyya b. Abba was very particular to get the exact teachings of Rabbi Yohanan his teacher. He used to go over what he learned from Rabbi Yohanan every thirty days." (*Berachot* 38b; *Keritut* 27a)

Repent
A man who was a thief wanted to repent and return all the stolen objects. His wife said to him: "If you repent, then even your belt is not yours." He changed his mind and did not repent. (*Bava Kamma* 94b)

✿ Repentance
One of Rabbi Eliezer's famous sayings was: "Let the honor of your fellow-man be as precious as your own; be not easily provoked to anger; repent one day before you die, warm yourself at the fire of the Sages, but beware of their glowing coals." (*Avot* 2:15)

Repentance
Rabbi Amram said in the name of Rav: "Happy is a person who repents while still in full vigor." (*Avodah Zarah* 19a)

Repentant
R. Shimon b. Yohai said: "If a person is righteous all his life but rebels at the end, he destroys all his former good deeds. On the other hand, if the person is completely wicked but repents at the end, he is not reproached for his misdeeds. (*Kiddushin* 40b)

✿ Repentant is on a high level
R. Avohu said: "In the place where the *baalei teshuva* stand, even the most righteous cannot stand." (*Berachot* 34b; *Sanhedrin* 99a)

Repentant sinners
When a sinner is sincerely repentant, Hashem forgives that person. (*Yevamot* 21a)

Repenting
The whole matter of *teshuva* depends on me alone. (*Avodah Zarah* 17a)

📖 Reprieved from dying at this time
Once R. Huna b. Yehoshua was very ill, and R. Papa went to visit him. When he saw that he was very sick, he said to the people:

"Make ready for his trip to heaven."

R. Huna recovered and R. Papa was embarrassed for thinking it was the end. He asked him: "What did you see?"

He answered him: "You were right, it was indeed my end, but the Almighty said to the angels: 'He deserves to live longer, because he never insisted on his rights and is a forgiving person.'" (*Rosh Hashana* 17a)

✿ Reproval accepted
The great R. Huna accepts reproval from the rabbis

Once R. Huna had a great loss: 400 jars of wine turned sour. He was visited by Rav Yehuda, the brother of R. Sala Hasida and the other rabbis. But some say it was R. Adda b. Ahava and other rabbis who visited him. They said to him;

"Master, you ought to examine your actions."

He asked them: "Am I suspicious in your eyes?"

They replied: "We heard that the master does not give his tenant his lawful share of vine twigs."[218]

---

218. See entry, Humble.

He replied; "Does he leave me any? He steals all of them."

They said to him: "That is exactly what the proverb says: 'If you steal from a thief, you also have a taste of it.'" (*Berachot* 5b)

Reptiles and frogs
Dead reptiles in the public domain (*Taharot* 5:1–4)

Requests from heaven
Rava said: "Three requests I made from Heaven – two were granted and one was not. I prayed I should acquire the scholarship of R. Huna, and the wealth of R. Hisda which were granted to me, but the modesty of Rabbah b. Huna was not granted to me." (*Moed Katan* 28a)

Rescue
To rescue oneself with money or the means of another's property (*Bava Kamma* 60b)

Rescuing from a lion
A person rescuing an object that is not his from a lion or other dangerous animals or places (*Avodah Zarah* 43a)

📖 Resh Lakish dies
R. Yohanan grieves
Resh Lakish and R. Yohanan had a disagreement and the quarrel got out of hand; words were exchanged. A short time later, Resh Lakish died and R. Yohanan was plunged into deep depression. The rabbis sent R. Eleazar b. Pedat to comfort him. He went and sat before him and they learned together. Every dictum which R. Yohanan uttered, he was supported by R. Eleazar with the remark: "There is a Beraita which supports you."

"You are no replacement for Resh Lakish," he complained. "When I stated a law, Resh Lakish raised twenty-four questions and objections, to which I gave twenty-four answers. This led to understanding

the law fully. While you tell me that a Beraitha supports me. Do I not know myself that what I said is correct?"

R. Yohanan went on rending his garments and weeping. "Where are you Resh Lakish, where are you Resh Lakish?" He grieved and cried and he also died from grief. (*Bava Metzia* 84a)

📖 Resh Lakish meets R. Yohanan
One day, Rabbi Yohanan was bathing in the Jordan River and Resh Lakish also happened to be there. Resh Lakish jumped into the river next to R. Yohanan. R. Yohanan said to him: "Your strength should be used for learning Torah."

Resh Lakish returned the compliment by saying: "Your good looks should be for women."

Rabbi Yohanan replied: "I have a sister who is more beautiful than I am. If you repent, I will give you my sister in marriage."

Resh Lakish agreed to repent,[219] and subsequently Rabbi Yohanan taught him the Torah and Mishna. After years of study, Resh Lakish became a great scholar. (*Bava Metzia* 84a)

Residence of Rebbe
Rabbi Yehuda HaNasi lived in splendor and there were guards at his residence which the Roman authorities placed there. (*Berachot* 16b)

📖 Resistance
Rabbi Yehuda ben Bava became a martyr[220] when he disobeyed the decree of the Roman authorities banning the ordination of rabbis. (*Sanhedrin* 14a)

📖 Resisting immorality
It is related that a woman once tried to seduce R. Hanina b. Papi. He pronounced

---

219. See entry, Baal teshuva.
220. See entry, Martyrdom.

a magic formula which made his body full of scabs and undesirable, but she also pronounced a magic formula and his scabs were removed. He fled to a bathhouse. In those days it was not safe to enter a bathhouse alone. The next day the rabbis asked him: "Who guarded you?"

He answered: "Two imperial armored guards."

They said to him: "Perhaps you were guarded because you resisted an immoral act?" As it is written: "Miracles happen to people who resist immoral acts." (*Kiddushin* 39b)

📖 Respect

Rabbi Yehuda HaNasi was giving his students a halachic decision. Rabbi Yishmael b. R. Yosi b. Halafta was present and he said: "My father ruled to the contrary."

To this R. Yehuda replied: "In that case, if the old man has already ruled, then the ruling is retracted."

R. Papa observed: "Come and see how much they loved each other! Had R. Yosi been alive, he would have sat before R. Yehuda with respect, but now that his son is occupying his father's place and sits before R. Yehuda with utmost respect, R. Yehuda says because your father already decided, my ruling is retracted." (*Shabbat* 51a; *Sanhedrin* 24a)

Respect

Once Ravin and Abbaye were traveling together and Ravin's donkey went ahead in front of Abbaye. Ravin did not apologize, and Abbaye was annoyed, and thinking to himself: *Since this student came up from Eretz Yisrael, he became haughty.* When they arrived at the door of the synagogue, Ravin said to Abbaye: "Rabbi, would you please enter."

Abbaye answered him: "And until now, was I not your rabbi?" (*Berachot* 47a)

Respect

Two scholars trembled in admiration for each other

Whenever R. Hisda and R. Sheshet met each other, they trembled in admiration of each other. R. Hisda admired R. Sheshet's extensive knowledge of Mishna. R. Sheshet admired R. Hisda for his deep penetrating mind in *pilpul*. (*Eruvin* 67a)

Respect among scholars

Rav and Shemuel and R. Assi once met at a *brit*. Rav did not want to enter before Shemuel, and Shemuel did not want to enter before R. Assi. Finally, it was decided that Rav and R. Assi would enter together first, and Shemuel would enter last. (*Bava Kamma* 80a; *Gittin* 6a)

✿ Respect everyone

R. Eleazar b. Shammua said: "Let the honor of your student be as precious as your own, the honor of your colleague as your teacher, and the honor of your teacher as the honor of God." (*Avot* 4:12)

Respect for a father

R. Avohu said: "One may give his father pheasants as food and not fulfill the mitzvah of honoring your father, while another may make him grind in a mill and yet fulfill the mitzvah, because he does it with respect. A good example is my son Avimi who has fulfilled the commandment '*honor thy father*.' Every time when R. Avohu visited his son Avimi, he himself ran to the door to open it, and while running he was calling out loud, "Yes, yes," until he reached the door. Even though R. Avimi had five sons who were already ordained rabbis in his father's lifetime.

One day, his father asked him for a glass of water. While he went to bring him the water, he fell asleep. He stood there in place with the water in his hand until he woke up. (*Kiddushin* 31 a–b)

📖 Respect for a mother

R. Assi had an old mother. He left her and moved to Eretz Yisrael. When he heard that she is following him to Eretz Yisrael, he went to R. Yohanan and asked him: "May I leave Eretz Yisrael to go abroad?" He answered him that it is forbidden.

"May I leave to meet my mother?"

He answered, "I do not know."

He waited a while and asked him again. R. Yohanan answered:

"Assi, I see you are determined to go, may God bring you back in peace." (*Kiddushin* 31b)

✡ Respect for a wife

R. Helbo said: "One must always give high respect to his wife, because all the blessings in one's home are on account of his wife." (*Bava Metzia* 59a)

Respect for colleagues

R. Ulla once visited Pumbedita and they brought some blood for him to examine, but he refused to see it. The town was under the jurisdiction of R. Yehuda. He explained. "If R. Eleazar, who was the supreme authority in the Land of Israel, refused to examine blood when he visited the town of R. Yehuda, how could I do it?" (*Niddah* 20b)

Respect for local rabbi

One time, Rav visited a certain place and he didn't abide by his own rulings out of respect for the local rabbis, and who were they? R. Kahana and R. Assi. (*Shabbat* 146b)

Respect for scholars

R. Hezkiya stated: "R. Hanina b. R. Avohu said it to me in the name of R. Avdimi from Haifa that when a scholar passes, one should rise before him within four cubits; when the head of the court walks in, one should rise while he is in sight; when the president of the Sanhedrin walks in,

one should rise when he is in sight and should be seated only after he is seated. (*Kiddushin* 33b)

📖 Respect in the Sanhedrin

Rabbis rise to show respect to the leaders according to the office they hold

It is related in the Talmud that Rabbi Yohanan stated: In the days when Rabbi Shimon ben Gamliel was president, instructions were issued as follows:

"It was the custom that whenever the President of the Sanhedrin, R. Shimon b. Gamliel entered, everyone would stand up;[221] when R. Meir the Hacham and R. Nathan the Av Bet Din entered, all the people stood up for them also."

Said R. Shimon b. Gamliel: "Should there be no distinction between my office and theirs?" Therefore, he issued instructions that when the President enters, everyone should stand up, but when the Hacham and Av Bet Din enter, only a limited number of the assembly should rise. (*Horayot* 13b)

Responsible for an act

Sometimes a person is responsible for damages done by his oxen, but is not responsible for his own acts, and sometimes it is the reverse. (*Bava Kamma* 34b)

📖 Responsible for sins committed

The Emperor Antoninus was having a discussion with Rebbe.

The Emperor asked: "The body and soul have a good argument to escape punishment. The body can plead that the soul has sinned, and the proof of it is that since the soul left me, I lie in the ground like a stone in the grave, while the soul can plead that the body has sinned, and the proof of it is that since I left the body, I fly in the air without committing sins."

---

221. Sanhedrin decorum.

Rebbe replied: "It is compared to two watchmen – one is blind and one is lame. The lame one is telling the blind one: 'I see beautiful figs in the orchard. Take me on your shoulders and I will pick some for us to eat.' The blind one carried the lame and they ate the figs. Some time later, the owner of the orchard inquired from his watchmen: 'Where are those beautiful figs you were supposed to watch in my orchard?' The lame watchman replied: 'Do I have feet to walk with?' And the blind man asked: 'Do I have eyes to see with?' The owner of the orchard told the lame one to ride on the shoulder of the blind and he judged them together." (*Sanhedrin* 91 a–b)

Responsible for one another
כל ישראל ערבים זה בזה
All Israelites are responsible for one another. (*Shevuot* 39a; *Sanhedrin* 27b)

Responsibility אחריות
Depositing money with someone – that person undertakes responsibility. (*Bava Metzia* 43a)

Resting from secular activities שבות
Abstention from secular activities on Shabbat (*Shabbat* 89a, 97a)

Restrictions on wine and meat
During the week of Tisha Be'Av, it is forbidden to cut the hair, to wash one's clothes, eat meat, or drink wine. (*Taanit* 26b)

Rests until doubt is gone
מונח עד שיבוא אליהו
It rests until Eliyahu comes. It rests until the doubt disappears. (*Bava Metzia* 3a, 37a)

Resurrection
Rabbi Gamliel was asked by a sectarian: "How do we know that the dead will be resurrected?" He replied: "We know it from the Torah, from the Prophets, and from the Hagiographa. In the Torah in *Devarim* (31:16) it says: 'You shall die and rise.'" (*Sanhedrin* 90b)

Resurrection
Rabbi Meir was asked: "When the dead will arise, will they come forth nude or clothed?"

He replied: "They surely will be clothed for if a wheat grain is buried nude and comes up wrapped in several garments, how much more so a righteous person." (*Sanhedrin* 90b)

Resurrection
R. Meir said: "Where do we know that resurrection is from the Torah? From the song that Moshe sang at the splitting of the sea. It does not say 'he sang,' but 'he will sing.'" (*Sanhedrin* 91b)

Resurrection
Rava said: "How do we know that resurrection is hinted in the Torah? It is written (*Devarim* 33:6) 'May Reuven live and not die.'" (*Sanhedrin* 91a)

Resurrection
Rabbi Simai said: "How do we know that resurrection is hinted in the Torah? It is written: 'I will give them (the Patriarchs) the land of Cannan.'" (*Sanhedrin* 90b)

Resurrection
The emperor asked R. Gamliel: "You maintain that the dead will be resurrected, but they turn to dust, and can dust come to life?"

The emperor's daughter was present, and she answered: "If God can create humans from water, he surely can create them from dust." (*Sanhedrin* 91a)

Resurrection
One who says that resurrection is not

in the Torah will not have a share in the World to Come. (*Sanhedrin* 90a)

Retained by the court
יהא מונח עד שיבוא אליהו
Retained by the court until the coming of Eliyahu (*Bava Metzia* 3a, 37a)

Retraction of ruling – refused
Sticking to principles
Shila b. Avina decided a matter according to Rav.

After Rav passed away, R. Assi asked him to retract, because Rav had retracted his ruling.[222]

R. Shila said: "If Rav had retracted, he would have told me," and refused to retract. Thereupon R. Assi put him under the ban. (*Niddah* 36b)

Return of lost animal (*Bava Metzia* 28b; *Shabbat* 105b)

Returning lost object
Even many times (*Bava Metzia* 30b, 31a)

Reuven
About sinning (*Shabbat* 55b)

Reuven b. Istroboli[223] (*Meilah* 17b)

Revival of Torah
Rabbi Shimon ben Lakish said that in ancient times, when the Torah was forgotten, Ezra came up from Babylon and re-established it. Then it was forgotten again, and Hillel the Babylonian came up and re-established it. Yet again, some of it was forgotten and Rabbi Hiyya and his sons came up from Babylonia and re-established it again. (*Sukkah* 20a)

Revived
The dead revived by Yechezkel
R. Eliezer b. R. Yosi HaGlili said: "The dead whom the Prophet Yehezkel revived went to Israel, married wives, and had children."

R. Yehuda b. Betera rose up and said: 'I am one of their descendants, and these are the *tefillin* which my grandfather left for me. It was passed on from them." (*Sanhedrin* 92b)

Revival of R. Kahana
R. Yohanan looked at R. Kahana and noticed that R. Kahana's lips were parted. He thought that he is laughing at him. For this, R. Yohanan felt insulted. In consequence, R. Kahana died. The next day, R. Yohanan said to the rabbis: "Did you notice how the Babylonian insulted us?"

But they said to him: "Not so, that is his natural appearance."

R. Yohanan went to the cave of R. Kahana and prayed for mercy and he revived him. He said to R. Kahana: "Had I known that is your natural appearance, I would not have taken offense." (*Bava Kamma* 117a)

Reward
Reward for a mitzvah commanded is greater than one not commanded. (*Bava Kamma* 87a)

Reward
Ben Hei Hei said: "The reward is in proportion to the exertion." (*Avot* 5:26)

Reward for commandments (*Hullin* 142a)

Rewarded in this world
R. Papa and R. Huna b. Yehoshua once came before Rava, and he asked them: "Have you learned this particular tractate and the other tractate?"

They replied in the affirmative.

"Are you a little richer?"

---

222. See entry, Principles to uphold.
223. See entry, Demons.

"Yes," they replied, "because we bought some land."

Rava exclaimed in happiness: "Happy are the righteous who are rewarded also in this world." (*Horayot* 10b)

Rewards

Antigonus Ish Socho said in the name of Shimon HaTzaddik: "Be not like servants who serve for the expected reward, but be like servants who don't expect rewards." (*Avot* 1:3)

✡ Rewards in both worlds

R. Yehuda b. Shila said in the name of R. Assi in the name of R. Yohanan: "There are six good deeds from which one can derive benefits in this world and still get the rewards in the World to Come: hospitality to guests, visiting the sick, concentration during prayer, rising early for prayer, bringing up a son with Torah study, and judging everyone as being upright." (*Shabbat* 127a)

Ribit   ריבית

Money lent with interest (*Bava Metzia* 63a)

Ribit Meuheret   ריבית מאוחרת

Postpaid interest (*Bava Metzia* 75b)

Ribit Mukdemet   ריבית מוקדמת

Prepaid interest (*Bava Metzia* 75b)

Ribui Ahar Ribui   ריבוי אחר ריבוי

In the Torah, when amplification follows amplification (*Bava Kamma* 45b; *Menahot* 89a)

Ribui U-Miut   ריבוי ומיעוט

Amplifications and limitations (*Shevuot* 37b)

Rice on Pesach

R. Yohanan b. Nuri forbade rice on Pesach. (*Pesahim* 35a, 114b; *Berachot* 37a)

Rich

Who is rich? (*Shabbat* 25b)

Rich and poor litigants

A student who is present when his Rebbe mistakenly decides for the rich man, and the student knows that the poor man is right, should not keep quiet? (*Shevuot* 31a; *Sanhedrin* 6b)

Rich and righteous

Aibu, the father of Rav, stated: "I was next to Rabbi Eleazar ben Tzadok when a certain man came to ask him this question: 'I possess cities, vineyards, and olive trees, and the inhabitants of the cities come and work the fields and eat the olives. Is this proper in a Shemittah year or improper?' He answered him that it is improper. When the man left, Rabbi Eleazar remarked: 'It is now forty years that I live here and I have never seen as righteous a man as this one.' The man returned to ask. 'What should I do?' Rabbi Eleazar told him: 'Abandon the olives to the poor and pay for the labor from your own money.'" (*Sukkah* 44b)

📖 Rich charitable person

Rabbi Ulla and Rabbi Hisda were walking and they passed the house of R. Hana b. Hanilai. R. Hisda sighed.

Asked R. Ulla: "Why are you sighing?"

He answered him: "How can I refrain from sighing? He used to have sixty cooks by day and sixty cooks by night that cooked for every one in need. He always had his purse ready to give charity. The house had four doors one on each side. Whoever went in hungry, came out full. In time of scarcity, he put the grain and barley outside at nighttime for anyone to take — he did not want people to have to come inside to be embarrassed. Now it is all in ruins – shall I not sigh?" (*Berachot* 58b)

Rich daughter

The daughter of the richest man in Jerusalem had to sell her hair for food.[224] (*Shabbat* 156b; *Nedarim* 50a)

Rich man

Carries poor scholars tools

R. Hana b. Hanilai – who was a very rich man – was a great follower of Rabbi Huna. When he saw Rabbi Huna carry his tools on his shoulder, he would take it from him and carry it. (*Megillah* 28a)

Rich men

Rabbi Akiva showed respect to rich men, so did Rabbi Yehuda HaNasi. (*Eruvin* 86a)

Rich son

Rabbi Kahana's son was very rich. R. Zevid told R. Kahana that his daughter-in-law throws around gold as if it is worthless. (*Meilah* 19a)

Rich; who is considered to be rich
איזהו עשיר השמח בחלקו

Ben Zoma used to say: "Who is wise? One who learns from all people. Who is strong? One who subdues his passions. Who is rich? One who is happy with his portion. Who is honored? One who honors his fellow-men." (*Avot* 4:1)

Riding on the king's horse

It is not permissible to ride on the king's horse. (*Sanhedrin* 22a)

Riding on a donkey

Time for praying

When praying time arrives and one is riding on a donkey is discussed in the 4th *perek* of *Berachot*. (*Berachot* 28b)

Right of a king

R. Huna said: "When David was at war

with the Philistines, they hid themselves in stacks of barley belonging to Israelites. David asked the rabbis whether it is permissible to destroy another's property in order to save his army. He was told that it was not permissible. 'However, you are a king and a king has the right to break the fences and go through another's property to make way for his army and nobody is entitled to stop him.'" (*Bava Kamma* 60b)

Right shoe first

Our rabbis taught: "When one puts on shoes, he should put on his right shoe first." (*Shabbat* 61a)

Righteous

R. Yohanan said: "The righteous are greater than the ministering angels." (*Sanhedrin* 93a)

Righteous

R. Hanina said: "Everything is in the hand of Heaven except the fear of Heaven." (*Berachot* 33b)

Righteous

Legacy of a righteous person remains even after his death

R. Eleazar said in the name of R. Hanina" "When a righteous person dies, it is a great loss to his generation, but is not really lost because his legacy remains. It is like when one loses a precious pearl; it is a loss only to the owner, but the pearl remains a pearl wherever it is." (*Megillah* 15a)

Righteous

When a righteous person leaves this world, he is replaced with another righteous person.

It was learned by an authority that on the day that Rabbi Akiva died, Rebbe was born, and on the day that Rebbe died, Rav Yehuda was born. When Rav Yehuda, died Rava was born; when Rava died, Rav Ashi was born. This is to teach us that when a

---

224. See story under, Akiva's wife.

righteous person leaves this world, he is replaced with another righteous person. (*Kiddushin* 72a)

Righteous

The righteous promise little
R. Eleazar said: "The righteous promise little and perform much; the wicked promise much and do not perform even little." (*Bava Metzia* 87a)

Righteous but sins at his end of life

R. Shimon b. Yohai said: "If a person is righteous all his life but rebels at the end, he destroys all his former good deeds. On the other hand, if the person is completely wicked but repents at the end, he is not reproached for his misdeeds." (*Kiddushin* 40b)

Righteous men

R. Yohanan said in the name of R. Shimon b. Yehotzedek: "There are forty-five righteous men in every generation: thirty are in Israel and fifteen are in exile. By virtue of these men the world continues to exist. (*Hullin* 92a)

Righteous men, Lamed Vav Tzaddikim
תלתין ושיתא צדיקי
Abbaye said: "In each generation, the world must contain no less than thirty-six righteous men who merit the sight of the Shechina." (*Sanhedrin* 97b; *Sukkah* 45b)

Righteous will be rewarded

R. Tarfon said: "It is not your obligation to complete the job, but neither are you at liberty to be idle. If you studied much Torah, you will have great reward, because your Employer is faithful and you should know that the righteous will be rewarded in the time to come." (*Avot* 2:16)

Ring found by Eleazar HaKappar

R. Eleazar HaKappar found a ring with idol images on it. (*Avodah Zarah* 43a)

Rinse with salt and rinse again

Shemuel said: "The blood is not extracted from the meat unless it is salted very well." (*Hullin* 113a)

Rinsing the mouth

The rinsing and cleaning of the mouth between eating meat and milk (*Hullin* 104b)

✿ Rise to the challenge

R. Hillel said: "Where there are no men to lead, strive to be a competent leader." (*Avot* 2:5)

✿ Rising before scholars

R. Hezkiya said: "R. Hanina b. Avohu told me in the name of R. Avdimi deman Haifa: 'When a scholar passes, one should rise for him from a distance of four cubits. When the head of a Bet Din enters the room, one should rise as soon as he is seen and should sit down when he passes four cubits. When the Nasi enters the room, one rises when he is seen and sits down only after he is seated.'" (*Kiddushin* 33b)

📖 Risked being arrested

R. Meir risked being arrested to save his sister-in-law from captivity
The Talmud relates that the sister of Berurya was captured and placed in a brothel. Berurya was Rabbi Meir's wife and the daughter of Rabbi Hanania b. Teradion.

Berurya told her husband: "I am ashamed to have my sister in a brothel. Can you do something to get her out of there?"

So he took a bag full of *dinarim* and set out to ransom her. He said to himself *If she is clean then a miracle will happen.* He disguised himself as a knight and came to the place where she was kept. He said to her: "Get ready for me."

She replied: "I am menstruating."

He answered: "I am prepared to wait."

She replied: "But there are many prettier women here than me."

He determined that she probably had the same excuse for others. He offered the money to the watchman and he released her. The government found out what he had done and they were looking to arrest him. For that reason he had to leave Eretz Yisrael and move to Babylonia. (*Avodah Zarah* 18a)

Ritual uncleanness and its origin
Av Ha-Tumah   אב הטומאה
Original uncleanness (*Kelim* 1:1)

📖 River Ginai split
R. Pinhas b. Yair was on his way to redeem captives, when he came to the Ginai River. He said: "O Ginai, split your waters for me so I can pass."

The river replied: "You are on the way to do the will of your Maker, and I, too, am doing the will of my Maker. You may or may not accomplish your mission, but I am sure I am accomplishing my mission."

R. Pinhas declared: "If you don't split the waters, I will decree that no waters ever pass through this river." After this declaration by R. Pinhas, the river split[225] and R. Pinhas was able to pass. (*Hullin* 7a)

Roasting the Pesach offering
The procedure for roasting the Pesach offering (*Pesahim* 74a)

📖 Robbed of redemption money
Money was entrusted to him to redeem captives
The Talmud relates that a certain man was traveling to redeem some captives. He had a purse of money with him, which was the ransom money, but he was attacked by robbers. He handed over to them the

money as they demanded and they let him go. On his return, he was summoned before Rabbah for using the money to redeem himself, but Rabbah found him not guilty of negligence.

Abbaye said to Rabbah: "Didn't this man rescue himself with another man's money?"

Rabbah replied: "There could hardly be a case of redeeming captives more urgent than this." (*Bava Kamma* 117b)

Robbed one of five people
A person robbed one of five people, but did not know from whom he robbed. (*Bava Kamma* 103b; *Yevamot* 118b; *Bava Metzia* 37a)

Robbing
R. Yohanan said: "To rob a fellow man even of a small amount is like taking away his life." (*Bava Kamma* 119a)

Robbing a non-Jew
R. Akiva said: "Whence can we learn that robbing a non-Jew is forbidden?" He quotes a passage in the Torah. (*Bava Kamma* 113a, b)

📖 Roman soldier is granted heaven
Our rabbis taught that when the Roman soldiers came upon R. Hanania b. Teradion sitting and teaching Torah in public, they took him and his scroll of Torah and wrapped the scroll around his body, placed bundles of wood around him, and set it on fire. They soaked cloth of wool in water and placed it over his heart, in order to prolong his agony. The executioner asked him:

"Rabbi, if I remove the wool from your heart, will you take me with you to heaven?"

He said: "Yes." The executioner removed the wool, increased the flames, and his soul departed speedily. The executioner then threw himself into the fire.

---

225. See entry, Redeeming captives.

Rabbi Hanania ben Teradion became one of the Ten Martyrs.[226] (*Avodah Zarah* 18a)

📖 Romans study in Israel

The government of Rome sent two commissioners to Israel to learn Torah from the Jewish Sages. The Torah was read to them three times. Before leaving they remarked: "We are not happy with the law of an ox belonging to a Jew goring an ox belonging to a non-Jew." (*Bava Kamma* 38a)

Romanus   רומנוס

Amora from Eretz Yisrael
Lived in the 3rd century CE, a student of Rebbe (*Shabbat* 47a)

📖 Rome

Herod asked for Consent from Rome to build the Temple

Herod asked Rabbi Bava ben Buta: "What could I do to amend for the sin of killing all the scholars?"

R. Bava answered: "You have extinguished the light of the world by killing the rabbis; you should attend to the other light of the world – the Temple."

Herod told him: "I am afraid of the government in Rome."

Bava b. Buta advised him to send an envoy to Rome to ask permission, and let the envoy take a year on the way, and let him stay a year in Rome and another year to come back. In the meantime, Herod should rebuild the Temple.

Herod followed his advice. He received the following reply from Rome:

"If you have not yet pulled down the old one, do not do so; if you have pulled it down, do not rebuild it. If you have pulled it down and already rebuilt it, you are one of those bad servants who do first and ask permission afterwards." (*Bava Batra* 4a)

Rome

Rome is asking a share in the World to Come. (*Avodah Zarah* 2b)

Rome academy

R. Matya was born in Eretz Yisrael, and was a student of Rabbi Yohanan ben Zakkai, but in his later years he established a great academy in Rome. (*Sanhedrin* 32b)

Rome ruled in Israel

R. Yishmael b. Yosi b. Halafta was ill. The rabbis sent word to him: "Tell us a few things you heard from your father."

He told them: "One hundred and eighty years before the Temple was destroyed Rome was ruling over Israel. The Persian rule lasted thirty-four years after the building of the Temple, Greece ruled 180 years during the existence of the Temple. (*Avodah Zarah* 9a)

Rome visit by R. Shimon b. Yohai

One time, the Roman authorities issued a decree against Jewish religious practices. They forbade Jews to observe the Shabbat, or to circumcise their sons, or to observe the practice of family purity. When the edict was issued, the Jewish leadership decided to send a delegation to Rome[227] to find a way for the law to be rescinded, and R. Shimon ben Yohai and R. Eleazar b. Yosi were chosen to travel to Rome. (*Meilah* 17b; *Yoma* 57a)

Roof collapses

Student dies

R. Rehumei was at the school of Rava at Mehuza and he was sitting and studying on the roof, and suddenly the roof collapsed and killed him. (*Ketubbot* 62b)

---

226. See entry, Burned with his Torah together.

227. See entry, Delegation sent to Rome to rescind.

Roosters
It is improper to breed roosters or hens in Jerusalem. (*Bava Kamma* 79b, 82b; *Taanit* 25a; *Temurah* 15b)

Rose gardens
The garden of roses, which existed in Jerusalem from the days of the former Prophets. (*Bava Kamma* 82b)

Rosh Hashana   ראש השנה
R. Keruspedai said in the name of R. Yohanan: "Three books are opened in heaven on Rosh Hashana: one for the completely wicked, one for the completely righteous, and one for those in between. The completely righteous are forthwith inscribed to life, the completely wicked are forthwith inscribed to death, and the fate of those in between is suspended from Rosh Hashana till Yom Kippur. If they deserve it, they are inscribed to life; if not, they are inscribed to death. (*Rosh Hashana* 16b)

Rosh Hashana on Shabbat
Is the *shofar* blown when Rosh Hashana falls on Shabbat? (*Rosh Hashana* 29b)

Rosh Hashana prayers
The proper order for the prayers on Rosh Hashana (*Rosh Hashana* 32a)

Rosh Hashana Torah reading
(*Megillah* 30b)

Rosh Hodesh, New month   ראש חודש
During the prayers of Rosh Hodesh, where is one to add the mention of Rosh Hodesh? During the blessing after the meal, should one mention Rosh Hodesh? (*Shabbat* 24a)

Rosh Hodesh Torah reading
(*Megillah* 30b)

Roughnecks
Once there were some Biryoni in the neighborhood of R. Meir who caused him a lot of aggravation. R. Meir wanted to pray for them to die. But his wife Berurya said to him: "It is not a good idea. Rather pray for them they should repent." He did pray and they repented. (*Berachot* 10a)

Ruined building dangerous to enter
R. Yosi said: "I was once traveling on the road and I entered a ruin in Jerusalem in order to pray. Eliyahu, of blessed memory, appeared and guarded me until I finished praying. After I finished he said to me: 'Peace be with you, my Rebbe.'

"I replied to him, 'Peace shall be with you, my Rebbe and teacher.'

"He said to me, 'My son, why did you enter this ruin?'

"I answered him, 'I went in to pray.'

"He said, 'You should have prayed on the road.'

"I said to him, 'I feared that I would be interrupted by passersby.'

"Eliyahu told me, 'You should have said an abbreviated prayer.'

"From this, I learned three things: one should not enter a ruin, one may pray on the road, and the prayer on the road should be a short one.'" (*Berachot* 3a)

Ruling of one's Rebbe should not be questioned
R. Hisda said: "Whoever contends against the ruling of his Rebbe is as though he contends against the Shechina." (*Sanhedrin* 110a)

Running
Two guys running who cause injury (*Bava Kamma* 32a)

Ruth   רות
The biblical Ruth lived to see Shlomo's

kingdom. Shlomo was the grandson of her grandson. (*Bava Batra* 91b)

Ruth – the author of the book
The author of the book of Ruth was the Prophet Shemuel. (Others name different authors.) (*Bava Batra* 15a)

S

Sabbatical flax
If a person is under suspicion of ignoring the Shemittah year, one may not buy from him flax. (*Bechorot* 29b)

Sabbatical year violation
Avak Shevi'it אבק שביעית
Shade of violating the Sabbatical year (*Sukkah* 40b; *Kiddushin* 20a; *Arachin* 30b)

Sacred scrolls
What renders sacred scrolls and hands unclean (*Yadayim* 3:5)

Sacred writings
Can sacred writings be saved on Shabbat from a fire? (*Shabbat* 115a)

Sacrifices to be read daily
R. Ammi said: "The Patriarch Avraham spoke to God and said: 'What will happen to my children when the Temple is no more – how will their sins be forgiven?'

"Hashem answered him: 'Whenever they will read the passages that deal with the sacrifices, I will consider it as if they brought an offering and will forgive their iniquities." (*Megillah* 31b; *Taanit* 27b)

Safekeeping
A man once deposited seven pearls, wrapped in a sheet, with R. Miasha, the grandson of R. Yehoshua b. Levi. When R. Miasha died, without a will, they came before R. Ammi to claim the pearls. R. Ammi

said to them: "I know that R. Miasha was not a wealthy man and secondly, the man did give recognizable clues. (*Ketubbot* 85b)

Safekeeping
A man left his money with his neighbor for safekeeping. When he asked for the money, he was told: "I don't know where I put it." (*Bava Metzia* 42a)

Safra ספרא
Amora from Babylonia
4th century CE (*Pesahim* 51b; *Avodah Zarah* 4a)

Safra and the lion
A caravan, in which R. Safra was traveling, was followed by a lion. Every night, they had to abandon one donkey to satisfy the lion. When it came to give up R. Safra's donkey, the lion would not eat it, and R. Safra reclaimed his donkey. (*Bava Kamma* 116a)

Sages exaggerate sometimes
R. Ammi said: "The Sages spoke sometimes in exaggerated terms." (*Hullin* 90b)

Saintly person
R. Pinhas b. Hama said: "When there is a sick person in the house, one should go to a scholar who is a Saint who will pray on behalf of the sick person." (*Bava Batra* 116a)

Sale transaction complete
Sale is complete when the object was drawn
What is required to complete a sale, the buyer must draw the object. (*Bava Metzia* 44a)

Salmon Peloni Almoni
R. Hanan b. Rava said in the name of Rav: "Elimelech, Salmon, and Peloni Almoni, and the father of Naomi were all the children of Nahshon b. Aminadav." (*Bava Batra* 91a)

Salting meat on a vessel with holes

R. Shemuel said: "One may not salt raw meat except in a vessel with holes in it." R. Shemuel said: "Flesh cannot be drained of its blood, unless it has been salted very well and rinsed very well." (*Hullin* 113a)

Salt on steps on Shabbat

Can salt be sprinkled on Shabbat to prevent slipping? (*Eruvin* 104a)

📖 Samaritans

The Talmud relates: "It was taught that the twenty-fifth of Tevet, is the day of Mount Gerizim. On that day, no mourning is permitted. It is the day in which the Samaritans asked Alexander the Macedonian to give them permission to destroy the Temple, and he granted their request. Shimon HaTzaddik dressed up in his high priestly garments, and took with him the noblemen of Israel. When Alexander saw the lit torches in the night from a distance, he asked the Samaritans. "Who are those people walking?"

They told him that those are the Jews who had rebelled against him.

When Shimon HaTzaddik and his group met Alexander,[228] he asked them for what reason they had come to see him.

They said to him, "Is it possible that you would listen to the advice of star-worshippers to destroy the Temple in which we pray for you and your kingdom that it should never be destroyed?"

"Who are those star-worshippers?"

"They are the Samaritans who stand before you."

He answered, "They are delivered in your hands."

That day was made into a festive day. (*Yoma* 69a)

Samaritans and R. Eleazar b. Yosi

It has been taught: R. Eleazar b. Yosi said: "I refuted the books of the Samaritans, who maintained that resurrection is not deducible from the Torah." R. Eleazar pointed out to them that they falsified the Torah. (*Sanhedrin* 90b)

📖 Sambatyon River

On Shabbat the river is quiet

Tinnius Rufus or Turnus Rufus, the Roman governor of Judea, asked R. Akiva: "In what way is the Jewish Shabbat different from any other day of the week?"

R. Akiva asked in turn: "In what way is one man different from any other man, as for instance, you?"

Rufus answered: "I am different because the Emperor wants it that way."

R. Akiva rejoined: The Shabbat is different because the Master of the world wants it that way."

Rufus asked: "How do you know for certain which day is Shabbat, perhaps you are mistaken and another day of the week is the real Shabbat?"

R. Akiva answered: "The River Sambatyon is proof." Rashi comments that this river of stones is turbulent every day of the week, except on Shabbat, when it rests. (*Sanhedrin* 65b)

Same day

When it is stated "the same day" concerning the slaughtering of an animal and its young, the day follows the preceding night. (*Hullin* 83a)

Sanctity may be elevated

But not degraded   מעלין בקודש ואין מורידין

Sanctity may be elevated to a higher degree of sanctity, but not degraded. (*Berachot* 28a; *Megillah* 9b, 21b; *Yoma* 12b)

---

228. See entry, Alexander and the Samaritans.

Sandals and shoes
The susceptibility of sandals and shoes to uncleanness (*Kelim* 26:1–4)

Sanhedrin
R. Akiva said: "The Sanhedrin rabbis do not eat on the day of the execution of a condemned person." (*Sanhedrin* 63a; *Moed Katan* 14b)

Sanhedrin
Members of the Sanhedrin witnessing a murder (*Bava Kamma* 90b; *Rosh Hashana* 25b)

Sanhedrin
Admission as a student to the Sanhedrin (*Berachot* 27b)

Sanhedrin
Eleazar b. Azariah said: "A Sanhedrin that puts to death one person in seventy years is termed a tyrannical court." (*Makkot* 1:10)

📖 Sanhedrin Decorum
It is related in the Talmud that Rabbi Yohanan said: "The following instructions were issued in the days when Rabbi Shimon ben Gamliel was president of the Sanhedrin: Whenever the president of the Sanhedrin enters into the assembly, everyone should stand up, but when the Hacham and the Av Bet Din enter, only a limited number of the assembly should rise. Rabbi Meir was the Hacham and Rabbi Nathan was the Av Bet Din. Rabbi Meir and Rabbi Nathan were not present when the instructions were issued. The next day, when Rabbi Meir and Rabbi Nathan entered the Sanhedrin hall, they noticed the lack of respect being given to them. When they asked why the change, they were told that those were the instructions of Rabbi Shimon.

Rabbi Meir and Rabbi Nathan decided to engage in a discourse, in which Rabbi Shimon was not familiar. When Rabbi

Yaakov ben Korshai found out what was planned, he reasoned that this might lead to a disgrace to the presidency of the Sanhedrin. He therefore started to study that subject just outside Rabbi Shimon's chamber. He did it loudly, again and again. When R. Shimon heard him, he perceived that something was happening in the Sanhedrin. He concentrated on the subject and familiarized himself with it. The next day, they approached him to discuss the subject. He agreed and he was able to hold his ground. When they finished, he said to them: "Had I not familiarized myself with the subject, you would have disgraced me." He issued an order to have them removed from the Sanhedrin.

When they were on the outside, they wrote down difficult scholastic questions on slips of paper, which they threw inside. Many of the questions could not be answered inside, and they were sent back outside unanswered. They wrote down the answer and sent it back inside. Rabbi Yosi said to the assembly: "The Torah is outside and we are sitting inside." Rabbi Shimon changed his mind and said: "We shall readmit them, but impose on them this penalty. No traditional statement will be quoted in their names." Rabbi Meir received the designation to be quoted as "others say" and Rabbi Nathan as "some say." (*Horayot* 13b)

Sanhedrin heads
It is stated that Rabbi Hillel and his descendants Shimon, Gamliel, and his son Shimon were the heads of the Sanhedrin for one hundred years during the Temple's existence. (*Shabbat* 15a)

Sanhedrin membership qualification
Essential requirements to be a member of the Sanhedrin
R. Yohanan said: "The men appointed to the Sanhedrin are to be men of stature,

wisdom, good appearance, mature age, with knowledge of sorcery. Also knowledge of seventy languages, in order there will be no need for an interpreter." (*Sanhedrin* 17a)

Sanhedrin members were multilingual
It was taught: A Sanhedrin that has two members who are able to speak seventy languages and the rest of the Sanhedrin are able to understand those languages, that body is a fit Sanhedrin. If there are three who can speak the seventy languages, that body is a middling Sanhedrin. If there are four who can speak the seventy languages, that body is a wise Sanhedrin. In Yavne, there were four: Ben Azzai, Ben Zoma, Ben Hachinai, and R. Eleazar b. Matya. (JT *Shekalim* 5:1)

Sanhedrin seating
The members of the Sanhedrin were seated in a semi-circle in order for them to see one another. (*Sanhedrin* 36b; *Hullin* 5a)

Sanhedrin, the Great סנהדרין גדולה
The Great Sanhedrin was composed of seventy-one members. (*Sanhedrin* 2a)

Sanhedrin, the Small סנהדרין קטנה
The Small Sanhedrin consisted of twenty-three members. (*Sanhedrin* 2a)

Sanhedrin, unanimous decision voided
R. Kahana said: "If the Sanhedrin unanimously finds the defendant guilty, he is acquitted." (*Sanhedrin* 17a)

Sanheriv
King of Assyria
Sanheriv was an enemy of Judea. During the reign of Hezkiyahu King of Judea, he attacked Jerusalem. (*Sanhedrin* 94a, 94b, 96b)

Sanheriv
Shemaya and his colleague Avtalyon were

descendants of Sanheriv. They became converts and the greatest scholars in Judaism in that period. Rabbi Hillel was one of their students. (*Gittin* 57b)

Sanheriv
The difference between the great Jewish leaders and the non-Jewish leaders like Sanheriv – the Jewish leaders showed humility while Sanheriv was haughty. (*Hullin* 89a)

Sanitation in Jerusalem
Dung hills were not permitted in Jerusalem. (*Bava Kamma* 82b)

Saris סריס
A person lacking procreative powers (*Bava Batra* 155b)

Saris
R. Eliezer said: "A certain kind of *saris*[229] needs to submit to *halitza*, because cases of this nature are cured in Alexandria, Egypt. (*Yevamot* 80a)

Satan
Resh Lakish said: "Satan, the evil instigator, and the Angel of Death are one and the same. (*Bava Batra* 16a)

✡ Satisfied with his lot
Rav Yehuda said in the name of Rav: "Every day a Bat Kol went out from Mount Horev and proclaimed: 'The whole world is being fed for the merits of my son Hanina and yet my son Hanina is satisfied with a small measure of carobs from one Friday to the next Friday.'" (*Berachot* 17b)

Saul
King Saul spared some Amalekites
Rabbi Mani had an explanation as to why King Saul did not kill all the Amalekites.

---

229. Emasculated man.

He reasoned that since the children were innocent they should be spared. (*Yoma* 22b)

Save a life on Shabbat
Violating Shabbat to save a life
Shimon b. Menasia said: "In order to save a life, one may violate the Shabbat, because it is better to profane one Shabbat in order to be able to keep many Shabbats." (*Yoma* 85b; *Shabbat* 151b)

Saves boat and passengers
His action causes a donkey of another man to drown
A certain man pushed his donkey on a ferry boat before the passengers had a chance to disembark. The boat started to shake and was about to be turned over. Another man who was on the boat came and pushed the donkey overboard, saved the boat,[230] but the donkey drowned. (*Bava Kamma* 117b)

Saving a life transcends Shabbat
Rabbi Yonatan derived from the Torah that saving a life transcends the Shabbat. (*Yoma* 85b)

Saving face of a colleague
R. Gamliel asked for seven rabbis to meet with him in the morning in the upper chamber to intercalate the year. When he came into the chamber, he found eight rabbis. He asked: "Who came to this meeting uninvited? Let him leave."

R. Shemuel HaKatan rose and said: "I am the one who came uninvited. I came only to learn the practical application of the law."

R. Gamliel responded: "Sit down my son. You are well qualified to intercalate all the years." It turned out that it was not R. Shemuel who came without an invitation,

but he wanted to spare that person from humiliation. (*Sanhedrin* 11a)

Saving from a fire
Rabbi Meir said: "One can put as many cloths on himself as possible in order to save them from a fire on Shabbat." (*Shabbat* 120a; *Eruvin* 95b)

Saving from fire on Shabbat
What may be saved from a fire on Shabbat? (*Shabbat* 115a)

Saw Holy vessels
Holy vessels plundered from the Temple
While Rabbi Eleazar was in Rome, he saw the vessels plundered from the Temple. He also saw the splattered blood from the sacrifices on the curtain that separated the Holy of Holies. (*Meilah* 17a–b)

✿ Say little and do much
One of R. Shammai's dictums was: "Make the study of Torah a steady habit, say little and do much, and receive every person with a cheerful countenance." (*Avot* 1:15)

Sayings
Rava quoted some sayings by the rabbis to Rabbah b. Mari. (*Bava Kamma* 92b)

Scales for weighing
Different types of scales with regards to being susceptible to uncleanness (*Kelim* 29: 3, 4, 5, 6)

Scapegoat ceremony
The ceremony for the two goats on Yom Kippur (*Yoma* 39a)

Scholar
R. Ashi stated: "A scholar who is not as hard as iron is not a scholar." (*Taanit* 4a)

---

230. See entry, Boat endangered by a donkey.

Scholar

A dedicated scholar who died in his middle age (*Shabbat* 13a)

✿ Scholar blacksmith

When Rabbi Gamliel saw the great respect the Sanhedrin accorded to Rabbi Yehoshua, he decided to go to him to apologize. When he reached his house, he saw that the walls were black from charcoal. He said to him:

"I can tell by your walls that you are a blacksmith."

Rabbi Yehoshua replied: "Pity for our generation, of which you are the leader, that you know nothing of the problems, struggles and difficulties the scholars have in order to sustain themselves."

He said to him: "I apologize, forgive me." But Rabbi Yehoshua ignored him. "Do it out of respect for my father." Rabbi Yehoshua accepted it and they were reconciled. (*Berachot* 28a)

Scholar aging acquires more wisdom

R. Yishmael stated: "The older the scholars get, the more wisdom they acquire. But the reverse is true about the ignorant: the older they get, the more foolish they become." (*Shabbat* 152a)

Scholar to learn three things

R. Yehuda said in the name of Rav: "A scholar must learn three things: writing, *shehita*, and circumcision." (*Hullin* 9a)

Scholars

R. Yosi b. R. Yehuda said: "Warning to a scholar about a transgression is not needed." (*Sanhedrin* 41a)

Scholars

Two scholars when they argue and at the same time are amiable (*Shabbat* 63a)

Scholars beware

One of R. Avtalyon's sayings was: "Scholars, be careful with your words, lest you incur the penalty of exile into a place of evil waters, and the disciples who follow you are likely to drink of them and die." (*Avot* 1:11)

▭ Scholars had privileges

It is related that R. Dimi from Nehardea brought a load of figs in a boat. The Exilarch said to Rava, "Go and see if he is a scholar, and if so, reserve the market for him." The scholars had privileges; they could dispose of their merchandise ahead of the rest of the merchants, in order they could then go and study.

Rava sent R. Adda b. Abba to test his scholarship. He put to him the following question. "If an elephant swallows a basket and then passes it out with excrement, is it still considered to be a basket?"

R. Dimi could not give an answer. He asked R. Adda: "Are you Rava?"

R. Adda answered: "Between Rava and me there is a great difference, but at any rate, I can be your teacher, and therefore, Rava is the teacher of your teacher." Consequently, they did not reserve the market for him, and his figs were a total loss. He appealed to Rabbi Yosef, by saying: "See how they have treated me?"

It so happens that shortly afterwards R. Adda died. R. Dimi aggravated himself and said: "It is through me that he has been punished, because he made me lose my figs." (*Bava Batra* 22a)

Scholars of earlier times

R. Zera said in the name of Rava b. Zimuna: "If the earlier scholars were children of angels, then we are children of humans, and if the earlier scholars were children of humans, then we are like children of donkeys. But not like donkeys of

R. Hanina b. Dosa or R. Pinhas b. Yair, but like common donkeys." (*Shabbat* 112b)

School of Hillel changed their views
The school of Hillel changed their views and agreed with the school of R. Shammai in several matters. (*Eduyot* 3a)

School of Shammai prevailed
On one occasion, the school of R. Hillel was outnumbered by the disciples of R. Shammai. They took a count and the view of R. Shammai prevailed. (*Shabbat* 16b)

✿ Schoolchildren
Rabbi Shimon ben Lakish said in the name of Rabbi Yehuda Nesiah: "The world endures only for the sake of the breath of schoolchildren."

Resh Lakish also said in the name of R. Yehuda Nesiah: "Schoolchildren may not be allowed to neglect their studies even for the building of the Temple."

Resh Lakish also said to R. Yehuda Nesiah: "I have a tradition from my fathers – others say from your fathers – every town in which there are no schoolchildren, deserves to be destroyed." (*Shabbat* 119b)

Schooling system
Introduced in Israel by R. Yehoshua b. Gamla
A universal system of education[231] was introduced by R. Yehoshua b. Gamla which was adopted and took root in Israel. (*Bava Batra* 21a)

Schools in Israel
Ratio of teachers and students
Rava said: "The number of students per teacher should be twenty-five; for fifty, we assign two teachers; for forty, we

---

231. See entry, Children's education; Introduced in Israel.

appoint one teacher and an assistant." (*Bava Batra* 21a)

Sciatic nerve   גיד הנשה
There is a prohibition to eat the sciatic nerve. It is discussed in Tractate *Hullin*. (*Hullin* 89b)

Science
In the Mishna, Rabbi Eleazer ben Hisma said: "Bird offerings and the onset of menstruation are principal ordinances, while calculations of the seasons and *gematria* are trivia compared to the laws of Torah." (*Avot* 3:18)

▭ Scientific knowledge by rabbis
R. Gamliel and R. Yehoshua once traveled on a boat. R. Gamliel had some bread with him while R. Yehoshua had other provisions. When R. Gamliel's bread was consumed, he had to rely on the provisions of R. Yehoshua. He asked R. Yehoshua: "How did you know to bring adequate provisions?"

He answered: "A certain comet appears every seventy years and confuses the sailors. I suspected that it will appear about this time."

"You possess so much knowledge and yet you travel on board a ship."

"Don't marvel at me, rather be surprised at two of your students who live on land, like Rabbi Eleazar ben Hisma and Rabbi Yohanan ben Nuri, who can calculate how many drops of water there are in the sea, and yet they have neither bread to eat nor clothing to put on."

Rabbi Gamliel decided to appoint them as supervisors, and sent for them when he landed. They were reluctant to accept on account of their humility. But Rabbi Gamliel told them: "Do you imagine that I offer you rulership? It is servitude that I offer you." (*Horayot* 10a)

Scissors
Using a scissors to cut the beard? (*Makkot* 21a)

Scorpions
The pit in which Yosef was thrown had scorpions in it. (*Shabbat* 22a)

Scoundrel
Hanan the scoundrel slapped a person in the face. The court ordered him to pay the man half a *zuz*. However, he paid with a *zuz* that was damaged and could not be exchanged. So Hanan slapped him again and told him he can keep the whole *zuz*. (*Bava Kamma* 37a)

Scribe
Rabbi Yehoshua ben Levi said: "Whenever you find the statement in the Talmud, 'a student said it in the name of Rabbi Yishmael, in front of Rabbi Akiva,' it refers to Rabbi Meir, who was an attendant to both Rabbi Akiva and Rabbi Yishmael."

It was taught that Rabbi Meir said: "When I was with Rabbi Yishmael, I used to put a chemical called *kankantum* into the ink, and he never told me not to do it. But when I was with Rabbi Akiva and I tried to do the same thing, he forbade it."

A similar story was related by Rav Yehuda in the name of Rabbi Shemuel in the name of Rabbi Meir: "When I was a student at Rabbi Akiva, I used to put *kankantum* into the ink and he never told me not to do it. But when I came to study at Rabbi Yishmael, he asked me: 'What is your profession?'

"I answered him: 'I am a scribe.'

"Upon this, Rabbi Yishmael said to me: 'Be meticulous in your work, because your work is heavenly sacred. Should you omit one letter or add one letter, you could cause a situation where a world is destroyed.'[232]

"I told him I put *kankantum* in the ink, which makes the ink permanent immediately." (*Eruvin* 13a)

📖 Scribe
The Talmud relates a story: Rabbi Nahman said: "My father was a scribe for the court of Rabbi Shemuel. When I was about six or seven years old, I remember that they used to make an announcement in public that any deed document found on the street should be returned to the owners." (*Bava Metzia* 16b)

Scribe and Pen
A scribe should not go out Friday afternoon carrying his pen. (*Shabbat* 11a)

Scribe's error   אחריות טעות סופר היא
Omission of mortgaging the debtor's property is an error of the scribe. (*Bava Metzia* 14a, 15b; *Bava Batra* 169b)

Scrolls
Rav said: "I found secret scrolls of the school of R. Hiyya in which it is written that Issi b. Yehuda discusses the thirty-nine principal labors forbidden on Shabbat.

Rabbi Issi must have kept secret scrolls of traditions. (*Shabbat* 6b)

✡ Scrupulous
Be as scrupulous in performing a minor good deed as a major one
R. Yehuda HaNasi said: "Which path is the proper one to choose? Whatever is honorable to you and earns you the esteem of your fellow-men. Be as scrupulous in performing a minor good deed as a major one, for one does not know which one has a greater reward. Consider three

---

232. Rashi comments, by adding one letter to a

word one can change that word from singular to plural, and when speaking of God that would be blasphemous.

things and you will avoid sinning: Know what is above you; an eye that sees an ear that hears, and all your deeds are recorded in a book." (*Avot* 2:1)

Sea

The sea is a special domain with respect to Shabbat. (*Shabbat* 6a)

Sea of Tiberias

The Sea of Tiberias was given to the tribe of Naphtali as their portion when they divided the land. (*Bava Kamma* 81b)

Seal of Hashem

Resh Lakish said: "The last letter of Hashem's seal is *tav*, as R. Hanina said: 'The seal of Hashem is *Emet*." (*Shabbat* 55a; *Yoma* 69b; *Sanhedrin* 64a)

Seals preserving wine or food

One seal or two seals placed on the wine are needed to preserve the wine or food, however rabbis differ on this. (*Avodah Zarah* 31a)

Search

Your clothing should be searched on Erev Shabbat. (*Shabbat* 12a)

Searching for Hametz

What is the blessing when one does the *Bedikat Hametz*? (*Pesahim* 7a)

Searching for leavened bread   בודק חמץ
(*Pesahim* 2a)

Seat that is fixed in the Synagogue
מקום קבוע
R. Helbo said in the name of R. Huna: "A person who has a fixed place when he prays has the God of Avraham as his helper." (*Berachot* 6b)

Seated according to his function

When they were sitting together in the academy, Mar Ukva was sitting in front of R. Shemuel at a distance of four cubits, because R. Shemuel was the head of the academy. When they were sitting together at a court session, R. Shemuel sat in front of Mar Ukva at a distance of four cubits, because Mar Ukva was the Exilarch. The place where Mar Ukva sat was dug out and lined with matting. (*Moed Katan* 16b)

Seating in the Sanhedrin

The members of the Sanhedrin were seated in a semicircle, in order for them to see each other. (*Sanhedrin* 36b)

Sechar Halicha   שכר הליכה

Reward for going to do a mitzvah or to go to the Synagogue. (*Avot* 5:14)

Second day of Yom Tov

During one of the Festivals, a deer was served at the table of the Exilarch. This was on the second day of the festival, but the deer was caught on the first day by a non-Jew and slain on the second day. Among the guests at the table were R. Nahman, R. Hisda, and R. Sheshet. R. Nahman and R. Hisda ate from the deer, but R. Sheshet would not eat from it. "What can I do with R. Sheshet who does not want to eat from the deer?"

"How could I eat from it?" retorted R. Sheshet, in view of what R. Assi quoted R. Yosi? (*Eruvin* 39b)

Second tithing   מעשר שני
(*Pesahim* 35b, 38a; *Bava Metzia* 47b)

Second vessel and first vessel on Shabbat

With regards to cooking which is prohibited on Shabbat, one should take into consideration the vessel which is directly on the fire — called the first vessel. When the food is taken and placed in the next vessel — this is the second vessel. R. Yitzhak

b. Avdimi said: "I once followed Rebbe to the bath and wanted to give him heated oil, he told me to put it in a second vessel." (*Shabbat* 40b)

Secondary degree prohibition
איסור מצוה שניות
Secondary degree in relationship to what is forbidden (*Yevamot* 20a)

Secrets and wine
יין סוד
"When wine goes in, secrets come out."
The sons of R. Hiyya, Yehuda and Hezkiya, were having dinner with R. Yehuda HaNasi[233] and they said something improper. Rebbe was unhappy. R. Hiyya intervened and said: "Rebbe, be not angry: the numerical value of the Hebrew letters for 'wine' is the same as the Hebrew letters for 'secret.' You had them drink wine, when wine goes in the secret comes out." (*Sanhedrin* 38a)

Seder Eliyahu
A man once brought to R. Anan a load of fish. R. Anan asked him: "What is your business here?"

The man answered: "I have a lawsuit before you."

R. Anan did not accept the gift and told him: "I am now disqualified to try your case."

The man said to R. Anan: "I do not expect you to be the judge in my case, but I would like you to accept my gift in order to be a substitute for my first fruit offering."

"I had no intention to accept the gift, but since you have given me your reason I will accept."

He sent him to R. Nahman, who was also a judge, with a message: "Will you please try this case because I am disqualified to be his judge." After reading the message,

R. Nahman thought the man was his relative. R. Nahman postponed another case which was a lawsuit of orphans to take this one and showed great consideration to this man. The man was greatly astonished at the consideration he was shown.

Until this incident, Eliyahu was a frequent visitor to R. Anan, whom he was teaching the *Seder Eliyahu*. After this incident Eliyahu stopped his visits. R. Anan spent his time in fasting and in prayers. Eventually Eliyahu came to him again, but a fear came over R. Anan when Eliyahu appeared. In order not to be frightened, he made himself a box and he sat in it until he finished the *Seder Eliyahu*. This is the reason there is a *Seder Eliyahu Rabbah* and a *Seder Eliyahu Zuta* – one part is before this incident and one after. (*Ketubbot* 105b)

Seder Olam
The authorship of the book *Seder Olam* is attributed to Rabbi Halafta or to his son R. Yosi b. Halafta: "Come and hear, it was taught in the book *Seder Olam*," and so on. The book is a history in chronological order; it begins with Creation and ends with the Bar Kochva revolt. (*Shabbat* 88a; *Yevamot* 82b; *Niddah* 46b)

Seducer
מסית
A seducer to worship of idols (*Sanhedrin* 67a)

Seduction resisted
It is related that a woman once tried to seduce R. Hanina b. Papi. He pronounced a magic formula, which made his body full of scabs and undesirable, but she also pronounced a magic formula and his scabs were removed. He fled to a bathhouse. In those days, it was not safe to enter a bathhouse alone. The next day the rabbis asked him: "Who guarded you?"

He answered: "Two imperial armored guards."

They said to him: "Perhaps you were

---

233. See entry, Dining with R. Yehuda HaNasi.

guarded because you resisted an immoral act? As it is written, 'miracles happen to people who resist immoral acts.'" (*Kiddushin* 39b)

Segula סגולה
A safe investment; it refers to a custodian of a minor. (*Bava Kamma* 87b; *Bava Batra* 52a)

Sehora סחורה
Amora from Babylonia
3rd – 4th centuries CE (*Eruvin* 54b)

Selecting on Yom Tov
Selecting beans or other things on Yom Tov (*Betzah* 14b)

Selection ברירה
Bereira is an expression that a subsequent selection reveals retrospectively what the original intent was. (*Bava Kamma* 51b, 69b; *Bava Batra* 27b)

Self-incrimination
אין אדם משים עצמו רשע
No man may declare himself wicked. (*Yevamot* 25b; *Ketubbot* 18b; *Sanhedrin* 9b, 25a)

✿ Self-restraint
R. Pinhas b. Yair said: "Zeal leads to cleanliness, and cleanliness leads to purity; purity leads to self-restraint, and self-restraint leads to sanctity; sanctity leads to humility, and humility leads to fear of sin; fear of sin leads to piety, and piety leads to divine intuition; and divine intuition leads to resurrection of the dead, and the resurrection of the dead shall come through Eliyahu HaNavi, of blessed memory. (*Sotah* 9:15)

✿ Selfishness
R. Hillel said: "If I am not for myself, who will be, and if I am for myself only, what am I? And if not now, when?" (*Avot* 1:14)

Seller
According to R. Akiva, a seller interprets the terms of the sale liberally and the rabbis disagree. (*Bava Batra* 64b)

Selling a house
When a house is sold and there are no specifics, what is included? (*Bava Batra* 61a)

Selling a town
When a town is sold, what is included in the sale? (*Bava Batra* 68a)

Selling a ship
When one sells a ship, what is included in the sale? (*Bava Batra* 73a)

Selling fields
When selling fields, what is included in the sale? (*Bava Batra* 68b)

Selling fruit
When one sells fruit, when is the sale considered to be finalized? (*Bava Batra* 84b)

Selling Hametz to a Gentile (*Shabbat* 18b; *Pesahim* 21a)

Selling fruit
Not yet in existence (*Bava Metzia* 66b; *Yevamot* 93a)

Selling non-kosher
R. Idi bar Avin said: "A person who is suspected of selling non-kosher meat cannot be rehabilitated unless he moves to a place where he is unknown and finds an opportunity of returning a lost article of considerable value, or of taking a big loss when a piece of meat of his became *trefa*. (*Sanhedrin* 25a)

Selling on Friday to a gentile
It is discussed in the 1st *perek* of the Tractate *Shabbat*, יציאות השבת. (*Shabbat* 2a, 18b)

Semen flow (*Zavim* 1:2)

Semicha   סמיכה
The laying of the hands on the offerings in the Temple, or when ordaining rabbis. (*Menahot* 93a)

Sending the mother bird away   שלוח הקן
Letting the mother bird go from the nest (*Hullin* 138b)

Sentenced to die
Leaves to a friend a sizable inheritance
The Talmud relates that Geniva was unfortunately sentenced to die. When the sentence was about to be carried out, he instructed the people to give Rabbi Avina 400 *zuz* from his wine estate. (*Gittin* 65b)

Seorim
Rav Seorim was the brother of Rava
Rava had a brother by the name of Rav Seorim. It is stated that while Rav Seorim was sitting next to Rava's bedside, he noticed that Rava was going into a sleep to die. He bent over to him to hear him say something. Rava said to his brother: "Please tell the Malach HaMavet not to torment me." (*Moed Katan* 28a; *Bava Metzia* 73b)

Separation during menstrual period
Our rabbis taught: Husband and wife should separate during the menstrual period. (*Shevuot* 18b; *Niddah* 63b; *Yevamot* 62b)

✿ Separation from the community
Withdrawal from the community
"Do not separate yourself from the community, do not believe you know it all, and do not judge your friend until you have been in his position." (*Avot* 2:4)

Sepphoris   ציפורי
It is stated that Rabbi Yehuda lived in Bet Shearim, but when he fell ill he was brought to Sepphoris, because it was situated on higher ground and its air was fresher. (*Ketubbot* 103b)

Sepphoris academy
Sepphoris is an ancient city in Israel. It is located in the Galilee, north of Caesarea and south of Acco. During King Yannai's reign, it already had many inhabitants and was the administrative capital of the Galilee. It became the seat of the Patriarchate and the Sanhedrin under Rabbi Yehuda HaNasi. The Talmud advises scholars to follow their teachers to their locations, and mentions to follow Rabbi Yosi ben Halafta to Sepphoris. Elsewhere it is mentioned that Rabbi Yosi was exiled to his hometown Sepphoris.

The following were the heads of the academy in Sepphoris: Hanina bar Hama who lived in the 3rd century CE, and Mani who lived in the 4th century CE. (*Sanhedrin* 32b, 33b; *Shabbat* 33b)

Serah   סרח
Serah was the daughter of Asher, the son of Yaakov. She lived a long life and was still alive at the exodus from Egypt. She told Moshe where to find the remains of Yosef. (*Sotah* 13a)

Serpent's manipulations
Four biblical figures died through the serpent's manipulation. (*Shabbat* 55b)

Servant to be treated
The treatment of a servant should be on the same standard as himself: the quality food and drinks. (*Kiddushin* 20a)

Serve Hashem
Not for the reward
Antigonus Ish Socho said in the name of Shimon HaTzaddik: "Be not like servants

who serve for the expected reward, but be like servants who don't expect rewards." (*Avot* 1:3)

Set out on a ship
To set out on a ship before Shabbat (*Shabbat* 19a)

Seven blessings on Shabbat
During the Amidah
It was asked to what the seven blessings recited on Shabbat correspond. R. Halafta b. Shaul said: to the seven voices mentioned by King David in Psalm 29. (*Berachot* 29a)

Seven characteristics
There are seven characteristics in an uncultured person and seven in a wise man. (*Avot* 5:7)

Seven commandments
The seven commandments accepted by the descendants of Noah (*Bava Kamma* 38a; *Avodah Zarah* 2b; *Sanhedrin* 56a)

Seven gates to the Temple court
There were seven gates to the Temple court. Three were on the south and they were named: Gate of Kindling, Gate of Firstlings, and Gate of Water. On the east, they had one called the Gate of Nicanor, and three gates on the north. (*Middot* 1:4)

Seven things created
Seven things were created by God before he created the world: The Torah, Teshuva, the Garden of Eden, Gehinom, the Throne of Honor, the Holy Temple, and the name of Mashiach. (*Pesahim* 54a)

Seventh millennium
It has been taught according to R. Kattina: Just as the seventh year is one year of release, so is the world: 1,000 years out of seven shall be fallow.

D'bei Eliyahu teaches: The world is to exist 6,000 years. (*Sanhedrin* 97a)

Seventy languages
R. Yohanan said: "In order to qualify for a seat in the Sanhedrin, one must be a man of stature, wisdom, good appearance, mature age, knowledge of sorcery, and conversant in seventy languages. (*Sanhedrin* 17a; *Menuhot* 65a)

Seventy years Honi HaMaagel slept
R. Honi HaMaagel fell asleep and didn't wake up. He slept hidden in a cave for seventy years. When he awoke, he saw a man gathering the fruit from the carob tree. He asked him: "Are you the man who planted the tree?" The man replied: "I am his grandson." He came to the conclusion that he slept seventy years. When he returned home, he enquired: "Is the son of Honi HaMaagel still alive?" The people told him that his son is no longer alive, but his grandson is still living. He declared: "I am Honi HaMaagel," but no one believed him. He went to the house of study, where he overheard the rabbis say: "The Halachah is as clear as in the days of Honi HaMaagel, which he made very clear to us. When Honi HaMaagel used to come to the house of study he would settle every difficulty the rabbis had."

When he heard this he declared to the rabbis: "I am Honi," but the rabbis did not believe him, and they did not give him the honor due to him. This hurt him greatly and he prayed for death, and he died.[234] (*Taanit* 23a)

Shabbat
Two loaves of bread
R. Abba said: "On Shabbat, it is one's duty

---

234. See Honi HaMaagal.

to break bread over two loaves." R. Ashi said: "I saw R. Kahana holding two loaves, but he broke only one of them." (*Shabbat* 117b; *Berachot* 39b)

📖 Shabbat
Observance with zeal
R. Shimon b. Yohai and his son R. Eleazar were hiding in a cave. When they were coming out from the cave on Friday evening before sunset, they saw a man rushing with two bundles of myrtle in his hand. "What are these for?" they asked him.

"They are in honor of Shabbat."

"But would not one bundle be enough?"

"One is for remembering the Shabbat and one is for observing the Shabbat."

R. Shimon said to his son: "See how precious the *mitzvot* are to the people of Israel." (*Shabbat* 33b)

Shabbat   אין אבילות בשבת
There is no mourning on the Shabbat. (*Moed Katan* 24a)

Shabbat and Yom Kippur
When the day of Yom Kippur happens to fall on Shabbat and a person inadvertently does some prohibited work. (*Hullin* 101b)

Shabbat candles
Rav said: "Lighting Shabbat candles is an obligation." (*Shabbat* 25b)

Shabbat candles
Which oils can be used to light the Shabbat candles? (*Shabbat* 20b)

Shabbat candles
R. Tarfon said: "Only olive oil is to be used for the Shabbat candles." (*Shabbat* 24b)

Shabbat desecration
R. Shimon ben Gamliel said: "The Shabbat may be desecrated for a child one-day old, but it may not be desecrated for King David if he is dead." (*Shabbat* 151b)

Shabbat garments
Rabbi Hanina used to dress up in the finest garments on Friday evening and call out: "Let's go out and welcome the Queen Shabbat." (*Shabbat* 119a)

Shabbat honored
With finest cuts of meat
R. Abba used to buy thirteen cuts of the finest meat from thirteen different butchers, and then hand them over to his servants to prepare them for Shabbat. He was also a very charitable person. (*Shabbat* 119a)

Shabbat Kiddush before dark
May one make Shabbat *Kiddush* before dark? (*Berachot* 27b)

Shabbat – meal following Shabbat
R. Hanina said: "One should always set his table after the Shabbat is out – even if he requires only as much as an olive." (*Shabbat* 119b)

Shabbat meals
According to Rabbi Hidka, one is obligated to have four meals on Shabbat. (*Shabbat* 117b; *Ketubbot* 64b)

Shabbat observance
R. Yehuda said in Rav's name: "Had Israel kept the first Shabbat, no nation would have been able to rule over them." (*Shabbat* 118b)

Shabbat observance
R. Hiyya b. Abba said in the name of R. Yohanan: "Whoever observes the Shabbat according to its law, even if he worships idols like the generation of Enosh – he is forgiven." (*Shabbat* 118b)

Shabbat observance and redemption

R. Yohanan said in the name of R. Shimon b. Yohai: "If Israel were to keep two Shabbatot according to the laws, they would be redeemed immediately. (*Shabbat* 118b)

Shabbat prayers early Friday

The Shabbat prayers for Friday evening may one pray early in the afternoon? (*Berachot* 27a–b)

Shabbat preparation

Rabbah and R. Yosef used to get ready for Shabbat by chopping wood in honor of Shabbat. R. Huna would light lamps, R. Papa would twist the wicks, R. Hisda would mince vegetables, R. Zera would kindle the fire. These rabbis felt they had to do something physical to prepare themselves for Shabbat. (*Shabbat* 119a)

Shabbat walk limit   תחום שבת

Walking beyond the *tehum Shabbat* – a distance the rabbis set as a limit for what one may walk on Shabbat (*Eruvin* 52b, 105a)

Shade is more than the sun

צלתה מרובה מחמתה

(*Sukkah* 9b)

Shades of slander   אבק לשון הרע

Not real slander, but implied slander (*Bava Batra* 165a)

Shadow of the Temple

R. Yohanan b. Zakkai was sitting in the shadow of the Temple and teaching all day. (*Pesahim* 26a)

Shame, never to suffer shame

Once when Rabbi Shimon b. Halafta left Rebbe's house, Rebbe told his son: "Go after him in order for him to bless you."

He blessed him with this blessing: "May God grant you his grace that you would never be put to shame and not feel ashamed yourself."

When he came back to his father, he asked him: "What did he say to you?"

He replied: "He said some common remarks to me," and he quoted the blessing.

Said Rebbe to his son: "He blessed you with the blessing God blessed Israel twice." (*Moed Katan* 9b)

Shame not another person in public

R. Zutra b. Toviya said in the name of Rav; according to others, R. Hana b. Bizna said it in the name of R. Shimon Hasida, and others say it was said by R. Yohanan in the name of R. Shimon b. Yohai: "It is preferable for a person to jump into a fiery furnace than to shame another person in public." (*Berachot* 43b; *Bava Metzia* 59a)

Shaming a person

R. Abbaye asked R. Dimi: "What do people in Eretz Yisrael try to avoid the most?"

He answered, "Putting another person to shame." (*Bava Metzia* 58b)

Shaming a person in public

A Tanna said before R. Nahman b. Yitzhak: "Anyone who shames another person in public is equal to shedding the blood of another person." (*Bava Metzia* 58b)

Shaming a sleeping person

המביש את הישן

(*Bava Kamma* 8:1)

Shaming publicly another person

המלבין את פני חבירו ברבים אין לו חלק לעוה"ב

Rava said: "One who publicly puts to shame another person has no portion in the wold to come." (*Bava Metzia* 59a; *Sanhedrin* 99a, 107a)

Shaming another person

R. Eliezer HaModai said: "Anyone who

shames another person in public, even if he is a great scholar and has done good deeds, he will not have a share in *Olam Haba*." (*Sanhedrin* 99a; *Avot* 3:11)

Shamir שמיר
A worm called *shamir* was used to cut stones. It disappeared when the Temple was destroyed. (*Sotah* 48a)

Shammai שמאי
Tanna from Eretz Yisrael
1st century BCE — 1st century CE (*Hagigah* 2:2, 16a–b)

Shammai and Hillel
On one particular day, R. Hillel sat submissive before R. Shammai, like one of his students. (*Shabbat* 17a)

Shammai and Hillel stringencies
R. Yehuda lists six cases in which the school of R. Hillel is more stringent than the school of Shammai. R. Yosi also lists six different cases in which the school of Shammai is more lenient than the school of Hillel. R. Yishmael lists three cases in which the school of Shammai are more lenient than the school of Hillel, and R. Eliezer lists two cases in which the school of Shammai are more lenient. (*Eduyot* 5:1, 2, 3, 4)

Shamta שמתא
To put a ban on a person or to excommunicate (*Moed Katan* 17a; *Nedarim* 7b)

Shapur King of Persia
R. Shemuel used to juggle with eight glasses of wine before King Shapur, and Abbaye used to juggle before Rabbah with eight eggs, or some say with four eggs. (*Sukkah* 53a)

Shapur King of Persia
King Shapur of Persia interacted and had discussions with Rabbi Hama. (*Sanhedrin* 46b)

Shapur King of Persia
King Shapur gave a big compliment to Resh Lakish. (*Bava Metzia* 119a)

Shapur King of Persia dreams
King Shapur I asked R. Shemuel: "Can you tell me what I will dream about?"

R. Shemuel answered him: "You will see the Romans taking you captive and making you grind date pits in a golden mill."

He thought about it all day, and at night that was what he dreamt. (*Berachot* 56a)

Shapur's mother
Ifra Hormizd, the mother of King Shapur, sent a chest of gold coins to R. Yosef and requested that it should be used for a very important religious mitzvah. R. Yosef was thinking hard what the mitzvah should be, when his student Abbaye said to him: "Perhaps the mitzvah of redeeming captives would be a good choice." (*Bava Batra* 8a)

Sharing a Lulav
The Talmud relates that R. Gamliel, R. Yehoshua, R. Eleazar b. Azariah, and R. Akiva were traveling together on a ship. Only R. Gamliel owned a *lulav* which he bought for 1,000 *zuz*. R. Gamliel performed the mitzvah of waving the *lulav*. When he finished, he gave it as a gift to R. Yehoshua. R. Yehoshua did likewise and then gave it as a gift to R. Eleazar b. Azariah who performed the mitzvah. When he finished, he gave it as a gift to R. Akiva. R. Akiva performed the mitzvah and then returned it to R. Gamliel. (*Sukkah* 41b)

Sharing tenant אריס
A tenant who tills the land for a share of the produce. (*Bava Metzia* 74b)

📖 Sharp student

Rabbi Kahana had to flee Babylonia, because of an incident. Rav advised Rabbi Kahana to move to Eretz Yisrael and to study at Rabbi Yohanan, but he also made him promise that for seven years he would not give Rabbi Yohanan a hard time with his sharp questions. When he arrived, he found Resh Lakish with the young rabbis going over the lecture. He sat down to listen and pointed out to them the difficult points in the lecture. He also gave some of the answers.

Resh Lakish went before R. Yohanan and told him: "A lion has come up from Babylonia, be well prepared for tomorrow's lecture." The next day, R. Kahana was seated in the first row, because Resh Lakish thought he was a scholar. But he kept quiet for a long while, as he had promised Rav. Consequently, they demoted him and seated him in the seventh row, which happened to be the last row.

R. Yohanan said to Resh Lakish: "The lion turns out to be a fox."

Rabbi Kahana prayed that the insult of the demotion to the seventh row would be considered like the seven years he had promised. The next day, R. Kahana said to R. Yohanan: "Would the Master repeat the lecture from the beginning?" When Rabbi Yohanan started to lecture again, R. Kahana threw out one question after another, quoting sources in contradiction.

After this, they seated him again in the first row. R. Yohanan was sitting on seven cushions. Whenever R. Yohanan made a statement and R. Kahana pointed out the difficulty, they pulled out one cushion. As he continued to lecture, all seven cushions were removed and R. Yohanan was now sitting on the floor. R. Yohanan looked at R. Kahana and noticed that R. Kahana's lips were parted. He thought that he was laughing at him. For this, R. Yohanan felt insulted. In consequence, R. Kahana died.

The next day, R. Yohanan said to the rabbis: "Did you notice how the Babylonian insulted us?" But they said to him: "This is not so, that is his natural appearance." R. Yohanan went to the cave of R. Kahana and prayed for mercy and he revived him. He said to R. Kahana: "Had I known that is your natural appearance, I would not have taken offense." (*Bava Kamma* 117a)

Shas

R. Kahana finished the *Shas* at age eighteen. (*Shabbat* 63a)

Shav Veyativ שף ויתיב
A synagogue in Nehardea by that name

It was stated that the fathers of Shemuel and Levi were sitting in the synagogue Shav Veyativ in Nehardea. While they were in the synagogue, the Shechina came and they heard a sound of tumult. They rose from their seats and went out. Tradition has it that the synagogue in Nehardea was built during the first exile from stones brought by the exiles from Jerusalem. The name Shav Veyativ means "moved and settled." (*Megillah* 29a; *Avodah Zarah* 43b)

Shavuot Torah reading (*Megillah* 30b)

Shearing sheep
The practice of shearing sheep is discussed. (*Shabbat* 54b)

Shechina
R. Halafta Ish Kefar Hanania is quoted as saying: "If a group of people sit and study Torah, the Shechina is present among them." (*Avot* 3:6)

Shechina
R. Hanania b. Teradion said: two people who sit together and discuss Torah, the Shechina is present with them. (*Avot* 3:2)

Shechina in exile

R. Shimon b. Yohai said: "Come and see how beloved Israel is in the sight of God – for wherever Israel was exiled to, the Shechina went with them. They were exiled to Egypt and the Shechina was with them, as it is written. They were exiled to Babylon and the Shechina was with them, as it is written. And when they will be redeemed in the future, the Shechina will be with them, as it is written. Abbaye said: "In Babylonia, the Shechina is in the synagogue of Huzal, and in the synagogue of Shav Veyativ, which is in Nehardea. But do not think it is in both places, but rather it is sometimes in one and sometimes in the other." R. Abbaye always prayed in that synagogue when he was in that town. (*Megillah* 29a)

Shechina is present

The Shechina is present only where there is joy in performing a mitzvah. (*Shabbat* 30b; *Pesahim* 117a)

Shechiv Mera   שכיב מרע

A dying person
A dying person left his property to strangers, but then recovered. (*Bava Batra* 146b, 148b; *Bava Metzia* 19b, 66a)

Shehakol

The blessing on food that is not grown in the earth is the blessing of *Shehakol*. (*Berachot* 40b)

Shehita

A Jewish scholar must learn three things
R. Yehuda said in the name of Rav: "A scholar must learn three things: writing in Torah script, *shehita* (kosher slaughtering), and circumcision." R. Hanania b. Shalmaya said in the name of Rav: "They also have to know how to make a knot in the *tefillin*, the blessings at a wedding, and binding the *tzitzit*. (*Hullin* 9a)

Shehita over water

Is it permissible to slaughter an animal over water? (*Hullin* 41a)

Shekalim

When do they read *Parshat Shekalim*? (*Megillah* 29a)

Shells of fruits

Shells of fruits can acquire uncleanness (*Uktzin* 2:4)

Shema at bedtime

Rabbi Yitzhak said: "If one recites the *Shema* before going to sleep, the demons keep away from him." (*Berachot* 5a)

Shema and Ehad

Sumchos said: "Anyone who stretches out the word *Ehad* will have his days lengthened." (*Berachot* 13b)

Shema and the silent Baruch

ברוך שם כבוד מלכותו לעולם ועד

R. Shimon b. Lakish said: "Yaakov wanted to reveal to his sons the end of days . . ." (*Pesahim* 56a)

Shema and Ve-Haya

These two chapters of the Torah are read next to each other during prayer services. One is the acceptance of the yoke of God, and the other is the acceptance of God's commandments. (*Berachot* 13a)

Shema in time

R. Mani said: "He who says the *Shema* in its proper time is greater than the one who studies Torah." (*Berachot* 10b)

Shema on R. Akiva's lips when he died

When R. Akiva was taken out to be executed, it was the time for the recital of *Shema*. While they were tearing his flesh with iron combs, he was accepting upon himself the kingship of Heaven. His students asked him: "Rabbi, do you have to go to such extremes?"

He answered: "All my life I have been troubled by a verse in the Torah, which says 'with all your soul.' I wondered when I would have the opportunity to fulfill this commandment. Now that I have the opportunity – shall I not fulfill it?" (*Berachot* 61b)

Shema recital

R. Shimon said: "Be heedful how you read the *Shema*." (*Avot* 2:13)

Shema recital language

In what language may the *Shema* be recited? (*Sotah* 32a; *Berachot* 13a, 40b; *Shevuot* 39a)

Shema recital time

The proper time to recite *Shema* (*Berachot* 2a)

Shema without Tefillin

R. Ulla said: "If one recites the *Shema* without *tefillin*, he is compared to one bearing false witness against himself." (*Berachot* 4b)

Shema words

When reciting the *Shema*, one should be careful to separate words from each other, to avoid running together two words where the first ends with the same letter as the second begins with. (*Berachot* 15b)

Shemaya   שמעיה

Tanna from Eretz Yisrael
1st century BCE (*Yoma* 35b)

Shemaya and Avtalyon

The story of Shemaya and Avtalyon administering the waters of a *sotah* to a freed maiden servant. (*Berachot* 19a)

📖 Shemittah year debt payment

Repayment of debt in a Shemittah year
R. Abba b. Marta owed money to Rabbah. Rabbah asked him for his money, but he was slow. Finally, some years later, he came with the money during a Shemittah year.

The Halachah is that in a Shemittah year all debts are cancelled. Rabbah said to him: "It is cancelled." So R. Abba took the money, put it in his pocket and went home. Afterwards, R. Abbaye met Rabbah and found him to be in a bad mood.

"Why are you in a bad mood?" Rabbah told him what happened with R. Abba.

R. Abbaye went to R. Abba and asked him: "When you took the money to Rabbah, what did you say to him?"

"I offered to pay back the money I owed."

"And what did he say?"

"He said: 'It is cancelled.'"

"Did you say to him: 'Even so, take it?'"

"No, I did not."

Abbaye said to him: "If you had said to him: 'All the same, take it,' he would have taken it. Now go to him and offer him the money again, but make sure you say to him: 'All the same, take it.'"

He did as he was advised. Rabbah took it from him and said: "This rabbinical student did have the sense to see this from the beginning." (*Gittin* 37b)

Shemittah year produce

A person who deals in Shemittah year produce (*Shevuot* 45a)

Shemona Esrei   שמונה עשרה

It has been taught: Shimon HaPakuli formulated the proper order of the eighteen blessings of the *Amidah* in the presence of R. Gamliel in Yavne. R. Yohanan said that it was stated in a Beraita: "A hundred and twenty elders – among them were many prophets – drew up eighteen blessings in a fixed order." (*Megillah* 17b; *Berachot* 28b)

Shemuel
The sons of the Prophet Shemuel are discussed. (*Shabbat* 56a)

Shemuel   שמואל
Amora from Babylonia
  Head of the academy in Nehardea
3rd century CE (*Shabbat* 108b)

Shemuel and Avlat
Shemuel and Avlat were sitting together, and boiled wine was being served. Avlat withdrew his hand.[235] Shemuel said to him: "Boiled wine is not suspected of idolatrous use." (*Avodah Zarah* 30a)

Shemuel and Pinhas
R. Shemuel had a brother by the name of Pinhas. They married two sisters. (*Sanhedrin* 28b)

Shemuel bar Nahmeni   שמואל בר נחמני
Amora from Eretz Yisrael
3rd – 4th centuries CE (*Berachot* 63a)

Shemuel HaKatan   שמואל הקטן
Tanna from Eretz Yisrael
1st – 2nd centuries CE (*Berachot* 28b)

Shemuel mourns the passing of Rav
When they informed Shemuel that Rav has passed away, he rent thirteen garments on account of him, and declared: "Gone is the man before whom I trembled." (*Moed Katan* 24a)

Shemuel the physician
The Talmud states that Shemuel Yarchinah was the physician of R. Yehuda HaNasi. Rebbe suffered from an eye disease. Shemuel suggested treating it with a certain lotion. (*Bava Metzia* 85b)

Shemuel the Prophet
Shemuel the Prophet was a Nazirite according to the opinion of R. Nehorai. (*Nazir* 66a)

Shemuel's father
He was strict with his daughters. (*Shabbat* 65a)

Shemuel's grandson
R. Mari, the son of the daughter of R. Shemuel, pointed out to Rava a contradiction with regards to prayer, but he gave him no answer. Later he said to him: "Did you hear any statement on this subject?"
  He answered: "Yes, I heard R. Sheshet clarify this contradiction." (*Berachot* 16a)

Shepherd
A shepherd who was breeding small animals does *teshuva*. (*Bava Kamma* 80a)

Shepherd
A shepherd was pasturing his herd on the banks of the Papa River when one of his animals slipped and fell into the river and drowned. He came before Rabbah who exempted him from liability. (*Bava Metzia* 93a)

Shepherd selling merchandise
We may not buy from a shepherd: wool, milk, or goats. (*Bava Kamma* 118b)

Sheshet   ששת
Amora from Babylonia
3rd – 4th centuries CE (*Eruvin* 67a)

Shetar Zeifa   שטר זייפא
A forged document (*Bava Batra* 32b)

Shetia stone   אבן שתייה
A stone was under the Temple ark and its name was Shetia. (*Sanhedrin* 26b)

Shetuki   שתוקי
A *shetuki* is one who knows who his

---

235. Avlat was not Jewish.

mother is, but does not know who his father is. (*Kiddushin* 69a)

Sheva Berachot   שבע ברכות
R. Ashi came to the wedding feast of R. Kahana. On the first day, he said all the benedictions, but on the following days he said them all only if there were new guests at the table. (*Ketubbot* 8a)

Shevut
Work forbidden on Shabbat by the rabbis – it does not apply in the Temple. (*Pesahim* 85a)

Shewbread in the Temple   לחם הפנים
(*Menahot* 95b)

Shifra and Puah
Rav and Shemuel say Shifra and Puah are Yocheved and Miriam. (*Sotah* 11b)

Shila   שילא
Amora from Babylonia
3rd century CE (*Yoma* 20b)

Shiloh   שילה
The Tabernacle was moved from Gilgal to Shiloh. (*Zevahim* 112b)

Shimi bar Ashi   שימי בר אשי
Amora from Babylonia
4th – 5th centuries CE (*Berachot* 31a)

Shimi bar Hiyya   שימי בר חייא
Amora from Babylonia
3rd century CE (*Berachot* 47a)

Shimon Ahi Azariah   שמעון אחי עזריה
Tanna from Eretz Yisrael
1st – 2nd centuries CE (*Zevahim* 1:2, 2a; *Taharot* 8:7)

Shimon and Levi
R. Levi and R. Shimon son of Rebbe studied together (*Avodah Zarah* 19a)

Shimon bar Abba   שמן בר אבא
Amora from Babylonia
3rd century CE (*Ketubbot* 23a)

Shimon ben Akashia   שמעון בן עקשיה
Tanna from Eretz Yisrael
2nd century CE (*Kinnim* 3:6)

Shimon ben Eleazar   שמעון בן אלעזר
Tanna from Eretz Yisrael
2nd century CE (*Shabbat* 134a)

Shimon ben Gamliel   שמעון בן גמליאל
Tanna from Eretz Yisrael
1st century CE (*Sukkah* 53a)

Shimon ben Gamliel
Since R. Shimon b. Gamliel passed away, troubles multiplied in the world. (*Sotah* 49a)

Shimon ben Gamliel
R. Yohanan said: "The Halachah is like R. Shimon b. Gamliel – except in three cases." (*Bava Kamma* 69a; *Gittin* 38a, 75a; *Ketubbot* 77a; *Bava Metzia* 38b; *Bava Batra* 174a *Sanhedrin* 31a)

Shimon ben Gamliel
Tanna from Eretz Yisrael
2nd century CE (*Taanit* 29a)

Shimon b. Gamliel said
The mule came into existence during the days of Anah. That was said by R. Shimon b. Gamliel. (*Pesahim* 54a)

Shimon ben Halafta   שמעון בן חלפתא
Tanna from Eretz Yisrael
2nd century CE (*Moed Katan* 9b)

Shimon ben HaSegan   שמעון בן הסגן
Tanna from Eretz Yisrael
1st – 2nd centuries CE (*Ketubbot* 2:8, 23b)

Shimon ben Lakish   שמעון בן לקיש
Amora from Eretz Yisrael
3rd century CE (*Bava Metzia* 84a)

Shimon ben Menasye   שמעון בן מנסיא
2nd – 3rd centuries CE (*Yoma* 85b)

Shimon ben Nanas   שמעון בן ננס
Tanna from Eretz Yisrael
2nd century CE (*Bava Batra* 10:8, 175b)

Shimon ben Nathanel   שמעון בן נתנאל
Tanna from Eretz Yisrael
1st – 2nd centuries CE (*Avot* 2:13)

Shimon ben Pazi   שמעון בן פזי
Amora from Eretz Yisrael
3rd century CE (*Berachot* 61a)

Shimon ben Shetah   שמעון בן שטח
Tanna from Eretz Yisrael
1st century BCE (*Avot* 1:8)

Shimon ben Shetah and Honi HaMaagel
Shimon b. Shetah sent word to Honi HaMaagel: "You deserve to be excommunicated, but what can I do, I see that you are a favorite of Hashem." (*Berachot* 19a; *Taanit* 19a)

Shimon ben Yehotzedek   שמעון בן יהוצדק
Tanna from Eretz Yisrael
2nd – 3rd centuries CE (*Sukkah* 11b)

Shimon ben Yehuda HaNasi   שמעון בן יהודה הנשיא
Tanna from Eretz Yisrael
2nd – 3rd centuries CE (*Ketubbot* 103b)

Shimon ben Yohai   שמעון בן יוחאי
Tanna from Eretz Yisrael
2nd century CE (*Sanhedrin* 14a)

Shimon ben Yohai in Rome
When Rabbi Shimon ben Yohai visited Rome, Rabbi Matya consulted him on an important halachic issue. (*Meilah* 17a)

Shimon ben Yohai was the student
A student asked Rabbi Gamliel and Rabbi Yehoshua: "Is the *Maariv* service obligatory or not?" The student asking the question was Rabbi Shimon b. Yohai. (*Berachot* 28a)

Shimon b. Yosi Lekunia (*Bechorot* 38b)

Shimon HaPakuli   שמעון הפקולי
Tanna from Eretz Yisrael
1st – 2nd centuries CE (*Berachot* 28b)

Shimon HaTimni   שמעון התימני
Tanna from Eretz Yisrael
2nd century CE (*Sanhedrin* 17b)

Shimon HaTimni
R. Shimon HaTimni was multi-lingual. (*Sanhedrin* 17b)

Shimon HaTzaddik   שמעון הצדיק
Pre-Tannaic
3rd century BCE (*Avot* 1:2)

Shimon Ish HaMitzpah   שמעון איש המצפה
Tanna from Eretz Yisrael
1st century CE (*Yoma* 14b)

Shimon Shezuri   שמעון שזורי
Tanna from Eretz Yisrael
2nd century CE (*Demai* 4:1; *Hullin* 4:5, 74b)

Shimshon
Shimshon's eyes were gouged out by the Philistines (*Sotah* 9b)

Shimshon's mother
The name of David's mother was Nitzevet, and she was the daughter of Adael.

The mother of Shimshon was Tzelalfonit, and his sister's name was Nashyan. (*Bava Batra* 91a)

Shin ש
Abbaye said the *shin* of the *tefillin* was given to Moshe on Sinai. (*Shabbat* 62a)

Shinena שיננא
Shemuel called R. Yehuda "Shinena"; it was a term of endearment. (*Bava Kamma* 14a; *Berachot* 36a)

Shir HaShirim שיר השירים
Song of Songs (*Shevuot* 35b)

Shiva sitting not observed
When is sitting *shiva* and observance of mourning annulled? (*Moed Katan* 19a)

Shizbi שיזבי
Amora from Babylonia
3rd – 4th centuries CE (*Eruvin* 80b)

Shizbi
R. Hisda used to pass the house of the parents of Shizbi. He predicted that a great scholar would be born to them. (*Shabbat* 23b)

Shlomo
About sinning (*Shabbat* 56b)

Shlomo
Marries Pharaoh's daughter (*Shabbat* 56b)

Shlomo and the Torah
Ulla said in the name of R. Eleazar: "Before Shlomo, the Torah was like a basket without handles. When Shlomo came, he affixed handles to it." This means he added restrictions to it. (*Yevamot* 21a; *Eruvin* 21b)

Shlomo attends to David's body
David died on Shabbat; Shlomo inquired what to do with David's body on Shabbat. (*Shabbat* 30b)

Shoes
Putting on shoes (*Shabbat* 61a)

Shoes
Do not walk without shoes.[236] (*Pesahim* 112a)

Shoes for a mourner (*Pesahim* 4a)

Shoes of Kohanim to be removed
The Kohanim have to remove their shoes when they ascend the *bimah*. This is one of the ordinances instituted by R. Yohanan b. Zakkai. (*Sotah* 40a)

Shofar blasts
Six blasts were blown on the *shofar* on Erev Shabbat to bring in the Shabbat. (*Shabbat* 35b)

Shofar blasts in the Temple
The number of *shofar* blasts in the Temple, minimum and maximum blasts (*Sukkah* 53b; *Arachin* 10a)

Shofar blasts on Rosh Hashana
The number of blasts on Rosh Hashana and the proper order of the blasts (*Rosh Hashana* 27a, 33b)

Shofar blowing on Shabbat
It once happened that Rosh Hashanah fell on a Shabbat and Rabbi Yohanan ben Zakkai said to Bnai Betera: "Let us blow the *shofar*."

They said: "Let us discuss the matter." He said: Let us first blow the *shofar* and then discuss the matter.

After they blew the *shofar*, they asked to discuss the matter.

He replied: "The *shofar* has already been heard in Yavne and what has been done is no longer open for discussion." (*Rosh Hashana* 29b)

Shofar blowing time
When is the proper time to blow the *shofar*? (*Megillah* 20b)

---

236. See entry, Akiva's instructions to his son.

Shofar on fast days
The Talmud relates that in the town of Sepphoris in the days of Rabbi Halafta and Rabbi Hanania ben Teradion, they prayed special prayers and blew the *shofar* on fast days. (*Taanit* 2:5)

Shofar that is proper
What kind of *shofar* is proper to use on Rosh Hashana? (*Rosh Hashana* 26b)

Shoftim book author
The author of the book of *Shoftim* was the Prophet Shemuel.[237] (*Bava Batra* 14b)

Shohet ignorant
R. Yehuda said in the name of R. Shemuel: "One may not eat the animal slaughtered by a butcher who does not know the laws of *shehita*." (*Hullin* 9a)

Shohet knife
R. Yohanan said: "The knife of the *shohet* should be shown to the Sage out of respect to him." (*Hullin* 10b)

Shohet knife damaged   סכין מסוכסכת
A knife with one-edge notch   סכין אוגרת
A knife with several notches (*Hullin* 17b)

Shohet knife examined
Once it happened that Ravina examined the shohet knife in Babylonia, but R. Ashi, who was the halachic authority in the area, was offended and said to him:

"Why are you acting in this manner?" Ravina answered: "Did not R. Hamnuna decide legal matters at Harta di Argiz during the lifetime of R. Hisda? And just like in their case I am also your colleague and your student." (*Eruvin* 63a)

Shohet to examine organs
R. Yehuda said in the name of R. Shemuel:

"The *shohet* or the butcher must examine the organs after the slaughtering." (*Hullin* 9a, 32a)

Shomer Hinam   שומר חנם
Unpaid watchman (*Bava Metzia* 82b, 93a, 94b)

Shomer Sachar   שומר שכר
Paid watchman (*Bava Metzia* 82b, 93a, 94b)

Short and burned leg
R. Zera acquired a nickname after an incident. When R. Zera emigrated to Eretz Yisrael, he was fasting a hundred fasts to forget the method of how he had learned the Gemara in Babylonia. He also endured a hundred fasts for R. Eleazar to stay alive, and that the burden of the community should not fall on his (R. Zera's) shoulder. He also endured a hundred fasts that the Gehinom fire would be powerless against him. Every thirty days, he would heat an oven and test the power of the fire on him. The fire did not burn him. But one day, the rabbis cast an envious eye upon him and his legs were singed. From that day, he was nicknamed "Short and burned leg." (*Bava Metzia* 85a; *Sanhedrin* 37a)

Shoshbina   שושבינא
Best man at a wedding (*Bava Batra* 144b)

Shoulder or foreleg, the two cheeks, and the maw   זרוע לחיים והקבה
The shoulder and the two cheeks and the maw that were given to the Kohen (*Hullin* 130a)

Shover   שובר
A receipt document (*Bava Metzia* 13a, 18a, 19b; *Gittin* 27a)

Showing off
Rebbe and R. Hiyya were once walking on the road. They turned off the main road and walked on private property to avoid

---

237. Others name different authors.

Showing respect

the pegs on the road. This is according to
the Halachah established during the time
of Yehoshua. But R. Yehuda b. Kenosa
stayed on the main road. Rebbe asked R.
Hiyya: "Who is that man in front of us
who is showing off?" R. Hiyya answered"
"I think it is R. Yehuda b. Kenosa, who is
a student of mine, who does everything
out of piety." When they caught up with
him, R. Hiyya said to him: "If you were
not Yehuda b. Kenosa, I would have cut
your joints off with an iron saw." (*Bava
Kamma* 81b)

Showing respect

Rava was serving drinks at his son's wedding. When he offered drinks to R. Papa
and to R. Huna b. Yehoshua, they stood
up before him out of respect. (*Kiddushin* 32b)

Shti Va-Erev　　שתי וערב

Lengthwise and crosswise, warp and woof
(*Bava Batra* 168b)

Sichnin; Academy　　סיכני

Sichnin or Sikni was located in the Galilee
in Israel. The Talmud advises scholars to
follow their teachers to their locations,
and mentions to follow Rabbi Hanania
ben Teradion to Sikni. (*Sanhedrin* 32b)

Sick person

When praying, pray for every Jewish person
When one prays for a sick person, one
should pray for the person together
with prayers for all the Jewish people.
(*Shabbat* 12b)

Side post　　לחי

Side post used to make an *eruv* for Shabbat
(*Sukkot* 16b; *Eruvin* 12b)

Side post using Lavud
　　לחי פחות משלשה כלבוד דמי
A post for an *eruv* less than three handbreadths is halachically considered like it

is wide enough by using the principle of
lavud. (*Sukkot* 16b; *Eruvin* 12b)

Sifra anonymous

Rabbi Yohanan said: "The author of an
anonymous Mishna is Rabbi Meir; of an
anonymous Tosefta, Rabbi Nehemia; of
an anonymous Sifra, Rabbi Yehuda b. Illai; of an anonymous Sifri, Rabbi Shimon;
and all are taught according to the views
of Rabbi Akiva." (*Sanhedrin* 86a)

Sighing

Rabbi Ulla and Rabbi Hisda were walking
and they passed the house of R. Hana b.
Hanilai. R. Hisda sighed.
　R. Ulla asked: "Why are you sighing?"
　He answered him: "How can I refrain
from sighing? He used to have sixty cooks
to cook and bake for the poor. He always
had his purse ready to give charity. In time
of scarcity, he put the grain and barley
outside at nighttime for anyone to take –
he did not want people to have to come
inside to be embarrassed. Now it is all in
ruins, shall I not sigh?" (*Berachot* 58b)

Signature verification

Documents produced or found – the
signatures on them must be verified.
(*Ketubbot* 20b)

Sikra

Abba Sikra
The Talmud relates that Abba Sikra, the
head of the Jewish guards, was a nephew of
Rabbi Yohanan ben Zakkai. R. Yohanan
sent for him to come to visit in secrecy.
(*Gittin* 56a)

✡ Silence

Rabbi Shimon ben Gamliel is quoted
as saying: "I was brought up all my life
amongst the Sages and I have found nothing as essential as silence. Also, the study
is not the important thing, but the deeds.

Anyone who talks too much brings on sins." (*Avot* 1:17)

✿ Silence is precious
When R. Dimi came to Babylon, he said: "A word is worth the monetary value of a *sela*, and silence is worth two *sela*." (*Megillah* 18a)

Silent when hearing obscene language
R. Nahman b. Yitzhak said: "When one hears obscene language and is silent, he will wind up in the Gehinom." (*Shabbat* 33a)

Silly questions
Silly questions were asked of R. Hillel to try to make him angry. (*Shabbat* 31a)

Silver cup story
R. Ahi b. R. Yoshiah – who lived in Israel – had a silver cup stored with someone in Babylonia. He asked R. Dostai b. Yannai and R. Yosi b. Kipar who were traveling to Babylonia to get it from the person and bring it to him . . . (*Gittin* 14a–b)

Simlai   שמלאי
Amora from Babylonia
3rd century CE (*Bava Batra* 111a)

Simphon   סימפון
A receipt or something similar (*Sanhedrin* 31b)

Sin fearing
R. Shimon and R. Eleazar were sitting when R. Yaakov b. Ahai was walking by. One said to the other: "Let us arise before him, because he is a sin fearing man." (*Shabbat* 31b)

Sin in public
R. Illai said: "If one has a great urge to sin and one cannot overcome his urges, rather than sin publicly, one should go to a place where no one knows him, put on black garments and let him satisfy his urges, but do not profane the Name of Heaven publicly. (*Hagigah* 16a; *Moed Katan* 17a; *Kiddushin* 40a)

Sin offering
R Yitzhak said: "A person that occupies himself with the study of the laws of sin-offering is considered as if he offered a sin-offering." (*Menahot* 110a)

Sinai
The Talmud says that R. Avdimi b. Hama b. Hasa stated that when the Jewish people stood at Har Sinai, the Almighty uprooted the mountain and held it over their heads and said to them: "If you accept the Torah it is well, if not, there will be your burial place." (*Shabbat* 88a; *Avodah Zarah* 2b)

Sinai
Torah hints that all was given on Sinai
R. Levi b. Hama said in the name of R. Shimon b. Lakish that the words in the Torah ואתנה לך את לוחות האבן והתורה והמצוה אשר כתבתי להורותם, "I have given you the following." Each word represents something: the לוחות are the Tablets, והתורה the Five Books of Torah, והמצוה is Mishna, אשר כתבתי is for the Prophets, and להורותם is for the Gemara. (*Berachot* 5a)

📖 Sinai student choice
Or uprooter of mountains
The Talmud relates that they were about to choose a leader for the yeshiva in Pumbedita – the choice was between Rabbah and Rabbi Yosef. The elders of Pumbedita sent a query to Eretz Yisrael asking which one to choose. One is "Sinai," which is R. Yosef, and the other is an "up-rooter of mountains," which is Rabbah.[238]

---

238. Resh Lakish explained his point of view with such excitement, as if he were "uprooting mountains" – *oker harim*.

The answer came from Eretz Yisrael that Sinai is preferred, because everyone is in need of the knowledge of Sinai. However, R. Yosef declined, because the astrologers told him that he would serve as head of the yeshiva for only two years. Rabbah took the position and he served for twenty-two years. After that, R. Yosef served for two and a half years. During the whole term of Rabbah as head of the academy, R. Yosef did not summon anyone to his house, but went to the person himself. (*Berachot* 64a)

Since   הואיל

The rabbis used the term "since" in certain instances. Since under different conditions he could have performed the mitzvah, therefore under these circumstances he can perform the mitzvah even now. (*Pesahim* 62a)

Singing voice

R. Hamnuna must have had a good singing voice, because the Talmud relates that at the wedding of Mar, Rabbi Ravina's son, they asked Rabbi Hamnuna Zuta to sing a song, and he obliged them. (*Berachot* 31a)

Single person affects the whole world

R. Eleazar b. Shimon said: "Every individual person has the opportunity to affect the whole world for good or bad, because the world is judged by its majority of good people and not so good, and an individual is judged by the majority of his deeds – good or bad." (*Kiddushin* 40b)

Sinner

A Jew is a Jew is a Jew

R. Abba b. Zavda said: "A Jew who has sinned is still a Jew; as it is said, a myrtle

---

In this case, "Sinai" means a rabbi who has at his command and in his memory a vast amount of laws given at Sinai.

among reeds is still a myrtle and so it is called." (*Sanhedrin* 44a)

Sinning via an agent (*Bava Kamma* 51a)

Sins of executed person are forgiven

When a person is executed, his sins are forgiven. It happened once that a man was taken out to be executed and he declared: "If I am guilty of this sin, may my death not atone for any of my sins; but if I am innocent, may my death expiate all my sins. The court and all Israel are guiltless, but may the witnesses never be forgiven." (*Sanhedrin* 44b)

Sisters of R. Shemuel

Shemuel's father was very strict with his daughters. (*Shabbat* 65a)

Sit and do not do it   שב ואל תעשה

Sit and do not do it, concerning transgressions (*Makkot* 13b)

Sitting Shiva

When a stranger dies and there is no one to mourn

There was a man who died in the neighborhood where R. Yehuda lived, but there was no one to mourn after him. R. Yehuda assembled ten men every day and they sat *shiva* for seven days. After seven days, the man who died appeared to R. Yehuda in a dream and told him: "Your mind will be at peace because you have set my mind at peace." (*Shabbat* 152a–b)

Sitting Shiva after a teacher

When Rabbi Yohanan passed away, Rabbi Ammi sat *shiva* and observed *sheloshim* for him. (*Moed Katan* 25b)

Six hundred and thirteen commandments   תרי״ג מצוות

R. Simlai said: Six hundred and thirteen

precepts were given to Moshe, 365 negative precepts, corresponding to the number of solar days in the year, and 248 positive precepts, corresponding to the number of organs in the human body. (*Makkot* 23b)

Six leniencies of R. Shammai (*Eduyot* 7a)

Six stringencies
Six cases where Hillel is more stringent
R. Yehuda lists six cases in which the school of R. Hillel is more stringent than the school of Shammai. R. Yosi also lists six different cases in which the school of Shammai is more lenient than the school of Hillel. R. Yishmael lists three cases in which the school of Shammai is more lenient than the school of Hillel, and R. Eliezer lists two cases in which the school of Shammai is more lenient. (*Eduyot* 5:1, 2, 3, 4; *Shabbat* 77a)

Sixtieth part for Teruma
Rav and Shemuel both ruled: The proper measure to be given to the priest for the first of the fleece is one-sixtieth part; for *teruma*, one-sixtieth part, and for the corner of the field to the poor, one-sixtieth part. (*Hullin* 137b)

Size of Torah scroll
The Talmud discusses the size of a Torah scroll. R. Aha wrote a Torah scroll on calfskin and hit it exactly to the right measurement. (*Bava Batra* 14a)

Skeptic
R. Ameimar had debates with a prominent Zoroastrian priest about belief in God. (*Sanhedrin* 39a)

Skeptic debates with R. Avohu
R. Avohu had debates with a prominent skeptic about belief in God. (*Sanhedrin* 39a)

Skin-disease expert
A Kohen who is not an expert in the various skin diseases is not competent to inspect them. (*Shevuot* 6a; *Arachin* 3a)

Skin diseases
Various symptoms for skin diseases (*Negaim* 3:4, 5, 6)

Skins of animals
Skins susceptibility to uncleanness (*Kelim* 26:5)

✿ Slander
Rav taught his students against listening to slander, warning them of its grave consequences. (*Shabbat* 56b)

✿ Slanderer
R. Aha b. Hanina said: "A slanderer has no remedy." (*Arachin* 15b)

Slanderer
R. Hisda said in the name of Mar Ukva: "Of a slanderer, Hashem says: 'He and I cannot live in the same world.'" (*Arachin* 15b)

Slanderers
R. Hama b. Hanina said: "What is the remedy for slanderers? If he is a scholar, he should engage in learning Torah, but if he is an ignorant person, he should become a humble person." (*Arachin* 15b)

Slapping someone in the face (*Bava Kamma* 36b, 90a; *Kiddushin* 11b; *Bechorot* 20b)

Slaughterer in Sepphoris
Nathan b. Shila was the chief slaughterer in Sepphoris. (*Hullin* 50b)

Slaughtering kosher שחיטה
Rebbe said: "וזבחת כאשר צויתך (*Devarim* 12:21) From these words, we learn that Moshe received instructions on Sinai how

to do proper kosher slaughtering." (*Hullin* 28a, 85a; *Yoma* 75b)

Slaughtering
Slaughtering an animal on Yom Tov (*Eduyot* 6a)

Slaughtering
An animal slaughtered on Shabbat or Yom Kippur, is the meat kosher? (*Hullin* 14a; *Bava Kamma* 71a)

Slaughtering
On Shabbat for a sick person (*Hullin* 15b)

Slaughtering a dying animal (*Hullin* 37a)

Slaughtering at night
Is slaughtering at night kosher? (*Hullin* 13b, 37a)

Slaughtering by a blind person
(*Hullin* 13b)

Slaughtering by a minor (*Hullin* 13a)

Slaughtering by cutting neck
Kosher slaughtering is performed on the neck (*Hullin* 27a)

Slaughtering by cutting organs
To slaughter in a kosher way, one must cut certain organs. (*Hullin* 27a)

Slaughtering knife examination
(*Hullin* 17b)

Slaughtering instruments
Instruments permissible to use for kosher slaughtering (*Hullin* 15b)

Slaughtering kosher animals
Who may slaughter kosher animals? (*Hullin* 2a)

Slaughtering over water (*Hullin* 41a)

Slaughtering poultry
אין שחיטה לעוף מן התורה
Some rabbis hold that *shehita* for a bird is not required in the Torah, only by rabbinic enactment. (*Hullin* 20a, 27b, 28a)

Slaughtering without intent
Slaughtering without intent (*Hullin* 31a)

Slave
A Jewish slave carrying on Shabbat (*Shabbat* 58a)

Slave
If one left his property to a slave (*Bava Batra* 150a)

Slaves and a Mezuza
Is a Jewish slave obligated to have a *mezuzah*? (*Berachot* 17b, 20a)

Slaves and Grace after a Meal
Is a Jewish slave obligated to say Grace after a Meal? (*Berachot* 17b, 20a)

Slaves and prayers
Is a Jewish slave obligated to pray? (*Berachot* 17b, 20a)

Slaves and Shema
Is a Jewish slave obligated to recite the Shema? (*Berachot* 17b, 20a)

Slaves and Tefillin
Is a Jewish slave obligated to wear *tefillin*? (*Berachot* 17b, 20a)

Slave's property
The property of a slave is considered equal to real estate or equal to movable property R. Ikka R. Ammi said: "All authorities agree that a slave is considered equal to real estate property." (*Bava Kamma* 12a; *Bava Batra* 68a; *Gittin* 39a)

Sleep

Before one goes to sleep, one should recite the prayer *Ha-Mapil*. (*Berachot* 60b)

Sleep for a long time

When the daughter of R. Hisda, asked her father to take a nap, he answered her: "Soon the days in the grave shall be long and short, and I shall have plenty of time to sleep long." (*Eruvin* 65a)

Sleep not with Tefillin

One should not sleep while wearing *tefillin*. (*Shabbat* 49a)

✿ Sleeping in the Bet Midrash

The students once asked R. Adda b. Ahava: "To what do you attribute your longevity?"

He replied: "I have never displayed my impatience at home, I have never walked in front of a man greater than myself, I have never had thoughts about Torah in a dirty place, I have never walked four *amot* without Torah thoughts, and I never fell asleep in the Bet Midrash. I never rejoiced at the embarrassment of my friends, and I never called my friends by a nickname." (*Taanit* 20b)

Sleeping in the sun

Avlat found Shemuel sleeping in the sun. He said to him: "My Jewish sage, can something that is injurious be possibly beneficial?"

Shemuel answered: "It is the day of bloodletting." (*Shabbat* 129a)

Slow teacher

R. Dimi from Nehardea said: "It is preferable to appoint a teacher who teaches slowly, but makes no mistakes, over one who teaches fast, but with mistakes." (*Bava Batra* 21a)

Small cattle breeding

It is not proper to breed small cattle in Eretz Yisrael. (*Bava Kamma* 79b)

📖 Smart young boy

R. Yehoshua b. Hanania remarked: "No one has ever had the better of me except a woman, a little boy, and a little girl."

What was the incident with the little boy? "I was once walking on the road, when I noticed a little boy sitting at a crossroad. 'Which road leads to the town?' I asked.

"He replied: 'This one is short but long, and that one is long but short.'

"I took the short but long road. When I got to the town, I discovered that gardens and orchards fenced the town in. I returned to where the boy was sitting and said to him:

"'My son, didn't you tell me that this road was short?'

"'Yes,' he answered, 'but didn't I tell you that it is also long?'

"I kissed him on his forehead and told him: 'Happy are you, Israel, all of you are wise, both young and old.'" (*Eruvin* 53b)

📖 Smell of garlic

It happened once that when Rabbi Yehuda was delivering a lecture, he noticed a smell of garlic in the room. He told his students: "Let the person who ate garlic leave the room." R. Hiyya stood up and left the room, and then all the students left the room. The next morning, R. Hiyya was asked by R. Shimon, the son of R. Yehuda: "Was it you that caused annoyance to my father? Heaven forbid that such a thing should happen in Israel." (*Sanhedrin* 11a)

📖 Smuggled out from Jerusalem

The Talmud relates that Abba Sikra, the head of the Jewish guards, was a nephew of Rabbi Yohanan ben Zakkai.

Rabbi Yohanan told him to devise a plan, which would enable him to escape in order to meet with Vespasian, the Roman general. Abba Sikra suggested that he should pretend to be dead and that his students should smuggle him out in a coffin. He took his advice and the two students who smuggled him out were Rabbi Eliezer ben Horkynos and Rabbi Yehoshua ben Hanania. When he was out from Jerusalem, he met with Vespasian.[239] (*Gittin* 56a)

Snake
A snake is considered to be *muad* (warned). (*Bava Kamma* 15b)

Snakes in the pit
Snakes and scorpions were in the pit where Yosef was thrown. (*Shabbat* 22a; *Hagigah* 3a)

Snares
To set snares on Erev Shabbat? (*Shabbat* 17b)

Sodom
The men of Sodom have no portion in the World to Come. (*Sanhedrin* 108a, 109a–b)

📖 Sold as slaves
Brother and sister, children of R. Yishmael were sold as slaves
Rav Yehuda related in the name of Rav: "The son and the daughter of Rabbi Yishmael ben Elisha were carried off and sold as slaves to two masters. Some time later, the two masters met and discussed their two slaves and how good-looking they were. One suggested marrying them to each other and sharing their children.

"They placed them in one room for a whole night. The boy sat in one corner and the girl in another. The boy was talking to himself, saying: 'I am a descendant of the High Priests, how could I marry a slave girl?'

"The girl was saying to herself: 'I am a descendant of the High Priests, how could I marry a slave?'

"They passed that night in tears. In the morning, they recognized each other, and fell upon each other's necks and cried with tears until their souls departed." (*Gittin* 58a)

Sold father's estate
It happened in Bene Berak that a person sold his father's estate and then died. The members of his family protested and claimed that he was still a minor. They came to R. Akiva and asked that the body be exhumed. He told them that it is not permitted to dishonor the dead; furthermore, the signs after death undergo a change. (*Bava Batra* 154a)

Solomon
The *eruv* which permits halachically to perform prohibited things on Shabbat was instituted by King Solomon. (*Shabbat* 14b; *Eruvin* 21b)

Solomon
R. Shemuel b. Nahmaini said in the name of R. Yonatan: "Whoever maintains that King Solomon sinned is making an error." (*Shabbat* 56b)

Some say
(*Hullin* 3b)   איכא דאמרי א״ד

Son and grandson
Of R. Yehoshua b. Levi
R. Yehoshua b. Levi had a son by the name of R. Yosef and a grandson by the name of Meyasha. (*Berachot* 24b; *Pesahim* 50a)

Son of David
R. Hama b. Hanina said: "The Son of David will not come until all kingdoms will lose their power over Israel."

R. Zeiri said: "The Son of David will not come until there are no conceited men in Israel."

---

239. See entry, Escape from besieged Jerusalem.

R. Simlai said in the name of R. Eleazar b. Shimon: "The Son of David will not come until all the judges are removed from Israel."

R. Yohanan said: "The Son of David will come only in a generation that is all righteous or all wicked." (*Sanhedrin* 98a)

Son of David will come

Eliyahu spoke of Mashiach

Eliyahu said to Rav Yehuda the brother of R. Sala Hasida: "The world will last not less than eighty-five Jubilees and in the last Jubilee, the Son of David will come."

Eliyahu was asked: "Will it be in the beginning or in the end?"

He answered: "I do not know."

R. Ashi said that his answer was: "Do not expect him before, but afterwards expect him." (*Sanhedrin* 97b)

Son of holy people   בנן של קדושים

Son of the holy: The Talmud says that R. Menahem son of R. Simai is called "the son of holy people" because he did not look at the effigy of a coin. (*Avodah Zarah* 50a; *Pesahim* 104a)

Son of R. Eleazar repented

R. Yehuda HaNasi visited the town of R. Eleazar b. Shimon. He inquired: "Did that *tzaddik* leave a son?"

"Yes," they replied, "and every harlot whose hire is two *zuz* is willing to hire him for herself for eight *zuz*."

R. Yehuda summoned him, ordained him as a rabbi in order to bestow respect on him, and entrusted him to be educated by R. Shimon b. Issi b. Lakonia, his mother's brother.

Every day, the young man would say: "I am going back to my town," and the teacher would reply: "They made you a sage and they spread a gold-trimmed cape on you and they call you rabbi, and in spite of it, you say 'I am going back to my town'?"

The young man answered his teacher: "I swear that I am cured, that my desires have been abandoned."

Some years later when he became a great scholar, he went to Rebbe's academy and participated in the discussions. On hearing his voice Rebbe observed: "This voice is similar to the voice of R. Eleazar b. Shimon."

"He is the son of R. Eleazar," said the students of the academy. Rebbe was very pleased and cited a verse from Scripture in praise. He also complimented R. Shimon b. Issi b. Lakonia for accomplishing his mission.

When he died, they buried him next to his father. (*Bava Metzia* 85a)

Son of R. Mereimar

R. Mereimar had one son – R. Yehuda – who was a colleague of Mar b. Rav Ashi and R. Aha. (*Berachot* 45b)

Son of R. Yosi b. Halafta

One time R. Yosi b. Akavia failed to attend the academy of Rabbi Yosi ben Halafta for three days. Wardimus, the son of Rabbi Yosi ben Halafta, happened to meet him outside and asked:

"Why have you not shown up at the academy for the past three days?"

He answered him: "Because I didn't get a proper explanation from your father for the rulings he made." (*Nedarim* 81a)

Son who follows in his ways lives on

Pinhas b. Hama HaKohen states that if one leaves behind a son who follows in his ways, when that person dies, he is considered as going to sleep. A person who does not leave behind a son who follows him in his ways – when he dies, he can be considered to be dead. (*Bava Batra* 116a)

Song of Az Yashir   שירה אז ישיר

R. Akiva expounded: "When Moshe sang

the *Az Yashir* song, the congregation of Israel responded to him verse after verse." (*Sotah* 27b)

Song of the day   שיר של יום
R. Yehuda said in the name of R. Akiva: "The reasons the songs by the Levites were sung on the particular days." (*Rosh Hashana* 31a)

Songs of thanksgiving
We have learned that the songs of thanksgiving were accompanied by lutes, lyres, and cymbals. (*Shevuot* 15b)

Songs of the Levites
Every day the Levites sang to the words of a different Psalm. (*Tamid* 33b; *Rosh Hashana* 31a)

Sons inherit
When a man dies leaving sons and daughters, if the inheritance is large, the sons inherit, and the daughters receive maintenance. (*Bava Batra* 139b; *Ketubbot* 108b)

Sons of R. Akiva died in his lifetime
Rabbi Akiva lost two sons – both of them were bridegrooms. People came from all over Israel to lament for them. Rabbi Akiva stood on a podium and addressed the people: "Even though these two sons were bridegrooms, I am consoled on account of the honor you have done to them." (*Moed Katan* 21b)

Sons of R. Ashi
Rabbi Ashi had two sons: Mar b. Rav Ashi, and Sama, and also a daughter, as mentioned in the Talmud. (*Berachot* 45b; *Ketubbot* 106a)

Sons of R. Hiyya b. Abba
R. Hiyya had many sons: Rabbi Abba, Rabbi Yirmiyahu, Rabbi Kahana, and Rabbi Nehemia. (*Berachot* 5a; *Moed Katan* 22a)

Sons of R. Mari
Two sons of Rabbi Mari are mentioned: Mar Zutra and Rabbi Adda Saba. (*Kiddushin* 65b)

Sons of R. Nahman b. Yaakov
And his daughters
R. Nahman had four sons who are mentioned in the Talmud: Rabbah, Hon, Mar Zutra, and Hiyya. Rabbi Nahman also had two daughters. (*Shabbat* 119a; *Yevamot* 34b; *Bava Batra* 7a, 46a; *Gittin* 45a)

Sons of R. Papa
רבי אחא בר פפא, רבי אבא בר פפא, רבי אדא בר פפא, רבי חייא בר פפא, רבי חנינא בר פפא
(*Bava Kamma* 80b)

Sotah   סוטה
The *sotah* ceremony takes place when a husband is suspicious of his wife's fidelity and they go through the ceremony of *sotah*. (*Sotah* 2a, 7a, 8a; *Berachot* 63a)

Sotah at Nikanor gate
The ceremony of drinking the *sotah* water took place opposite the Nikanor Gate. (*Sotah* 7a, 8a)

Sound, sight, and smell
R. Shimon b. Pazi said in the name of R. Yehoshua b. Levi: "There is no violation of *meilah* if one benefits from enjoying the voice, sight or smell of holy objects." (*Pesahim* 26a; *Keritut* 6a)

Soup kitchen   תמחוי
Public soup kitchen (*Bava Batra* 8b)

Soup kitchen overseer   גבאי תמחוי
Overseer of the soup kitchen (*Bava Metzia* 38a; *Bava Batra* 8b; *Pesahim* 13a)

South gate to the Temple
The south gate to the Temple was not

used. No man was allowed to enter through the south gate. (*Tamid* 30b)

Spare Israel unnecessary expense
התורה חסה על ממונן של ישראל
The Torah wished to spare Israel unnecessary expense. (*Rosh Hashana* 27a; *Hullin* 49b)

Spark
A spark flying off a hammer causing damages (*Bava Kamma* 62b)

Speaking not with his full heart
המדבר אחד בפה ואחד בלב
One who speaks one thing with his mouth and another in his heart. (*Pesahim* 113b)

Specification needing generalization
פרט הצריך לכלל
(*Bechorot* 19a)

✿ Speech, refined
R. Huna said in Rav's name, others say R. Huna said in Rav's name, which he heard from R. Meir:
  "One should always teach his student to use concise language and refined speech." (*Pesahim* 3b; *Hullin* 63b)

Speeches of R. Meir and their content
Rabbi Yohanan said: "When Rabbi Meir used to deliver his public discourses, it would consist of one-third Halachah, one-third Aggadata, and one-third of parables." (*Sanhedrin* 38b)

Spices at Shabbat ending   בשמים
Blessing over spices at the end of Shabbat during *Havdalah* (*Berachot* 51b; *Pesahim* 103a)

Spilling water
On the public street, thereby causing damages (*Bava Kamma* 30a)

Spinal cord
Hut Ha-Shidra חוט השדרה (*Hullin* 42a, 45a)

📖 Spiritual advancement preferred
Rabbi Ilfa and Rabbi Yohanan studied together, but they had no income. They spoke to each other about going into business, but Rabbi Yohanan had a dream not to do it and therefore he continued to study. However, Rabbi Ilfa decided to go to earn a living.

Years later when Rabbi Ilfa returned to the community, Rabbi Yohanan presided already over his academy. The scholars were teasing him by telling him: "Had you remained here to study, you might have been presiding over the academy."

To prove to the scholars that he did study, Ilfa suspended himself from the mast of a ship and exclaimed: "If there is any one who will ask me a question from a Beraita of Rabbi Hiyya and Rabbi Oshaya, if I fail to know the subject, then I will throw myself into the water to drown." An old man came forward and asked him a question. Rabbi Ilfa had the right answer for the question. (*Taanit* 21a)

Spit
The penalty for spitting at someone (*Bava Kamma* 90a; *Ketubbot* 66a)

Spitting at Halitza ceremony
When spitting at the ceremony of *halitza* – what is required to make it valid? (*Yevamot* 104a)

Spoilage   מבעה
Spoilage caused by animals eating up someone's crop (*Bava Kamma* 2a)

Spring of water at the Temple
R. Pinhas said it in the name of R. Huna from Sepphoris: "The spring which comes out from the Holy of Holies resembles the

horns of locusts, and further on when it reaches the entrance to the Temple court, it becomes as large as the mouth of a small bottle." (*Yoma* 77b)

Stalks of fruits and vegetables

Stalks of fruits and vegetables can acquire uncleanness. (*Uktzin* 1:6)

S'tam Mishna   סתם משנה

R. Yohanan said: "The Halachah is in agreement with the anonymous Mishna." (*Yevamot* 42b; *Shabbat* 46a)

Standing in a private domain

While standing in a private domain on Shabbat drinking a liquid located in a public domain (*Eruvin* 98b)

Standing on one foot

It was said of R. Hanina that at the age of eighty, he could stand on one foot and put on and take off his shoe on the other foot. (*Hullin* 24b)

📖 Standing on one leg learning Torah

A heathen came before Shammai and asked him to convert him to Judaism and to teach him the Torah while he stands on one leg. Shammai chased him away with a builder's ruler.

The man came to Hillel with the same request. Rabbi Hillel told him:

"Yes, I will convert you to Judaism, and this is what the Torah teaches: 'What is hateful to you, do not impose on your neighbor.' That is the whole Torah and the rest is commentary. Now go and learn the rest." (*Shabbat* 31a)

Standing up for a scholar (*Shabbat* 31b; *Gittin* 62a)

Standing up for a pious

Standing up for a sin-fearing person (*Shabbat* 31b; *Gittin* 62a)

📖 Star appears every 70 years

Rabbi Gamliel and Rabbi Yehoshua once traveled on board a ship. The food supply of Rabbi Gamliel was quickly consumed and he had to rely on the food which Rabbi Yehoshua brought with him.

"Did you know that we would be delayed so much that you brought additional food with you?" asked Rabbi Gamliel.

"A certain star appears every seventy years and leads sailors to miscalculate their position and I calculated that it was due to appear," said Rabbi Yehoshua.

"You posses so much knowledge," complimented him Rabbi Gamliel, "and yet you travel on board a ship."

"Don't marvel at me, rather be surprised at two of your students who live on land, like Rabbi Eleazar Hisma and Rabbi Yohanan ben Nuri, who can calculate how many drops of water there are in the sea and yet they have neither bread to eat nor clothing to put on."

Rabbi Gamliel decided to appoint them as supervisors,[240] and sent for them when he landed. They were reluctant to accept on account of their humility. But Rabbi Gamliel told them: "Do you imagine that I offer you rulership? It is servitude that I offer you." (*Horayot* 10a)

Stars visible

R. Yehuda said in the name of R. Shemuel: "Three stars that are visible indicate that it is night." (*Shabbat* 35b)

📖 Starvation

A woman and children starving

It has been taught that R. Binyamin the Tzaddik was the supervisor of the charity fund. One day, a woman came to him during a year of great famine and asked him for help. He said to her: "There is no money in the charity basket."

---

240. See entry, Jobs offered.

She replied to him: "Rabbi, if you don't help me then a mother and her seven children will die." When he heard this, he took his own money and gave her what she needed.

Some time at a later period, he became dangerously ill. The angels addressed the Holy One: "You have decreed that he who saves one soul of Israel is equal to saving a whole world. Binyamin the Tzaddik saved a mother and her seven children. Is it right that he should die at such a young age?" His sentence to die was immediately torn up and he lived another twenty-two years. (*Bava Batra* 11a)

📖 Starving for a principle
Not to derive benefit from learning Torah
R. Yehuda HaNasi opened his storehouse of produce to the public with a proclamation: "The storehouse is open to all who studied the Scripture, the Mishna, the Gemara, the Halachah, or the Aggadah. There is no admission for the ignorant." R. Yonatan b. Amram entered the storehouse and asked for food.

Rebbe asked him: "My son, have you studied Scripture and Mishna?"

"No," he answered.

"How can I feed you, you don't qualify."

"Feed me as a dog or as a raven is fed." He gave him some food.

After he left, Rebbe regretted giving him food, saying to his son, "I have broken my principle in giving food to an ignorant." R. Shimon his son said to him: It was your student R. Yonatan b. Amram who made it his principle not to derive material benefit from learning Torah."[241] (*Bava Batra* 8a)

Statements made by R. Akiva (*Eduyot* 4a)

Statements by R. Dosa b. Horkynos
R. Dosa b. Horkynos ruled with regards to purity. (*Eduyot* 4b)

Statements made by R. Eleazar b. Azaria (*Eduyot* 6a)

Statements made by R. Gamliel (*Eduyot* 5b)

Statements made by R. Tzadok (*Eduyot* 5b)

Statements made by R. Yishmael
R. Yishmael made a statement in front of the Sages in the vineyard of Yavne about three matters. (*Eduyot* 3b)

Statements by R. Yehoshua b. Hanania (*Eduyot* 5a)

Stealing a palm tree
The consequences of the deed (*Bava Kamma* 96a)

Stealing a purse on Shabbat
If one steals a purse on Shabbat, is his transgression for Shabbat or for stealing? (*Bava Batra* 86a)

Steal from people
R. Levi also stated: "To rob a human is worse than the robbery of holy things." (*Bava Batra* 88b)

Stealing from parents (*Sanhedrin* 71a)

Stealing from a thief
"The proverb says: "If you steal from a thief, you also have a taste of it." (*Berachot* 5b; *Bava Kamma* 62b, 67b)

Steals
If one steals and sells it on Shabbat (*Bava Kamma* 70a–b)

---

241. See entry, Feeding the hungry.

Steals a field

If one steals a field and bandits steal it from him (*Bava Kamma* 116b)

Stipulations contrary to Torah

כל המתנה על מה שכתוב בתורה

Stipulations in a contract contrary to Torah commandments are considered null and void. (*Ketubbot* 83a; *Bava Metzia* 94a)

Stole

A stolen animal was slaughtered on Yom Kippur. (*Bava Kamma* 70a, 71a)

Stole a cow

If one stole a cow and the stolen cow became pregnant (*Bava Kamma* 93b, 95b)

Stole a yoke of oxen

A man stole a yoke of oxen. He used the oxen to work the land. He was brought to the court of R. Nahman and he judged against the thief very harshly. The thief had to pay also for the improvement of the land. Rava objected. But R. Nahman said to Rava: "When I sit in judgment, do not interrupt me. As you know, R. Huna said of me: 'R. Nahman and King Shapur are like brothers with respect to civil law.'" (*Bava Kamma* 96b)

Stole and converted

The stolen object was converted to another object. (*Bava Kamma* 65b, 66a, 93b; *Temurah* 6a)

Stole and swore

If one stole even the worth of a *peruta* and swore he didn't steal (*Bava Kamma* 103a; *Bava Metzia* 55a)

Stolen

An item entrusted to a guardian and the guardian claims it was stolen (*Bava Kamma* 62b, 63b, 106b)

Stolen Arava

Is a stolen *arava* (one of the Four Species) fit for performing the mitzvah of *arba minim*? (*Sukkah* 33b)

Stolen Etrog

Is a stolen *etrog* fit for performing the mitzvah? (*Sukkah* 34b)

Stolen Hadas

Is a stolen *hadas* fit for performing the mitzvah? (*Sukkah* 34b)

Stolen Lulav

Is a stolen *lulav* fit for performing the mitzvah? (*Sukkah* 29b)

Stolen Torah

It has been taught: If a Torah – belonging to the inhabitants of the town – was stolen, the judge of that town may not judge the case, nor may the inhabitants of the town give testimony. (*Bava Batra* 43a)

Stomach ailment

Rabbi Ashi's daughter had a stomach ailment, and Rabin from Naresh cured her with herbal medicines. (*Gittin* 69b)

Stone of claims for lost objects

Our rabbis taught: "A stone of claims was in Jerusalem for lost and found objects." (*Bava Metzia* 28b)

Stone on the coffin

R. Eleazar b. Hanoch was excommunicated, and when he died they placed a large stone on his coffin. (*Berachot* 19a)

Stones at the Jordan

There were three different stones erected: one set of stones erected by Moshe, the other set erected by Yehoshua at the Jordan, and a third erected at Gilgal. (*Sotah* 35b)

Stones at the Jordan
R. Yosi b. Halafta said: "My father R. Halafta and R. Eliezer b. Matya and R. Hanania b. Hachinai were standing next to the stones that were erected at the Jordan and they were trying to estimate the weight of those stones." (*Sotah* 34a)

Stones of the altar stored away
The Hasmoneans stored away the altar stones which the Greeks made abominable. (*Avodah Zarah* 52b)

Stoning
The somber procedure that is followed when a person is condemned to die by stoning. (*Sanhedrin* 42b)

Stoning
R. Hiyya b. Ashi said in the name of R. Hisda: "When a person is taken out to be executed, he is given a goblet of wine spiced with frankincense, in order to benumb his senses." (*Sanhedrin* 43a)

Store in a courtyard
A store in a courtyard where business is done; the noise it causes. What are its limitations? (*Bava Batra* 20b)

Stories recalled
R. Kahana said: "When R. Yishmael became ill, he was asked to recall stories from his father, R. Yosi b. Halafta." (*Shabbat* 15a; *Avodah Zarah* 8b)

Storing food on Shabbat
Storing food on Shabbat to keep the food warm (*Shabbat* 47b; *Bava Batra* 19a; *Nedarim* 2b; *Nazir* 2a)

Stove on Shabbat
A stove heated with stubble can one put a dish on it to warm the food? (*Shabbat* 36b)

Strangers eating at the same table
R. Shimon b. Gamliel deals with a case where two people who do not know each other eat at the same table – one eating meat and the other eating dairy. (*Shabbat* 13a; *Hullin* 107b)

Straw
Straw left on the street, causing damage or straw thrown on a public street injuring a person (*Bava Kamma* 30a)

Stream reversing direction
R. Eliezer had disputes with the rabbis; to prove his point, he said if I am right, let the river flow in the opposite direction.[242] (*Bava Metzia* 59b)

✡ Strife
Abbaye Kashisha spoke out against controversy and dissention: "Strife is like planks in a wooden bridge, the longer you let them lie, the stronger they get." (*Sanhedrin* 7a)

✡ Strife
If not stopped, it increases
R. Huna said: "Strife is similar to an opening made by a rush of water that widens as the water pushes through the opening." (*Sanhedrin* 7a)

📖 Strife in Israel
We have learned: R. Yosi said: "Originally, there were not many disputes in Israel, and therefore it was sufficient to have one Bet Din of seventy-one members who sat in the hall of the Lishkat HaGazit and two courts of twenty-three each who sat at the entrance of the Temple Mount and at the door of the Temple court. There were also other courts of twenty-three in all Jewish cities. Any inquiry that arose was directed to the local Bet Din. If they

---

242. See entry, Bat Kol.

heard and had a tradition, they ruled; if not, they went to the nearest Bet Din; if they had an answer, they ruled, if not, they went to the Bet Din at the entrance to the Temple Mount; if they heard and had a tradition, they ruled. However, if one of the rabbis did not agree, they went to the court sitting at the entrance of the court; the rabbi who disagreed declared: 'This is my view on the matter and this is the view of my colleagues.' If this court heard and had the tradition related to this case, they ruled, if not, they proceeded to the Sanhedrin where the seventy-one members sat from the morning until the evening. The question was put to them; if they had the tradition for a similar case at hand, they ruled, if not, they took a vote and it was decided by a majority, and the ruling was given.

However, later on, when the disciples of R. Shammai and the disciples of R. Hillel had many disagreements and the rulings became contradictory, and it looked as if there were two Torahs, they changed the system. From the Sanhedrin hall, they sent out instructions to all the communities in Israel, appointing men of wisdom and humility and who were esteemed by their fellowmen to be the judges of the community. From there, if merited, they were promoted to the Temple Mount and from there, they were further promoted to the Sanhedrin of seventy-one." (*Sanhedrin* 88b; *Sotah* 47b)

Striking with a hammer   מכה בפטיש
Striking with a hammer;[243] it is the last strike with the hammer indicating the utensil is finished. (*Shabbat* 73a, 75b, 102b)

Stringencies
Greater stringency applies to the

rabbinical teachings than to the teachings of the Torah. (*Sanhedrin* 88b)

Stringencies of R. Hillel
Six cases where Hillel is more stringent
R. Yehuda lists six cases in which the school of R. Hillel is more stringent than the school of Shammai. R. Yosi also lists six different cases in which the school of Shammai is more lenient than the school of Hillel. R. Yishmael lists three cases in which the school of Shammai is more lenient than the school of Hillel, and R. Eliezer lists two cases in which the school of Shammai is more lenient. (*Eduyot* 5:1, 2, 3, 4)

Stripes
When flogging is ordered, it applies for certain transgressions and for certain persons. (*Makkot* 13a)

Stripes
When flogging is ordered, how many lashes are given? (*Makkot* 22a)

Stripped of its hide
An animal that was stripped of its hide, is it rendered not kosher? There is a disagreement between the rabbis. (*Hullin* 55b)

✡ Strong
Who is strong?
Ben Zoma used to say: "Who is wise? One who learns from all people. Who is strong? One who subdues his passions. Who is rich? One who is happy with his portion. Who is honored? One who honors his fellow-men." (*Avot* 4:1)

✡ Strong as a lion
Rabbi Yehuda b. Tema is quoted as saying: "Be strong like a leopard, light like an eagle, run like a deer, and be powerful like a lion when you do God's will." (*Avot* 5:20)

---

243. A Talmudic expression.

📖 Struggles of scholars for sustenance

There was another halachic dispute between Rabbi Gamliel and Rabbi Yehoshua. It concerned the Ammonites, and whether they can be accepted into the Jewish community. Rabbi Yehoshua was in favor and Rabbi Gamliel was against. The Sanhedrin sided with Rabbi Yehoshua. When Rabbi Gamliel saw the great respect the Sanhedrin accorded to Rabbi Yehoshua, he decided to go to him to apologize. When he reached his house, he saw that the walls were black from charcoal. He said to him: "I can tell by your walls that you are a blacksmith."

Rabbi Yehoshua replied: "Pity for our generation, of which you are the leader, that you know nothing of the problems, struggles, and difficulties the scholars have in order to sustain themselves."

He said to him: "I apologize, forgive me." But Rabbi Yehoshua ignored him. "Do it out of respect for my father." Rabbi Yehoshua accepted it and they were reconciled. (*Berachot* 28a)

📖 Stuck on the road before Shabbat

Rabbah and R. Yosef were traveling together on a Friday evening, but it was getting close to Shabbat. Rabbah said to R. Yosef: "Let our Shabbat resting place be under that particular palm tree which is leaning on another tree."

"I do not know that tree," said R. Yosef. "Rely on me and make me your messenger, and I will declare our Shabbat resting place." (*Eruvin* 51a)

Student asking the question

The student asking the question about the evening prayer was R. Shimon b. Yohai. He asked the question from R. Yehoshua and from R. Gamliel. (*Berachot* 28a)

Student deciding Halachah

A student may not decide matters of Halachah without the permission of his teacher. (*Sanhedrin* 5b; *Eruvin* 63a)

Student identified

Rabbi Yehoshua ben Levi said: "Whenever you find a statement in the Talmud, 'a student said it in the name of Rabbi Yishmael in front of Rabbi Akiva' – it refers to Rabbi Meir, who was an attendant to both Rabbi Akiva and Rabbi Yishmael."

It was taught that Rabbi Meir said: "When I was with Rabbi Yishmael, I used to put a chemical called *kankantum* into the ink, and he didn't object to it. But when I was with Rabbi Akiva and I tried to do the same thing, he forbade it." (*Eruvin* 13a; *Sotah* 20a)

Student of exceptional mind

Rabbi Abba b. Hanina said: "In the generation of Rabbi Meir, there was none equal to him. Then why was the Halachah not fixed in agreement with his views? Because his colleagues could not fathom the depth of his mind." (*Eruvin* 13b, 53a)

Student of R. Eliezer deciding Halachah

A story of a student of R. Eliezer who made a halachic ruling in the presence of his teacher and died that year. (*Eruvin* 63a)

📖 Student prayers answered

R. Hanina a student of R. Gamliel prays for R. Gamliel's son recovery

Our rabbis taught: "Once the son of R. Gamliel became ill. He sent two scholars to R. Hanina b. Dosa to ask him to pray. R. Hanina went up to the upper chamber and prayed. When he came down, he said to them: "Go home, the fever has left him."

They asked him: "Are you a prophet?"

He replied: "I am neither a prophet, nor the son of a prophet, but I learnt this from experience. If my prayer is fluent in my mouth, I know that my prayers are accepted, but if the prayers are not smooth then I know that my prayers have not been accepted." The rabbis made a note of the exact time when he said the fever left him. When they returned to the house of R. Gamliel, he confirmed to them that the fever left the child exactly at that moment. (*Berachot* 34b)

Student refugee
A student who has to exile to a town of refuge, his teacher goes with him. (*Makkot* 10a)

Student to be a witness to his Rebbe
The Rebbe tells his student: "You know that I am honest, but I have only one witness. I want you to be my second witness. Be my second witness just by standing there, you don't have to say anything." (*Shevuot* 31a)

☐ Students
It is related that R. Avdan and the students of the academy at Rabbi Yehuda HaNasi were discussing a halachic subject. In the middle of their talking, Rebbe entered. They all hurried to their seats, except R. Yishmael ben Yosi. Due to his corpulent body, he could not reach his seat in time.

He climbed over the seats of other students to get to his seat.

"Who is this man who climbs over the heads of the holy people?" asked Avdan.

"I am Yishmael, son of Rabbi Yosi. I have come to learn Torah from Rebbe."

R. Avdan asked him:

"Are you fit to learn Torah from Rebbe?"

"Was Moshe fit to learn Torah from God?"

"Are you Moshe?" he retorted.

"Is your teacher God?" asked R. Yishmael.

In the meantime, Rebbe sent Avdan to take care of some other matter at hand and

while he went out, R. Yishmael quoted his father in this matter. Avdan was called back because the matter was settled.

When Avdan returned, he had to climb over other students. R. Yishmael called out. "The person for whom the holy people have a need, he may climb over their heads, but you for whom the holy people have no need how dare you climb over?" (*Yevamot* 105b)

Students choosing subjects to study
Two students choosing subject for study with different emphasis of interest (*Bava Kamma* 60b)

☐ Students of R. Akiva died
It is stated that Rabbi Akiva had 12,000 pairs of students. All of them died at the same time, because they did not treat each other with respect. A Tanna taught that all of them died between Pesach and Shavuot. And these were the remaining students of Rabbi Akiva who revived the Torah at that time: Rabbi Meir, Rabbi Yehuda bar Illai, Rabbi Yosi ben Halafta, Rabbi Shimon bar Yohai, and Rabbi Eleazar ben Shammua. (*Yevamot* 62b)

☐ Students of R. Akiva traveling
Students of R. Akiva were traveling on the road and they were overtaken by highway robbers.

They asked: "Where are you traveling to?"

They replied: "We are traveling to Acco," but when they reached Kheziv they stopped. The students have learned that when encountering robbers it is best to tell them that their destination is further than the one actually planned.

The robbers asked: "Whose students are you?"

They answered: "We are students of R. Akiva."

They said: "Happy are R. Akiva and his

students for no evil will encounter them."
(*Avodah Zarah* 25b)

📖 Students of R. Meir excluded

It is related that after Rabbi Meir passed away, Rabbi Yehuda b. Illai told his students: "Do not allow the students of Rabbi Meir to enter our academy, because they come only for disputations and to overwhelm me with citations from traditions, but not to learn Torah." Rabbi Sumchos forced his way into the academy. He quoted Rabbi Meir on an important halachic issue. Rabbi Yehuda became very angry and told his students: "Didn't I instruct you not to admit any of Rabbi Meir's students?"[244]

Rabbi Yosi b. Halafta responded: "People will say: 'Rabbi Meir is dead, Rabbi Yehuda is angry, and Rabbi Yosi is silent.'" (*Nazir* 49b; *Kiddushin* 52b)

Students of R. Yehuda b. Illai

R. Shemuel b. Nahman said in the name of R.Yonatan: "The students of R. Yehuda b. Illai were so poor that six of his students had to cover themselves with one garment, yet they studied the Torah." (*Sanhedrin* 20a)

Studied Greek wisdom

R. Yehuda said in the name of R. Shemuel that R. Shimon b. Gamliel said: "One thousand students were in my father's house: 500 studied Torah and 500 studied Greek wisdom." (*Bava Kamma* 83a; *Sotah* 49b; *Gittin* 58a)

📖 Studied Talmud with a partner

When Rabbi Yehuda HaNasi died, R. Afes became president of the academy.

R. Hanina did not attend the studies inside the academy, but instead studied outside in the company of Rabbi Levi. When Rabbi Afes passed away, R. Hanina

---

244. See also entry, Barred from the academy.

bar Hama took over the presidency, and R. Levi was left without a partner to study. As a consequence, he moved to Babylonia. (*Ketubbot* 103b)

Study and prayer

R. Hamnuna held that the time for prayer and the time for Torah study are distinct from each other. It happened once that Rabbi Yirmiyahu was studying with Rabbi Zera and it was getting late for the prayer service. Rabbi Yirmiyahu asked his teacher R. Zera to interrupt the study so he could pray. (*Shabbat* 10a)

Study of Torah

R. Shemuel b. Inia stated in the name of Rav: "The study of Torah is more important than the offering of the daily sacrifices." (*Eruvin* 63b)

Studies Torah daily   כל השונה הלכות

It was taught in the Tanna D'bei Eliyahu: He who studies Torah Laws every day will be destined to have a place in the World to Come. (*Megillah* 28b)

✿ Study in the synagogue preferred

Abbaye said: "At one time, I used to study at home and pray in the synagogue, but when I noticed the words of David, I began to study also in the synagogue." (*Megillah* 29a; *Berachot* 8a)

Study or practice, which is greater?

Rabbi Tarfon and the Elders were once reclining in the upper floor of a house in Lydda. They were asked: "Which is greater, study or practice?"

Rabbi Tarfon said that practice is greater. Rabbi Akiva said that study is greater. Then all agreed that study is greater, because it leads to action. (*Kiddushin* 40b)

Study revised every thirty days

R. Hiyya b. Abba used to go over his

learning with R. Yohanan every thirty days. (*Hullin* 86b; *Berachot* 38b)

📖 Study Talmud with a partner

When R. Shimon b. Lakish died, R. Yohanan became grief-stricken. The rabbis sent R. Eleazar b. Pedat to comfort him. He went and sat before him and they learned together. Every dictum which R. Yohanan uttered, he was supported by R. Eleazar with the remark: "There is a Beraita which supports you."

"You are no replacement for Resh Lakish," he complained. "When I stated a law, Resh Lakish raised twenty-four objections, to which I gave twenty-four answers. It led to a fuller understanding of the law. While you tell me that a Beraita supports me. Do I not know myself that what I said is correct?" (*Bava Metzia* 84a)

Study time

R. Tanhum said: "One should divide his time of study into three: one-third Scripture, one-third Mishna, and one-third in Talmud." (*Avodah Zarah* 19b; *Kiddushin* 30a)

Study Torah

Is one obligated to interrupt for the *Shema* or for the *Shemona Esrei*? (*Shabbat* 11a)

✿ Studying method; no cramming

Rava said in the name of R. Sehora in the name of R. Huna: "If a person studies too much at a time, his learning decreases, but if he studies a little at a time, his knowledge increases."

Rabbah remarked: "The rabbis were aware of this advice, but disregarded it."

R. Nahman b. Yitzhak said: "I acted on this advice and it benefited me greatly." (*Eruvin* 54b; *Avodah Zarah* 19a)

Studying Torah by a non-Jew

R. Meir said: "If a non-Jew occupies himself with studying the Torah, his status is equal to the High Priest." (*Bava Kamma* 38a; *Avodah Zarah* 3a; *Sanhedrin* 59a)

Studying Torah in poverty

R. Yehuda b. Hiyya said: "A Torah scholar who occupies himself studying Torah in poverty will have his prayers heard."

Rabbi Aha b. Hanina added: "And neither will they draw the veil before him." (*Sotah* 49a)

Submissive

On that day R. Hillel sat submissive before R. Shammai like one of his students. (*Shabbat* 15a, 17a)

Substances of different kind

מין בשאינו מינו

Substances of different kind mixed together (*Hullin* 97b; *Avodah Zarah* 66a)

Substances of like kind

מין במינו

Substances of like kind mixed together (*Hullin* 97b, 100a)

Substances of the like kind are . . .

מין במינו במשהו

A mixture of the same species becomes disqualified by a drop of a forbidden substance mixed into it. (*Avodah Zarah* 73a)

Substituting dedicated animals

Exchanging an unconsecrated animal for a consecrated animal (*Temurah* 2a; *Hullin* 2a)

Sucking animal

A sucking animal bought from a non-Jew is not under suspicion that the calf is from another mother animal. (*Bechorot* 23b)

📖 Suffering

R. Yohanan fell ill and R. Hanina went to visit him. He said to him: "Are your sufferings welcome to you?"

He answered him: "No, neither the suffering nor their reward are welcome."

R. Hanina told him: "Give me your hand." He gave him his hand and he cured him. R. Yohanan cured others, so why couldn't he cure himself? The rabbis replied: "A prisoner cannot free himself." (*Berachot* 5b)

Suffering
R. Ashi said: "When there was suffering in the world, I saw R. Kahana remove his cloak, clasp his hands, and pray." (*Shabbat* 10a)

Suffering of an animal צער בעלי חיים
The suffering of an animal; cruelty to animals (*Shabbat* 128b, 154b; *Bava Metzia* 32b, 33a)

📖 Sukkah
R. Gamliel and R. Akiva were on a journey on a ship during the Sukkot holiday. R. Gamliel declared that a *sukkah* on a boat is invalid; R. Akiva declared it valid. During this trip, R. Akiva erected a *sukkah* on the deck of the ship. The next day a wind tore the *sukkah* and blew it away. R. Gamliel asked R. Akiva: "Akiva where is your *sukkah*?" (*Sukkah* 23a)

Sukkah covering
R. Hanina was told by an old man that to use reeds to cover the Sukkah is a proper covering. R. Yehoshua, his uncle, agreed. (*Sukkah* 20b)

Sukkah for an infant
R. Shammai broke an opening of the roof and covered it with proper *sukkah* covering in order that his infant grandchild could be under the *sukkah*. (*Yevamot* 15a; *Sukkah* 28a)

Sukkah height
What are the height requirements for a *sukkah*? (*Sukkah* 2a)

Sukkah offerings in the Temple
The number of offerings in the Temple on the holiday of Sukkot (*Sukkah* 55b)

Sukkah, old
Is an old *sukkah* fit to be used? (*Sukkah* 2a)

Sukkah on a vehicle
A *sukkah* built on a vehicle is it fit to be used. (*Sukkah* 22b)

Sukkah ornaments (*Shabbat* 22a, 45a; *Betzah* 30b; *Sukkah* 10a)

Sukkah shade
What are the shade requirements for a *sukkah*? (*Sukkah* 2a, 22b)

Sukkah under a tree
A *sukkah* built under a tree – is it fit to be used? (*Sukkah* 9b)

Sukkot holiday, one is to sleep in the Sukkah
R. Hisda and Rabbah b. Huna slept on the river bank of Sura when they were visiting the Exilarch during the Sukkot holiday, saying: "We are engaged in a religious errand and therefore we are exempt from the mitzvah of sleeping in the *sukkah*." (*Sukkah* 26a)

Sukkot Torah reading (*Megillah* 30b)

Sumchos ben Yosef סומכוס
Tanna from Eretz Yisrael
2nd – 3rd centuries CE (*Bava Metzia* 80a)

Summer solstice; vernal equinox
R. Shemuel discussed when the vernal equinox and summer solstice occur. (*Eruvin* 56a)

Summons
A summons can't be given to a person during the month of Nisan or Tishrei. (*Bava Kamma* 113a)

Summons
A summons can't be given to a person on Erev Shabbat. (*Bava Kamma* 113a)

📖 Sumptuous dining
R. Hiyya b. Abba related a story: "I was once a guest in a house in Lodokia where they served the host on a golden table which was carried by sixteen men with sixteen silver chains. On it were plates, goblets, pitchers, and bottles. In those utensils were all kinds of delicious foods and spices. I said to him: 'What did you do to merit all this?'

"He replied: 'I was a butcher, and every time I came across a fine piece of meat, I put it aside for Shabbat.'" (*Shabbat* 119a)

Sun is more than the shade
חמתה מרובה מצלתה

(*Sukkah* 2a, 9b, 22b)

Sun stood still
The sun stood still in the time of Yehoshua. (*Avodah Zarah* 25a; *Taanit* 20a)

Sunrise and sunset prayers
R. Hiyya b. Abba said in the name of R. Yohanan: "It is a mitzvah to pray with the first and last appearance of the sun." (*Berachot* 29b; *Shabbat* 118b)

Sunset
הערב השמש

(*Yoma* 6a)

📖 Supreme authority on blood
R. Ulla once visited Pumbedita and they brought some blood for him to examine, but he refused to see it. The town was under the jurisdiction of R. Yehuda. He explained: "If R. Eleazar, who was the supreme authority in the Land of Israel, refused to examine blood when he visited the town of R. Yehuda, how could I do it?"

Why was R. Eleazar described as the supreme authority in the Land of Israel? Because a woman once brought to R. Eleazar some blood to be examined, while R. Ammi was present. R. Eleazar smelled it and declared:

"This is blood of lust." After this, she went out. R. Ammi followed to question her, and she admitted: "My husband was away on a trip and I desired him." (*Niddah* 20b)

Supreme knowledge in Torah
Rabbi Aha son of Rava said: "Between Rabbi Yehuda HaNasi and Rabbi Ashi there was no one who was supreme in Torah and in worldly affairs."

He was asked: "Is that really so? Wasn't there Rabbi Huna ben Nathan?"

He answered: "That is different, because Rabbi Huna deferred to Rabbi Ashi." (*Gittin* 59a)

Supersedes the day of Shabbat
Certain work required to do for the Pesach offering does supersede Shabbat. (*Pesahim* 65b, 69b; *Eruvin* 103a)

Sura; Academy
סורא

Sura is a town in Babylonia south of Baghdad. It is situated on the banks of the Euphrates River where it divides into two rivers. It was an important Torah center for several centuries. It was also an important agricultural area, where the rabbis of the Talmud were active in farming, planting vineyards, producing wine, raising cattle, and engaging in trade.

Sura became a famous Torah center when Rav moved to the town in the year 219, and established the famous yeshiva there. Rav's yeshiva attracted hundreds of students and scholars.

When Rav passed away in 247, the academy lost its preeminence to Nehardea for seven years. However, when Rabbi

Shemuel from Nehardea passed away in 254, Sura regained its role under the leadership of Rabbi Huna.

The following were the heads of the academy in Sura: Rav, who lived in the 3rd century CE; Huna, who lived in the 3rd century CE; Rabbah bar Huna, who lived in the 3rd – 4th centuries CE; Hamnuna, who lived in the 3rd century CE; Hisda, who lived in the 3rd – 4th centuries CE; Mereimar, who lived in the 4th – 5th centuries CE; Ashi, who lived in the 4th – 5th centuries CE; Rava Tosfaah, who lived in the 5th century CE; Mar b. R. Ashi, who lived in the 5th century CE; Ravina II, who lived in the 5th century CE. (*Hullin* 110a)

Sura and Pumbedita

The Talmud states that when the majority of the rabbis departed from the academy of Rav in Sura, there still remained behind 1,200 students. When the students left the academy of R. Huna in Sura, there remained behind 800 students.

When R. Huna delivered a lecture, thirteen interpreters assisted him.

When the students left the academy of Rabbah and R. Yosef in Pumbedita, there remained 400 students, and they described themselves as orphans.

When the students left the academy of R. Abbaye in Pumbedita, others say from the academy of R. Papa, in Naresh, and still others say from the academy of R. Ashi in Mata Mehasya 200 rabbis remained, and they described themselves as orphans of the orphans. (*Ketubbot* 106a)

Suspicion ignoring Teruma

If a person is under suspicion of selling *teruma* as *hullin*. (*Bechorot* 29b)

Suspicion of firstborn blemishes

If a person is under suspicion of causing blemishes in firstborn animals (*Bechorot* 29b)

Swallowing a leech

If one swallows a leech, it is permitted to heat water in order to try to save him on Shabbat. (*Avodah Zarah* 12b)

Swift as a deer

Yehuda b. Tema said: "Be bold as a leopard, light as an eagle, swift as a deer, and strong as a lion – to carry out the will of your Father in Heaven." (*Avot* 5:20)

Swimming on Shabbat (*Shabbat* 40b)

Swindlers on the increase

Our rabbis taught: In former times when one lost an article, he gave identifying marks and was given the article, but when swindlers increased, they instituted that the claimant must bring witnesses. (*Bava Metzia* 28b)

📖 Swine to the besieged

The Hasmonean House divided

When the two brothers Hyrcanus and Aristobulus of the Hasmonean House[245] were contending for the crown, war broke out between them. Hyrcanus was outside the city wall and Aristobulus was within the city of Jerusalem. They had no animals inside the city for sacrifices. Those on the inside lowered down money inside buckets and in return they received cattle for the sacrifices. One day when the bucket came down with the money, they sent up a swine. It was proclaimed on that occasion: "Cursed be the man who breeds swine." (*Sotah* 49b)

Synagogue   בית הכנסת
(*Berachot* 6a; *Megillah* 27a)

Synagogue

R. Hisda said: "A synagogue should not be

---

245. See entry, Hasmonean house divided.

demolished before another one has been built to take its place." (*Bava Batra* 3b)

Synagogue attendance daily

Ravin b. Rav Adda said in the name of R. Yitzhak: "If a man is accustomed to attend the synagogue daily and one day does not attend, God asks for him." (*Berachot* 6b)

Synagogue to be sold

Can a synagogue be sold? (*Megillah* 27b)

Synagogue transplanted

R. Eliezer HaKappar states that the synagogues and houses of learning from Babylon in the time to come will be transplanted into Eretz Yisrael. (*Megillah* 29a)

Synagogue windows

R. Hiyya b. Abba said: "A person should always try to pray in a house with windows." (*Berachot* 31a, 34b)

Syria

To breed small animals in Syria

It is proper to breed small animals in Syria. (*Bava Kamma* 79b; *Temurah* 15b; *Taanit* 25a)

Syrian language

R. Yehuda HaNasi was against using the Syrian language in Israel. (*Bava Kamma* 83a)

T

Tabernacle destroyed

R. Yohanan b. Torta said: "Why was the Tabernacle at Shiloh destroyed? Because of two sinful things: immorality and contemptuous treatment of Holy objects." (*Yoma* 9a)

Table replica

Can one make a replica of the table used in the Temple? (*Avodah Zarah* 43a; *Rosh Hashana* 24a; *Menahot* 28b)

Tablets

R. Hanina b. Agil asked R. Hiyya b. Abba: "Why is there no mention of Tov in the first Tablets given to Moshe, but it is mentioned in the second Tablets?" (*Bava Kamma* 54b, 55a)

Tablets

Rabbi Hisda stated: "The letters *mem* and *samech* which were in the Tablets were suspended by miracle and the writing on the Tablets could be read from within and without or from both sides." (*Shabbat* 104a)

Tablets

The whole Tablets and the broken Tablets were placed in the Holy Ark. (*Berachot* 8b; *Bava Batra* 14b)

Taf

R. Abba b. Hanina quoted from the prophet Yehezkel, chapter nine, the following: "The angel Gabriel was told to go and inscribe with ink the letter *taf* upon the forehead of the righteous so that the destroying angel would have no power over them, and inscribe the letter *taf* with blood on the wicked so that the destroying angel would have power over them." (*Shabbat* 55a)

Tahash

R. Ellai quotes Rabbi Shimon ben Lakish as saying, Rabbi Meir said:

"The animal '*tahash*' mentioned in the Torah was a separate species particular to those days; it had one horn in its forehead and it came to Moshe providentially, just for that occasion. Moshe made the Tabernacle cover from its skin." After that period the animal disappeared. (*Shabbat* 28b)

✿ Tail to lions or head to foxes

R. Matya ben Heresh said: "Be first to extend greetings to all people, be rather a tail to lions than a head to foxes." (*Avot* 4:15; *Sanhedrin* 37a)

✿ Take charge when needed
R. Hillel said: "Where there are no men to lead, strive to be a competent leader." (*Avot* 2:5)

Taking a pledge for a loan
If one lends money to another person, can he take a pledge to secure the loan? (*Bava Metzia* 113a)

📖 Taking a wife under false pretenses
A man bought a boatload of wine and was looking for a place to store it. A certain woman had a storage room, but she was not willing to rent it to him. He decided to marry her and was able to use her storage room for his wine. Soon after the marriage, he wrote her a bill of divorce and sent it to her.[246] She hired carriers, paying them money from selling some of this man's wine, and had the wine put out on the street.

The matter came before R. Huna b. Yehoshua, who said: "As he did, so shall be done to him." She can say to him: 'To anybody else I am willing to rent out the place, but not to you, because you are like a lion in ambush.'" (*Bava Metzia* 101b)

Taking mother bird with the chicks
נוטל אם על הבנים
Taking the mother bird together with the young (*Hullin* 141a)

📖 Talking only about health matters
Rabbi Huna asked his son Rabbah: "Why are you not attending the lectures of Rabbi Hisda, whose lectures are so sharp and enlightening?"

"Why should I attend? He talks about secular matters most of the time. He

---

246. See entry, Dishonest marriage.

speaks about how one should behave in the toilet, not to sit down abruptly, not to force the rectum, because the glands might be dislocated."

R. Huna became annoyed with his son and said to him: "He is discussing health matters and you call them secular? There is even more reason that you should attend his lectures." (*Shabbat* 82a)

📖 Talking with demons
The Talmud relates that certain people were carrying a barrel of wine and they put the barrel under a drainpipe to take a rest. While resting, some demon caused the barrel to burst. The people came to R. Mar b. Ashi. He brought trumpets and exorcised the demon, which now stood before him. "Why did you break the barrel?"

The demon replied: "What else could I do? They placed the barrel on my ear."

R. Mar asked him: "What business do you have in a public place? You are in the wrong and you must pay for the damage."

The demon asked for time to pay. A day was fixed for the payment to be made, but the demon did not keep his promise with the excuse that he can acquire only things which are not tied, sealed or measured or counted, and he could not find other things." (*Hullin* 105b)

Tall rabbis
Abba Shaul was considered to be one of the tallest men in his generation, and R. Tarfon reached to his shoulder. R. Tarfon was considered to be one of the tallest men in his generation, and R. Meir reached to his shoulder. Rebbe was considered to be one of the tallest men in his generation, and R. Hiyya reached to his shoulder. R. Hiyya was considered to be one of the tallest men in his generation, and Rav his nephew reached to his shoulder. Rav was considered to be one of the tallest men in his generation and R. Yehuda b. Yehezkel,

his student, reached to his shoulder. R. Ye-huda was considered to be one of the tallest men in his generation and his assistant Abba reached to his shoulder. (*Niddah* 24b)

Talmid Hacham
R. Hisda said: "He who declares his own animal *trefa* is a *talmid hacham*." (*Hullin* 44b)

Talmud – he learned all of it at eighteen
When R. Kahana was eighteen, he had already studied the whole Talmud. He was a student of Rabbah in Pumbedita and he lived in the 4th century. (*Shabbat* 63a)

Talmud redaction
Rabbi Ashi is credited with the redaction of the Babylonian Talmud. The Talmud states: Rebbe and Rabbi Nathan completed the Mishna, and Rav Ashi and R. Ravina completed the Talmud. Later on, Ravina b. Huna edited it to its final completion. (*Bava Metzia* 86a)

Tamed animal   תם
An animal that never caused damages (*Bava Kamma* 15a, 16b)

Tamed animal
What is considered to be a *tam* with regards to causing damages (*Bava Kamma* 23b)

Tangible property   קרקע
Immovable property, for instance a field, land, or real estate (*Bava Metzia* 11b, 31a, 48b; *Bava Batra* 84b; *Ketubbot* 87b)

Tanhum bar Abba   תנחום בר אבא
Amora from Eretz Yisrael
4th century CE (*Sanhedrin* 39a)

Tanhum bar Hanilai   תנחום בר חנילאי
Amora from Eretz Yisrael
3rd century CE (*Bava Kamma* 55a)

Tanhum bar Hiyya   תנחום בר חייא
Ish Kefar Acco
Amora from Eretz Yisrael
3rd – 4th centuries CE (*Moed Katan* 16b)

Tanna and also an Amora
Rav was an Amora and also a Tanna
The Talmud says that Rav has a right to differ because he is a Tanna. (*Ketubbot* 8a; *Eruvin* 50b)

Tanner
It is discussed whether one can prepare skins on Shabbat. (*Shabbat* 17b)

Tanner of skins
R. Yosi b. Halafta
R. Yosi b. Halafta made a living as a tanner of skins. As is mentioned in the Talmud, Rabbi Yishmael the son of Rabbi Yosi said: "My father worked on animal hides and he would ask me to fetch a hide for him so that he may sit on it."

R. Yosi b. Halafta married his deceased brother's wife, with whom he had five sons: Rabbi Yishmael and Rabbi Eleazar are two of them. (*Shabbat* 49a–b)

Tarbu
The goats of Bei Tarbu used to cause damage to the property of R. Yosef. He said to Abbaye: "Go and tell the owners they should keep them fenced in." But R. Abbaye said to him: "What is the use of telling them? They will say that we should build a fence around our property." (*Bava Kamma* 23b)

Tarfon   טרפון
Tanna from Eretz Yisrael
1st century CE (*Ketubbot* 84b)

Targum Onkelos
R. Yirmiyahu said, some say R. Hiyya b. Abba said: "The Targum on the Torah was authored by Onkelos the proselyte

under the guidance of R. Eliezer and R. Yehoshua." (*Megillah* 3a)

Targum translation on the Prophets

The Talmud states: The Targum on the Prophets was authored by R. Yonatan b. Uzziel under the guidance of Haggai, Zechariah, and Malachi. After the Targum was finished, there was an earthquake in the Land of Israel over an area of 400 by 400 *parsi*, and a Bat Kol came forth and exclaimed:

"Who is responsible for revealing my secrets to mankind?"

R. Yonatan b. Uzziel stood up and declared: "It is I who revealed the secret to mankind. It is fully known to You Hashem that I did not do it for my honor or for the honor of my father's house, but for Your honor so that dissension will not increase among Jews." R. Yonatan b. Uzziel wanted to reveal also the inner meanings of the Ketuvim, but a Bat Kol was heard that said: "Enough." What was the reason? Because the date of when Mashiach is coming would have been revealed. (*Megillah* 3a)

Tasty, strong wine – Mar Ukva drank

R. Yosef said: "Once I entered the baths and Mar Ukva was present, and on leaving I was offered a cup of his wine. After drinking, I experienced a terrific cooling sensation from the hair of my head to the toe nails; had I drank another glass I would have feared I would lose some merits in the World to Come. I am told Mar Ukva drank it every day." (*Shabbat* 140a)

Tattooing   קעקע

An incised imprint in the flesh

  Disfiguring the body with tattoos (*Makkot* 21a)

Tavla

R. Tavla was a student of Rav. (*Bava Metzia* 94a)

Tax collector

R. Zera's father was a tax collector for thirteen years. When the chief of the district came to town, R. Zera's father would tell the scholars: "Come with me and go into your chambers." When he saw the town's people, he would tell them: "The district chief is coming to the town. He will slaughter the father in the presence of the son, and the son in the presence of the father." They all hid themselves. When the chief arrived, he rebuked him for failing in his duty and not collecting enough taxes. (*Sanhedrin* 25b)

Taylor with his needle

On Friday just before Shabbat, a tailor with his needle (*Shabbat* 11a)

✿ Teach concise language

R. Huna said in Rav's name, others say R. Huna said in Rav's name, which he heard from R. Meir:

"One should always teach his student to use concise language and refined speech." (*Hullin* 63b; *Pesahim* 3b)

✿ Teach slowly without mistakes

R. Dimi said: "It is better to appoint a teacher who teaches slowly, but makes no mistakes; because once a mistake is implanted in a child it is difficult to erase." (*Bava Batra* 21a)

✿ Teach your son a clean, easy trade

R. Bar Kappara stated: "When the merchandise is cheap, hurry to buy. In a place where there is no man, you be the man. A man should always teach his son a clean and easy trade." (*Berachot* 63a)

Teach your student four times

R. Eliezer said: "It is an obligation to teach your student Torah four times. (*Eruvin* 54b)

Teacher and student

It was learned that a very great teacher has precedence over one's father. R. Huna was R. Hisda's teacher. R. Hisda asked him: "What about a case where a student is needed by his teacher?"

R. Huna took offense and exclaimed: "Hisda, Hisda, I do not need you, but you need me." They bore resentment against each other for a long time and did not visit each other. R. Hisda kept forty fasts because R. Huna felt humiliated, and R. Huna kept forty fasts because he unjustly suspected R. Hisda. (*Bava Metzia* 33a)

📖 Teacher and student

Once R. Shimi ben Ashi came to Abbaye and asked him to give him lessons. He answered him: "I have no time; I need my time to study for myself."

The other asked him: "Then teach me at night."

Abbaye answered: "At night, I am also busy. I have to water my fields."

R. Shimi offered to water his fields during daytime and to get lessons at nighttime. Abbaye agreed and he studied with him.

However, one incident did not please Abbaye at all. R. Shimi went to the owners of the fields which were located above R. Abbaye's fields, declared that the field-owners below have first right to water the fields. He then went to the field-owners below Abbaye's fields and told them the field-owners above have the first right to water the fields. In the meantime, R. Shimi had all the water available for himself to irrigate the fields of Abbaye. When Abbaye found out what he had done, it displeased him very much, and he refused to eat of that year's produce. (*Gittin* 60b)

📖 Teacher and students

The Talmud relates that when R. Ammi and R. Assi were sitting before R. Yitzhak Nepaha,[247] one of them said to him: "Would you please tell us some Halachah?" The other one said: "Would you please tell us some Aggadata?" (*Bava Kamma* 60b)

✿ Teacher to advise you

R. Gamliel said: "Provide yourself a teacher and you will avoid making mistakes. Train yourself to be accurate and not to estimate." (*Avot* 1:16)

✿ Teaching a son Torah

R. Yehoshua b. Levi said: "If a person teaches his son Torah, it is as if he had received it at Mount Horev." (*Berachot* 21b; *Kiddushin* 30a)

✿ Teaching children to believe in God

Abbaye and Rava were sitting before Rabbah when they were still young boys. Rabbah wanted to test them, and he asked: "To whom do we say the benedictions?"

They both answered: "To God."

"And where is God?"

Rava pointed to the roof, and Abbaye went outside and pointed to the sky. Rabbah said to them: "Both of you will become rabbis." (*Berachot* 48a)

Teaching Torah

R. Hiyya b. Abba said in R. Yohanan's name, some say, R. Yishmael b. Nahmani said it in the name of R. Yonatan: "Anyone who teaches Torah to the children of his friend, will have the merit to sit in the heavenly yeshiva." (*Bava Metzia* 85a)

Teaching Torah

Rabbi Meir also used to say: "He who studies Torah but does not teach it to others – puts the words of the Torah to shame." (*Sanhedrin* 99a)

---

247. See entry, Aggadata.

📖 Teaching Torah

Resh Lakish was marking the burial caves of the rabbis in order to prevent the priests from becoming defiled. But he could not locate the grave of R. Hiyya. Feeling humiliated, he called out: "Sovereign of the Universe, did I not debate on the Torah like R. Hiyya did?"

A heavenly voice responded: "You did indeed debate like he did, but you did not spread the Torah as he did."

R. Hiyya went out and sowed flax, made nets from the flax, and trapped deer. He gave the venison to orphans, and from the skins he prepared scrolls upon which he wrote the Five Books of Moshe. Then he went to a town which had no teachers and taught to five children the Five Books of Moshe, and to six children the Six Orders of the Mishna.

When he left, he told the children: "Until I return, I want you to teach each other what I have taught you."

And thus he preserved the Torah from being forgotten by the Jewish people.

This is what Rebbe meant when he said: "How great are the works of R. Hiyya."

"Are they greater than yours?" asked R. Yishmael b. R. Yosi.

"Yes," replied Rebbe. (*Bava Metzia* 85b; *Ketubbot* 103b)

Teachings

The Talmud states that Rabbi Shimon ben Azzai said: "I found a roll of genealogical records in Jerusalem and therein was written a Halachah. In addition, it said that the teachings of R. Eliezer b. Yaakov are small in quantity, but thoroughly sifted." (*Yevamot* 49b)

Tear not legal ruling

Rava instructed R. Papa and R. Huna b. Yehoshua: "When a written legal decision of mine comes before you and you find objection to it, do not tear it up before you speak to me. If I have valid reasons for my decision, I will tell it to you, and if not, I will withdraw it. After my death, you shall neither tear it up nor draw any conclusions from it. You shall not tear it up, because had I been there, I might have given you my reasons, and do not draw any conclusions, because a judge must be guided by what he sees with his eyes." (*Bava Batra* 130b)

Techelet, Blue fringes   תכלת

The absence of blue fringes (*Menahot* 38a)

Tefillat Ha-Derech   תפלת הדרך

R. Yaakov said in the name of R. Hisda: "When one is on the road traveling, a special prayer should be said which is called *Tefillat Ha-Derech*. (*Berachot* 29b)

Tefillin

Putting on *tefillin* and reading the *Shema* (*Berachot* 14b)

Tefillin

The *shin* on the *tefillin*, its rectangular shape, the *retzuot*, and the black color for the *tefillin* are a law given to Moshe on Sinai. Abbaye said: "The *shin*, *daled*, and *yud* of the *tefillin* are commanded through Moshe from Sinai." (*Shabbat* 28b, 62a, 108a; *Makkot* 11a)

Tefillin

Rabbah b. R. Huna said: "*Tefillin* should be touched from time to time." (*Shabbat* 12a; *Yoma* 7b; *Menahot* 36b)

Tefillin

R. Yosef said: "*Tefillin* should be made of a kosher animal." (*Shabbat* 28b)

Tefillin

The parchments inside the *tefillin* must be written in Hebrew. (*Megillah* 8b)

Tefillin
Is Shabbat the time for *tefillin*? This is a disagreement between R. Gamliel and the rabbis. (*Eruvin* 95b; *Shabbat* 60a, 61a)

📖 Tefillin
R. Yannai said, "*Tefillin* require a pure body like Elisha, the man of wings." He was called "the man of wings" because the Roman government once decreed a prohibition on wearing *tefillin*. Elisha put them on anyhow. A Roman soldier ran after him and caught him. He removed them and held them in his hand.

"What is that in your hand?"

"They are wings of a dove." He opened his hand and there were wings of a dove in his hand. (*Shabbat* 49a, 130a)

Tefillin
Michal, the daughter of King Saul, wore *tefillin*. (*Eruvin* 96a)

Tefillin bag
A bag made specifically for *tefillin* – can one use it to hold money? (*Sanhedrin* 48b)

Tefillin found on Shabbat
What is one to do when finding *tefillin* on Shabbat in the street? (*Eruvin* 95a; *Shabbat* 62a; *Betzah* 15a)

Tefillin, four sections
Four sections are required for the *tefillin* that are placed on the head. (*Sanhedrin* 4b)

Tefillin knots
R. Yehuda b. R. Shemuel b. R. Shilat said: "The shapes of the *tefillin* knots are an Halachah from Sinai." (*Eruvin* 97a; *Menahot* 35b)

Tefillin knots
R. Hana b. Bizna said in the name of R. Shimon Hasida: "Hashem showed Moshe the knot of the *tefillin*." (*Berachot* 7a)

Tefillin to be removed
When nature calls, the *tefillin* are to be removed. (*Shabbat* 62a)

Tefillin worn by Hashem
R. Avin b. Rav Adda said in the name of R. Yitzhak: "How do we know that Hashem puts on *tefillin*? We know it from a passage in Yeshaya 62:8."

The great scholar, Rabbi Nahman ben Yitzhak, asked Rabbi Hiyya b. Avin to explain to him a question that bothered him: "What is inscribed on the *tefillin* worn by the Ruler of the Universe?"

R. Avin replied: "These words are written: 'And who is like your people Israel?'"(*Berachot* 6a)

Tehilla Le-David
R. Eleazar said in the name of Rabbi Avina: "Whoever recites *Tehilla Le-David* – which is preceded by the verse *Ashrei* – three times a day, is sure to inherit the World to Come. (*Berachot* 4b)

Tehillim author
The author of the book of Tehillim was King David. (*Bava Batra* 15a)

Tehum Shabbat   תחום שבת
A distance that is permitted to walk on Shabbat. (*Eruvin* 52b, 58a, 105a; *Hagigah* 15a)

📖 Tehum Shabbat
Elisha b. Avuyah was a great scholar, and R. Meir was one of his students. In his later years, he became a non-believer.

Our rabbis taught: Once Aher[248] was riding a horse on the Shabbat, and Rabbi Meir was walking behind him to learn Torah from him. When they had gone a distance, Aher said to R. Meir: "Turn back, because by my measurement, we

---

248. See also entry, Aher.

have gone already to the limit of the *te-hum-Shabbat*." (*Hagigah* 15a)

Tekoa תקוע

R. Yehuda HaNasi related that when he studied at R. Shimon b. Yohai in Tekoa, he and the students used to carry oil and towels from roof to roof and from the roof to the courtyard, from the courtyard to another courtyard and from there to a *karpaf* until they arrived to the well where they bathed. (*Eruvin* 91a)

Tekoa, academy

Tekoa is a small town in Israel south of Jerusalem and Bethlehem. R. Shimon b. Yohai established an academy there. R. Yehuda HaNasi studied in that academy.

Shimon bar Yohai lived in the 2nd century CE. (*Eruvin* 91a)

Telescope

R. Gamliel already used a telescope to observe the stars and the planets, and had copies of shapes of the moon hung on his wall in his office for witness examination. (*Eruvin* 43b)

✡ Temperaments

There are four types of people:

Easy to anger and easy to pacify – for such a person, his gain disappears in his loss;

Hard to anger and hard to pacify – His loss is offset by his gain;

A person who is hard to anger and easy to pacify is an extraordinary person;

A person who is easy to anger but hard to pacify is a wicked person. (*Avot* 5:11)

Temple – the First and Second differed

There were five differences between the First and the Second Temple. (*Yoma* 21b)

Temple building at night

The Temple in Jerusalem cannot be built at night. (*Shevuot* 15b)

Temple building on Shabbat

Building the Temple does not supersede the Shabbat. (*Yevamot* 6a)

Temple chambers

There were six chambers in the Temple for storing things and other uses: the salt chamber, the Parvah chamber, the rinsing chamber, the wood chamber, the diaspora chamber, and the Gazit chamber. (*Middot* 5:3)

Temple court measurements

The whole Temple court measured 187 cubits long by 135 cubits wide. (*Middot* 5:1)

Temple destroyed
Remember destruction of the Temple

After the destruction of the Temple, the rabbis felt that one should not have a house which is very ornate. Therefore the rabbis declared that a house may be plastered, but one should leave a small area bare. How much of an area? R. Yosef said: "It should be a cubit square."

R. Hisda added: "It should be by the entrance." (*Bava Batra* 60b)

Temple furnishing measurements

Vessels and furnishing measurements used in the Temple (*Menahot* 96a)

📖 Temple Herod built

Herod asked Rabbi Bava ben Buta: "What could I do to amend for the sin of killing all the scholars?"

R. Bava answered: "You have extinguished the light of the world by killing the rabbis; you should attend to the other light of the world – the Temple."

Herod told him: "I am afraid of the government in Rome."

Bava b. Buta advised him to send an envoy to Rome to ask permission, and let the envoy take a year on the way, and let him stay a year in Rome and another year to come back. In the meantime, Herod should rebuild the Temple. (*Bava Batra* 4a)

Temple in Jerusalem most beautiful
בית המקדש
Our rabbis taught: "Anyone who has not seen the Water-drawing at the Temple in Jerusalem has not seen rejoicing in his life. Anyone who has not seen Jerusalem in its splendor has never seen a lovely city. Anyone who has not seen the Temple in Jerusalem when it was fully rebuilt has never seen a beautiful building in his life."

The Talmud asks: Which Temple? Abbaye said, and some say R. Hisda said: "This refers to the building that Herod built."

The Talmud asks: What kind of material did he use to build it?

Rabbah answered: "He built it of yellow and white marble." Some differ and say that it was built of yellow, blue, and white marble. The building was constructed in tiers: one row was projecting out and one row was receding inward. His intention was to overlay the marble stones with gold, but the rabbis advised him to leave the marble as is, because it had the appearance of the waves of the sea." (*Sukkah* 51b; *Bava Batra* 4a)

Temple Mount
A person should not enter the Temple Mount with his cane. (*Yevamot* 6b; *Berachot* 54a)

Temple Mount
R. Eleazar said: "All three Patriarchs, Avraham, Yitzhak, and Yaakov prayed on Temple Mount. Avraham called the mountain Mountain, Yitzhak called it

Field, and Yaakov called it the House of God. (*Pesahim* 88a)

Temple Mount size
The size of the Temple Mount was 500 by 500 cubits. (*Middot* 2:1)

Temple Mount spitting forbidden
R. Bibi said in the name of R. Yehoshua b. Levi: "Anyone who spits these days on the Temple Mount, is as if he spat in the pupil of His eye. One should not spit when standing on the Temple mount, it is a violation. (*Berachot* 54a, 62b)

Temple priests of Onias in Egypt
The priests that served in the Temple erected by Onias in Leontopolis, Egypt[249] were not permitted to serve in the Temple in Jerusalem. (*Avodah Zarah* 52b; *Menahot* 109a)

Temple replica
One may not build a house in the same design as the Temple in Jerusalem. (*Avodah Zarah* 43a; *Rosh Hashana* 24a; *Menahot* 28b)

Temple sacrifices and its replacement
Avraham our ancestor spoke to God: "How do I know I shall inherit it, suppose my children will sin, and You will do to them as You did to the generation of the flood?"

He answered: "Take me a heifer, three years old."

Avraham said: "This is very well for the time when the Temple will be standing, but in the time when there will be no Temple, what will happen to them?"

Hashem answered: "I have already fixed for them the order of the sacrifices; whenever they will read them, it will be counted as offerings." (*Megillah* 31a; *Taanit* 27b)

---

249. Jews in Egypt erected a replica of the Temple in Jerusalem. The priests performed services and offerings similar to services in Jerusalem.

Temple Sanctuary measurements
The Heichal measured 100 by 100 cubits. (*Middot* 4:6)

Temple Water-drawing
Our Rabbis taught: "Anyone who has not witnessed the rejoicing at the Water-drawing in Jerusalem has never seen rejoicing in his life." (*Sukkah* 51b)

Temples destroyed
The First Temple and the Second Temple were destroyed on the ninth day of Av. (*Taanit* 26b; *Rosh Hashana* 18b)

Temple's holy vessels
While Rabbi Eleazar was in Rome, he saw the vessels plundered from the Temple. He also saw the splattered blood on the curtain, which separated the Holy of Holies. The blood was from the sacrifice offerings.

He also states that he saw in Rome the *tzitz*[250] with the inscription Holy to God, and that it was all inscribed in one line.[251] (*Meilah* 17b; *Sukkah* 5a)

Temurah   תמורה
Substituting dedicated animals (*Temurah* 2a)

Ten Commandments
During daily prayers
Rabbah b. Huna wanted to institute the practice of saying the Ten Commandments during the prayer service, but R. Hisda said to him: "It had long been abolished on account of the *minim* who were bad-mouthing the Torah. They stated that the Ten Commandments are the only ones to be obeyed, and as proof that the whole Torah is not read daily." (*Berachot* 12a)

Ten Commandments
The difference between the two written Ten Commandments (*Bava Kamma* 54b)

Ten days between Rosh Hashana
During the ten days between Rosh Hashana and Yom Kippur, the words are changed in the prayers of the *Amidah* (*Berachot* 12b)

Ten enactments by Ezra
Ezra the Sofer ordained ten enactments. (*Bava Kamma* 82a)

Ten people learning Torah
R. Halafta of Kfar Hanania said: "Ten people that sit together and study Torah, the Divine presence is sitting with them." (*Avot* 3:6)

Ten regulations
Ten regulations were enacted in the city of Jerusalem. (*Bava Kamma* 82b; *Yoma* 23a; *Arachin* 32b)

Ten requirements
For a city
A city has to have ten things before a Torah scholar may live in it. (*Sanhedrin* 17b)

Ten sons of Rabbi Yohanan died
Rabbi Yohanan's own life was a sad one. He lost ten of his sons in his lifetime. However, he had several daughters who survived. (*Berachot* 5b; *Bava Batra* 116a)

Ten stipulations
Made by Yehoshua
When Yehoshua entered the Land of Israel, he laid down ten stipulations. (*Bava Kamma* 80b; *Eruvin* 17a)

Ten things bring back the illnesses
(*Avodah Zarah* 29a)

---

250. Head plate of the high priest.
251. There was a disagreement whether one line or two lines.

Ten tribes of Israel cut off

Rabbi Helbo said the wines of Perugitha and the water of Diomsith caused the ten tribes of Israel to be cut off from their brethren. R. Eleazar b. Arach visited that place, was attracted and stayed there. Consequently, he forgot his learning. When he returned to his former home, he tried to read from the Torah but didn't remember, and read incorrectly. The rabbis who were his colleagues prayed for him and his memory returned. We have learned, R. Nehorai said: "If you have to move to another location, be sure you move to a place of Torah and do not say that Torah will follow you, and do not rely on your own understanding of the Torah." Some say his name was not Nehorai but R. Nehemia, others say his name was Eleazar b. Arach, and why was he called Nehorai? Because he enlightened the eyes of the Sages with his knowledge of the law. (*Shabbat* 147b; *Sanhedrin* 110b; *Yevamot* 16b)

Tenai   תנאי

On condition (*Ketubbot* 19b)

Tending to sheep on Shabbat

R. Huna owned sheep that needed shade during daytime and open air at nighttime. On weekdays, it was arranged by spreading a mat over the area and removing it for the night, but on Shabbat, he was concerned this might be an act of building. He came to his teacher, Rav, and asked him what to do. Rav advised him to roll up the mat on Friday evening before Shabbat, but to leave a handbreadth unrolled, and the next morning when the mat is unrolled he will only add to an existing temporary tent. (*Eruvin* 102a)

Tent of meeting vessels hidden

The vessels were stored beneath the crypts of the Temple

Rabbi Hisda transmitted a tradition in the name of Rabbi Avimi: The Tent of Meeting built by Moshe during their wanderings in the wilderness including its boards, hooks, bars, pillars, and sockets were stored away after the First Temple was erected by King Solomon. Where were they stored? R. Hisda said in the name of R. Avimi: "They stored them beneath the crypts of the Temple." (*Sotah* 9a)

Tents of Israel admired

Bilam admired the tents of Israel because of how modestly they were set up to protect privacy. (*Sanhedrin* 105b)

Teruma

Rav and Shemuel both ruled: The proper measure to be given to the priest for the first of the fleece is one-sixtieth part, for *teruma* one-sixtieth part, and for the corner of the field, one-sixtieth part. (*Hullin* 137b)

Teruma

A man told a story: "When I was a child I remember my father taking me out of school, and making me immerse in a *mikveh* in order to be able to partake in *teruma*. (*Bava Kamma* 114b; *Ketubbot* 26a)

Teruma   תרומה עין יפה אחד מארבעים

We have learnt: The proper measure for *teruma* for a man with a generous eye is one-fortieth part. (*Hullin* 137b)

Teshuva

Rebbe said: "Some need many years to acquire the World to Come, a *baal teshuva* acquires it in one hour.

   R. Levi said: "Great is *teshuva* for it reaches up to the Throne of Glory." (*Yoma* 86a; *Avodah Zarah* 10b, 17a, 18a)

📖 Teshuva

R. Yehuda HaNasi visited the town of R.

Eleazar b. Shimon. He inquired: "Did that *tzaddik* leave a son?"

"Yes," they replied, "and every harlot whose hire is two *zuz* is willing to hire him for herself for eight *zuz*."

R. Yehuda summoned him, ordained him as a rabbi in order to bestow respect on him, and entrusted him to be educated by R. Shimon b. Issi b. Lakonia, his mother's brother.

Every day the young man would say: "I am going back to my town," and the teacher would reply: "They made you a sage and they spread a gold-trimmed cape on you and they call you rabbi, and in spite of this you say, 'I am going back to my town'?"

The young man answered to his teacher: "I swear that I am cured, that my desires have been abandoned."

Some years later when he became a great scholar, he went to Rebbe's academy and participated in the discussions. On hearing his voice, Rebbe observed: "This voice is similar to the voice of R. Eleazar b. Shimon."

"He is the son of R. Eleazar," said the students of the academy. Rebbe was very pleased and cited a verse from scripture in praise. He also complimented R. Shimon b. Issi b. Lakonia for accomplishing his mission.

When he died, they buried him next to his father. This was R. Yosi b. Eleazar b. R. Shimon. (*Bava Metzia* 85a)

Testimony
R. Yehoshua b. Hanania gave testimony in the name of R. Yohanan b. Zakkai. (*Eduyot* 9b)

Testimony
Testimony for a widow whose husband's death is uncertain (*Bava Metzia* 27b)

Testimony
Testimony by R. Akiva in the name of R. Nehemia Ish Bet Deli (*Eduyot* 9b)

Testimony about five things
R. Nahman said: "R. Yehuda ben Bava testified about five things: that they instruct an orphan girl who is a minor to refuse marriage; a woman may remarry on the evidence of one witness; a rooster was stoned in Jerusalem because it killed a human being; that wine forty days old was poured as an offering on the altar; that the daily offering was brought at four hours in the morning." (*Berachot* 27a; *Eduyot* 6:1; *Niddah* 8a)

Testimony annulled
Any testimony that a part of it was annulled becomes annulled altogether. (*Bava Kamma* 73a)

Testimony by R. Menahem b. Signai
(*Eduyot* 9a)

Testimony by R. Nehunia b. Gudgeda
(*Eduyot* 9a)

Testimony by R. Papayas (*Eduyot* 8b)

Testimony by R. Yakim (*Eduyot* 8b)

Testimony by R. Yehoshua b. Betera
(*Eduyot* 9a)

Testimony by R. Yehuda b. Betera
(*Eduyot* 9a)

Testimony by R. Yehuda HaKohen
(*Eduyot* 9a)

Testimony by R. Yosi b. Yoezer
(*Eduyot* 9a)

Testimony by Shimon b. Guda
(*Avodah Zarah* 32a)

Testimony of R. Hanina
R. Hanina Segan HaKohanim testified about four matters. (*Eduyot* 3b)

Testing his patience
Two men wagered that if anyone can anger R. Hillel, he will receive 400 *zuz*. (*Shabbat* 31a)

Tevi Rishba   טבי רישבא
Tevi Rishba was a student of Shemuel; he quoted Shemuel that a derivative of *teruma* is also *teruma*. (*Shabbat* 17b)

Teyomet   תיומת
The central part of a *lulav* (*Bava Kamma* 96a)

That same day   בו ביום
A Tanna taught: Whenever the Talmud speaks of "that day" it refers to the day when R. Eleazar b. Azariah was elected as Nasi of the Sanhedrin. On that day, every Halachah that was in question before the rabbis was resolved. Even R. Gamliel didn't stay away from the assembly even for one hour, in spite of him being removed as president. (*Berachot* 28a; *Yadayim* 4:4)

Theodos the physician
Theodos said: "No cow or pig left Alexandria, Egypt without its uterus being cut out – to prevent reproduction." (*Sanhedrin* 33a, 93a)

Think before you do
R. Yohanan b. Zakkai had five outstanding students: R. Eliezer b. Horkynos, R. Yehoshua b. Hanania, R. Yosi HaKohen, R. Shimon b. Netanel, R. Eleazar b. Arach.

He said to them: "Go and discern which is the proper way that a person should follow."

R. Eliezer said a good eye; R. Yehoshua said a good friend; R. Yosi said a good neighbor; R. Shimon said one who considers the outcome of his actions; and R. Eleazar said a good heart.

On this, R. Yohanan b. Zakkai remarked: "I prefer the words of R. Eleazar b. Arach, because all your words are included in his words." (*Avot* 3:1)

Third cup at the Seder (*Pesahim* 117b)

Thirteen
R. Yehuda b. Tema said: "At the age of thirteen, it is the time for a young man to fulfil the Torah commandments." (*Avot* 5:21)

Thirty-nine principal labors
The principal labors on Shabbat are thirty-nine. (*Shabbat* 49b)

Thirty-six righteous men   ל״ו צדיקים
Abbaye said: "In each generation, the world must contain no less than thirty-six righteous men who merit the sight of the Shechina." (*Sanhedrin* 97b; *Sukkah* 45b)

This applies only   במה דברים אמורים בד״א
The above can be said only. (*Hullin* 3a)

Thorns
Whenever R. Hisda had to walk between thorns, he lifted up his garments, saying: "If I hurt my body it will heal, but for garments there is no cure." (*Bava Kamma* 91b; *Taanit* 23a)

Thoughts beyond our understanding
One time, Rabbi Yehoshua was standing on the Temple Mount and Ben Zoma saw him, but did not stand up before him. Rabbi Yehoshua asked him: "What are you thinking about?"

He replied: "I was gazing between the upper and the lower waters, and there is barely three fingers breadth between them." Thereupon, R. Yehoshua said to his disciples: "Ben Zoma is still outside." (*Hagigah* 15a)

Three by three
A three by three fingerbreadth square of cloth is liable to become unclean. (*Shabbat* 26a–b, 27a)

Three dining together   שלושה שאכלו
This is discussed in the 7th *perek* of Berachot. (*Berachot* 45a)

Three generations of Torah scholars
R. Parnach said in R. Yohanan's name: "A scholar in Torah who has a son a scholar and his son's son also a scholar will never have Torah absent from his seed." (*Bava Metzia* 85a)

Three gifts from God
R. Shimon b. Yohai said: "Three precious gifts were given to Israel by God and all of them through sufferings." They are: the Torah, the Land of Israel, and the World to Come. (*Berachot* 52a)

Three liquids prohibited
We have learned: Three liquids are prohibited to drink if left uncovered: water, wine, and milk. (*Hullin* 10a, 49b; *Terumot* 8:4)

Three meals on Shabbat   שלש סעודות
R. Yose said: "May my portion be with those who eat three meals on Shabbat." (*Shabbat* 118b)

✿ Three persons are loved by God
Three kinds of people are loved by God: one who does not display a temper, one who does not become intoxicated, and one who does not insist on his full rights. (*Pesahim* 113b; *Megillah* 28a)

Three stars
R. Yehuda said in the name of R. Shemuel: "One star visible indicates it is still daylight, two stars indicate it is *ben ha-shma-shot*,[252] three stars visible indicate it is already night. (*Shabbat* 35b)

Three stringencies
In three matters R. Gamliel was stringent in accordance and agreeing with the views of Bet Shammai. (*Betzah* 21b; *Eduyot* 3:10)

Three who dine together
שלשה שאכלו זימון
When three dine together, they must say the After-meal blessing together. (*Berachot* 45a)

Three wishes by Moshe
R. Yohanan said in the name of R. Yosi: "Three things did Moshe ask from Hashem, and they were granted to him: He asked that the Divine presence should rest upon Israel; that the Divine presence should not rest upon the idolaters; and that He should show him the ways of Hashem. All three requests were granted to him. (*Berachot* 7a; *Bava Batra* 15b)

Threefold cord
Rami b. Hama said the following: "A threefold cord is not easily broken." This is exemplified by R. Oshaya, who is the son of R. Hama, the son of R. Bisa. (*Bava Batra* 59a)

Threshold   איסקופה
A threshold serves two domains on Shabbat. (*Shabbat* 6a, 9a)

Throwing
Throwing on Shabbat from one domain to

---

252. Between day and night.

another is discussed in *Hazorek*, the 11th *perek* in *Shabbat*. (*Shabbat* 4a, 96a)

📖 Throwing stones
Into the public street

A man was removing stones from his own ground into the public street. A Hasid said to him "Fool, why do you remove stones from the ground that is not yours into the ground which is yours?"[253] (*Bava Kamma* 50b)

Thunder

The blessing over thunder – when one hears it – is discussed in the 9th *perek* of *Berachot, Haroeh* הרואה. (*Berachot* 54a)

Tiberias

One of the ten stipulations Yehoshua laid down on entering the Land of Israel was that fishing with an angle in the Sea of Tiberias be permitted. (*Bava Kamma* 81a; *Eruvin* 17a)

Tiberias

A pipe was conducted in Tiberias from the hot springs to heat the water. (*Shabbat* 38b, 39a–b)

Tiberias

The inhabitants of Tiberias are not students of Torah. (*Avodah Zarah* 58a)

Tiberias

R. Hanania ben Akavya permitted the people of Tiberias three things. (*Eruvin* 87b)

Tiberias; Academy   טבריא

Tiberias is a city in Eretz Yisrael on the western shore of Lake Kinneret. In Hebrew, the city is called Teveryah. Herod Antipas, the son of Herod, founded the city in the first century CE. The city is built on steep slopes spread over a wide

area, and it rises from below sea level to approximately 800 ft. above sea level. The city is famous for its hot springs, where the temperature reaches boiling point. Rabbi Shimon ben Yohai lived there for a while, and the Sages of the time established the seat of the Sanhedrin there. Tiberias was also the seat of the famous rabbinical academy in Eretz Yisrael.

The graves of several great Sages are in Tiberias, among them Rabbi Yohanan ben Zakkai, Rabbi Meir Baal HaNes, Rabbi Akiva, Rabbi Ammi, and Rabbi Assi. Several of the great Amoraim taught there, including R. Yohanan, R. Shimon b. Lakish, R. Eleazar b. Pedat, R. Ammi b. Nathan, and R. Assi.

The following were the heads of the academy in Tiberias: Yohanan ben Nepaha, 3rd century CE; Eleazar ben Pedat, 3rd century CE; Yehuda Nesiah, 3rd century CE; Ammi bar Nathan, 3rd – 4th centuries CE; Assi, 3rd – 4th centuries CE; Yehuda Nesiah III, 3rd – 4th centuries CE; Hillel 2nd, 4th centuries CE; Yirmiyahu b. Abba, 4th century CE; Yonah, 4th century CE; Yosi, 4th century CE.

The following are a few of many sources where the academy is mentioned in the Talmud: *Shabbat* 38b, 39a–b; *Betzah* 16b.

Tikkun Olam   תיקון עולם

Improving the world, attending to the well-being of the world and preventing abuses. (*Gittin* 32a)

✿ Time and labor ethics

R. Tarfon said: "The day is short, and the task is great, and the laborers are sluggish, the compensation is ample, and the master is pressing." (*Avot* 2:15)

Time before Mashiach

R. Zera said in the name of R. Yirmiyahu b. Abba: "In the time just before

---

253. See entry, Hasid.

the Mashiach will come, the scholars of the generation will be persecuted. When I repeated this statement in front of R. Shemuel, he exclaimed: 'There will also be test after test.'" (*Ketubbot* 112b)

Time-bound Mitzvah
מצוות עשה שהזמן גרמא
(*Shabbat* 62a; *Kiddushin* 29a)

Time-bound Precept
כל מצות עשה שהזמן גרמא נשים פטורות
All affirmative precepts bound by a stated time are not incumbent upon women. (*Kiddushin* 29a; *Berachot* 20b; *Eruvin* 27a; *Shabbat* 62a; *Menahot* 43a; *Rosh Hashana* 30a)

Time for sacrificial offerings
The appointed time for the various sacrifice offerings (*Pesahim* 58a)

✿ Time is now
R. Hillel said: "If I am not for myself, who will be; and if I am for myself only, what am I? And if not now, when?" (*Avot* 1:14)

📖 Time just before Mashiach comes
R. Nehorai said: "In the generation when Mashiach comes, young men will insult the old, old men will stand before the young, daughters will rise against their mothers, and daughters-in-law against their mothers-in-law. The people will be dog-faced and a son will not be embarrassed in his father's presence."

R. Nehemia said: "In the generation just before Mashiach is coming, impudence will increase, esteem will be considered wrong, the vine will yield its fruit, but wine will be expensive, and the kingdom will become non-believers and no one to rebuke them."

R. Zera said: "Three things come unawares: Mashiach, finding a lost article, and a scorpion." (*Sanhedrin* 97a; *Sotah* 49a)

Time lapse between cheese and meat
How long must one wait after eating cheese to eat meat? (*Hullin* 105a)

📖 Time of day
In Jerusalem, they recorded on contracts the time of the day
The mother of Rami b. Hama gave her property in writing to Rami b. Hama in the morning, but in the evening she gave it in writing to Mar Ukva b. Hama. Rami b. Hama came to R. Sheshet, who confirmed his inheritance. Mar Ukva then went to R. Nahman, who confirmed Mar Ukva in his inheritance.

R. Sheshet thereupon went to R. Nahman and said to him: "What is the reason you acted this way in this matter?"

R. Nahman replied: "And what is the reason you acted in this matter this way?"

R. Sheshet answered: "Because the will of R. Rami was written first."

R. Nahman replied: "Are we living in Jerusalem, where the hours are recorded? We live in Babylonia, where the hours are not recorded."

R. Sheshet asked: "And why did you act the way you did?"

"I treated it as a case to be decided at the discretion of the judges," replied R. Nahman.

R. Sheshet then retorted: "I also treated it as a case to be decided at the discretion of the judges."

But R. Nahman replied: "I am a judge, and you are not, and furthermore, you did not at first say that you treated it as a case to be decided by a judge." (*Ketubbot* 94b; *Bava Batra* 151a)

📖 Time of scarcity
R. Hana b. Hanilai fed the poor without embarrassing them
Rabbi Ulla and Rabbi Hisda were walking and they passed the house of R. Hana b.

Hanilai. R. Hisda sighed. R. Ulla asked: "Why are you sighing?"

He answered him: "How can I refrain from sighing? He used to have sixty cooks to cook and bake for the poor. He always had his purse ready to give charity. In time of scarcity, he put the grain and barley outside at nighttime for anyone to take, since he did not want people to have to come inside to be embarrassed. Now it is all in ruins, shall I not sigh?" (*Berachot* 58b)

Time proscribed for praying

Morning Prayer is discussed in *Tefillat Ha-Shachar* תפלת השחר, the 4th *perek* in Tractate *Berachot*. (*Berachot* 26a)

Tinnius Rufus and R. Akiva

Tinnius Rufus or Turnus Rufus, the governor of Judea, asked R. Akiva: "In what way is the Jewish Shabbat different from any other day of the week?"

R. Akiva asked in turn: "In what way is one man different from any other man, as for instance you?"

Rufus answered: "I am different because the Emperor wants it that way."

R. Akiva rejoined: "The Shabbat is different because the Master of the world wants it that way."

Rufus asked: "How do you know for certain which day is Shabbat, perhaps you are mistaken and another day of the week is the real Shabbat?"

R. Akiva answered: "The River Sambatyon is proof."

Rashi comments that this river of stones is turbulent every day of the week, except on Shabbat when it rests. (*Sanhedrin* 65b)

Tinnius Rufus or Turnus Rufus

R. Akiva on seeing the wife of Tinnius Rufus, spat, laughed, and then wept. He foresaw that she would become a convert to Judaism and that he would marry her. (*Avodah Zarah* 20a)

Tisha Be'Av on Friday

The fast day on the ninth of the month Av

R. Yehuda stated: "We were once sitting in the presence of R. Akiva, and that day was the ninth of the month of Av that occurred on a Friday. They brought him a lightly roasted egg and he ate it without salt. He did this not because he had an appetite for it, but to show the students what the Halachah was. (*Eruvin* 41a)

Tisha Be'Av   תשעה באב

During the week of Tisha Be'Av, it is forbidden to cut hair, to wash one's clothes, eat meat, or drink wine. (*Taanit* 26b; *Yevamot* 43a)

Tithing   מעשר

(*Pesahim* 35b; *Berachot* 47a; *Shabbat* 127b; *Eruvin* 31b; *Betzah* 13b)

Tithing

Erev Shabbat (*Shabbat* 34a)

Tithing

The tithe of R. Eleazar b. Azariah's flocks amounted to 13,000 calves annually. (*Shabbat* 54b)

Tithing cattle

When does the law of tithing cattle apply? (*Bechorot* 53a)

Tithing exemption

Lands exempt from tithing

R. Yehuda said in R. Shemuel's name: "All the lands God showed to Moshe are subject to tithing. These are excluded: Kenite, Kenizite, and Kadmonite."

R. Meir said: "These are the Nabateans, Arabians, and Salmoeans."

R. Eliezer said: "They are Mount Seir, Ammon, and Moab."

R. Shimon said: "They are Ardiskis, Asia, and Aspamia." (*Bava Batra* 56a)

Tithing in secret

R. Yohanan said: "Three kinds of people earn special approval from Hashem: a bachelor who lives in a large city and does not sin, a poor man who returns lost property to its owner, and a rich man who tithes his produce in secret." (*Pesahim* 113a)

Tithing method

What method was used to tithe the animals? (*Bechorot* 58b)

Tithing periods

There are three periods for tithing cattle. (*Bechorot* 57b)

Title to land

Undisputed title to a house and other properties requires occupying it for a certain amount of time. (*Bava Batra* 28a)

Titus

During the wars which Titus conducted against the Land of Israel, the rabbis issued decrees against ornaments (*Sotah* 49a)

Toast on wine by R. Akiva

R. Akiva made a banquet for his son and he made a toast over every glass, saying: "Wine and health to the mouth of our teachers and their students." (*Shabbat* 67b)

Toch Kedei Dibbur   תוך כדי דיבור

Statements spoken one after another within the minimum of time (as for instance the utterance שלום עליך רבי ומורי). Such statements have halachic consequences. (*Bava Kamma* 73a; *Nedarim* 87a; *Nazir* 20b; *Bava Batra* 129a; *Makkot* 6a; *Shevuot* 32a)

Tofes   טופס

The general part of a document, which may be written in advance. It does not include the name or the date. (*Bava Metzia* 7b)

Toilet

Praying or wearing *tefillin* when entering a toilet (*Shabbat* 10a)

Toilet

R. Yohanan said: "It is a blessing to have a toilet close to your house." (*Bava Metzia* 107a)

⌨✡ Tolerant for peace sake

Once a woman broke two candles on R. Bava b. Buta's head. When he asked her why she did it, she answered: "My husband ordered me to do it." He blessed her; he didn't want to cause trouble between her and her husband. (*Nedarim* 66b)

⌨ Tongue can be good or bad

The Midrash relates that R. Shimon b. Gamliel once sent his servant Tavi to buy a good piece of meat. Tavi returned with a tongue. The next time he sent him to buy meat – but not the best piece of meat. When he returned, he again brought back a tongue. R. Shimon asked him to explain how the same food could be good and bad. Tavi explained that when the tongue speaks well, there could be nothing better, but when the tongue speaks evil things, there could be nothing worse. (*Berachot* 16b; *Keritut* 1:7, 8a)

Tongue guarded   נצור לשוני

Mar the son of Ravina concluded the *Amidah* with the prayer of נצור לשוני. (*Berachot* 17a)

✡ Tongue guarded

Rabbi Yohanan said in the name of R. Yosi b. Zimra: "The tongue is guarded by two walls, one of bone and one of flesh, in order to guard it from speaking evil." He also said: "One who bears evil tales is almost as bad as the one who denies the foundation of faith." (*Arachin* 15b)

Tongue licking the dust

R. Yosef said: "Had Aher (Elisha b. Avuyah) not seen the fate of Hutzpit, he wouldn't have sinned." He saw the tongue of Hutzpit dragged along by a swine, and he exclaimed: "The mouth that uttered pearls licks the dust." This had such an effect on him that he became a changed man. (*Kiddushin* 39b; *Hullin* 142a)

Toothache

A toothache on Shabbat is discussed in *Shemona sheratzim*, the 14th *perek* in *Shabbat*. (*Shabbat* 111a; *Avodah Zarah* 28a)

Torah

Studying Torah is the greatest mitzvah because it leads to doing *mitzvot*. (*Bava Kamma* 17a; *Megillah* 27a; *Kiddushin* 40b)

Torah and its plain meaning
אין מקרא יוצא מידי פשוטו

One cannot depart from the plain meaning of the Torah. (*Shabbat* 63a; *Yevamot* 11b, 24a)

Torah and knowledge of the world

Knowledge of Torah and worldly affairs all in one person

Rabbi Aha son of Rava said: "Between Rabbi Yehuda HaNasi and Rabbi Ashi, there was no one who was supreme in Torah and in worldly affairs."

He was asked: "Is that really so, wasn't there Rabbi Huna ben Nathan?"

He was answered: "That was different, because Rabbi Huna deferred to Rabbi Ashi." (*Gittin* 59a; *Sanhedrin* 36a)

Torah chronological or not (*Pesahim* 6b)

Torah decree

By R. Ammi

R. Ammi once sent out a decree in Israel with these words: "I Ammi son of Nathan issue a Torah decree to all of Israel with regards to a law about slaves." (*Gittin* 44a)

Torah language and language of Sages
לשון תורה לעצמה לשון חכמים לעצמו

The Torah language is distinct, and the language of the Sages is distinct. (*Avodah Zarah* 58b; *Hullin* 137b)

Torah Law and Rabbinic Law

R. Yehoshua b. Korha said: "When two rabbis differ, we follow the stricter view in laws of the Torah, and the more lenient laws of the Sofrim." (*Avodah Zarah* 7a)

Torah on one leg

There are many stories which illustrate the patience of Rabbi Hillel. One such story is that a heathen who came before Shammai and asked him to convert him to Judaism and to teach him the Torah while he stands on one leg. Shammai chased him away with a builder's ruler. The man came to Hillel with the same request. Rabbi Hillel told him: "I will convert you and this is what the Torah and Judaism are all about. 'What is hateful to you, do not impose on your neighbor.' That is the whole Torah, while the rest is commentary. Now go and learn the rest." (*Shabbat* 31a)

Torah Parsha of the week

R. Huna b. Yehuda said in the name of R. Ammi: "One should complete reading the *parsha* of the week twice in Hebrew and once in Aramaic." (*Berachot* 8a)

Torah reading

Ezra HaSofer ordained that the Torah should be read on Mondays and on Thursdays, in addition to Shabbat. Three days should not pass without Torah. A minimum of ten *pesukim* (verses) should be read for the three *aliyot*. (*Bava Kamma* 82a)

Torah reading, minimum required

When the Torah is read, the required minimum is for three sentences to be read for each *aliyah*. (*Megillah* 23b)

Torah script

Mar Zutra said, some say Mar Ukva said: "Originally the Torah was given to Israel in the Hebrew language and Hebrew letters. Later, in the time of Ezra, it was also given in Assyrian square letters and Aramaic language. Finally, they selected the Assyrian script and the Hebrew language."

It has been taught that Rebbe said: "The Torah was originally given to Israel in the *Ashurit* writing. When they sinned it was changed into *Roetz* writing. When they repented the old writing was reintroduced. Why was it called *Ashurit*? Because its script was upright.[254]

R. Shimon b. Eleazar said in the name of R. Eliezer b. Parta, who said it in the name of R. Eleazar HaModai: The writing of the Torah script was never changed." (*Sanhedrin* 21b, 22a)

Torah scroll

The size of a Torah scroll (*Bava Batra* 14a)

Torah study

R. Shemuel b. Onia said in the name of Rav: "The study of Torah is more important than the offering of the Tamid." (*Sanhedrin* 44b; *Eruvin* 63b; *Megillah* 3b)

Torah study

R. Yehuda b. Hiyya said: "A Torah scholar who occupies himself studying Torah in poverty will have his prayers heard." R. Aha b. Hanina added: "And neither will they draw the veil before him." (*Sotah* 49a)

Torah study

R. Avdimi b. Hama said: "A person who occupies himself with the study of Torah will have his wishes granted by God." (*Avodah Zarah* 19a)

Torah study at night

Resh Lakish said: "One who is engaged in the study of Torah by night – Hashem extends His grace to him by day." (*Avodah Zarah* 3b)

Torah study blessings

Blessings over Torah study (*Berachot* 11b)

Torah study delays death

R. Hisda was studying when his time came to depart from this world.[255] (*Makkot* 10a)

Torah study surpasses all

We have learned: The following are *mitzvot* for which one gets enjoyment in this world and will also receive rewards in the World to Come: honoring parents, practice of loving-kindness, and making peace between people – while the study of Torah surpasses them all. (*Shabbat* 127a; *Kiddushin* 39b)

Torah taught on Shabbat in open field

Rabbah quoted R. Hiyya: "R. Yehuda HaNasi once went to a certain place to teach there on Shabbat, but the place was too small. He therefore went out to the field to lecture there. However, the field was not suitable, it was full of sheaves. He removed the sheaves to make the field clear."

R. Yosef related a similar story about R. Hiyya. He said it in the name of R. Oshaya. (*Shabbat* 127a)

Torah to be sold

Can a Torah be sold? (*Megillah* 26a, 27a)

Torah to endure

Resh Lakish said: "Torah will endure with those who are willing to sacrifice themselves for Torah." (*Shabbat* 83b)

---

254. "*Ashurit*" is from the same root as "*yashar*," Hebrew for "upright."

255. See entry, Angel of death.

Torah touching
It is not proper to touch the Torah with bare hands. (*Taanit* 29b)

Torah transferred from Moshe
The Torah was given to Moshe on Sinai and he transferred it to Yehoshua and then to the Elders, to the Prophets and to the Great Assembly (*Avot* 1:1)

📖 Torah used for own glorification
R. Zadok said: "Do not separate yourself from the community. When you are appointed as judge, do not act as a lawyer. Do not use the Torah as a crown for self-glorification, nor should you use the Torah as a spade to dig." (*Avot* 4:7)

Torah uses ordinary language
דברה תורה בלשון בני אדם
The Torah uses the ordinary form of expression used by human beings. (*Berachot* 31b; *Bava Metzia* 31b, 94b)

Torah vs. rabbinic commandments
Greater stringency applies to the rabbinical teachings than to the teachings of the Torah. (*Sanhedrin* 88b)

✿ Torah with no work
R. Gamliel b. R. Yehuda HaNasi said: "Torah study together with an occupation is excellent. All Torah study that is not in combination with work is for naught. All who occupy themselves with community needs should do it for the sake of heaven." (*Avot* 2:2)

✿ Torah with occupation
Our rabbis taught: One should combine the study of Torah with a worldly occupation. This is the view of R. Yishmael. However, Rabbi Shimon b. Yohai said: "If you plow in its season, and reap in its season, and so on, what will become of studying Torah – there

wil be no time left to study Torah?"
  R. Abbaye said: "Many have followed the advice of R. Yishmael and it worked well. Others have followed R. Shimon b. Yohai, and it has not been successful." (*Berachot* 35b)

✿ Torah with ulterior motive
R. Yehuda said in the name of Rav: "A person should always engage in Torah and the performance of commandments even though it is done for ulterior motives, because eventually it will lead to performance for its own sake." (*Horayot* 10b)

✿ Torah without food
R. Eleazar b. Azariah said: "Where there is no Torah, there is no proper conduct; where proper conduct is absent, there is no Torah. If there is no wisdom, there is no fear of God; if there is no fear of God, there is no wisdom. Where there is no knowledge, there is no understanding; where there is no understanding, there is no knowledge. If there is no bread, there is no Torah; if there is no Torah there is no bread." (*Avot* 3:21)

Torch lighting at Shabbat ending הבדלה
Blessing over a lit torch at the end of Shabbat during *Havdalah*. (*Berachot* 51b; *Pesahim* 103a)

Toref תורף
The essential part of a document, which includes the name and the date. (*Bava Metzia* 7b; *Hagigah* 6b)

Torts
R. Shimon b. Eleazar stated four general rules which apply to the laws of Torts. (*Bava Kamma* 14a)

Tosefta, anonymous
Rabbi Yohanan said: "The author of an anonymous Mishna is Rabbi Meir; of an

anonymous Tosefta, Rabbi Nehemia; of an anonymous Sifra, Rabbi Yehuda; of an anonymous Sifri, Rabbi Shimon; and all are taught according to the views of Rabbi Akiva. (*Sanhedrin* 86a; *Eruvin* 96b; *Gittin* 4a; *Kiddushin* 53a)

Touching
Touching your own body below the waist (*Shabbat* 41a)

Touching one's purse
R. Yitzhak said: "A man usually touches his purse at frequent intervals." (*Bava Metzia* 21b)

Touching parchment
Touching the Torah parchment (*Shabbat* 14a)

Tov   טוב
If one sees the letter *tet* in a dream, as the first letter of the word "*tov*," this is a good omen. (*Bava Kamma* 55a)

Tovi
It happened that R. Gamliel accidentally put out the eye of his slave Tovi. It made R. Gamliel happy, because he wanted to free his very faithful slave. When he met R. Yehoshua and told him: "Do you know that my slave Tovi has obtained his freedom?", R. Yehoshua told R. Gamliel that he disagrees with his conclusion and a discussion developed. (*Bava Kamma* 74b)

Tower of Babel
The generation of the dispersion (*Sanhedrin* 109a)

Town sold
When a whole town is sold, what is included in the sale? (*Bava Batra* 68a; 150a)

Town to be squared
Our rabbis taught: When a town is

planned, it should be squared to correspond to the four directions of the world; and use as a guide the planets and the sun. (*Eruvin* 56a)

Trade that is clean
Rabbi Meir said: "A man should always teach his son a clean trade." (*Kiddushin* 4:14)

Tradition   יש אם למסורת
Tradition is a determinant in biblical exegesis. (*Kiddushin* 18b; *Sukkah* 6b)

Tradition from our fathers
       מסורת בידינו מאבותינו
R. Levi said: "This is a tradition transferred to us from our fathers." (*Sotah* 10b)

Trajan coins and Hadrianic coins
Abbaye said: "The rabbis wanted to store away every Hadrianic and Trajan coin, because they were coined in Jerusalem." (*Avodah Zarah* 52b)

Transfer nonexistent item
     אדם מקנה דבר שלא בא לעולם
One can transfer that which did not yet come to this world, the opinion of R. Meir. (*Bava Metzia* 16b, 33b; *Bava Batra* 79b, 127b, 131a; *Yevamot* 93a; *Kiddushin* 62b; *Gittin* 13b)

Transferring a nonexistent item
     אין אדם מקנה דבר שלא בא לעולם
One cannot transfer that which did not yet come to this world, the opinion of the rabbis. (*Bava Metzia* 16b, 33b; *Bava Batra* 79b, 127b, 131a; *Yevamot* 93a; *Kiddushin* 62b; *Gittin* 13b)

Transgressing the words of rabbis
Whosoever transgresses the words of the rabbis, deserves to die. (*Berachot* 4b; *Eruvin* 21b)

Transgression through a messenger
       אין שליח לדבר עבירה
One cannot appoint a messenger to

commit a transgression. (*Bava Kamma* 51a, 79a; *Bava Metzia* 10b; *Kiddushin* 42b)

✿ Transgression to save your life

R. Yohanan said in the name of Shimon b. Yehotzedek: "The rabbis met in the upper chamber of Nitzah in Lydda. By a majority vote they resolved that one may save his life and transgress on every commandment of the Torah, except idol worship, incest, and murder." (*Sanhedrin* 74a)

Transgressions

Rabin said in the name of R. Yohanan: "There is a difference in transgressions if committed in public or in private." (*Sanhedrin* 74a)

Transgressions

R. Amram said in the name of Rav: "Three transgressions are hard to avoid: sinful thoughts, insincere prayers, and slander or shades of slander." (*Bava Batra* 164b, 165a)

✿ Transgressions עבירות שבין אדם לחבירו עבירות שבין אדם למקום

Committing a transgression against a fellow man is not forgiven.

One of R. Eleazar b. Azariah's quotations is: "On Yom Kippur, God forgives transgressions between man and God, but transgressions between man and his fellow-man are not forgiven – until he has placated his fellow-man." (*Yoma* 85b)

Translator unqualified

R. Yehuda b. Nahmeni was the interpreter for Rabbi Shimon ben Lakish. It happened once that the office of the Nasi appointed an unqualified person to lecture at the academy. They asked Rabbi Yehuda to stand by him and interpret. Rabbi Yehuda bent down to listen to what the lecturer had to say, but he made no attempt to say anything. Thereupon, Rabbi Yehuda delivered his own lecture.

He was saying: "Woe into him who talks to wood or to a silent stone. It is overlaid with gold and silver, but there is no breath in it." (*Sanhedrin* 7b)

Transmission of Temple service

Having been in that exalted office, R. Hanina was able to transmit many details of the Temple service and customs prevalent during the Temple period. (*Pesahim* 1:6)

Transplanted in time to come to Israel

Eliezer HaKappar states that the synagogues and houses of learning from Babylon will in time to come be transplanted to Eretz Yisrael. (*Megillah* 29a)

Traveler

A traveler finding himself Friday night at dusk; the object he is carrying is discussed in *Mi she-hehshich*, the 24th *perek* in *Shabbat*. (*Shabbat* 153a)

Traveler in the Desert

A story about a traveler in the desert (*Taanit* 5b)

Traveling

Praying on the road (Berachot 4th *perek*)

Traveling on a ship and praying

Praying on a ship is discussed in the 4th *perek* of *Berachot*. (*Berachot* 26a)

Travels of the Ark ויהי בנסוע הארון

Our Rabbis taught: Hashem provided signs for this *parsha* at the beginning and at the end, because it ranks as a separate book. (*Shabbat* 115b, 116a)

Tree

Tree hanging over a neighbor's field (*Bava Kamma* 82a)

✿📖 Tree overhanging

It happened that Rabbi Yannai had a tree,

which overhung on a public road. Another man also had a tree hanging over a public street. Some people who used the street objected, and the man was summoned to the court of R. Yannai.

R. Yannai said to them: "Go home and come back tomorrow." During the night, he had his workers cut down his own tree.

On the next day when they came back for a decision, he ordered the man to cut down his tree. The man objected, saying to the rabbi: "But you, sir, also have a tree hanging over the street?"

R. Yannai answered: "Go and see. If mine is cut down, then cut yours; if it is not, you need not cut yours."

What was R. Yannai's thinking? At first he thought that people would be happy to sit in the shade of the tree. (*Bava Batra* 60a)

Tree planting
Planting trees next to a neighbor's property (*Bava Batra* 26a)

Tree Uprooting[256] (*Bava Metzia* 59b)

Trefa   טרפה
An animal afflicted with a fatal organic disease is not kosher The following defects make an animal *trefa*: the gullet pierced, the windpipe severed, etc. (*Hullin* 32a, 42a, 52b)

Trefa and kosher meat shops
In a case where there were nine kosher meat shops and one *trefa* – if one bought from one of them but does not remember from which . . . (*Hullin* 95a)

Trefot   טרפות
We have learned in D'bei Yishmael: Eighteen *trefot* were told to R. Moshe on Mount Sinai.

Eight types of *trefot* were communicated to Moshe on Mount Sinai. (*Hullin* 42a, 43a)

Trefot   טרפות
One suspected of selling unkosher meat (*Sanhedrin* 25a)

Trembling before Rebbe
On one occasion when Rav was still very young, he and R. Hiyya were having dinner at Rabbi Yehuda HaNasi's table. Rebbe said to Rav: "Get up and wash your hands." R. Hiyya saw that Rav was trembling. He said to him: "Son of Princes, he is telling you to prepare yourself to lead in the blessings after the meal." (*Berachot* 43a)

Trembling in awe of each other
Whenever R. Hisda and R. Sheshet met each other, they trembled in awe of each other. R. Hisda admired R. Sheshet's extensive knowledge of Mishna, and R. Sheshet admired R. Hisda's keen dialectics. (*Eruvin* 67a)

Tribe of Benjamin
Rabbah bar b. Hana said in the name of R. Yohanan: "The fifteenth day of Av was the day when the tribe of Benjamin was allowed to rejoin the rest of the tribes of Israel." (*Bava Batra* 121a)

Tribe to be judged
To judge a whole tribe of Israel, a court of seventy-one is required. (*Sanhedrin* 2a)

Triple twisted cord
חוט המשולש לא במהרה ינתק
A triple twisted cord will not break easily. (*Kiddushin* 1:10, 40b)

Triple twisted cord will not break
רבי ביסא רבי חמא רבי אושעיא
The Talmud tells us that Rabbi Hama left his home and spent twelve years in the academy to study Torah. When he

---

256. See story under, Bat Kol.

returned home, he stopped at the local academy before going home. A young man entered the academy and sat down next to him and asked him a question on the subject of study. When R. Hama saw the great knowledge this young man possessed, he became depressed. He was thinking, *Had I been here, I also could have had such a son.* After he finally went home, the young man followed him and knocked on the door. Believing that he came to ask him another question, he rose before him as he entered the house. His wife broke out in laughter: "What kind of father stands up before his son?" The young man that followed him happened to be Rabbi Oshaya, his son. It was said of them: A threefold cord is not quickly broken." (*Ketubbot* 62b; *Bava Batra* 59a)

📖 Troops in Jewish homes on Pesach

The government placed troops in the town of Mehuza and the Jews had to give them quarters in their homes.

Rava told the townspeople of Mehuza: "Remove the leavened bread belonging to the troops from your homes, because it is in your possession, and if lost or stolen, you will be responsible for the loss. Therefore, it is considered to be your property and your *hametz.* (*Pesahim* 5b)

✿ Truth

R. Shimon b. Gamliel said: "The world rests on three foundations: truth, justice, and peace." (*Avot* 1:18)

Truth, Truth   אמת אמת

Repeating the word "*Emet*" (*Berachot* 14b)

Trying to do too much
תפסת מרובה לא תפסת

If you try to grasp a lot, you will not be able to hold on to it. If you try to do too much, you won't accomplish anything.

(*Rosh Hashana* 4b; *Hagigah* 17a; *Yoma* 80a; *Sukkah* 5b; *Kiddushin* 17a; *Hullin* 138a)

Tumtum

A person whose genitals are hidden or underdeveloped, hence of unknown sex. (*Sanhedrin* 66a)

Tumtum

A person whose sex is uncertain – the inheritance of such a *tumtum* is discussed. (*Bava Batra* 140b)

Tur Malka was destroyed

It was the custom that when a bride and groom were escorted to the wedding canopy, a rooster and a hen were carried before them. One day a band of Roman soldiers passed by and they took away the rooster and chicken. The Jews at the wedding fell upon the soldiers and beat them. The soldiers reported to the Emperor that the Jews were rebelling. R. Assi said: "Three hundred thousand men with drawn swords went into Tur Malka and they slaughtered the population for three days." (*Gittin* 55b)

Turned face away

Rav turned his face away, when he heard Shemuel's ruling. (*Eruvin* 94a)

Tutoring

Once R. Shimi ben Ashi came to Abbaye and asked him to give him lessons in Torah.[257] R. Abbaye answered him: "I have no time; I need my time to study for myself."

The other asked him:

"Then teach me at night." (*Gittin* 60b)

Twenty-four-hour period   מעת לעת

From time to time, a twenty-four-hour period (*Shabbat* 15a; *Niddah* 2a)

---

257. See story under, Correct and scrupulous.

Twenty-four priestly endowments

There are twenty-four priestly endowments all bestowed upon Aharon and his sons – first in general terms and then specified separately. Whosoever observes them is as though he observes the whole Torah. Ten are to be eaten within the precincts of the Temple; four are to be enjoyed in Jerusalem, and ten given to them to be within the borders of Israel. (*Hullin* 133b; *Bava Kamma* 110b)

Twenty-four principal damages

R. Hiyya taught: "There are twenty-four kinds of principal damages." (*Bava Kamma* 4b; *Keritut* 2b)

Twilight   בין השמשות

(*Shabbat* 34a, 35b; *Eruvin* 76a; *Berachot* 2b)

Twin animals' firstlings

Both are males, which one belongs to the Kohen? (*Bechorot* 17a)

Twin animals' firstlings

One is a male and one is female – is there an exemption? (*Bechorot* 17a)

Twins three months apart

R. Avin b. R. Adda quoted R. Menahem as saying: "It once happened that a child was born to the same mother three months after the first one, and both of those students were sitting in our academy."

Who were these students? They were Rabbi Yehuda and Rabbi Hezkiya, the sons of Rabbi Hiyya. But didn't we learn that a woman couldn't conceive twice during one pregnancy? Rabbi Abbaye explained: "It was semen which split into two. After it split, the features of one were completed at the beginning of the seventh month, and the features of the other were completed at the end of the ninth month." (*Niddah* 27a; *Yevamot* 65b)

Two chests in the wilderness

All those years that the Israelites were in the wilderness, two chests preceded them – one of the Shechina and one of the corpse of Yosef. (*Sotah* 13a)

Two contingencies simultaneously

אין אדם מתנה על שני דברים כאחד

R. Ayyo taught that R. Yehuda said: "A person cannot conditionally reserve two contingencies simultaneously." (*Hullin* 14b; *Eruvin* 36b; *Betzah* 37b)

Two goat offerings

Specifications for the two goats offered on Yom Kippur (*Yoma* 62a)

✿ Two have turned into three

Rebbe[258] asked R. Shimon b. Halafta: "Why didn't we have the pleasure of your visit on the festival as our parents used to receive your parents?"

He replied: "The rocks have grown tall, the near has become distant, two have turned into three, and the peacemaker of my home has ceased." (*Shabbat* 152a)

Two loaves in the Temple   שתי הלחם

The two loaves in the Temple

The time to consume the two loaves which were offered on Shavuot. (*Arachin* 8b; *Menahot* 94a)

✿ Two on the road

Two are traveling on the road far away from civilization – one has a pitcher of water. If both drink from it, they will both die; but if one only drinks, he can reach civilization and survive. Ben Petura taught that it is better that both should drink and die rather than one should see his companion die. R. Akiva taught that if the water is yours, your life takes precedence over the life of the other. (*Bava Metzia* 62a)

---

258. Rabbi Yehuda HaNasi.

Two persons finding object
An object is found by two people, and each claims that he found it first. (*Bava Metzia* 2a; *Bava Batra* 170a)

Two-story building
Two partners owning a two-story building and the building collapses. (*Bava Kamma* 20b; *Bava Metzia* 117a)

📖 Two Torahs
The written Torah and the oral Torah
A non-Jew came to Shammai and asked him: "How many Torahs do you have?"

Shammai answered: "We have two: the written Torah and the oral Torah."

The non-Jew said to Shammai: "I accept the written Torah, but not the oral Torah. Make me a Jew on condition that you teach me only the written Torah."

R. Shammai became angry and chased him out of his house. The same man came to Hillel with the same request and Hillel accepted him. On the first day, he taught him *aleph*, *bet*, *gimmel*, *dalet*, but the following day he taught him the reverse; *dalet*, *gimmel*, *bet*, *aleph*.

The non-Jew complained to Hillel: "Yesterday you taught me differently?"

Hillel replied: "You must rely on me not only on what is written, but also on what I tell you. The same is with the Torah. You must rely not only on the written Torah, but also on the oral Torah." (*Shabbat* 31a)

Two verses   שני כתובין הבאין כאחד
Two verses which teach the same thing (*Hullin* 113b; *Kiddushin* 24a)

Tyranical court
Eleazar b. Azariah said: "A Sanhedrin that puts to death one person in seventy years is termed a tyrannical court." (*Makkot* 1:10)

Tyrian money   כסף צורי
Rav Yehuda said in the name of Rav:

"Wherever the Torah speaks of money, it is Tyrian." (*Bava Kamma* 36b; *Kiddushin* 11a)

Tzadoki
R. Gamliel related that a Tzadoki once lived in the same alley with them in Jerusalem. (*Eruvin* 61b)

Tzadoki and Rebbe
A certain Tzadoki said to Rebbe: "It seems to me that if one reads the Scriptures, the mountains and the wind was not created by the same God."

Rebbe told him: "You are a fool. Read the end of the verse." At the end of the discussion, Rebbe asked him to stay for dinner, and he accepted. After the meal, Rebbe asked him: "Would you rather drink the cup of wine over which the benedictions after the meal have been said, or would you prefer forty gold coins?"

He replied: "I would rather drink the cup of wine." The family of that Tzadoki is still to be found amongst the notables of Rome; their name is Bar Levianus.[259] (*Hullin* 87a; *Sanhedrin* 39a)

Tzadukim
The Tzadukim were debating R. Yohanan b. Zakkai regarding inheritance for a daughter. (*Bava Batra* 115b)

Tzavua
An animal which changes every seven years (*Bava Kamma* 16a)

Tzedaka   צדקה
R. Assi said: "Giving charity is equivalent to all other religious precepts combined." (*Bava Batra* 9a)

Tzidkiyahu   צדקיהו
Tzidkiyahu is also called Shalom. (*Horayot* 11b)

---

259. The story in *Sanhedrin* is slightly different.

Tzitz צִיץ

It was taught that the *tzitz* which was worn by the High Priest on his forehead was in the shape of a plate of gold. Its size was two fingerbreadths broad and stretching from ear to ear. Upon it were engraved two lines: "*Kodesh*" above and followed by "*lamed* and *yud hei*" below. (*Sukkah* 5a; *Shabbat* 63b)

Tzitz צִיץ

The golden plate worn by the High Priest on his head atones for sacrifices offered in a state of uncleanness. (*Sanhedrin* 12b; *Pesahim* 77a; *Yoma* 7b)

Tzitz in Rome צִיץ

R. Eleazar b. Yosi said: "I saw in Rome the *tzitz*[260] with the inscription "Holy to God," and that it was all inscribed on one line.[261] (*Shabbat* 63b; *Sukkah* 5a)

Tzitzit

It was learned that the precept of *tzitzit* equals all the precepts together. (*Shevuot* 29a; *Shabbat* 32b)

Tzitzit

Five reasons explaining why the *parsha* of *tzitzit* is part of the *Shema* reading. (*Berachot* 12b)

Tzitzit from mixed yarns (*Yevamot* 4a)

Tzitzit removing

Removing *tzitzit* from one garment to another (*Shabbat* 22a; *Menahot* 41b)

Tzon Barzel צאן ברזל
Sheep of iron

It is a type of contract that when a flock of sheep is sold, there is a condition of payment in full, also a wife's estate being held by the husband. In case of death or divorce, the husband must restore loss of deterioration. (*Yevamot* 66a; *Bechorot* 16b; *Bava Metzia* 70b)

Tzurba Me-Rabanan צורבא מרבנן

It is not the nature of a Talmudic scholar to do such a thing. (*Bava Batra* 168a; *Shevuot* 41a)

U

Ukva, Mar מר עוקבא
Amora from Babylonia

Exilarch 3rd century CE (*Eruvin* 81a)

Ukvan b. Nehemia

Ukvan b. Nehemia was Resh Galuta during the lifetime of Rabbah and R. Zera. (*Shabbat* 56b)

Ulla עולא
Amora from Eretz Yisrael
3rd century CE (*Shabbat* 83b; *Eruvin* 21b)

Ulla b. R. Illai

Ulla had a case before R. Nahman. (*Shevuot* 30a)

✿ Ulterior motives

R. Yehuda said in the name of Rav: "A person should always engage in Torah and the performance of commandments even though it is done for ulterior motives, because eventually it will lead to performance for its own sake." (*Horayot* 10b)

📖 Unable to speak

There were two mute men unable to speak in the neighborhood of Rebbe. They were the sons of R. Yohanan b. Gudgeda's daughter. Others say they were his sister's sons. They sat in the academy of Rebbe and nodded their heads and moved their

---

260. Head plate of the High Priest.
261. There was a disagreement, one line or two lines.

lips. Rebbe prayed for them and they were cured. It was found out that they were versed in Halachah and in the whole Talmud. (*Hagigah* 3a)

Unanimous Sanhedrin

R. Kahana said: "If the Sanhedrin decided unanimously to find the accused guilty, the verdict was voided and the accused acquitted." (*Sanhedrin* 17a)

Unavoidable accident

Responsibility of a guardian in an unavoidable accident (*Bava Metzia* 93b)

Unaware

R. Zera said: "Three things come unawares: Mashiach, finding a lost article, and a scorpion." (*Sanhedrin* 97a)

Unawareness   בהעלם אחד

In one state of unawareness (*Keritut* 11b; *Shabbat* 70b)

Unawareness multiplied

R. Akiva said: "I asked R. Eliezer this question: If one does many labors on many Shabbatot – all in one state of unawareness." (*Keritut* 16a)

Uncertain of who was the seller

A pious man bought an article from one of two persons. When he was ready to pay, he was uncertain from which one he had bought it. (*Bava Kamma* 103b)

Uncircumcised Jew

An Israelite whose brothers died as a result of circumcision, consequently he was not circumcised. (*Hullin* 5a)

Uncleanness by carrying (*Ohalot* 2:3)

Uncleanness by touch (*Ohalot* 2:3)

Uncleanness unawares
(*Shevuot* 14a)

📖 Uncomplimentary words

R. Ulla once visited R. Nahman and they dined together. When they finished, R. Ulla made the after-meal blessings over a cup of wine. R. Ulla passed the cup of wine to R. Nahman. R. Nahman said to him: "Please pass the cup to my wife, Yalta."[262] Words were exchanged between R. Ulla and R. Nahman which were not complimentary to women. When Yalta heard the exchange, she got up in anger and went to the wine storage and broke 400 jars of wine. (*Berachot* 51b)

✿ Uncontrolled rage

Leads to disaster

Rabbi Kahana had to flee Babylonia, because of an incident. A man was brought before Rav. He wanted to denounce another Jew to the Persian authorities and to show them where the Jew was hiding his straw. Rav ordered the man not to show it, but the man insisted: "I will show it." Rabbi Kahana was present during this incident and he became enraged[263] at the man that he was defying Rav. In the argument, he accidentally killed the man. Rav advised Rabbi Kahana to move to Eretz Yisrael and to study at Rabbi Yohanan, but he also made him promise that for seven years he would not give Rabbi Yohanan a hard time with his sharp questions. (*Bava Kamma* 117a)

Uncovered head

A person removed the covering of the head of a woman. (*Bava Kamma* 90b)

---

262. See entry, Yalta.
263. See entry, Rage can lead to ugly consequences.

Uncultured person   עם הארץ
Rabbi Akiva said: "When I was still an uncultured person, I said to myself that if I would get hold of a scholar I would maul him like an ass." (*Pesahim* 49b)

Undergarments for a scholar
R. Yohanan asks R. Banaah: "What kind of undergarments should a Torah scholar wear?" (*Bava Batra* 57b)

✿ Understanding and wisdom
R. Hillel said: "The more Torah, the more life; the more thought, the more wisdom; the more counsel, the more understanding; the more righteousness, the more peace." (*Avot* 2:8)

Undertake to do the possible
         תפסת מועט תפסת
If you grasp a little, you can hold on to it. (*Rosh Hashana* 4b; *Hagigah* 17a; *Yoma* 80a; *Sukkah* 5b; *Kiddushin* 17a; *Hullin* 138a)

📖✿ Unethical behavior
Once R. Shimi ben Ashi came to Abbaye and asked him if he could get lessons from him. Abbaye answered: "I have no time; I need my time to study for myself."

The other asked him: "Then teach me at night."

Abbaye answered: "At night I am also busy I have to water my fields."

R. Shimi offered to water his fields during daytime and to get lessons at nighttime. Abbaye agreed and he studied with him.

However, one incident did not please Abbaye at all. R. Shimi went to the field-owners which were located above R. Abbaye's fields and declared to them that the field-owners below have the first right to water the fields. He then went to the field-owners below Abbaye's fields and told them the field-owners above have the first right to water the fields. In the meantime, R. Shimi had all the water available for himself to irrigate the fields of Abbaye. When Abbaye found out what he had done, it displeased him very much, and he refused to eat of that year's produce. (*Gittin* 60b)

Unintentional
Unintentional actions on Shabbat (*Shabbat* 41b; *Betzah* 23b)

Unintentional cooking
Can food be eaten if it was cooked on Shabbat unintentionally? (*Shabbat* 38a; *Bava Kamma* 71a; *Hullin* 15a; *Gittin* 53b; *Betzah* 17b)

📖 Unintentional insult
One time Rabbi Yohanan inadvertently insulted Resh Lakish by a slip of the tongue, when he expressed himself thus: "A robber knows his trade." One word led to another and they hurt each other's feelings. Resh Lakish fell ill. His wife came to R, Yohanan, who was her brother, and cried – asking him to forgive her husband. She pleaded: "Forgive him for the sake of my son." (*Bava Metzia* 84a)

📖 Unknown brother
A man came to Mari b. Isaac from Be-Hozai claiming that he is his brother, and he wanted to share in the inheritance of their father. "I do not know you," said R. Mari. The case came before R. Hisda. R. Hisda said to R. Mari: "He speaks the truth," but R. Hisda also said to the brother: "Go and produce witnesses that you are his brother."

"I have witnesses, but they are afraid to testify on account of his being a powerful man."

R. Hisda then said to R. Mari: "You go and bring witnesses that you are not his brother."

"Is that justice?" exclaimed R. Mari.

Subsequently, witnesses came to testify that he was his brother. (*Bava Metzia* 39b; *Ketubbot* 27b)

📖 Unmarried

R. Hisda was praising R. Hamnuna to R. Huna, saying that he is a great man. Said R. Huna: "When he comes to you, bring him to me!"

When he came, he didn't wear a cap, which is customarily worn by married men. "Why have you no head cap?"

"I have no head cap, because I am not married."

R. Huna turned his face away from him and said: "See to it that you do not come before me before you are married." (*Kiddushin* 29b)

Unmarried

R. Eleazar said: "Any man who has no wife is not a complete man." (*Yevamot* 63a)

✿ Unmarried

R. Tanhum declared in the name of Rabbi Hanilai, his father: "Any man who has no wife lives without joy, without blessing, and without goodness." (*Yevamot* 62b)

Unplastered area

The Sages ordained: It is permissible to plaster ones house, but a small area should be left bare to mourn the destruction of the Temple.

R. Yosef said that the size of the unplastered area should be one square cubit square.

R. Hisda said: "The unplastered area should be at the entrance." (*Bava Batra* 60b)

📖 Unselfish R. Hanina b. Hama

When Rabbi Yehuda HaNasi died, he left instructions. One of them was: R. Hanina bar Hama shall preside at the academy. However R. Hanina did not accept because R. Afes was two and a half years

older. Hence R. Afes became president of the academy. R. Hanina did not attend inside the academy, but instead studied outside in the company of Rabbi Levi. When Rabbi Afes passed away, R. Hanina bar Hama took over the presidency. Rabbi Levi had no one to study with, as a consequence he moved to Babylonia. (*Ketubbot* 103b)

✿ Unselfish R. Avohu

The rabbis decided to appoint R. Avohu as head of the academy in Acco, but when R. Avohu saw that R. Abba of Acco had numerous creditors asking for payment, he said to the rabbis: "There is a greater scholar more suitable for the office." (*Sotah* 40a)

Unthinkable of excommunication

R. Yehuda said: "It is unthinkable that Akaviah b. Mehalalel was excommunicated, for there was no equal to him in wisdom, in purity and in fear of sin." (*Berachot* 19a; *Pesahim* 64b)

Until

When a time is specified with a limit expressed by the word "until" – is "until" inclusive or not? (*Berachot* 26b)

Unusual handling   כלאחר יד

The back of the hand, not in the usual way (*Shabbat* 92a, 153b)

Unworthy judges

R. Shimon b. Lakish said: "Whoever appoints unworthy judges is as bad as planting the idol Asherah." (*Avodah Zarah* 52a)

Unworthy student

R. Yehuda stated in the name of Rav: "Whosoever teaches an unworthy student will fall into the Gehinnom." (*Hullin* 133a)

✿ Upbuilding the world
R. Yohanan said: "A Torah scholar is one who upbuilds the world." (*Shabbat* 114a)

Uprooting mountains during study
Ulla said: "Watching Resh Lakish in the Bet Midrash engaged in debate – one would think he is uprooting mountains and grinding them together." (*Sanhedrin* 24a)

Upside down world
R. Yosef the son of R. Yehoshua b. Levi became ill and lost consciousness. When he came around, his father asked him:
  "What did you see?"
  "I saw an upside down world – the upper class was down, and the people who are ignored in this world were on top."
  "My son," said R. Yehoshua, "you have seen a clear world." (*Pesahim* 50a)

Uriah the Hittite
The affair is being discussed. (*Shabbat* 56a)

Urim Ve-Tumim　　אורים ותומים
We have learned: The Land of Israel was divided among the tribes by the signs from the *Urim Ve-Tumim*. Eleazar the High Priest was dressed with the *Urim Ve-Tumim* on his chest. Yehoshua and all Israel stood before him. An urn containing the names of the tribes and another urn contained the boundaries. Eleazar was inspired by the *Ruah Ha-Kodesh* and gave instructions which tribe gets which land. (*Bava Batra* 122a)

Urim Ve-Tumim　　אורים ותומים
David and his Sanhedrin consulted the *Urim Ve-Tumim*. (*Sanhedrin* 16a)

Urinating
The distance required to avoid urinating on property of others (*Bava Batra* 17a, 19b)

Urinating from private into public
While one is standing in a private domain on Shabbat and is urinating into a public domain. (*Eruvin* 98b)

Urns of gold donated
The two he-goats were waiting and an urn containing two lots was nearby. The urns were made of box-wood, but Ben Gamla donated gold urns to replace the wooden ones. For this, he was praised. (*Yoma* 37a)

Usha; Academy　　אושא
Usha is a town in Israel south of Acco and west of Tiberias. After the suppression of the Bar Kochva revolt, the rabbis of the time convened a meeting at Usha. They enacted far-reaching legislation, which was urgently needed for a defeated people. Some of these enactments are mentioned in the Talmud. Present at the meeting were such luminaries as Rabbi Yehuda bar Illai, R. Nehemia, R. Meir, R. Yosi ben Halafta, R. Shimon ben Yohai, R. Eliezer b. Yosi HaGlili, and R. Eliezer b. Yaakov. Rabbi Shimon b. Gamliel was the head of the Sanhedrin, but he was still in hiding. (*Sanhedrin* 14a; *Ketubbot* 49b, 50a; *Bava Kamma* 89b)

Usha enactments
R. Yosi b. Hanina said: "When they convened in Usha, they enacted many new laws." (*Bava Metzia* 35a; *Bava Batra* 50a)

Usurer　　מלוה ברבית
The testimony of a witness who is a usurer is not accepted. (*Sanhedrin* 24b; *Shevuot* 45a)

Usurers
R. Yosi said: "Come and see the blindness of a usurer." (*Bava Metzia* 71a)

Usury
What is the difference between נשך and תרבית? (*Bava Metzia* 60b)

Usury

Usury (*Bava Metzia* 70b)

Usury
Usury is forbidden to the lender and to the borrower. (*Bava Metzia* 62a, 71b, 75b)

Usury
Charging interest to a non-Jew (*Bava Metzia* 70b, 71a)

Usury indirect
Avak Ribit אבק רבית
Indirect interest, shade of usury (*Bava Metzia* 67a, 61b)

Usury transgressors
Who is considered a transgressor of the usury prohibition? (*Bava Metzia* 75b)

Utensils bought from a heathen (*Avodah Zarah* 75b)

Utensils to rest שביתת כלים
Should utensils rest on Shabbat? (*Shabbat* 18a)

Utensils susceptible
Which utensils are susceptible to uncleanness? (*Kelim* 2:1)

V

Valuation
Property is being valuated. (*Bava Kamma* 58b)

Valuation for dedication
All persons are fit for dedication evaluation. (*Arachin* 2a)

Valuation minimum and maximum
(*Arachin* 7b)

📖 **Vanity and idle gossip**
Once the wife of the interpreter of R. Avohu said to the wife of R. Avohu:

"My husband has no need to get instructions from your husband, and when he bows down to your husband he is merely being courteous."
His wife told R. Avohu what she said. He said to her: "Why should we worry about it? All that matters is that through the two of us God is praised." (*Sotah* 40a)

Vatikin ותיקין
People who are punctilious (*Berachot* 9b)

Va-yachulu ויכולו השמים
Rava said, some say R. Yeoshua b. Levi said: "When praying Friday evening – even without a *minyan* – one is supposed to say '*Va-yachulu*.'" (*Shabbat* 119b)

✿ **Vegetables**
Leftover vegetables on Friday afternoon
The Talmud relates that Rabbah said to Rafram b. Papa: "Tell me some of the good deeds Rabbi Huna had done."
He replied: "On Friday afternoons, he would send messengers to the market and buy all the leftover vegetables." (*Taanit* 20b)

Vegetables
The blessing on vegetables is *pri haadama*. (*Berachot* 35a)

Vegetables
Blessing over boiled vegetables and raw vegetables (*Berachot* 38b, *perek* 6)

Vegetables
R. Huna: "A scholar should not dwell in a place where vegetables are unobtainable." (*Eruvin* 55b)

Ve-Haloh Din Hu והלא דין הוא
This cannot be so because a fortiori would point us to a different conclusion. (*Hullin* 22b)

Vendor interprets the sale liberally
מוכר בעין יפה מוכר
The vendor interprets the sale liberally, according to R. Akiva. The rabbis disagree. (*Bava Batra* 64b)

Vendor is very strict מוכר בעין רעה מוכר
The vendor interprets the sale strictly. (*Bava Batra* 64b)

Vendors
Four rules apply to vendors (*Bava Batra* 83b)

📖 Venomous serpent protected coat
It was said of R. Eleazar b. Pedat that he studied Torah in the lower market of Sepphoris, but he left his coat in the upper market of the town. R. Yitzhak b. Eleazar told a story:

"Once a man wanted to take the coat for himself and found a venomous serpent inside the coat." (*Eruvin* 54b)

Venus
It was recorded in R. Yehoshua b. Levi's notebook that the day of the week a person was born determines his fate. When R. Hanina heard this, he said to his people: "Go and tell the son of Levi: Not the *mazal* of the day, but the *mazal* of the hour influences the fate."

A person born under the influence of the sun will be distinguished; he will eat and drink from his own provisions and his secrets will be revealed. If he becomes a thief, he will not succeed.

A person who is born under Venus will be wealthy and immoral.

A person born under Mercury will have a retentive memory and will be wise.

A person born under the moon will suffer, he will build and demolish, he will eat and drink that which is not his own, his secrets will remain hidden, and if he chooses to be a thief he will be successful.

A person born under Saturn will have his plans frustrated. (*Shabbat* 156a)

Verbal transaction
A dispute between Rav and R. Yohanan on whether a broken verbal transaction is considered a breach of faith (*Bava Mertzia* 49a; *Bechorot* 13b)

Verbal-will on Shabbat (*Bava Batra* 156b)

Verbal wrongdoing
R. Yohanan said in the name of R. Shimon b. Yohai: "To wrong another person verbally is worse than monetary cheating." (*Bava Metzia* 58b)

Vernal equinox, summer solstice
R. Shemuel discussed when the vernal equinox and summer solstice occur. (*Eruvin* 56a)

Verse's real meaning
אין מקרא יוצא מידי פשוטו
The Torah never departs from its plain meaning. (*Yevamot* 11b)

Veshet ושט
The gullet in a bird, it can also refer to the windpipe of an animal. (*Hullin* 10a)

Veshet has two skins
Rabbah said: "The gullet has two skins." (*Hullin* 43a)

📖 Vespasian
Rabbi Yohanan asked Abba Sikra to devise a plan, which would enable him to escape[264] in order to meet with Vespasian, the Roman general. Abba Sikra suggested that his students should smuggle him out in a coffin. He took his advice and the two students who smuggled him out were Rabbi Eliezer ben Horkynos and Rabbi

---

264. See entry, Escape from besieged Jerusalem.

Yehoshua ben Hanania. When he was out from Jerusalem, he met with Vespasian. After a lengthy conversation, Vespasian told Rabbi Yohanan: "I must leave now, but make a request of me and I will grant it to you."

Rabbi Yohanan said: "Give me Yavne and its wise men, and a physician to heal Rabbi Tzadok." The wish was granted, and the Yeshiva in Yavne was spared. (*Gittin* 56a)

Vespasian wars

During Vespasian's invasion of Israel, they prohibited the wearing of garlands. (*Sotah* 49a; *Gittin* 7a; *Niddah* 61b)

Vessels of the Temple

R. Hanina said: "All the Mishkan vessels which Moshe made, he received their measurements from the Torah: their length, their width and their height. (*Sukkah* 5a; *Menahot* 96a)

Vessels plundered from the Temple

Rabbi Eleazar who accompanied Rabbi Shimon b. Yohai to Rome describes what he saw in Rome:

"It was the vessels plundered from the Temple." He also saw the splattered blood on the veil, and the High Priest's gold head plate inscribed. (*Meilah* 17b)

Vessels' use after twelve months

Vessels belonging to non-Jews (*Avodah Zarah* 34a; *Taanit* 11b)

Vestibule to the next world

R. Yaakov said: This world is like a vestibule to the World to Come. (*Avot* 4:16)

Vidui ודוי

Confession (*Shabbat* 32a)

Village dogs

Breeding village dogs (*Bava Kamma* 80a)

📖 Vinegar son of wine

R. Eleazar b. Shimon was arresting thieves by the order of the Roman authorities. R. Yehoshua b. Korha sent a reproving message to him: "Vinegar, son of wine, how long will you deliver the people of our God to slaughter?"

R. Eleazar sent a reply: "I weed out thorns from the vineyard."

R. Yehoshua retorted: Let the owner of the vineyard come and weed out the thorns." (*Bava Metzia* 83b)

Vineyard

If one is lost in someone else's vineyard (*Bava Kamma* 81a–b)

📖 Vineyards of Yavne

It is stated that when the rabbis entered the vineyard of Yavne, among them were Rabbi Yehuda, Rabbi Yosi, Rabbi Nehemia, and Rabbi Eliezer ben Yosi HaGlili. They all spoke in honor of hospitality and they expounded on the text of the Torah. When it came to Rabbi Nehemia's turn, he also praised hospitality and cited texts from the Torah and the book of Shmuel. (*Berachot* 63b)

✿ Violating Shabbat to save a life

Shimon b. Menasia said: "In order to save a life one may violate the Shabbat, because it is better to profane one Shabbat in order to be able to keep many Shabbatot." (*Yoma* 85b; *Avodah Zarah* 28a)

Violating Shabbat

(*Sanhedrin* 66a; *Shabbat* 153a)

Violating Shabbat in public (*Hullin* 5a)

Violating Shabbat to heal

(*Avodah Zarah* 28a)

✿ Virtue leads to virtue

R. Pinhas b. Yair said: "Zeal leads to

cleanliness, and cleanliness leads to purity; purity leads to self-restraint, and self-restraint leads to sanctity; sanctity leads to humility, and humility leads to fear of sin; fear of sin leads to piety, and piety leads to divine intuition, and divine intuition leads to resurrection of the dead, and the resurrection of the dead shall come through Eliyahu HaNavi of blessed memory." (*Sotah* 9:15)

Visit
With R. Dosa b. Horkynos (*Yevamot* 16a)

📖 Visit by R. Yehoshua b. Hanania
Rabbi Yehoshua traveled to Alexandria, Egypt, where the Jewish community received him with great honor. They put before him twelve questions: Three were of a scientific nature, three were matters of Aggadah, three were silly questions, and three were matters of human conduct. (*Niddah* 69b)

Visit by Rabbah b. Yirmiyah
(*Avodah Zarah* 50b)

📖 Visit to Babylonia by Rav
Shemuel and Karna were sitting by the bank of the Nahar Malka. They saw the water rising and becoming discolored.

When R. Shemuel saw the water, he said to Karna: "I can tell by the water rising that a great man is arriving from Eretz Yisrael, who suffers from stomach trouble. Go and smell his bottle."[265] It was Rav who arrived in Babylonia. Karna went and asked Rav several tricky Talmudic questions to test his knowledge. Subsequently, Shemuel took him into his house and gave him barley bread, fish, and strong liquor, but did not show him where the outhouse was. Rav was suffering from stomach trouble

and was annoyed with Shemuel because of it. (*Shabbat* 108a)

Visiting the sick   ביקור חולים
Visiting the sick is one of the great *mitzvot*. (*Bava Kamma* 100a; *Bava Metzia* 30b)

Visiting the sick
When visiting the sick – where to be seated and where not to be seated. (*Shabbat* 12b)

Visiting the sick
R. Aha b. Hanina said: "He who visits the sick removes one-sixtieth from their suffering." (*Nedarim* 39b; *Bava Metzia* 30b)

Visiting the sick
Rewarded in both worlds
R. Yehuda b. Shila said in the name of R. Assi in the name of R. Yohanan: "There are six good deeds from which one can derive benefits in this world and still get the rewards in the World to Come: hospitality to guests, visiting the sick, concentration during prayer, rising early for prayer, bringing up a son with Torah study, and to judge everyone as being upright." (*Shabbat* 127a)

📖 Visiting the sick
R. Helbo became ill, and R. Kahana announced it publicly. However, no one came to visit him. He said to them: "It happened that a student of R. Akiva became sick and none of the students visited him." R. Akiva was upset, and he himself went to visit. And because they swept and sprinkled the ground before him, he recovered.

He said to R. Akiva: "My Rebbe, you have revived me."

Thereupon, R. Akiva lectured: "He who does not visit the sick is considered as though he shed blood." (*Nedarim* 39b, 40a)

---

265. This means to find out how much learning he acquired.

Visiting the sick on Shabbat
When visiting the sick on Shabbat, what does one say? (*Shabbat* 12a)

Vomit on the street
R. Yehuda said, others say R. Nehemia said: "One must not cause himself to vomit in the street, out of decency." (*Shabbat* 12a)

Vows
Better not to make vows; the view of R. Meir. (*Hullin* 2a)

Vows annulled   הפרת נדרים
Vows annulled by a close relative (*Nedarim* 76b)

Vows invalidated   התרת נדרים
Vows invalidated by a court (*Nedarim* 20b, 21a)

Vows to be annulled
Can vows be annulled on Shabbat? (*Shabbat* 157a)

Vows to be annulled
Three persons are required to annul a vow when no scholar is present. (*Bechorot* 36b)

V'ridin   וורידין
R. Yehuda said that one must cut through the jugular vein (*v'ridin*) when slaughtering for kosher meat. (*Hullin* 27a, 28b)

Vulgar
R. Yehuda said in the name of Rav: "Some men of Jerusalem were vulgar." (*Shabbat* 62b)

✡ Vulgar language
On account of obscene language, troubles multiply, etc. (*Shabbat* 33a)

✡ Vulgar language
Two students were sitting before Rav discussing a difficult subject.
One of them made a remark: "This discussion has exhausted me like a swine."
The other remarked; "This discussion made me tired like a kid."
Upon hearing this, Rav would not speak to the one who used vulgar language. (*Pesahim* 3b)

W

Wagon sold
What is included in a sale of a wagon? (*Bava Batra* 77b)

Wakeup blessings
Blessings to be recited when waking up (*Berachot* 60b)

✡ Walk at night
R. Yitzhak said: "A *talmid hacham* should not walk alone at night." (*Hullin* 91a; *Berachot* 43b; *Pesahim* 112b)

✡ Walk on the right
The Master said: "Whoever walks on the right of his teacher is an uncultured person." (*Hullin* 91a)

Wall collapsed next to neighbor (*Bava Metzia* 117b)

✡ Wall unpainted as a reminder
After the destruction of the Temple, the rabbis felt that one should not have a house which is very ornate. Therefore, the rabbis declared that a house may be plastered, but one should leave a small area bare.
How much of an area? R. Yosef said: "It should be a cubit square."
R. Hisda said it should be by the entrance." (*Bava Batra* 60b)

Walled city house sale
Selling a house in a walled city (*Arachin* 31a)

Walls inclined for R. Eliezer

Rabbi Eliezer had halachic differences with the rabbis. He brought forth every argument to prove his point, but the rabbis did not accept them.

He declared: "If I am right, then let the walls of this school prove it."

Thereupon, the walls began to incline.[266]

Rabbi Yehoshua spoke up and rebuked the walls. "When scholars are in a holy dispute, what business do the walls have to interfere?" The walls stopped to incline, but did not straighten out either. (*Bava Metzia* 59b)

Walls unsafe, Rabbi Huna rebuilt

The Talmud relates that Rabbah said to Rafram b. Papa: "Tell me some of the good deeds that Rabbi Huna has done."

He replied: "On cloudy days they used to drive him in his golden carriage to survey every part of the city of Sura. When he saw walls that were unsafe, he would order them to be demolished, and if the owner could not afford to rebuild them, he would rebuild them at his own expense." (*Taanit* 20b)

War leader anointed

The person anointed to lead soldiers into battle addresses the people. (*Sotah* 42a)

War of Gog U'Magog

Self-made proselytes in the time of the war of Gog U'Magog are discussed. (*Avodah Zarah* 3b)

War of free choice

To go to war of free choice can only be waged by the authority of a court of seventy-one judges. (*Sanhedrin* 2a)

Warming food

Warming food on Shabbat is discussed in *Kira*, the 3rd *perek* in *Shabbat*. (*Shabbat* 36b)

Warming on Shabbat

A pot on a preheated stove to be used on Shabbat. (*Shabbat* 36b)

Warning to an offender   התראה

According to Torah Law, a death sentence may be executed only by a court of twenty-three. In addition, to execute a death sentence, it is required to have proper eyewitness testimony, proper warning given to the offender, and the warners must advise the person that a death sentence may follow. (*Sanhedrin* 8b, 41a, 72b; *Makkot* 6b, 9b)

Warning to a scholar

R. Yosi b. R. Yehuda said: "Warning a scholar is not needed." (*Sanhedrin* 41a)

Warning to a Sotah

Before the Sotah ceremony can take place, the husband must give a warning to his wife before witnesses. (*Sotah* 2a)

Wars of David

R. Shemuel b. Nahmeni said in the name of R. Yonatan: "Soldiers who fought in the wars of David wrote a divorce to their wives." (*Shabbat* 56a; *Ketubbot* 9b)

Washing

Washing one's own body on Shabbat (*Shabbat* 39b)

Washing for Shabbat

It was the custom of R. Yehuda b. Illai to wash his face, hands and feet on Erev Shabbat. He wrapped himself in Shabbat clothing. (*Shabbat* 25b)

Washing hands   נטילת ידים

Ordained by King Solomon
R. Yehuda stated in the name of R. Shemuel: "When King Solomon ordained the

---

266. See entry, Bat Kol.

laws of making an *eruv* and the washing of hands before eating bread, a heavenly voice proclaimed: "My son, if your heart be wise, my heart will be glad, even mine." (*Eruvin* 21b; *Shabbat* 14b)

Washing hands
Vessels that may be used to wash hands (*Yadayim* 1:2)

Washing hands
After using the toilet, one must wash hands and recite a blessing. (*Bava Kamma* 17a)

Washing hands
The amount of water to be used (*Yadayim* 1:1)

Washing hands
R. Idi b. Avin said in the name of R. Yitzhak b. Ashyan: "Washing hands before eating is a meritorious act." (*Hullin* 105a)

Washing hands after a meal
מים אחרונים חובה
Washing hands after the meal is an obligation. (*Hullin* 105a)

📖 Washing hands in prison
R. Akiva insisted on washing hands[267] before eating a meal, while there was barely enough water for drinking. (*Eruvin* 21b)

Washing hands and making Kiddush
Washing for bread and making Kiddush
R. Berona said in the name of Rav: "If one washed his hands for bread, he should not make *Kiddush* over wine."

R. Yitzhak b. Shemuel b. Mata said to them: "Rav has barely died and we have already forgotten his ruling? I stood many times before Rav – sometimes he preferred bread and made *Kiddush* over bread,

and at other times he preferred wine and made *Kiddush* over wine." (*Pesahim* 106a–b)

Washing hands Asmachta
R. Eleazar b. Arach said that the Sages found biblical support for washing hands. (*Hullin* 106a)

Washing hands in the morning
Rav said: "One may wash his hands in the morning and stipulate that it shall serve him for the whole day long." (*Hullin* 106b)

Washing hands up to what point
Our rabbis taught: The washing of hands for common food must reach up to the joint. (*Hullin* 106a–b)

Washing hands – what vessels to use
What kind of vessels may be used to wash hands for a meal? (*Hullin* 107a)

📖 Wasting bread or food
The Talmud relates: R. Gamliel was riding on a donkey from Acco to Kheziv immediately after Pesach and R. Illai was behind following him. R. Gamliel saw an expensive loaf of bread on the ground and he said to R. Illai:

"Please pick up the loaf of bread."

On the road further on, they met a non-Jew by the name of Mavgai. R. Gamliel called out: "Mavgai! Take away the loaf of bread."

R. Illai approached the stranger and asked him: "Where are you from?"

"I am an attendant at the station-house." "And what is your name?"

"My name is Mavgai."

"Did you ever meet R. Gamliel?"

'No,' answered Mavgai.

From this experience we became aware that R. Gamliel had *Ruah Ha-Kodesh*. We also learned three things: One may not leave eatables on the road, we also learned that we assume the food was left on the

---

267. See also entry, Akiva's water spilled.

road by the majority of the travelers who are non-Jews, and we also learned that after Pesach, one may derive benefit from leavened bread which belongs to a non-Jew. (*Eruvin* 64b)

Watchman
Paid watchman and unpaid watchman handing over his charge to another watchman. (*Bava Kamma* 11b; *Bava Metzia* 36a)

Watchmen at the Temple
Three places in the Temple where the Kohanim kept watch during the night: Bet Avtinos, Bet HaNitzotz and Bet HaMoked. (*Tamid* 2a)

Watchmen at the Temple
Twenty-one places in the Temple were watched by the Levites. (*Middot* 1:1)

Water and milk benediction
A *Shehakol* benediction is made on water, milk, and food that is not grown in the earth. (*Berachot* 40b)

Water-drawing rejoicing
שמחת בית השואבה

At the Temple in Jerusalem
Our rabbis taught: "Anyone who has not seen the Water-drawing at the Temple in Jerusalem has not seen rejoicing in his life. Anyone who has not seen Jerusalem in its splendor has never seen a lovely city. Anyone who has not seen the Temple in Jerusalem when it was fully rebuilt has never seen a beautiful building in his life."

The Talmud asks, which Temple? R. Abbaye said, and some say R. Hisda said: "This refers to the building Herod built."

The Talmud asks, what kind of material did he use to build it? Rabbah answered: "He built it of yellow and white marble." Some differ and say that it was built of yellow, blue, and white marble. The building

was constructed in tiers – one row was projecting out and one row was receding inward. His intention was to overlay the marble stones with gold, but the rabbis advised him to leave the marble as is, because it had the appearance of the waves of the sea. (*Sukkah* 51b; *Shabbat* 21a)

📖 Water-drawing festivities
When Rabbi Shimon ben Gamliel rejoiced at the Water-drawing festivities, he used to take eight lit torches, throw them up in the air and catch them one after another, and they did not touch one another. And when he prostrated himself, he used to dig his two thumbs into the ground, bend down, kiss the ground, and draw himself up again – a feat no one else could duplicate. (*Sukkah* 53a)

Water drawn
The amount of drawn water to make a *mikveh* unfit (*Shabbat* 15a)

Water left uncovered
How may one dispose of water which was left uncovered? (*Avodah Zarah* 30b)

✿ Water spilled
R. Yosef said: "Rebbe taught us a lesson: 'A person should not spill water when others need it.'" (*Yevamot* 11b)

📖 Water stream flowing in reverse
Rabbi Eliezer had halachic differences with the rabbis; he brought forth every argument to prove his point, but the rabbis did not accept them. He declared: "If the Halachah agrees with me, let this carob tree prove it." The carob tree uprooted itself. The rabbis retorted: "The carob tree couldn't prove the argument."

He then said to them: "If I am right, then let the stream of water prove it." Thereupon, the stream of water started flowing in the opposite direction. The rabbis retorted: "The stream of water couldn't prove anything in this matter."

Rabbi Yirmiyahu arose and declared: "The Torah has already been given on Mount Sinai, it belongs here on earth and we do not pay attention to heavenly voices." He continued to say: "It has been written in the Torah that the majority decides." (*Bava Metzia* 59b)

Watering
The question of starting to water the garden on Erev Shabbat (*Shabbat* 18a)

Waving the Lulav
Where in the prayers do they wave the *lulav*? (*Sukkah* 37b)

✿ Way of life
Our rabbis taught: When R. Eliezer fell ill, his students came to visit him. They said to him: "Teach us the way of life so that we should merit the World to Come."

He advised them: "Give honor to your colleagues, keep your children from nonsense, and place them between the knees of scholars. When you pray, know before Whom you are standing. In this way, you will merit the World to Come." (*Berachot* 28b)

✿ Wealth
R Hillel said: "The more flesh, the more worms; the more possessions, the more anxiety." (*Avot* 2:7)

Wealthy
The annual tithing of the flock of R. Eleazar b. Azariah was 13,000. (*Shabbat* 54b)

✿ Wealthy
Who is considered to be wealthy?
  R. Meir said: "He who enjoys his wealth."
  R. Tarfon said: "He who has many properties."

R. Akiva said: "He who has a righteous woman for a wife."

R. Yosi said: "He who has a toilet near his dwelling." (*Shabbat* 25b)

📖 Wealthy man's daughter starving
The Talmud relates that once Rabbi Yohanan ben Zakkai left Jerusalem riding on a donkey while his students followed him. They saw a girl picking barley grain in the dung of Arab cattle. When she saw him, she approached and said: "Master, feed me."

He asked: "Who are you?"

"I am the daughter of Nakdimon ben Gurion."

"My daughter," he asked, "what happened to the wealth of your rich father?"

"It is gone."

"And where is the wealth of your father-in-law?"

"One came and destroyed the other."

She further said to him: "Do you remember when you signed my *ketubbah*?"

"I remember," he said. "There was in your *ketubbah* one million *dinarim* from your father's house, in addition to that from your father-in-law."

Rabbi Yohanan wept, and said: "How happy are Israel when they do the will of God; no nation on earth has any power over them, but when they defy the will of God they are delivered into the hands of a low people." (*Ketubbot* 66b)

Wealthy person who honored Shabbat
A wealthy person attributed his wealth to his honoring the Shabbat. (*Shabbat* 119a)

📖✿ We all make mistakes
Regretting the derogatory remark made
R. Eleazar b. Shimon was coming home from the house of his teacher in Migdal Gedor. He was riding leisurely on his donkey by the riverside, and he was feeling happy and elated because he studied a lot

of Torah. A man, who was very ugly-looking, was passing him, and he greeted him with: "Peace shall be upon you."

He did not return the greeting. Instead, he said to him:

"Raca, how ugly you are. Are all your townspeople as ugly as you are?"

"I do not know," he answered. "But go and tell the craftsman who made me."

When R. Eleazar realized that he had done wrong he dismounted from the donkey and bowed down before the stranger and said to him. "I am in your debt, please forgive me."

Soon afterwards, R. Eleazar entered the Bet Midrash and delivered a speech on the subject.

"A man should always be gentle[268] as a reed and let him never be unyielding as the cedar." (*Taanit* 20a)

Weather watching
R. Yitzhak b. Avdimi said: "At the termination of the last day of Sukkot, people were watching for signs of rain. They watched the smoke from the Temple altar to see in which direction the wind was blowing it." (*Bava Batra* 147a)

Weaving
Weaving on Shabbat is discussed in *Haoreg*, the 13th *perek* in *Shabbat*. (*Shabbat* 105a)

Wedding
R. Assi came to the wedding feast of Mar, the son of R. Ashi, and recited six benedictions. (*Ketubbot* 8a)

Wedding
R. Ashi came to the wedding feast of R. Kahana. On the first day, he said all the benedictions, but the following days he said all the blessings only if there were new guests at the table. (*Ketubbot* 8a)

Wedding feast
R. Shemuel said to R. Yehuda: "Hurry and eat, hurry and drink, because this world is a wedding feast." (*Eruvin* 54a)

✿ Weddings
Rabbi Helbo said in the name of Rabbi Huna: "A person should partake of the wedding meal and felicitate the newlyweds."

Rabbi Ammi and Rabbi Assi are mentioned in the Talmud as decorating the *huppah* for Rabbi Eleazar's wedding. (*Berachot* 16a)

✿ Weddings for 300 brides
Paid by R. Tarfon
R. Tarfon was a wealthy person, and very charitable. Once he made a wedding for 300 brides, who were poor, because it was a year of severe drought. (*Nedarim* 62a)

Weep for the mourners
בכו לאבלים ולא לאבידה
Weep for the mourners and not for the deceased. (*Moed Katan* 25b)

Welcoming the Shabbat
Rabbi Hanina used to dress up in the finest garments on Friday evening and call out: "Let's go out and welcome the Bride and the Queen." (*Shabbat* 119a; *Bava Kamma* 32b)

Welcoming the Shabbat
R. Yannai used to dress up in Shabbat attire and say: "Come Bride, come Bride."

He also used to welcome the Shabbat by saying: "Welcome Queen." (*Bava Kamma* 32b; *Shabbat* 119a)

Well
Well belonging to partners; they were supposed to use the well on alternate days. However, one of them used it on a day that was not his day. (*Bava Kamma* 27b)

---

268. See entry, Gentle as a reed.

Well between two courtyards
In what manner can it be used on Shabbat? (*Eruvin* 86a)

Well-lit house of R. Avin the Carpenter
R. Huna used to say: "A person who lights his house well will have scholarly sons." R. Huna used to frequently pass the house of R. Avin the carpenter. He noticed that many lights were always lit in the house. He remarked: "Two great men will be born to him," and so it was: R. Idi b. Avin and R. Hiyya b. Avin were born to him. (*Shabbat* 23b)

Well-sifted teachings
The Talmud states that Rabbi Shimon ben Azzai said I found a roll of genealogical records in Jerusalem and therein was written a Halachah. In addition, it said that the teachings of R. Eliezer b. Yaakov are small in quantity, but thoroughly sifted. (*Yevamot* 49b)

Well water for a Mikveh (*Mikvaot* 5:1)

Wells
A well in a public domain during Shabbat (*Eruvin* 17b)

Western Wall
R. Aha was quoted as saying: "The Divine Presence never departed from the Western Wall of the Temple." (*Yerushalmi Yoma* 6:4)

What can be said?
מאי איכא למימר
If that is the case, what can be said? (*Shabbat* 6a)

▯ Whatever happened, Hashem did it for something good
R. Huna said in the name of Rav, who learned it from R. Meir, who learned it from R. Akiva: "A person should always say: 'Whatever happened, Hashem did it for my benefit.'"

The following story illustrates it: R. Akiva was on the road traveling. He traveled with a rooster, a donkey, and a lamp. He arrived in a certain town and he looked around for lodging, but none was available. He said to himself, *Whatever Hashem does, it will be for my good*, and he slept in the open field. A strong wind came and blew out the lamp, a wild cat came and ate the rooster, and a lion came and ate the donkey. He said again, *Whatever Hashem does, it is for the good*. During the same night, a gang of terrorists came and captured all the inhabitants of the town and carried them away. He expressed himself thus: "Did I not say, '*Whatever Hashem does, it is for the good*'?"

He must have learned it from R. Nahum Ish Gam Zu, who was the teacher of R. Akiva for many years. (*Berachot* 60b)

Wheat is claimed
Wheat is claimed by plaintiff but defendant admits to barley (*Bava Kamma* 35b)

✿ When there is no leader
Strive to be a leader
Rabbi Hillel said: "Where there are no men to lead, strive to be a leader." (*Avot* 2:5)

▯ Where is God
Abbaye and Rava were sitting before Rabbah when they were still young boys. Rabbah wanted to test them and he asked: "To whom do we say the benedictions?" They both answered: "To God."

"And where is God?"

Rava pointed to the roof and Abbaye went outside and pointed to the sky. Rabbah said to them: "Both of you will become rabbis."

This is why people say: "Every pumpkin can be told from its stalk." (*Berachot* 48a)

✿ Where there is no man, you be the man

R. Bar Kappara stated: "When the merchandise is cheap, hurry to buy. In a place where there is no man, you be the man. A man should always teach his son a clean and easy trade." (*Berachot* 63a)

Whip for lashes

A whip for administering lashes ordered by the court (*Makkot* 23a)

White garments

R. Shimon b. Gamliel said: "In my father's house, it was a practice to give to a gentile the white garments to be washed three days before Shabbat. (*Shabbat* 18a, 19a)

✿ White lie

For the sake of peace a white lie is permitted
Rabbi Illai said in the name of Rabbi Eleazar ben Shimon: "One may modify a statement in the interest of peace." Rabbi Nathan said: "It is a commandment." (*Yevamot* 65b)

Who is like your people Israel?"

R Hiyya b. Avin said: "The writing on the *tefillin* of Hashem are 'Who is like Thy people Israel.'" (*Berachot* 6a)

Whole Talmud at eighteen

By the time R. Kahana (4th century) was eighteen, he had already studied the whole Talmud. His close associates were Rabbi Aha b. Huna, Rabbi Rama b. Hama, and Rabbi Safra. (*Shabbat* 63a)

✿ Wicked person   רשע
Pious man   חסיד
Average person   מדת כל אדם

The rabbis taught: One who invests the money of orphans at risk to the orphans, but no risk to himself is called a wicked man, and one who invests the money of orphans so that they will receive profits only but will not share in the losses, is called a pious man, and one who invests to share both in profits and losses is an average person. (*Bava Metzia* 70a)

Widow of R. Huna

The widow of R. Huna had a case before R. Nahman. (*Shevuot* 30b)

Widow's maintenance   אלמנה ניזונת

A widow is to be maintained of the estate from the deceased husband. (*Ketubbot* 95b)

Widow's recourse

When a brother dies childless, then one of the remaining brothers must marry the widow. However, if the brother refuses, he must perform the ceremony of *halitza* in place of *yibbum*. It also involves taking off the shoe. (*Yevamot* 2a, 106b)

Wife

R. Yohanan said: "The death of a first wife is so much grief to a husband that it is compared to the destruction of the Temple in its days." (*Sanhedrin* 22a)

Wife encouraging husband to study

The Talmud says that the wife of Ben Azzai, who was the daughter of Rabbi Akiva, acted in a similar manner as her mother, insisting that he go to study. He had a reputation as an outstanding scholar. (*Ketubbot* 63a)

Wife found

In the West, they used to ask a man מצא או מוצא. He who finds a wife finds a great good. (*Berachot* 8a; *Yevamot* 63b)

Wife from Khuzestan

Ameimar permitted R. Huna b. Nathan to take a wife from Khuzestan, even though it is not within the boundaries of Babylon as defined by the rabbis. R. Ashi questioned R. Ameimar on this. He answered that this is the view of R. Meir. (*Kiddushin* 72b)

Wife injured
When one injures his wife during intercourse (*Bava Kamma* 32a)

✿ Wife loved by husband as himself
Our rabbis taught: One who loves his wife as himself, who honors his wife more than himself, is a very virtuous man. (*Yevamot* 62b; *Sanhedrin* 76b)

✿ Wife not to be wronged with words   אונאת אשתו
Rav said: "One should be very careful not to wrong his wife with inappropriate words." (*Bava Metzia* 59a)

Wife of R. Akiva
R. Akiva on seeing the wife of Tinnius (Turnus) Rufus, spat, laughed, and then wept. He foresaw that she would become a convert to Judaism and that he would marry her. She was the second wife of R. Akiva; his first wife was Rachel, daughter of Kalba Savua.[269] (*Avodah Zarah* 20a)

Wife traveled overseas
A man's wife traveled overseas, and the husband was informed that she died. (*Yevamot* 94a)

✿ Wife's blessings
R. Helbo said: "One must always give high respect to his wife, because all the blessings in one's home are on account of his wife." (*Bava Metzia* 59a)

Wife's duties
What are the duties that a wife has to perform? (*Ketubbot* 59b)

---

269. Most likely she passed away.

Wife's property   נכסי מלוג
A wife's estate in which the husband is entitled to the usufruct, but the property itself is not his and has no responsibility for the losses. (*Bava Kamma* 88b, 90a; *Bava Batra* 50a, 139b)

Wife's property   נכסי צאן ברזל
A wife's property, which the husband can enjoy the usufruct, but he is also responsible for maintaining it intact. If it gains, it is his gain but also his loss. (*Bava Kamma* 89a)

Will
How to write a proper will (*Bava Batra* 136a)

Winding staircases in the Temple
(*Middot* 4:5)

Windows
R. Hiyya b. Abba said: "A person should always try to pray in a house with windows." (*Berachot* 31a, 34b)

Wine
R. Hiyya said: "Anyone who can keep a clear mind under the influence of wine has the characteristics of the seventy elders. The numerical value of *yayin* is seventy." (*Eruvin* 65a)

Wine
On wine one makes the blessing *Pri Hagefen*. (*Berachot* 35a)

Wine
Rava said: "Wine which does not have three parts of water and one-part of concentrated wine is not wine." (*Shabbat* 77a)

📖 Wine and secrets   סוד יין
Have the same numerical value
R. Hiyya and his children, R. Yehuda and R. Hezkiya were having dinner with Rebbe, when they were still very young.

The sons did not utter a word during the meal. Whereupon Rebbe said:

"Give the young men plenty of strong wine, so that they will open up and say something."

When the wine was having its effect, they started talking, and they said:

"The son of David cannot come until the two ruling houses of Israel shall come to an end."

"My children, you throw thorns in my eyes." R. Hiyya intervened and said. "Rebbe, do not angry: the numerical value of the Hebrew letters for 'wine' is the same as the Hebrew letters for 'secret.' When wine goes in the secret comes out."[270] (*Sanhedrin* 38a)

Wine belonging to a non-Jew (*Avodah Zarah* 29b)

Wine cooked
Rava said: "Cooked wine is not rendered unfit by being left uncovered nor is it suspected of idolatrous use." (*Avodah Zarah* 30a)

▭ Wine for Kiddush
Once there was no rain and Rabbi Yehuda HaNasi ordained a fast, but no rain fell. R. Ilfa went before the ark and recited the prayers for rain and rain fell.

Rebbe asked him: "What is your special merit?"

He answered: "I live in a poverty-stricken remote neighborhood, where wine for *Kiddush* and *Havdalah* is hard to come by. I make sure that I have wine and this way I help others to fulfill the mitzvah of *Kiddush*." (*Taanit* 24a)

Wine not kosher   יין נסך
Wine of libation; wine known or suspected to have been dedicated or manipulated

---

270. See entry, Dining with R. Yehuda HaNasi.

for idolatrous libation. (*Hullin* 4b; *Avodah Zarah* 65b)

Wine pitchers broken (*Bava Kamma* 28a)

Wine poured by a non-Jew
(*Avodah Zarah* 58a)

Wine purchase retracted
A man gave money in advance to a wine merchant for wine he intended to buy. However, the buyer found out that the government intends to seize the wine; he asked the seller to return his money. (*Bava Metzia* 49b)

Wine sold
If one sold wine or oil and the price went up or it went down. (*Bava Batra* 87a)

Wine store and a non-Jew attendant
If a wine store owner left a non-Jew in his store and an Israelite was going in and out. (*Hullin* 3a)

▭ Wine turned sour
A man asked his friend to buy him 400 barrels of wine. When he brought him the wine, it turned out to be sour. The man came to Rava to claim that his friend bought him sour wine. Rava said to the man who bought the wine: "Go and bring proof that when you bought the wine it was good wine, and then will you be free from liability." (*Bava Metzia* 83a)

Wipe with the left hand
Ben Azzai said: "Once I went after R. Akiva in a privy and I learned from him three things: one of them was that it is proper to wipe with the left hand and not with the right hand." (*Berachot* 62a)

✿ Wisdom followed by deeds
Rabbi Hanina used to say: "He whose

deeds exceed his wisdom, his wisdom will endure, but he whose wisdom exceeds his deeds, his wisdom will not endure." (*Avot* 3:9)

Wisdom to be acquired
R. Yishmael said: "If one desires to be wise from learning, then one should study the Halachah on monetary judgment, since no subject in the Torah surpasses this. It is like a perpetual fountain." (*Berachot* 63b; *Bava Batra* 175b)

✡ Wise
Who is wise?
Ben Zoma used to say: "Who is wise? One who learns from all people. Who is strong? One who subdues his passions. Who is rich? One who is happy with his portion. Who is honored? One who honors his fellow-men." (*Avot* 4:1)

Wise person
Ameimar said: "A wise man is even superior to a prophet. (*Bava Batra* 12a)

✡ Wise sayings
R. Eliezer HaKapar said: "The newborn are destined to die, the dead will live again, and the living will be judged. Know that everything is according to the reckoning. Let not your evil inclination mislead you that your grave will be an escape for you. You were created against your will, you were born against your will, against your will you live, against your will you will die and against your will you are destined to give an account before the King of Kings." (*Avot* 4:29)

Wise scholars
It was Rabbi Eleazar who transmitted in the name of Rabbi Hanina the famous saying:
"The wise scholars of Torah increase peace in the world." (*Berachot* 64a; *Yevamot* 122b; *Nazir* 66b *Tamid* 32b)

Witchcraft
On one occasion, Rabbi Shimon ben Shetah took drastic action to eradicate witchcraft. In Ashkelon, he ordered eighty witches to be hanged. (*Sanhedrin* 6:4, 45b)

✡ Withholding wages
Delaying payment to a hired laborer (*Bava Metzia* 112a; *Bava Kamma* 119a)

Without reward
One should do Hashem's commandments without thinking of the reward. (*Avodah Zarah* 19a)

Witness
R. Yehoshua said: "A witness who refuses to testify is exempt from judgments by men, but is liable to the judgment of Heaven." (*Bava Kamma* 55b)

Witness
One witness only (*Eduyot* 8:5)

Witness examination
Procedure established and followed for witness examination (*Sanhedrin* 37a, 40a)

Witness for pay (*Bechorot* 29a)

Witness; one witness only
Rabbi Shimon ben Gamliel said in the name of R. Shimon b. HaSegan: "One witness is sufficient to accept a person as a Kohen." (*Ketubbot* 2:8, 23b)

✡ Witness to a murder
R. Shimon b. Shetah said: "May I never see comfort if I did not see a man pursuing another man into a ruin. When I ran after him, he had a sword in his hand with blood dripping from it. I exclaimed: 'Wicked

man, you slew this man.' It is related that before they left the ruin, a serpent bit the man and he also died." (*Sanhedrin* 37b)

Witnesses

R. Yohanan b. Beroka said: "A woman or a child can testify in certain cases." (*Bava Kamma* 114a)

✿ Witnesses
Do not lead witnesses

Shimon ben Shetach said: "Question witnesses thoroughly, and do not lead them to false testimony." (*Avot* 1:9)

Witnesses

If one witness turns out to be false, then all the witnesses are considered false. (*Makkot* 5b)

Witnesses don't sign for a minor

It is an established fact that witnesses do not sign to validate a contract of a minor unless they know that the minor is of age. (*Bava Batra* 155a; *Ketubbot* 19a; *Sanhedrin* 29b)

✿ Witnesses ineligible

The following are ineligible for testifying as witnesses: A dice- or card player, a usurer, a person who flies pigeons, and a person who deals in produce of the Shemittah year. (*Rosh Hashana* 22a; *Sanhedrin* 24b)

Witnesses to the new moon

Profaning the Shabbat while being a witness to the new moon. (*Rosh Hashana* 21b, 19b)

Wolf

The wolf is considered to be *muad*.[271] (*Bava Kamma* 15b)

---

271. To be warned of being dangerous.

Wolf attack

Animals attacked by a wolf that caused wounds in the animals (*Hullin* 52b)

Wolves

How many wolves are considered to be a danger? (*Bava Metzia* 93b)

Woman
Without a hand

Our rabbis taught: There was a man who married a woman who had one hand missing. He didn't notice that until the day she died.

Rebbe remarked: "Come and see the modesty of this woman."

R. Hiyya said: "For her it was natural, but the modesty of the man is amazing that he did not scrutinize the looks of his wife during her lifetime." (*Shabbat* 53b)

Woman in childbirth

R. Haviva said: "The Elders of Pumbedita ruled one additional ruling." Rava had said that they ruled on two matters and R. Haviva added one more. The additional ruling was that it is permitted to light a fire on Shabbat for a woman in childbirth. It was Rav Yehuda who said it in R. Shemuel's name. (*Eruvin* 79b)

Woman's own declaration

A woman declares" "I was married, but I am divorced." It is a dispute between R. Gamliel and R. Yehoshua. (*Bechorot* 36a; *Ketubbot* 22a)

Woman tried to seduce R. Kahana

The Talmud relates that R. Kahana came to the house of a Roman woman to sell the baskets and she tried to seduce him. He excused himself to clean up first. He went to the roof and jumped. The Angel Eliyahu flew towards him and caught him in mid-air and saved him from being killed.

Eliyahu complained to him: "I had to fly 400 *parsi* to save you." (*Kiddushin* 40a)

Women סדר נשים
The Tractate Nashim contains laws concerning women, family life, marriage, and divorce.

Women
Are women obligated to light Chanukah candles? (*Shabbat* 23a)

Women
Women's responsibility for damages (*Bava Kamma* 14b, 15a)

Women
One may buy from women. (*Bava Kamma* 118b, 119a)

Women
A woman vowing she will marry the first man who makes her an offer (*Bava Kamma* 80a)

Women and Grace after a Meal (*Berachot* 17b, 20b)

Women and Kiddush
Are women obligated to make *Kiddush*? (*Berachot* 20b; *Shevuot* 20b)

Women and a Mezuzah (*Berachot* 17b, 20b)

Women and prayers (*Berachot* 17b, 20b)

Women and Shema (*Berachot* 17b, 20b)

Women and Tefillin (*Berachot* 17b, 20b)

Women in captivity
Rabbi Abba was the father of Rabbi Shemuel. Certain women captives came once to Nehardea, and R. Shemuel's father placed watchmen over them. R. Shemuel asked his father: "And who

watched over them until now?"

His father answered him: "If they had been your daughters, would you have spoken so lightly of them?" R. Abba devoted a lot of time and resources to redeeming many Jewish captives.

Women on Chanukah (*Shabbat* 23a)

Women's hall in the Temple
The Women's hall was 135 cubits long and 135 cubits wide, and it had four chambers at its four corners. (*Middot* 2:5)

Wooden utensils
Found wooden utensils – can they be used? (*Bava Metzia* 30a)

Wool
Buying wool from a wool processor (*Bava Kamma* 119b)

Wool tearing
Rav holds that torn wool from a sheep is not considered as shorn wool, it is considered shorn in an unusual manner. (*Bechorot* 25a)

Word comes to cancel a word
אתי דיבור ומבטל דיבור
(*Gittin* 32b; *Kiddushin* 59b)

Word of Torah, its numerical value
It is stated that Moshe brought down from Mount Sinai 613 commandments. The numeric value of the word "Torah" is 611. The two missing commandments are the first two, which the people of Israel heard from Hashem himself. (*Makkot* 23b)

Words of God
Both are the words of the living God
Rabbi Abba said in the name of Rabbi Shemuel: "For three years there was a dispute between Bet Shammai and Bet Hillel, each one claiming the Halachah is

in agreement with their views. Then a Bat Kol (heavenly voice) was heard announcing that both are the words of the living God, but the Halachah is in agreement with the rulings of Bet Hillel." (*Eruvin* 13b; *Gittin* 6b)

✿ Work is respectful
Rabbi Kahana had a hard time making a living. Rav advised him: "Flay carcasses in the marketplace and earn a living. Do not say: 'I am a priest and a great man; this type of work is beneath my dignity.'" (*Pesahim* 113a)

Work on Erev Shabbat
It was taught: Anyone who does work on Erev Shabbat or Erev Yom Tov from Minha onwards will never see a blessing from that work. (*Pesahim* 50b)

Work on Shabbat
R. Akiva said: "Any work that could have been done before Shabbat does not override Shabbat." (*Pesahim* 66a)

Work on Tisha Be'Av
Is it permitted to work on Tisha Be'Av? (*Pesahim* 54b)

✿ Worked hard and found success
R. Yitzhak said: "If a man says to you: 'I have worked hard but I have not found,' do not believe him. If he says: 'I have not worked, but still I have found,' do not believe him. If he says: 'I have worked hard, and I have found,' you may believe him." (*Megillah* 6b)

Working man
R. Hiyya b. Ammi said in the name of R. Ulla: "A man who lives from the labor of his hands is greater than one who fears God." (*Berachot* 8a)

World exists in the merit of the great
Rava said or R. Yohanan said: "The world exists only in the merit of Moshe and Aharon." (*Hullin* 89a)

✿ World is based on three things
R. Shimon HaTzaddik stated: "The world is based on three things: the Torah, Divine service, and charity." (*Avot* 1:2)

✿ World of Mashiach
The difference between our time and Mashiach's time
R. Shemuel said: "The difference between this world and the world of Mashiach is that in this world, there is exile and servitude, and during Mashiach's time, there will be freedom." (*Sanhedrin* 91b, 99a; *Shabbat* 63a, 151a; *Berachot* 34b; *Pesahim* 68a)

✿ World rests on three things
R. Shimon b. Gamliel said: "The world rests on three things: on judgment, on truth, and on peace." (*Avot* 1:18)

World to Come   עולם הבא
All Jews have a share in the World to Come. (*Sanhedrin* 90a)

World to Come   עולם הבא
R. Yehuda b. Shila said in the name of R. Assi, in the name of R. Yohanan: "There are six things which a person can benefit from in this world while the principal remains to be benefited from in the World to Come: hospitality to wayfarers, visiting the sick, mediation in prayer, arriving early at the Bet Midrash, teaching a son Torah, and judging everyone as being upright. (*Sanhedrin* 90a; *Shabbat* 127a; *Kiddushin* 39b)

World to Come   עולם הבא
Is there anyone here who merits the World to Come?
R. Beroka used to frequent the market

in Be-Lapat where he frequently met with Eliyahu.[272] Once he asked Eliyahu: "Is anyone in this market who merits the World to Come?"

Eliyahu pointed out a man and said: "That man has a share in the World to Come."

R. Beroka ran after him and asked him: "What is your occupation?"

The man told him: "Go away and come back tomorrow."

The next day he asked him again: "What is your occupation?"

"I am a jailer, and I keep the men and women separated, and I place my bed between them." (*Taanit* 22a)

World trembled

When Hashem said at Sinai: "Do not take My name in vain" the whole world trembled. (*Shevuot* 39a)

World upside down

R. Yosef b. R. Yehoshua was ill and became unconscious. When he recovered, his father asked him: When you were unconscious, did you have any visions?"

He said: "I saw an upside down world; those who are up were down, and those who are down in this world are up in the World to Come."

His father told him: "You saw a true and well-regulated world." (*Bava Batra* 10b)

World was created

It was taught that R. Eliezer said: "The world was created in Tishrei. R. Yehoshua said: "The world was created in Nisan." (*Rosh Hashana* 11a)

World was created

Rav said: "The world was created in the merit of David."

Shemuel said: "In the merit of Moshe."

R. Yohanan said: "The world was created in the merit of Mashiach." (*Sanhedrin* 98b)

✿ Worldly occupation

Our rabbis taught: One should combine the study of Torah with a worldly occupation. This is the view of R. Yishmael.

However, Rabbi Shimon b. Yohai said: "If you plow in its season, and reap in its season, and so on, what will become of studying Torah?"

R. Abbaye said: "Many have followed the advice of R. Yishmael and it worked well. Others have followed R. Shimon b. Yohai, and it has not been successful." (*Berachot* 35b)

Worms painful

R. Yitzhak said: "Worms are as painful to the dead as needles are to the living." (*Shabbat* 13b)

Worst quality property   זיבורית

(*Bava Kamma* 7b; *Gittin* 48b)

📖 Wrapped in a Torah and burned

Our rabbis taught: When Rabbi Yosi b. Kisma was ill, R. Hanania b. Teradion went to visit him.

R. Yosi said to him: "Don't you know that Heaven ordained that the Romans would destroy our Temple and rule over us? I heard that you are defying them and teach Torah in public."

R. Hanania answered: "Heaven will show mercy."

R. Yosi said to him: "I am telling you plain facts and you tell me 'Heaven will show mercy?' I would not be surprised if they burn you and the scroll of Torah together with you in one fire."

R. Hanania asked R. Yosi: "How do I stand in the World to Come?"

"Is there any particular act you are concerned about?"

"Yes, once I mistakenly mixed up the

---

272. See entry, Eliyahu.

Purim money with the ordinary charity."

Rabbi Yosi replied: "I wish your portion would be my portion."

Within a few days, R. Yosi b. Kisma died and all the great men of Rome came to his funeral and eulogized him. On their return they came upon R. Hanania b. Teradion sitting and teaching Torah in public. They took him and his scroll of Torah and wrapped the scroll around his body,[273] placed bundles of wood around him and set it on fire. They soaked cloth of wool in water and placed it over his heart, in order to prolong his agony. When his daughter saw him, she exclaimed: "Father! Woe to me to see you in this state."

He told her: "If it would be just me, it would be hard to bear, but being burned with the Torah is more comforting."

His students asked him: "Rabbi, what do you see?"

He answered: "The parchment I see burning, but the letters are soaring high." The executioner asked him:

"Rabbi, if I remove the wool from your heart will you take me with you to heaven?"

He said: "Yes." The executioner removed the wool, increased the flames, and his soul departed speedily. The executioner then threw himself into the fire.

When R. Yehuda HaNasi heard the news, he cried and said: One may acquire *Olam Haba* in a single hour; others after many years.

Rabbi Hanania ben Teradion became one of the Ten Martyrs. (*Avodah Zarah* 18a)

Write a Torah

Rabbah said: "It is a mitzvah for each individual to write a Torah, even if one inherits a Torah from one's parents; as it is written." (*Devarim* 31:19; *Sanhedrin* 21b)

Writing on Shabbat

Writing on Shabbat in any form is discussed in *Ha-boneh*, the 12th *perek* in *Shabbat*. (*Shabbat* 103a)

Written contract
Even between friends

R. Ashi sent word to Ravina, asking for a loan of ten *zuz*, so he could buy a small parcel of land. His reply was: "Bring witnesses and we will draw up a contract."

R. Ashi was surprised. "I am one of your best friends, and even from me you want a written contract?"

Ravina answered: "Especially from you I want a contract. You are so immersed in the study of Torah, you are bound to forget, thus causing you to sin and bring a curse on me." (*Yoma* 86a)

Written text determinant יש אם למקרא

The written and read text is a determinant in biblical exegesis. (*Kiddushin* 18b; *Sukkah* 6b; *Sanhedrin* 4a; *Pesahim* 86b; *Bechorot* 34a; *Keritut* 17b; *Makkot* 7b)

Wrong decision by the Bet Din
(*Horayot* 2a)

Wronging wife with words אונאת אשתו

Rav said: "One should be very careful not to wrong his wife with angry words." (*Bava Metzia* 59a)

Y

Yaakov יעקב
Amora from Babylonia
3rd – 4th centuries CE (*Berachot* 29b)

Yaakov
Yaakov our patriarch established Maariv prayers. (*Berachot* 26b)

---

273. See also entry, Burned with his Torah together.

Yaakov and the House of God

Yaakov called Jerusalem "Bet El," the house of God. (*Pesahim* 88a)

Yaakov spent fourteen years at Ever

When Yaakov ran away from his brother Eisav and was traveling to the house of Lavan, he stopped at the Yeshiva of Ever and studied there for fourteen years. (*Megillah* 17a)

Yaakov's funeral

A Tanna taught: When they carried Yaakov's coffin from Egypt to Hevron in Israel, Yosef placed his crown on the coffin to show respect to his father. When the kings from the other nations saw Yosef's crown, they all placed their crowns on the coffin to show respect to Yaakov.

R. Abbahu said: "Hushim, the son of Dan and grandson of Yaakov, was at the funeral. He was hard of hearing and heard a commotion. When he found out that Eisav the brother of Yaakov showed up and caused the commotion and wanted to prevent the burial, he took a club and killed Eisov. Thus Yaakov and Eisav were buried on the same day. (*Sotah* 13a)

Yaakov bar Aha   יעקב בר אחא
Amora from Eretz Yisrael
3rd century CE (*Berachot* 49a)

Yaakov bar Idi   יעקב בר אידי
Amora from Eretz Yisrael
3rd century CE (*Hullin* 98a)

Yaakov ben Karshai   יעקב בן קרשי
Tanna from Eretz Yisrael
2nd century CE (*Horayot* 13b)

Yaakov from Nehar Pakod

יעקב מנהר פקוד

(*Avodah Zarah* 72a)

Yaaleh VeYavo in   ברכת המזון

On the days of Rosh Hodesh, one should mention *Yaaleh VeYavo* in the After-meal blessing. (*Shabbat* 24a)

Yaazek court

There was a court in Jerusalem called Yaazek. All the witnesses assembled there to give testimony. (*Rosh Hashana* 23b)

Yad   יד

A *yad* is a handle. Stalks of fruit are considered handles. It has halachic ramifications regarding impurity. (*Hullin* 118a)

Yaddua HaBavli   ידוע הבבלי
Tanna from Eretz Yisrael
2nd century CE (*Bava Metzia* 7:9)

Yakim Ish Hadar   יקים איש הדר
Tanna from Eretz Yisrael
1st – 2nd centuries CE (*Eduyot* 7:5)

Y'AL K'GaM   י״על ק״גם

Initials indicating where we rule like Abbaye in these six cases: יאוש עד זומם לחי קדושין גלוי דעתא מומר (*Bava Metzia* 22b; *Kiddushin* 52a; *Bava Kamma* 73a; *Sanhedrin* 27a)

Yalta   ילתא

R. Nahman b. Yaakov was married to Yalta, the daughter of the Exilarch. (*Hullin* 124a)

📖 Yalta   ילתא

R. Ulla once visited R. Nahman and they dined together. When they finished, R. Ulla made the After-meal blessings over a cup of wine. R. Ulla passed the cup of wine to R. Nahman. R. Nahman said to him: "Please pass the cup to my wife, Yalta." Words were exchanged between R. Ulla and R. Nahman which were not complimentary to women. When Yalta heard the exchange, she got up in anger and went to the wine storage and broke 400 jars of wine.

R. Nahman said to R. Ulla: "Please send her another cup of wine."

R. Ulla sent her a cup with a message: "All that wine can be counted as a blessing."

She sent back a message: "Peddlers spread gossip and rags make vermin." (*Berachot* 51b)

Yalta ילתא

Yalta once said to R. Nahman, her husband: "For everything that the Divine Law has forbidden us, it has permitted us an equivalent . . ." (*Hullin* 109b)

Yannai

King Yannai was the same as King Yohanan. It is a dispute between Abbaye and Rava. (*Berachot* 29a)

Yannai ינאי

Amora from Eretz Yisrael
3rd century CE (*Ketubbot* 62b)

Yannai

R. Yannai was the teacher of R. Yohanan. (*Bava Batra* 154b)

Yannai bar Yishmael ינאי בר ישמעאל

Amora from Eretz Yisrael
3rd century CE (*Taanit* 14a)

Yannai King of Judea

The rabbis enacted a rule that a king may not be judged nor be a judge

A king of Israel may not be a judge nor be judged, but the kings of the House of David can be both.

King Yannai's slave killed a man. R. Shimon b. Shetah said to the assembled rabbis: "Set your eyes boldly upon him and let us judge him."

They sent a messenger to the king

saying: "Your slave has killed a man." He sent the slave to be tried, but the rabbis insisted that the king himself must come. The king came and sat down. R. Shimon b. Shetah said to him: "Stand on your feet and let the witnesses testify against you."

The king replied: "I will not do what you tell me to do; let your colleagues give instructions." The king looked at them, and they turned their gaze to the ground.

After this incident, they enacted the rule that a king may not be judged nor be a judge. (*Sanhedrin* 18a, 19a)

Yannai King of Judea

When Ravin came from Eretz Yisrael to Babylonia, he stated: "There was a city belonging to King Yannai in the King's mountain where they were chopping down fig trees. They needed a great amount of salted fish to feed the workers."

He also stated: "King Yannai had a tree on the king's mountain, from which they used to take down every month forty young pigeons from three broods." (*Berachot* 44a)

Yannai's palace

After the reign of King Yannai ended, his palace was destroyed and idolators came and set up Mercurius idol worshipping in the building. Subsequently, other idolators came that did not worship Mercurius, and they removed the stones and paved the road with them. Some rabbis abstained from walking on the stones. (*Avodah Zarah* 50a)

Yanuka

Mar Yanuka and Mar Kashisha were the sons of R. Hisda. (*Bava Batra* 7b)

Yarden River

Rabbi Abba said to Rabbi Ashi: "The Jordan is called Yarden, because it originates its flow from Dan, a place formerly called Leshem (Yered Dan, Yehoshua 19:47). R. Yitzhak said Leshem is Pameas. (*Bechorot* 55a)

Yarhina

R. Shemuel was called Yarhinah, because he was knowledgeable in astronomy which helped him in halachic matters.
What is *zikin*?
R. Shemuel said it is a comet. R. Shemuel also said: "I am as familiar with the paths of heaven as with the streets of Nehardea." (*Berachot* 58b; *Bava Metzia* 85b)

Yarmulke

The mother of R. Nahman b. Yitzhak was told by astrologers that her son will be a thief. For that reason, she did not let him go bareheaded, saying to him: "Cover your head so that the fear of Heaven will be upon you. (*Shabbat* 156b)

✡ Yarmulke

R. Huna b. Yehoshua said: "May I be rewarded for never walking four cubits bareheaded." (*Shabbat* 118b)

📖 Yavne

R. Yohanan b. Zakkai met with Vespasian who was the commander of the troops besieging Jerusalem. He was trying to save something for the Jewish people. They had a long discussion and shortly thereafter a messenger arrived to inform Vespasian that the Emperor died and that the Senate wants Vespasian to be the next Emperor of Rome. Vespasian told Rabbi Yohanan: "I must leave now, but make a request of me and I will grant it to you."
Rabbi Yohanan said: "Give me Yavne[274] and its wise men, and a physician to heal Rabbi Tzadok." The wish was granted, and the Yeshiva in Yavne was spared. (*Gittin* 56a)

Yavne

There were four people in Yavne who could speak seventy languages. (*Sanhedrin* 17b)

Yavne; Academy   יבנה

Yavne is an ancient biblical city located south of Yaffa and north of Ashdod. During the Hasmonean period, it had its share of conflict. Yonatan the Hasmonean fought one of the decisive battles near the city. Shimon the Hasmonean also fought nearby and captured the city. After the fall of Jerusalem, the Sanhedrin moved its location from Jerusalem to Yavne. At first the Sanhedrin was under the leadership of Rabbi Yohanan ben Zakkai, but later Rabbi Gamliel II became Nasi.
The academy in Yavne was called The Sanhedrin. It served not only as an academy of learning, but also as the highest court in the land. It was an institution where the law was promulgated. The Sanhedrin met in the upper floor of a certain house in a vineyard; hence the academy was called "The Vineyard at Yavne" (Kerem Be-Yavne). Yavne at one time was a thriving city with its own cattle market and wheat market. It was already a center for Torah study even before the destruction of the Second Temple. Even in the old days, it had a Bet Din of twenty-three members, which decided capital cases. The following were the heads of the academy in Yavne: Eleazar ben Azariah, who lived in the 1st – 2nd centuries CE, and Gamliel ben Shimon De-Yavne, who lived in the 1st – 2nd centuries CE. (*Sanhedrin* 89a)

Yayin Mevushal   יין מבושל

Boiled wine (*Avodah Zarah* 30a)

---

274. See entry, Escape from besieged Jerusalem.

Yayin Nesech יין נסך, Not kosher wine
Wine of libation; wine known or suspected to have been dedicated or manipulated for idolatrous libation. (*Hullin* 4b; *Avodah Zarah* 65b)

Years before the Jubilee
The years before and after the Jubilee have to be taken into account in all transactions. (*Arachin* 24a)

Yehei Shemei Rabba מברך יהא שמיה רבא
May His great name be blessed
R. Yehoshua ben Levi said: "If a person responds with the above blessing in a loud voice, his decreed sentence is torn up." (*Shabbat* 119b)

Yehezkel
R. Yehuda said in Rav's name: "Hanania b. Hezkiya is to be remembered for blessing; if not for him the book of Yehezkel would have been hidden." (*Shabbat* 13b)

📖 Yehezkel
The dead Yehezkel revived
R. Eliezer b. R. Yosi HaGlili said: "The dead whom the Prophet Yehezkel revived went to Israel, married wives, and had children."
R. Yehuda b. Betera rose up and said: "I am one of their descendants, and these are the *tefillin* which my grandfather left me from them." (*Sanhedrin* 92b)

Yehezkel author
The authors of the book Yehezkel were the Men of the Great Assembly.[275] (*Bava Batra* 15a)

Yehoshafat יהושפט
King of Judea
Every time King Yehoshafat saw a Torah scholar, he got up from his throne and

---

275. Others name different authors.

called the scholar: "Father, Father, *Rebbe Mori*." (*Makkot* 24a)

Yehoshua
R. Yehoshua was in disagreement with R. Eliezer. (*Eduyot* 8a; *Bava Metzia* 84b)

Yehoshua יהושע
Since R. Yehoshua b. Hanania passed away goodness ceased to exist.
Rabbi Yehoshua was multi-lingual. (*Sanhedrin* 17b; *Sotah* 49a)

Yehoshua ben Akiva יהושע בן עקיבא
Tanna from Eretz Yisrael
2nd century CE (*Pesahim* 112a)

Yehoshua ben Gamla יהושע בן גמלא
High Priest, Jerusalem
1st century CE (*Yevamot* 61a; *Bava Batra* 21a)

Yehoshua ben Hanania יהושע בן חניא
Tanna from Eretz Yisrael
1st – 2nd centuries CE (*Sukkah* 53a)

Yehoshua ben Horkynos
יהושע בן הורקנוס
Tanna from Eretz Yisrael
2nd century CE (*Sotah* 5:5, 27b)

Yehoshua ben Korha יהושע בן קרחה
Tanna from Eretz Yisrael
2nd century CE (*Bava Metzia* 84b)

Yehoshua ben Levi יהושע בן לוי
Amora from Eretz Yisrael
Head of the academy in Lydda
3rd century CE (*Zevahim* 88b)

Yehoshua ben Matya יהושע בן מתיא
Tanna from Eretz Yisrael
2nd century CE (*Eduyot* 2:5)

Yehoshua ben Perahia יהושע בן פרחיא
Tanna from Yerushalayim
2nd – 1st centuries BCE (*Avot* 1:6)

Yehoshua HaGarsi   יהושע הגרסי
Tanna from Eretz Yisrael
2nd century CE (*Eruvin* 21b)

Yehoshua's ten stipulations
Yehoshua, the Prophet and leader of the Jewish people, laid down ten stipulations upon entering the land. (*Bava Kamma* 80b; *Eruvin* 17a)

Yehoyakim
King of Judea (*Sanhedrin* 104a)

Yehuda ben Bava   יהודה בן בבא
Tanna from Eretz Yisrael
2nd century CE (*Sanhedrin* 14a)

Yehuda ben Bava lists five matters
R. Yehuda b. Bava gave testimony about five matters. (*Eduyot* 8a)

Yehuda ben Betera I   יהודה בן בתירא
Tanna from Eretz Yisrael and Babylon
1st century CE (*Peah* 3:6)

Yehuda ben Betera II   יהודה בן בתירא
Tanna from Eretz Yisrael
2nd century CE (*Shabbat* 96b, 97a)

Yehuda ben Betera   יהודה בן בתירא
A Syrian non-Jew used to go to Jerusalem on Pesach time. He boasted to R. Yehuda b. Betera when he returned that he ate from the very best of the Paschal lamb in spite of the prohibition.

R. Yehuda b. Betera said to him: "Did they supply you with the fat-tail?"

"No," he replied."

The next time he was in Jerusalem on Pesach time he said to them: "Supply me with the fat-tail."

"But the fat-tail belongs to the Most High." they said to him. "Who told you to ask for it?"

He answered that it was R. Yehuda b. Betera. They investigated and found out that he was not an Israelite. They sent a message to R. Yehuda b. Betera: "Peace be with you, even though you are in Nisibis, your net is spread over Jerusalem." (*Pesahim* 3b)

Yehuda ben Dostai   יהודה בן דוסתאי
Tanna from Eretz Yisrael
1st century CE (*Makkot* 7a)

Yehuda ben Gerim   יהודה בן גרים
Tanna from Eretz Yisrael
2nd century CE (*Moed Katan* 9a)

Yehuda ben Hiyya   יהודה בן חייא
Amora from Eretz Yisrael
3rd century CE (*Niddah* 27a)

Yehuda ben Illai   יהודה בן אלעי
Tanna from Eretz Yisrael
2nd century CE (*Menahot* 18a)

Yehuda ben Nahmeni   יהודה בר נחמני
Amora from Eretz Yisrael
3rd century CE (*Sanhedrin* 7b)

Yehuda ben Shammua   יהודה בן שמוע
Tanna from Eretz Yisrael
2nd century CE (*Rosh Hashana* 19a)

Yehuda ben Simon   יהודה בר סימון
Amora from Eretz Yisrael
3rd – 4th centuries CE (*Sanhedrin* 100a)

Yehuda ben Tabbai   יהודה בן טבאי
Tanna from Eretz Yisrael
1st century BCE (*Avot* 1:8)

Yehuda ben Teima   יהודה בן תימא
Tanna from Eretz Yisrael
2nd century CE (*Avot* 5:20)

Yehuda ben Yehezkel   יהודה בר יחזקאל
Amora from Babylonia
Head of the Academy in Pumbedita
3rd century CE (*Berachot* 36a)

Yehuda HaKohen　　יהודה הכהן
Tanna from Eretz Yisrael
2nd century CE

Yehuda HaNasi　　יהודה הנשיא
President of the Sanhedrin
Tanna from Eretz Yisrael
2nd – 3rd centuries CE (*Kiddushin* 72b)

Yehuda HaNasi
Since R. Yehuda HaNasi died, humility and fear of sin ceases. (*Sotah* 49a)

Yehuda HaNasi's son
The son of R. Yehuda HaNasi was married to the daughter of R. Yosi b. Zimra. (*Ketubbot* 62b)

Yehuda Nesiah　　יהודה נשיאה
Amora from Eretz Yisrael
3rd century CE (*Avodah Zarah* 36a)

Yehuda Nesiah　　יהודה נשיאה
Amora from Eretz Yisrael
3rd – 4th centuries CE (*Rosh Hashana* 20a)

Yehuda Nesiah
Yehuda Nesiah and R. Oshaya were sitting at the house of R. Yehuda. They were discussing the case of an animal knocking over items belonging to others. (*Bava Kamma* 19b)

Yehuda Nesiah III　　יהודה נשיאה
Resh Lakish and R. Yehuda Nesiah had a disagreement about building a wall and who should pay for it. (*Bava Batra* 7b)

Yehudit
Wife of R. Hiyya
R. Hiyya and his wife Yehudit had twin sons: Yehuda and Hezkiya. They also had twin daughters: Pazi and Tavi. Rabbinai was Rabbi Hiyya's brother. (*Yevamot* 65b; *Berachot* 21b)

Yericho
In Yericho, they could hear the noises of the gate openings and also smell the spices that were offered in the Temple. (*Tamid* 30b)

Yerovam ben Nevat　　ירבעם בן נבט
First king of Israel (*Berachot* 35b; *Rosh Hashana* 17a)

Yerushalayim academy
Yerushalayim was for many years the seat of the Sanhedrin and the academy of learning.
　The following were the heads of the academy in Yerushalayim: Shemaya, 1st century BCE; Avtalyon, 1st century BCE; Hillel HaZaken, 1st century BCE – 1st century CE; Menahem, 1st century BCE; Shammai, 1st BCE – 1st century CE; Gamliel HaZaken, 1st century CE; Shimon ben Gamliel, 1st century CE. (*Yoma* 35b; *Shabbat* 31a; *Pesahim* 66a; *Sanhedrin* 11b; *Bava Metzia* 84b)

Yes or no
R. Yosi b. Yehuda said: "When you say yes, it should be justifiable, and when you say no, it should be justifiable." (*Bava Metzia* 49a)

Yesh Em La-Masoret　　יש אם למסורת
The rabbis hold that Traditional Scriptural text is authoritative. (*Sukkah* 6b)

Yesh Em La-Mikra　　יש אם למקרא
R. Shimon holds that Traditional reading – irrespective of spelling with vowels – is authoritative, etc. (*Sukkah* 6b)

Yeshayahu was killed by Menashe
R. Shimon b. Azzai said: "I found a roll of genealogical records in Jerusalem and therein was written 'So and so is a bastard, having been born from a forbidden union with a married woman.' In the records was also written: 'The teaching of R. Eliezer b. Yaakov is small in quantity but thoroughly sifted.' In the records was

also written: 'Menashe killed Yeshayahu.'"
(*Yevamot* 49b)

Yeshevav   ישבב
Tanna from Eretz Yisrael
1st century CE (*Hullin* 2:4, 32a)

📖 Yezdegird
The rabbis and King Yezdegird had cordial relations
It is related in the Talmud that R. Ameimar, Mar Zutra, and R. Ashi were sitting at the gate of the Persian king Yezdegird – with whom they had a cordial relationship – when the king's steward passed them by. Just then, R. Ashi noticed that Mar Zutra turned pale. R. Ashi dipped his finger into the dish the steward was carrying and put it in the mouth of Mar Zutra.

The officers asked him: "Why did you do that? You have rendered the meal unsuitable for the king."

R. Ashi answered them: "I noticed a piece of contaminated meat in the dish." They examined the dish, but found nothing contaminated.

He pointed with his finger to a part of the dish, and asked: "Did you examine this part?"

They examined that part and found it contaminated.

The rabbis asked him: "Why did you rely on a miracle?"

He answered them: "I saw a sickness hovering over Mar Zutra." (*Ketubbot* 61a)

Yiba Saba   ייבא סבא
Amora (*Bava Kamma* 49a)

Yibbum   יבום
Levirate marriage (*Yevamot* 2a)

Yirmiyahu bar Abba   ירמיה בר אבא
Amora from Babylonia
Head of academy in Tiberias
4th century CE (*Megillah* 4a; *Moed Katan* 4a)

Yishmael   ישמעאל
Tanna from Eretz Yisrael
1st – 2nd centuries CE (*Gittin* 58a)

📖 Yishmael
Descendants of Yishmael claim the Land of Israel belongs also to them
The rabbis taught: "The children of Yishmael[276] came before Alexander the Macedonian to make a claim against Israel." (*Sanhedrin* 91a)

Yishmael
Rabbi Yohanan stated that Rabbi Yishmael served and studied under Rabbi Nehunia b. HaKana, who expounded the Torah on the principles of generalization and specification, and he also expounded by the same principles. (*Shevuot* 26a; *Sotah* 16a)

Yishmael ben Yohanan ben Beroka   ישמעאל בנו של רבי יוחנן בן ברוקא
Tanna from Eretz Yisrael
2nd century CE (*Sanhedrin* 11:1, 85b)

Yishmael ben Yosi ben Halafta   ישמעאל בן יוסי בן חלפתא
Tanna from Eretz Yisrael
2nd – 3rd centuries CE (*Eruvin* 86b)

Yishmael ben Pavi
Since R. Yishmael ben Pavi died, the splendour of the priesthood ceased. (*Sotah* 49a)

Yitzhak   יצחק
Yitzhak was born to Avraham and Sarah when Avraham was one hundred years old. The gossipers were saying that Yitzhak was the child of Avimelech. But when Yitzhak grew up, he looked exactly like Avraham. Therefore, everyone agreed that Yitzhak was the son of Avraham. (*Bava Metzia* 87a)

---

276. See entry, Alexander the Macedonian.

Yitzhak   יצחק
Tanna from Eretz Yisrael and Babylonia
2nd century CE (*Berachot* 48b)

Yitzhak bar Avdimi   יצחק בר אבדימי
Amora from Babylonia
3rd – 4th centuries CE (*Berachot* 44a)

Yitzhak bar Eleazar   יצחק בן אלעזר
Amora from Eretz Yisrael
4th century CE (*Eruvin* 54b)

Yitzhak bar Rav Yehuda   יצחק בר יהודה
Amora from Babylonia
3rd – 4th centuries CE (*Shabbat* 35b)

Yitzhak bar Shemuel   יצחק בר שמואל
Amora from Babylonia
3rd century CE (*Berachot* 3a)

Yitzhak (Nepaha)   יצחק נפחא
Amora from Eretz Yisrael
3rd century CE (*Bava Kamma* 60b)

Yiush   יאוש
Renunciation, giving up hope of ever recovering the lost item. (*Bava Kamma* 66a, 67a,
68a; 114a; *Bava Metzia* 21b)

Yohanan and Simlai
R. Yohanan and R. Simlai were discussing
to study the Sefer Yohasin. (*Pesahim* 62b)

Yohanan ben Beroka   יוחנן בן ברוקא
Tanna from Eretz Yisrael
2nd century CE (*Avot* 4:4)

Yohanan ben Gudgeda   יוחנן בן גודגדא
Tanna from Eretz Yisrael
1st – 2nd century CE (*Arachin* 11b)

Yohanan ben HaHorani   יוחנן בן ההורני
Tanna from Eretz Yisrael
1st century CE (*Sukkah* 2: 7, 28a)

Yohanan ben Matya   יוחנן בן מתיא
Tanna from Eretz Yisrael
2nd century CE (*Bava Metzia* 83a)

Yohanan ben Nepaha   יוחנן בן נפחא
Amora from Eretz Yisrael
Head of the academy in Tiberias
3rd century CE (*Kiddushin* 31b)

Yohanan ben Nuri   יוחנן בן נורי
Tanna from Eretz Yisrael
2nd century CE (*Ketubbot* 1:10, 14b)

Yohanan ben Pinhas   יוחנן בן פינחס
Officer of the Temple (*Shekalim* 5:1)

Yohanan ben Torta   יוחנן בן תורתא
Tanna from Eretz Yisrael
2nd century CE (*Yoma* 9a)

Yohanan ben Yehoshua   יוחנן בן יהושע
Tanna from Eretz Yisrael
2nd century CE (*Yadayim* 3:5)

Yohanan ben Zakkai   יוחנן בן זכאי
Tanna from Eretz Yisrael
Head of the Sanhedrin in Yavne
1st century CE (*Rosh Hashana* 31b)

Yohanan ben Zakkai
Since R. Yohanan b. Zakkai died, the
glory of wisdom ceased to exist. (*Sotah* 49a)

Yohanan ben Zakkai's students
R. Yohanan b. Zakkai had five outstand-
ing students: R. Eliezer b. Horkynos, R.
Yehoshua b. Hanania, R. Yosi HaKohen,
R. Shimon b. Netanel, and R. Eleazar b.
Arach. (*Avot* 2:8)

Yohanan ben Zakkai's longevity
R. Yohanan lived to 120 years: forty years
he was a businessman, forty years he studied, and forty years he was teaching Torah.
(*Sanhedrin* 41a; *Rosh Hashana* 31b)

Yohanan HaSandler   יוחנן הסנדלר
Tanna from Eretz Yisrael
1st – 2nd centuries CE (*Shabbat* 19a;
Berachot 22a)

Yohanan Kohen Gadol   יוחנן כהן גדול
King of Judea, also called John Hyrcanus,
was king of Judea from 135–105 BCE. He
was the son of Simon the Hasmonean and
a grandson of the famous Matityahu, who
started the Chanukah revolt against Antiochus Epiphanies. (*Berachot* 29a)

Yohanan's mother
*R. Yohanan b. Nepaha's mother died giving
birth to him*
R. Yohanan's father died on the day he was
conceived, and his mother died in childbirth on the day he was born. He inherited
fields and vineyards from his parents, using the income for his livelihood, which
allowed him free time to study Torah.

He was raised by his grandfather. He
studied in the academy of Rabbi Yehuda
HaNasi. (*Kiddushin* 31b)

Yohanan's strength
R. Yohanan was ascending a staircase
while R. Ammi and R. Assi were supporting him, and then the staircase collapsed
under them. R. Yohanan rose up and carried with him both R. Ammi and R. Assi
to the top.

The rabbis asked him: "Since your
strength is all there, why do you need to
be supported?"

He answered them: "If I use up my
strength, what will I keep for my old age?"
(*Ketubbot* 62a)

Yocheved
R. Hama b. Hanina said: "Yocheved, the
mother of Moshe and daughter of Levi,
was born when Yaakov and his family of
seventy entered the walls of Egypt." (*Sotah*
12a; *Bava Batra* 122a–b)

Yoke of heaven
R. Yohanan said: "If one wants to accept
upon himself the yoke of the Kingdom
of Heaven in the most complete manner,
he should first use the toilet, wash his
hands, put on *tefillin*, recite the *Shema*,
and say the *Amidah*. This is the complete
acknowledgement of the Kingdom of
Heaven." (*Berachot* 15a)

Yom Kippur
When Yom Kippur falls on Shabbat,
do we mention Shabbat in the prayers?
(*Shabbat* 24a)

Yom Kippur
R. Papa said: "The service of Yom Kippur
in the Temple was prescribed in a particular order." (*Sanhedrin* 49b; *Yoma* 60a)

Yom Kippur
R. Eleazar b. Azariah expounded: "Yom
Kippur effects atonement for transgressions from man towards God, but forgiveness for transgressions between man and
his fellow-man are not forgiven until it is
asked of the person offended." (*Yoma* 85b)

Yom Kippur
Eating and drinking well on the ninth day
of Tishrei is equal to fasting. (*Berachot* 8b)

Yom Kippur brings atonement
Rebbe said: "For all transgressions committed, whether the person repented or
not, Yom Kippur brings atonement except
for three things." (*Shevuot* 13a; *Yoma* 85b, 86a;
Keritut 7a)

Yom Kippur Eve prayers
How many prayers are recited on Yom
Kippur eve? (*Pesahim* 3a; *Yoma* 87b; *Niddah* 8b)

📖 Yom Kippur, the happiest day
R. Shimon b. Gamliel said: "There
were no happier days for Israel than the

fifteenth day of Av and the day of Yom Kippur, for on those days the daughters of Jerusalem used to go out dressed in white garments, borrowed in order not to shame the ones who had none. They went out and danced in the vineyards. They called out: 'Young man, lift up your eyes and see what you will select for yourself. Set not your eyes on beauty. but fix your eyes on family. For grace is deceitful and beauty is vain.'" (*Taanit* 26b; *Bava Batra* 121a)

✿ **Yom Kippur Musaf**
When R. Aha finished the *Musaf* service on Yom Kippur, he would urge the congregation with these words: "People who have children, go out and feed them and give them to drink to avoid exposing them to danger." (Yerushalmi *Yoma* 6:4)

Yom Kippur Torah reading (*Megillah* 30b)

Yom Tov enjoyment
It is a Torah commandment to enjoy the Sukkah holidays all eight days. (*Sukkah* 48a)

Yom Tov on Erev Shabbat
When Yom Tov falls on Erev Shabbat, what is permitted and what is not permitted to prepare for Shabbat? (*Betzah* 15b)

Yom Tov on Sunday יין נר קידוש הבדלה
When Yom Tov falls on Sunday, one needs to make several blessings on Motzei Shabbat: on wine, on a candle, *Kiddush*, and *Havdalah*. The order in which the blessings are made is disputed among the rabbis — each has a formula in abbreviated letters.
  The abbreviated formulas are as follows: ינהק יקנה יהנק קניה נהיק יקנהז יקזנה
(*Pesahim* 103a)

Yonah יונה
Amora from Eretz Yisrael
Head of the academy in Tiberias
4th century CE (*Taanit* 23b)

Yonah's wife
The Prophet Yonah's wife made a Festival pilgrimage to Jerusalem. (*Eruvin* 96a)

Yonatan יונתן
Tanna from Eretz Yisrael
2nd century CE (*Avot* 4:9)

Yonatan ben Amram יונתן בן עמרם
Tanna from Eretz Yisrael
2nd – 3rd centuries CE (*Bava Batra* 8a)

Yonatan ben Eleazar יונתן בן אלעזר
Amora from Babylonia
3rd century CE (*Gittin* 78b)

Yonatan ben Uzziel יונתן בן עוזיאל
Tanna from Eretz Yisrael
1st century BCE — 1st century CE (*Bava Batra* 134a)

Yosef and Rabbah
R. Yosef was a well-read scholar, and Rabbah was a keen dialectician who debated as long as it took to arrive at the truth. (*Horayot* 14a)

Yosef bar Hiyya יוסף בר חייא
Amora from Babylonia
Head of the Academy in Pumbedita
3rd – 4th centuries CE (*Berachot* 64a)

Yosef ben Ailim יוסף בן אילים
Yosef b. Ailim from Sepphoris once substituted for the Kohen Gadol who was unable to perform the service. When the Kohen Gadol returned to his duties, Yosef b. Ailim was not permitted to serve in any capacity." (*Horayot* 12b)

Yosef
R. Yosef answered a question after 22 years
Rabbah pointed out a difficult question to R. Yosef, but did not receive an answer until twenty-two years later when R. Yosef became the head of the

academy in Pumbedita. (*Bava Kamma* 66b; *Ketubbot* 42b)

Yosef the son of Yaakov
Yosef was privileged to bury his father. (*Sotah* 9b)

Yosef's coffin
How did Moshe know where to find the coffin of Yosef? Our Rabbis taught: Moshe went to Serah, the daughter of Asher, who was a survivor from that generation and asked her if she knew where Yosef was buried. She told him that the Egytians had placed him in a metal coffin and lowered him into the Nile River so that the river would be blessed.

Moshe stood on the bank of the Nile River and called out: "The time has arrived for me to fulfill the oath of delivering you to the Land of Israel. "If you show yourself, then I can be true to the oath, if not we are free of the oath." Immediately, the coffin floated to the surface. (*Sotah* 13a)

Yoshaya   יאשיה
Tanna from Babylonia
2nd century CE (*Gittin* 61a)

Yoshaya Rabbah   אושעיא רבה
Amora from Eretz Yisrael
2nd – 3rd centuries CE (*Moed Katan* 24a)

Yoshiyahu
R. Shemuel b. Nahmaini said in the name of R. Yonatan: "Whoever maintains that King Yoshiyahu sinned is making an error." (*Shabbat* 57b)

Yoshiyahu hid away the oil
King Yoshiyahu hid away the anointing oil, the Holy Ark, the jar of manna, Aharon's rod with the almond' blossoms, and also the coffer that the Philistines had sent as a gift to Israel. He did not want

these precious things to be taken by the enemy. (*Horayot* 12a)

Yosi   יוסי
Amora from Eretz Yisrael
Head of the academy in Tiberias
4th century CE (*Menahot* 70b)

Yosi bar Dormaskit   יוסי בר דורמסקית
Tanna from Eretz Yisrael
1st – 2nd centuries CE (*Yadayim* 4:3)

Yosi ben Akavia   יוסי בן עקביא
Tanna from Babylonia
2nd century CE (*Nedarim* 81a)

Yosi ben HaMeshullam   יוסי בן המשולם
or Yosi ben Meshullam
Tanna from Eretz Yisrael
2nd – 3rd centuries CE (*Bechorot* 3:3, 24b)

Yosi ben Halafta   יוסי בן חלפתא
Tanna from Eretz Yisrael
2nd century CE (*Yevamot* 62b)

Yosi ben Hanina   יוסי בר חנינא
Amora from Eretz Yisrael
3rd century CE (*Bava Bastra* 90b)

Yosi ben Kippar   יוסי בן כיפר
Tanna from Eretz Yisrael
2nd century CE (*Berachot* 63a)

Yosi ben Kisma   יוסי בן קיסמא
Tanna from Eretz Yisrael
2nd century CE (*Avot* 6:9)

Yosi ben Yehuda   יוסי בן יהודה
Tanna from Eretz Yisrael
2nd – 3rd centuries CE (*Pesahim* 112b)

Yosi ben Yehuda Ish Kefar HaBavli
יוסי בן יהודה איש כפר הבבלי
Tanna from Eretz Yisrael
2nd century CE (*Avot* 4:20)

Yosi ben Yoezer יוסי בן יועזר
Tanna from Eretz Yisrael
2nd century BCE (*Bava Batra* 133b)

Yosi ben Yohanan יוסי בן יוחנן
Tanna from Eretz Yisrael
2nd century BCE (*Avot* 1:5)

Yosi ben Zimra יוסי בן זימרא
Tanna from Eretz Yisrael
2nd century CE (*Yoma* 78a)

Yosi HaGlili יוסי הגלילי
Tanna from Eretz Yisrael
2nd century CE (*Eruvin* 53b)

Yosi HaGlili
Fowl and milk prohibition excluded
In the place of R. Yosi HaGlili, they used
to eat fowl's flesh cooked in milk. "He
learned that since a fowl has no mother's
milk, it is excluded from the prohibition."
(*Hullin* 116a)

Yosi HaKohen יוסי הכהן
Tanna from Eretz Yisrael
1st – 2nd centuries CE (*Shabbat* 19a)

Yosi Hali Kofri יוסי חלי קופרי
Tanna from Eretz Yisrael
1st century CE (*Machshirin* 1:3)

Yosi Katnuta יוסי קטנתא
Since R. Yosi Katnuta died, the pious
ceased to exist. (*Sotah* 49a)

Yotzeh Dofen יוצא דופן
A child born by caesarean section.
(*Niddah* 40a)

You be the man
R. Bar Kappara stated: "When the merchandise is cheap, hurry to buy. In a place
where there is no man, you be the man. A
man should always teach his son a clean
and easy trade." (*Berachot* 63a)

Young women אלו נערות
These are the young women that are being
discussed. (*Ketubbot* 29a)

Yud י
Abbaye said the *shin*, *dalet*, and *yud* of
the *tefillin* were given to Moshe on Sinai.
(*Shabbat* 62a)

Yudan Berebi (*Bechorot* 37b)

Z

Zachin זכין לאדם שלא בפניו
A benefit can be conferred on a per-
son in his absence. (*Eruvin* 81b; *Gittin* 11b;
Kiddushin 23a)

Zachor זכור
When do they read *Parshat Zachor*?
(*Megillah* 29a)

Zadok צדוק
Tanna from Eretz Yisrael
1st century BCE – 1st century CE (*Gittin* 56b)

Zadok II צדוק
Tanna from Eretz Yisrael
2nd century CE (*Kiddushin* 40a)

Zav זב
Discharge from a male (*Niddah* 68b)

Zavah זבה
Discharge from a female (*Niddah* 68b)

Zechariah ben Avkulos זכריה בן אבקולוס
Tanna from Eretz Yisrael
1st century CE (*Gittin* 55b, 56a)

Zechariah ben HaKatzav זכריה בן הקצב
Tanna from Eretz Tisrael
1st century CE (*Sotah* 5:1)

Zechariah ben Kavutal זכריה בן קבוטל
Tanna from Eretz Yisrael
1st century CE (*Yoma* 1:6, 18b)

Zeiri זעירי
Amora from Babylonia
3rd century CE (*Sanhedrin* 98a)

Zelophehad
R. Akiva stated: "The gatherer of wood on
Shabbat was Zelophehad."

R. Yehuda b. Betera told R. Akiva: "Either way, you will have to answer to the
Heavenly Court; if you are correct, you
revealed a matter the Torah kept hidden,
and if you are wrong you slandered a *tzaddik*." (*Shabbat* 96b)

Zeman Gerama
כל מצוות עשה שהזמן גרמא נשים פטורות
All affirmative precepts bound by a stated
time are not incumbent upon women.
(*Kiddushin* 29a; *Berachot* 20b; *Eruvin* 27a; *Shabbat*
62a; *Menahot* 43a; *Rosh Hashana* 30a)

Zera זירא
Amora from Babylonia
3rd – 4th centuries CE (*Berachot* 39a)

Zerika זריקא
Amora from Babylonia
4th century CE (*Taanit* 23b)

זביד **Zevid**
Amora from Babylonia
4th century CE (*Meilah* 19a)

Ziborit זיבורית
Worst quality land (*Bava Kamma* 7b)

Zika זיקה
A widowed woman waiting to be mar-
ried to the brother of her dead husband.[277]
(*Yevamot* 17b)

Zimri ben Salu
Zimri is the one and the same as Shelum-
iel ben Tzurishadai. (*Sanhedrin* 82b)

Zimun זימון
Three men eating together and saying
Grace after a Meal. (*Berachot* 45a)

Zimun cup זימון
The cup of wine for *Zimun* has to be lifted
with both hands and then passed to the
right hand. (*Berachot* 51a)

Zimun formula זימון
(*Berachot* 49b)

Zimun with ten men or more
Formula for saying Grace after a Meal
eaten together by ten or more people.
(*Berachot* 49b)

Zutra bar Tovya זוטרא בר טוביה
Amora from Babylonia
3rd century CE (*Berachot* 43b)

Zutra, Mar מר זוטרא
Amora and Exilarch in Babylonia
4th – 5th centuries CE (*Bava Kamma* 81b)

Zutra, Mar II מר זוטרא
Exilarch from Babylonia
5th – 6th centuries CE

---

277. See entry, Levirate marriage.

An Overview of the Order of the Talmud

The Talmud was redacted and arranged in a certain order by Rabbi Yehuda HaNasi and Rabbi Nathan. That part of the Talmud is called the Mishna. All those quoted in the Mishna were called Tannaim. Later on, Rabbi Ashi and Rabbi Ravina added a large amount of comments and debates made by the rabbis who followed the Tannaim – they were called Amoraim. That part of the Talmud is called the Gemara. Those comments and debates are inserted after each Mishna. The following is a general review of the subjects included in the Talmud. (*Bava Metzia* 86a)

*

The Talmud consists of six orders, *Sedarim*, which are then subdivided into sixty-three volumes or tractates.

The tractates are further subdivided into smaller sections called *perek*. Each *perek* is further subdivided into smaller units called Mishna.

These are the six orders of the Talmud:

ZERAIM / סדר זרעים
Literally meaning Seeds; the laws of cultivation of the soil and agriculture

MOED / סדר מועד
Holiday; The laws of Shabbat and other Festivals

NASHIM / סדר נשים
Women; the laws concerning women, family life, marriage, and divorce

NEZIKIN / סדר נזיקין
Damages; the laws concerning damages, criminal, and civil law

KEDOSHIM / סדר קדשים
Holy things; the laws concerning Holy things, sacrifices, and Temple services

TAHAROT / סדר טהרות
Purity; the laws concerning purity and impurity

The following are the tractates in *Seder Zeraim* זרעים

Berachot   ברכות
The Tractate *Berachot* deals with blessings and benedictions.

Peah   פאה
The Tractate *Peah* deals with the commandment of leaving the corners in the fields for the poor. The tractate has no Gemara.

Demai   דמאי
The Tractate *Demai* deals with doubtful tithing. The tractate has no Gemara.

Kilayim   כלאים
The Tractate *Kilayim* deals with prohibited plant mixtures, mixtures in clothing, and crossbreeding of animals. The tractate has no Gemara.

Shevi'it   שביעית
The Tractate *Shevi'it* deals with the Sabbatical year, which is every seven years. That year is called Shemittah. The tractate has no Gemara.

Terumot   תרומות
The Tractate *Terumot* deals with separating the Kohen's share. The tractate has no Gemara.

Maasrot   מעשרות
The Tractate *Maasrot* deals with tithing the portion for the Levites. The tractate has no Gemara.

Maaser Sheni   מעשר שני
The Tractate *Maaser Sheni* deals with second tithing. The tractate has no Gemara.

Hallah   חלה
The Tractate *Hallah* deals with the portion of the dough given to the Kohen. The tractate has no Gemara.

Orlah   ערלה
The Tractate *Orlah* deals with fruits grown on trees the first three years after planting. They are called *orlah*, meaning "uncircumcised" and are forbidden to be eaten. The tractate has no Gemara.

Bikkurim   בכורים
The Tractate *Bikkurim* deals with First Fruits to be brought to the Temple. The tractate has no Gemara.

These tractates are in *Seder Moed* מועד

Shabbat   שבת
The Tractate *Shabbat* deals with the laws of Shabbat: the permitted and forbidden things on Shabbat.

Eruvin   ערובין
The Tractate *Eruvin* deals with the Shabbat boundaries regarding walking a certain distance on Shabbat and carrying objects on Shabbat.

Pesahim   פסחים
The Tractate *Pesahim* deals with Pesach laws, forbidden breads and foods, and other laws pertaining to the holiday of Pesach.

Shekalim   שקלים
The Tractate *Shekalim* deals with monetary issues, as they apply to collecting the funds for the Temple.

Yoma   יומא
The Tractate *Yoma* deals with the Day of Atonement, which is Yom Kippur, and with the laws pertaining to Yom Kippur.

Sukkah   סוכה

The Tractate *Sukkah* deals with the holiday of Sukkot, the *sukkah* tent, and the Four Species consisting of the *lulav, etrog, hadas,* and *arava* which are used during the prayer services.

Betzah   ביצה

The Tractate *Betzah* deals with the laws of Yom Tov, an egg laid on Yom Tov, and what kind of work is prohibited on Yom Tov.

Rosh Hashana   ראש השנה

The Tractate *Rosh Hashana* deals with the holiday of New Year, the laws as they apply to that holiday, and the dates of the other New Years that were established in the Jewish calendar.

Taanit   תענית

The Tractate *Taanit* deals with the laws of public fast days.

Megillah   מגילה

The Tractate *Megillah* deals with Purim and the reading of the *Megillah*.

Moed Katan   מועד קטן

The Tractate *Moed Katan* deals with minor holidays such as Hol Hamoed.

Hagigah   חגיגה

The Tractate *Hagigah* deals with the pilgrimage to Jerusalem and the offerings made in the Temple during the Festivals.

The following tractates are in *Seder Nashim* נשים

Yevamot   יבמות

The Tractate *Yevamot* deals with levirate marriages for childless widows.

Ketubbot   כתובות

The Tractate *Ketubbot* deals with marriage contracts and marriage settlements.

Nedarim   נדרים

The Tractate *Nedarim* deals with the laws of vows.

Nazir   נזיר

The Tractate *Nazir* deals with the laws of a Nazarite. A person who makes a vow to abstain from certain foods or actions is called a Nazarite.

Sotah   סוטה

The Tractate *Sotah* deals with the laws of a married woman under suspicion of adultery.

Gittin   גיטין

The Tractate *Gittin* deals with the laws of divorces and the manner the divorce is to be executed.

Kiddushin   קדושין

The Tractate *Kiddushin* deals with betrothals and the laws that apply to it.

The following tractates are in *Seder Nezikin* נזיקין

Bava Kamma   בבא קמא

The Tractate *Bava Kamma*[1] deals with civil law and damages and injuries.

Bava Metzia   בבא מציעא

The Tractate *Bava Metzia* deals with found property, and with buying, selling, and hiring.

---

1. *Bava Kamma* is the first part of a three part volume; *Bava Metzia* is the second, and *Bava Batra* is the third.

Seder Kodashim

Bava Batra בבא בתרא

The Tractate *Bava Batra* deals with commerce, inheritance, and real estate.

Sanhedrin סנהדרין

The Tractate *Sanhedrin* deals with various courts in the Land of Israel, the size of the courts, and the administration of justice in criminal and capital crimes.

Makkot מכות

The Tractate *Makkot* deals with crimes punishable by lashes.

Shevuot שבועות

The Tractate *Shevuot* deals with oaths and the different kind of oaths.

Eduyot עדיות

The Tractate *Eduyot* deals with various testimonies.

Avodah Zarah עבודה זרה

The Tractate *Avodah Zarah* deals with the prohibition of idol worship.

Avot אבות

The Tractate *Avot* discusses ethics of our fathers and quotes many wise sayings.

Horayot הוריות

The Tractate *Horayot* deals with wrongful and erroneous decisions by the courts.

These are the tractates in *Seder Kodashim* קדשים

Zevahim זבחים

The Tractate *Zevahim* deals with the sacrifices in the Temple.

Menahot מנחות

The Tractate *Menahot* deals with the meal offerings in the Temple.

Hullin חולין

The Tractate *Hullin* deals with slaughtering unsanctified animals.

Bechorot בכורות

The Tractate *Bechorot* deals with the firstborn, as it applies to men or animals.

Arachin ערכין

The Tractate *Arachin* deals with the valuation and appraising for dedication purposes.

Temurah תמורה

The Tractate *Temurah* deals with substitution for sanctified animals.

Keritut כריתות

The Tractate *Keritut* deals with excision laws concerning sins punishable by excision.

Meilah מעילה

The Tractate *Meilah* deals with misappropriation, sacrilege, and bad faith as it applies to sacrifices in the Temple.

Tamid תמיד

The Tractate *Tamid* deals with the daily sacrifices in the Temple.

Middot מדות

The Tractate *Middot* deals with measurements concerning the courtyards of the Temple and the Temple building.

Kinnim קנים

The Tractate *Kinnim* deals with the sacrifices of birds in the Temple.

The following tractates are in *Seder Taharot* טהרות

Kelim כלים

The Tractate *Kelim* deals with utensils in

general: their cleanness or uncleanness, cleanness of garments. What causes vessels or garments to become unclean?

Ohalot   אהלות

The Tractate *Ohalot* deals with tents and the uncleanness inside them caused by a dead body.

Negaim   נגעים

The Tractate *Negaim* deals with afflictions and leprosy.

Parah   פרה

The Tractate *Parah* deals with the red heifer, the burning of the heifer, the water treated with the ashes of the heifer, and the laws pertaining to it.

Taharot   טהרות

The Tractate *Taharot* deals with ritual impurity of various degrees and periods.

Mikvaot   מקואות

The Tractate *Mikvaot* deals with pools, reservoirs, and ritual wells.

Niddah   נדה

The Tractate *Niddah* deals with the laws concerning the period of menstruation.

Machshirin   מכשירין

The Tractate *Machshirin* deals with liquids that will render food susceptible to become impure.

Zavim   זבים

The Tractate *Zavim* deals with ailments and laws concerning ill people who suffer from gonorrhea.

Tevul Yom   טבול יום

The Tractate *Tevul Yom* deals with the status of a person who was impure, but had immersed himself in a *mikveh* on that same day.

Yadayim   ידים

The Tractate *Yadayim* deals with purification of hands and the amount of water required for purification.

Uktzin   עוקצין

The Tractate *Uktzin* deals with fruit shells and stalks, with their cleanness and uncleanness.

Perakim of the Talmud

The Talmud tractates are subdivided into chapters called *perek*. In plural, they are called *perakim*.

The following *perakim* are in the Tractate *Berachot* ברכות

Me-aimatai   מאימתי
The first *perek* in *Berachot* is *Me-aimatai*. It deals with the proper time for the *Shema* prayer and how many benedictions are recited before the *Shema*. (*Berachot* 2a)

Hayah Koreh   היה קורא
The 2nd *perek* in *Berachot* is *Hayah Koreh*. It deals with permissible and forbidden interruptions during prayer. (*Berachot* 13a)

Mi She-meto   מי שמתו
The 3rd *perek* in *Berachot* is *Mi She-meto*. It deals with religious obligations and exemptions for mourners, women, minors, and Jewish slaves. (*Berachot* 17b)

Tefillat Ha-Shahar   תפילת השחר
The 4th *perek* in *Berachot* is *Tefillat Ha-Shahar*. It deals with the morning service, abbreviated prayers, prayer time, praying while riding on a donkey or traveling on a ship. (*Berachot* 26a)

Ein Omdin   אין עומדין
The 5th *perek* in *Berachot* is *Ein Omdin*. It deals with having a reverend frame of mind during prayers. It also deals with when to insert additional prayers and how to correct making a mistake in the prayer. (*Berachot* 30b)

Keitzad Mevarchin   כיצד מברכין
The 6th *perek* in *Berachot* is *Keitzad Mevarchin*. It deals with blessings on fruits, vegetables, and on food not grown in the earth. (*Berachot* 35a)

Shelosha She-achlu   שלשה שאכלו
The 7th *perek* in *Berachot* is *Shelosha She-achlu*. It deals with three people eating together, the format of the blessing for three. (*Berachot* 45a)

Eilu Devarim   אלו דברים
The 8th *perek* in *Berachot* is *Eilu Devarim*. It deals with the differences between Bet Shammai and Bet Hillel with regards to a blessing before a meal. It also deals with washing hands before a meal, *Havdalah* blessings, and with forgetting to say the blessing after the meal. (*Berachot* 51b)

Haroeh   הרואה
The 9th *perek* in *Berachot* is *Haroeh*. It deals with a blessing to be said when one visits a site where miracles happened to the Jewish people. It also deals with blessings for an earthquake, thunder, lightning, mountains, the sea, when bad things happen, and how to enter the Temple Mount. (*Berachot* 54a)

The following *perakim* are in the Tractate *Shabbat* שבת

Yetziat Ha-Shabbat   יציאות השבת
The 1st *perek* in *Shabbat* deals with moving objects from one domain to another, visiting a barber shop on Friday, preparing work on Friday, selling things on Friday, and laundering on Friday. (*Shabbat* 2a)

Bameh Madlikin   במה מדליקין
The 2nd *perek* in *Shabbat* deals with what oil may be used to light the *Shabbat* candles. It also deals with utensils for candles, extinguishing candles, and reminders before Shabbat. (*Shabbat* 20b)

Kira   כירה
The 3rd *perek* in *Shabbat* deals with warming food on a stove already heated before Shabbat. (*Shabbat* 36b)

Bameh Tomnin   במה טומנין
The 4th *perek* in *Shabbat* deals with how to keep food warm on Shabbat. (*Shabbat* 47b)

Bameh Beheimah   במה בהמה
The 5th *perek* in *Shabbat* deals with what an animal can wear on Shabbat if owned by a Jew. (*Shabbat* 47a)

Bameh Isha   במה אישה
The 6th *perek* in *Shabbat* deals with the kind of accessories a woman may carry on Shabbat. (*Shabbat* 57a)

Kelal Gadol   כלל גדול
The 7th *perek* in *Shabbat* deals with the principles of Shabbat, violating the Shabbat more than once, also the thirty-nine main labors forbidden on Shabbat. (*Shabbat* 67b)

Ha-Motzi Yayin   המוציא יין
The 8th *perek* in *Shabbat* deals with the size and volume of objects one may or may not carry from one domain to another on Shabbat. (*Shabbat* 76b)

Amar Rabbi Akiva   אמר רבי עקיבא
The 9th *perek* in *Shabbat* deals with moving objects from one domain to another. It also deals with purities and impurities. (*Shabbat* 82a)

Hamatznia   המצניע
The 10th *perek* in *Shabbat* deals with moving stored away items and carrying objects in an unusual way on Shabbat. (*Shabbat* 90b)

Hazorek   הזורק
The 11th *perek* in *Shabbat* deals with throwing objects on Shabbat from one domain to another. (*Shabbat* 96a)

Haboneh   הבונה
The 12th *perek* in *Shabbat* deals with the prohibited labors on Shabbat such as building, plowing, and writing. (*Shabbat* 102b)

Haoreg   האורג
The 13th *perek* in *Shabbat* deals with weaving on Shabbat, rending one's cloth, bleaching, and hunting. (*Shabbat* 105a)

Shemona Sheratzim   שמונה שרצים
The 14th *perek* in *Shabbat* discusses the eight unclean reptiles mentioned in the Torah, also a toothache on Shabbat. (*Shabbat* 107a)

Eilu Kesharim   אלו קשרים
The 15th *perek* in *Shabbat* deals with making knots on Shabbat and folding cloths. (*Shabbat* 111b)

Kol Kitvei   כל כתבי
The 16th *perek* in *Shabbat* discusses saving holy objects from a fire on Shabbat, saving

food, saving garments, telling a non-Jew what to do when there is a fire. (*Shabbat* 115a)

Kol Hakelim כל הכלים
The 17th *perek* in *Shabbat* deals with moving utensils on Shabbat, crushing nuts, and broken utensils. (*Shabbat* 122b)

Mefanin מפנין
The 18th *perek* in *Shabbat* deals with clearing away straw or grain on Shabbat to prepare for when guests arrive, delivering a newborn animal, delivering a newborn human baby. (*Shabbat* 126b)

Rabbi Eliezer De-Milah רבי אליעזר דמילה
The 19th *perek* in *Shabbat* discusses circumcision on Shabbat, bathing a new baby. (*Shabbat* 130a)

Tolin תולין
The 20th *perek* in *Shabbat* discusses the act of suspending a strainer and moving straw on the bed. (*Shabbat* 137b)

Notel נוטל
The 21st *perek* in *Shabbat* deals with using a child to carry objects, removing bones from the table on Shabbat. (*Shabbat* 141b)

Havit חבית
The 22nd *perek* in *Shabbat* discusses saving food from a broken barrel, warming food, breaking a barrel, placing food in a pit to preserve it, bathing in the waters of Tiberias, and anointing on Shabbat. (*Shabbat* 143b)

Shoel שואל
The 23rd *perek* in *Shabbat* discusses borrowing food on Shabbat, hiring employees, and arranging funerals. (*Shabbat* 148a)

Mi She-hehshich מי שהחשיך
The 24th *perek* in *Shabbat* deals with a

traveler finding himself Friday night at dusk in the middle of nowhere, what to do with the objects he is carrying. It also deals with feeding animals on Shabbat and the vows to be annulled. (*Shabbat* 148a)

The following *perakim* are in the Tractate *Eruvin* עירובין

Mavoi מבוי
The 1st *perek* in *Eruvin* deals with alleys and their heights, markers for alleys, caravans in a valley making a circle on Shabbat. (*Eruvin* 2a)

Osin Passin עושין פסין
The above is the 2nd *perek* in *Eruvin* which deals with wells and gardens on Shabbat. (*Eruvin* 17b)

Bakol Me'arvin בכל מערבין
The 3rd *perek* in *Eruvin* deals with making an *eruv* in partnership with someone and what food may be used for it. It also deals with where one can place the *eruv* and making conditions for the *eruv*. (*Eruvin* 26b)

Mi She-Hotziuhu מי שהוציאוהו
The 4th *perek* in *Eruvin* deals with a situation of being in one place when Shabbat started, but due to circumstances winding up in another place. It also deals with how a traveler is to make an *eruv*. (*Eruvin* 41b)

Keitzad Me'avrin כיצד מעברין
The 5th *perek* in *Eruvin* deals with making an *eruv* for a town and how to measure the boundaries for an *eruv*. (*Eruvin* 52b)

Hadar הדר עם הנכרי
The 6th *perek* in *Eruvin* deals with making an *eruv* in a courtyard where non-Jews reside. It also deals with forgetting to make an *eruv*. Also when several courtyards are

open to each other, or two courtyards are one in front of the other. (*Eruvin* 61b)

Halon   חלון
The 7th *perek in Eruvin* deals with a window or other separations between two courtyards, adding food on Shabbat when the existing one is diminished, and what kind of food is to be used to make an *eruv*. (*Eruvin* 76a)

Keitzad Mishtatfin   כיצד משתתפין
The 8th *perek in Eruvin* deals with how to make a joint *eruv*, how much food is necessary to make an *eruv*, and how to deal with a well between two courtyards. (*Eruvin* 82a)

Kol Gagot   כל גגות
The 9th *perek* in *Eruvin* deals with an *eruv* for roofs, also with a breach in the walls of a courtyard. (*Eruvin* 89a)

Hamotzeh Tefillin   המוצא תפילין
The 10th *perek* in *Eruvin* deals with finding *tefillin* on Shabbat, how to handle it. It also discusses what one can do when reading a rolled parchment and one end rolls away to another domain, standing in a private domain and drinking outside it, and what is permitted to do for the Temple but not for other places. (*Eruvin* 95a)

The following *perakim* are in the Tractate Pesahim פסחים

Ohr Le'arbaah Asar   אור לארבעה עשר
The 1st *perek* in *Pesahim* deals with searching for unleavened bread on the fourteenth day of the month of Nisan. (*Pesahim* 2a)

Kol Shaah   כל שעה
The 2nd *perek* in *Pesahim* deals with feeding *hametz* to animals, what kind of grain is permissible to use for *matzot*, which

vegetables are suitable to fulfill the obligation at the Seder. (*Pesahim* 21a)

Eilu Ovrin   אלו עוברין
The 3rd *perek* in *Pesahim* deals with food which must be removed to get rid of it by burning the *hametz*. It also discusses how one prepares for Pesach when the 14th of Nisan falls on a Shabbat, also when one is on his way to perform a mitzvah like circumcising his son – what one is required to do about other commandments. (*Pesahim* 42a)

Makom She-nahagu   מקום שנהגו
The 4th *perek* in *Pesahim* deals with doing work on the 14th of Nisan, selling small or large animals to a non-Jew, performing labor on Tisha Be'Av. It also discusses the six things the people of Yericho did in observance – three of them the rabbis approved. It also discusses the six things King Hizkiyahu did. (*Pesahim* 50a)

Tamid Nish'hat   תמיד נשחט
The 5th *perek* in *Pesahim* deals with the daily offerings and the manner in which the Pesach offering is slaughtered. (*Pesahim* 58a)

Eilu Devarim   אלו דברים
The 6th *perek* in *Pesahim* deals with the Pesach offering overriding Shabbat and who may eat of the Pesach offering. (*Pesahim* 65b)

Keitzad Tzolin   כיצד צולין
The 7th *perek* in *Pesahim* deals with the Pesach offering and how it is to be roasted. It also discusses five offerings and impurities, and what is to be burned. (*Pesahim* 74a)

Ha-Isha   האשה
The 8th *perek* in *Pesahim* deals with a woman's obligation to eat the Pesach offering. It also discusses whether one can delegate the slaughter of the Pesach offering, the

obligations of a mourner, a sick person, an old person, a freed prisoner, and a single person. (*Pesahim* 87a)

Mi She-hayah   מי שהיה

The 9th *perek* in *Pesahim* deals with observing the second Pesach in the following month as a makeup for people who were unclean, the difference between the first and second Pesach, a mix-up of sacrifices, and groups joining to eat the Pesach. (*Pesahim* 92b)

Arvei Pesahim   ערבי פסחים

The 10th *perek* in *Pesahim* deals with eating before the Seder. It also discusses how to conduct a Seder, the four cups of wine, the asking of the Four Questions, *Hallel*, and the *afikomon*. It also teaches the recitation of the three essential words which are: *Pesach*, *Matzah* and *Maror*. (*Pesahim* 99b)

The following *perakim* are in the Tractate *Shekalim* שקלים

Be-Ehad Be-Adar   באדר באחד

The 1st *perek* in *Shekalim* deals with making proclamations regarding the donation of the *Shekel*. It also deals with the reading of the Megillah, repairing roads, water reservoirs and marking the graves, and taking *Shekel* pledges from women and minors. (*Shekalim* 1)

Metzarfin   מצרפין

The 2nd *perek* in *Shekalim* deals with exchanging the *Shekel* to other currency, what to do if the *Shekel* was stolen, what is permitted with the excess money. (*Shekalim* 2)

Bi-shelosha Perakim   בשלושה פרקים

The 3rd *perek* in *Shekalim* deals with appropriations for the Temple. (*Shekalim* 3)

Ha-Terumah   התרומה

The 4th *perek* in *Shekalim* deals with purchases of holy needs for the Temple, what to do with the excess of funds from *terumah* and what to do with dedicated items to the Temple. (*Shekalim* 4)

Eilu Hen   אלו הן

The 5th *perek* in *Shekalim* deals with the functions of the officers who served in the Temple, the treasurers, the seals of the Temple with the names of the sacrifices inscribed on them, and the secret chamber of charity. (*Shekalim* 5)

Shelosha Asar   שלושה עשר

The 6th *perek* in *Shekalim* deals with prostrations, the hidden ark, with the tables in the Temple, the storage chests and with the inscriptions on them. (*Shekalim* 6)

Ma'ot   מעות

The 7th *perek* in *Shekalim* deals with money found in the Temple, what to do with it and a non-Jew who sent an offering to the Temple. (*Shekalim* 7)

Kol Harokin   כל הרוקין

The 8th *perek* in *Shekalim* deals with spit found in the Temple, whether it contaminates or not, vessels found, whether they are pure or not, flesh found in the Temple grounds, and the curtain in the Temple. (*Shekalim* 8)

The following *perakim* are in the Tractate *Yoma* יומא

Shivat Yamim   שבעת ימים

The 1st *perek* in the tractate *Yoma* deals with the preparations of the Kohen Gadol for Yom Kippur, the appointment of a deputy Kohen Gadol. (*Yoma* 2a)

Be-Rishona   בראשונה

The 2nd *perek* in *Yoma* deals with clearing the ashes from the altar, the rush of several Kohanim to be the first to make the offering. It discusses an incident that occurred during a rush, and lots were taken to determine which Kohen performs the service, the daily offering, and the number of Kohanim that merit to perform the various daily offerings. (*Yoma* 22a)

Amar Ha-Memuna   אמר להם הממונה

The 3rd *perek* in *Yoma* discusses the procedure of an officer telling the Kohanim to check the time for the offerings, the immersion required before entering the Temple court, the clothing that were worn by the Kohen Gadol, the confession he recited, the two sacrificial goats, the golden vessels donated by King Monbaz, the golden tablet for the sotah which was donated by queen Helen, the doors donated by Nicanor, and several personalities who were in disgrace. (*Yoma* 28a)

Taraf Ba-Kalpi   טרף בקלפי

The 4th *perek* in *Yoma* deals with the lots taken for the two goats and the crimson strip of wool. (*Yoma* 39a)

Hotziu Lo   הוציאו לו

The 5th *perek* in *Yoma* deals with how the utensils were handled, the curtain dividing the Holy of Holies and also the Holy Ark, and the proper order of performance. (*Yoma* 47a)

Shnei Se'irei   שני שעירי

The 6th *perek* of *Yoma* discusses the looks of the two goats. It discusses the scapegoat, the person who leads the goat away, and the way the Kohen Gadol was informed of the arrival of the goat to its destination. (*Yoma* 62a)

Ba Lo Kohen Gadol   בא לו כהן גדול

The 7th *perek* of *Yoma* deals with the readings for the Kohen Gadol, the exit of the Kohen Gadol from the Temple after he finished the service, and the eight garments worn by him. (*Yoma* 68b)

Yom Ha-Kippurim   יום הכפורים

The 8th *perek* of *Yoma* deals with the forbidden things on Yom Kippur, like eating, bathing, etc, who may eat, and which transgressions are forgiven and which are not. (*Yoma* 73b)

The following *perakim* are in the Tractate Sukkah סוכה

Sukkah   סוכה

The 1st *perek* in the tractate *Sukkah* deals with the height of the *sukkah* and the walls of a *sukkah*, a *sukkah* under a tree, and improper coverings for the *sukkah*. (*Sukkah* 2a)

Hayashen   הישן תחת המיטה

The 2nd *perek* in *Sukkah* deals with sleeping in the *sukkah*, with a *sukkah* built on a wagon, a boat or between trees. It also deals with how many meals is one obligated to eat in the *sukkah*, and when only part of the body is in the *sukkah*, who is obligated to eat in the *sukkah*, and what to do if it rains. (*Sukkah* 20b)

Lulav Ha-Gazul   לולב הגזול

The 3rd *perek* in *Sukkah* deals with the *lulav*, the *hadas*, the *arava*, and the *etrog* — what makes them valid for performing the mitzvah. It deals with a *lulav* that was stolen or dried out. It deals with how many branches of the *hadas* and *arava* are to be taken, how to tie the *lulav*, how many days the *lulav* is to be waved, and the case when the first day of Yom Tov falls on Shabbat. (*Sukkah* 29b)

Betzah

Lulav Ve-Arava   לולב וערבה

The 4th *perek* in *Sukkah* deals with the days the *lulav* and *arava* are to be taken, *Hallel*, water libation, and the flute playing. It also describes the *arava* and the water libation ceremonies. (*Sukkah* 42a)

He-Halil   החליל

The 5th *perek* in *Sukkah* deals with the flute playing, a description of the ceremony, the number of sacrifices, and the duty shifts for the Kohanim. (*Sukkah* 50a)

The following *perakim* are in the Tractate *Betzah* ביצה

Betzah   ביצה

The 1st *perek* in the tractate *Betzah* deals with an egg laid on the day of Yom Tov, slaughtering animals on Yom Tov, moving a step ladder, giving to the Kohen his due gifts, pounding spices, selecting beans. (*Betzah* 2a)

Yom Tov   יום טוב

The 2nd *perek* in the tractate *Betzah* deals with cooking when the first day of Yom Tov falls on Friday or on a Sunday. It also deals with heating water for the feet, sweeping the room, what animals may carry, and whether it is permissible to drag an object on Shabbat. (*Betzah* 15b)

Ein Tzadin   אין צדין

The 3rd *perek* in *Betzah* deals with catching fish on Yom Tov, hunting wild animals, moving a dead animal, sharpening knives, and measuring out a quantity of food. (*Betzah* 23b)

Ha-Mevi   המביא

The 4th *perek* in *Betzah* deals with moving jars of wine, moving wood, splitting wood, handling a lamp, breaking a vessel, cutting paper, leading an animal with a staff, producing fire from stones, etc. (*Sukkah* 29b)

Mashilin   משילין

The 5th *perek* in *Betzah* deals with throwing down fruit through a trapdoor, climbing a tree, riding on an animal, swimming in the water, sitting in judgment, perform betrothals, and borrowing utensils. (*Betzah* 35b)

The following *perakim* are in the Tractate *Rosh Hashana* ראש השנה

Arbaah Rashei Shanim   ארבעה ראשי שנים

The 1st *perek* in *Rosh Hashana* deals with the four new years in the Jewish calendar, messengers sent out to the country to inform the people, witnesses who saw the new moon, ineligible witnesses, and handicapped witnesses. (*Rosh Hashana* 2a)

Im Einan Makirin   אם אינן מכירין

The 2nd *perek* in *Rosh Hashana* deals with a witness who is unknown, the signals of light beacons on top of the hills for people who live at a distance, the courtyard for witness examination, the manner in which witnesses were examined, the diagrams of the moon. It also discusses the dispute between R. Gamliel and R. Yehoshua and their reconciliation. (*Rosh Hashana* 22a)

Rauhu Bet Din   ראהו בית דין

The 3rd *perek* in *Rosh Hashana* deals with sanctifying the new month, the valid shofar, and the raised hands of Moshe. (*Rosh Hashana* 25b)

Yom Tov   יום טוב

The 4th *perek* in *Rosh Hashana* deals with Yom Tov and Shabbat coinciding on the same day, accepting witnesses all day, the order of the prayers, and the manner and order of sounding the *shofar*. (*Rosh Hashana* 29b)

The following *perakim* are in the Tractate *Taanit* תענית

Me-aimatai מאמתי
The 1st *perek* in *Taanit* deals with when to start saying the prayer for rain, fasting for rain, restrictions during fast days. (*Taanit* 2a)

Seder Taaniyot Keitzad סדר תעניות כיצד
The 2nd *perek* in *Taanit* deals with the order and procedure of praying for rain, taking out the Ark to an open space in the town, which prayer is recited, and which are the days of no fasting. (*Taanit* 15a)

Seder Taaniyot Eilu סדר תעניות אילו
The 3rd *perek* in *Taanit* deals with the order of the fasts and when the shofar is sounded. (*Taanit* 18b)

Be-shelosha Perakim בשלושה פרקים
The 4th *perek* in *Taanit* deals with the blessings of the Kohanim, the lay divisions (the Israelites), fasting, carrying wood offerings to the Temple, Tisha Be'Av coinciding with Shabbat, and describing the fifteenth of Av and Yom Kippur night as special events. (*Taanit* 26a)

The following *perakim* are in the Tractate *Megillah* מגילה

Megillah Nikraat מגילה נקראת
The first *perek* in *Megillah* deals with reading the Megillah, and when it is read in large towns and walled cities. What are the differences between the first month of Adar and the second, between Yom Tov, Shabbat, and Yom Kippur. The difference between holy books, *tefillin* and *mezuzahs*, between Kohanim, between Shiloh and Jerusalem. (*Megillah* 2a)

Ha-Koreh Le-Mafrea הקורא למפרע
The 2nd *perek* in *Megillah* deals with the proper way to read the Megillah, who qualifies to read, time of the day to read the Megillah, time of the day to say Hallel, Temple functions. It also deals with the Omer. (*Megillah* 17a)

Ha-Koreh Omed הקורא עומד
The 3rd *perek* in *Megillah* deals with reading the Megillah – sitting or standing, the blessing before reading the Megillah. It also deals with how many *aliyot* on Mondays and Thursdays, Shabbat *Minha*, on Rosh Hodesh, Hol Hamoed, the requirement of a *minyan* of ten men, the minimum of sentences per *aliyah*, a person not properly dressed, a blind person. (*Megillah* 21a)

Benai Ha'ir בני העיר
The 4th *perek* in *Megillah* deals with what can be sold and exchanged for another holy item, a synagogue which became a ruin. It discusses *Parshat Shekalim*, *Parshat Zachor*, *Parshat Parah Adumah*, and *Parshat Ha-Hodesh*. Reading for Pesach, Shavuot, Rosh Hashana, and Yom Kippur, Sukkot, Chanukah, and Rosh Hodesh, *Maamodot*, and fast days. (*Megillah* 25b)

The following *perakim* are in the Tractate *Moed Katan* מועד קטן

Mashkin Bet Ha-Shalhin משקין בית השלחין
The 1st *perek* in *Moed Katan* deals with irrigation during Hol Hamoed and the kind of work one is permitted during Hol

Hamoed. It deals with marriage. (*Moed Katan* 2a)

Mi She-Hafach   מי שהפך
The 2nd *perek* in *Moed Katan* deals with agriculture and emergency work on Hol Hamoed, purchasing a home or purchasing animals. (*Moed Katan* 11b)

Ve-Eilu Megalhin   ואלו מגלחין
The 3rd *perek* in *Moed Katan* deals with Hol Hamoed: cutting one's hair, washing, writing, mourning, the status of holidays after the destruction of the Temple, and rending garments. (*Moed Katan* 13b)

The following *perakim* are in the Tractate *Hagigah* חגיגה

Ha-Kol Hayavin   הכל חייבין
The 1st *perek* in *Hagigah* deals with the obligation of appearing in the Temple during the holidays. It also deals with a person who didn't celebrate Sukkot, sins that cannot be corrected, and how to be released from vows. (*Hagigah* 2a)

Ein Dorshin   אין דורשין
The 2nd *perek* in *Hagigah* deals with forbidden teachings, leaning hands over sacrifices on Yom Tov, and contamination of cloths. (*Hagigah* 11b)

Homer BaMikdash   חומר במקדש
The 3rd *perek* in *Hagigah* deals with stringencies of sanctified food, immersing utensils, and the procedure for immersing. (*Hagigah* 20b)

The following *perakim* are in the Tractate *Yevamot* יבמות

Chamesh-esrei Nashim   חמש עשרה נשים
The 1st *perek* in *Yevamot* deals with who is

exempt from the ceremony of *halitza*, and certain stringencies applied to six particular women. (*Yevamot* 2a)

Keitzad   כיצד
The 2nd *perek* in *Yevamot* deals with exemptions for *halitza*, a man betrothing one of two sisters, or two brothers betrothing two sisters, and bringing a bill of divorce from overseas. (*Yevamot* 17a)

Arbaah Ahin   ארבעה אחין
The 3rd *perek* in *Yevamot* deals with four brothers of which two were married to two sisters, three brothers of which two were married to two sisters, two men marrying two sisters, and when the brides were mistakenly switched. (*Yevamot* 26a)

Ha-Holetz Le-yevimto   החולץ ליבמתו
The 4th *perek* in *Yevamot* deals with pregnancies from a prior husband, a woman waiting for *yibbum*, the obligation falls on the oldest brother to perform *halitza*, a minor and *halitza*, waiting period for *halitza*, four brothers marrying four sisters and then died, also when is a child considered a *mamzer*. (*Yevamot* 35b)

Rabban Gamliel   רבן גמליאל
The 5th *perek* in *Yevamot* deals with divorces and *maamar*s.[2] (*Yevamot* 50a)

Haba al Yevimto   הבא על יבמתו
The 6th *perek* in *Yevamot* deals with one having intercourse with his sister-in-law. It also deals with all of the forbidden marriages of the Jewish people in general, or the Kohanim. It also deals with the Kohen Gadol and whom he cannot marry, and with the commandment to be fruitful. (*Yevamot* 53b)

---

2. Statement of betrothal.

Almana Le-Kohen Gadol
אלמנה לכהן גדול

The 7th *perek* in *Yevamot* deals with restrictions on the Kohanim and whom they can marry, and also financial matters of a marriage. (*Yevamot* 66a)

He-Arel
הערל

The 8th *perek* in *Yevamot* deals with people unqualified to eat *terumah*. (*Yevamot* 70a)

Yesh Mutarot
יש מותרות

The 9th *perek* in *Yevamot* deals with marriages which are permitted or forbidden. (*Yevamot* 84a)

Ha-Isha Rabbah
האשה רבה

The 10th *perek* in *Yevamot* deals with a man who traveled overseas and his wife was told he died. She married another man and the first husband came home. It also deals with a father and son who went overseas and the wife was told that they died. It also discusses when a wife went overseas and the husband was told she had died, but actually she didn't die and then returned home. It discusses the age that one is considered to be a minor and its consequences. (*Yevamot* 87b)

Nosin Al Ha-Anusah
נושאין על האנוסה

The 11th *perek* in *Yevamot* deals with Jewish people in general and whom they are permitted to marry. It discusses also a converted woman and her children, and whom they can marry. It deals with the children of five women that were mixed up, and the real mother is not known. Other mix-ups are also discussed. (*Yevamot* 97a)

Mitzvat Halitza
מצוות חליצה

The 12th *perek* in *Yevamot* deals with how many judges need to be present for the ceremony of *halitza*, the valid shoe for the ceremony, and the proper way to do the ceremony. (*Yevamot* 101a)

Bet Shammai
בית שמאי

The 13th *perek* in *Yevamot* deals with the prerogative of refusal, and with two brothers married to two sisters. (*Yevamot* 107a)

Heresh She-nasa
חרש שנשא

The 14th *perek* in *Yevamot* deals with a deaf-mute who married, also with two deaf-mutes brothers marrying two sisters of sound hearing, and similar cases. (*Yevamot* 112b)

Ha-Isha Shalom
האשה שלום

The 15th *perek* in *Yevamot* deals with a husband and wife who went overseas, she returned alone claiming her husband died. It also deals with credible witnesses, and conflicting statements of the witnesses. (*Yevamot* 114b)

Ha-Isha Batra
האשה בתרא

The 16th *perek* in *Yevamot* deals with a couple traveling overseas and one of them died – what kind of testimony is acceptable. It also deals with a man who fell into the water – the kind of testimony required, and whether one witness is acceptable.
(*Yevamot* 119a)

The following *perakim* are in the Tractate *Ketubbot* כתובות

Betula Niset
בתולה נשאת

The 1st *perek* in *Ketubbot* deals with the monetary value of a *ketubbah* and different categories of *ketubbot*, disputes over issues of virginity, and pregnant women. (*Ketubbot* 2a)

Ha-Isha She-nitarmela
האשה שנתארמלה

The 2nd *perek* in *Ketubbot* deals with a woman that became a widow, financial disputes of a widow, forced witnesses, and the testimony of captive women. It deals with a grown person testifying about matters he saw when he was still a minor. (*Ketubbot* 15b)

Elu Naarot   אלו נערות
The 3rd *perek* in *Ketubbot* deals with compensation for misdeeds, and indemnity for a disgrace. (*Ketubbot* 29a)

Naara She-nitpateta   נערה שנתפתתה
The 4th *perek* in *Ketubbot* deals with seduction of a girl, proselytized women, and with the father's right to a daughter's property. (*Ketubbot* 41b)

Af Al Pi   אף על פי
The 5th *perek* in *Ketubbot* discusses the monetary settlement for a virgin girl, a woman's obligation to her husband, and a wife refusing to have intercourse with her husband. (*Ketubbot* 54b)

Metziat Ha-Isha   מציאת האשה
The 6th *perek* in *Ketubbot* deals with monetary matters in marital affairs. (*Ketubbot* 65b)

Ha-Madir   המדיר
The 7th *perek* in *Ketubbot* deals with vows of a wife. It also deals with finding flaws in the husband or wife after they were married. (*Ketubbot* 70a)

Ha-Isha She-naflu   האשה שנפלו
The 8th *perek* in *Ketubbot* deals with a woman inheriting property and possessions from her family. (*Ketubbot* 78a)

Ha-Kotev Le-Ishto   הכותב לאשתו
The 9th *perek* in *Ketubbot* discusses a case of a husband declaring in writing to his wife that he has no right or title to her property. It also deals with a husband that died, a husband who puts in writing a promise not to impose an oath on her, a widow who returned to her father's house and other claims in a marriage. (*Ketubbot* 83a)

Mi She-haya Nasui   מי שהיה נשוי
The 10th *perek* in *Ketubbot* deals with a man, who married two or more wives — how the inheritance is settled. (*Ketubbot* 90a)

Almanah Nizanet   אלמנה ניזונת
The 11th *perek* in *Ketubbot* deals with maintenance for a widow, with her rights to a *ketubbah* settlement, the judge's valuation of the property, and the prerogative of refusing to be married. (*Ketubbot* 95b)

Ha-Noseh Et Ha-Isha   הנושא את האשה
The 12th *perek* in *Ketubbot* deals with a wife who made a condition that her daughter will be fed, and a widow who refuses to leave the home of her former husband. (*Ketubbot* 101b)

Shenai Dayanai   שני דייני
The 13th *perek* in *Ketubbot* deals with Admon and Hanan, the two judges of civil law and their rulings — in Yerushalayim, the three provinces of Judea, beyond the Yarden and the Galilee, and their status in marital cases. (*Ketubbot* 104b)

The following *perakim* are in the Tractate *Nedarim* נדרים

Kol Kinuyai   כל כנויי
The 1st *perek* in *Nedarim* deals with different kinds of vows. (*Nedarim* 2a)

Ve-Eilu Mutarin   ואלו מותרין
The 2nd *perek* in *Nedarim* deals with vows that are not binding. (*Nedarim* 13b)

Arbaah Nedarim   ארבעה נדרים
The 3rd *perek* in *Nedarim* deals with four kinds of vows permitted to be annulled. It also discusses the greatness of the mitzvah of circumcision. (*Nedarim* 20b)

Ein Ben Ha-Mudar אין בין המודר

The 4th *perek* in *Nedarim* deals with things that are under a vow and the prohibition to benefit from them. (*Nedarim* 32b)

Ha-Shutfin השותפין

The 5th *perek* in *Nedarim* deals with partners making vows. (*Nedarim* 45b)

Ha-Noder Min Ha-M'vushal הנודר מן המבושל

The 6th *perek* in *Nedarim* discusses a vow against eating cooked foods, different foods that are similar or a derivative of the food under a vow. (*Nedarim* 49a)

Ha-Noder Min Ha-Yerek הנודר מן הירק

The 7th *perek* in *Nedarim* discusses vows to abstain from vegetables, houses, beds, and fruits. (*Nedarim* 54a)

Konam Yayin קונם יין

The 8th *perek* in *Nedarim* discusses vows against wines and vows with a time limit. (*Nedarim* 60a)

Rabbi Eliezer רבי אליעזר

The 9th *perek* in *Nedarim* discusses reasons for annulment of a vow, and also vows which are against Torah Law. (*Nedarim* 64a)

Naarah Ha-M'orasa נערה המאורסה

The 10th *perek* in *Nedarim* deals with vows of a betrothed, vows of a *bogeret*,[3] and a woman waiting for a levirate marriage. (*Nedarim* 66b)

Ve-elu Nedarim ואלו נדרים

The 11th *perek* in *Nedarim* deals with vows made against doing things, but the consequences would cause afflictions, it also deals with vows made by a person ignorant in vows, a widow and a divorcee and nine instances of women's vows. (*Nedarim* 79a)

---

3. A girl 12.5 years or older.

The following *Perakim* are in the Tractate *Nazir* נזיר

Kol Kinuye Nezirot כל כנויי נזירות

The 1st *perek* in *Nazir* deals with the form of words used to become a Nazir, and it also deals with the specified and unspecified duration of a Nazir's vow. (*Nazir* 2a)

Hareni Nazir הריני נזיר

The 2nd *perek* in *Nazir* discusses a Nazir's vow which would make specific items prohibited to him. (*Nazir* 9a)

Mi She-Amar מי שאמר

The 3rd *perek* in *Nazir* discusses when a Nazir can cut his hair. (*Nazir* 16a)

Mi She-Amar מי שאמר

The 4th *perek* in *Nazir* discusses a case of a second man hearing a man making a vow to become a Nazir and the second man declares: "I also." It also discusses a father making his son a Nazir. (*Nazir* 20b)

Bet Shammai בית שמאי

The 5th *perek* in *Nazir* deals with errors made in the declaration. (*Nazir* 30b)

Shelosha Minin שלשה מינין

The 6th *perek* in *Nazir* deals with forbidden things for a Nazir, and the time period when an unspecified time to be a Nazir is declared. (*Nazir* 34a)

Kohen Gadol כהן גדול

The 7th *perek* in *Nazir* Discusses a case where a Kohen Gadol or a Nazir need to attend to a dead person. (*Nazir* 47a)

Shnei Nezirim שני נזירים

The 8th *perek* in *Nazir* deals with the doubtful uncleanness of a Nazir. (*Nazir* 47a)

Ha-Kutim Ein Lahem   הכותים אין להם

The 9th *perek* in *Nazir* deals with the eligibility of non-Jews to become Nazirs, the eligibility of a servant to become a Nazir, and a Nazir finding a corpse. (*Nazir* 61a)

The following *perakim* are in the Tractate *Sotah* סוטה

Ha-M'kaneh   המקנא

The 1st *perek* in *Sotah* deals with a husband giving notice to his wife about his suspicion. It also deals with how notice is given, the number of witnesses, where the *sotah* is taken, and how the *sotah* is dressed. It also comments on Shimshon. (*Sotah* 2a)

Haya Mevi   היה מביא

The 2nd *perek* in *Sotah* deals with the proper writing of the *sotah* scroll. (*Sotah* 14a)

Haya Notel   היה נוטל

The 3rd *perek* in *Sotah* deals with the *korban* offering brought by the *sotah*, and the different requirements between a man and a woman. (*Sotah* 19a)

Arusah   ארוסה

The 4th *perek* in *Sotah* deals with a betrothed woman and a woman awaiting levirate marriage. It also deals with women not required to drink the water. (*Sotah* 23b)

Ke-Shem She-Hamayim   כשם שהמים

The 5th *perek* in *Sotah* deals with the husband of the *sotah*, and several comments of the Tannaim. (*Sotah* 27b)

Mi She-Kineh   מי שקנא

The 6th *perek* in *Sotah* deals with the testimony of only one witness, testimony of a slave and other witnesses, and contradictory testimony. (*Sotah* 31a)

Elu Ne'emarin   אלו נאמרין

The 7th *perek* in *Sotah* deals with the language permitted to use when writing a *sotah* scroll and other instances, blessings and curses, the Priestly Blessings, and the readings of the King. (*Sotah* 32a)

Mashuah Milhamah   משוח מלחמה

The 8th *perek* in *Sotah* deals with the anointed person to lead the soldiers into battle and his speech to the people. It also deals with persons exempt from military duty, with the duties the exempted have to perform, and the difference between an optional war and a war of duty. (*Sotah* 42a)

Eglah Arufa   עגלה ערופה

The 9th *perek* in *Sotah* deals with the language to be used when the ceremony of breaking a heifer's neck is performed. It also discusses instances when the breaking of the heifer's neck is not performed, the measuring of the distance from the towns, contradictory testimony, ceremonies which were suspended after the Temple was destroyed and other calamities, things that ceased when some of the scholars died. It also discusses Eliyahu HaNavi, divine intuition, and resurrection. (*Sotah* 44b)

The following *perakim* are in the Tractate *Gittin* גיטין

Ha-Mevi Get   המביא גט

The 1st *perek* in *Gittin* deals with bringing a letter of divorce from overseas, bringing a *get* in Eretz Yisrael, and a non-Jewish witness for a *get*. (*Gittin* 2a)

Ha-Mevi Get   המביא גט

The 2nd *perek* in *Gittin* deals with the testimony of the witnesses. It also deals with the ink that can be used to write the *get* and who is eligible to write the *get*. (*Gittin* 15a)

Kol Ha-Get   כל הגט

The 3rd *perek* in *Gittin* deals with the intention of the person when writing a *get*. It deals with blank sheets of *get* scrolls and blank contracts with spaces to be filled and how to prepare them. It also discusses *get* papers lost and found, a town under siege, a ship that is in a storm tossed at sea, and lending money. (*Gittin* 24a)

Ha-Sholeah   השולח

The 4th *perek* in *Gittin* deals with a man changing his mind after sending a *get*, changing one's name, property of orphans, the status of a slave, a slave who is half free, a Jewish slave sold to a non-Jew. It deals with selling himself and his children as slaves to a non-Jew. (*Gittin* 32a)

Ha-Nizokin   הניזקין

The 5th *perek* in *Gittin* deals with valuation and compensation, maintenance of orphans, with a deaf-mute, confiscated property, and *darchei shalom*.[4] (*Gittin* 48b)

Ha-Omer   האומר

The 6th *perek* in *Gittin* deals with sending a *get* with a messenger. (*Gittin* 62b)

Mi She-ahazu   מי שאחזו

The 7th *perek* in *Gittin* deals with one who has hallucinations while writing a *get*, and a *get* that has conditions. (*Gittin* 67b)

Ha-Zorek   הזורק

The 8th *perek* in *Gittin* deals with throwing a *get* to his wife, or if the husband told his wife to take this bond and it happened to be her *get*, or if she found the *get* but did not receive it from her husband. It also deals with dating the *get* according to the date system of other nations, or a mix-up in the writing of a *get*. (*Gittin* 77a)

---

4. For the sake of peace.

Ha-M'garesh   המגרש

The 9th *perek* in *Gittin* deals with a *get* that has conditions attached to it, with two *get* scrolls mixed up, a get that was written differently from the standard *get*, a *get* that was written in Hebrew, but the witnesses signed in a different language. (*Gittin* 82a)

The following *perakim* are in the Tractate *Kiddushin* קידושין

Ha-Isha Niknet   האשה נקנית

The 1st *perek* in *Kiddushin* deals with what action is necessary to make a marriage valid, and a Jewish bondman and a non-Jewish bondman and their marriage. It also deals with the sale of property and what makes it binding, father and son, and father and daughter obligations, commandments which are obligated upon men but not on women, and Commandments applying only to the Land of Israel. (*Kiddushin* 2a)

Ha-Ish Mekadesh   האיש מקדש

The 2nd *perek* in *Kiddushin* deals with marrying through an agent, a father giving his daughter in betrothal, and sanctified money used for betrothal. (*Kiddushin* 41a)

Ha-Omer   האומר

The 3rd *perek* in *Kiddushin* deals with a man appointing an agent to acquire him a wife, a man marrying a woman with conditions, a man claiming he married a woman and she claims it is not true. It also deals with a child, which parent it goes after, and what is a *mamzer*. (*Kiddushin* 58b)

Asara Yohasin   עשרה יוחסין

The 4th *perek* in *Kiddushin* deals with ten classes of people that returned from Babylon. It also deals with a class called *shetuki*, and with classes that need examination, a full Jew intermarrying with the other classes, a couple traveling overseas coming back with children, a bachelor teaching young children, a bachelor with the occupation of a shepherd, a father teaching his son an occupation. (*Kiddushin* 69a)

The following *perakim* are in the Tractate *Bava Kamma* בבא קמא

Arbaah Avot   ארבעה אבות
The 1st *perek* in *Bava Kamma* discusses the principal causes of damages, and what makes an animal to be considered warned as dangerous. (*Bava Kamma* 2a)

Keitzad Ha-Regel   כיצד הרגל
The 2nd *perek* in *Bava Kamma* deals with how to determine which constitutes a dangerous animal as far as damages are concerned. (*Bava Kamma* 17a)

Ha-Meniah   המניח
The 3rd *perek* in *Bava Kamma* discusses vessels broken, public street injury caused by a person, and two oxen injuring each other. (*Bava Kamma* 27a)

Shor She-nagah arbaah שור שנגח ארבעה
The 4th *perek* in *Bava Kamma* discusses multiple stabbings by an ox, and an ox goring a person to death. (*Bava Kamma* 36a)

Shor She-nogach   שור שנגח את הפרה
The 5th *perek* in *Bava Kamma* discusses the subject of an ox goring a pregnant cow, goring a pregnant woman, and an open pit belonging to partners. (*Bava Kamma* 46a)

Ha-Kones   הכונס
The 6th *perek* in *Bava Kamma* deals with animals locked up properly but they broke loose and caused damage. It also discusses leaving animals out in the sun, stacking sheaves in another's property without

permission, causing a fire through another person, and a spark causing fire. (*Bava Kamma* 55b)

Meruva   מרובה
The 7th *perek* in *Bava Kamma* discusses restitution and penalties. It also discusses what kind of animals one may raise in Israel, Syria, and in the wilderness. (*Bava Kamma* 62b)

Ha-Hovel   החובל
The 8th *perek* in *Bava Kamma* discusses what a person may be charged with when causing injury; it also discusses hitting one's parents. It is pointed out that payment of penalty does not absolve the person; one must ask for forgiveness. (*Bava Kamma* 83b)

Ha-Gozel Etzim   הגוזל עצים
The 9th *perek* in *Bava Kamma* deals with items stolen and converted to other uses, giving vessels to a craftsman for repair and the vessels were ruined while at the craftsman, and stealing from a proselyte. (*Bava Kamma* 93b)

Ha-Gozel U-maachil   הגוזל ומאכיל
The 10th *perek* in *Bava Kamma* deals with a person stealing and feeding his children with the stolen items. It also discusses finding and recognizing one's belongings at another person, robbing a field from another person, and then the property was taken by the tax collector, buying wool from a shepherd, and buying fruits from a field guard. (*Bava Kamma* 111b)

The following *perakim* are in the Tractate *Bava Metzia* בבא מציעא

Shnayim Ohazin   שנים אוחזין
The 1st *perek* in *Bava Metzia* discusses a

case when two people found an object and each claims he found it first, and objects found by a person's dependents. (*Bava Metzia* 2a)

Elu Metziot   אלו מציאות

The 2nd *perek* in *Bava Metzia* deals with objects found that need to be publicized, for how long a period, and what is considered lost property. (*Bava Metzia* 21a)

Ha-Mafkid   המפקיד

The 3rd *perek* in *Bava Metzia* discusses when objects left at a friend to watch were stolen, hiring a cow from a friend and then lending it to another friend, leaving perishable food at a friend to be watched, leaving money at a friend to be watched, and a guard using the items himself. (*Bava Metzia* 33b)

Ha-Zahav   הזהב

The 4th *perek* in *Bava Metzia* deals with the exchange of gold and silver, the penalty for overcharges, both the buyer and seller have recourse, fraud in words, substituting another person's fruit for his, and buying from five granaries and mixing them together. (*Bava Metzia* 44a)

Eizehu Neshech   איזהו נשך

The 5th *perek* in *Bava Metzia* discusses the difference between usury and overcharging, the lender dwelling free in the house of the borrower, forbidden business deals, dealing in futures, and people who could be considered as transgressors of usury. (*Bava Metzia* 60b)

Ha-Socher Et Ha-Umnin   השוכר את האומנין

The 6th *perek* in *Bava Metzia* discusses the hiring of craftsmen, and hiring animals for one type of work and using them for another. (*Bava Metzia* 75b)

Ha-Socher Et Ha-Poalim   השוכר את הפועלים

The 7th *perek* in *Bava Metzia* deals with employees and what one may expect from them to do, what they can eat, what is considered an unavoidable mishap, animals dying under his charge, and making conditions contrary to Torah Law. (*Bava Metzia* 83a)

Ha-Shoel Et Ha-Parah   השואל את הפרה

The 8th *perek* in *Bava Metzia* discusses hiring an animal with its owner to do work, exchanging one animal for another, exchanging one field for another, and renting out a house to another person. (*Bava Metzia* 94a)

Ha-M'kabel Sadeh Me-Havero   המקבל שדה מחבירו

The 9th *perek* in *Bava Metzia* deals with leasing a field from another person, the lessee's obligations, when wages should be paid to an employee, and taking a pawn from a borrower. (*Bava Metzia* 103a)

Ha-Bayit Ve-Haaliyah   הבית והעלייה

The 10th *perek* in *Bava Metzia* discusses partnership in a house, a collapsed wall on the neighbor's property, and two adjoining gardens. (*Bava Metzia* 116b)

The following *perakim* are in the Tractate *Bava Batra*   בבא בתרא

Ha-Shutafin   השותפין

The 1st *perek* in *Bava Batra* discusses partners in a house or garden. (*Bava Batra* 2a)

Lo Yahpor   לא יחפור

The 2nd *perek* in *Bava Batra* deals with digging ditches, water canals, and cisterns; placing stoves in the house, opening business shops in the house, ladders, the distance of trees, and a threshing house. (*Bava Batra* 17a)

Hezkat Ha-Batim   חזקת הבתים
The 3rd *perek* in *Bava Batra* deals with the time needed to have undisputed ownership for houses and other real estate, the three provinces of Yisrael, what constitutes possession or ownership, and in what direction windows should face. (*Bava Batra* 28a)

Ha-Mocher Et Ha-Bayit   המוכר את הבית
The 4th *perek* in *Bava Batra* discusses the sale of a house and what is normally included in the sale, sale of a courtyard, sale of an olive press, sale of a bath house, sale of a whole town, and sale of a field. (*Bava Batra* 61a)

Ha-Mocher Et Ha-S'fina
המוכר את הספינה
The 5th *perek* in *Bava Batra* deals with the sale of a boat and what is included in the sale, the sale of an ass, buying trees, and the four rules that apply to vendors. (*Bava Batra* 73a)

Ha-Mocher Perot   המוכר פירות
The 6th *perek* in *Bava Batra* discusses the sale of produce, sale of property for building a house on it, properties adjacent to each other, property with a public street running through it, and the sale of property for a grave. (*Bava Batra* 92a)

Bet Kur   בית כור
The 7th *perek* in *Bava Batra* deals with selling a piece of arable property, and measuring a *bet kur*. It also discusses property that has rocks and ditches, the sale that includes the rocks, and ditches up to a certain size. (*Bava Batra* 102b)

Yesh Nohalin   יש נוחלין
The 8th *perek* in *Bava Batra* deals with issues of inheritance. (*Bava Batra* 108a)

Mi She-Met   מי שמת
The 9th *perek* in *Bava Batra* deals with issues of inheritance for children of different ages, with two brothers, with joint ownership, a father-in-law, a man sick and dying, and a house that collapsed and killed the father or the mother. (*Bava Batra* 139b)

Get Pashut   גט פשוט
The 10th *perek* in *Bava Batra* deals with documents and contracts, divorces, betrothal documents, partial repayment of a debt, contracts which became effaced, two brothers – one rich and one poor, two people with the same name living in the same town, and lending money with a contract. (*Bava Batra* 160a)

The following *Perakim* are in the Tractate *Sanhedrin* סנהדרין

Dinei Mamonot   דיני ממונות
The 1st *perek* in *Sanhedrin* deals with the judicial system. Different cases require different numbers of judges. Capital cases require more judges then monetary cases. It discusses the number of judges required when judging a whole tribe, false prophets, the Kohen Gadol, the act to go to war, permission to enlarge a city, and the number of judges required for the Sanhedrin. (*Sanhedrin* 2a)

Kohen Gadol   כהן גדול
The 2nd *perek* in *Sanhedrin* discusses what the Kohen Gadol can do and what he cannot. It also discusses the duties and honors of a king. (*Sanhedrin* 18a)

Zeh Borer   זה בורר

The 3rd *perek* in *Sanhedrin* deals with how the judges are selected and that each party selects a *borer*.[5] It also discusses gamblers and people ineligible to be selected as judges, relatives, and how witnesses are examined. (*Sanhedrin* 23a)

Ehad Dinei Mamonot   אחד דיני ממונות

The 4th *perek* in *Sanhedrin* discusses the procedure and formalities of the court, the seating arrangement of the Sanhedrin. (*Sanhedrin* 32a)

Hayu Bodkin   היו בודקין

The 5th *perek* in *Sanhedrin* deals with the examination of witnesses and the kind of question they are asked. It also discusses how contradictory testimony is dealt with. (*Sanhedrin* 40a)

Nigmar Ha-Din   נגמר הדין

The 6th *perek* in *Sanhedrin* describes the procedure for a condemned person. (*Sanhedrin* 42b)

Arba Mitot   ארבע מיתות

The 7th *perek* in *Sanhedrin* describes the four kinds of death sentences, and how the death sentences are carried out. It also discusses which of the four death penalties is applied to a particular crime, what constitutes idol worship, what is the penalty for desecrating the Shabbat, and the penalty for witchcraft. (*Sanhedrin* 49b)

Ben Sorer U-Moreh   בן סורר ומורה

The 8th *perek* in *Sanhedrin* deals with a rebellious son, what a son has to do to be considered rebellious, it also deals with breaking into a house to steal. (*Sanhedrin* 68b)

Ha-Nisrafin   הנשרפין

The 9th *perek* in *Sanhedrin* deals with what crime deserves the death penalty of burning, and when guilty of two death penalties – which one is applied. (*Sanhedrin* 75a)

Eilu Hen Ha-Nehnakin   אלו הן הנחנקין

The 10th *perek* in *Sanhedrin* deals with the crimes for which the penalty is death by strangling, and the subject of violating an injunction by the scribes is in some cases more stringent. It also deals with false prophets. (*Sanhedrin* 84b)

Helek   חלק

The 11th *perek* called *Helek* discusses the World to Come, who deserves and who does not deserve a portion in the World to Come, and a condemned town. (*Sanhedrin* 90a)

The following *perakim* are in the Tractate *Makkot* מכות

Keitzad Ha-Edim   כיצד העדים

The 1st *perek* in *Makkot* deals with what kind of punishment is taken against false witnesses. (*Makkot* 2a)

Elu Hen Ha-Golin   אלו הן הגולין

The 2nd *perek* in *Makkot* deals with unintentional killing, and with towns of refuge. (*Makkot* 7a)

Elu Hen Ha-Lokin   אלו הן הלוקין

The 3rd *perek* in *Makkot* deals with the punishment of stripes. It also discusses the reason God gave us many commandments. (*Makkot* 13a)

---

5. Selected judge.

The following *Perakim* are in the Tractate *Shevuot* שבועות

Shevuot Shtayim   שבועות שתים
The 1st *perek* in *Shevuot* deals with the different kind of oaths. It also deals with the animal sacrifices for the holidays. (*Shevuot* 2a)

Yediot Ha-Tumah   ידיעות הטומאה
The 2nd *perek* in *Shevuot* deals with awareness of uncleanness, creeping insects and their uncleanness. (*Shevuot* 14a)

Shevuot Shetayim   שבועות שתים
The 3rd *perek* in *Shevuot* deals with oaths, when one is liable many times for one oath, what is deemed a false oath, and what is a vain oath. (*Shevuot* 19b)

Shevuot Ha-Edut   שבועות העדות
The 4th *perek* in *Shevuot* deals with what constitutes an oath. (*Shevuot* 30a)

Shevuot Ha-Pikadon   שבועות הפיקדון
The 5th *perek* in *Shevuot* deals with an oath concerning a deposit, and an accusatory oath. (*Shevuot* 36b)

Shevuot Ha-Dayanin   שבועות הדיינין
The 6th *perek* in *Shevuot* deals with the oath imposed by the judges on the other party to the claim. It also deals in cases where an oath is not required, in cases of a loan, and a pledge for the loan. (*Shevuot* 38b)

Kol Ha-Nishba'in   כל הנשבעין
The 7th *perek* in *Shevuot* deals with oaths in order not to have to make restitution. It deals with different kinds of cases, like lenders and borrowers, store keepers and customers, partners and tenants. (*Shevuot* 44b)

Arbaah Shomrin   ארבעה שומרין
The 8th *perek* in *Shevuot* deals with four classes of guardians. (*Shevuot* 49a)

The following *perakim* are in the Tractate *Eduyot* עדויות

Shammai Omer   שמאי אומר
The 1st *perek* in *Eduyot* deals with the time of uncleanness for women, the size of the dough to be liable for taking *hallah*, drawn water rendering the *mikveh* unfit, the majority of judges to prevail, bones of a corpse making objects unclean. It discusses the matters in which the school of Hillel changed their views to teach like the school of Shammai, and a person who is half free and half slave. (*Eduyot* 2a)

Rabbi Hanina   רבי חנינא
The 2nd *perek* in *Eduyot* relates that R. Hanina, the deputy High Priest, testified about four matters. It also relates that R. Yishmael told the Sages three things in the vineyard of Yavne; three matters were told to R. Yishmael, also three matters in which R. Akiva and R. Yishmael disagreed. R. Akiva said three things. In addition, he made five statements about the length of time certain events lasted. (*Eduyot* 3b)

Kol Ha-M'tamin   כל המטמאין
The 3rd *perek* in *Eduyot* deals with uncleanness under a roof. It also deals with other unclean objects, a captive woman eating *terumah*, doubtful situations, and the disagreement among the rabbis about unclean objects. (*Eduyot* 4b)

Elu Devarim   אלו דברים
The 4th *perek* in *Eduyot* discusses the leniencies of Bet Shammai and the stringencies of Bet Hillel. It also discusses two brothers marrying two sisters, vows of a

Nazir, and the status of a woman who had a miscarriage. (*Eduyot* 6a)

Rabbi Yehuda   רבי יהודה

The 5th *perek* in *Eduyot* discusses the six stringencies of Rabbi Hillel and the testimony of R. Akavia b. Mahalalel. (*Eduyot* 7a)

Rabbi Yehuda b. Bava   רבי יהודה בן בבא

The 6th *perek* in *Eduyot* states that R. Yehuda testified about five matters and it discusses the testimony of several Sages. (*Eduyot* 7a)

He'id Rabbi Yehoshua   העיד רבי יהושע

The 7th *perek* in *Eduyot* describes the testimony of several Sages. (*Eduyot* 8b)

He'id R. Yehoshua ben Betera
העיד רבי יהושע בן בתירא

The 8th *perek* in *Eduyot* describes the testimony of R. Yehoshua ben Betera. Also R. Eliezer said that he heard details about the building of the Temple. It also discusses Eliyahu HaNavi. (*Eduyot* 9a)

The following *perakim* are in the Tractate *Avodah Zarah* עבודה זרה

Lifnei Idihen   לפני אידיהן

The 1st *perek* in *Avodah Zarah* deals with interaction of a Jew with idol worshippers during their festivals. It lists the idol worshippers' holidays. (*Avodah Zarah* 2a)

Ein Maamidin   אין מעמידין

The 2nd *perek* in *Avodah Zarah* lists what business one is fobidden to do with an idol worshipper. It discusses deriving any benefit from objects belonging to idol worshippers, and items permitted under supervision by a Jew. (*Avodah Zarah* 22a)

Kol Ha-Tzlamim   כל הצלמים

The 3rd *perek* in *Avodah Zarah* discusses

the prohibition of images. It also relates a story about R. Gamliel and the son of a philosopher. It deals with worshippers of mountains and hills, and houses close to a house of idol worshipping. (*Avodah Zarah* 40b)

Rabbi Yishmael   רבי ישמעאל

The 4th *perek* in *Avodah Zarah* discusses stones that might belong to idol worshippers, a garden belonging to an idol worshipper, and how to annul an idol object. It also discusses wines. (*Avodah Zarah* 49b)

Ha-Socher Et Ha-Poel   השוכר את הפועל

The 5th *perek* in *Avodah Zarah* deals with hiring a non-Jew to prepare non-kosher wine and wine prohibitions in general. (*Avodah Zarah* 62a)

The following *perakim* are in the Tractate *Avot* אבות

The 1st *perek* in *Avot* discusses how the Torah and traditions were handed down from generation to generation. It enumerates the wise sayings of our Sages.

The 2nd *perek* in *Avot* repeats the advice of the Sages on how to live a life worth living.

The 3rd *perek* in *Avot* advises to be a good citizen in the country where you live, to study Torah all the time – even at mealtime, to be sociable and friendly with your fellow-men. It also states that if there is no food, there is no Torah.

The 4th *perek* in *Avot* advises to learn from everyone, to learn and to teach, that everyone has their own hour, not to be judgmental, to have respect for your fellow-men, that this world is like a vestibule for the World to Come, that learning when one is young is more endurable than at an older age.

The 5th *perek* in *Avot* discusses the

creation of the world, the generations from Adam to Avraham, the miracles that happened to the Jewish people. It also discusses the character traits of mankind.

The 6th *perek* in *Avot* deals with the advantages of studying Torah. It also describes a Bat Kol, a heavenly voice, reminding the world about studying Torah. It also advises to honor your teacher and not to chase after honor.

The following *perakim* are in the Tractate *Horayot* הוריות

Horu Bet Din   הורו בית דין
The 1st *perek* in *Horayot* deals with a Bet Din giving a ruling which led to transgressions. (*Horayot* 2a)

Hora Kohen Mashiach   הורה כהן משיח
The 2nd *perek* in *Horayot* deals with the Kohen Gadol making decisions contrary to Torah Law. It discusses the conduct of the Kohen Gadol in the Temple. (*Horayot* 6b)

Kohen Mashiach   כהן משיח
The 3rd *perek* in *Horayot* deals with who is considered to be the Kohen Mashiach, and it discusses who takes precedent – a Kohen over a Levi and in some cases, a woman over a man. (*Horayot* 9b)

The following *perakim* are in the Tractate *Zevahim* זבחים

Kol Ha-Zevahim   כל הזבחים
The 1st *perek* in *Zevahim* deals with offerings in the Temple. (*Zevahim* 2a)

Kol Ha-Zevahim She-kibbel Daman
כל הזבחים שקבל דמן
The 2nd *perek* in *Zevahim* deals with an offering attended to by a person other than

a qualified Kohen, or offered in the wrong location. (*Zevahim* 15b)

Kol Ha-P'sulin   כל הפסולין
The 3rd *perek* in *Zevahim* deals with who is qualified to slaughter the offering. It also deals with the intention of the slaughterer when making the offering. (*Zevahim* 31b)

Beis Shammai   בית שמאי
The 4th *perek* in *Zevahim* deals with *pigul*, meaning the offering was offered with the wrong intention. It also deals with offerings by a non-Jew. (*Zevahim* 36b)

Eizehu Mekoman   איזהו מקומן
The 5th *perek* in *Zevahim* deals with the proper place and direction where the priest is to make the offerings. It also deals with the various offerings on different holidays, the burnt offering, and the peace offering. (*Zevahim* 47a)

Kodshei Kodashim   קדשי קדשים
The 6th *perek* in *Zevahim* deals with the altar and the proper way to approach and depart from the altar. (*Zevahim* 58a)

Hatat Ha-Off   חטאת העוף
The 7th *perek* in *Zevahim* deals with the red-line marking painted on the center of the altar, using the wrong hand, and making the offering at night. (*Zevahim* 66a)

Kol Ha-Zevahim   כל הזבחים
The 8th *perek* in *Zevahim* deals with cases where the offerings were mixed up. (*Zevahim* 70b)

Ha-Mizbeah Mekadesh   המזבח מקדש
The 9th *perek* in *Zevahim* deals with anything that was brought up on the altar and is automatically sanctified. (*Zevahim* 83a)

Kol Ha-Tadir   כל התדיר
The 10th *perek* in *Zevahim* deals with which

offering precedes others. It also deals with the portions of the priests and in what manner they can be eaten. (*Zevahim* 89a)

Dam Hatat   דם חטאת
The 11th *perek* in *Zevahim* deals with the clothing of the priest and if they got soiled. (*Zevahim* 92a)

Tevul Yom   טבול יום
The 12th *perek* in *Zevahim* deals with who can participate in the holy food that was on the altar, a person who immersed that day in the *mikveh*. It deals with the skins of the animals. (*Zevahim* 98b)

Ha-Shohet Ve-Hamaaleh   השוחט והמעלה
The 13th *perek* in *Zevahim* deals with offerings made outside the Temple. (*Zevahim* 106a)

Parat Hatat   פרת חטאת
The 14th *perek* in *Zevahim* deals with the sin offering, the offering of the scapegoat, and an invalid animal brought to the altar. It also discusses the periods before the Temple was built during which time the altars were located in Gilgal, Shiloh, Nov, and Givon. (*Zevahim* 112a)

The following *perakim* are in the Tractate *Menahot* מנחות

Kol Ha-Menahot   כל המנחות
The 1st *perek* in *Menahot* deals with the meal offerings, and the intent of the person making the offering. (*Menahot* 2a)

Ha-Kometz Et Ha-Minha   הקומץ את המנחה
The 2nd *perek* in *Menahot* deals with the fistful of meal offerings taken by the Kohen, and violations that make the offering invalid. (*Menahot* 13a)

Ha-Kometz Rabbah   הקומץ רבה
The 3rd *perek* in *Menahot* deals with the larger fistful of meal offerings taken by the Kohen, the intent of the offering, a mix-up of offerings, validation or the lack of it, and the *menorah* candles. (*Menahot* 17a)

Ha-Techelet   התכלת
The 4th *perek* in *Menahot* deals with the *tzitzit*, the *tefillin*, and impairment of the offerings. (*Menahot* 38a)

Kol Ha-Menahot Baot   כל המנחות באות
The 5th *perek* in *Menahot* deals with the meal offering made of *hametz* or matzah, the ingredients added in the mixture of the offering, and the lifting of the offering. (*Menahot* 52b)

Rabbi Yishmael   רבי ישמעאל
The 6th *perek* in *Menahot* deals with the amount required for the offering, the Omer, the procedure of how the Omer was brought from the fields, the new crop and when it is permissible to eat it, and the obligation to take *hallah*. (*Menahot* 63b)

Elu Menahot   אלו מנחות נקמצות
The 7th *perek* in *Menahot* deals with which meal offering requires a fistful to be taken. (*Menahot* 72b)

Ha-Todah Haitah Baah   התודה היתה באה
The 8th *perek* in *Menahot* deals with the size and shape of the meal offering. (*Menahot* 76b)

Kol Korbanot Ha-Tzibbur   כל קרבנות הצבור
The 9th *perek* in *Menahot* deals with the community offerings, the quality and the source of the grain brought for the meal offering, and the quality of the oil used. (*Menahot* 83b)

Shtei Middot   שתי מדות
The 10th *perek* in *Menahot* deals with the scales used in the Temple, which offering requires libation, which require leaning of hands, who is unqualified to lean hands (*Menahot* 87a)

Shetei Ha-Lehem   שתי הלחם
The 11th *perek* in *Menahot* deals with the loaves of bread and the showbread. It describes the tables in the Temple and the time when the loaves can be eaten. (*Menahot* 94a)

Ha-Menahot Ve-Han'sachim
המנחות והנסכים
The 12th *perek* in *Menahot* deals with the offering becoming unclean, and using the wrong vessels or the wrong grain. (*Menahot* 100b)

Harei Alai Isaron   הרי עלי עשרון
The 13th *perek* in *Menahot* deals with offerings that are to be the correct number offered, and an offering that contracted a blemish. (*Menahot* 104b)

The following *perakim* are in the Tractate *Hullin* חולין

Ha-Kol Shohatin   הכל שוחטין
The 1st *perek* in *Hullin* deals with who may slaughter an animal to be kosher, an animal slaughtered on Shabbat, what tools may be used. It also deals with *Havdalah*, Yom Tov on Friday, the format of the *Havdalah*. (*Hullin* 2a)

Ha-Shohet   השוחט
The 2nd *perek* in *Hullin* deals with the manner of slaughtering, slaughtering for a non-Jew, slaughtering in worship of mountains, seas, and rivers. (*Hullin* 27a)

Elu Terefot   אלו טרפות
The 3rd *perek* in *Hullin* deals with what is considered to be not kosher and what is considered to be kosher, kosher in fowls, and distinguished features of kosher and non-kosher animals and locusts. (*Hullin* 42a)

Beheima Ha-Maksha   בהמה המקשה
The 4th *perek* in *Hullin* deals with the birth of a calf, miscarriage of an animal, finding a calf inside the womb after it was slaughtered. (*Hullin* 68a)

Oto V'et B'no   אותו ואת בנו
The 5th *perek* in *Hullin* deals with the commandment prohibiting the "mother and child" to be slaughtered on the same day. It also deals with the obligation of informing the buyer when both mother and lamb were sold to be slaughtered. It also clarifies when the day begins for this commandment of "mother and child." (*Hullin* 78a)

Kissuy Ha-Dam   כסוי הדם
The 6th *perek* in *Hullin* deals with the law of covering the blood, a minor and a mentally defective person slaughtering, and what can be used to cover the blood. (*Hullin* 83b)

Gid Ha-Nasheh   גיד הנשה
The 7th *perek* in *Hullin* deals with the prohibition of eating the sinew of the thigh vein, the punishment for eating the sinew, and meat cooked with the sinew in it. (*Hullin* 89b)

Kol Ha-Basar   כל הבשר
The 8th *perek* in *Hullin* deals with mixing meat and milk, and to what extent do they have to be separated. (*Hullin* 103b)

Ha-Or Ve-Harotev   העור והרוטב
The 9th *perek* in *Hullin* deals with parts of the animal such as the skin and the bones,

that when combined make a prohibited size. (*Hullin* 117b)

Ha-Z'roa Ve-hal'hayim הזרוע והלחיים
The 10th *perek* in *Hullin* deals with the gifts of the shoulder, the two cheeks, the maw, and sanctified animals. (*Hullin* 130a)

Reshit Ha-Gez ראשית הגז
The 11th *perek* in *Hullin* deals with the law of "the first of the fleece." (*Hullin* 135a)

Shiluah Ha-Ken שלוח הקן
The 12th *perek* in *Hullin* deals with the commandment of birds and letting the mother bird leave the nest, and the punishment for violating the law (*Hullin* 138b)

The following *perakim* are in the Tractate *Bechorot* בכורות

Ha-Lokeah Ubar Hamoro הלוקח עובר חמורו
The 1st *perek* in *Bechorot* deals with a firstborn animal, in what circumstances is the animal exempt from the law of the firstling. (*Bechorot* 2a)

Ha-Lokeah Ubar Parato הלוקח עובר פרתו
The 2nd *perek* in *Bechorot* deals with buying an unborn animal from a non-Jew, blemished animals, abnormal looking animals, a calf born not in the regular way – but was extracted. (*Bechorot* 13a)

Ha-Lokeah Beheimah הלוקח בהמה
The 3rd *perek* in *Bechorot* deals with buying an animal from a non-Jew and it is unknown if the animal had a firstling. It also deals with blemished animals. (*Bechorot* 19b)

Ad Kamah עד כמה
The 4th *perek* in *Bechorot* deals with the length of time an owner must tend to the firstling, and finding a blemish after it was slaughtered. It also deals with a person who is paid to inspect the firstling, a judge who is being paid to give legal decisions, and people who are suspect of being transgressors. (*Bechorot* 26b)

Kol Pesulei כל פסולי המוקדשין
The 5th *perek* in *Bechorot* deals with invalidated firstlings. (*Bechorot* 31a)

Al Elu Mumin על אלו מומין
The 6th *perek* in *Bechorot* deals with blemishes in the firstling. (*Bechorot* 37a)

Mumin Elu מומין אלו
The 7th *perek* in *Bechorot* deals with blemishes in a firstling and in people. (*Bechorot* 43a)

Yesh Bechor יש בכור
The 8th *perek* in *Bechorot* deals with human beings and their firstborn, miscarriages, caesarean birth, a man having two wives and both had firstborns, the amount to give the priest, and what currency may be used for the redemption. (*Bechorot* 46a)

Maaser Beheimah מעשר בהמה
The 9th *perek* in *Bechorot* deals with tithing animals, the periods for tithing, and the proper procedure for tithing. (*Bechorot* 53a)

The following *perakim* are in the Tractate *Arachin* ערכין

Ha-Kol Maarichin הכל מעריכין
The 1st *perek* in *Arachin* deals with who is fit to dedicate another person or to be dedicated himself. (*Arachin* 2a)

Ein Ne'archin אין נערכין
The 2nd *perek* in *Arachin* deals with valuation and the minimum amount of the valuation. It also deals with intercalation

of the months, the number of *shofar* blasts in the Temple, when the flute was played and who played it, the amount of animals to be prepared for the holidays, and how many Levites would serve in the Temple. (*Arachin* 7b)

Yesh Be-Arachin   יש בערכין
The 3rd *perek* in *Arachin* deals with the leniencies and restrictions when making valuations. (*Arachin* 13b)

Heseg Yad   השג יד
The 4th *perek* in *Arachin* deals with what determines the valuations. (*Arachin* 17a)

Ha-Omer Mishkali Alai
האומר משקלי עלי
The 5th *perek* in *Arachin* deals with a person making a vow of dedication and the valuation thereof. It also deals with the pledges taken. (*Arachin* 19a)

Shum Ha-Yitomim   שום היתומים
The 6th *perek* in *Arachin* deals with valuations of property belonging to orphans. It also deals with valuation of attached property. (*Arachin* 21b)

Ein Makdishin   אין מקדישין
The 7th *perek* in *Arachin* deals with valuations just prior to the Jubilee year, redemption during the Jubilee year. (*Arachin* 24a)

Ha-Makdish Et Sadehu
המקדיש את שדהו
The 8th *perek* in *Arachin* deals with dedicating his field and then wanting to redeem it. It also deals with renouncing his property. (*Arachin* 27a)

Ha-Mocher Et Sadehu   המוכר את שדהו
The 9th *perek* in *Arachin* deals with selling a property during a Jubilee year. It also deals with selling a house in a walled city, and inheritance. (*Arachin* 29b)

The following *perakim* are in the Tractate *Temurah* תמורה

Ha-Kol Memirin   הכל ממירין
The 1st *perek* in *Temurah* deals with exchanging sanctified animals. (*Temurah* 2a)

Yesh Be-Korbanot   יש בקרבנות
The 2nd *perek* in *Temurah* deals with the differences between a community and an individual offering. (*Temurah* 14a)

Elu Kodashim   אלו קדשים
The 3rd *perek* in *Temurah* deals with offerings and what animal offerings can be substituted. (*Temurah* 17b)

Velad Hatat   ולד חטאת
The 4th *perek* in *Temurah* deals with an animal designated for an offering but was lost, or if money set aside for the offering was lost. It also discusses if the offering develops a blemish after it was set aside. (*Temurah* 21b)

Keitzad Maarimim   כיצד מערימים
The 5th *perek in Temurah* deals with how to make substitutes for offerings and what would constitute circumventing the law. (*Temurah* 24b)

Kol Ha-Issurin   כל האסורין
The 6th *perek* in *Temurah* deals with forbidden sacrifices on the altar and what renders items forbidden on the altar. It also deals with what is considered a harlot's hire and what is considered a dog's hire. It also deals with the status of the offsprings of the invalidated offerings. (*Temurah* 28a)

Yesh Be-Kodshei   יש בקדשי
The 7th *perek* in *Temurah* deals with the differences between animals on the altar and the animals belonging to the Temple

treasury. It also deals with how to dispose of forbidden things, and with sanctified items that were not offered on time or in the proper place. (*Temurah* 31a)

The following *perakim* are in the Tractate *Keritut* כריתות

Sheloshim Ve-shesh   שלושים ושש

The 1st *perek* in *Keritut* deals with the thirty-six transgressions entailing the penalty of excision, and the offerings which may be eaten. (*Keritut* 2a)

Arbaa Mehusarei   ארבעה מחוסרי כפרה

The 2nd *perek* in *Keritut* deals with transgressions whose atonement is not complete until more is done for atonement. It also deals with a maiden servant that is half-free. (*Keritut* 8b)

Amru Lo   אמרו לו

The 3rd *perek* in *Keritut* deals with eating forbidden fat, and eating several forbidden foods in one spell of forgetfulness. It also deals with the transgression of incest, slaughtering offerings outside the Temple area, and with doing several acts of work on Shabbat in one spell of unawareness. (*Keritut* 11b)

Safek Achal Helev   ספק אכל חלב

The 4th *perek* in *Keritut* deals with being in doubt about eating forbidden foods. (*Keritut* 17a)

Dam Shehita   דם שחיטה

The 5th *perek* in *Keritut* deals with the transgression of eating blood, eating one of two pieces of flesh — one of them being sanctified meat — but the person is in doubt which one was eaten, and also with two pieces of meat — one of them being a forbidden food. (*Keritut* 20b)

Ha-Mevi Asham   המביא אשם

The 6th *perek* in *Keritut* deals with bringing a doubtful guilt offering, yet before it was slaughtered it was revealed there was no guilt. It also discusses setting aside money to buy guilt offerings, but the prices have changed. It also deals with an offering that died. (*Keritut* 23b)

The following *perakim* are in the Tractate *Meilah* מעילה

Kodshei Kodashim   קדשי קדשים

The 1st *perek* in *Meilah* deals with the most holy sacrifices. It also deals with the lesser sacrifices and the sprinkling of the blood. (*Meilah* 2a)

Hatat Ha-Off   חטאת העוף

The 2nd *perek* in *Meilah* deals with fowl offerings. It also deals with sacrifices that are to be burned, the two loaves brought to the Temple, and the showbread and the meal offerings. (*Meilah* 8a)

Velad Hatat   ולד חטאת

The 3rd *perek* in *Meilah* deals with sacrilege or using the offspring of a sin offering, exchange offerings, making use of money set aside for an offering by a nazirite, the sanctified blood, and the ashes that the burning produced. It also deals with the milk or the egg of an offering and other offerings where the law of sacrilege applies. It also discusses the difference between donations to the upkeep of the Temple and offerings, and donating a whole field to the Temple. (*Meilah* 10b)

Kodshei Mizbeah   קדשי מזבח

The 4th *perek* in *Meilah* deals with several offerings joined together, and making the portion large enough for the law of sacrilege to be applied. It also deals with various instances of sanctified items joined together. (*Meilah* 15a)

Ha-Neheneh Min Ha-Hekdesh הנהנה מן ההקדש

The 5th *perek* in *Meilah* deals with the law of making use of holy items and the size of the item to be in violation. (*Meilah* 18a)

Ha-Shaliah She-Asa השליח שעשה

The 6th *perek* in *Meilah* deals with an agent who did the violation on behalf of his sender. It also deals with an agent who was a deaf-mute or mentally defective or a minor. It also deals with transgressing the law of sacrilege that applies to transactions between two civilian individuals. (*Meilah* 20a)

The following *perakim* are in the Tractate *Tamid* תמיד

Be-Shelosha Mekomot בשלושה מקומות

The 1st *perek* in *Tamid* deals with the places where the guards of the Temple were watching and the performance of their jobs, with Kohanim who volunteered, and those who were assigned by the appointed chief to clean the ashes of the altar. (*Tamid* 25b)

Rauhu Ahiv ראוהו אחיו

The 2nd *perek* in *Tamid* describes the competition among the Kohanim to perform the services. It also discusses the order of the service. (*Tamid* 28b)

Amar Lahem Ha-Mimuneh אמר להם הממונה

The 3rd *perek* in *Tamid* describes the lots that were cast to give assignments to the Kohanim to do the services in the Temple. It also describes the ceremony of taking out the golden and silver vessels for the

service, and opening the tremendous gates to the Temple. (*Tamid* 30a)

Lo Hayu Koftin לא היו כופתין

The 4th *perek* in *Tamid* describes the proper procedure for bringing the offerings on the altar. (*Tamid* 30b)

Amar Lahem Ha-Mimuneh אמר להם הממונה

The 5th *perek* in *Tamid* describes how the appointed chief instructed the Kohanim what prayers and blessings to say during the service, the incense offering, the firepan offering, and the musical instruments used. The noise they produced signaled a reminder to the other Kohanim and Levites when to start their services. (*Tamid* 32b)

Hehelu Olim החלו עולים

The 6th *perek* in *Tamid* describes the Kohanim walking up the stairs of the porch, clearing the ashes, cleaning and preparing the *menorah*. (*Tamid* 33a)

Be-Z'man She-Kohen Gadol בזמן שכהן גדול

The 7th *perek* in *Tamid* describes how the Kohen Gadol was assisted when he prostrated himself and the manner in which he performed his part of the service. It also describes the singing of the Levites: each day of the week was assigned a different song. (*Tamid* 33b)

The following *perakim* are in the Tractate *Middot* מידות

Be-Shelosha Mekomot בשלושה מקומות

The 1st *perek* in *Middot* describes the responsibilities of the watchmen in the Temple. There were three watch stations assigned to the Kohanim and twenty-one for the Levites. It describes how the appointed chief made the rounds. It also describes the various gates in the Temple. (*Middot* 1st *perek*)

Har HaBayit   הר הבית
The 2nd *perek* in *Middot* describes the measurements of the Temple area and where the main entrance was. It also describes the measurements of the ladies hall. (*Middot* 2nd *perek*)

Ha-Mizbeah   המזבח
The 3rd *perek* in *Middot* describes the measurements of the altar, its ramp and its pavement. It also describes the laver. (*Middot* 3rd *perek*)

Pitho Shel Heichal   פתחו של היכל
The 4th *perek* in *Middot* describes the measurements of the Sanctuary. (*Middot* 4th *perek*)

Kol Ha-Azarah   כל העזרה
The 5th *perek* in *Middot* describes the measurements of the Temple court and the various storage rooms. (*Middot* 5th *perek*)

The following *perakim* are in the Tractate *Kinnim* קינים

Hatat Ha-Off   חטאת העוף
The 1st *perek* in *Kinnim* deals with sin offerings, using a bird as a *korban*. It also deals with a mix-up of offerings. (*Kinnim* 22b)

Ken Setuma   קן סתומה
The 2nd *perek* in *Kinnim* deals with bird offerings, and the birds flying away. (*Kinnim* 23a)

Ba-Meh Dvarim Amurim   במה דברים אמורים
The 3rd *perek* in *Kinnim* deals with bird

offerings, a mix-up, and the inquiry of the priest. (*Kinnim* 23b)

The following *perakim* are in the Tractate *Kelim* כלים

Avot Ha-Tumot   אבות הטומאות
The 1st *perek* in *Kelim* deals with the primary sources of uncleanness and what is above or below others in uncleanness to transfer it by contact. It also discusses the ten grades of uncleanness and ten grades of holiness. (*Kelim* 1st *perek*)

Kli Etz   כלי עץ
The 2nd *perek* in *Kelim* deals with utensils of wood, leather or bone, and also utensils of glass and earthenware. (*Kelim* 2nd *perek*)

Shiur Kli Heres   שיעור כלי חרס
The 3rd *perek* in *Kelim* deals with sizes of various kinds, with broken earthenware vessels and the size of the breach, repairs by plastering, jugs that developed a hole and were repaired. (*Kelim* 3rd *perek*)

Ha-Heres   החרס
The 4th *perek* in *Kelim* deals with broken and defective utensils. (*Kelim* 4th *perek*)

Tanur   תנור
The 5th *perek* in *Kelim* deals with what would make an oven susceptible to uncleanness. It also discusses if an oven became unclean, and how to render it clean again. (*Kelim* 5th *perek*)

Ha-Oseh   העושה
The 6th *perek* in *Kelim* discusses ovens made of stone in various forms and the combination of forms. (*Kelim* 6th *perek*)

Ha-Kalatut   הקלתות
The 7th *perek* in *Kelim* deals with stoves

Kelim

and their supporting bases, with projecting shelves, and the distances required between unclean and clean vessels. (*Kelim* 7th *perek*)

Tanur   תנור

The 8th *perek* in *Kelim* discusses unclean creeping insects found in an oven. It also discusses if a person touched another person who became unclean from a corpse. (*Kelim* 8th *perek*)

Mahat   מחט

The 9th *perek* in *Kelim* discusses finding needles or rings in the oven, if a cask full of clean liquid was placed in a room where there was a corpse, a sponge soaking up unclean liquid, and a hole in the oven under various scenarios. (*Kelim* 9th *perek*)

Elu Kelim   אלו כלים

The 10th *perek* in *Kelim* discusses vessels that can be protected from uncleanness, and with what can they be sealed for protection. (*Kelim* 10th *perek*)

Klei Matachot   כלי מתכות

The 11th *perek* in *Kelim* discusses metal vessels. (*Kelim* 11th *perek*)

Tabaat Adom   טבעת אדם

The 12th *perek* in *Kelim* deals with rings or chains with regards to susceptibility to uncleanness, also metal coverings, nails and instruments of all sorts. (*Kelim* 12th *perek*)

Ha-Sayef Ve-Hasakin   הסייף והסכין

The 13th *perek* in *Kelim* discusses swords and knives with regards to susceptibility to uncleanness and various other instruments. (*Kelim* 13th *perek*)

Klei Matachot   כלי מתכות

The 14th *perek* in *Kelim* deals with metal utensils and the size required for them to retain their uncleanness. It also discusses

wagons, basket lids, and keys. (*Kelim* 14th *perek*)

Klei Etz   כלי עץ

The 15th *perek* in *Kelim* discusses wooden utensils, leather utensils, and musical instruments with regards to retaining their uncleanness. (*Kelim* 15th *perek*)

Kol Klei Etz   כל כלי עץ

The 16th *perek* in *Kelim* deals with wooden utensils broken in two, and whether they retain their uncleanness. It also deals with wooden baskets, reed baskets, leather utensils, gloves, and the sheath of a sword. (*Kelim* 16th *perek*)

Kol Klei Baalei Batim   כל כלי בעלי בתים

The 17th *perek* in *Kelim* discusses the various sizes of halachic measurements: the size of a pomegranate, an egg, a dried fig, an olive, and a cubit. It also discusses creatures of the sea. (*Kelim* 17th *perek*)

Ha-Shida   השידה

The 18th *perek* in *Kelim* deals with chest cabinets, with beds and with *tefillin*. (*Kelim* 18th *perek*)

Ha-Mifarek   המפרק

The 19th *perek* in *Kelim* deals with dismantling a bed, a man with gonorrhea who is carried on a bed, a box that was open on the top or open on the side. (*Kelim* 19th *perek*)

Ha-Karim   הכרים

The 20th *perek* in *Kelim* deals with mattresses, pillow cases, bags, chairs and stools, troughs, sheets, and mats. (*Kelim* 20th *perek*)

Ha-Nogea   הנוגע

The 21st *perek* in *Kelim* discusses touching items that are unclean. (*Kelim* 21st *perek*)

Ha-Shulhan · השולחן

The 22nd *perek* in *Kelim* deals with unclean tables, stools, bridal chairs, and cabinets. (*Kelim* 22nd *perek*)

Ha-Kadur · הכדור

The 23rd *perek* in *Kelim* discusses unclean balls, a *kamea*, and *tefillin*. It also discusses the difference between riding upon and sitting. (*Kelim* 23rd *perek*)

Shelosha Trisin · שלושה תריסין

The 24th *perek* in *Kelim* deals with unclean shields, wagons, kneading troughs, boxes, leather chests, bases, beds, waste baskets, mats, goatskin bottles, hides, sheets, wrappings, leather gloves, and headcovers. (*Kelim* 24th *perek*)

Kol Ha-Kelim · כל הכלים

The 25th *perek* in *Kelim* discusses the inside and the outside of vessels, and measuring devices for wine and oil. (*Kelim* 25th *perek*)

Sandal Amaki · סנדל עמקי

The 26th *perek* in *Kelim* deals with specific sandals, gloves, damaged sandals, hides, skins belonging to owners of different occupations, and changing the use of the animal skin to something different. (*Kelim* 26th *perek*)

Ha-Beged · הבגד

The 27th *perek* in *Kelim* discusses clothing that can become unclean under various circumstances. (*Kelim* 27th *perek*)

Shalosh Al Shalosh · שלוש על שלוש

The 28th *perek* in *Kelim* deals with the uncleanness of cloth three by three fingerbreadth, a ball or stuffing inside a ball, bands for parchment scrolls, kerchiefs, and garments of poor people with patches. (*Kelim* 28th *perek*)

Numei Ha-Sadin · נומי הסדין

The 29th *perek* in *Kelim* discusses the fringes hanging out from a sheet. It also deals with several woolen pillow cases – if they are touching each other, measuring cords, and scales. (*Kelim* 29th *perek*)

Klei Zechuchit · כלי זכוכית

The 30th *perek* in *Kelim* deals with glassware, mirrors and small flasks. (*Kelim* 30th *perek*)

The following *perakim* are in the Tractate *Ohalot* אהלות

Shnayim Teme'im · שנים טמאים

The 1st *perek* in *Ohalot* discusses uncleanness by a corpse and how contact with a person or utensils that touched a corpse transfer the uncleanness by touch. It also discusses the organs of human beings. (*Ohalot* 1st *perek*)

Elu Metamin · אלו מטמאין

The 2nd *perek* in *Ohalot* discusses the status of tents or anything with a roof over a corpse. It also discusses areas where bones of a dead person have been found. (*Ohalot* 2nd *perek*)

Kol Ha-Metamin · כל המטמאין

The 3rd *perek* in *Ohalot* discusses different situations of a corpse in a tent. (*Ohalot* 3rd *perek*)

Migdal · מגדל

The 4th *perek* in *Ohalot* discusses uncleanness in the house, also cabinets and door openings. (*Ohalot* 4th *perek*)

Tanur · תנור

The 5th *perek* in *Ohalot* discusses how an oven in the house is affected by uncleanness, and different vessels and their uncleanness. (*Ohalot* 5th *perek*)

Adam Ve-kelim   אדם וכלים
The 6th *perek* in *Ohalot* discusses being
under the shadow of human beings or the
shadow of vessels, and causing uncleanness to that which is under the shadow. It
also discusses a wall separating two houses
and a corpse being inside one of them.
(*Ohalot* 6th *perek*)

Ha-Tumah Be-Kotel   הטומאה בכותל
The 7th *perek* in *Ohalot* discusses different shapes of houses and how they are
affected by uncleanness. It also discusses
a child being born dead in a house and the
consequences. (*Ohalot* 7th *perek*)

Yesh Mevi'in   יש מביאין
The 8th *perek* in *Ohalot* discusses screens
that can shield the area from uncleanness.
(*Ohalot* 8th *perek*)

Kaveret   כוורת
The 9th *perek* in *Ohalot* discusses large
vessels in various positions with regards
to uncleanness. (*Ohalot* 9th *perek*)

Arubah   ארובה
The 10th *perek* in *Ohalot* discusses hatches
in the house with different size openings
and the way they are situated. (*Ohalot* 10th
perek)

Ha-bayit She-nisdak   הבית שנסדק
The 11th *perek* in *Ohalot* discusses a house
with a roof that is split, a porch with a split
roof, and also a situation where a dog eats
a corpse. (*Ohalot* 11th *perek*)

Neser   נסר
The 12th *perek* in *Ohalot* discusses boards
lying on top of a stove and different situations of boards causing uncleanness.
(*Ohalot* 12th *perek*)

Ha-Oseh Maor   העושה מאור
The 13th *perek* in *Ohalot* discusses making
new openings in the house to let in the
light. It also discusses windows and their
size, and holes in the doors. (*Ohalot* 13th
perek)

Ha-Ziz   הזיז
The 14th *perek* in *Ohalot* discusses projec-
tions in the door, walls or windows that
can have an affect on uncleanness. (*Ohalot*
14th *perek*)

Sagos   סגוס
The 15th *perek* in *Ohalot* discusses using
heavy garments or wood to block a split
in the roof, also wooden boards touching
each other, and wine casks they touching
each other. It also discusses rooms separated with boards, a room full of straw or
pebbles, also a situation where a person
touches a corpse and then touches utensils. (*Ohalot* 15th *perek*)

Kol Ha-Metaltelin   כל המטלטלין
The 16th *perek* in *Ohalot* discusses movable objects with regards to uncleanness,
also finding a grave when plowing a field,
and how to inspect a field for graves.
(*Ohalot* 16th *perek*)

Ha-Horesh   החורש
The 17th *perek* in *Ohalot* discusses how to
go about plowing a field with a grave in it.
(*Ohalot* 17th *perek*)

Keitzad Botzrim   כיצד בוצרים
The 18th *perek* in *Ohalot* deals with a vineyard in a grave field, a grave that is lost
in a field, how to render an unclean field
clean, and walking in a grave field. It also
deals with buying a field in Syria and enumerates ten places that are not considered
dwellings of Canaanites. (*Ohalot* 18th *perek*)

The following *perakim* are in the Tractate *Negaim* נגעים

Marot Negaim   מראות נגעים
The 1st *perek* in *Negaim* deals with colors of leprosy and the various symptoms of the disease. (*Negaim* 1st *perek*)

Baheret Aza   בהרת עזה
The 2nd *perek* in *Negaim* deals with what time of the day the leprosy should be inspected, and with the person inspecting the disease and his qualifications. (*Negaim* 2nd *perek*)

Ha-Kol Metamin   הכל מיטמאין
The 3rd *perek* in *Negaim* deals with who might contract uncleanness from a person with leprosy, the duration of uncleanness for leprosy, and the duration of leprosy in a house. (*Negaim* 3rd *perek*)

Yesh Be-Se'ar   יש בשער
The 4th *perek* in *Negaim* deals with the symptoms, signs, and conditions in the hair of a leper. (*Negaim* 4th *perek*)

Kol Safek   כל ספק
The 5th *perek* in *Negaim* deals with doubtful leprosy. (*Negaim* 5th *perek*)

Gufa   גופה
The 6th *perek* in *Negaim* deals with the size of the affliction of leprosy. It describes twenty-four organs in the human body that will not become unclean. (*Negaim* 6th *perek*)

Elu Beharot   אלו בהרות
The 7th *perek* in *Negaim* deals with prior signs of leprosy and with the color of the leprosy changing its appearance. (*Negaim* 7th *perek*)

Ha-Poreah   הפורח
The 8th *perek* in *Negaim* deals with the leprosy disappearing but then returning. (*Negaim* 8th *perek*)

Ha-Shehin   השחין
The 9th *perek* in *Negaim* deals with various kinds of sore spots on the body and the duration of their uncleanness. (*Negaim* 9th *perek*)

Ha-Netakim   הנתקים
The 10th *perek* in *Negaim* deals with *netakim* (a kind of leprosy), signs of thin hairs, and how to shave the hair. Baldness is also discussed. (*Negaim* 10th *perek*)

Kol Ha-Bigadim   כל הבגדים
The 11th *perek* in *Negaim* deals with the uncleanness of garments, and with dyed skins. (*Negaim* 11th *perek*)

Kol Ha-Batim   כל הבתים
The 12th *perek* in *Negaim* deals with houses contracting uncleanness from leprosy, and houses made of stones or of wood. (*Negaim* 12th *perek*)

Asara Batim   עשרה בתים
The 13th *perek* in *Negaim* deals with the ten rulings that apply to houses. (*Negaim* 13th *perek*)

Keitzad Metaharin   כיצד מטהרין
The 14th *perek* in *Negaim* describes how the priest cleansed the leper. (*Negaim* 14th *perek*)

The following *perakim* are in the Tractate *Parah* פרה

Rabbi Eliezer   רבי אליעזר
The 1st *perek* in *Parah* deals with the heifer.[6] When a murdered person was found

---

6. A calf.

between two towns, they used a heifer to atone for the town that was guilty. It also deals with the age of the heifer. (*Parah* 1st *perek*)

Rabbi Eliezer　　　　רבי אליעזר
The 2nd *perek* in *Parah* deals with the red heifer as a sin offering – what makes it valid or invalid. (*Parah* 2nd *perek*)

Shivat Yamim　　　　שבעת ימים
The 3rd *perek* in *Parah* deals with the Kohen who will handle the red heifer and how he will prepare himself for the job. It also discusses the Temple mount and the leaning of hands on the heifer. (*Parah* 3rd *perek*)

Parat Hatat　　　　פרת חטאת
The 4th *perek* in *Parah* deals with whether the red heifer was slaughtered with the wrong intention. It also deals with the burning of the heifer and with the persons handling the heifer. (*Parah* 4th *perek*)

Ha-Mevi　　　　המביא
The 5th *perek* in *Parah* deals with the person handling the vessels and his immersion. (*Parah* 5th *perek*)

Ha-Mekadesh　　　　המקדש
The 6th *perek* in *Parah* deals with handling the ashes from the burnt offering. (*Parah* 6th *perek*)

Hamisha　　　　חמשה
The 7th *perek* in *Parah* deals with mingling the ashes of the red heifer. (*Parah* 7th *perek*)

Shnayim　　　　שניים
The 8th *perek* in *Parah* deals with mixing the water and ashes from the burned heifer. It also deals with the cloth worn by the mixer, immersion, and which water is considered a *mikveh*. (*Parah* 8th *perek*)

Tzelohit　　　　צלוחית
The 9th *perek* in *Parah* deals with a creature falling into the water of the red heifer, animals drinking from the water of the heifer, what kind of transportation is not permitted, as for instance across a river, and when water from the heifer got mixed up with other water. (*Parah* 9th *perek*)

Kol Ha-Ra'ui　　　　כל הראוי
The 10th *perek* in *Parah* deals with the vessel of the red heifer being touched by an unclean object, and the water touching an oven. (*Parah* 10th *perek*)

Tzelohit She-heniha　　　　צלוחית שהניחה
The 11th *perek* in *Parah* deals with covering the vessel which holds the water, and with invalid hyssop. It also deals with Torah prohibitions vs. prohibitions enacted by the scribes. (*Parah* 11th *perek*)

Ha-Ezov　　　　האזוב
The 12th *perek* in *Parah* deals with hyssop in different situations and how it is sprinkled. (*Parah* 12th *perek*)

The following *perakim* are in the Tracate *Taharot* טהרות

Shelosha Asar　　　　שלשה עשר
The 1st *perek* in *Taharot* deals with thirteen rules with regards to uncleanness in fowl and cattle, and with dough and loaves belonging to the priest. (*Taharot* 1st *perek*)

Ha-Isha　　　　האשה
The 2nd *perek* in *Taharot* deals with uncleanness of a pot with vegetables in it. (*Taharot* 2nd *perek*)

Ha-Rotev　　　　הרוטב
The 3rd *perek* in *Taharot* deals with food like broth, milk, and oil. It deals with a

person who was deaf or mentally defective, and with children. (*Taharot* 3rd *perek*)

Ha-Zorek   הזורק
The 4th *perek* in *Taharot* deals with unclean reptiles, corpses, spit, liquids, and with unclean hands. (*Taharot* 4th *perek*)

Ha-Sheretz   השרץ
The 5th *perek* in *Taharot* deals with a dead reptile or frog, and with two alleys – one clean and one not clean. (*Taharot* 5th *perek*)

Makom   מקום
The 6th *perek* in *Taharot* deals with private and public domains, trees, two shops – one clean and one not, fields in the summer and winter, and a colonnade – private or public. (*Taharot* 6th *perek*)

Ha-Kadar   הקדר
The 7th *perek* in *Taharot* deals with a potter, and with an uneducated person in Jewish law. (*Taharot* 7th *perek*)

Hadar   הדר
The 8th *perek* in *Taharot* deals with one living in the same courtyard with a person ignorant in Jewish law. It also deals with losing an object and finding it the next day. (*Taharot* 8th *perek*)

Zeitim   זיתים
The 9th *perek* in *Taharot* deals with olives – their cleanness or uncleanness, and with reptiles found in the grinding stone. (*Taharot* 9th *perek*)

Ha-Noel   הנועל
The 10th *perek* in *Taharot* deals with an olive press and workers in the press, and with spit falling into the olive press. (*Taharot* 10th *perek*)

The following *perakim* are in the Tractate *Mikvaot* מקוואות

Shesh Maalot   שש מעלות
The 1st *perek* in *Mikvaot* deals with various grades of uncleanness in a bathhouse, what must be done to make the bath clean again, and rain water flowing into the *mikveh*. (*Mikvaot* 1st *perek*)

Ha-Tameh   הטמא
The 2nd *perek* in *Mikvaot* deals with doubtful immersion in the *mikveh*, with a *mikveh* that was measured and found short of the required measurement, how it affects objects immersed into the *mikveh*, and mud inside the *mikveh*. (*Mikvaot* 2nd *perek*)

Rabbi Yosi   רבי יוסי
The 3rd *perek* in *Mikvaot* deals with two *mikvaot* adjacent to each other, but neither has the required adequate water. It deals also with cisterns. (*Mikvaot* 3rd *perek*)

Ha-Meniah   המניח
The 4th *perek* in *Mikvaot* deals with utensils under a rain gutter catching the water, with drawn water and rain water, well water and sea water. (*Mikvaot* 4th *perek*)

Maayan   מעין
The 5th *perek* in *Mikvaot* deals with well water conducted into several channels, and with the sea being used as a *mikveh*. (*Mikvaot* 5th *perek*)

Kol Ha-Me'urav   כל המעורב
The 6th *perek* in *Mikvaot* deals with three *mikvaot* that are adjacent to each other – two contained valid water and the third containing drawn water. It also deals with two *mikvaot* next to each other – neither having enough required valid water, but they are connected with

a hole in the wall between them. (*Mikvaot* 6th *perek*)

Yesh Maalin   יש מעלין

The 7th *perek* in *Mikvaot* deals with snow, hail, ice, wine, and other fluids mixed with the valid water. (*Mikvaot* 7th *perek*)

Eretz Yisrael   ארץ ישראל

The 8th *perek* in *Mikvaot* deals with *mikvaot* in the Eretz Israel and those outside of Eretz Israel. It also deals with what act or condition requires immersion. (*Mikvaot* 8th *perek*)

Elu Hotzetzin   אלו חוצצין

The 9th *perek* in *Mikvaot* deals with interventions of things between the person and the water. (*Mikvaot* 9th *perek*)

Kol Yadot   כל ידות

The 10th *perek* in *Mikvaot* deals with vessels and their handles, which vessels when immersed need to have the *mikveh* water enter inside the vessel. (*Mikvaot* 19th *perek*)

The following *perakim* are in the Tractate Niddah נדה

Shammai   שמאי

The 1st *perek* in *Niddah* deals with women during the period of impurity, and with four categories of women. (*Niddah* 1st *perek*)

Kol Ha-Yad   כל היד

The 2nd *perek* in *Niddah* deals with the time period when a woman is considered impure. (*Niddah* 2nd *perek*)

Ha-Mapelet Haticha   המפלת חתיכה

The 3rd *perek* in *Niddah* deals with a woman who lost her child at birth. (*Niddah* 3rd *perek*)

Benot Cuthites   בנות כותים

The 4th *perek* in *Niddah* deals with the daughters of the Cuthites and with the daughters of the Tzadokis. (*Niddah* 4th *perek*)

Yotzeh Dofen   יוצא דופן

The 5th *perek* in *Niddah* deals with birth by caesarean section. It also deals with the different status of children – female or male – at a certain age. (*Niddah* 5th *perek*)

Ba Siman   בא סימן

The 6th *perek* in *Niddah* deals with the signs required to be considered an adult. (*Niddah* 6th *perek*)

Dam Ha-Niddah   דם הנידה

The 7th *perek* in *Niddah* deals with the blood of menstruation, and with blood stains. (*Niddah* 7th *perek*)

Ha-Roeh Ketem   הרואה כתם

The 8th *perek* in *Niddah* deals with the distinction of blood from a wound or menstruation. (*Niddah* 8th *perek*)

Ha-Isha She-Hi Osah   האשה שהיא עושה

The 9th *perek* in *Niddah* deals with women who lent their underwear to a non-Jewish woman and blood was found on them, and with three women who slept in one bed. It also deals with methods of testing the blood and with women who have a regular date for menstruation. (*Niddah* 9th *perek*)

Tinoket   תינוקת

The 10th *perek* in *Niddah* deals with a girl who had not yet attained her age, and her status. It deals with different times of examinations for all women. (*Niddah* 10th *perek*)

The following *perakim* are in the Tractate *Machshirin* מכשירין

Kol Mashkeh   כל משקה
The 1st *perek* in *Machshirin* deals with liquids transferring uncleanness to food when the food becomes wet. It also deals with "*bechi yutan*," a Talmudic term for a situation where there was no intention to make the food wet, but if it fell upon it, it is welcome. (*Machshirin* 1st *perek*)

Zeyat Batim   זיעת בתים
The 2nd *perek* in *Machshirin* deals with cleanness, uncleanness of the drippings of houses, ditches and caves, and with sweat of a person. It also deals with a Jewish town having also non-Jews as residents and how this affects the bathhouse as well as finding meat on the street and other objects. It also deals with fruits found on the street – are they subject to tithing? (*Machshirin* 2nd *perek*)

Sack   שק
The 3rd *perek* in *Machshirin* deals with a sack full of fruit placed next to a stream or other wet areas. It also deals with various situations where foodstuff can come in contact with liquids. (*Machshirin* 3rd *perek*)

Ha-Shoheh   השוחה
The 4th *perek* in *Machshirin* deals with rain falling on a person in his impurity, and with various situations of food coming in contact with liquids. (*Machshirin* 4th *perek*)

Mi She-taval   מי שטבל
The 5th *perek* in *Machshirin* deals with a person immersing in a stream, and with a person swimming in a stream. (*Machshirin* 5th *perek*)

Ha-Maaleh   המעלה
The 6th *perek* in *Machshirin* deals with fruits on the roof and when dew fell upon the fruit. It deals with eggs and fish. It lists seven types of liquids, and liquids which carry uncleanness. (*Machshirin* 6th *perek*)

The following *perakim* are in the Tractate *Zavim* זבים

Ha-Roeh   הרואה
The 1st *perek* in *Zavim* deals with a man having a discharge of gonorrhea or a discharge of semen. (*Zavim* 1st *perek*)

Ha-Kol Metamin   הכל מיטמאין
The 2nd *perek* in *Zavim* deals with how to examine the discharge, and what objects become unclean by contact. (*Zavim* 2nd *perek*)

Ha-Zav   הזב
The 3rd *perek* in *Zavim* deals with two persons – one clean and one not clean – sitting together on a boat or on an animal. It deals with the difference between a small or large boat. (*Zavim* 3rd *perek*)

Rabbi Yehoshua   רבי יהושע
The 4th *perek* in *Zavim* deals with two women – one clean one not – sitting together on a bed. It also deals with an unclean person sitting on several bags or in other ways that are in contact with utensils. (*Zavim* 4th *perek*)

Ha-Nogea   הנוגע
The 5th *perek* in *Zavim* deals with a clean person touching a person with a discharge of gonorrhea. It also gives a general principle about uncleanness from gonorrhea. It deals with reptiles and birds with regards to uncleanness. (*Zavim* 5th *perek*)

The following *perakim* are in the Tractate *Tevul Yom* טבול יום

Ha-Mechanes המכנס
The 1st *perek* in *Tevul Yom* deals with food being touched by an unclean person who immersed himself the same day. (*Tevul Yom* 1st *perek*)

Mashkeh משקה
The 2nd *perek* in *Tevul Yom* deals with the fluid of a person immersed on the same day. (*Tevul Yom* 2nd *perek*)

Kol Yadot כל ידות
The 3rd *perek* in *Tevul Yom* deals with stalks of fruits being touched by an immersed person the same day he was immersed. (*Tevul Yom* 3rd *perek*)

Ochel Maaser אוכל מעשר
The 4th *perek* in *Tevul Yom* deals with tithed produce that was rendered susceptible to uncleanness by a liquid and was touched by a person immersed the same day. It deals with a woman immersed the same day as she was kneading dough. It deals with an *am haaretz*, meaning an uneducated person in Halachah. (*Tevul Yom* 4th *perek*)

The following *perakim* are in the Tracate *Yadayim* ידים

Mei Revi'it מי רביעית
The 1st *perek* in *Yadayim* deals with cleaning hands, how much water is required, and what kind of vessels may be used to clean hands. (*Yadayim* 1st *perek*)

Natal Le-Yado נטל לידו
The 2nd *perek* in *Yadayim* deals with how to pour water on the hands to cleanse them. It also deals with doubts of clean hands. (*Yadayim* 2nd *perek*)

Ha-Machnis המכניס
The 3rd *perek* in *Yadayim* deals with a person putting his hands inside a house affected by leprosy, the straps of *tefillin*, and the sacred scrolls of Shir HaShirim and Kohelet. (*Yadayim* 3rd *perek*)

Bo Be-Yom בו ביום
The 4th *perek* in *Yadayim* deals with Halachah rulings issued the same day when R. Eleazar ben Azariah was elected Nasi of the Sanhedrin. It discusses Ammonites, Moabites, and Egypt. A story is told about an Ammonite who converted to Judaism. Ezra and Daniel is discussed as well as the Tzadokis and Pharisees. (*Yadayim* 4th *perek*)

The following *perakim* are in the Tractate *Uktzin* עוקצין

Kol She-Hu כל שהוא
The 1st *perek* in *Uktzin* deals with roots of garlic and onions, stalks of edible plants, and stalks of figs. (*Uktzin* 1st *perek*).

Zeitim זיתים
The 2nd *perek* in *Uktzin* deals with olives, pomegranate, melons, and all shells. It also deals with eggs, green leaves, cucumbers, and clay vessels. (*Uktzin* 2nd *perek*)

Yesh Tzerichin יש צריכין
The 3rd *perek* in *Uktzin* deals with foods susceptible to uncleanness – intentional or not. It also deals with beasts, wild animals, birds, as well as discussing uncleanness in carcasses of animals, fish, beehives, and honeycombs. (*Uktzin* 3rd *perek*)

Abbreviations

א"א = אברהם אבינו
א"א = אי אמרת
א"א = אי אפשר
א"א = אשת איש
אא"ב = אי אמרת בשלמא
אא"כ = אלא אם כן
אב"א = אי בעית אימא
א"ד = איכא דאמרי
א"ה = אי הכי
אוה"ע = אומות העולם
אח"כ = אחר כך
א"י = ארץ ישראל
א"י = איני יהודי
א"נ = אי נמי
אע"ג = אף על גב
אע"פ = אף על פי
אפ"ה = אפילו הכי
א"ק = אמר קרא
אקב"ו = אשר קדשנו
במצוותיו וצוונו
א"ר = אמר רב אמר רבי
את"ל = אם תמצא לומר

ב"א = בני אדם
ב"ב = בבא בתרא
ב"ד = בית דין
בד"א = במה דברים אמורים
ב"ה = בית הלל
ב"ה = בעל הבית
בה"כ = בית הכנסת
בהמ"ד = בית המדרש
בהמ"ז = ברכת המזון
בהמ"ק = בית המקדש
בו"ד = בשר ודם

ב"ז = בן זכאי
בזה"ז = בזמן הזה
ב"ח = בעל חוב
ב"י = בני ישראל
ביה"ש = בין השמשות
ב"כ = ברכת כהנים
בכ"מ = בכל מקום
במ"מ = בורא מיני מזונות
במ"מ = במה מצינו
בנ"ט = בנותן טעם
בע"ה = בעל הבית
בע"כ = בעל כרחו
בע"פ = בעל פה
בפה"א = בורא פרי האדמה
בפה"ע = בורא פרי העץ
בפ"נ ובפ"נ = בפני נכתב
ובפני נחתם
בפ"ע = בפני עצמו
ב"ש = בית שמאי
בש"א = בית שמאי אומרים

גז"ד = גזר דין
גז"ש = גזירה שוה
ג"ח = גמילות חסדים
ג"ע = גילוי עריות
ג"ע = גן עדן

ד"א = דבר אחר
דא"א = דאמרי אינשי
ד"ה = דברי הכל
ד"ס = דברי סופרים
ד"ת = דבר תורה

הב"ע = הכא במאי עסקינן
ה"ד = היכי דמי

ה"ה = הוא הדין
ה"ז = הרי זה
הלמ"מ = הלכה למשה מסיני
ה"מ = הני מילי
המע"ה = המוציא מחבירו
עליו הראיה
ה"נ = הכי נמי
ה"ק = הכי קאמר

ואצ"ל = ואין צריך לומר
וא"ת = ואם תאמר
וגו' = וגומר
וח"א = וחד אמר
וחכ"א = וחכמים אומרים
וי"א = ויש אומרים
וכ"ת = וכי תימא

זא"ז = זה את זה
ז"ל = זכור לטוב
ז"ל = זכרונם לברכה

ח"א = חד אמר
חה"מ = חול המועד
ח"ו = חס ושלום
חכ"א = חכמים אומרים
ח"ל = חוצה לארץ
חש"ו = חרש שוטה וקטן

י"א = יש אומרים
יה"כ = יום הכפורים
י"ח = ידי חובתו
י"ט = יום טוב
יצה"ר = יצר הרע
יצ"ט = יצר טוב

כ"ג = כהן גדול

כדא"א = כדאמרי אינשי
כה"ג = כהן גדול
כה"ג = כי האי גונא
כה"ג = כנסת הגדולה
כו"כ = כמה וכמה
כ"ז = כל זמן
כ"כ = כל כך
כ"מ = כל מקום
כ"ע = כולי עלמא
כ"פ = כי פליגי
כ"ש = כל שכן

ל"א = לישנא אחרינא
להד"מ = לא היו דברים מעולם
לה"ק = לשון הקודש
לה"ר = לשון הרע
ל"ל = למה לי
ל"מ = לא מיבעי
למה"ד = למה הדבר דומה
לעה"ב = לעולם הבא
ל"צ = לא צריכא
ל"ק = לא קשיא
ל"ש = לא שנא
ל"ת = לא תעשה לא תימא

מא"ל = מאי איכא למימר
מבע"י = מבעוד יום
מ"ד = מן דאמר
מ"ה = מלאכי השרת
מה"ת = מן התורה
מו"מ = משא ומתן
מוצ"ש = מוצאי שבת
מ"ט = מאי טעמא
מלה"ד = משל למה הדבר דומה
מל"ת = מצוות לא תעשה
מ"מ = מכל מקום
ממ"נ = ממה נפשך
מנה"מ = מנא הני מילי
מ"ס = מר סבר
מ"ע = מצוות עשה
מע"ט = מעשים טובים
מע"ר = מעשר ראשון
מע"ש = מעשר שני
מע"ש = מערב שבת
מרע"ה = משה רבינו עליו השלום

מ"ש = מאי שנא
משא"כ = מה שאין כן
מש"ה = משום הכי

נ"ה = נמי הכי
נ"ט = נותן טעם
נט"י = נטילת ידים
נ"מ = נפקא מינה

ס"ד = סלקא דעתך
סד"א = סלקא דעתך אמינא
ס"ל = סבירא

עאכו"כ = על אחת כמה וכמה
ע"ג = על גב
ע"ד = על דבר
ע"ה = עם הארץ
עוה"ב = עולם הבא
עוה"ז = עולם הזה
עה"ר = עין הרע
ע"ז = עבודה זרה
עיו"ט = ערב יום טוב
ע"כ = עד כאן
ע"כ = על כורחו
עכו"ם = עובד כוכבים ומזלות
ע"מ = על מנת
ע"פ = על פי
ע"ש = על שם
ע"ש = ערב שבת

פ"א = פעם אחת

צ"ל = צריך לומר

קא"ל = קא אמר ליה
קה"ק = קודש הקדשים
קה"ת = קריאת התורה
קו"ח = קל וחומר
קי"ל = קיימא לן
קמ"ל = קא משמע לן
ק"ש = קריאת שמע

ר"א = ר' אליעזר
ר"א = ר' אלעזר
ראב"י = ר' אליעזר בן יעקב
ראב"ע = ר' אלעזר בן עזריה
רבש"ע = רבונו של עולם
ר"ג = רבן גמליאל
ר"ה = ראש השנה

רה"י = רשות היחיד
רה"ר = רשות הרבים
רוה"ק = רוח הקדש
ר"ז = רב זירא
ר"ח = ראש חודש
ר"ח = ר' חנינא
ר"ט = ר' טרפון
ר"י = ר' יהושע
ר"י = ר' יוחנן
ר"י = ר' יוסי
ריב"ז = רבן יוחנן בן זכאי
ריב"ל = ר' יהושע בן לוי
ר"ל = ריש לקיש
ר"מ = ר' מאיר
ר"נ = ר' נחמיה
ר"נ = רב נחמן
ר"פ = רב פפא
ר"ש = רב ששת = ר' שמעון
רשב"א = ר' שמעון בן אלעזר
רשב"ג = רבן שמעון בן
גמליאל
רשב"י = ר' שמעון בן יוחai
רשב"ל = ר' שמעון בן לקיש

ש"ד = שפיכות דמים
שהנ"ב = שהכל נהיה בדברו
ש"ח = שומר חינם
שט"ח = שטר חוב
ש"מ = שמע מינה
ש"ע = שמונה עשרה
ש"פ = שוה פרוטה
שפ"ד = שפיכות דמים
ש"צ = שליח צבור
ש"ש = שומר שכיר

ת"ה = תפילת הדרך
ת"ח = תלמיד חכם
תח"מ = תחיית המתים
ת"ל = תלמוד לומר
תנ"ה = תניא נמי הכי
ת"ק = תנא קמא
ת"ר = תנו רבנן
ת"ש = תא שמע
תש"ת = תקיעה שברים תקיעה
ת"ת = תלמוד תורה

Talmudic Expressions

Talmudic sayings, expressions, and axioms as used in the language of the Talmud

---

א

Head of the court   אב בית דין
Rabbi Nathan was the Av Bet Din of the Sanhedrin during the time when R. Shimon b. Gamliel was the Nasi. New protocol was established regarding the honor accorded to the Av Bet Din.
(*Horayot* 13b; *Taanit* 15a)

אב הטומאה
Source of original uncleanness (*Kelim* 1:1)

אב מלאכה
Principal labor forbidden on Shabbat.
(*Shabbat* 68a; *Keritut* 16b)

Principal labor categories   אבות מלאכות
R. Hanina b. Hama said: "The thirty-nine principal labor categories on Shabbat correspond to the forms of labor performed in the Tabernacle." (*Shabbat* 49b, 68a; *Bava Kamma* 2a)

אבילות
Mourning, and what is forbidden to a mourner. (*Moed Katan* 21a)

אבילות שבעה
Mourning time is seven days. (*Moed Katan* 24a; *Moed Katan* 20a; *Yevamot* 43b)

אבינו מלכנו
The Talmud states that R. Akiva prayed *Avinu Malkenu* during a severe drought. Since then, we recite those prayers during the ten days between Rosh Hashana and Yom Kippur, and also on fast days.
(*Taanit* 25b)

אבן שתייה
A stone was under the Temple ark and its name was Shetia. (*Sanhedrin* 26b; *Yoma* 53b)

אבק לשון הרע
Shade of slander (*Bava Batra* 165a)

אבק ריבית
Indirect interest, shade of usury (*Bava Metzia* 61b, 67a)

אבק שביעית
Shade of violating the Sabbatical year
(*Sukkah* 40b; *Kiddushin* 20a; *Arachin* 30b)

אבר מן החי

Eating a limb from a living animal (*Hullin* 101b; *Meilah* 16a)

אגב אורחא

Incidentally, by the way (*Sanhedrin* 95b)

אגדתא

Talmudic stories, sayings and interpretations of the Torah (*Sotah* 40a)

Hire and loss (*Bava Metzia* 69b)   אגרא פגרא

אדם חשוב

A distinguished person (*Avodah Zarah* 28a; *Berachot* 19a)

אדם מקנה דבר שלא בא לעולם

One can transfer that which did not yet come to this world. The opinion of R. Meir. (*Bava Metzia* 33b; *Bava Batra* 79b; *Yevamot* 93a; *Kiddushin* 62b; *Gittin* 13b)

אדם עשוי למשמש בכיסו בכל שעה ושעה

R. Yitzhak said: "A man usually touches his purse at frequent intervals." (*Bava Metzia* 21b; *Bava Kamma* 118b)

אדם קרוב אצל עצמו

A man is his own relative; a person is partial to himself. (*Yevamot* 25b; *Ketubbot* 18b; *Sanhedrin* 9b, 25a)

אדרבה איפכא מסתברא

On the contrary, the reverse stands to reason. (*Pesahim* 28a)

אדרכתא

A halachic document of authorization to seize property. (*Bava Batra* 169a; *Bava Kamma* 112b)

אהבה רבה אהבת עולם

The blessing just before the *Shema* during the morning service starts with two words.

The rabbis discuss which one is more appropriate to say. (*Berachot* 11b)

אהלא

An herb used for medicinal purposes. What is *borit*? It is *ahala* or aloe. (*Shabbat* 90a)

אונאה

Fraud, overcharging (*Bava Metzia* 49b, 55a)

אונאת אשתו

Rav said: "One should be very careful not to wrong his wife with angry words." (*Bava Metzia* 59a)

אונאת דברים

Wronging someone with words (*Bava Metzia* 58b)

Mourner (acute)   אונן, אוננת

The period of mourning immediately after the relative passes away. (*Ketubbot* 53a; *Bava Metzia* 18a; *Yevamot* 29b; *Sanhedrin* 28b; *Moed Katan* 14b)

אורים ותומים

Breastplate worn by the High Priest

We have learned: The Land of Israel was divided among the tribes by the signs from the *Urim Ve-Tumim*. Eleazar the High Priest was dressed with the *Urim Ve-Tumim* on his chest. Yehoshua and all Israel stood before him. One urn contained the names of the tribes and another urn contained the boundaries. Eleazar was inspired by the *Ruah Ha-Kodesh* and gave instructions which tribe gets which land. (*Bava Batra* 122a)

Usha; the academy of the rabbis   אושא

Usha is a town in Israel south of Acco and west of Tiberias. After the suppression of the Bar Kochva revolt, the rabbis of the time convened a meeting at Usha. Present at the meeting were such luminaries as R.

Yehuda bar Illai, R. Nehemia, R. Meir, R. Yosi ben Halafta, R. Shimon ben Yohai, R. Eliezer b. Yosi HaGlili, and R. Eliezer b. Yaakov. R. Shimon b. Gamliel was the head of the Sanhedrin, but he was still in hiding. (*Sanhedrin* 14a; *Ketubbot* 49b, 50a; *Bava Kamma* 89b)

Animal and its young אותו ואת בנו
Slaughtering an animal and its young on the same day is a transgression. (*Hullin* 78a)

Ehad *in the* Shema *prolonged* אחד
It has been taught, Sumchos said: "Whoever prolongs the word *Echad* will have his days prolonged." R. Abba b. Yaakov said the stress is on the *dalet*. R. Yirmiyahu was once sitting before R. Hiyya b. Abba, and R. Hiyya noticed that R. Yirmiyahu was prolonging the *Ehad* very much. He explained to him how long to prolong it. (*Berachot* 13b)

אחריות
Taking on responsibility and risk (*Bava Metzia* 14a, 43a)

אחריות טעות סופר היא
Omission of mortgaging the debtor's property is an error of the scribe. (*Bava Metzia* 14a, 15b; *Ketubbot* 104b; *Bava Batra* 169b)

אטב״ח
According to R. Hiyya, this is a code of the Aleph Bet which was used to keep secrets from the oppressive authorities. (*Sukkah* 52b)

אי אמרת בשלמא
I grant you if you were to say. (*Yoma* 17b)

אי אפשר לצמצם
Impossible to measure exactly (*Bechorot* 17a, 9a)

איגלאי מלתא
The fact became known. (*Sanhedrin* 109b)

איגרות מזון
Deeds of maintenance for widows, orphans (*Bava Metzia* 20a; *Ketubbot* 100b)

איגרות שום
Deeds of valuation (*Bava Metzia* 20a; *Ketubbot* 100b)

איזהו עשיר השמח בחלקו
Who is rich? One who is happy with his portion. (*Avot* 4:1)

איילונית
A woman incapable of bearing children A sexually underdeveloped woman (*Ketubbot* 11a, 100b *Yevamot* 113a; *Bava Metzia* 67a)

Some say (*Hullin* 3b) איכא דאמרי א״ד

אין אבילות בשבת
There is no mourning on the Shabbat. (*Moed Katan* 23b, 24a)

אין אדם אוסר דבר שאינו שלו
One cannot make anything prohibited if the thing does not belong to him. (*Avodah Zarah* 54b)

אין אדם מעיז פניו בפני בעל חובו
No man is so brazen as to deny a claim in the presence of a creditor. (*Bava Kamma* 107a; *Shevuot* 42b; *Bava Metzia* 3a, 5b; *Ketubbot* 18a; *Gittin* 51b)

אין אדם מקדיש דבר שאינו שלו
One cannot dedicate what does not belong to him. (*Arachin* 26b)

אין אדם מקנה דבר שלא בא לעולם
One cannot acquire or transfer that which did not yet come to this world. This is the opinion of the rabbis. (*Bava Metzia* 33b; *Bava*

Batra 79b, 127b; *Gittin* 13b, 42b; *Kiddushin* 62b; *Yevamot* 93a)

אין אדם משים עצמו רשע
Self-incrimination
No man may declare himself wicked. (*Yevamot* 25b; *Ketubbot* 18b; *Sanhedrin* 9b, 25a)

אין אדם מתנה על שני דברים כאחד
Two contingencies simultaneously
R. Ayyo taught that R. Yehuda said: "A person cannot use two contingencies simultaneously." (*Hullin* 14b; *Betzah* 37b; *Eruvin* 36b; *Yoma* 9b)

אין איסור חל על איסור
A prohibition does not apply on a prohibition already in force. (*Yevamot* 13b, 20a; *Hullin* 113b)

אין בגידין בנותן טעם
R. Yishmael b. Beroka said that sinews cannot impart a flavor. (*Hullin* 89b, 99b)

אין בין העוה"ז לימות המשיח אלא שעבוד מלכיות
R. Shemuel said: "There is no difference between this world and the world of Mashiach except bondage of foreign powers. (*Berachot* 34b; *Shabbat* 63a, 151b; *Pesahim* 68a)

אין בית דין יכול לבטל דברי בית דין חבירו אלא א"כ גדול הימנו בחכמה ובמנין
A court is unable to annul the decision of another court, unless it is superior to it in wisdom and numerical strength. (*Avodah Zarah* 36a; *Moed Katan* 3b; *Megillah* 2a; *Gittin* 36b)

אין בית דין שקול
A court is not constituted with even number members. (*Sanhedrin* 3b, 13b)

אין גוזרין גזירה על הצבור אלא אם כן רוב צבור יכולין לעמוד בה
No law may be imposed upon the public

unless a majority of the people can endure it. (*Avodah Zarah* 36a; *Horayot* 3b; *Bava Kamma* 79b; *Bava Batra* 60b)

אין דיחוי אצל מצוות
A positive precept cannot be disabled. (*Hullin* 87a; *Avodah Zarah* 47a; *Sukkah* 33a)

אין הדבר תלוי אלא בי
It all depends on me alone
Eleazar b. Dordia was a vulgar and sinful person. He repented and was granted forgiveness.

Rebbe remarked: "One may acquire eternal life after many years and another may acquire it in one hour." (*Avodah Zarah* 17a)

אין חבין לאדם שלא בפניו
No obligation may be imposed on a person in his absence. (*Eruvin* 81b; *Gittin* 11a; *Kiddushin* 23a)

אין מיעוט אחר מיעוט
We do not apply one limitation after another limitation. (*Yoma* 43a; *Bava Kamma* 86b; *Megillah* 23b; *Bava Batra* 14a; *Sanhedrin* 15a, 46a, 86a; *Shevuot* 7b; *Menahot* 9b; *Makkot* 9b, 67a; *Hullin* 132a)

אין מוקדם ומאוחר בתורה
The Torah is not written in chronological order. (*Pesahim* 6b)

אין מקרא יוצא מידי פשוטו
One cannot depart from the plain meaning of the Torah. (*Shabbat* 63a; *Yevamot* 11b, 24a)

אין סדר למשנה
Mishna is not in its original order
The Mishna has not retained its original order. A general statement is sometimes first, then there are different opinions quoted later. (*Avodah Zarah* 7a)

אין ספק מוציא מידי ודאי

A doubt cannot set aside a certainty.
(*Avodah Zarah* 41b; *Hullin* 10a; *Pesahim* 4b, 9a)

אין עשה דוחה לא תעשה ועשה

When two precepts coincide and one is expressed only in the positive language, it does not supersede a precept given in the positive and negative. (*Shabbat* 25a; *Sanhedrin* 19a; *Betzah* 8b)

אין קנין לנכרי בארץ ישראל

A non-Jew cannot acquire Land in Israel to free the crop from the obligation of tithing. (*Bava Metzia* 101a; *Gittin* 47a; *Menahot* 31a; *Bechorot* 11b)

אין שחיטה לעוף מן התורה

Slaughtering poultry
Some rabbis hold that *shehita* for a bird is not required in the Torah; it is only by rabbinic enactment. (*Hullin* 4a, 20a, 27b, 28a; *Kiddushin* 71a; *Nazir* 25a)

אין שליח לדבר עבירה

Messenger for a transgression
One cannot appoint a messenger to commit a transgression. (*Bava Kamma* 51a, 79a; *Bava Metzia* 10b; *Kiddushin* 42b)

איסור בישול בשר בחלב

Prohibition against cooking meat in milk (*Hullin* 115b; *Kiddushin* 57b)

איסור חל על איסור

A prohibition may apply on another prohibition already in force. (*Hullin* 113b, 114a, 116a; *Yevamot* 32a; *Kiddushin* 77b; *Sanhedrin* 81a; *Keritut* 14a; *Meilah* 16a)

איסור מצווה שניות

Secondary degree prohibition
Secondary degree in relationship to what is forbidden (*Yevamot* 20a)

איסקופה

A threshold
A threshold serves two domains on Shabbat. (*Shabbat* 6a, 9a)

איסרו לחג

Binding to the holiday, adding another day of joy to the holiday. (*Sukkah* 45b)

איפכא מסתברא

On the contrary, the reverse argument is more reasonable. (*Hullin* 20b; *Rosh Hashana* 20a; *Bechorot* 5a)

איתרע שטרא

Impaired document (*Shevuot* 42a)

אכילת עראי

Casual eating (*Sukkah* 25a, 26a)

אכסדרה

An open porch, it has halachic implications (*Bava Batra* 11b)

אלישע בעל כנפים

R. Yannai said: "When wearing *tefillin*, one needs to have a pure body like Elisha the man of wings." (*Shabbat* 49a, 130a)

אלמלא

If not (*Sanhedrin* 49a)

אלמנה ניזונת

A widow is to be maintained of the estate from the deceased husband. (*Ketubbot* 43a, 81a, 95b)

אל"ף בי"ת

The rabbis told R. Yehoshua b. Levi that Aleph Bet letters have special meanings. (*Shabbat* 104a)

אם אין אני לי מי לי

R. Hillel said: "If I don't look out for myself, who will?" (*Avot* 1:14)

אם לא עכשו אימתי

R. Hillel said: "If not now, when?" (*Avot* 1:14)

אם אין קמח אין תורה

R. Eleazar b. Azariah said: "If there is no Torah, there is no good conduct, if there is no good conduct there is no Torah. If there is no wisdom, there is no fear of God; if there is no fear of God, there is no wisdom. If there is no understanding, there is no knowledge; if there is no knowledge, there is no understanding. If there is no food, there is no Torah; if there is no Torah, there is no food." (*Avot* 3:21)

Guesswork (*Avot* 1:16) אמדות

אמן

Resh Lakish said: "He who responds Amen with all his might will have the gates of Gan Eden opened for him." (*Shabbat* 119b)

אמן

R. Hanina said: "'Amen' has the initials for **א״ל מלך נאמן**." (*Shabbat* 119b; *Sanhedrin* 111b)

אמר הממונה

The overseeing officer inquired whether the time has arrived for the morning sacrifices. (*Yoma* 28a)

אמר להם הממונה

The overseeing officer urged them to cast lots to see which Kohen is doing what. (*Tamid* 3rd *perek*)

אמר להם הממונה

The overseeing officer urged them to pronounce the blessing and the rest of the reading. (*Tamid* 5th *perek*)

אנינות

Grief, deep mourning (*Kiddushin* 80b)

אנשי כנסת הגדולה

Men of the Great Assembly (*Avot* 1:1)

אסופי

An *asufi* is one who was picked up from the street and knows neither his father nor his mother. (*Kiddushin* 69a, 74a; *Yevamot* 76a)

אסור בהנאה

It is forbidden to have any benefit or enjoyment from it. (*Bava Kamma* 41a; *Pesahim* 21b, 22a; *Kiddushin* 56b; *Hullin* 114b)

Asimon אסימון

An unofficial coin of metal (*Bava Metzia* 44a, 47b)

אסמכתא

An obligation undertaken in a commercial transaction (*Bava Batra* 168a; *Ketubbot* 67a; *Bava Metzia* 66b)

אסמכתא

Support from a biblical text; a rabbinic enactment which relies on a biblical text. (*Hullin* 64b)

Even though (*Shabbat* 7a) אף על גב

Although (*Yevamot* 54b) אף על פי

אף על פי שחטא ישראל הוא

A Jew is a Jew is a Jew
R. Abba bar Zavda said: "Even though a Jew sinned, he is still a Jew. Thus people say, a myrtle, even when it is mixed in with reeds is still a myrtle and is so called." (*Sanhedrin* 44a)

אפוטרופוס

A stewart appointed by the court (*Bava Metzia* 39a, 66b)

אפותיקי

Mortgaged a particular field (*Bava Kamma* 96a)

אפיקומן

Afikoman is a piece of matzah eaten at the end of the Seder. This matzah was set aside earlier in the Seder meal for this purpose and no food is eaten after the *afikoman*. (*Pesahim* 86a, 119b)

אפיקורוס

What is an *apikoros*? It is someone who does not accept the teachings of the rabbis. Rav and R. Hanina both say an *apikoros* is a person who insults a scholar. (*Sanhedrin* 38b, 90a, 99b)

אפשר לצמצם

It is possible to ascertain. (*Bechorot* 9a, 17b, 18a, 9a; *Shevuot* 32a; *Yevamot* 19a, 88a)

Four cubits　　　　　　　ארבע אמות
R. Abba Kohen Bardella is quoted by Rabbi Shimon ben Lakish that a man's four cubits acquire property for him everywhere. (*Bava Metzia* 10a–b)

ארבעים סאה

Forty *se'ah*, the reqired measurement for a *mikveh* when immersion is mandated. (*Avodah Zarah* 75b)

Distinguished scholar　　　　　ארי
A lion – a name bestowed upon a distinguished scholar. (*Yevamot* 122b)

אריוך

A title of dignity applied to R. Shemuel (*Hullin* 76b; *Shabbat* 53a)

אריס

A tenant who tills the land for a share of the produce. (*Bava Metzia* 74b)

אשם תלוי

Suspended guilt offering (*Keritut* 17b)

Watch of the night (*Berachot* 1a)　אשמורות

אשר יצר

A blessing recited after leaving the toilet. Abbaye composed the very profound blessing of *Asher Yatzar*. This blessing is said when one exits from the toilet after washing hands. (*Berachot* 60b)

אשרה

Certain trees made into idols (*Avodah Zarah* 48a)

את

The word "et" in the Torah adds something
R. Shimon Hamsoni or R. Nehemia Hamsoni derived from every *et* in the Torah to add something, but when he reached the *et* of "to fear God," he could not find anything to fit, and he stopped.

His students said to him: "What will happen to all the other expositions that you have already given?"

He answered them: "Just as I have received reward for the expositions, so will I get reward for withdrawing them." Until R. Akiva came and expounded the *et* to mean all the Torah scholars. (*Bava Kamma* 41b; *Pesahim* 22b; *Kiddushin* 27a; *Bechorot* 6b; *Hagigah* 12a)

א"ת ב"ש

A code written in cryptic letters based on the Hebrew alphabet of Aleph Bet. It exchanges the first letter with the last letter, and the second letter from the beginning with the second letter from the end and so on (Rashi, *Sanhedrin* 22a)

It is similar to *Ahas beta gif* אח"ס בט"ע גי"ף, a combination of letters in a code whereby the first letter is replaced with the eighth letter, as for instance, א is replaced with ח and so on. (*Shabbat* 104a)

אתי דיבור ומבטל דיבור

A word comes to cancel a word. (*Gittin* 32b; *Kiddushin* 59a)

Harlot's hire　　　　　　אתנן זונה
Money received by a harlot for her service. (*Temurah* 29a; *Avodah Zarah* 62b)

ב

בגרת

A young girl twelve and a half years old who is about to mature, adolescence. (*Ketubbot* 39a, 49a; *Sanhedrin* 66b)

בהמה בחייה בחזקת איסור עומדת

An animal while alive is presumed to be forbidden, and remains to be forbidden when dead until it becomes known that it was slaughtered ritually. (*Hullin* 9a; *Betzah* 25a)

בהמה שנשחטה הרי היא בחזקת היתר

An animal slaughtered ritually is presumed to be permitted. (*Hullin* 9a; *Betzah* 25a)

בהעלם אחד

In one state of unawareness (*Shabbat* 104b; *Keritut* 11b, 12b)

On that very day **בו ביום**

A Tanna taught: Whenever the Talmud speaks of "that day," it refers to the day when R. Eleazar b. Azariah was elected as Nasi of the Sanhedrin. On that day every Halachah that was in question before the rabbis was resolved. Even R. Gamliel didn't stay away from the assembly for one hour, in spite of him being removed as president. (*Berachot* 28a; *Yadayim* 4:4)

בודק חמץ

A search is made for leavened bread. (*Pesahim* 2a)

Borei Minei Mezonot **בורא מיני מזונות**

We make this blessing on cake and the like. (*Berachot* 36b)

Chosen judge **בורר**

Disputes in monetary matters are judged by three. Each litigant chooses one and the two choose a third one. (*Sanhedrin* 23a; *Bava Metzia* 20a)

ביטול מקח

A transaction in business that was nullified. (*Bava Metzia* 50b)

בין השמשות

Twilight (*Bava Kamma* 32a; *Shabbat* 34b, 35b, 137a)

בינונים בינונית

Medium quality (*Rosh Hashana* 16b; *Bava Kamma* 7b; *Gittin* 48b)

ביקור חולים

Visiting the sick (*Bava Kamma* 99b, 100a; *Bava Metzia* 30b)

בישולי נכרים

Cooked by non-Jews (*Avodah Zarah* 38a; *Betzah* 16a; *Shabbat* 20a; *Shevuot* 17b)

בית אבטינס

A chamber at the Temple that had an upper floor where the young priests kept watch. (*Tamid* 2a; *Shekalim* 5:1)

בית גרמו

Officer of the Temple (*Shekalim* 5:1)

בית דין

A court of judges (*Sanhedrin* 2a; *Bava Metzia* 32a; *Ketubbot* 97a)

בית דין הדיוטות

A court of non-expert judges (*Bava Metzia* 32a)

בית דין חצוף

An impudent court (*Sanhedrin* 3a, 5b, 30a, 87b; *Ketubbot* 22a)

בית דין מומחין

A court of expert judges (*Bava Metzia* 32a)

בית דין נוטה

A court with an odd number of judges (*Sanhedrin* 3b)

בית דין שקול
A court with an even number of judges
(*Sanhedrin* 3b, 13b)

בית הכנסת
Synagogue (*Berachot* 6a; *Megillah* 27a)

בית המדרש
House of study (*Megillah* 27a)

בית המוקד
A chamber in the Temple where the Elders of the priests slept. They had the keys to the different chambers. (*Tamid* 2a)

בית המקדש
Holy Temple (*Bava Batra* 60b)

בית הניצוץ
A chamber in the Temple that had an upper floor where the young priests kept watch during the night. (*Tamid* 2a)

בית הפרס
An area where graves might be located. (*Ohalot* 17:1; *Niddah* 57a; *Berachot* 19b; *Eruvin* 30b; *Moed Katan* 5b; *Hagigah* 25b; *Pesahim* 92b; *Ketubbot* 28b; *Bechorot* 29a)

בית חוניו
The Temple erected by Onias the 4th in Leontopolis Egypt. It was modeled after the Temple in Jerusalem. (*Menahot* 109a; *Avodah Zarah* 52b)

בית שערים
Bet Shearim is an ancient city in lower Galilee. It was the seat of the Sanhedrin during Rabbi Yehuda HaNasi's tenure. During the time of R. Yehuda there were hundreds of students studying in his academy. The Mishna – upon which the whole Gemara is based – was redacted by Rabbi Yehuda HaNasi and he did most of his editing in Bet Shearim. Rabbi Yehuda HaNasi is buried there. (*Sanhedrin* 32b; *Ketubbot* 103b)

ביתוסי
Bithusian, a sect similar to the Tzadokis
(*Shabbat* 108a)

בכו לאבלים ולא לאבידה
Weep for the mourners and not for the deceased. (*Moed Katan* 25b)

בכי יותן
Bechi yutan is a Talmudic term for a situation where food became wet unintentionally. However, the owner welcomes the liquid that fell upon the food. (*Hullin* 16a; *Shabbat* 11b; *Machshirin* 1:1)

בל יראה ובל ימצא
Regarding leavened bread on Pesach – it should not be seen and it should not be found. (*Pesahim* 46b)

בל תחסום
You shall not muzzle. (*Bava Metzia* 90a)

בל תשחית
A commandment; "You shall not destroy." (*Shabbat* 129a, 140b)

במה דברים אמורים בד"א
This applies only. (*Hullin* 3a)

בן סורר ומורה
A rebellious and disobedient son (*Sanhedrin* 68b; *Niddah* 52a)

בני ברק
During the 2nd century CE in Tannaic times, Bene Berak became a center of Jewish learning. Rabbi Akiva ben Yosef established his academy there. (*Sanhedrin* 32b)

Main rule בנין אב
It is one of the thirteen methods and principles of biblical interpretation by R. Yishmael. (*Bava Kamma* 77b; *Hullin* 78b)

בנין דכרין

Male children (*Bava Kamma* 89b; *Bava Batra* 131a; *Ketubbot* 52b)

בנן נוקבין

Female children (*Ketubbot* 52b; *Bava Batra* 131a)

בנן של קדושים

Sons of the holy. This referred to R. Menahem son of R. Simai. He would not gaze even at a coin that had an image on it. (*Avodah Zarah* 50a; *Pesahim* 104a)

בסיס לדבר האסור

A stand for that which is forbidden (*Shabbat* 117a)

בסיס לדבר המותר

A stand for that which is permitted (*Shabbat* 117a)

בעל תשובה

R. Avohu said: "In the place where the *baalei teshuva* stand, even the most righteous cannnot stand." (*Berachot* 34b; *Sanhedrin* 99a)

בפרהסיא

A prohibited act done in public (*Avodah Zarah* 27b, 54a)

בצנעא

A prohibited act done hidden from others (*Avodah Zarah* 27b, 54a)

ברוך שם

The rabbis were discussing how to recite the words "*Baruch Shem*." R. Avohu said it should be said aloud, because if it was said quietly, the heretics might accuse the worshippers of cursing them in quiet. But in Nehardea, where there were no heretics, they said it in a low voice. (*Pesahim* 56a)

ברוך שם כבוד מלכותו לעולם ועד

R. Shimon b. Lakish said: "Yaakov wanted

to reveal to his sons the end of days . . ." (*Pesahim* 56a)

ברוריה

The Talmud relates that Berurya, Rabbi Meir's wife was the daughter of Rabbi Hanania b. Teradion. (*Avodah Zarah* 18a)

ברייתא

Similar to a Mishna in learning, but not incorporated in the Talmud. (*Shabbat* 19b, 61a; *Eruvin* 19b; *Pesahim* 101b; *Gittin* 45a; *Arachin* 30a)

ברירה

A subsequent selection reveals retrospectively what the original intent was. (*Bava Kamma* 51b, 69b; *Bava Batra* 27b; *Betzah* 39b; *Nedarim* 45b)

ברית

ברית *to be mentioned in Haaretz of* ברכת המזון

R. Illai said in the name of R. Yaakov b. Aha, in the name of Rabbeinu: "Whoever omits the mention of *Brit* and *Torah* in the blessing of *Haaretz*, which is part of *Birkat Hamazon*, has not fulfilled his obligation." (*Berachot* 49a)

ברכו את ה' המבורך

In the synagogue, when there is a *minyan*, the *hazan* says: ברכו את ה' המבורך. (*Berachot* 49b)

ברכת המזון

On the days of Rosh Hodesh one should mention *Yaaleh Ve-Yavoh* in the After-meal blessing. (*Shabbat* 24a)

ברכת כהנים

The proper way of performing the Blessing of the Kohanim, what they should do and what they are not to do (*Sotah* 39b)

בשלמא
It is well; it can be acceptable. (*Shabbat* 7a)

בשמים
Blessing over spices at the end of Shabbat during *Havdalah* (*Berachot* 51b)

בשר בחלב
Boiling or eating meat and milk together (*Hullin* 103b, 104b, 107b)

בת קול
The rabbis were meeting in the upper chamber in Yavne when they heard a heavenly voice say: "There is one amongst you who is worthy that the Shechina should rest upon him." The rabbis present directed their gaze on Shemuel HaKatan (*Sanhedrin* 11a)

ג

גבאי צדקה
Charity overseer (*Bava Metzia* 38a; *Bava Batra* 8b; *Pesahim* 13a)

גבאי תמחוי
Overseer of the soup kitchen (*Bava Metzia* 38a; *Bava Batra* 8b; *Pesahim* 13a)

גבעון
The Tabernacle was moved from Shiloh to Givon. (*Zevahim* 112b; *Megillah* 10a)

גוג ומגוג
The wars of Gog U'Magog (*Sanhedrin* 95b, 97b)

גוד אחית
A wall or partition that is close to but does not reach the ground is deemed halachically as continuing downward and touching the ground. (*Eruvin* 87a; *Shabbat* 101a)

גוד אסיק
A wall or partition that is close to but does not reach the ceiling is deemed halachically as continuing upward and touching the ceiling. (*Sukkah* 4b)

גולל ודופק
Stone covering the grave (*Hullin* 72a)

גזירה
A decree or an ordinance
R. Yishmael b. Elisha said: "We do not issue a *gezera* on the community unless the majority can endure it." (*Bava Batra* 60b)

גזירה שוה
Word analogy, similar words – it is one of the thirteen methods and principles of biblical interpretation by R. Yishmael. (*Shabbat* 97a; *Pesahim* 66a; *Niddah* 19b)

גט
Divorce
If a messenger brings a document of divorce from overseas, he must state that it was signed in his presence. (*Gittin* 2a, 15a)

גט פשוט
A plain contract document (*Bava Batra* 160a; *Kiddushin* 49a)

גיד הנשה
Sciatic nerve
There is a prohibition to eat the sciatic nerve. (*Hullin* 89b)

גלגל
The Tabernacle was in Gilgal for fourteen years. (*Zevahim* 112b)

גלגל שבועה
A rollover oath – if by chance an oath is imposed by the court on a person in an unrelated case, the court can make him swear also in another case. (*Shevuot* 45a, 48b)

גלוי וידוע

The matter is open and revealed. (*Shabbat* 55a; *Berachot* 3b; *Sanhedrin* 16a)

Loving-kindness   גמילות חסדים

R. Eleazar stated: "The performance of charity is greater than offering all the sacrifices."

R. Eleazar further stated: "The act of *gemilut hasadim* is greater than charity."

He also stated: "The reward of charity is dependent on the kindness in it." (*Sukkah* 49b; *Bava Kamma* 100a)

גר תושב

A proselyte settler, a gentile who renounces idolatry. (*Avodah Zarah* 64b, 65a)

ד

דבי אליהו

It was taught in D'bei Eliyahu: The world is to exist 6,000 years; the first 2,000 years are to be void, the next 2,000 years are the period of Torah, and the following 2,000 years are the time of Mashiach. (*Avodah Zarah* 9a)

דבי חזקיה

Rabbi Hezkiya is the author of the *D'bei Hezkiya* (meaning, it was taught in the school of Hezkiya). (*Sanhedrin* 37b; *Ketubbot* 30a; *Sotah* 8b)

דבי רבי ישמעאל

The school of R. Yishmael taught: The Torah stated three times: "You shall not cook a kid in its mother's milk." One is a prohibition against eating, one against deriving benefit, and one against cooking it. (*Hullin* 115b; *Kiddushin* 57b)

דבר הגורם לממון כממון דמי

A matter where money is to be extracted is equivalent to money.

An act causing an outlay of money is considered in law as money. (*Bava Kamma* 71b, 98b; *Shevuot* 32a; *Pesahim* 29b)

דבר הלמד מעניינו

The meaning of a subject is deduced from its context. (*Hullin* 63a)

דבר שיש בו דעת לישאל

A being that is rational, has a mind and can be interrogated. (*Sotah* 28b; *Pesahim* 19b; *Niddah* 4b, 5b)

דברה תורה בלשון בני אדם

The Torah uses the ordinary form of expression used by human beings. (*Berachot* 31b; *Bava Metzia* 31b, 94b)

דברי הימים

The author of the book of Divrei Hayamim was the Prophet Ezra. Others name different authors. (*Bava Batra* 15a)

דברי סופרים

Enactment by the scribes, a ruling by the rabbis (*Yevamot* 84a; *Sanhedrin* 53b; *Kiddushin* 50a; *Bava Batra* 48a; *Hullin* 106a)

דוכסוסטוס

A parchment from which the upper layer has been removed. (*Shabbat* 78b, 79b)

דייתיקי

Disposition of property by a contract, by will and testament (*Bava Batra* 152b)

דינא דמלכותא דינא

R. Shemuel said: "The law of the land is the law." One has to obey the laws of the land in which he lives. (*Bava Kamma* 113a; *Bava Batra* 54b; *Gittin* 10b; *Nedarim* 28a)

דיעבד

An issue after the act was done or an act in unusual circumstances. (*Hullin* 2a)

דם הקזה

First blood (*Keritut* 22a)

דם התמצית

Secondary blood (*Keritut* 22a)

דמאי

Doubtful if tithed (*Pesahim* 35b; *Shabbat* 127b; *Berachot* 47a; *Eruvin* 37a)

דרישה וחקירה

The process of enquiry and examination of witnesses (*Sanhedrin* 32a; *Yevamot* 122b)

דרכי שלום

When the rabbis instituted the Halachah, they paid great attention for the sake of peace. (*Bava Metzia* 12a; *Gittin* 6a)

דררא דממונא

Monetary loss (*Bava Metzia* 2b)

ה

ה' שפתי תפתח ופי יגיד תהלתך

Amidah beginning
R. Yohanan said: "One begins the *Amidah* with the above words." (*Berachot* 4b, 9b)

הבדלה

Blessing over a lit torch at the end of Shabbat during *Havdalah* (*Berachot* 51b; *Pesahim* 103a)

הדיוט

Ordinary man (*Megillah* 12b)

הדרת פנים

A man with a beard, which enhances his looks (*Bava Metzia* 84a)

הודה במקצת

Admitting to a portion of it (*Shevuot* 38b, 40b)

הודה מקצת הטענה

Admitting to part of the claim (*Bava Metzia* 4b; *Bava Batra* 128b)

הוה אמינא אדרבה

I might have said on the contrary. (*Pesahim* 77a)

החדש הזה

When do they read *Parshat Ha-Hodesh Ha-Zeh*? (*Megillah* 29a)

החוזר בו ידו על התחתונה

Whichever party cancels the contract is at a disadvantage. (*Bava Metzia* 76a, 77b; *Bava Kamma* 102a; *Avodah Zarah* 7a)

הטוב והמטיב

The One Who is kind and Who deals with kindness. This is a blessing to be said on special occasions. (*Taanit* 31a; *Berachot* 48b)

היזק שאינו ניכר

A damage caused without a visible sign (*Gittin* 41a, 44b, 53a; *Moed Katan* 13a; *Bechorot* 35a; *Bava Kamma* 5a)

היסח הדעת

Mental neglect
Mental unawareness (*Pesahim* 34a)

הכל לפי המבייש והמתבייש

All according to the social position of the insulted and the insulter (*Bava Kamma* 83b; *Ketubbot* 40a)

הלכה למשה מסיני

It is a command by Moshe from Sinai. (*Kiddushin* 38b; *Orlah* 3:9)

המבייש את הישן

Shaming a sleeping person (*Bava Kamma* 8:1)

המדבר אחד בפה ואחד בלב

Speaking not with his full heart
One who speaks from both sides of his mouth — he speaks one thing with his mouth and another in his heart. (*Pesahim* 113b)

המוציא מחבירו עליו הראיה

Proving the case falls on claimant

The onus of proving the case falls on the claimant. He who claims from the other has to produce proof. (*Bava Kamma* 35a–b, 46a; *Bava Metzia* 2b; *Hullin* 134a)

המלבין את פני חבירו ברבים אין לו חלק לעוה"ב

One who publicly puts to shame another person has no portion in the World to Come. (*Bava Metzia* 59a)

המלבין פני חבירו ברבים כאילו שופך דמים

Shaming a person in public

A Tanna said before R. Nahman b. Yitzhak: "Anyone who shames another person in public is equal to shedding the blood of another person." (*Bava Metzia* 58b, 59a)

המלך הקדוש המלך המשפט

The text of the prayers changes during the days between Rosh Hashana and Yom Kippur. (*Berachot* 12b)

המשנה ידו על התחתונה

Whichever party changes the terms of the contract is at a disadvantage. (*Bava Metzia* 76a, 77b; *Bava Kamma* 102a; *Avodah Zarah* 7a)

המתנה על מה שכתוב בתורה

Making a condition in a contract contrary to that which is written in the Torah. (*Bava Metzia* 94a; *Ketubbot* 83a; *Kiddushin* 19b)

הנאה

Enjoyment – to enjoy or to get some benefit from a forbidden object. (*Bava Kamma* 41a; *Pesahim* 22b; *Kiddushin* 56b)

העלם אחד

All in one state of unawareness (*Shabbat* 70b; *Sanhedrin* 62a; *Shevi'it* 19a, 26a; *Keritut* 3b)

Sunset (*Yoma* 6a) הערב השמש

הפה שאסר הוא הפה שהתיר

The mouth that prohibited is the mouth that can permit it. (*Ketubbot* 16a)

Minor loss הפסד מועט
(*Bava Kamma* 117a; *Shabbat* 154b)

Major loss הפסד מרובה
(*Bava Kamma* 117a; *Shabbat* 154b)

הפקר

When property is declared abandoned, it has halachic consequences.[1] (*Bava Metzia* 30b; *Peah* 6:1)

Separation הפרשה
(*Yoma* 8b; *Demai, perek* 2)

הפרת נדרים

Vows annulled by a close relative (*Nedarim* 67 ff.; *Yevamot* 29b; *Ketubbot* 39a, 46b; *Kiddushin* 4a)

Common denominator הצד השוה שבהן
(*Bava Metzia* 4a; *Hullin* 114a; *Kiddushin* 5b)

הר גריזים

Blessings on Har Gerizim (*Sotah* 32a)

Curses on Har Eival (*Sotah* 32a) הר עיבל

השג יד

According to his means (*Arachin* 5a, 17a)

השמר פן אל

R. Avin said in the name of R. Illai: "Whenever it is written in the Torah the words: *hishamer, pen,* and *al* - it is a negative precept." (*Eruvin* 96a; *Makkot* 13b; *Shevuot* 4a, 36a; *Sotah* 5a; *Avodah Zarah* 51b; *Zevahim* 106a; *Menahot* 99b)

התורה חסה על ממונן של ישראל

The Torah wished to spare Israel

---

1. See entry, Hefker.

unnecessary expense. (*Rosh Hashana* 27a; *Yoma* 39a, 44b; *Menahot* 76b, 86b, 88b, 89a; *Hullin* 49b, 77a)

Warning to an offender התראה
According to the Torah, a death sentence may be executed only by a court of twenty-three. In addition, to execute a death sentence, it is required to have proper eyewitness testimony, proper warning given to the offender, and the warners must advise the person that a death sentence may follow. (*Sanhedrin* 8b, 80b)

התרת נדרים
Vows invalidated by a court (*Nedarim* 20b; *Nazir* 11b)

ו

והלא דין הוא
This cannot be so because a fortiori would point us to a different conclusion. (*Hullin* 22b, 23b)

ווֹרידין
R. Yehuda said one must cut through the jugular veins. (*Hullin* 19a, 27a, 28b)

Travels of the Ark ויהי בנסוע הארון
Our rabbis taught: Hashem provided signs for this *parsha* at the beginning and at the end, because it ranks as a separate book. (*Shabbat* 115b, 116a)

ויכולו השמים
When praying alone without a *minyan*, should this prayer also be recited? (*Shabbat* 119b)

Derivative uncleanness ולד הטומאה
A ritual uncleanness derived from an original uncleanness. (*Taharot* 1:5)

וסת
A woman who has a regular date for the menstrual period. (*Niddah* 2a, 63a)

ורפא ירפא
R. Yishmael said: From ורפא ירפא we learn that a doctor has the permission to heal the sick. (*Bava Kamma* 84a)

ושט
The gullet in a bird and animal (*Hullin* 10a, 28a)

ז

זאת אומרת
The subject or the rule discussed applies only. (*Hullin* 3a)

זב
Discharge from a male (*Niddah* 36b, 68b)

זבה
Discharge from a female (*Niddah* 36b, 68b)

זה וזה גורם
A product or an act of combined causes (*Avodah Zarah* 49a; *Temurah* 30b; *Pesahim* 27a)

זה נהנה וזה חסר
In a transaction, one party benefits and the other loses. (*Bava Kamma* 20a–b; *Yoma* 22b)

זה נהנה וזה לא חסר
In a transaction, one party benefits and the other is not losing anything. (*Bava Kamma* 20b; *Yoma* 22b)

Property of inferior quality זיבורית
(*Bava Kamma* 7b; *Gittin* 48b)

זימון
Three people eating together are to say the After-meal blessing together. (*Berachot* 45a)

Abbreviations

זיקה

A widowed woman waiting to be married to the brother of her dead husband, in a Levirate marriage. (*Yevamot* 17b, 30a, 51a, 53a)

זכין לאדם שלא בפניו

A benefit can be conferred on a person in his absence. (*Eruvin* 81b; *Gittin* 11b; *Kiddushin* 23a)

זקן ממרא

An elderly person rebelling against the ruling of the Bet Din (*Sanhedrin* 86b)

זרוע לחיים והקבה

The shoulder, the two cheeks, and the maw (*Hullin* 130a)

ח

חביתים

The griddle cakes in the Temple (*Menahot* 96a)

חבלו של משיח

The birth pangs before Mashiach comes (*Sanhedrin* 98b)

חג״בש (חלב גבינה בצלים שחלים)

After bloodletting, one should not eat milk, cheese, onions, and pepper. (*Avodah Zarah* 29a; *Nedarim* 54b)

החוט המשולש לא במהרה ינתק

A triple twisted cord will not break easily
The Talmud tells us that Rabbi Hama left his home and spent twelve years in the academy to study Torah. When he returned home, he stopped at the local academy before going home. A young man entered the academy and sat down next to him and asked him a question on the subject of study. When R. Hama saw the great knowledge this young man possessed, he became depressed. He was thinking, *Had I been here, I also could have had such a son.* After he finally went home, the young man followed him and knocked on the door. Believing that he came to ask him another question, he rose before him as he entered the house. His wife broke out in laughter: "What kind of father stands up before his son?" The young man that followed him happened to be Rabbi Oshaya, his son. It was said of them, a threefold cord is not quickly broken. (*Ketubbot* 62b; *Bava Batra* 59a) *Father and son disagreed about a halachic matter; the grandfather sides with grandson* There was a dispute between R. Hama and R. Oshaya. R. Hama, the father, ruled one way, and R. Oshaya, the son, ruled differently. They went to ask R. Bisa, the grandfather. He decided in favor of R. Oshaya, his grandson. Rami b. Hama applied to them the verse: "A threefold cord is not easily broken." This is exemplified by R. Oshaya, the grandson, R. Hama, the son, and R. Bisa, the grandfather. (*Bava Batra* 59a; *Ketubbot* 62b; *Kiddushin* 40b)

חוט השדרה

Spinal cord (*Hullin* 45b; *Ketubbot* 7a)

חזקה

Presumptive title to a property; a title to a property not supported by documents or witnesses, but based only on possession. (*Bava Batra* 28a)

חזקה אין אדם מעמיד עצמו על ממונו

No man will let his property be taken without resistance. (*Sanhedrin* 72a; *Yoma* 85b)

חיי שעה

Life of the hour (*Avodah Zarah* 27b)

חילול השם

Profanation of the Name (*Avodah Zarah* 28a)

חילוק מלאכות

Separation of labors for Shabbat and Yom Tov (*Makkot* 21b)

חליצה

When one brother dies childless, one of the remaining brothers must marry the widow. However, if he refuses, he must perform the ceremony of *halitza*. It also involves taking off the shoe. (*Yevamot* 2a)

Fifteenth day of Av   חמשה עשר באב

R. Shimon b. Gamliel said: "There were no happier days for Israel than the Fifteenth day of Av and the day of Yom Kippur. For on those days, the daughters of Jerusalem used to go out dressed in white garments, borrowed in order not to shame the ones who had none. They went out and danced in the vineyards. They called out: 'Young man, lift up your eyes and see what you will select for yourself. Set not your eyes on beauty but fix your eyes on family. For grace is deceitful and beauty is vain.'" (*Taanit* 26b; *Bava Batra* 121a)

חמתה מרובה מצלתה

The sun is more than the shade; it matters with regards to a *sukkah*.
(*Sukkah* 9b)

חציו עבד וחציו בן חורין

Half-servant and half-free – the servant belonged to two persons. One freed the slave, and the other did not. (*Gittin* 4a; *Pesahim* 88a; *Hagigah* 2a; *Bava Batra* 13a)

חציצה

A Talmudic term; when an object intervenes between the body and the water during immersion. (*Bava Kamma* 82a; *Sukkah* 6a; *Eruvin* 4b)

חצרו של אדם קונה לו שלא מדעתו

A man's courtyard acquires property for him even without his knowledge. (*Bava Metzia* 11a, 102a, 118a; *Bava Kamma* 49b; *Hullin* 141b)

חקירת עדים

The process of examining and investigating the witnesses for the purpose of establishing the new month. (*Rosh Hashana* 24a, 25b)

חקירות ובדיקות

R. Kahana and R. Safra studied at Rabbah. They encountered Rami b. Hama and they were discussing the difference between *hakirot* and *bedikot*. (*Sanhedrin* 41b)

Excommunication   חרם
A Rabbi was put in Herem

Shila b. Avina decided a matter according to Rav, but when Rav was on his deathbed, he said to R. Assi:

"Go and restrain him and if he does not listen, try to convince him." After Rav passed away R. Assi asked him to retract, because Rav had retracted his ruling.

R. Shila said: "If Rav had retracted he would have told me." He refused to retract. Thereupon, R. Assi put him under the ban.

R. Shila asked him: "Are you not afraid of the fire?" He answered: "I am Issi b. Yehuda, who is Issi b. Gur-aryeh, who is Issi b. Gamliel, who is Issi b. Mahalalel, a cooper mortar, which does not rust."

The other retorted: "I am Shila b. Avina, an iron mallet that breaks the cooper mortar."

Soon after this incident, R. Assi became very sick and died. R. Shila told his wife: "Prepare my shrouds, because I don't want him to have the opportunity to tell Rav things about me." When R. Shila departed, people saw a myrtle fly from one grave to the other. We may conclude that the rabbis have made peace. (*Niddah* 36b)

ט

טבול יום

Someone who requires immersion in the *mikveh* has a special status on the day of his immersion. After he immerses, he is called a *tevul yom*. (*Parah* 8:7)

Tiberias; Academy   טבריא

Tiberias is a city in Eretz Yisrael on the western shore of Lake Kinneret. Tiberias was also the seat of the famous rabbinical academy in Eretz Yisrael. The graves of several great Sages are in Tiberias, among them Rabbi Yohanan ben Zakkai, Rabbi Akiva, Rabbi Meir Baal HaNes, Rabbi Ammi, and Rabbi Assi. Several of the great Amoraim taught there, including R. Yohanan, R. Shimon b. Lakish, R. Eleazar b. Pedat, R. Ammi b. Nathan, and R. Assi.

The following were the heads of the academy in Tiberias: Yohanan ben Nepaha, 3rd century CE; Eleazar ben Pedat, 3rd century CE; Yehuda Nesiah, 3rd century CE; Ammi bar Nathan 3rd – 4th centuries CE; Assi, 3rd – 4th centuries CE; Yehuda Nesiah III, 3rd – 4th centuries CE; Hillel II, 4th century CE; Yirmiyahu b. Abba, 4th century CE; Yonah, 4th century CE; Yosi, 4th century CE. (*Shabbat* 38b, 39a–b; *Betzah* 16b)

טופס

The general part of a document; it may be written in advance. It does not include the name or the date. (*Bava Metzia* 7b; *Hagigah* 6b)

טעם לפגם

Imparts a worsened flavor (*Avodah Zarah* 36a, 39a–b, 75b)

טריפה

An animal afflicted with a fatal organic disease is not kosher and is called *terefa*. (*Hullin* 32a, 42a)

י

יאוש

Renunciation, giving up hope of ever recovering the item. (*Bava Kamma* 66a–b, 67a–b, 68a, 114a; *Bava Metzia* 21b)

יאוש שלא מדעת

Unconscious renunciation, giving up unconsciously (*Bava Metzia* 21b)

Levirate marriage   יבום

(*Yevamot* 2a)

Yavne; Academy   יבנה

Yavne is an ancient biblical city located south of Yaffa and north of Ashdod. After the fall of Jerusalem, the Sanhedrin moved its location from Jerusalem to Yavne. At first, the Sanhedrin was under the leadership of Rabbi Yohanan ben Zakkai, but later Rabbi Gamliel II became Nasi.

The academy in Yavne was called The Sanhedrin. It served not only as an academy of learning, but also as the highest court in the land. It was an institution where the law was promulgated. The Sanhedrin met in the upper floor of a certain house in a vineyard, hence the academy was called "The Vineyard at Yavne" (Kerem Be-Yavne, כרם ביבנה).

It is stated, when the rabbis entered the vineyard of Yavne, there were among them Rabbi Yehuda, Rabbi Yosi, Rabbi Nehemya, and Rabbi Eliezer ben Yosi HaGlili. They all spoke in honor of hospitality and they expounded on the text of the Torah. When it came to Rabbi Nehemya's turn, he also praised hospitality and cited texts from the Torah and book of Shmuel.

Yavne at one time was a thriving city and it had its own cattle market and wheat market. It was already a center for Torah study even before the destruction of the Second Temple. Even in the old days, it had a Bet Din of twenty-three members which decided capital cases. The following were the heads of the academy in Yavne: Eleazar ben Azariah, He lived in the 1st – 2nd centuries CE, and Gamliel ben Shimon De-Yavne. He lived in the 1st – 2nd centuries CE. (*Sanhedrin* 89a)

ידו של אדם חשובה לו כד' על ד'

A man's hand is equal to him as an area of four by four (*Shabbat* 5a; *Ketubbot* 31b)

יהא מונח עד שיבא אליהו

Retained by the court until the coming of Eliyahu (*Bava Metzia* 3a, 37a)

יהושפט

King of Judea

Every time King Yehoshafat saw a Torah scholar, he got up from his throne and called the scholar: "Father, Father, Rebbee Mori." (*Makkot* 24a; *Ketubbot* 103b)

יוחנן or יונתן

Rav and R. Hanina, R. Yohanan and R. Haviva learned the entire Seder of Moed. Whenever they learned the name of R. Yohanan, they substituted it to R. Yonatan (*Shabbat* 54b; *Sukkah* 4b; *Megillah* 7a)

יוחנן כהן גדול

King of Judea, also called John Hyrcanus, was king of Judea from 135 to 105 BCE. He was the son of Simon the Hasmonean and a grandson of the famous Matityahu, who started the Chanukah revolt against Antiochus Epiphanies. (*Berachot* 29a; *Yoma* 9a)

יוצא דופן

A child born by caesarean section. (*Niddah* 40 a,b, 41a)

יין מבושל

Boiled wine has halachic implications. (*Avodah Zarah* 30a)

יין נסך

Wine of libation, wine which is known or suspected of having been dedicated or manipulated for idolatrous libation. (*Hullin* 4b; *Avodah Zarah* 65b)

יין נר קידוש הבדלה

When Yom Tov falls on Sunday, one needs to make several blessings on Motzei Shabbat: on wine, on a candle, *Kiddush*, and *Havdalah*. The order in which the blessings are made is disputed among the rabbis – each has a formula in abbreviated letters.

The abbreviated formulas are as follows: ינהק יקנה יהנק קניה נהיק יקנהז יקזנה (*Pesahim* 103a; *Berochot* 51b, 52b)

יין סוד

When wine goes in the secret comes out.

The sons of R. Hiyya, Yehuda and Hezkiya, were having dinner with R. Yehuda HaNasi and they said something improper. Rebbe was unhappy. R. Hiyya intervened and said: "Rebbe, be not angry; the numerical value of the Hebrew letters for wine is the same as the Hebrew letters for Secret. You had them drink wine, when wine goes in, the secret comes out." (*Sanhedrin* 38a)

ילתא

R. Nahman b. Yaakov was married to Yalta, the daughter of the Exilarch. (*Berachot* 51b; *Hullin* 124a)

יעלקג"מ – יאוש לחי קדושין גלוי מומר

Initials indicating where we rule like Abbaye in these six cases: (*Bava Metzia* 22b; *Sanhedrin* 27a; *Bava Kamma* 73a; *Kiddushin* 52a)

ירעה עד שיסתאב

Left to pasture until it develops a blemish (*Yoma* 62a; *Shevuot* 12a; *Temurah* 22a, 23a)

יש אם למסורת

Tradition is a determinant in biblical exegesis. (*Kiddushin* 18b; *Sukkah* 6b)

יש אם למקרא

The written and read text is a determinant in biblical exegesis. (*Kiddushin* 18b; *Sukkah* 6b; *Sanhedrin* 4a; *Pesahim* 86b; *Bechorot* 34a; *Keritut* 17b; *Makkot* 7b)

יש קנין לנכרי בארץ ישראל

A non-Jew can acquire land in Israel to free the crop from tithing. The rabbis disagree. (*Bava Metzia* 101a; *Gittin* 47a; *Menahot* 31a; *Bechorot* 11b)

יש שחיטה לעוף מן התורה

Some rabbis hold that *shehita* for a bird is from the Torah. (*Hullin* 20b, 27b, 28a, 75b; *Kiddushin* 71a; *Nazir* 29a)

ישנה לשכירות מתחילה ועד סוף

There is liability for hire from the beginning to the end. (*Bava Kamma* 99a)

כ

כהן גדול

The procedure to prepare the High Priest for Yom Kippur. (*Yoma* 2a; *Horayot* 13a)

כהן משיח

The anointed High Priest; this title was given to the High Priest of the First Temple when he was anointed with the holy anointing oil. (*Horayot* 6b)

כוי

R. Yosi and R. Yehuda said: "A *quee* is a separate creature of animal; it is unusual and a strange animal." The rabbis differ on what it is. (*Hullin* 80a; *Yoma* 74a–b; *Keritut* 21a)

כוסו כיסו כעסו

R. Illai said: "One can recognize a person's character by three things: his cup, his purse, and his anger. (*Eruvin* 65b)

כופין אותו עד שיאמר רוצה אני

He is subjected to pressure until he says: "I am willing." This tactic is used by the rabbis in divorce cases and in *halitza*. (*Yevamot* 106a; *Arachin* 21a; *Kiddushin* 50a)

כותים גרי אריות הן

Sectarian non-Jews living in the Land of Israel; they are considered to be forced conversions. (*Hullin* 3b; *Kiddushin* 75b; *Bava Kamma* 38b; *Sanhedrin* 85b; *Niddah* 56b)

Like an olive **כזית**

A halachic measurement (*Eruvin* 4b; *Berachot* 41b; *Shabbat* 112b)

כי

Resh Lakish said: "The word '*ki*' can be used to have four meanings: if, perhaps, but, and because." (*Gittin* 90a; *Shevuot* 49b; *Rosh Hashana* 3b; *Taanit* 9b)

כי אזלינן בתר רובא באיסורא בממונא לא

Shemuel said: "We follow the majority only in ritual matters, but not in monetary matters." (*Bava Kamma* 27b, 46b; *Bava Batra* 92b)

כל איסורין שבתורה בטלין בשישים

R. Hiyya b. Abba said in the name of R. Yehoshua b. Levi who said it in the name of Bar Kappara: "All prohibited substances of the Torah are nullified by sixty-fold." (*Hullin* 98a)

כל איסורין שבתורה מצטרפין זה עם זה

R. Meir said: "All the prohibited things of the Torah are combinable together to create an amount required for transgressing." (*Avodah Zarah* 66a)

כל המתנה על מה שכתוב בתורה

Stipulations in a contract contrary to Torah commandments are considered null and void. (*Ketubbot* 83a; *Bava Metzia* 94a; *Kiddushin* 19b)

כל השונה הלכות בכל יום
It was taught in the Tanna D'bei Eliyahu: He who studies Torah Laws every day will be destined to have a place in the World to Come. (*Megillah* 28b; *Niddah* 73a)

כל ישראל ערבים זה בזה
All of Israel are guarantors one for another. (*Shevuot* 39a; *Sanhedrin* 27b)

כל שהוא
A minute quantity (*Shevuot* 21b, 24a; *Makkot* 17a; *Meillah* 18a; *Nazir* 4a)

כלאחר יד
The back of the hand; an act done not in the usual way. (*Shabbat* 92a, 153b)

כלי ראשון
The pot with food cooking directly on the fire is called the first vessel. (*Shabbat* 42b)

כלי שני
Food boiled in a vessel which was transferred to another vessel not directly on the fire – this vessel is called the second vessel. (*Shabbat* 42b)

Generalization and specification כלל ופרט
It is one of the thirteen methods and principles of biblical interpretation by R. Yishmael. (*Hullin* 88b; *Bechorot* 19a; *Bava Kamma* 54b, 62b, 64b; *Eruvin* 27b; *Nazir* 35b)

כלל ופרט אין בכלל אלא מה שבפרט
A general proposition followed by a specific instruction; in such a case, the scope of the proposition is limited to that of the specific.
This is one of the thirteen principles of biblical interpretation of R. Yishmael. (*Hullin* 88b; *Bechorot* 19a; *Bava Kamma* 54b, 62b, 64b; *Eruvin* 27b; *Nazir* 35b)

כלל ופרט וכלל
Generalization followed by a specification, which is then followed by another generalization; in such a case, it has an impact on the whole proposition.
This is one of the thirteen methods and principles of biblical interpretation of R. Yishmael. (*Bava Kamma* 54b, 62b, 64b; *Eruvin* 27b; *Nazir* 35b)

כסוי הדם
Covering the blood with sand or dirt after slaughtering (*Hullin* 31a, 83b, 87b)

כסף בידו ידו על העליונה
R. Shimon said: "He who has the money in his hand has the advantage." (*Bava Metzia* 44a, 47b, 49b, 74b)

Tyrian money כסף צורי
Rav Yehuda said in the name of Rav: "Wherever the Torah speaks of money, it is Tyrian." (*Bava Kamma* 36b; *Kiddushin* 11a; *Bechorot* 50b)

Excision כריתות
There are transgressions which are punishable by the penalty of excision, cutting off from the people of Israel, or extinction. (*Keritut* 2a)

כרמלית
A domain, neither private nor public (*Shabbat* 7a; *Eruvin* 87a)

ל

לא היה דברים מעולם
This never happened; what you claim never happened. (*Shevuot* 41b)

לא עביד איניש דינא לנפשיה
No man may take the law into his own hands for the protection of his interests. (*Bava Kamma* 27b)

לא תבשל גדי בחלב אמו

It was taught in the school of R. Yishmael: The prohibition of cooking a kid in its mother's milk is stated three times in the Torah: One is a prohibition against eating it, one a prohibition against deriving benefit from it, and one a prohibition against cooking it. (*Hullin* 115b; *Kiddushin* 57b)

לאו הבא מכלל עשה עשה

Negative injunction deduced from a positive injunction

A negative injunction deduced from a positive one is considered a positive injunction. (*Pesahim* 41b; *Yevamot* 54b, 68a, 73b; *Zevahim* 34a; *Hullin* 81a)

לאו שיש בו מעשה

A negative precept in the Torah that involves action. (*Shevuot* 21a)

לבוד

A halachic law; a gap in the wall which is less than three handbreadths apart is to be considered as connected. (*Shabbat* 97a; *Eruvin* 9a, 16a, 79b; *Sukkah* 6b)

לויתן

R. Yosi b. Durmaskith said: "The Leviathan is a clean fish."
Rabbah said in the name of R. Yohanan: "In the future, Hashem will make a banquet for the righteous, and will serve them the flesh of the Leviathan." (*Bava Batra* 74a–b, 75a; *Hullin* 67b)

ל״ו צדיקים

Abbaye said: "In each generation, the world must contain no less than thirty-six righteous men who merit the sight of the Shechina." (*Sanhedrin* 97b; *Sukkah* 45b)

לחי

The sidepost used to permit to make an *eruv* for an alleyway on Shabbat. (*Sukkot* 16b; *Eruvin* 12b)

לחי פחות משלשה כלבוד דמי

A post for an *eruv* less than three handbreadths is halachically considered like it is wide enough by using *lavud*. (*Sukkah* 16b; *Eruvin* 12b)

לחם הפנים

The showbread in the Temple (*Menahot* 95b)

לחם משנה

R. Abba said: "On Shabbat, it is one's duty to break bread over two loaves."
R. Ashi said: "I saw R. Kahana holding two loaves, but he broke only one of them." (*Shabbat* 117b; *Berachot* 39b)

למפרע

Retroactive (*Berachot* 13a)

לפנים משורת הדין

Above and beyond; within the margin of judgment (*Bava Kamma* 100a; *Bava Metzia* 30b)

לשון הרע

R. Shemuel said: "David did not listen to gossip." (*Shabbat* 56a; *Makkot* 23a; *Yoma* 22b)

לשון קודש

Holy tongue, words of Torah (*Shabbat* 40b)

לשון תורה לעצמה לשון חכמים לעצמו

The language of the Torah is distinct and the language of the Sages is distinct. (*Avodah Zarah* 58b; *Hullin* 137b)

מ

מאמר

Betrothal by word in connection with *yibbum* (*Yevamot* 17a, 18b)

מבוי

An entrance to a blind alley with a cross beam on top (*Eruvin* 2a)

מבטל

To annul; regarding idol images to be annulled (*Avodah Zarah* 43a)

מבטל את רשותו

One gives up the right to a thing or a courtyard. (*Eruvin* 68b)

מבעה

Spoilage caused by animals eating up someone's crop. (*Bava Kamma* 2a; *Shekalim* 8a; *Keritut* 2b)

מבקר חולים

Visiting the sick (*Nedarim* 39b; *Bava Metzia* 30b)

מה נפשך

Which way will you have it? Whatever your assumption is. (*Horayot* 5a; *Avodah Zarah* 31b)

מה נשתנה

Why is it different? These are the first words of the Four Questions a son is asking his father at the Seder table. (*Pesahim* 116a)

מודה במקצת

Admitting to part of the claim (*Bava Kamma* 107a; *Bava Metzia* 3a)

מוכר בעין יפה מוכר

The vendor interprets the sale liberally, according to R. Akiva. The rabbis disagree. (*Bava Batra* 64b)

מוכר בעין רעה מוכר

The vendor interprets the sale strictly. (*Bava Batra* 64b)

מוכת עץ

Loss of virginity through an accident (*Ketubbot* 11a)

מומחה לבית דין

An expert advisor to the court (*Sanhedrin* 5a, *Rosh Hashana* 25b)

מומר

An apostate; one who abandons his faith. (*Avodah Zarah* 26b; *Hullin* 3a)

מומר להכעיס

One who is an apostate in defiance to provoke anger. (*Avodah Zarah* 26b; *Hullin* 3a)

מומר לתיאבון

One who is an apostate only to satisfy his appetite. (*Avodah Zarah* 26b; *Hullin* 3a)

מונח עד שיבא אליהו

It rests until Eliyahu comes. It rests until the doubt disappears. (*Bava Metzia* 3a, 37a)

מועד

An animal which is on notice to cause damages. (*Bava Kamma* 15a, 16b)

מופנה

A Talmudic term meaning that a word or term is free and not used for other teachings. In a *gezera shava* where similar words are used to teach us a Halachah, the words must be *mufna* – free and not used for some other Halachah. (*Bava Kamma* 25b; *Sanhedrin* 40b; *Shabbat* 64a)

מוצאי שבת
לעולם יסדר אדם שולחנו במוצאי שבת

One should always have a nice meal the night after Shabbat ends. (*Shabbat* 119b)

מוקצה

Set aside; an object forbidden to handle on Shabbat for various reasons. (*Shabbat* 43b, 44a–b, 45b, 46b; *Betzah* 30b)

מזל מזלות

Planet, planets, constellations (*Avodah Zarah* 42b)

מחוזא

Mehuza; Academy

Mehuza is a town in Babylonia on the banks of the Tigris River. Rava lived in

Mehuza and headed the academy for fourteen years.

The following were the heads of the academy in Mehuza: Rabbah bar Avuha, who lived in the 3rd century CE; Rava, who lived in the 3rd – 4th centuries CE; Ameimar, who lived in the 4th – 5th centuries CE. (*Berachot* 59b; *Yoma* 11a; *Bechorot* 55b)

מחיר כלב

Price received for the sale of a dog; that money is not permitted to be used to buy an animal for a dedication in the Temple. (*Temurah* 30a)

Movables, vs. real estate   מטלטלין
(*Bava Metzia* 11b, 44a, 48b; *Kiddushin* 26b; *Bava Batra* 156b)

מיאון

Refusal; a fatherless girl of minor age who was given away by her mother or brother can at any time refuse the continuance of the marriage until she matures. (*Yevamot* 107b, 108a; *Sanhedrin* 2a; *Hullin* 26b)

מיאש

The owner of the object gave up of recovering it. (*Avodah Zarah* 43a; *Bava Metzia* 21b, 22a, 24a)

Since   מיגו
Since he could have claimed more, therefore, a lesser claim is convincing. (*Bava Metzia* 5b; *Sanhedrin* 24a)

מים אחרונים חובה

Washing hands after the meal is an obligation. (*Hullin* 105a)

מין במינו

Substances of like kind that are mixed together. (*Hullin* 97b, 100a)

מין במינו במשהו

Substances of like kind mixed together;

the forbidden substance disqualifies the larger quantity even if very small. (*Avodah Zarah* 73a)

מין בשאינו מינו

Substances of different kinds that are mixed together. (*Hullin* 97b; *Avodah Zarah* 66a)

מיעוט אחר מיעוט

A limitation followed by another limitation. (*Bava Kamma* 86b; *Yoma* 43a)

מכה בפטיש

Striking with a hammer; when a craftsman is working on a utensil, it is the last strike with the hammer that indicates that the utensil is completed. (*Shabbat* 73a, 102b)

מכות

The number of lashes administered, the place and position of the lashes (*Makkot* 22a)

Angel of Death (*Makkot* 10a)   מלאך המוות

Ministering angels (*Hullin* 91b) מלאכי השרת

מלאכי השרת

R. Yosi b. R. Yehuda said: "On Friday evening, two ministering angels accompany a man from the synagogue to his home." (*Shabbat* 119b)

מלוג

A wife's estate in which the husband is entitled to the fruits without the responsibility for the losses. (*Yevamot* 66a; *Ketubbot* 79b)

מלוה בריבית

Lending with charging interest, usury (*Shevuot* 45a)

מלחמות גוג ומגוג

The great wars of Gog and Magog (*Sanhedrin* 97b)

מליקה

Kosher slaughtering of a bird in the Bet HaMikdash (*Hullin* 19b, 28a)

מלשינים

Author of the prayer Ve-Lamalshinim
Rabbi Gamliel asked for a volunteer to compose a prayer which reflects Jewish opposition to the sectarians and non-believers. Rabbi Shemuel volunteered and composed the prayer called "*Ve-La-malshinim.*" This prayer with the other eighteen prayers constitute the *Amidah* prayers. (*Berachot* 28b)

ממאנת

Refusal; a minor who was given in marriage by her mother or brother has the right to repudiate the contract. (*Yevamot* 108a)

ממה נפשך

Dilemma; either way, in either case (*Bava Kamma* 31a, 38a)

ממזרים

Children born and conceived by forbidden sex. (*Yevamot* 44a, 49a; *Kiddushin* 74b)

מה"מ מנא הני מילי

How do we arrive at this conclusion (*Horayot* 10a)

מנחה *Minha services*
The afternoon services are called *Minha*, and were instituted by the Patriarch Yitzhak. (*Berachot* 26b)

מסורת בידינו מאבותינו

R. Levi said: "This is a tradition transferred to us from our fathers." (*Sotah* 10b)

מסירה משיכה הגבהה
How is movable property acquired
Abbaye and Rava stated that *mesirah*, meaning handing over, confers legal ownership in a public area or in a courtyard that belongs to neither of them. *Meshichah*, meaning pulling, confers ownership in an alley or in a courtyard owned by both of them, and *hagbahah*, meaning lifting, confers ownership everywhere. (*Bava Batra* 76b)

מסית

A seducer to worship idols (*Sanhedrin* 67a)

מעילה

Misappropriation or the slightest deviation from the prescribed ceremony is called *meilah*, desecration. (*Meilah* 2a)

מעלין בקודש ואין מורידין

Sanctity may be elevated to a higher degree of sanctity, but not degraded. (*Berachot* 28a; *Shabbat* 21b; *Megillah* 9b, 21b; *Horayot* 12b)

מעמדות

The early Prophets established twenty-four guard divisions consisting of Kohanim, Levites, and Israelites. When the time came for a particular guard division to go up, the Kohanim and the Levites went up to Jerusalem, while the Israelites of that division would assemble in their own towns and read the chapter of Creation. (*Taanit* 26a)

מעריב

The evening prayer was instituted by the Patriarch Yaakov. (*Berachot* 26b)

מעת לעת

From time to time, a twenty-four hour period (*Shabbat* 15a; *Niddah* 2a)

מצוה שהיא תלויה בארץ

Every precept which is dependent on the Land is practiced only in the Land. (*Kiddushin* 36b)

מצוות עשה שהזמן גרמא
A commandment that has to be performed at a particular time. (*Shabbat* 62a; *Eruvin* 96b)

מצוות עשה שהזמן גרמא נשים פטורות
All affirmative precepts bound by a stated time are not incumbent upon women. (*Kiddushin* 29a; *Shabbat* 62a)

מצרף
Combining two smaller amounts to make up the size required. (*Shevuot* 21b)

מקח טעות
An erroneous sale (*Avodah Zarah* 71b)

מקיל ומחמיר
Leniencies and stringencies (*Moed Katan* 20a)

מראית עין
The appearance of improper behavior. Do not flaunt doing things in public, which might be objectionable to your neighbors. (*Avodah Zarah* 12a; Shabbat 64b; *Betzah* 9a)

משהו
Very little, insignificant amount (*Hullin* 102b)

משום עינא
Harm may come to it through an evil eye. (*Bava Metzia* 30a)

משיכה קונה
Moving an object transfers possession. (*Bava Metzia* 46b; *Kiddushin* 1:4; *Eruvin* 81b; *Hullin* 83a)

משכון
Pledge; taking a pledge when lending money to another person. (*Bava Metzia* 48b, 49a, 113a)

משנכנס אדר מרבין בשמחה
Joyous month of Adar
R. Yehuda b. R. Shemuel b. Shilat in the name of Rav said: "Just as from the beginning of the month of Av we curtail rejoicing, so it is the opposite with the month of Adar: from the beginning of Adar, rejoicing is increased." (*Taanit* 29b)

מתוך שלא לשמה בא לשמה
R. Yehuda said in the name of Rav: "A person should always engage in Torah and the performance of commandments even though it is done for ulterior motives, because eventually it will lead to performance for its own sake." (*Horayot* 10b)

Giving charity in secret מתן בסתר
The Talmud relates: There was a poor man in Mar Ukva's neighborhood, and Mar Ukva used to throw four *zuz* at his door everyday in such a way that he would not be seen. Mar Ukva was the Exilarch of the Jewish community.

One day, the poor man was curious to see who this benefactor person was, and he waited for him. The next day when Mar Ukva and his wife were on their way home, they threw the coins at his door. As soon as the man saw people approaching his door, he went out after them to see who they were. They ran to hide in the furnace room, where his feet almost got burned. (*Ketubbot* 67b; *Bava Batra* 9b)

מתנה על מה שכתוב בתורה
Stipulations in a contract contrary to Torah commandments are considered null and void. (*Ketubbot* 83a; *Bava Metzia* 94a)

It was learned in a Beraita מתניתא
A Matnita is similar to a Mishna in learning, but not incorporated in the Talmud. (*Shabbat* 19b, 145b)

נ

נבלה

Non-kosher meat; it is so on account of being dead and not receiving a proper *shehita*. It also refers to decaying flesh. (*Hullin* 30b, 32a; *Bava Kamma* 15a, 34a)

נדה

The period and duration of menstrual uncleanness. (*Niddah* 2a)

Abstinence during the נדה *period* נדה
R. Meir said: "Why did the Torah ordain that the duration of uncleanness during the menstrual period be seven days? In order that the absence will make their love even greater." (*Niddah* 31b)

נוב

The Tabernacle was moved to from Shiloh to Nov. (*Zevahim* 112b)

נוגע בעדותו

A witness with interest in the matter (*Sanhedrin* 23b; *Bava Batra* 43a)

נוגעין בעדותן

Interested parties, prejudiced witnesses (*Bava Batra* 43a)

נוטל אם על הבנים

Taking the mother bird together with the young (*Hullin* 141a; *Makkot* 16a, 17a)

Imparts a taste (*Avodah Zarah* 66a) נותן טעם

נותר

Leftovers from the Temple offerings (*Meilah* 6b)

נטילת ידים

Before eating bread one must wash hands as instituted by Shlomo HaMelech (*Eruvin* 21b)

נכסי מלוג

A wife's estate in which the husband is entitled to the usufruct, but the property itself is not his and has no responsibility for the losses. (*Bava Kamma* 88b, 90a; *Bava Metzia* 35a; *Bava Batra* 50a; *Ketubbot* 50a, 78b)

Sheep of iron נכסי צאן ברזל
It is a type of contract they use when selling a herd of sheep. The sale is conditioned on payment in full. Similarly, a wife's estate held by the husband which the husband can enjoy the usufruct, but he is also responsible for maintaining it intact. In case of death or divorce, the husband must restore loss of deterioration. (*Yevamot* 66a; *Bechorot* 16b; *Bava Metzia* 69b, 70b; *Bava Kamma* 89a)

נעילה

The prayer services on Yom Kippur at the end of the day. (*Shabbat* 24b)

נערה מאורסה

Betrothed maiden (*Sanhedrin* 66b)

נעשה ונשמע

R. Simai lectured: "When the Israelites gave the answer 'We will do, we will listen," 600,000 angels placed two crowns on each person at Mount Sinai – one for 'we will do,' and one for 'we will listen.' But as soon as the Israelites sinned they were removed by the angels." (*Shabbat* 88a)

נפילת אפים

Falling with the face on the arms to pray (*Bava Metzia* 59b)

Sunrise (*Berachot* 9b) נץ החמה

נצור לשוני

Mar b. R. Avina used to finish the *Amidah* with a special prayer: "Keep my tongue from evil and my lips from speaking falsehood. May I be silent for those who curse me, and may I be to them like dust. Open my heart to Torah and may I pursue your commandments, etc." Most congregations have adopted this prayer and they recite it at the conclusion of the *Amidah*. (*Berachot* 17a)

נציבין

Nitzivin or Nisibis was a community in Northeastern Mesopotamia. R. Yehuda b. Betera established an academy there. Yehuda ben Betera II lived there in the 2nd century CE. (*Sanhedrin* 32b)

נשג״א (נדה שפחה עובדת כוכבים אשת איש)

R. Dimi said: "A Jew who has sexual relations with an idol worshipping woman transgresses four prohibitions." (*Avodah Zarah* 36b; *Sanhedrin* 82a)

נשג״ז (נדה שפחה עובדת כוכבים זונה)

Ravin said: "A Jew who has sexual relations with an idol worshipping woman transgresses four prohibitions." (*Avodah Zarah* 36b; *Sanhedrin* 82a)

נשך ותרבית

What is the difference between the two? (*Bava Metzia* 60b)

נשמת כל חי

This prayer is recited on Shabbat and Yom Tov. R. Yohanan called it the blessing of the song. (*Pesahim* 118a)

ס

סגולה

A safe investment; it refers to a custodian handling the money of a minor. (*Bava Kamma* 87b; *Bava Batra* 52a)

סוטה

When a husband is suspicious of his wife's

fidelity and they go through the ceremony of *sotah*. (*Sotah* 2a)

Sura; Academy   סורא

Sura is a town in Babylonia south of Baghdad. It is situated on the banks of the Euphrates River where it divides into two rivers. Sura became a famous Torah center when Rav moved to the town in 219, and established the famous Yeshiva there. Rav's yeshiva attracted hundreds of students and scholars.

When Rav passed away in 247, the academy lost its preeminence to Nehardea for seven years. However, when Rabbi Shemuel from Nehardea passed away in 254, Sura regained its role under the leadership of Rabbi Huna.

The following were the heads of the academy in Sura: Rav, who lived in the 3rd century CE; Huna, who lived in the 3rd century CE; Hamnuna, who lived in the 3rd century CE; Rabbah bar Huna, who lived in the 3rd – 4th centuries CE; Hisda, who lived in the 3rd – 4th centuries CE; Mereimar, who lived in the 4th – 5th centuries CE; Ashi, who lived in the 4th – 5th centuries CE; Rava Tosfaah, who lived in the 5th century CE; Mar b. R. Ashi, who lived in the 5th century CE; Ravina II, who lived in the 5th century CE. (*Hullin* 110a; *Shabbat* 37b; *Betzah* 29b)

A stubborn and rebellious son   סורר ומורה

R. Shimon said: "It never happened and will never happen. Why did the Torah write it? So that one studies it and receives a reward." (*Sanhedrin* 68b, 71a)

סימפון

A receipt or something similar (*Sanhedrin* 31b; *Bava Metzia* 21a)

סכין מסוכסכת

A knife with one edge notched (*Hullin* 17b)

סכין אוגרת

A knife with notches (*Hullin* 17b)

סמיכה

The laying of hands: What is meant by laying of hands? R. Yohanan said that it refers to the ordination of the Elders. (*Sanhedrin* 13b, 14a)

סמיכה

The laying on of the hands in the Temple on the sacrifices, or ordaining rabbis. (*Menahot* 93a; *Hullin* 2b; *Berachot* 42a; *Betzah* 20a; *Zevahim* 33a)

סנהדרין גדולה

The Great Sanhedrin was composed of seventy-one members. (*Sanhedrin* 2a, 3b)

סנהדרין קטנה

The Small Sanhedrin consisted of twenty-three members. (*Sanhedrin* 2a)

סריס

A person lacking procreative powers (*Bava Batra* 155b)

סתם משנה

R. Yohanan said: "The Halachah is in agreement with the anonymous Mishna." (*Yevamot* 42b; *Shabbat* 46a; *Bava Kamma* 69a)

ע

עבירות שבין אדם לחבירו

Transgressions between man and his fellow-man (*Yoma* 85b)

עבירות שבין אדם למקום

Transgressions between man and God (*Yoma* 85b)

עגונה

A deserted wife; a wife unable to get a divorce. (*Gittin* 33a)

עגל

Seal bearing the inscription
There were four seals in the Temple with these inscriptions: עגל זכר גדי חוטא (*Shekalim* 5:3)

עגלה ערופה

The heifer used in the ceremony when a person was found murdered between two communities. (*Parah* 1:1)

עד ועד בכלל

When the Talmud says: "It is up to a certain day or hour," is the day or hour included or excluded? (*Berachot* 26b; *Hullin* 46a)

עדשה

Lentil; a halachic measurement (*Bava Kamma* 25b; *Shabbat* 64a)

עובר במעי אשה

A live fetus or a dead fetus in the womb of its mother (*Hullin* 72a)

עולם הבא

World to Come
All Jews have a share in the World to Come.

R. Yehuda b. Shila said in the name of R. Assi, in the name of R. Yohanan: There are six things of which a person can benefit in this world while the principal remains to be benefited from in the World to Come: hospitality to wayfarers, visiting the sick, mediation in prayer, arriving early at the Bet Midrash, teaching a son Torah, and judging to judge everyone as being upright. (*Sanhedrin* 90a; *Shabbat* 127a; *Kiddushin* 39b)

עולם הבא

Acquiring Olam HaBa in a single hour
R. Hanania b. Teradion was condemned to die for violating the decree "not to teach Torah." While he was being burned to death, the executioner asked him: "If I ease your pain, would you take me to the next world with you?"

R. Hanania answered him in the affirmative. The executioner increased the flames and removed the wet cloth from his chest and his soul departed speedily. The executioner then jumped and threw himself into the fire. A Bat Kol exclaimed: "R. Hanania b. Teradion and the executioner have been assigned to the World to Come."

When R. Yehuda HaNasi heard the news, he cried and said: "One may acquire *Olam Haba* in a single hour, others after many years."

Rabbi Hanania ben Teradion became one of the Ten Martyrs. (*Avodah Zarah* 18a)

Depth and height　　עומקא ורומא
(*Bava Batra* 64a)

עומר

The meal offering in the Temple is called *omer*. (*Menahot* 76b)

Impudent person　　עזות פנים
Rebbe added this prayer to the morning service to save us from brazen and impudent men. (*Shabbat* 30b)

עידית

Property of the best quality (*Bava Kamma* 7b)

עין תחת עין

Eye for an eye; R. Shimon b. Yohai said: "An eye for an eye means pecuniary compensation." (*Bava Kamma* 84a; *Ketubbot* 38a)

עם הארץ

A person ignorant of Torah study (*Taharot* 8:1, 2; *Horayot* 11a)

עשה ולא תעשה

Positive and negative commandments (*Shabbat* 25a; *Betzah* 8b)

פ

Redeeming captives　　פדיון שבוים
Redeeming captives is a mitzvah of great importance. (*Bava Batra* 8b)

פוגם

A slaughtering knife with a notch in it (*Hullin* 10a; *Pesahim* 9a; *Avodah Zarah* 41b)

Pum Nahara; Academy　　פום נהרא
R. Kahana escorted R. Shimi b. Ashi from Pum Nahara to Bei Tzenitha of Babylonia. When they arrived he asked him: "Do people really say that these palm trees are from the time of Adam?"

R. Kahana V כהנא was the Head of the academy in Pum Nahara. He lived in the 4th century CE. (*Yevamot* 16b; *Hullin* 95b; *Berachot* 31a; *Sotah* 46b)

Pumbedita; Academy　　פומבדיתא
Pumbedita is a town in Babylonia northwest of Baghdad. It is situated on the bank of the Euphrates River, near the canal Shunya-Shumvatha, and near the canal Papa. According to some sources, the town had already a Jewish settlement in the time of the Second Temple. In 259 CE, Nehardea and its academy were destroyed by Papa ben Nasser, the commander in chief of Palmyra. The scholars from Nehardea fled and established an academy in Pumbedita under the leadership of Rabbi Yehuda b. Yechezkel. This academy was the central religious authority for the Babylonian Jewry for many centuries.

The following were the heads of the academy in Pumbedita: Yehuda bar Yehezkel, 3rd century CE; Rabbah, 3rd – 4th centuries CE; Yosef b. Hiyya, 3rd – 4th centuries CE; Abbaye, 3rd – 4th centuries CE; Bibi bar Abbaye, 4th century CE; Hama, 4th century CE; Dimi of Nehardea, 4th century CE; Rafram b. Papa, 4th – 5th centuries CE; Rehumei II, 5th century CE.

(*Gittin* 60b; *Yoma* 77b; *Bava Kamma* 12a; *Bava Metzia* 18b)

פיגול

Pigul is a term used for Temple offerings that were offered with the wrong intentions or not in their proper time, or proper place. (*Zevahim* 36b)

Saving a life　　　פיקוח נפש
R. Yohanan said: "One may do any work on Shabbat in order to save a life." (*Ketubbot* 5a)

Pesach one and Pesach two　　פסח שני
What differences are there between the first and the second Pesach? (*Pesahim* 95a)

A certainty!　　פסיק רישא ולא ימות
Let his head be cut off, but let him not die. This is a dialectic term for a sure consequence of an act. (*Shabbat* 75a, 103a, 111b, 117a, 120b, 133a, 143a; *Ketubbot* 6b; *Bechorot* 25a)

פצוע דכא
A man's testicles crushed or wounded (*Yevamot* 75a)

Ascetics (*Bava Batra* 60b)　　פרושין

פרי האדמה
On vegetables, one makes the blessing *pri haadama*. (*Berachot* 35a, 37a)

פרי הגפן
On wine, one makes the blessing *pri ha-gefen* (*Berachot* 35a)

פרי העץ
On fruits of the tree, one makes the blessing *pri ha-etz* (*Berachot* 35a)

פרסומי ניסא
Publicizing the miracle of Chanukah (*Shabbat* 23b)

פת הבאה בכסנין
Bread filled with sweets, like honey and raisins – there is a debate about whether the blessing is *ha-motzi*. (*Berachot* 41b)

פתיחא
A legal document like a warrant (*Bava Kamma* 112b)

צ

Sheep of iron　　צאן ברזל
An ironclad agreement. It is a type of contract they use when selling a herd of sheep; the sale is conditioned on payment in full. Similarly, a wife's estate held by the husband is conditioned. In case of death or divorce, the husband must restore loss of deterioration. (*Yevamot* 66a; *Bechorot* 16b; *Bava Metzia* 69b, 70b)

A Tzadoki (*Horayot* 11a)　　צדוקי

צדקה
R. Assi said: "Giving charity is equivalent to all other religious precepts combined." (*Bava Batra* 9a)

צורבא מרבנן
It is not in the nature of a rabbinic scholar to act this way. (*Shevuot* 41a; *Bava Batra* 168a)

Sepphoris academy　　ציפורי
The following were the heads of the academy in Sepphoris: Hanina bar Hama who lived in the 3rd century CE, and Mani who lived in the 4th century CE. (*Sanhedrin* 32b, 33b; *Shabbat* 33b)

ציץ
It was taught that the *tzitz* which was worn by the High Priest on his forehead was in the shape of a plate of gold. Its size was two fingerbreadths broad and it stretched from ear to ear, and upon it were engraved

two lines: *yud* and *hei* above, and *Kodesh* followed by *lamed* below.

R. Eleazar b. Yosi said: "I saw it in Rome and it had *Kodesh Lashem* in one line." (*Sukkah* 5a)

צלתה מרובה מחמתה

The shade is more than the sun; it matters in a *sukkah*. (*Sukkah* 9b)

Modest (*Avodah Zarah* 47b)　　　צנוע

צער בעלי חיים

Cruelty to animals (*Bava Metzia* 32b; *Shabbat* 128b)

ק

קבורה

Burial (*Bava Kamma* 100a; *Bava Metzia* 30b)

קדושה

The *Kedushah* prayer is to be said with a *minyan* of ten. (*Berachot* 21b)

קום עשה

A positive religious commandment that has to be done. (*Bava Metzia* 62a)

קורה

A cross beam used to correct or make for Shabbat an *eruv* for an alleyway. (*Eruvin* 12b)

קידוש לבנה

R. Aha b. Hanina said in the name of R. Assi in the name of R. Yohanan: "Whoever makes the blessing over the new moon in its proper time is equal to being in the presence of the Shechina." (*Sanhedrin* 42a)

קידוש לבנה

It was taught in the school of R. Yishmael: "If Israel had no other *zechut* but to greet the Heavenly Father once a month, it would have been sufficient."

Abbaye said: "Therefore, it should be said while standing." (*Sanhedrin* 42a)

קיום השטר

Attestation of a deed (*Bava Batra* 154a)

Light and stringent　　　קל וחומר

Fortiori = inference from minor to major It is one of the thirteen methods and principles of biblical interpretation of R. Yishmael. (*Hullin* 12:5; *Sanhedrin* 73a; *Bava Kamma* 25a; *Bava Metzia* 88b)

קלוטה כמי שהונחה

Interception in the air is equal as resting on the ground. It has halachic implications on Shabbat. (*Shabbat* 4b; *Bava Kamma* 70b;

Amulet (*Shabbat* 53b, 61a)　　　קמיע

קמיע מומחה

An approved amulet (*Shabbat* 61a)

Imposing a fine　　　קנס

R. Nahman b. R. Hisda asked R. Nahman b. Yaakov: "How many judges are required to levy a double-, four- or fivefold fine?" (*Sanhedrin* 8a)

קעקע

An incised imprint in the flesh (*Makkot* 21a)

Enclosure (*Shabbat* 7a)　　　קרפף

קרקע

Land, real estate (*Bava Metzia* 31a, 48b, *Bava Batra* 84b; *Ketubbot* 87b)

קשוט עצמך ואחר כך קשוט אחרים

Resh Lakish said: "Correct yourself first before you correct others." (*Bava Metzia* 107b; *Bava Batra* 60b; *Sanhedrin* 18a, 19a)

ר

ראיה
Who is obligated to appear in Jerusalem for the Three Festivals? (*Hagigah* 2a)

ראש השנה
R. Keruspedai said in the name of R. Yohanan: "Three books are opened in heaven on Rosh Hashana." (*Rosh Hashana* 16b)

New month (*Shabbat* 24a)　　**ראש חודש**

First of the fleece (*Hullin* 135a)　　**ראשית הגז**

ריבית
Money lent with interest (*Bava Metzia* 63a)

ריבית מאוחרת
Interest postpaid (*Bava Metzia* 75b)

ריבית מוקדמת
Interest prepaid (*Bava Metzia* 75b)

רוח הקודש
The Talmud relates that R. Gamliel was riding on a donkey – immediately after Pesach – from Acco to Kheziv. R. Illai was behind following him. R. Gamliel saw an expensive loaf of bread on the ground. He said to R. Illai: "Please pick up the loaf of bread." Riding on further on the road they met a non-Jew by the name of Mavgai.

R. Gamliel called Mavgai by name and told him to take away the loaf of bread. R. Illai approached the stranger and asked him: "Where are you from?"

"I am an attendant at the station-house."

"And what is your name?"

"My name is Mavgai."

"Did you ever meet R. Gamliel?"

"No," answered Mavgai.

From this experience, we become aware that R. Gamliel had *Ruah Ha-Kodesh*. We also learned three things: One may not leave eatables on the road; that we assume the food was left on the road by the majority of the travelers who are non-Jews, and that one may derive benefit after Pesach from leavened bread which belongs to a non-Jew. (*Eruvin* 64b)

רות
The biblical Ruth lived to see Solomon's kingdom. Solomon was the grandson of her grandson. (*Bava Batra* 91b)

ריבוי אחר ריבוי
An amplification following amplification. This is one of R. Yishmael's thirteen principles. (*Bava Kamma* 45b, 64b; *Shevuot* 5a)

ריבוי ומיעוט
Amplifications and limitations (*Shevuot* 37b)

ריבוי ומיעוט וריבוי
Amplification followed by a diminution followed in its turn by another amplification. (*Bava Kamma* 64b; *Shevuot* 5a)

Exilarch　　**ריש גלותא**
(*Shabbat* 48a; *Zevahim* 19a)

ורפא ירפא
R. Yishmael said: "From this, we learn that a doctor has the permission to heal the sick." (*Bava Kamma* 84a)

רשע
The rabbis taught: one who invests the money of orphans at risk to the orphans but no risk to himself is called a wicked man; one who invests the money of orphans so that they will receive profits only but will not share in the losses, is called a pious man, and one who invests to share both in profits and losses is an average person. (*Bava Metzia* 70a)

ש

ש
The Letter Shin in the Aleph Bet
Abbaye said that the *shin* of the *tefillin* was given to Moshe on Sinai. (*Shabbat* 28b, 62a; *Menahot* 35a)

שב ואל תעשה
Sit and do not do it, concerning transgressions (*Makkot* 13b)

שבועה זו תקנת חכמים היא
This oath is an institution of the rabbis. (*Bava Metzia* 3a, 5b, 60b)

שבות
Abstention from secular activities on Shabbat (*Shabbat* 89a, 97a)

שביתת כלים
Should utensils rest on Shabbat? (*Shabbat* 18a)

שבע ברכות
R. Ashi came to the wedding feast of R. Kahana. On the first day he said all the benedictions, but the following days he said all the blessings only if there were new guests at the table. (*Ketubbot* 8a)

שבע מצוות נצטוו בני נח: דינין וברכת השם ע"ז גילוי עריות ושפיכות דמים וגזל ואבר מן החי
Seven commandments were given to the children of Noah. (*Sanhedrin* 56a; *Avodah Zarah* 2b)

שדים
Demons (*Sanhedrin* 67b)

שואלין ודורשין בהלכות הפסח
Questions are asked and lectures are given on the laws of Pesach. (*Pesahim* 6a)

שובר
A receipt document; a receipt for payment of the *ketubbah* (*Bava Metzia* 19b)

שומא
Evaluation (*Bava Metzia* 35a)

שומר אבידה
Keeper of a lost article waiting for its owner (*Bava Metzia* 29a, 82a; *Bava Kamma* 56b; *Shevuot* 44a; *Nedarim* 33b)

שומר חינם
Unpaid watchman (*Bava Metzia* 82b, 93a)

שומר שכר
Paid watchman (*Bava Metzia* 82b, 93a)

שושבין שושבינא
Groomsmen, best man (*Bava Batra* 144b)

שחיטה
Rebbe said: "וזבחת כאשר צויתך" (*Devarim* 12:21). From those words, we learn that Moshe received instructions on Sinai how to do proper kosher slaughtering." (*Hullin* 28a, 85a; *Yoma* 75b)

שחרית
Morning services were instituted by Avraham. (*Berachot* 26a)

שטר זייפא
A forged document (*Bava Batra* 32b)

שטר שכתוב בו ריבית
Contract that includes interest
A contract which has a clause with forbidden interest written into it. (*Bava Kamma* 30b, 72a; *Bava Batra* 94b)

Antedated notes **שטרי חוב המוקדמין**
(*Bava Metzia* 17a, 72a; *Bava Batra* 157b, 171b; *Sanhedrin* 32a)

שילוח הקן
Letting the mother bird go from the nest (*Hullin* 138b)

שינוי קונה

A change transfers ownership; this is debated. (*Bava Kamma* 66a)

שיננא

R. Shemuel called R. Yehuda by that name; it was an endearing term. (*Bava Kamma* 14a; *Berachot* 36a)

Casual sleeping (*Sukkah* 26a) **שינת ארעי**

שיר השירים

Song of Songs composed by King Solomon (*Shevuot* 35b)

שכיב מרע

A dying person (*Bava Metzia* 19b, 66a)

שכר הליכה

Reward for going to do a mitzvah or going to the synagogue (*Avot* 5:14)

שלוחו של אדם אינו כמותו

A man's agent is not as himself. (*Bava Metzia* 96a)

שלוחו של אדם כמותו

A man's agent is as himself. (*Bava Metzia* 96a; *Berachot* 34b)

שלושה שאכלו

When three dine together, they must say the After-meal blessing together. (*Berachot* 45a, 50a)

שמונה עשרה

It has been taught: Shimon HaPakuli formulated in the proper order the eighteen blessings of the *Amidah* in the presence of R. Gamliel in Yavne. R. Yohanan said that it was stated in a Beraita: "A hundred and twenty elders —among whom were many prophets— drew up eighteen blessings in a fixed order." (*Megillah* 17b; *Berachot* 28b)

שמחת בית השואבה

Water-drawing rejoicing (*Shabbat* 21a)

שמיני עצרת

The eighth day of Sukkot (*Rosh Hashana* 4b; *Hagigah* 17a; *Sukkah* 48a)

שמיר

A worm called *shamir* was used to cut stones. It disappeared when the Temple was destroyed. (*Sotah* 48a)

שמתא

To put a ban on a person or to excommunicate (*Moed Katan* 17a)

שני כתובין הבאין כאחד

Two verses which teach the same thing (*Hullin* 24a, 113b)

שף ויתיב

A synagogue in Nehardea was called Shaf Yativ. It was very old, some say it was from the period before the destruction of the Temple. (*Avodah Zarah* 43b)

שתוקי

A *shetuki* is one that knows his mother, but does not know his father. (*Kiddushin* 69a)

שתי הלחם

The two loaves in the Temple (*Menahot* 94a)

שתי וערב

Lengthwise and crosswise, warp and woof (*Bava Batra* 168b)

ת

The Letter Tav in the Aleph Bet **ת**

R. Aha b. Hanina quoted the following from the Prophet Yehezkel chapter 9: The angel Gabriel was told to go and inscribe with ink the letter **ת** *tav* upon the forehead of the righteous in order that the destroying angel would have no power over them, and inscribe the letter *tav* with blood on the wicked in order that the destroying angel would have power over them. (*Shabbat* 55a)

תדיר ושאינו תדיר תדיר קודם
Whatever is more frequent takes precedence over something that is non-frequent. (*Horayot* 12b)

תוך כדי דיבור
Statements following one another within the minimum of time as for instance שלום עליך רבי ומורי. (*Bava Kamma* 73a; *Nedarim* 87a; *Nazir* 20b; *Bava Batra* 129a; *Makkot* 6a; *Shevuot* 32a; *Temurah* 25b)

תוכו כבורו
כל תלמיד שאין תוכו כבורו לא יכנס
Students whose exterior appearance does not match their interior intellect may not enter. (*Berachot* 27b; *Yoma* 72b)

תולדות מלאכות *Derivative labors on Shabbat*
These are labors that are derived from the main categories of labors which are forbidden on Shabbat. (*Shabbat* 68a)

תחום שבת
Walking beyond the *tehum Shabbat*, which is a distance the rabbis ordained as a limit, is a violation of Shabbat. (*Eruvin* 52b)

תורף
The essential part of a document, which includes the name and the date. (*Bava Metzia* 7b; *Gittin* 21b)

תיומת
The central part of a *lulav* (*Bava Kamma* 96a; *Sukkah* 32a–b)

תינוק שנשבה לבין הנכרים
An infant child that was taken into captivity among idol worshippers (*Shevuot* 5a)

תיקון עולם
Improving the world, working for the well-being of the world and preventing abuses. (*Gittin* 32a)

תלתין ושיתא צדיקי
Abbaye said: "In each generation, the world must contain no less than thirty-six righteous men who merit the sight of the Shechina." (*Sanhedrin* 97b; *Sukkah* 45b)

תם
What is considered to be a Tam in an animal (*Bava Kamma* 23b; *Yevamot* 65a)

תמורה
Substituting dedicated animals with another animal (*Temurah* 2a)

תמחוי Public soup kitchen (*Bava Batra* 8b)

תנאי On condition (*Ketubbot* 19b)

תפילת הדרך
R. Yaakov and R. Hisda said: "When one travels on the road, one should say the prayer *Tefillat Ha-Derech*. (*Berachot* 29b)

תפילת השחר
Morning Prayer time is until . . . (*Berachot* 26a)

תפסת מועט תפסת
If you grasp little, you can hold on to it. (*Rosh Hashana* 4b)

תפסת מרובה לא תפסת
If you try to grasp a lot, you cannot hold on to it. If you try to do too much, you won't accomplish anything. (*Rosh Hashana* 4b)

תקוע *Tekoa; Academy*
Tekoa is a small town in Israel south of Jerusalem and Bethlehem. R. Shimon b. Yohai established an academy there. R. Yehuda HaNasi studied in that academy. (*Eruvin* 91a)

תקנה גדולה

A great enactment was established with regards to misappropriated articles. (*Bava Kamma* 103b)

אושא תקנת

Enactments of the rabbis when they met in Usha (*Bava Kamma* 89a–b; *Bava Batra* 139b)

תקנת השבים

Enactment of the rabbis for the repentant; to make it easier for them (*Bava Kamma* 94a)

תקנת חכמים

Ordinance of the Sages (*Ketubbot* 10a)

תרומה עין יפה אחד מארבעים

We have learnt: The proper measure for *terumah* for a man with a generous eye is one-fortieth part. (*Hullin* 137b)

תרי"ג מצוות

R. Simlai said: Six hundred and thirteen precepts were given to Moshe, 365 negative precepts corresponding to the number of solar days in the year, and 248 positive precepts corresponding to the number of organs in the human body. (*Makkot* 23b)

תשעה באב

During the week of Tisha Be'Av, it is forbidden to cut the hair, wash one's clothes, eat meat, or drink wine. (*Taanit* 26b)

About the Author

MORDECHAI (MARTIN) JUDOVITS is a longtime student of the Talmud, a retired businessman, and a Holocaust survivor.

He grew up in the town of Dej, in Transylvania, Romania, and studied for several years in the Yeshivas of Dej.

He is the grandson of Rebbe Moshe Paneth, the rabbi of Dej, and a great-grandson of Rabbi Yechezkel Paneth, the author of *Sefer Mareh Yechezkel* and former Chief Rabbi of Transylvania.

His mother, Nechama Reizel, a Holocaust martyr, was the daughter of the Dejer Rebbe, Moshe Paneth.

His father, Shlomo ben Mordechai Judovits, also a Holocaust martyr, was a landowner and businessman.

In March 1944, German troops marched into Hungary, at which time the Jews from Hungary and Transylvania were deported to Auschwitz and other concentration camps. Mordechai, his parents, his brothers and sister were carried away to Auschwitz. The last time Mordechai saw his parents was when he was separated from the rest of his family in Auschwitz.

Liberated in 1945, he returned to Dej to be reunited with his family, soon realizing that he was the only survivor of his family.

In 1947, he immigrated to the U.S., where he married his wife Helen and raised a family.

Since 1978, upon retiring from business, he has been very active in Jewish organizations, in particular the Boca Raton Synagogue. He served as president of the Boca Raton Synagogue. As chairman of the building committee, he supervised the construction of the Mikvah and the synagogue buildings.

He is also the author of *Sages of the Talmud*, published by Urim Publications in 2009.